Thomas Usk

The Testament of Love

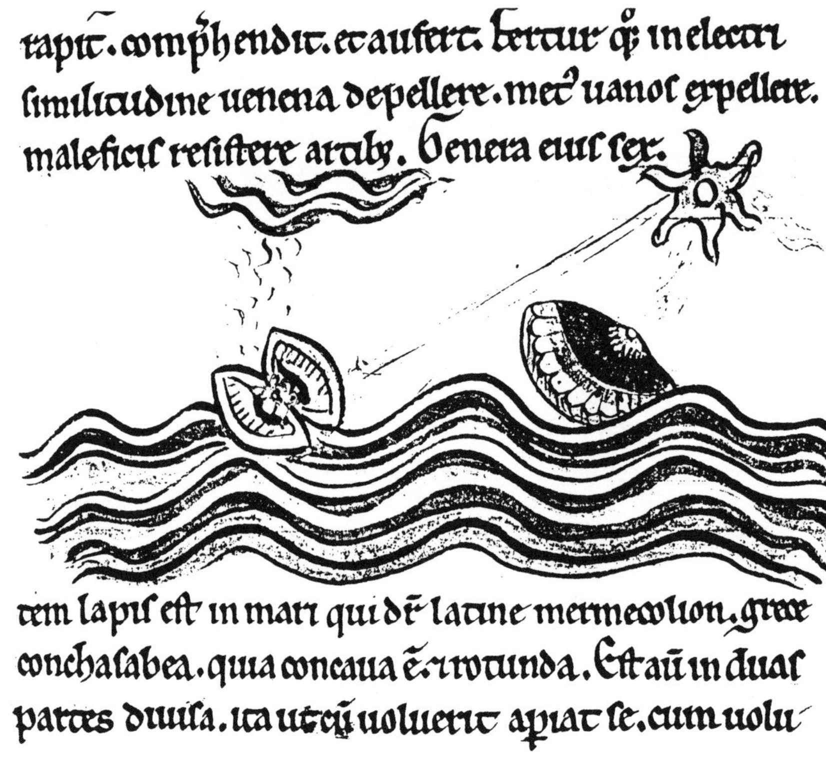

rapit. comprehendit. et aufert. Fertur quod in electri
similitudine uenena depellere. metus uanos expellere.
maleficiis resistere artibus. Genera eius sex.

tem lapis est in mari qui dicitur latine mermecolion, grece
concha sabea. quia concaua est et rotunda. Est autem in duas
partes diuisa. ita ut cum uoluerit aperiat se. cum uolu-

Pearl Oyster (*mermecolion*). Oxford, Bodleian Library, MS Bodley 602 (Bestiary and other texts), fol. 34. Photo: The Bodleian Library, Oxford. Permission granted by The Bodleian Library.

Thomas Usk

The Testament of Love

Edited by
R. Allen Shoaf

Published for TEAMS
(The Consortium for the Teaching of the Middle Ages)
in Association with the University of Rochester

by

Medieval Institute Publications

WESTERN MICHIGAN UNIVERSITY

Kalamazoo, Michigan — 1998

Library of Congress Cataloging-in-Publication Data

Usk, Thomas, d. 1388.
Testament of love / Thomas Usk ; edited by R. Allen Shoaf.
p. cm. -- (Middle English texts)
Text in Middle English; introduction and summary in English.
Includes bibliographical references.
ISBN 1-58044-001-0 (alk. paper)
1. London (England)--History--To 1500--Poetry. 2. Political prisoners--England--London--Poetry. 3. Christian poetry, English (Middle) 4. Politicians--England--London--Poetry. 5. Philosophy, Medieval--Poetry. 6. Autobiography--Poetry. 7. Love--Poetry. 8. Usk, Thomas, d. 1388. Testament of love. I. Shoaf, R. A. (Richard Allen), 1948- . II. Title. III. Series: Middle English texts (Kalamazoo, Mich.)
PR2148.U75T47 1998 98-9895
821'.1--dc21 CIP

ISBN 1-58044-001-0

Printed in the United States of America

Cover design by Elizabeth King

Middle English Texts

The Middle English Texts Series is designed for classroom use. Its goal is to make available to teachers and students texts which occupy an important place in the literary and cultural canon but which have not been readily available in student editions. The series does not include those authors such as Chaucer, Langland, or Malory, whose English works are normally in print in good student editions. The focus is, instead, upon Middle English literature adjacent to those authors that teachers need in compiling the syllabuses they wish to teach. The editions maintain the linguistic integrity of the original work but within the parameters of modern reading conventions. The texts are printed in the modern alphabet and follow the practices of modern capitalization and punctuation. Manuscript abbreviations are expanded, and u/v and j/i spellings are regularized according to modern orthography. Hard words, difficult phrases, and unusual idioms are glossed on the page, either in the right margin or at the foot of the page. Textual notes appear at the end of the text, along with a glossary. The editions include short introductions on the history of the work, its merits and points of topical interest, and also include briefly annotated bibliographies.

To the Memory of

Judson B. Allen

Richard H. Green

David W. Hadley

Robert E. Kaske

Contents

Preface

Seven years ago I began this project with two goals in mind. One, I wanted to realize the aspiration of METS to provide a reliable text of an important Middle English work for purposes of teaching that work, hitherto comparatively neglected, in the undergraduate as well as graduate classroom. Two, I wanted to continue my researches into the image of the knot in medieval and early modern literature — an image, I am convinced, of far greater importance than has hitherto been appreciated.

Others ultimately will judge how successful I have been in attaining the first goal — teachers of Middle English literature in North America and abroad. I am better able to judge of the second, at least initially, and, as I hope my notes will show, I have made progress in my study of the knot, a crucial image in the *Testament of Love* where God is called "the knotte of all goodnesse"— although I can report that the image is even more vast than I had thought, in its complexity and dissemination alike.

But a third goal has emerged in the past three years, one entirely unanticipated in the early stages of my work. Briefly, I have in recent years become interested — perhaps "concerned" is the better word — with the nature of editing as such; and I have it in mind now, in the introduction to this edition especially, to enter some tentative comments on what editing has come to seem to me to be.

Editing is not a science. It may be an art. It certainly is an exercise in subjectivity. And if socially constrained, it is also highly individualized. Whether reading Greetham, McGann, Tanselle, or others, I have become convinced that the most enduring impact of literary theory and its ferment in the last decades of the twentieth century on the future of literary studies will be felt in the interrogation of what constitutes a text as such. The realization that, as I now think of it, editing is originary deconstruction is both exciting and daunting. And for me at least, it will require much further reflection, both on my craft and on my professional identity.

In a historical moment when much furor is heard over changing the canon, so that courses in Chaucer, Shakespeare, and Milton are no longer "requirements" in undergraduate English majors, some may find it shocking, others liberating, to be asked to contemplate that the works of Chaucer, Shakespeare, and Milton do not exist; that copies of them exist, to be sure, in defiant abundance, but the works themselves? That's another matter (consider, for example, the many revisions of his poems by W. H. Auden). Over the past few years, my early training in philosophy, in America and Britain, my studies in aesthetics — reading Wollheim, for example, on the question of what the work of art is — has come to have a new coherence with my career as a whole. Literature and theory have been inseparable in my thought throughout my career, I see now, because literature has always been involved in theorizing its own ontology, asking itself what it is. Usk, too, manifests the same impulse (see Book 1, chapter 6 and Book 3, chapter 1). I offer the following, then, very much as work in progress, progress toward what I am not sure; but if asked to speculate, I would say now: the text as pretext and annotation as alternotation.

Acknowledgments

In the seven years I have worked on this project, I have incurred a large number of debts.

For sharing their scholarly knowledge with me, I want to thank John A. Alford, John Bowers, Robert R. Edwards, Andrew Galloway, Steven Justice, Kathryn Kerby-Fulton, John F. Leyerle, Maud Burnett McInerney, Stephen Medcalf, Annabel Patterson, Andrew Prescott, and Paul Strohm.

For help with the arduous and time-consuming tasks of typing, proofing, photocopying, and the like, I thank Joan Crawford, Marie Gill, George Kingson, and my research assistants over the past several years — Wim De Groote, Angelika Ilg, Jennifer M. Johnson, Teresa P. Reed, Dina Smith, and Margit Wogowitsch. At the University of Rochester, Mara Amster gave my transcription a careful reading and identified several errors that others had missed. She also performed the arduous task of formatting the volume and preparing the camera-ready copy. I am particularly grateful to her.

For assistance in the library, I would like to thank the staff of Interlibrary Loan in the George A. Smathers Library of the University of Florida; I would like also to thank the Acquisitions Librarian for my department, John Van Hook, and his supervisor, Frank Di Trolio, and, in cataloguing, where I received much valuable help, Marianne Waltz.

For help with computers and questions of electronic textuality, I am grateful, here at the University of Florida, to Michael Conlon, Patricia Sivinski, Nancy Sorkin, and the late Wayne Wolfe; further afield but still close in many ways, Hoyt N. Duggan and Roy C. Flannagan shared their knowledge and experience of computers with me — I am indeed grateful to them, as much for the model of collegiality they have shown me as for the information they have given me.

For indispensable support in funds and sabbatical leave, I am grateful to the University of Florida and especially those officers of the University who helped me in my various applications for support — Ira Clark, Chair of English; Patricia Craddock, immediate past Chair of English; Karen Holbrook, Vice President for Research and Dean of the Graduate School; and Willard W. Harrison, Dean of the College of Liberal Arts and Sciences. Likewise, I am grateful to the National Endowment for the Humanities which supported the work at the University of Rochester that brought the volume to completion.

Acknowledgments

I am grateful to Russell A. Peck for help in making hard editorial decisions about how we would format the new edition in relation to Thynne's text. I am also grateful for his assiduous help in pointing the text, for his insights into textual glosses, and for the writing of several textual notes and a few of the explanatory notes. Also, he and Alan Lupack of the Robbins Library gave the volume a meticulous reading in its penultimate stage and eliminated many errors that had escaped my, by this time, inevitably flagging attention — I am especially grateful for this intervention. Finally, I appreciate suggestions made by Tom Seiler and Juleen Eichinger at Medieval Institute Publications after they received camera-ready copy from Amster and Peck and saw the volume through the press.

For moral support in moments of doubt (and there were quite a few of these), I thank Mario A. Di Cesare, Teresa Kennedy, and Russell Peck, and, most especially, my family — Judy, my wife, and our children, Brian, and Elaine — whose love, in this as in everything, sustains me.

I cannot leave these acknowledgments without one final expression of gratitude. It is now 100 years since Walter W. Skeat published his edition of *The Testament of Love* (1897). In my work on this project I have found him often wrong, but I have found him more often right — and right frequently when all he had to go on was native genius. In closing, then, I would like, joining Derek A. Pearsall (in his edition of *Piers Plowman* C), to honor Skeat, acknowledging that, in Pearsall's words, "the magnitude of his contribution to the understanding of the [*The Testament of Love*], in the midst of all his many other labours, remains a cause for wonderment."

Gainesville, Florida
October 7, 1997

The Testament of Love

Introduction

i. Nature of the Project

Reader, take note, *The Testament of Love* by Thomas Usk does not exist. *The Testament of Love* by Thomas Usk as printed in 1532 (nearly 150 years after Usk's death) by William Thynne,[1] who thought it was a work by Chaucer, exists.[2] These two data, reader, must govern everything that follows in this book. Thus, for example, in the absence of any manuscript witness to *TL*,[3] no editor can practice "traditional" editing techniques for the work in any systematic way (see Jellech [1970], p. 9). Expressed more theoretically, in contemporary terms of literary and editorial theory, the gap in the case of *TL* between the work and the text that conveys the work is extreme to the point of impasse.[4] If every work is only imperfectly realized in the text(s) of its conveyance, then *TL* must stand in Middle English literature as the perfect paradigm of this

---

[1] On William Thynne (d. 1546), see the helpful essay by Blodgett, pp. 35–52. I quote briefly from this essay (p. 37) to introduce Thynne's biography:

> [He] was a functionary in the royal household [of Henry VIII]. Surviving records trace his rise through the bureaucratic ranks. In a document from 1524, the earliest containing a definite reference to Thynne, he is called second clerk of the kitchen. By 1526 he had become the chief clerk of the kitchen, his title in household records dating through 1533 as well as in the preface to the edition of 1532. In documents from 1536 and 1538, Thynne is referred to as clerk controller of the king's household. By the end of 1540 he was one of the masters of the household, a position that he retained until his death in August, 1546.

Blodgett goes on to note that "the court in the 1520s and 1530s might even be considered an unofficial center for Chaucer studies" (p. 38), and it was in such a milieu that Thynne edited Chaucer's works. See, further, on Francis Thynne, William's son, and the political circumstances of editing and publishing in the period, Patterson, pp. 262–63.

[2] See *The Works of Geoffrey Chaucer and Others*. And see Greetham (1994), p. 363:

> indeed . . . the printing of a work in the fifteenth or sixteenth centuries typically entailed the loss of exemplars and other sources upon which the printing depended.

[3] From here on, I will use the abbreviation *TL* to refer to *The Testament of Love*.

[4] For terminology here and elsewhere in the Introduction, I follow the definitions of Peter L.

imperfection (see Greetham [1994], pp. 326 and 352; Machan, pp. 181 and 193). And it is thus paradigmatic not only because of temporal lag but also because of the pervasive corruption in Thynne's edition, acknowledged and lamented by readers for centuries. Thus comparison, the "traditional" editor's most reliable tool, is literally impossible in the case of *TL*: there are no witnesses to compare. Hence reconstruction from texts imperfectly realizing the work is equally impossible. So Skeat, note well, openly admits that he re-writes Thynne's Renaissance English into his, Skeat's, idea of fourteenth-century English expressly and solely from his own experience and invention.[5] The reader should note that the present editor does *not* presume to do likewise.

Rather, I have decided upon the following, different expedient. In this edition, I print Thynne in a diplomatic transcription (see below, note 8) and, contrapuntally with it, a pointed version of the work representing my efforts at construing it. Thus, I offer the contemporary reader the constant choice, in the absence of any other choice, between the sixteenth-century editor's, Thynne's, construction of Usk and the twentieth-century editor's construction of Usk, mine.[6] That this is a compromise we will all readily agree. However, it has one real virtue.

And that is the reader's constant awareness of the track of Thynne's text which I am at

---

Shillingsburg as I have found these quoted in Machan, pp. 6–7. Abbreviated they are: *work*, the intellectual product, "'the message or experience implied by the authoritative versions of a literary writing'" (p. 6); *version*, an instance of a work, "'one specific form of a work — the one the author intended at some particular point in time'" (p. 7); *text*, "in a bibliographic sense . . . 'the actual order of words and punctuation as contained in any one physical form'" (p. 7); and *document*, "'the physical material, paper, and ink, bearing the configuration of signs that represent a text'" (p. 7). Machan is quoting from *Scholarly Editing in the Computer Age* (Athens: University of Georgia Press, 1986).

[5] "Many of these things I have attempted to set right" (Skeat, p. xix). And see further Edwards, p. 186:

> In this conviction he was further sustained by the comforting knowledge that if fifteenth-century scribes did not know how to spell Chaucer's works, he did. He is quite frank about this:
>
> > There can be no harm in stating the simple fact, that a long and intimate acquaintance, extending over many years, with the habits and methods of the scribes of the fourteenth [*sic*] century, has made me almost as familiar with the usual spelling of the period as I am with that of modern English.
> >
> > It is little more trouble for me to write a passage of Chaucer from dictation than one from Tennyson. It takes me just a little longer, and that is all.

[6] There is other access to *TL* in the form of the two facsimiles and Virginia Jellech and John Leyerle's unpublished theses (see Select Bibliography).

pains to punctuate and redirect into my construction of its sense.[7] I have transcribed Thynne as accurately as I could[8] and then, on the same page, "edited" that transcription so that my reader can both experience Thynne's text and see, in the *mise en page*, my manipulation of that text. I mean by this expedient to provide readers with a device that will facilitate by comparison and contrast their own construction of Usk's sense even as it instructs them in my editorial theory and practice.

As for my theory and practice, readers should take note of the following. My assumption, after years of reading in editorial theory, is that the work is always deconstructed or, as I would prefer to say, disseminated, in the vehicle(s) of its conveyance (see Greetham [1994], p. 296, and [1996], pp. 32–33). Every text is a pretext for some agenda supererogatory to the work (see Sturges, p. 128). John Dagenais (pp. 16–17) expresses best, to my mind, the particular medieval circumstance of this condition:

> The keystone of modern medievalism, the idea that we must have "coherent" texts before we can begin to talk about medieval literature, is absolutely at odds with the object medievalism pretends to treat. Incoherence is a powerful force in the medieval textual world, and a recognition (not suppression) of its power is fundamental to any understanding of that world. In order to understand ethical reading, then, it is imperative that we explore the textual culture that supported it. It is the culture of the handwritten word: manuscript culture.

Readers of the present edition should bear in mind that I consider the *incoherence* of *TL* to be not its "fault" but the "fault" (if this is the word for it) of its cultural imbeddedness. Everything I attempt here, from identification of sources to speculations about the state of the manuscript Thynne had at his disposal to my deliberately minimal(-ist) punctuation, I undertake in the understanding that coherence is not the primary aim of my efforts: I am not trying to clear the text up but to clear a space around it in which readers can confront its alterity and, in confronting it, arrive at their own constructions of its meanings (see further Bruns, pp. 55–56).[9]

---

[7] See the article by Heyworth for suggestions on how re-punctuation should be undertaken in *TL*. Leyerle's critical edition, his PhD thesis, is an attempt at a global punctuation of *TL*.

[8] I have not altered capitalization of words or punctuation in Thynne. Thus I present here a sixteenth-century reading of *TL* according to the conventions of that age. I have left, unemended, the numerous compiler's errors. On diplomatic transcriptions, see Greetham (1994), p. 350; quoted below at page 18.

[9] Nor should anyone for a moment consider this sentence innocent. I know that I am, in Hanna's words, "substitut[ing] a certain modern neatness — partially driven by a sense of how canonized texts should work — for manuscript material evincing a much more various author (and far

A second major consequence of the data with which I began may already have dawned on readers, but I want to make it explicit. I do not know what Thomas Usk wrote in *TL*. I only know what William Thynne printed. To my knowledge no one knows what Thomas Usk wrote in *TL*. We can perhaps follow Paul Strohm in inferring what Usk said and might have said from the Middle English and Latin documents still extant from his trial.[10] But we have no way, short of a new manuscript suddenly appearing, of knowing what Usk wrote in *TL* — and even then we would still face many severe problems, even if it were a holograph (see Strohm [1990], p. 105).

Because I do not know what Usk wrote but only what Thynne printed, my practice in this edition has been, in a very literal sense, conservative, even as, theoretically, my position is radical. My conservatism is evident on two scores. First, I eschew speculative construal — whether in emendation or punctuation or re-ordering of the text — to a far greater extent than Skeat or Jellech or Leyerle: many are the times I simply leave *TL* obscure at the level of the sentence or even allusion, conceding that it suffers from severe corruption.[11] At the same time, however, and here is the second score on which my conservatism will be evident, I focus insistently and consistently on the vocabulary of *TL*; and I gloss liberally throughout (there are approximately 3000 glosses in this edition) because the words, the lexicon, are the only arguably reliable evidence we have for *TL*, far more reliable than the sentences, paragraphs, or sections — and this even though they, the words, are often formidable in their resistance to comprehension (the word *will*, as in "free will," in Book 3 is an excellent example; another, in the same book, is *commodité*). As difficult as the words sometimes are to understand, I have

more various reception)" (p. 178). Hanna's words are more than just a re-phrasing of Dagenais's; they point, additionally, to the bias, potentially even violence, of editorial "clearing." Call it colonizing, call it territoriality, call it what you will, editing remains appropriation by the editor of the text to his or her meaning and thus expropriation of the text from others who read it differently. But it also offers a direct presentation of the editor's hard choices in understanding the text and presenting it, as responsibly as possible, to the modern reader.

[10] See Strohm (1992), pp. 145–60, especially p. 157, quoted below at p. 24.

[11] See Jellech (1970), p. 3, on the corruption of Thynne's imprint. Jellech, like Skeat and others, also recognizes and reports the commonly acknowledged fact that all subsequent imprints of *TL*, depending as they do on Thynne, are of no use in establishing a text — worse, in fact, they only introduce more corruption into *TL*: "I have examined in microfilm each of these later printings and found none which contains a text superior to the 1532 edition."

As a control for my project, I examined the text of *TL* in the copy of Speght's 1598 edition, *The Workes of our Antient and Learned English Poet, Geffrey Chavcer*, in the Smathers Library of the University of Florida, checking one chapter per each book of *TL*; my findings in this experiment were

nevertheless, in the past seven years of work, slowly become convinced that, more frequently than has hitherto been realized, *TL* is comprehensible on the level of its lexicon, if one patiently works through the options that that lexicon presents. It is often difficult to be certain what a sentence or paragraph in *TL* means, as many before me have lamented, but it is often more possible than many have appreciated to know what the words of a sentence say (I am fully aware of the literary-theoretical controversiality of this distinction). I have therefore concentrated the greater part of my energies on glossing *TL*, and I present this edition to my readers in the conviction that my most important contribution to scholarship in it (after the computer transcription of Thynne's edition itself) is the work of glossing I have done.

ii. Usk's Biography

I call the reader's attention next to the biography of Usk and the relationship of the present edition to twentieth-century efforts to reconstruct or, in some cases, construct that biography. The first and most important fact that the reader should note is that I am not undertaking to write, narrate, or historicize the biography of Usk in this edition. This is an edition of *TL* and not a history of England in the 1380s or a biography of Usk or Brembre or Northampton. Ramona Bressie, Andrew Galloway, Virginia Jellech, Paul Strohm, among others, have all worked on these initiatives, most especially Paul Strohm whose neo-historicist narrations of Usk's life and career have attracted widespread attention in recent years. I, however, am doing something different and, ultimately, far less ambitious. I am trying to provide scholars such as these a working version of *TL* both more accessible and more reliable than has hitherto been available; while, at the same time, I am also trying to provide a tool that optimally helps all readers of Middle English to follow and appreciate *TL*. Thus, for example, I include as an Appendix the Middle English text of Usk's "Appeal" because it is materially useful to the reader's immediate construal of *TL* Book 1, chapters 6–8; but I do not include the Latin texts related to Usk's trial because, although they are of unquestionable importance to understanding Usk's biography and certainly therefore of importance in interpreting *TL*, they are not as immediately necessary to the reader's construal of *TL*. I base this opinion on my translation of the Latin text of Usk's "Appeal" as printed in Powell and Trevelyan; I have not, however, consulted this text in manu-

---

the same as those Jellech reports for her more elaborate undertaking — the text had obviously degenerated; and I conclude, therefore, that it is safe to assume no later printing need figure in my work.

script nor have I examined the manuscripts of other possibly relevant documents. At such time as I or other scholars studying those texts discover in them materials that are relevant to *TL*, I hope we will be able to post the findings to the World Wide Web in links to the hypertext version of *TL* that I am launching as a complement to this edition (see below, p. 25).

The decisions I have made in this regard and the judgments leading to them have various impulses, availability of time and space being principal ones (the edition needs to be finished and it can be only so long[12]). But one motive that I wish to make clear, just because I could well be wrong, is my sense, tentative as it may be, that *TL* is something more than Usk's autobiography. I do not mean for a moment that *TL* is not autobiographical — it most assuredly is. But only one book of the three is autobiographical as such, and only part of it (Book 1, chapters 6–8). Thus I have resisted the temptation to overwhelm the edition of *TL* with the (fascinating) work of constructing Usk's biography. If this proves to have been an error in judgment, corrections to this edition can be made electronically at a speed and with a degree of precision that should compensate in corrigibility for lapses in initial editorial judgment.

With these explanations in place, let me summarize what we currently assume we know of Usk's life. I base these remarks primarily on the researches of Paul Strohm, supplemented by the studies of Bird, Bressie, Galloway, Jellech and Leyerle. Thomas Usk was a scrivener and largely self-taught. A Londoner all his life, his origins were modest — his father a cap maker (Leyerle [1989], p. 333). He emerges into view in the 1380s as a player in the tortuous political factionalism of the period, what Ruth Bird aptly epitomizes as the "turbulent London of Richard II." Initially he sided with the faction of John of Northampton, a draper (craft guildsman) and mayor of London, but after being arrested and detained for his association with Northampton, he turned against him in 1384 and allied himself with Nicholas Brembre, a wealthy merchant ("often called simply a merchant [mercator], more often a grocer" — Bird, p. 4) who had defeated Northampton in the 1383 election for mayor of London. While in Brembre's custody, he experienced his change of heart and wrote his *Appeal* against Northampton and his associates (Appendix 2 below). His new allegiance, which eventually cost him his life, initially brought him under the patronage of the king and the royal faction generally. Between 1384 and 1387, when he appears as under-sheriff of Middlesex, appointed at the request of the King, he wrote *TL*: "For simplicity, we might simply think of the work as having been composed in 1385–86" (Strohm [1990], pp. 97–98 n18). But his fortunes deteriorated rapidly in late 1387. By Novem-

[12] See Machan, p. 190: "The Middle English canon . . . is very much a canon shaped by economics."

ber 1387 the Lords Appellant, as they came to be called, were underway with plans that would lead to the notorious Merciless Parliament of 1388. In this Parliament, the King and his faction suffered brutal defeat.[13] Among the numerous victims were Brembre (executed February 20, 1388) and Usk. Despised as a traitor, "faux and malveise" (Strohm [1990], p. 87), Usk

> was sentenced to be drawn, hanged, and beheaded. The sentence was carried out [on March 4, 1388] in a particularly brutal fashion. After being drawn and hanged, he was cut down while still alive and beheaded with agonizing slowness; records show that it took nearly thirty strokes of the sword. (Leyerle [1989], p. 334)

iii. Overview of *The Testament of Love*

If *TL* is autobiographical but also something more, the more consists in actually a wide variety of materials. For purposes of this introduction, I have elected to present these materials in the following outline: Plot, Sources, Imagery, Themes, Ideology. Of these five categories, the easiest to organize and describe is Imagery, the most difficult is Ideology (just because *TL* is often very confused, indeed frequently corrupt beyond construal).

Plot. The plot of *TL* in one sense is simple, in another frustrating. The Prologue and three Books comprise almost no action. Love descends into Usk's prison cell (the obvious model is Lady Philosophy coming to Boethius in the *Consolation*), and there they talk a good, long while. That's the "action." But the talk narrates other actions that are often frustratingly unclear — those surrounding Usk's arrest and imprisonment, for example — or represents ideas that sometimes seem to be hopelessly confused — free will and God's foreknowledge, for example. Below (pp. 44–45) I print a helpful summary, developed by Stephen Medcalf, of the progress of the chapters in each book, and I recommend that readers consult these summaries as they begin each book.

Sources. Usk's sources, the main ones, are fairly easy to identify: Boethius's *Consolation*, Anselm's *De Concordia*, and various works of Chaucer and Gower. He may have known *Piers Plowman*,[14] and other contemporary works may be conjectured as well (e.g., *The Cloud of*

---

[13] Richard would, of course, suffer even more brutal defeat some dozen years later when Bolingbroke deposed him. We have here, I strongly suspect, the main reason that no manuscripts of *TL* survive: it was perceived as Ricardian work by a Ricardian man — why would Lancastrians want copies of it circulating? Below I offer a conjecture as to why at least one copy of *TL* might have been preserved — see Section vi f, "The Problem of the Broken Sequence of Book 3."

[14] See pages 14–17 below, Section iv, "Usk and His Contemporaries."

Unknowing). But after these sources, the picture becomes obscure. Much about *TL* suggests that Usk was an autodidact; and I would be surprised if we were to find that he was able to avail himself of a stable library for long (which does not mean, of course, that he did not from time to time frequent libraries). Jellech plausibly adduces Vincent of Beauvais's *Speculum Majus* for many of her annotations, and it could be that Usk knew the four *specula* that make up this monumental medieval encyclopedia.[15] Clearly, he knew much of the kinds of lore that are found in such encyclopedias. He had, I now think, some access to several major works of St. Augustine (my notes will show extensive allusions and references), though I would hesitate to say that he knew these works firsthand. My suspicion is that he does use dictionaries, encyclopedias, or *florilegia* for many of his classical and patristic allusions and that these latter are garbled or weird or both because his source is abbreviated or incomplete or fragmented by imperfect recall from memory.[16]

Imagery. *TL*'s imagery, I should note at the outset, is the principal reason I first became interested in the work. Although much of it is obviously derivative (from Boethius and Chaucer, especially), there is also much that is idiosyncratic in fascinating and, I think, important ways. I wish to pause over this matter a moment to observe that the generalized sense widespread among medievalists that medieval literature is *un*original — i.e., topical and conventional — in the case of Usk finds peculiar exception. If we read in the Prologue to *TL* the phrase, "to pul up the spere that Alisander the noble might never wagge" (Prologue, lines 62–63), we may legitimately be perplexed at the apparent conflation of Arthur and Alexander: either this is just sloppy, which is always possible, or it represents a kind of idiosyncratic inventiveness[17] (the more likely case, I now think) that both provokes and dismays us — we wonder what it can mean, and we fear it may be garbled to the point of meaninglessness. I should observe that this is hardly an isolated case. I urge the reader to consider, as a sort of charitable minimum, that many of the

---

[15] See Twomey, pp. 182–215, for a helpful introduction to medieval encyclopedias.

[16] Jellech addresses Usk's sources at great length ([1970], pp. 53–118), some 65 pages. I have made no attempt to duplicate that work in this edition. In particular, and especially given also Leyerle's work with Usk's sources, I have deliberately chosen to minimize references wherever they are not instrumental for readers of this edition.

[17] On Usk's inventiveness, see Schaar, p. 13; Leyerle (1977), p. 325; and Medcalf, pp. 182, 194. C. S. Lewis (1936), p. 228, on the other hand, is as hard on Usk as Medcalf is approving of him:

> But Usk remains, even when we have made every allowance for a corrupt text, a clumsy and sometimes an unintelligible dialectician. All that he has to say can be found, much better, elsewhere.

Compare Lewis here with Medcalf ([1989], p. 182):

more impenetrable moments in *TL* may actually be the result of a quirky and unpolished learning that cobbles words together haphazardly but not without some degree of what we today would call imagination.

Be that as it may, there is much imagery in *TL* that can be accounted for. The most distinctive and widely documentable image is that of the pearl, the Margarite. Margarite is the beloved whom Usk serves and, at one point, he defines her allegorical significance thus: "Margarite a woman betokeneth grace, lernyng, or wisdom of God, or els holy church" (Book 3, lines 1123–24). This definition both helps and hinders. It helps in that in its simplicity and straightforwardness, it tells us who the Margarite is; it hinders in that, as the reader will soon learn, there are other "meanings" of the Margarite that do not quite square with this global definition (see especially Book 1, chapter 9). My sense of the matter is that the significance of the Margarite is so fluid that Usk himself is finally forced into the rather loose and baggy list of equivalents quoted above — he has as much difficulty as his reader controlling the sense, containing it, of his principal image.

Nor, in one regard at least, should this surprise us. The image of the pearl is both ancient and vast in its dissemination. The reader will find entire, lengthy articles devoted to it listed in Appendix 1, and I can hardly "cover" the matter in so brief a space as I have at my disposal here. But a few remarks do seem called for. First and foremost, the reader should be aware that Usk's use of the pearl in *TL* is far from an isolated instance in medieval English literature. The anonymous *Pearl* and the Marguerite tradition in French and English poetry are just two examples of contemporary dissemination (see Andrew and Waldron's edition for the former; Wimsatt's study for the latter). Next, the reader should note that the image and its allegorical significance have deep and important Scriptural warrant, most notably in Jesus's parable (Matthew 13.46).[18] The reader should also pay particular attention to the lapidary tradition which is

---

> Perhaps because Usk presumes in the book a dizzyingly analogical pattern in the universe, but more because his book is an exaltation of love and the new world which love has revealed to him, it is written, where it is engaged in philosophic argument, in a high style by no means as crabbed as it has sometimes appeared. It is in fact not only the first book of original philosophy in English, but also the first book in which English prose is made to have something of the pattern, gorgeousness and poignancy of poetry.

In the contrast between these two opinions, the reader will find why I have *not* attempted to "reconstruct" the *TL* in this edition. For more on this point, see below, page 18.

[18] See Vona for a massive compilation of patristic commentary; see also Ohly; and Wailes, pp. 120–24.

ubiquitous in medieval Europe and which features the pearl prominently. As examples of the sorts of information provided about the pearl, I have elected to cite in Appendix 1 several texts from different periods and languages; I include some brief commentary on them as well, plus additional bibliography. Note, in particular, when consulting them, the synonym "union" for the pearl — this word and the idea it conveys go a long way toward explaining the feel of the image of the pearl in *TL*.[19]

Before leaving the image of the pearl, it is necessary to comment on one feature of *TL* intimately connected with the pearl that is also a notorious crux. As the reader will learn at more length later in this introduction and in the annotations to the edition, *TL* is noteworthy for containing a famous acrostic formed of the initial letters of the chapters of each book. When restored (see below, vi c, for further discussion of this crux), the acrostic reads: MARGARETE OF VIRTW HAVE MERCI ON THIN USK.[20] The very progress of the chapters of *TL*, then, depend on the pearl, the Margarite, so completely does Usk invest his work with the image.

After the Margarite, the most important as it is also the most unusual image in *TL* is that of the knot. The knot figures centrally and extensively in Book 2 and serves there, as Jellech observes ([1970], pp. 99–100), as an equivalent to Boethius's *summum bonum* and *beatitudo*: at one point, God himself is said to be the "knotte of al goodnesse" (Book 2, line 1286). And yet this is hardly all that can be said, especially if one simply lists all the definitions of the knot in *TL* Book 2, chapters 4 and following. J.A.W. Bennett makes the very important observation (p. 350) that as a scrivener, Usk would have been intimately familiar with the practice of flourishing signatures with knots so as to make them unique and immune to forgery.[21] I suspect that

---

[19] The reader may also want to reflect on the history of the image of the pearl by recalling Claudius at the end (*Hamlet* V. ii. 271–74; Evans, p. 1184):

> The King shall drink to Hamlet's better breath,
> And in the cup an [union] shall he throw
> Richer than that which four successive kings
> In Denmark's crown have worn.

And see further V. ii. 282 and 326.

[20] Skeat opines (Thynne [1905], p. xl) "how Usk came to think of this curious device. . . .

> We may feel sure that Usk must have been acquainted with Higden's *Polychronicon*. . . . But this very device, of indicating the name of the author of a work by means of the initial letters of the chapters had already been adopted by Higden. . . . We see that Usk simply copied Higden's device.

For further comment, see Leyerle (1977), pp. xxviii–xxix, and Galloway, pp. 303–04.

[21] Bennett also cites a quotation from Butler in the *OED*:

Bennett is right and that corroboration can be found in other medieval and early modern artifacts and evidence. Perhaps the most famous knots in Middle English literature are those of *Sir Gawain and the Green Knight*; and in that poem, the pentangle (called a knot at lines 630 and 662) is not only a *summum bonum* of sorts but also a signature — as is also the green girdle (called a knot at lines 2376 and 2487), at the end of the poem especially, when it is adopted as a heraldic device by the whole court.[22]

But perhaps more important than sources or analogues or origins is the extraordinary history of the image of the knot. From Horace's *Ars poetica*[23] to the modern French denouement ("unknotting"), the knot has played an enduring and extensive role as an image of the specific complexity of life and man's search for meaning in life, as through literature. John Donne's "subtle knot, which makes us man"[24] or "knotty Trinity,"[25] or Dante's vision of God, "la forma universal di questo nodo,"[26] or Chaucer's Squire's "The knotte why that every tale is toold" (V F 401–08) or the Parson's attempt "To knytte up al this feeste and make an ende" (X [I] 47) are

---

As Scriveners take more pains to learn the slight
Of making knots, than all the hands they write.

For examples of such signature knots, see Preston and Yeandle, pp. 53, 61, 63, 65 (Queen Elizabeth I), and 79.

[22] See further Shoaf (1984), pp. 70 and 75; (1988), pp. 164–67.

[23] *Ars Poetica* 189–93:

Neve minor neu sit quinto productior actu
fabula quae posci volt et spectata reponi.
nec deus intersit, nisi dignus vindice nodus inciderit.

[A play should not be shorter or longer than five acts if, once it has been seen, it wishes to remain in demand and be brought back for return engagements. Nor should any god intervene unless a knot show up that is worthy of such a liberator (trans. Hardison and Golden, p. 13).]

[24] "The Ecstasy," line 64 (Carey, p. 123).

[25] See Holy Sonnet #12 (1–4) in Carey, p. 178:

Father, part of his double interest
Unto thy kingdom, thy Son gives to me,
His jointure in the knotty Trinity
He keeps, and gives me his death's conquest.

[26] "The universal form of this knot" — *Paradiso* 33.91 (trans. Singleton, p. 377); and see the perhaps even more famous "nodo" in Bonagiunta da Lucca's response to Dante's famous description of his poetics in *Purgatorio*, canto 24 (lines 55–57):

"O frate, issa vegg'io," diss' elli, "il nodo
che 'l Notaro e Guittone e me ritenne

all examples, among a great many,[27] of the same intellectual impulse that is at work in *TL*. The knot and meaning are felt in the human imagination as correlative. Meaning is a knot, it is knotty, and so when Usk comes in Book 2 to speak of the highest meaning, he calls it a knot, the substantative form of what has been knitted.

The Margarite and the knot are the most extensive and fully developed of Usk's images. Other images are important as well. Probably most significant in this latter group is the image of the "testament" itself. We should keep in mind how widespread this idea actually was in medieval and early modern literature: Henryson has his *Testament of Cresseid*; Villon, his *Testament*; and Gower, in *Confessio Amantis* (rather notoriously, given that *TL* was long thought to be by Chaucer), urges Chaucer to write his "testament of love" in his old age.[28] I have not pursued the "sub-genre" of medieval and early modern testaments, but I suspect we would learn a lot about *TL* from a systematic study of it.[29]

To look at representative examples of other images in *TL*, we may note, in Book 1 (line 270), the image of a ship wandering on the ocean (and conflated curiously with a wood full of wild animals — for the probable connection with Gower's *Vox Clamantis*, see below, p. 320, the note to 1.258ff.). In Book 2, we find an image of pillars in the sea to suggest strong or, to the contrary, unstable foundations (lines 490ff.). Agricultural imagery is frequent (Book 3, chapter 6, for example), and so are clouds (to suggest ignorance or confusion — Prologue, line 14). In Book 2 (chapter 4), we find a very elaborate image of the "three lives," which probably owes much to several different old and complex lores (see below the note at Book 2, lines 330ff.). Images from Scripture are not infrequent but usually left un- or underdeveloped.[30]

---

di qua dal dolce still nuovo ch'i'odo."

"O brother, now I see," he said, "the knot
that kept the Notary, Guittone, and me
short of the sweet new manner that I hear."

[27] A brief list of other examples might include Geoffrey of Vinsauf, *Poetria Nova* 1643–44 (trans. Nims, p. 74); *T&C* 5.766–70; Petrarch's *Rime sparse* 25, 59, 71, 196, 271, and 283; *Antony and Cleopatra* V.ii.301–03; and *Paradise Lost* 4.347–50. Then, too, there is the phenomenon of "entrelacement"/"interlace" — see the essay by Leyerle (1976); other helpful studies include Day and Evans.

[28] For Gower, see 8.2941–57 (Macaulay, vol. 2, p. 466); for Henryson, see the edition by Kindrick (pp. 147–86); and for Villon, see Sargent-Baur, pp. 51–193.

[29] See, among others, the studies by Perrow, Rice, and Sargent-Baur in her edition of Villon, p. 196 n 73.

[30] Here I list vocabulary items that signal main images in *TL*: beest, burjonen, cloud, clips, con-

Themes. *TL* is prolific in themes. Indeed, one underlying cause of its incoherence and occasional incomprehensibility is its prolixity in themes. Thus, for example, we find an elaborate defense of women at one point (Book 2, chapter 3); at another, we find an extraordinary excursus into the law, its kinds and functions (Book 3, chapters 1 and 2); a long and often vehement attack on avarice (Book 2, chapter 5); a sermonette on "gentilesse" (Book 2, chapter 2); a discourse on free will and God's foreknowledge (Book 3, throughout, but especially chapters 3, 4, 7, 8, 9). The list goes on. The reader must be perpetually prepared for the twists and turns, the incompletions, of many themes,[31] even as some others, the panegyric and defense of women, for example, are relatively shaped and even pointed. The effect of *TL* at the thematic level resembles a dilettantism of sorts, although, to be fair to Usk, I should temper that judgment by observing that he may have known more than he was capable always of expressing in his prose (this, of course, being a very uncertain matter because of the corruption of Thynne's edition).

Ideology. I have somewhat hesitantly chosen the term "ideology" to account for effects of *TL* I am insecure about otherwise categorizing. The term should be understood to cover "ideas" in some very basic sense, but I also include under it what I will call, for lack of a better term, sentiments — I do find the language of *TL* at times sentimental. Certainly, in a basic sense, Usk's ideology is Christian: he appears throughout the work a pious Christian (and is said to have gone to his death penitently and devoutly [Strohm (1990), p. 89]). But it is difficult, I think, to dispense with Usk's character or the ideology of *TL* as simply Christian. Obviously, Usk is also attuned to ideas of "courtly love" (Lewis [1936], pp. 222–31). He is deeply familiar with Boethius's *Consolation* and often clearly is to be understood as a student of Boethius. According to Jellech, following Conley and others, Usk, especially in his vocabulary and in his mode of argumentation as well, is "scholastic" (p. 98). Like many Christians of the Middle Ages, he feels the attraction and the ambiguity of the uneasy couple, Christianity and Philosophy.[32] He feels it acutely in his attempts rationally to reconcile concepts of a good God and an evil world or concepts of predestination and free will, especially since his rationality and his

founded, cosinage, crommes, daunger, ebbinge, endite, fantasye, fruite, graffed, jangeleres, knit, knot, pearl, prison, pyles, shyppe, styred, testament, tillers, tilth, wilde.

In the hypertext version of the edition that I plan to launch on the World Wide Web, I will index, key and "hotlink" these items.

[31] Medcalf speaks, in a felicitous phrase, of Usk's "lateral habits of mind" (1997), p. 251.

[32] The most eloquent witness is Dante — see Freccero, p. 24, for helpful comment.

prose are not always concordant (see especially Book 3).

Then, too, Usk was, in some sense, a politician, and as far as we can see, a failed one. His disappointments and disillusionments account for many of his ideas and expressions, though by no means all of them (Book 2 especially exceeds such an explanation). He ended up on the wrong side twice, in effect: with Northampton whom he subsequently turned against, and then with Brembre and the king when the Merciless Parliament turned against them. His complaints about his treatment at the hands of powerful individuals in the government of the 1380s sometimes elicit keen sympathy, for it seems clear, to me at least, that he had not grasped either the game he was playing or the players he was playing with. It is difficult to disagree with Paul Strohm: "A decent and epistemologically humble stab at comprehension, rather than judgment, is what we can offer poor Usk now" ([1992], p. 160). But a "decent and epistemologically humble stab at comprehension," to my mind, has to admit of some room for a lingering sense of unease about the intelligence of a man so distraught if not also distracted (see further, Galloway, p. 305).

My case could be illustrated with the example of Book 3's attempt at the problem of free will and God's foreknowledge, but in some ways that would be unfair — greater minds than Usk's have been defeated by this problem. Let me rather cite his curious quasi-feminism (Book 2, chapter 3). Here I am less interested in sources or even context than I am in sentiment. Usk celebrates and defends women in this longish passage in ways that are thoroughly traditional and patriarchal, seeming at times to want to say something about women as unique as it is important (for him), and yet all the while oblivious, as far as I can tell, to the massive institutionality underwriting what he says. It is perhaps not quite sentimentality, but it is an expression of emotion — a kind of "pitee," perhaps[33] — that is distracted from its bearer as much as it is from its bearer's desperate situation.

iv. Usk and His Contemporaries

Recent years have witnessed a stark increase in scholarly interest in this issue. In particular, numerous Langland scholars have revisited the question of Usk's first-hand knowledge of *Piers Plowman* C, which used to be assumed axiomatically (Donaldson, *The C-Text*, p. 19, following Devlin, "The Date of the C-Version"), and some have argued against such knowledge while others, just as vigorously, are arguing for it. John Bowers is a prominent Langland scholar of

[33] "Pitee renneth soone in gentil herte" — *CT* I A 1761.

the former persuasion; Kathryn Kerby-Fulton, one of the latter.[34] At this time, in my own researches, having read both Bowers ("Testing") and Kerby-Fulton and Justice ("Langlandian Reading Circles"), as well as others, I am of Bowers' persuasion — I doubt Usk knew *Piers* C at all and, even if he did, he would not, as I argue below, have cared to show it. This much said, however, I should acknowledge that this is a complex matter in need of much more elaborate treatment than I can afford it here. But I must, all the same, register my opinions and tentative conclusions if only to help users of this edition get their bearings in the matter.

In her 1970 thesis-edition of *TL* (pp. 77–81), Virginia Jellech argues that

> all of the passages cited by Skeat as indications that Usk had read *Piers Plowman* come under the category of the anonymous and conventional dicactic [*sic*] literature of the period or are attributable to St. Anselm. (p. 81)

At first, I was hesitant to accept Jellech's conclusion, seeing it as part of her general dissatisfaction with Skeat's work, which she is on occasion rather mordant in expressing (see below the note at Book 1, line 771). However, after long and systematic comparison of Usk's citations of Chaucer's *Troilus and Criseyde* with the proposed citations of *Piers*, I have come to agree with Jellech's position. The evidence for Usk's familiarity with *Piers* is questionable when compared with the evidence for his familiarity with *Troilus and Criseyde*. So far I have found nothing in *TL* proposed as an allusion to *Piers* as precise or as obvious as the allusions to *Troilus and Criseyde* in the following examples (of which there are some twenty more in the text):

Book 1, line 6: *Certes, her absence is to me an hell.* Compare *Trolius and Criseyde* 5.1396: "For though to me youre absence is an helle."

Book 1, lines 375–76: *O where haste thou be so longe commensal that hast so mykel eeten of the potages of foryetfulnesse*. Compare the identical phrasing in *Troilus and Criseyde* 4.496–97:

> "O, where hastow be hid so longe in muwe,
> That kanst so wel and formerly arguwe?"

Book 1, lines 443–44: *For this is sothe: betwixe two thynges lyche, ofte dyversité is required.* See *Troilus and Criseyde* 3.404–06:

> "Departe it so, for wyde-wher is wist
> How that ther is diverite requered

[34] I would like to take this occasion to thank John Bowers and Kathryn Kerby-Fulton and her co-author, Steven Justice, for their scholarly collegiality in sharing with me their work in progress or in press. Their goodwill has ensured that the METS *TL* is better informed than it otherwise could have been.

Bytwixen thynges like, as I have lered."

Book 1, lines 903–06: *What, trowest thou every ideot wotte the menynge and the privy entent of these thynges? They wene, forsothe, that suche accorde may not be, but the rose of maydenhede be plucked. Do waye, do waye. They knowe nothyng of this; for consente of two hertes alone maketh the fastenynge of the knotte*. Compare *Troilus and Criseyde* 2.890–94 (emphasis added):

"But wene ye that every wrecche woot
The parfit blisse of love? Why, nay, iwys!
They wenen all be love, if oon be hoot.
Do wey, do wey, they woot no thyng of this!"

These and many other passages show incontrovertible intimacy with *Troilus and Criseyde*,[35] almost as if Chaucer's poetry were a "second language" for Usk, and I hesitate to accord much credence to the *Piers* C argument until and unless similar intimacy with *Piers* C can be shown.[36] My own reading to date suggests anything but such intimacy. Of the 33 total references Skeat lists, for example, nine are actually to the notes in his edition of *Piers*, seven are mere "*cf.*"s or suggestions to compare *TL* and *Piers*, and the remainder are, with a few exceptions, instances where one can easily argue for the likelihood of a common source (e.g., *TL*, Book 2, line 618, and *Piers* C.7.225).

Thus, like Professor Bowers, I also incline to agree with Anne Hudson, in her comments on *TL* and *Piers* in her study, "The Legacy of *Piers Plowman*" that "some of the parallels produced seem unconvincing" (p. 253). Even she, though, goes on to write that "the echoes of the Tree of Charity are more persuasive." They may indeed seem so at first, but, as it turns out, Skeat's case may be weakest just here. There is abundant evidence, as Jellech suggests and my own researches also confirm now, that Usk may have developed his image from other sources, sources much more proximate, including possibly St. Anselm's *De Concordia*, which we know Usk was translating throughout large sections of Book 3 (see my notes below to Book 3, lines 576–77 and lines 806–07, especially, for more on this matter). I agree with Jellech (pp. 79–80) and Bowers ("Testing," typescript, p. 22) that a careful comparison of the tree images in *TL*

---

[35] Compare Bennett (Gray), p. 347: "The apparent familiarity with the *Troilus* and the *Boece* that he shows in his *Testament* may be due simply to his general recollection of passages that he had copied."

[36] Kerby-Fulton is at work on a list of parallels she proposes between *TL* and *Piers Plowman*; I have seen only a preliminary, incomplete version of this list that includes the passages in *TL* but not those in *Piers* supposed to be parallel.

and *Piers* shows not only that there are few similarities between them but indeed also radical differences.[37]

Professor Bowers shows in his forthcoming study that the effect of such conclusions, if they hold, will have crucial ramifications for the question of using *TL* as a *terminus ante quem* for the C-text of *Piers*. In conclusion, I would observe, for my part, that even if it were to turn out that Usk was aware of *Piers*, he perhaps would have had cause to mute any connection with it — where Usk stood politically, *Piers* was probably, as we would say today, "incorrect." This matter needs more careful attention, naturally, but I can easily imagine the case that Usk would have felt uncomfortable through any association with Langland's politics (see also Bowers, "Testing," typescript, p. 29); whereas, as Strohm has shown ([1989], p. 106), Usk would have wanted very much to associate himself with Chaucer and Chaucer's politics. It should be observed, too, that this argument also cuts the other way: Langland may have eschewed any reference to or implication in *TL* because involvement would have been for him as well politically inexpedient, especially after Usk's brutal execution.[38]

v. Importance of *The Testament of Love*

The importance of *TL* in English literary history can and should be measured from a variety of perspectives. Narrowly, it tells us something about politics and society in England in the 1380s. Also it records early, perhaps first, mentions of major contemporary works, especially Chaucer's *Trolius and Criseyde*. More broadly viewed, it is perforce a key document in the history of the development of English prose. And it is equally an important document in our

---

[37] See, further, Lewis (1995), pp. 432–33; see also Medcalf (1997), p. 248: "Given their common religion and their common culture, it must remain uncertain whether Usk took the image of the tree from Langland."

[38] My positions here depend primarily on Strohm and Bressie, although I am very pleased to acknowledge my several conversations with Bowers which helped me refine my thought. I also want to record my debt to Leyerle's work. I find his arguments on the distinctiveness of the mode and idiom of the *Testament* congenial (p. 393):

> Idioms appropriate to a man's political service to his lord had been transferred since the twelfth century to the situation of a lover's service to his lady. In the *Testament* Usk does the reverse: idioms appropriate to a lover's service to a lady are applied to Usk's political service to his lord. Usk's intentional application of the language of love service to his situation in London politics is central to an understanding of the mode and idiom of the *Testament*.

This argument has merit. And I find it helpful in understanding the vexed issue of Usk and Langland's

assessment of the kinds of learning or scholarship that were attainable in the 1370s and 1380s in England. (By contrast with Usk, Chaucer is not only more learned but also more conscious of what it means to be learned — more "disenchanted," in H. Marshall Leicester's sense of the term [pp. 26–27, especially]). More broadly still, *TL* is witness to something like a newly emerging idea of the relationship between self, society, and writing that we experience repeatedly in other monuments of fourteenth-century English culture (Strohm [1990], [1992]; Galloway).

vi. Guide to this Edition

Here I offer the reader a fuller guide to this edition as a tool. I want to emphasize that this edition is designed for the full range of students of Middle English culture — hence this elaboration.

The Transcription. In this edition I undertake a diplomatic transcription:

> The diplomatic transcript . . . dispenses with any attempt at such scrupulous fidelity to appearance, and concentrates primarily on the textual content of the original, reproducing the exact spelling, punctuation, and capitalization (usually) of the *diploma* (the document), but transcribing the text into a different type-face, with different lineation (except in verse, of course) and different type-sizes. (Greetham [1994], p. 350)

My reason for approaching *TL* in this way is simple. We have only one text — we need a faithful transcription of it into modern typography (electronic and print alike). That one text is severely corrupt, so corrupt that emendation as such would have to be so global as to arouse nothing but controversy (see Medcalf [1989], p. 188). Hence I emend sparingly and only when I feel the weight of probability is preponderant that I will help matters by doing so. I am not suffering from what E.Talbot Donaldson called the "editorial death-wish" (quoted in Greetham [1994], p. 296), "the desire to pretend that one's handiwork as editor is invisible" — to the contrary, my handiwork is evident everywhere in the glosses and in my re-presentation of the text. And yet, this is *not* a translation — it is an edition, if an edition only loosely speaking. It is a diplomatic transcription, with my deliberately minimal(-ist) construal of the work running contrapuntally to the transcription, supplemented by glosses and a confessed minimum of annotation. Thus it aspires to be, approximately, an *editio in usum scholarium*.

---

possible relationship. If Leyerle and Strohm are right, there would have been, I conjecture, a real antipathy between Usk and Langland, deriving from their very different political agenda.

Transcription Conventions. Folio numbers in Thynne are marked in the following manner: **<337rb><337va>**, to be read thus: here column b of folium 337 recto concludes and column a of folium 337 verso begins. Abbreviations are expanded and marked by italics. Virgules are included along with the other minimal punctuation that Thynne marks. Hyphenation is silently closed up, as are unmarked columnar spillovers. I have not reproduced Thynne's spacing.

How to Read this Edition. As an *editio in usum scholarium* this is not the definitive, final, once-and-for-all version of *TL*. It is a device for scholars and students to construct their own sense of *TL* from the accumulated information, recognizing always that what they will have as a result is a construct — i.e., something subject constantly to revision. To read the text, then, under these constraints, I would hope that the reader would proceed as follows. Start with Thynne. Read his text with the help of the glosses and the notes, *experimenting with punctuation options as these emerge principally from the lexicon* (do not ignore the virgules — they are on occasion helpful[39]). Use my pointing of the text only as an aid to construal, always remembering that it is conjectural and deliberately minimal(-ist). In the case of Book 1, chapters 6–8 and Book 3, chapters 3 and following, the material in Appendices 2 and 3 will help but can not be treated as substitutes for the text of *TL* or as furloughs from having to think about the text. And thinking about *TL* can, as Medcalf (1989) has shown, have its rewards.

Glosses and Glossary. The reader will notice not only that there are a lot of glosses, but also that there is considerable repetition. The reason for this is simple. Many are the second and subsequent instances of a term that I gloss not because I doubt the reader's memory but because I am trying to help the reader in this or that passage to understand the passage in its own particular recalcitrances. The reader may well remember what this or that word meant in other contexts but I want to help the reader understand the whole passage in which that word is met again. The Glossary makes no pretensions to exhaustiveness; rather it includes only those words which may be difficult, but which have not always been glossed. Hence if I have failed to repeat a gloss when it is needed, the reader can have recourse to the Glossary. If the hard word appears only a few times in the text and is always glossed, it will not appear in the glossary.

Annotations. I have freely borrowed from Jellech, Leyerle, Schaar, and Skeat in the annotations where their work in my judgment clearly will help the reader of *TL*.

My own contributions to the annotations may be classified as follows. First and foremost,

[39] Leyerle reports (p. x) that in his text, "extensive use was made of Thynne's punctuation, which is usually helpful, but occasionally mistaken." I tend to disagree with Thynne's punctuation somewhat more often than Leyerle.

where I think I can, I clarify the sense of passages corrupt or otherwise likely to confuse the reader — bear in mind, though, as I have already said, that I eschew conjectural construal in many cases of corruption because of the peculiar nature of *TL*'s transmission. Next, I offer many more references to Chaucer's *Troilus and Criseyde* than do my predecessors, believing that I have identified many hitherto undetected echoes. I also include references to Boethius's *Consolation*, though this matter is vexed. I disagree with Skeat who finds Boethius and/or Chaucer's *Boece* practically everywhere in *TL*, but I also disagree with Jellech who dismisses Skeat's opinion. My own position most closely resembles that of the editors of *Boece* for the *Riverside Chaucer*:

> Our independent examination of Usk convinces us that he did use *Boece*, although Skeat exaggerates the extent of that use; we disagree with Virginia Jellech's conclusion . . . that he used only Jean de Meun.[40]

Hence the reader will notice that often in my annotations, where Boethius is involved, I include reference to the *Riverside Chaucer* edition of *Boece* as a help toward exploring Usk's use of Chaucer's translation; but I make no effort to tabulate every reference to the *Consolation* or the *Boece*.

Where the historical context of *TL* is concerned, I have adopted two approaches. On the one hand, I depend on Paul Strohm's researches since it seems generally agreed that his constructions of the available evidence are the best we currently have. On the other, I include in an Appendix the Middle English text that comes down to us on the trial of Usk, "The Appeal." My recommendation to the reader is to read *TL* Book 1, chapters 6–8 first, then the Appendix; then re-read Book 1, chapters 6–8 with the Appendix in mind and to hand. A student of Usk in the 1380s will want to consult Strohm's studies at length for a fully documented and nuanced account of the matter.

The Problem of the Broken Sequence of Book 3. In section iii c (Imagery), I called attention to the famous acrostic in *TL* (MARGARETE OF VIRTW HAVE MERCI ON THIN USK) and to the crux surrounding it. That crux involves the order or sequence of chapters in Thynne's edition. For efficiency's sake, it will be best initially to quote the main part of Skeat's explanation ([1897], pp. xix-xx):

> . . . the initial letters of the various chapters were certainly intended to form an acrostic. Unfortunately, Thynne did not perceive this design, and has certainly begun some of the

[40] Hanna and Lawler (p. 1003); Siennicki provides an elaborate table of correspondences between *TL* and *Boece* in her thesis (pp. 225–63).

> chapters either with the wrong letter or at a wrong place. The sense shews that the first letter of Book I. ch. viii. should be E, not O . . . and, with this correction, the initial letters of the First Book yield the words — MARGARETE OF. In Book II, Thynne begins Chapters XI and XII at wrong places, viz. with the word "Certayn" . . . [line 1048] and the word "Trewly" . . . [below, Book 2, line 1127]. He thus produces the words — VIRTW HAVE MCTRCI. It is obvious that the last word ought to be MERCI, which can be obtained by beginning Chapter XI with the word "Every," which suits the sense quite as well. For the chapters of Book III, we are again dependent on Thynne. If we accept his arrangement as it stands, the letters yielded are — ON THSKNVI; and the three books combined give us the sentence: — MARGARETE: OF VIRTW, HAVE MERCI ON THSKNVI. Here "Margarete of virtw" means "Margaret endued with divine virtue"; and the author appeals either to the Grace of God, or to the Church. The last word ought to give us the author's name; but in that case the letters require rearrangement before the riddle can be read with certainty. After advancing so far towards the solution of the mystery, I was here landed in a difficulty which I was unable to solve. But Mr. H. Bradley, by a happy inspiration, hit upon the idea that the text might have suffered dislocation; and was soon in a position to prove that no less than six leaves of the MS. must have been out of place, to the great detriment of the sense and confusion of the argument. He very happily restored the right order, and most obligingly communicated to me the result. I at once cancelled the latter part of the treatise . . . and reprinted this portion in the right order, according to the sense. With this correction, the unmeaning THSKNVI is resolved into the two words THIN USK, i.e. "thine Usk". . . .

One crucial modification is immediately necessary here. Jellech ([1970], pp. 12–14) explains it most efficiently:

> Skeat made two different sets of changes in the order of the text in Thynne. The first set of changes was that recommended by Bradley in working out the acrostic. In them Skeat merely placed the parts of the latter half of the third book so as to make the parts conform to the demands of the acrostic. In addition, however, Skeat made a second set of changes. He interchanged portions of Chapters 5 and 6 of Book III to conform to his notion of the development of Usk's argument. That is, I assume this to be the case, for he makes no note or mention of such change in his edition. I find this interchange of Chapters 5 and 6 to be wholly unjustified and in my text they appear just as they do in Thynne. The gist of the matter is Usk's use of the metaphor of the tree of bliss, which is grounded in free choice and grows in the fruit of joy. As Miss Bressie has pointed out, the order in Thynne (after

> the chapters have been arranged in accordance with the acrostic) is logical: first the ground, then the spire, and finally the fruiting branches. Skeat would reverse the spire and the ground . . . .

Readers will find, therefore, that, to be completely accurate, I refer to the Bradley-Skeat order, *as modified by Bressie* (see her explanation, quoted on the next page). My edition, in offering the Bradley-Skeat order as modified by Bressie, also follows Jellech and Leyerle. Finally, I have provided the readers of my edition the elements necessary to test for themselves this reconstruction of the sequence of Book 3 — *i.e.*, both texts in parallel.

Having adopted the Bradley-Skeat order, as modified by Bressie, for Book 3, I proceed to explain my decision. The solution I offer here to the question of the order or arrangement of Book 3 depends mainly on Ramona Bressie's arguments, partly on Paul Strohm's, and partly on the general, diffuse sense of several scholars who recently have recorded Lancastrian behavior following the deposition of Richard II. My position can best be grasped by acknowledging the seeming tautology that if we can re-order Book 3 to accord with the acrostic, then it must have been at one time ordered to accord with the acrostic: that is, there was once something visible there that became invisible through the disordering of the Book's chapters.

I propose then, following Bressie and Strohm, that the part of the manuscript containing Book 3 was deliberately mutilated in order to erase the name of Usk and any possible allusion to Richard II; this mutilation was a Lancastrian agenda, like the obliteration of Richard's portrait from Bodley MS 581 (Bennett [1992], p. 16); and its motive was the new regime's systematic desire to legitimate itself (Hanawalt, p. xiii). Hence also the preservation of at least the one manuscript, rather than its total obliteration, since the new king, the usurper, might someday avail himself of a treatise in support of royalty against unruly Londoners just as usefully and conveniently as his deposed predecessor could have done.[41] The treatise and its arguments were worth preserving, in other words, if only as one of many possible hedges against future conflict with Londoners (and if thus in one copy only), but minus any references to Usk and Richard.

Key to my arguments are Bressie's conclusions which I, therefore, feel obliged to quote here at considerable length, with emphasis added to crucial phrases (p. 28):

[41] Consider, in this light, how attractive to any sovereign the following would appear (Book 1, lines 105–08): *For I trowe this is wel knowe to many persones that otherwhyle, if a man be in his soveraignes presence, a maner of ferdenesse crepeth in his herte not for harme but of goodly subjection, namely as men reden that aungels ben aferde of our savyour in heven.*

> It may be that the problem of Margarite may be solved through the text of the *TL*, for there is a chance that *it is not complete*, and that the missing portion contains definite information on the King and Margarite. I have tried in vain to reconstruct the quires of the manuscript on the assumption that it is complete. Skeat's reconstruction in his edition (pp. xxi–xxii) is certainly wrong, for by actually counting the lines in Thynne's edition I find that Skeat assigned to the "first 10 quires" what is contained in 5, 556 lines of the Thynne text, while the rest of the text, amounting to 1, 374 lines in Thynne, Skeat assigns to one quire and 2 folios of another, or to 10 folios in all. The first 10 quires would contain 80 folios in all. But the ration of 10 to 80 is not the ratio of 1, 374 to 5, 556. Also Skeat's scheme for the arrangement of the manuscript is wrong, for it accounts for the disarrangement of seven parts, which he numbered as they are printed in Thynne, 1, 2, 3, 4, 5, 6, 7. These, he believed, took in the manuscript in order 5, 3, 6, 2, 4, 1, 7. According to this scheme, 6 and 2 make up Thynne's chap. v which is Skeat's chap. vi, while 3 is Thynne's chap. vi which is Skeat's chap. v. But Thynne'sorder is correct in these two chapters, and Skeat's is wrong, because while chap. v in Skeat discusses the trunk of the tree, chap. vi discusses the ground in which the tree grows, although logically and by indications in the text such as the summary of the allegory (p. 133, II. 10ff.), "First the ground, etc.; and the stocke, etc.," the order should be as in Thynne, i.e., the chapter on the ground first and then the chapter on the tree. With this error corrected Skeat's seven parts take the order 5, 6, 2, 3, 4, 1, 7, indicating that there are really only four parts, viz., 5 and 6; 2, 3, and 4; 1; and 7. *This shows that the quire was turned inside out and reversed.* But the apparent halves will not match up evenly. The first part contains 512 lines, the second 494 lines, the third 378, and the fourth 80 lines, of the Thynne text, and these will not balance unless we assume that part of the text is missing. There seems to be some ground for such an assumption in two facts: (1) that of the three books of the *TL*, the third alone lacks a lyrical chapter after the Prologue; and (2) that in II, iv, 121, Love says: "To the gracious king art thou mikel holden of whos grace and goodnesse somtyme hereafter I thinke thee enforme, whan I shew the ground whereas moral virtue groweth"; yet when in Book III Love discusses the ground wherein moral virtue groweth, there is nothing about the King, nor is there such a passage, to the best of my knowledge, in the whole of the *TL*. If it ever existed, it may have been a poem, and a poem would be more likely *to be torn out entire than any one of the prose chapters*. Such a poem might possibly contain a full explanation of who Margarite is; so would the treatise on Margarite which, in II, i, 125–28, Usk proposed to write.

Note, especially, that my argument does not hinge on Bressie's speculation about a poem.

Whether or not there was a poem is less relevant than the possibility that there was some allusion to Richard II: such an allusion would have led to a section of the manuscript being "torn out entire." We may add to Bressie's conclusion Strohm's regarding the effacement of Usk from the records of Northampton's trial ([1992], p. 157):

> Apparent as we move through these three documents is a progressive effacement of Usk's role, a process in which our would-be appellant becomes a mere witness and finally ends up as a minor participant, glancingly mentioned, far short of eligibility to stand with Northampton and his confederates in the dock there at the Tower in September 1384, so small a fish that he was not even physically present in the room!

It will be evident now why I start with the seeming tautology: in the hypothesis that I offer, there must have been something there in the first place to mutilate, something offending that some prejudiced reader/user wished to remove — namely, references or allusions to Usk and Richard II repugnant to a Lancastrian;[42] and the easiest means of removal would have been mangling the quire and re-inserting it in the manuscript.[43] Hence, as well, an explanation of Thynne's imprint: Thynne and his printer simply printed what they had in hand; they are not responsible for the mangling — Thynne's reverence for Chaucer would not have countenanced that anyway; neither Thynne or any of the sixteenth-century readers, I hypothesize, noticed the

---

[42] The offending matter may once have been even more obvious (Skeat, [Thynne, 1905], p. xl):

> Mr. Bradley has since kindly pointed out to me [*viz.*, Skeat] that Usk's first design seems to have been to make his sentence end with THOMAS VSK instead of THIN VSK. There is a conspicuous O in Chapter IV of Book III, and a conspicuous M in Chapter V. . . . The A at . . . and the S at . . . are less certain, and the reading THIN certainly sounds better, and is more convincing.

The reader may find these letters in the METS edition below: O, at Book 3, line 497; M, at Book 3, line 709; A, at Book 3, line 798; S, at Book 3, line 662 (but in Skeat's order, not out of sequence). I am not so confident as Skeat that THIN "is more convincing"; but, be that as it may, if the acrostic once read THOMAS, all the more reason a Lancastrian would then have had to mutilate the offending section of the manuscript.

[43] Leyerle's conclusions are relevant here. He reports (p. xxii):

> I had worked out the correction to the Bradley shift completely before noticing that Ramona Bressie had come to much the same conclusion, although her analysis does not correspond in all the details to the one presented here.

The main difference between Leyerle and Bressie is Leyerle's hypothetical reconstruction of the gatherings of Book 3 and the explanation therefrom of the disordering that occurred. Although his argument is far too long to cite (it runs to many pages, complete with figures and tables), the conclusion he reaches is worth quoting (p. xxi):

> Gatherings o, p, and q contained the dislocation. Stripped of the unnecessary complexities introduced by Bradley and compounded by Skeat, the dislocation of texts in the *Testament*

acrostic nor therefore did they bother with the arrangement of the chapters of Book 3. Of this matter, Thynne is innocent, if also therefore ignorant.[44]

In conclusion, I would like to say that if a better, demonstrably more complete and accurate account of the disordering of Book 3 of *TL* should be proposed, I will be among the first to embrace it. I am not so enamored of the arguments above as to cling to them unreasonably. But I would like to say, after years of struggling with this problem, that the arguments I have put forth do seem to me at least to be credible and at best "to save the appearances" of such evidence as we have.

Hypertext Version. The entire edition exists also in electronic form. Out of this electronic archive, I have created a tagged version of Thynne's edition. This tagged version has been launched on the World Wide Web, and it will eventually be supplemented by the glosses and the annotations (expanded). The hypertext version on the WWW will, of course, be accessible via the Internet to all users in the world interested in *TL*; and I invite them to post to me their additions, suggestions, desiderata, corrigenda, and complaints (exempla@nervm.nerdc.ufl.edu). I will for several years to come regularly update the project and I expect to include, with full acknowledgment, any contributions received from the scholarly community.

---

is, thus, very simple: gatherings o and q were interchanged.

If this is correct — a big "if," to be sure, given the complexity of the matter — it would tend to favor my own hypothesis: someone simply switched the two gatherings.

[44] I could be wrong, however, I admit. It is conceivable that Thynne is, in fact, the culprit. Thynne may have recognized the acrostic and deliberately mangled Book 3 to conceal Usk's name, the better therefore to pass the work off as Chaucer's — we know what "Chaucer-olatry" flourished in Henry VIII's court (see above Blodgett, note 1). I am not reluctant to assign such a dark motive to Thynne out of any sentimentality: it is possible that he mutilated the text, indeed mutilated it even out of a reverence for Chaucer (to augment him in the eyes of Henry's court), placing *TL* after the *House of Fame*, definitively Chaucer's, as a kind of extension of that poem's argument, which in a great many ways it is (see especially the note to Book 1, line 652, below). But of the two interpretations of the available evidence, I think at this time that the one I have offered above is much more likely to approximate the truth: the motive is clear, the result comprehensible, the politics altogether (alas) explicable.

Select Bibliography (with Annotations)

Alford, John A. *Piers Plowman: A Guide to the Quotations*. Binghamton: MRTS, 1991.

Dante Alighieri. *The Divine Comedy*. Trans. Charles S. Singleton. 3 vols. in 6. Bollingen Series 80. Princeton: Princeton University Press, 1970–75.

———. *Monarchia*. Ed. Prue Shaw. Cambridge: Cambridge University Press, 1995.

Allen, Don Cameron. *The Legend of Noah: Renaissance Rationalism in Art, Science, and Letters*. Urbana: University of Illinois Press, 1963.

Anselm, St. *Works*. Ed. and trans. Jasper Hopkins and Herbert Richardson. 4 vols. New York: Edwin Mellen Press, 1975–76.

Aquinas, St. Thomas. *Nature and Grace: Selections from the Summa Theologica of Thomas Aquinas*. Ed. and trans. A. M. Fairweather. Philadelphia: Westminster Press, 1954.

Aristotle. *Nicomachean Ethics*. Trans. H. Rackham. Cambridge: Harvard University Press, 1926.

———. *Peri Hermenias*. *On Interpretation*. Trans. Harold P. Cooke. Cambridge: Harvard University Press, 1938.

———. *De Partibus Animalium* I and *De Generatione Animalium* I. Trans. with notes by D. M. Balme. Oxford: Clarendon Press, 1992.

Augustine, St. *Enarrationes in Psalmos*. "Expositions on the Book of Psalms." In 6 vols. Trans. by Members of the English Church. Oxford: John Henry Parker, various dates. Vol. 4, 1850; vol. 6, 1857.

———. *De Natura Boni*. "The Nature of the Good Against the Manichees." Trans. John H. S. Burleigh. Philadelphia: Westminster Press, 1953.

———. *Confessions*. Trans. R. S. Pine-Coffin. Harmondsworth: Penguin, 1961.

———. *De Trinitate*. Trans. Stephen McKenna. Washington, DC: Catholic University of America Press, 1963.

———. *City of God*. Ed. and introduction by David Knowles. Trans. Henry Bettenson. Harmondsworth: Penguin, 1972.

Baldwin, John W. *The Language of Sex: Five Voices from Northern France around 1200*. Chicago: University of Chicago Press, 1994.

Barber, Richard. *Henry Plantagenet*. Ipswich, Suffolk: Boydell Press, 1972.

Bassett, Steven, ed. *The Origins of Anglo-Saxon Kingdoms*. London: Leicester University Press, 1989.

Bennett, J. A. W. *Middle English Literature*. Ed. and completed by Douglas Gray. Oxford: Clarendon Press; New York: Oxford University Press, 1986.

Bennett, Michael J. "The Court of Richard II and the Promotion of Literature." In Hanawalt. Pp. 3–20.

Bible. *The Holy Bible*. Douay-Rheims Translation. Rockford, IL: Tan Books and Publishers, Inc., 1971.

Bird, Ruth. *The Turbulent London of Richard II*. London: Longman, Green and Co., 1949.

Blodgett, James E. "William Thynne." In *Editing Chaucer: The Great Tradition*. Ed. Paul G. Ruggiers. Norman, OK: Pilgrim Books, 1984. Pp. 35–52.

Boethius. *Philosophiae consolatio*. Ed. Ludwig Bieler. CCSL (Corpus Christianorum Series Latina) 94. Turnhout: Brepols, 1957.

———. *De institutione arithmetica*. Trans. Michael Masi. Amsterdam: Rodopi, 1983.

The Testament of Love

Bowers, John. "Dating *Piers Plowman*: Testing the Testimony of Usk's *Testament*." Unpublished typescript, 1997.

Bressie, Ramona. "A Study of Thomas Usk's 'Testament of Love' as an Autobiography." Ph.D. Diss., University of Chicago, 1928. [An early, still very important study of the life of Usk, with much information about his immediate historical context.]

———. "The Date of Thomas Usk's *Testament of Love*." *Modern Philology* 26 (1928), 17–29. [Argues, drawing on research for the thesis mentioned in the item above, for a date of composition for *TL* of December 1384–June 1385.]

Brooks, Nicholas. "The Creation and Early Structure of the Kingdom of Kent." In Bassett. Pp. 55–74.

Bruns, Gerald L. "The Originality of Texts in a Manuscript Culture." In *Inventions: Writing, Textuality, and Understanding in Literary History*. New Haven: Yale University Press, 1982. Pp. 44–59.

Burnley, J. D. "Chaucer, Usk, and Geoffrey of Vinsauf." *Neophilologus* 69 (1985), 284–93. [A study of the writers' interest in and use of rhetorics and *artes poeticae*, such as Geoffrey of Vinsauf's.]

Burns, J. H., ed. *The Cambridge History of Medieval Political Thought c.350–c.1450*. Cambridge: Cambridge University Press, 1988.

Burrow, John. *The Ages of Man: A Study in Medieval Writing and Thought*. Oxford: Clarendon Press, 1986.

Canning, J. P. "Law, Sovereignty and Corporation Theory, 1300–1450." In Burns. Pp. 454–76.

Carlson, David R. "Chaucer's *Boethius* and Thomas Usk's *Testament of Love*: Politics and Love in the Chaucerian Tradition." In *The Centre and Its Compass: Studies in Medieval Literature in Honor of Professor John Leyerle*. Ed. Robert Taylor, James Burke, Patricia Eberle, Ian Lancashire, and Brian Merrilees. Kalamazoo: Medieval Institute Publications, 1993. Pp. 29–70.

[Attempts a global assessment of the *Testament*, drawing on the work of Leyerle, and argues in particular, among many other points, for close affinities between the *TL* and Chaucer's *Troilus and Criseyde* and *Boece.*]

Cary, George. *The Medieval Alexander*. Ed. D. J. A. Ross. Cambridge: Cambridge University Press, 1956.

Catholicon Anglicum, an English-Latin Wordbook, dated 1483. Ed. Sidney J. H. Herrtage. EETS o.s. 75. London: N. Trübner, 1881.

Chance, Jane. *Medieval Mythography: From Roman North Africa to the School of Chartres, A.D. 433–1177*. Gainesville: University Press of Florida, 1994.

Chaucer, Geoffrey. *The Riverside Chaucer*. Gen. ed. Larry D. Benson. Boston: Houghton Mifflin, 1987.

The Cloud of Unknowing and the Book of Privy Counselling. Ed. Phyllis Hodgson. EETS o.s. 218. London: Oxford University Press, 1944.

Cole, Andrew W. "Trifunctionality and the Tree of Charity: Literary and Social Practice in *Piers Plowman*." *ELH* 62 (1995), 1–27.

Conley, John. "Scholastic Neologisms in Usk's *Testament of Love*." *Notes & Queries* 11 (1964), 209.

———. "The Lord's Day as the Eighth Day: A Passage in Thomas Usk's 'The Testament of Love'." *Notes & Queries* 17 (1970), 367–68.

Cursor Mundi (The cursur o the world). A Northumbrian poem of the XIVth century in four versions. Ed. Richard Morris. EETS o.s. 57, 59, 62, 66, 68, 99, 101. London: K. Paul, Trench, Trübner & Co., 1874–93.

Curtius, E. R. *European Literature and the Latin Middle Ages*. Trans. W. R. Trask. Princeton: Princeton University Press, 1953.

Dagenais, John. *The Ethics of Reading in a Manuscript Culture: Glossing the "Libro de buen amor."* Princeton: Princeton University Press, 1994.

Day, Cyrus L. *Quipus and Witches' Knots: The Role of the Knot in Primitive and Ancient Cultures*. Lawrence, KS: University of Kansas Press, 1967.

Devlin, Sister Mary Aquinas. "The Date of the C Version of *Piers Plowman*." Ph.D. Diss., University of Chicago, 1925.

Dictionary of the Middle Ages. Gen. ed. Joseph R. Strayer. New York: Scribner, 1982–89.

Donaldson, E. Talbot. *Piers Plowman: The C-Text and its Poet*. New Haven: Yale University Press, 1949.

Donati, Renzo. "The Threefold Concept of Love in Usk's *Testament*." In *Genres, Themes, and Images in English Literature from the Fourteenth to the Fifteenth Century*. Ed. Piero Boitani and Anna Torti. Beiträge zur Anglistik, 11. Tübingen: Günter Narr, 1988. Pp. 59–72. [Analyzes the degree of coherence of Usk's notion of love and its relationship to his allegory; frequent comparisons to Dante's *Commedia*.]

Donne, John. *John Donne*. Ed. John Carey. Oxford: Oxford University Press, 1990.

Dove, Mary. *The Perfect Age of Man's Life*. Cambridge: Cambridge University Press, 1986.

Downing, Christine. "Athena." In *Encyclopedia of Religion*. Volume 1. Ed. Mircea Eliade. New York: Macmillan, 1987. Pp. 490–91.

Destruction of Troy. The "Gest Hystoriale" of the Destruction of Troy: An Alliterative Romance translated from Guido de Colonna's "Hystoria Troiana." Ed. George A. Panton and David Donaldson. EETS o.s. 39 and 56. London: N. Trübner & Co., 1869–74.

Dronke, Peter. "Arbor Caritatis." In Heyworth. Pp. 207–53.

Eco, Umberto, and Constantina Marmo, eds. "Denotation." In *On the Medieval Theory of Signs*. Amsterdam: John Benjamins, 1989. Pp. 43–77.

Eco, Umberto, Roberto Lambertini, Constantino Marmo, and Andrea Tabarroni. "On Animal Language in the Medieval Classification of Signs." In Eco and Marmo. Pp. 3–41.

Edwards, A. S. G. "Walter Skeat." In *Editing Chaucer: The Great Tradition*. Ed. Paul G. Ruggiers. Norman, OK: Pilgrim Books, 1984. Pp. 171–89.

Evans, G. Blakemore. "Donne's 'Subtile Knot'." *Notes & Queries* 34 (1987), 228–30.

Evans, Joan, and Mary S. Serjeantson. *English Mediaeval Lapidaries*. EETS o.s. 190. London: Oxford University Press, 1933.

Farmer, David Hugh. *The Oxford Dictionary of Saints*. Third ed. Oxford: Oxford University Press, 1992.

Forni, Kathleen. "The Chaucerian Apocrypha: Did Usk's 'Testament of Love' and the 'Plowman's Tale' Ruin Chaucer's Early Reputation?" *Neuphilogische Mitteilungen* 98 (1997), 261–72.

Fowler, Alastair. *Spenser and the Numbers of Time*. New York: Barnes & Noble, 1964.

Freccero, John. *Dante: The Poetics of Conversion*. Ed. Rachel Jacoff. Cambridge: Harvard University Press, 1986.

Galfridus Anglicus (fl. 1440). *The Promptorium Parvulorum. The First English-Latin Dictionary*. Ed. A.L. Mayhew. EETS e.s. 102. London: K. Paul, Trench, Trübner & Co., 1908.

Galloway, Andrew. "Private Selves and the Intellectual Marketplace in Late Fourteenth-Century England: The Case of the Two Usks." *New Literary History* 28 (1997), 291–318. Also URL http://www.georgetown.edu/labyrinth/conf/cs95/papers/galloway.html. [Similar to Strohm's studies; argues for the cultural production of the self in the autobiographical elements of *TL*.]

Geoffrey of Vinsauf. *Poetria Nova*. Trans. Margaret F. Nims. Toronto: PIMS, 1967.

Gibbon, Edward. *The History of the Decline and Fall of the Roman Empire*. 6 vols. in 3. Ed. David Womersley. London: Allen Lane, Penguin Press, 1994.

Gilby, Thomas. *The Political Thought of Thomas Aquinas*. Chicago: University of Chicago Press, 1958.

Glossa Ordinaria. Biblia sacra, cum glossa ordinaria et expositione Lyre litterali et morali, quinta pars. Basel, 1498.

Gower, John. *The Complete Works of John Gower*. Ed. G. C. Macaulay. 4 vols. Oxford: Clarendon Press, 1899–1902.

Greetham, D. C. *Textual Scholarship: An Introduction*. New York: Garland, 1992; rpt. 1994.

———. *Scholarly Editing: A Guide to Research*. New York: MLA, 1995.

———. "Textual Forensics." *PMLA* 111 (1996), 32–51.

Hallmundsson, May Newman. "The Community of Law and Letters: Some Notes on Thomas Usk's Audience." *Viator* 9 (1978), 357–65. [Argues that the intended audience of *TL* consisted in the "clerks, lawyers, and judges of Chancery" to whom Usk was justifying his actions.]

Hanawalt, Barbara, ed. "Introduction." In *Chaucer's England: Literature in Historical Context*. Minneapolis: University of Minnesota Press, 1992. Pp. xi–xxii.

Hanna, Ralph III. *Pursuing History: Middle English Manuscripts and Their Texts*. Stanford: Stanford University Press, 1996.

Hanna, Ralph III, and Traugott Lawler, eds. *Boece*. In *The Riverside Chaucer*. Ed. Larry D. Benson. Boston: Houghton Mifflin Co., 1987. Pp. 395–469, 1003–19 and 1151–60.

Hanrahan, Michael. "Traitors and Lovers: The Politics of Love in Chaucer's *Legend of Good Women*, Gower's *Confessio Amantis*, and Usk's *Testament of Love*." Ph. D. Diss., Indiana University, 1995.

Heninger, S. K., Jr. "The Margarite-Pearl Allegory in Thomas Usk's *Testament of Love*." *Speculum* 32 (1957), 92–98.

Henryson, Robert. *The Poems of Robert Henryson*. Ed. Denton Fox. Oxford: Clarendon Press, 1981.

———. *The Poems of Robert Henryson*. Ed. Robert Kindrick. Kalamazoo: Medieval Institute Publications, 1997.

Hertz, R. "The Pre-eminence of the Right Hand: A Study in Religious Polarity." In Needham. Pp. 3–31.

Heyworth, P. L. "The Punctuation of Middle English Texts." In *Medieval Studies for J. A. W. Bennett*. Ed. P. L. Heyworth. Oxford: Clarendon Press, 1981. Pp. 139–57. [Argues that *TL* can often be understood by means of more careful punctuation — his examples are cited in the notes to this edition.]

Hicks, Michael. *Bastard Feudalism*. London: Longman, 1995.

Higden, *Polychronicon Ranulphi Higden monarchi Cestrensis*; together with the English translations of John Trevisa and of an unknown writer of the fifteenth century. 9 vols. London: Longman & Co., 1865–86.

Hirsh, John C. "Thomas Usk." In *Dictionary of Literary Biography*. Volume 146. *Old and Middle English Literature*. Ed. Jeffrey Helterman and Jerome Mitchell. Detroit: Gale Research, Inc., 1994. Pp. 305–11.

Horace. *Ars Poetica*. In *Horace for Students of Literature: The "Ars Poetica" and its Tradition*. Ed. and trans. O. B. Hardison, Jr., and Leon Golden. Gainesville: University Press of Florida, 1995.

Horrox, Rosemary, ed. "Service." In *Fifteenth-Century Attitudes: Perceptions of Society in Late Medieval England.* Cambridge: Cambridge University Press, 1994. Pp. 61–78.

Hudson, Anne. "Epilogue: The Legacy of *Piers Plowman.*" In *A Companion to Piers Plowman.* Ed. John A. Alford. Berkeley: University of California Press, 1988. Pp. 251–66.

Hugh of St. Cher. *Opera omnia in universum Vetus et Novum Testamentum*. Venice: N. Pezzana, 1732.

Isaac, Jean, O. P. *Le "Peri Hermeneias" en Occident de Boèce à Saint Thomas*. Bibliothèque Thomiste, 29. Paris: J. Vrin, 1953.

St. Isidore. *Etymologiarum sive Originum Libri XX.* Ed. W. M. Lindsay. Oxford: Oxford University Press, 1971.

Jellech, Virginia Boarding. *"The Testament of Love" by Thomas Usk: A New Edition*. Ph.D. Diss., Washington University, 1970. Ann Arbor: UMI, 1993.

Kerby-Fulton, Kathryn and Steven Justice. "Langlandian Reading Circles and the Civil Service in London and Dublin, 1380–1427." *New Medieval Literatures* 1 (1997), 59–83.

King, P. D. "The Barbarian Kingdoms." In Burns. Pp. 123–53.

Langland, William. *Piers Plowman*: *An Edition of the C-text*. Ed. Derek Pearsall. Berkeley: University of California Press, 1978.

Leicester, H. Marshall, Jr. *The Disenchanted Self: Representing the Subject in the Canterbury Tales.* Berkeley: University of California Press, 1990.

Lewis, C. S. *The Allegory of Love: A Study in Medieval Tradition.* Oxford: Clarendon Press, 1936.

———. *The Discarded Image: An Introduction to Medieval and Renaissance Literature*. Cambridge: Cambridge University Press, 1964.

Lewis, Lucy. "Langland's Tree of Charity and Usk's Wexing Tree." *Notes & Queries* (December 1995), 429–33.

Leyerle, John F. "Thematic Interlace in *The Canterbury Tales*." *Essays and Studies* 29 (1976), 107–21.

———. "Thomas Usk's *Testament of Love*: A Critical Edition." Ph.D. Diss. Harvard University 1977. [This thesis is the most recent and the most extensive effort at a critical edition of *TL*. Containing over 500 pages (more than 200 pages of which are notes), it is a massive compilation of information, particularly rich in proposed emendations and in glosses of difficult words. In addition, broad and frequently complex hypotheses are entered on many of the cruces in *TL*.]

———. "Thomas Usk." In *Dictionary of the Middle Ages*. Vol. 12. Ed. Joseph R. Strayer. New York: Scribner, 1982–89. Pp. 333–35.

Lindberg, David C. *The Beginnings of Western Science: The European Scientific Tradition in Philosophical, Religious, and Institutional Context, 600 B.C. to A.D. 1450*. Chicago: University of Chicago Press, 1992.

Little, Lester K. *Religious Poverty and the Profit Economy in Medieval Europe*. Ithaca: Cornell University Press, 1978.

de Lorris, Guillaume, and Jean de Meun. *The Romance of the Rose*. Trans. Charles Dahlberg. Third ed. Princeton: Princeton University Press, 1995.

Luria, Maxwell S., and Richard L. Hoffman, eds. *Middle English Lyrics*. New York: Norton, 1974.

Lydgate, John. *The Minor Poems of John Lydgate*. Part 2. *Secular Poems*. Ed. H. N. MacCracken. EETS o.s. 192. London: Oxford University Press, 1934.

Machan, Tim William. *Textual Criticism and Middle English Texts*. Charlottesville: The University Press of Virginia, 1994.

Mandeville, Sir John. *Mandeville's Travels*. Ed. M. C. Seymour. Oxford: Clarendon Press, 1967.

Manning, Stephen. "'I Sing of a Myden.'" *PMLA* 75 (1960), 8–12. Rpt. in Luria and Hoffman. Pp. 330–36.

Markus, R. A. "The Latin Fathers." In Burns. Pp. 92–122.

Martin, Ellen E. "Chaucer's Ruth: An Exegetical Poetic in the *Prologue* to the *Legend of Good Women*." *Exemplaria* 3 (1991), 467–90.

McInerney, Maud Burnett. "Opening the Oyster: Pearls in *Pearl*." *Aestel* 1 (1993), 19–54.

Medcalf, Stephen. "Inner and Outer." In *The Later Middle Ages*. Ed. Stephen Medcalf. New York: Holmes & Meier, 1981. Pp. 108–71. [Brief comment on *TL* under the rubric of "The Universe of Symbol: Thomas Usk" (pp. 140–49).]

———. "Transposition: Thomas Usk's *Testament of Love*." In *The Medieval Translator: The Theory and Practice of Translation in the Middle Ages*. Ed. Roger Ellis. Woodbridge, Suffolk: D. S. Brewer, 1989. Pp. 181–95. [A vigorous and often warm defense of *TL*; pays particular, close attention to Usk's relationship in Book 3 to Anselm's *De Concordia*.]

———. "The World and Heart of Thomas Usk." In Minnis, *et al*. Pp. 222–51. [An in-depth study of *TL*, offering several new hypotheses about its composition and meaning.]

Meyer, Heinz. *Die Zahlenallegorese im Mittelalter: Methode und Gebrauch*. Münstersche Mittelalter-Schriften. Munich: Wilhelm Fink Verlag, 1975.

Michel, Dan. *Dan Michel's Ayenbite of Inwyt*. Ed. Pamela Gradon. Rev. of Richard Morris edition of 1866. EETS o.s. 278. Oxford: Oxford University Press, 1979.

Middle English Dictionary. Ed. Hans Kurath and Sherman M. Kuhn. Ann Arbor: University of Michigan Press, 1952–.

Introduction

Milton, John. *Paradise Lost.* Ed. Roy Flannagan. New York: Macmillan, 1993.

Minnis, A. J. *Medieval Theory of Authorship: Scholastic Literary Attitudes in the Later Middle Ages.* Second ed. Philadelphia: University of Pennsylvania Press, 1988.

Minnis, A. J., with Charlotte C. Morse and Thorlac Turville-Petre, eds. *Essays on Ricardian Literature in Honour of J. A. Burrow.* Oxford: Clarendon Press, 1997.

Needham, Rodney, ed. *Right and Left: Essays on Dual Symbolic Classification.* Chicago: University of Chicago Press, 1973.

North, J. D. *Chaucer's Universe.* Oxford: Clarendon Press, 1988.

Ohly, Friedrich. "Die Geburt der Perle aus dem Blitz." In *Strukturen und Interpretationen: Studien zur deutschen Philologie gewidmet Blanka Horacek zum 60. Geburtstag.* Ed. Alfred Ebenbauer, Fritz-Peter Knapp, Peter Kramir. Philologica Germanica 1. Vienna: Wilhelm Braumüller, 1974. Pp. 263–78.

Oresme, Nicole. *Le Livre de éthiques d'Aristote.* Ed. Albert Douglass Menut. New York: G. E. Stechert & Co., 1940.

Ovid. *Ex Ponto.* Trans. Arthur Leslie Wheeler. Second ed. Rev. by G. P. Goold. Cambridge: Harvard University Press, 1988.

Oxford English Dictionary. Second ed. Oxford: Clarendon Press; New York: Oxford University Press, 1989.

Patience. In *The Poems of the Pearl Manuscript: Pearl, Cleanness, Patience, Sir Gawain and the Green Knight.* Ed. Malcolm Andrew and Ronald Waldron. Berkeley: University of California Press, 1979.

Patterson, Annabel. *Reading Holinshed's Chronicles.* Chicago: University of Chicago Press, 1994.

Pearl. In *The Poems of the Pearl Manuscript: Pearl, Cleanness, Patience, Sir Gawain and the Green Knight*. Ed. Malcolm Andrew and Ronald Waldron. Berkeley: University of California Press, 1979.

Pennington, K. "Law, Legislative Authority and Theories of Government, 1150–1300." In Burns. Pp. 424–53.

Perrow, E. C. "The Last Will and Testament as a Form of Literature." *Transactions of the Wisconsin Academy of Sciences, Arts, and Letters* 17 (1914), 682–753.

Petrarca, Francesco. *Petrarch's Songbook = Rerum Vulgarium Fragmenta*. Trans. James Wyatt Cook. Binghamton: MRTS, 1995.

Piltz, Anders. *The World of Medieval Learning*. Trans. David Jones. Oxford: Basil Blackwell, 1981.

Powell, Edgar, and G. M. Trevelyan, eds. *The Peasants' Rising and the Lollards*. London: Longmans, Green, and Co., 1899.

Preston, Jean F., and Laetitia Yeandle. *English Handwriting 1400–1650: An Introductory Manual*. Binghamton: MRTS, 1992.

Raymo, Robert. "The Testament of Love." In "Works of Religious and Philosophical Instruction." In *A Manual of the Writings in Middle English 1050–1500*. Vol. 7. Ed. Albert E. Hartung. New Haven: Connecticut Academy of Arts and Sciences, 1986. Pp. 2346–47 and 2551–52.

Reiss, Edmund. "The Idea of Love in Usk's *Testament of Love*." *Mediaevalia* 6 (1980), 261–77. [Explores *TL* as combining different notions of love into an idea that includes them all but is unique.]

Richard of St. Victor. *Liber Exceptionum*. Ed. Jean Chatillon. Paris: J. Vrin, 1958.

Rice, W. H. *The European Ancestry of Villon's Satirical Testaments*. New York: The Corporate Press, 1941.

Sanderlin, George. "Usk's *Testament of Love* and St. Anselm." *Speculum* 17 (1942), 69–73. [Demonstrates the relationship between Book 3 of *TL* and St. Anselm's *De Concordia.*]

The Sarum Missal. Ed. J. Wickham Legg. Oxford: Clarendon Press, 1969.

———. *The Sarum Missal in English.* Trans. Vernon Staley. In Two Parts. London: Alexander Moring, Ltd., 1911.

Saul, Nigel. *Richard II.* New Haven: Yale University Press, 1997.

Schaar, Claes. *Notes on Thomas Usk's "Testament of Love."* Lund: C. W. K. Gleerup, 1950.

———. "Usk's 'Knot in the hert'." *English Studies* 37 (1956), 260–61. [Argues that Usk's "knot" depends in part on Alan of Lille's "nodo dilectionis praecordialis" in *De Planctu Naturae.*]

Schlauch, Margaret. "Thomas Usk as Translator." In *Medieval Literature and Folklore Studies: Essays in Honor of Francis Lee Utley.* Ed. Jerome Mandel and Bruce Rosenberg. New Brunswick, NJ: Rutgers University Press, 1971. Pp. 97–103.

Seneca, *De Ira.* In *Moral Essays.* Trans. John W. Basore. Cambridge: Harvard University Press, 1964–70.

Shakespeare, William. *The Riverside Shakespeare.* Ed. G. Blakemore Evans. Boston: Houghton Mifflin Co., 1974.

Shoaf, R. Allen. *Dante, Chaucer, and the Currency of the Word: Money, Images, and Reference in Late Medieval Poetry.* Norman, OK: Pilgrim Books, 1983. [Available as an electronic postprint at http://www.clas.ufl.edu/~rashoaf/dccw.html.]

———. *The Poem as Green Girdle: "Commercium" in "Sir Gawain and the Green Knight."* Humanities Monographs Series of the University of Florida, Number 55. Gainesville: University Press of Florida, 1984.

———. “The ‘Syngne of Surfet’ and the Surfeit of Signs in *Sir Gawain and the Green Knight*.” In *The Passing of Arthur: New Essays in Arthurian Tradition*. Ed. Christopher Baswell and William Sharpe. New York: Garland, 1988. Pp. 152–69.

———. “Medieval Studies After Derrida After Heidegger.” In *Sign, Sentence, Discourse: Language in Medieval Thought and Literature*. Ed. Julian N. Wasserman and Lois Y. Roney. Syracuse: Syracuse University Press, 1989. Pp. 9–30.

———. *Milton, Poet of Duality: A Study of Semiosis in the Poetry and the Prose*. 1985; reissued, with a new Preface, by the University Press of Florida, 1993.

Siennicki, Barbara Lorraine. “No Harbour for the ‘Shippe of Traveyle’: A Study of Thomas Usk’s *Testament of Love*.” Ph.D. Diss., Queen’s University, 1985. [A book-length study (299 pages) surveying many features of *TL*, arguing in particular that “Margarite is Usk’s own sovereign, King Richard II.”]

Singer, Samuel. *Sprichwörter des Mittelalters III. Das 13. und 14. Jahrhundert*. Bern: Verlag Herbert Lang & Cie., 1944–47.

Skeat, Walter W., ed. *Wars of Alexander: An Alliterative Romance translated chiefly from the “Historia Alexandri Magni de preliis.”* EETS e.s. 47. London: N. Trübner, 1886.

———, ed. *Chaucerian and Other Pieces*. Vol. 7 of *The Complete Works of Geoffrey Chaucer*. Oxford: Clarendon Press, 1897.

———. “Thomas Usk and Ralph Higden.” *Notes & Queries* 10 (1904), 245.

———, ed. *Early English Proverbs of the Thirteenth and Fourteenth Centuries*. Oxford: Clarendon Press, 1910.

Speght, Thomas. *The Workes of our Antient and Learned English Poet, Geffrey Chavcer, newly printed*. London: Printed by Adam Islip, 1598.

Steele, Robert. *The Earliest Arithmetics in English.* EETS e.s. 118. London: Oxford University Press, 1922.

Stevenson, Burton. *The Home Book of Proverbs, Maxims, and Familiar Phrases.* New York: Macmillan, 1948.

Stokes, Myra, and John Scattergood. "Travelling in November: Sir Gawain, Thomas Usk, Charles of Orleans, and the *De Re Militari.*" *Medium Aevum* 53 (1984), 78–83. [Demonstrates that November was a "fitting moment" for "difficult transitions, marking as it did that time of year after which all 'passage' was necessarily difficult."]

Strohm, Paul. *Social Chaucer.* Cambridge: Harvard University Press, 1989. [Passing remarks on Usk and his attitude towards Chaucer.]

———. "Politics and Poetics: Usk and Chaucer in the 1380s." In *Literary Practice and Social Change in Britain, 1380–1530.* Ed. Lee Patterson. Berkeley: University of California Press, 1990. Pp. 83–112. [Detailed study of Usk's career; argues, in particular, the relationship between political factionalism and Usk's writings.]

———. "The Textual Vicissitudes of Usk's 'Appeal'." In *Hochon's Arrow: The Social Imagination of Fourteenth-Century Texts.* Princeton: Princeton University Press, 1992. Pp. 145–60. [Continues the work of the previous article and develops an idea of the effacement of Usk from the subsequent versions of his "Appeal."]

Sturges, Robert S. "Textual Scholarship: Ideologies of Literary Production." *Exemplaria* 3.1 (1991), 109–31.

Suetonius. *The Twelve Caesars.* Trans. Robert Graves. Rev. Michael Grant. New York: Penguin, 1989.

Taylor, Eva G. R. *The Haven-Finding Art: A History of Navigation from Odysseus to Captain Cook.* London: Hollis and Carter for the Institute of Navigation, 1958; second ed., 1971.

Thynne, Francis. *Animadversions upon Speght's First (1598 A.D.) Edition of Chaucers Workes*. Ed. G. H. Kingsley. EETS o.s. 9. London: N. Trübner & Co., 1865.

Thynne, William. *The Works of Geoffrey Chaucer and Others; being a reproduction in facsimile of the first collected edition 1532, from the copy in the British museum*. Introduction by W. W. Skeat. London: A. Moring, Ltd., H. Frowde, 1905.

———. *The Works, 1532 (with supplementary material from the editions of 1542, 1561, 1498 and 1602*). Ilkley: Scolar Press, 1969.

Tilley, Morris Palmer. *A Dictionary of the Proverbs in England in the Sixteenth & Seventeenth Centuries*. Ann Arbor: University of Michigan Press, 1950.

Twomey, Michael W. "Appendix: Medieval Encyclopedias." In *Medieval Christian Literary Imagery: A Guide to Interpretation*. Ed. R. E. Kaske in collaboration with Arthur Groos and Michael W. Twomey. Toronto Medieval Bibliographies 11. Toronto: University of Toronto Press, 1988. Pp. 182–215.

Usk, Thomas. *The Testament of Love*. Ed. William Thynne. fol. 325^{r}–361^{r}. [1532.]

———. *The Testament of Love*. Ed. Walter W. Skeat. In *Chaucerian and Other Pieces*. Vol. 7 of *The Complete Works of Geoffrey Chaucer*. Oxford: Clarendon Press, 1897. Pp. xviii–xxxi; 1–145; 451–84.

———. "The Appeal of Thomas Usk against John Northampton." In *A Book of London English 1384–1425*. Ed. R. W. Chambers and Marjorie Daunt. Oxford: Clarendon Press, 1967. Pp. 22–31.

———. "Extracts from Inquisitions Taken at the Trial of John Northampton" (in Latin). In *The Peasants' Rising and the Lollards*. Ed. Edgar Powell and G. M. Trevelyan. London: Longmans, Green, and Co., 1899. Pp. 27–38.

Villon, François. *François Villon: Complete Poems*. Ed. with English translation and commentary by Barbara N. Sargent-Baur. Toronto: University of Toronto Press, 1994.

Vincent of Beauvais. *Speculum quadruplex; sive, Speculum maius: naturale, doctrinale, morale, historiale*. Graz, Austria: Akademische Druck- u. Verlaganstalt, 1964–65.

Vitto, Cindy L. *The Virtuous Pagan in Middle English Literature*. Transactions of the American Philosophical Society, vol. 79, pt. 5. Philadelphia: The American Philosophical Society, 1989.

Vona, Costantino. "La *Margarita Pretiosa* nella interpretazione di alcuni scrittori ecclesiastici." *Divinitas* 1 (1957), 118–60.

Wagner, David, ed. *The Seven Liberal Arts in the Middle Ages*. Bloomington: Indiana University Press, 1983.

Wailes, Stephen L. *Medieval Allegories of Jesus' Parables*. Berkeley: University of California Press, 1987.

Walther, Hans. *Proverbia Sententiaeque Latinitatis Medii Aevi*. 6 vols. Göttingen: Vandenhoeck & Ruprecht, 1963–69.

Wimsatt, James I. *The Marguerite Poetry of Guillaume de Machaut*. Chapel Hill: University of North Carolina Press, 1970.

Yeager, R. F. "Literary Theory at the Close of the Middle Ages: William Caxton and William Thynne." *Studies in the Age of Chaucer* 6 (1984), 135–64.

Yunck, John A. *The Lineage of Lady Meed: The Development of Mediaeval Venality Satire*. Notre Dame: University of Notre Dame Press, 1963.

Summary of The Testament of Love

(from Stephen Medcalf [1997], pp. 229–31)

Usk dedicates the book to Margaret . . . by the prayer formed in the initial letters of its chapters, MARGARETE OF VIRTW HAVE MERCI ON THIN VSK. From this point on I shall include in my chapter-references to the *Testament* these initials, since I have found this practice useful in recalling the book's sequence of thought, which is as follows:

Book 1

Prologue	M	A formal apologia for the book, and especially for writing in English.
I	A	Usk in prison laments the absence of Margaret,
II	R	and is visited by the lady Love,
III–IV	GA	to whom he confesses in an allegory of a ship voyage how she showed him the pearl Margaret: but two difficulties destroy his hopes of Margaret, first false slanders and secondly her preciousness compared with his unworthiness.
V	R	Love assures him of her help.
VI–VII	ET	Usk outlines the slanders against him in a fairly literal account of his dealings with Northampton.
VIII	E	Love assures him that these slanders are no barrier between himself and Margaret.
IX	O	As for his unworthiness, Love assures him of the dignity of man,
X	F	and of the value of ill fortune in discriminating virtue and truth.

Book 2

I	V	Usk outlines the book to come, and speaks of a future book in which he will praise Margaret.
II	I	Love sings of her (i.e., Love's) rejection in the Church and the world.

III	R	She and Usk together praise women and lament the faithlessness of men.
IV–VIII	TW HAV	Usk's early life is analysed as an attempt to achieve love by means of riches, dignities, power, and renown, all four of which Love shows to be external and false means.
IX–X	EM	Love exalts the harmony of heaven as the lover's true end, and assures Usk that he is now in the true way to it,
XI	E	which is by virtue and reason,
XII	R	of which Margaret is the source.
XIII	C	Through Margaret comes good, which is a participation in God, while evil is only negation.
XIV	I	Usk's fortunes are retold in a parable (based on Proverbs) of a lover led astray by "fayned love" but delivered.

Book 3

I	O	The three books of the *Testament* are shown by Usk to correspond to the three ages of the world, Error, Grace, and Joy, and the subject of the whole book to be involved in other triads, such as Law, Philosophy, and Love.
II	N	Love promises Usk that he will be rewarded for his good service, which she shows to be good acts freely chosen and performed with a good heart.
III–IV	TH	She shows how the will is free in relation to necessity and eternity.
V–VII	INU	In the image of a tree, the interdependence of free will, love and grace is shown, and how love is its own reward. The lady Love enters Usk's heart.
VIII–IX	SK	Usk recapitulates in his own voice what love has taught him about the workings of grace and the will in love, truth, and righteousness.

The Testament of Love

Prologue

Many men there ben that with eeres openly sprad so moche swalowen the delyciousnesse of jestes and of ryme by queynt knyttyng coloures that of the goodnesse or of the badnesse of the sentence take they lytel hede or els none. Sothely, dul wytte and a thoughtful soule so sore have myned and graffed in my spyrites that suche craft of endytyng wol not ben of myn acqueyntaunce. And, for rude wordes and boystous, percen the herte of the herer to the inrest poynte and planten there the sentence of thynges, so that with lytel helpe it is able to spring, this boke, that nothyng hath of the great floode of wyt ne of semelych colours, is dolven with rude wordes and boystous, and so drawe togyder to maken the catchers therof ben the more redy to hent sentence.

Some men there ben that peynten with colours ryche and some with vers as with red

---

<325ra>MANY men there ben/ that w*ith* eeres openly sprad so moche swalowen the delyciousnesse of iestes and of ryme/ by queynt knyttyng coloures/ that of the goodnesse or of the badnesse of the sentence take they lytel hede or els none. Sothely dul wytte and a thoughtful soule/ so sore haue myned and graffed in my spyrites/ that suche craft of endytyng wol not ben of myn acqueyntau*n*ce. And for rude wordes and boystous percen the herte of the herer to the inrest poynte/ and planten there the sentence of thynges/ so that with lytel helpe it is able to spring. This boke that nothyng hath of the great floode of wyt/ ne of semelych colours/ is doluen with rude wordes and boystous/ and so drawe togyder to maken the catchers therof ben the more redy to hent sente*n*ce.

Some men there ben that peynten with colours ryche/ and some with vers/ as with red

1 eeres, ears; **sprad**, spread; **swalowen**, swallow. **2 queynt knyttyng coloures**, strange (curious) complex (intricate) rhetorical figures. **3 hede**, heed; **els**, else; **Sothely**, Truly. **4 myned**, undermined; **graffed in**, dug down (lit., dug a grave). **5 endytyng**, writing (composition); **boystous**, plain. **6 herer**, hearer; **inrest**, innermost. **7 spring**, grow. **8 semelych colours**, decorous rhetoric; **dolven**, cultivated. **9 catchers**, auditors; **hent sentence**, grasp meaning. **10 peynten**, paint; **vers**, special, distinct modes of communication (such as verse), ornate composition.

ynke and some with coles and chalke; and yet is there good matere to the leude people of thilke chalky purtreyture, as hem thynketh for the tyme; and afterwarde the syght of the better colours yeven to hem more joye for the first leudenesse. So, sothly, this leude clowdy occupacion is not to prayse but by the leude; for comenly leude leudenesse commendeth. Eke it shal yeve syght that other precious thynges shal be the more in reverence. In Latyn and French hath many soverayne wyttes had gret delyte to endyte and have many noble thynges fulfylde; but, certes, there ben some that speken their poysye mater in Frenche of whiche speche the Frenche men have as good a fantasye as we have in heryng of Frenche mennes Englysshe. And many termes there ben in Englysshe whiche unneth we Englysshmen connen declare the knowlegynge: howe shulde than a Frenche man borne suche termes conne jumpere in his mater, but as the jay chatereth Englyssh? Right so, trewly, the understandyng of Englysshmen wol not stretche to the

---

ynke/ and some with coles and chalke: and yet is there good matere to the leude people of thilke chalky purtreyture/ as hem thynketh for the tyme/ and afterwarde the syght of the better colours yeuen to hem more ioye for the first leudenesse. So sothly this leude clowdy occupacion is not to prayse/ but by the leude: for comenly leude leudenesse co*m*mendeth. Eke it shal yeue syght that other precious thynges shal be the more in reuerence. In latyn and french hath many souerayne wyttes had gret delyte to endyte/ and haue many noble thynges fulfylde/ but certes there ben some that speken their poysye mater in frenche/ of whiche speche the frenche men haue as good a fantasye as we haue in heryng of frenche mennes englysshe. And many termes there ben in englysshe/ whiche vnneth we englysshmen connen declare the knowlegynge: howe shulde than a frenche man borne/ suche termes conne iumpere in his mater/ but as the iay chatereth englyssh. Right so trewly the vnderstandyng of englysshmen wol not stretche to the

11 coles, charcoal; **leude**, lay, uneducated. **12 thilke**, that same; **purtreyture**, portraiture; **as hem thynketh**, as it seems to them. **13 yeven**, gives; **hem**, them; **for the first leudenesse**, on account of the former lack of skill; **sothly**, truly; **leude**, uncultured. **14 clowdy**, obscure, confused; **to prayse**, to be praised. **14–15 leude leudnesse commendeth**, the uneducated commend uncultured [matters]. **15 Eke**, Also; **yeve**, give. **16 endyte**, compose. **17 fulfylde**, accomplished; **speken**, speak. **18 poysye mater**, poetry. **19 heryng**, hearing. **20 unneth**, scarcely; **connen**, know how to; **knowlegynge**, comprehension of. **21 conne jumpere**, know how to assemble; **chatereth**, chatters. **22 stretche**, stretch.

privy termes in Frenche whatsoever we bosten of straunge langage. Let than clerkes endyten in Latyn, for they have the propertie of science and the knowynge in that facultie; and lette Frenchmen in their Frenche also endyten their queynt termes, for it is kyndely to their mouthes; and let us shewe our fantasyes in suche wordes as we lerneden of our dames tonge.

And although this boke be lytel thankeworthy for the leudnesse in travaile, yet suche writynges exciten men to thilke thynges that ben necessarie. For every man therby may, as by a perpetual myrrour, sene the vyces or vertues of other in whiche thyng lightly may be conceyved to eschewe peryls and necessaryes to catche after as aventures have fallen to other people or persons. Certes, the soveraynst thing of desyre and moste creature reasonable have, or els shulde have, ful appetyte to their perfection; unresonable beestes mowen not, sythe reason hath in hem no werkyng. Than reasonable that wol not is comparysoned to unresonable and made lyke hem. Forsothe the most soverayne and

---

priuy termes in frenche/ what so euer we bosten of straunge langage. Let than clerkes endyten in latyn/ for they haue the propertie of science**<325ra><325rb>**and the knowynge in that facultie: and lette frenchmen in their frenche also endyten their queynt termes/ for it is kyndely to their mouthes/ and let vs shewe our fantasyes in suche wordes as we lerneden of our dames tonge.

And although this boke be lytel thanke worthy for the leudnesse in trauaile/ yet suche writynges exciten men to thilke thynges that ben necessarie: for euery man therby may as by a perpetual myrrour sene the vyces or vertues of other/ in whiche thyng lightly may be conceyued to eschewe peryls/ and necessaryes to catche/ after as auentures haue fallen to other people or p*er*sons. Certes the souerAynst thing of desyre and moste creature reasonable/ haue or els shulde haue ful appetyte to their perfection: vnresonable beestes mowen not/ sythe reason hath in hem no werkyng. Than reasonable that wol not/ is comparysoned to vnresonable/ and made lyke hem. Forsothe the most souerayne and

23 privy, most peculiar; **bosten**, boast. **24 endyten**, compose. **25 queynt**, unfamiliar. **26 kyndely**, natural; **lerneden**, learned. **27 dames**, mothers'. **28 thankeworthy**, praiseworthy; **travaile**, labor. **29 exciten**, excite; **thilke**, those same. **30 perpetual**, ever-available. **31 eschewe**, avoid; **catche after as**, catch accordingly as. **32 Certes**, Certainly. **34 mowen**, may; **werkyng**, function; **reasonable**, [a] reasonable [person]. **35 hem**, them.

fynal perfection of man is in knowyng of a sothe, withouten any entent disceyvable, and in love of one very God that is inchaungeable; that is, to knowe and love his creatour.

Nowe, principally, the meane to bringe in knowlegyng and lovyng his creatour is the consyderacion of thynges made by the creatour, wherthrough be thylke thynges that ben made understonding here to our wyttes arne the unsene privytees of God made to us sightful and knowyng in our contemplacion and understondyng. These thynges than, forsoth, moche bringen us to the ful knowlegynge sothe and to the parfyte love of the maker of hevenly thynges. Lo, David sayth, "Thou haste delyted me in makynge," as who sayth to have delyte in the tune, how God hath lent me in consyderacion of thy makynge. Wherof Aristotle in the boke *de Animalibus* saythe to naturel phylosophers: "It is a great lykyng in love of knowynge their creatour, and also in knowynge of causes in kyndely thynges consydred." Forsoth, the formes of kyndly thynges and the shap, a great kyndely love me shulde have to the werkman that hem made. The crafte of a werkman is shewed in the werke. Herfore, truly the phylosophers with a lyvely studye

---

fynal perfection of man is in knowyng of a sothe/ withouten any entent disceyuable/ and in loue of one very god/ that is inchaungeable/ that is to knowe and loue his creatour.

Nowe principally the meane to bringe in knowlegyng and louyng his creatour/ is the consyderacion of thynges made by the creatour/ wherthrough be thylke thynges that ben made vnderstonding here to our wyttes/ arne the vnsene priuytees of god made to vs sightful and knowyng/ in our co*n*templacion *and* vnderstondyng. These thynges than forsoth moche bringen vs to th*e* ful knowlegynge sothe/ and to the parfyte loue of the maker of heuenly thynges. Lo Dauid sayth: thou haste delyted me in makynge/ as who sayth/ to haue delyte in the tune how god hath lent me in consyderacion of thy makynge. Wherof Aristotle in the boke de Animalibus/ saythe to naturel phylosophers: It is a great lykyng in loue of knowynge their creatour: and also in knowynge of causes in kyndely thyng*es* co*n*sydred. Forsoth the formes of kyndly thynges and the shap/ a great kyndely loue me shulde haue to the werkman th*at* hem made. The crafte of a werkman is shewed in the werke. Herfore truly the phylosophers with a lyuely studye

36 sothe, truth; **entent disceyvable**, intent to deceive. **37 inchaungeable**, constant. **38 meane**, means. **39 thylke**, those same. **40 understonding**, comprehensible; **unsene privytees**, unseen secrets. **42 sothe**, truth. **44 tune**, sense: harmonious totality of composition (see note). **46 lykyng**, desire (affinity). **47 kyndely**, natural. **48 me**, men (one). **49 Herfore**, Therefore; **lyvely studye**, animated and committed scholarship.

many noble thynges ryght precious and worthy to memory writen, and, by a great swetande travayle, to us leften of causes the propertyes in natures of thynges. To whiche, therfore, Phylosophers it was more joy, more lykynge, more herty lust in kyndely vertues and matters of reason, the perfection by busy study to knowe, than to have had al the treasour, al the richesse, al the vainglory that the passed emperours, prynces, or kynges hadden. Therfore the names of hem in the boke of perpetual memory in vertue and peace arn wryten; and, in the contrarye, that is to sayne, in Stixe, the foule pytte of helle, arn thilke pressed that suche goodnesse hated. And bycause this boke shal be of love and the pryme causes of sterynge in that doynge, with passyons and dyseases for wantynge of desyre I wyl that this boke be cleped *The Testament of Love*.

But nowe, thou reder, who is thylke that wyl not in scorne laughe to here a dwarfe or els halfe a man, say he wyl rende out the swerde of Hercules handes, and also he shulde set Hercules Gades a myle yet ferther; and over that, he had power of strengthe to pul up the spere that Alisander the noble might never wagge?

---

many noble thynges/ ryght**<325rb><325va>**precious and worthy to memory writen/ *and* by a great swetande trauayle to vs leften of causes the propertyes in natures of thynges. To whiche therfore Phylosophers it was more ioy/ more lykynge/ more herty lust in kyndely vertues and matters of reason the perfection by busy study to knowe/ than to haue had al the treasour/ al the richesse/ al the vainglory th*at* the passed Emperours/ prynces/ or kynges hadden. Therfore the names of hem in th*e* boke of perpetual memory in vertue and peace arn wryten/ and in the contrarye/ that is to sayne/ in stixe the foule pytte of helle arn thilke pressed that suche goodnesse hated. And bycause this boke shal be of loue/ and the pryme causes of sterynge in that doynge with passyons and dyseases for wantynge of desyre/ I wyl that this boke be cleped th*e* Testament of loue.

But nowe thou reder/ who is thylke that wyl not in scorne laughe/ to here a dwarfe or els halfe a man/ say he wyl rende out the swerde of Hercules handes/ and also he shulde set Hercules gades a myle yet ferther/ and ouer that he had power of strengthe to pul vp the spere/ that Alisander the noble might neuer wagge.

51 swetande travayle, sweating labor; **leften of**, bequeathed the knowledge of. **52 herty lust**, healthy desire. **53 kyndely**, natural. **53 busy**, intensive. **54 passed**, past. **56 arn**, are. **58 sterynge**, guidance. **59 for wantynge of**, i.e., lack of obtaining [the object] of; **cleped**, called. **60 thylke**, that one. **61 rende out the swerde of Hercules handes**, rip the sword from Hercules' hands. **62 Hercules Gades**, the pillars of Hercules at Cadiz. **63 spere that**, spear that; **wagge,** wield (lit., wage).

And that passyng al thynge to ben mayster of Fraunce by myght, thereas the noble gracyous Edwarde the thyrde, for al his great prowesse in victories, ne myght al yet conquere?

Certes, I wote wel there shal be made more scorne and jape of me, that I, so unworthely clothed altogyder in the cloudy cloude of unconnynge, wyl putten me in prees to speke of love or els of the causes in that matter, sythen al the grettest clerkes han had ynough to don and, as who sayth, gathered up clene toforne hem, and with theyr sharpe sythes of connyng al mowen, and made therof great rekes and noble ful of al plentyes to fede me and many another. Envye forsothe commendeth nought his reason that he hath in hayn, be it never so trusty. And althoughe these noble repers, as good workmen and worthy theyr hyer, han al drawe and bounde up in the sheves and made many shockes, yet have I ensample to gader the smale crommes and fullyn my walet of tho that fallen from the borde amonge the smale houndes, notwithstandynge the travayle of

---

And that passyng al thynge to ben mayster of Fraunce by myght/ there as the noble gracyous Edwarde the thyrde for al his great prowesse in victories ne myght al yet co*n*quere.

Certes I wote wel/ there shal be made more scorne *and* iape of me/ that I so vnworthely clothed al togyder in the cloudy cloude of vnconnynge wyl putten me in prees to speke of loue/ or els of the causes in that matter/ sythen al the grettest clerkes han had ynough to don/ and as who sayth gathered vp clene toforne hem/ and with theyr sharpe sythes of connyng al mowen and made therof great rekes and noble/ ful of al plentyes to fede me and many another. Enuye forsothe co*m*mendeth nought his reason/ that he hath in hayn/ be it neuer so trusty. And al thoughe these noble repers/ as good workmen and worthy theyr hyer/ han al drawe and bounde vp in th*e* sheues/ *and* made many shockes/ yet haue I ensample to gader the smale cro*m*mes/ and fullyn my walet of tho that fallen from the borde amonge the smale houndes/ notwithstandynge the trauayle of**<325va>**

64 mayster, master. **67 Certes**, Certainly; **wote**, know; **jape**, jest. **68 unconnynge**, unknowing, ignorance; **in prees**, in competition. **69 els**, else; **sythen**, since; **grettest**, greatest; **han had**, have had. **70 clene toforne**, thoroughly before and in front of; **sythes**, scythes, mowers. **71 connyng**, intelligence; **mowen**, mowed; **rekes**, rakes, piles of hay; **plentyes**, plenties; **fede**, feed. **73 hayn**, hatred; **repers**, reapers. **74 hyer**, hire; **sheves**, sheaves; **shockes**, stacks. **75 ensample**, example; **crommes**, crumbs; **fullyn**, fill; **tho**, those. **76 borde**, table.

the almoygner that hath drawe up in the cloth al the remyssayles as trenchours and the relyef to bere to the almesse. Yet also have I leve of the noble husbande Boece, although I be a straunger of connynge, to come after his doctryne and these great workmen and glene my handfuls of the shedynge after theyr handes; and, if me fayle ought of my ful, to encrease my porcyon with that I shal drawe by privytyes out of the shocke. A slye servaunt in his owne helpe is often moche commended; knoweyng of trouth in causes of thynges was more hardyer in the first sechers, and so sayth Aristotle, and lyghter in us that han folowed after. For theyr passyng study han fresshed our wyttes, and our understandynge han excyted in consideracion of trouth by sharpnesse of theyr reasons. Utterly, these thynges be no dremes ne japes to throwe to hogges. It is lyfelyche meate for chyldren of trouthe, and as they me betiden whan I pilgrymaged out of my kyth in

---

<325vb>the almoygner/ that hath drawe vp in th*e* cloth al the remyssayles/ as trenchours/ and the relyef to bere to the almesse. Yet also haue I leue of the noble husbande Boece/ al though I be a straunger of connynge to come after his doctryne/ and these great workmen/ and glene my handfuls of the shedynge after theyr handes/ *and* if me fayle ought of my ful/ to encrease my porcyon with that I shal drawe by priuytyes out of the shocke/ a slye seruaunt in his owne helpe is often moche co*m*mended/ knoweyng of trouth in causes of thynges/ was more hardyer in the first sechers/ and so sayth Aristotle/ *and* lyghter in vs that han folowed after. For theyr passyng study han fresshed our wyttes/ and our vnderstandynge han excyted in consideracion of trouth by sharpnesse of theyr reasons. Utterly these thynges be no dremes ne iapes/ to throwe to hogges/ it is lyfelyche meate for chyldren of trouthe/ and as they me betiden whan I pilgrymaged out of my kyth in

77 almoygner, almsman, who distributes the alms of another; **remyssayles**, leftovers; **trenchours**, brown-bread, in thick slices, serving as plates for food. **78 relyef**, the rest (possibly, "succeeding dishes"); **bere**, carry; **almesse**, those deserving of alms; **leve**, permission; **husbande**, cultivator. **79 connynge**, knowledge. **80 glene**, glean; **shedynge**, leavings. **81 by privytyes**, privately, by myself; **shocke**, stacked sheaves of grain. **81–82 A slye . . . owne helpe**, a servant expedient in helping himself. **83 more hardyer**, more difficult; **sechers**, seekers; **lyghter in**, easier for. **84 passyng**, surpassing, i.e., inimitably excellent; **fresshed**, refreshed. **86 Utterly**, Absolutely; **dremes**, dreams; **japes**, jests; **hogges**, hogs; **lyfelyche meate**, living food. **87 me betiden**, befell me; **kyth**, native land.

wynter, whan the wether out of measure was boystous and the wylde wynde Borias, as his kynde asketh, with dryenge coldes maked the wawes of the occian see so to aryse unkyndely over the commune bankes that it was in poynte to spyl al the erthe.

Thus endeth the prologue, and hereafter foloweth the fyrst boke of *The Testament of Love.*

---

wynter/ whan the wether out of measure was boystous/ *and* the wylde wynde Borias as his kynde asketh with dryenge coldes/ maked the wawes of the occian see so to aryse vnkyndely ouer the co*m*mune bankes that it was in poynte to spyl al the erthe.

Thus endeth the prologue/ and here after foloweth the fyrst boke of the Testament of Loue.**<325vb>**

88 wether, weather; **boystous**, rough. **89 kynde**, nature; **wawes**, waves; **occian see**, ocean. **90 unkyndely**, unnaturally; **commune**, universal, i.e., all its banks (so that it was about to destroy all the earth); **spyl**, destroy.

The Testament of Love

Book 1

Chapter I

Alas, Fortune, alas; I that somtyme in delycyous houres was wont to enjoy blysful stoundes am nowe dryve by unhappy hevynesse to bewayle my sondrye yvels in tene. Trewly, I leve in myn herte is writte of perdurable letters al the entencyons of lamentacion that nowe ben ynempned, for any maner disease outwarde in sobbyng maner sheweth sorowful yexynge from within. Thus from my comforte I gynne to spylle syth she that shulde me solace is ferre fro my presence. Certes, her absence is to me an hell; my sternyng dethe thus in wo it myneth that endelesse care is throughout myne herte clenched; blysse of my joye that ofte me murthed is turned into galle to thynke on thyng that may not at my wyl in armes me hent. Myrth is chaunged into tene, whan swynke is there contynually that reste was wont to sojourne and have dwellynge place. Thus

---

<326ra>ALAS Fortune alas/ I that som tyme in delycyous houres was wont to enioy blysful stoundes/ am nowe dryue by vnhappy heuynesse to bewayle my sondrye yuels in tene. Trewly I leue/ in myn herte is writte of perdurable letters al the entencyons of lamentacion that nowe ben ynempned/ for any maner disease outwarde in sobbyng maner/ sheweth sorowful yexynge from within. Thus from my comforte I gynne to spylle/ syth she that shulde me solace/ is ferre fro my presence. Certes her absence is to me an hell/ my sternyng dethe thus in wo it myneth/ that endelesse care is throughout myne herte clenched/ blysse of my ioye/ that ofte me murthed is turned in to galle/ to thynke on thyng that may not at my wyl in armes me hent. Myrth is chaunged in to tene/ whan swynke is there contynually/ that reste was wont to soiourne and haue dwellynge place. Thus

2 stoundes, times; **tene**, sorrow. **3 leve**, believe. **4 ynempned**, named. **5 yexynge**, sobbing; **gynne**, begin; **spylle syth**, decline since. **7 sternyng**, languishing (see note); **myneth**, means. **8 murthed**, gave me mirth. **9 hent**, take; **swynke**, labor. **10 that**, where.

wytlesse, thoughtful, syghtlesse lokynge, I endure my penaunce in this derke prisone, caytisned fro frendshippe and acquayntaunce, and forsaken of al that any wode dare speke. Straunge hath by waye of intrucyoun made his home there me shulde be if reason were herde as he shulde. Neverthelater, yet hertly, lady precious Margarit have mynde on thy servaunt and thynke on his disease how lyghtles he lyveth, sithe the beames brennende in love of thyn eyen arn so bewent that worldes and cloudes atwene us twey wol nat suffre my thoughtes of hem to be enlumyned. Thynke that one vertue of a Margarite precious is amonges many other the sorouful to comforte, yet wyl of that me sorouful to comforte is my luste to have nought els at this tyme; dede ne dethe, ne no maner traveyle hath no power myne herte so moche to fade as shulde to here of a twynckelynge in your disease. Ah, God forbede that; but yet lette me dey, lette me sterve withouten any measure of penaunce, rather than myne hertely thynking comforte in ought were diseased. What maye my servyce aveyle in absence of her that my servyce shulde accepte? Is this nat endlesse sorowe to thynke? Yes, yes, God wote;

---

wytlesse thoughtful/ syghtlesse lokynge/ I endure my penaunce in this derke prisone/ caytisned fro frendshippe and acquayntaunce/ and forsaken of al that any wode dare speke. Strau*n*ge hath by waye of intrucyoun made his home/ there me shulde be/ if reason were herde as he shulde. Neuer the later yet hertly lady p*re*cious Margarit/ haue mynde on thy seruaunt/ and thynke on his disease/ how lyghtles he lyueth/ sithe the beames bre*n*nende in loue of thyn eyen arn so be we*nt*/ that worldes *and* cloudes atwene vs twey wol nat suffre my thoughtes of hem to be enlumyned. Thynke that one vertue of a Margarite precious is amonges many other the sorouful to comforte yet wyl of that me sorouful to comforte is my luste to haue nought els at this tyme/ dede ne dethe/ ne no maner traueyle hath no power myne herte so moche to fade/ as shulde to here of a twynckelynge in your disease. Ah/ god forbede that/ but yet lette me dey/ lette me sterue withouten any measure of penaunce/ rather than myne hertely thynking comforte in ought were diseased. What maye my seruyce aueyle in absence of her/ that my seruyce shulde accepte? is this nat endlesse sorowe to thynke? Yes/ yes god wote/

11 thoughtful, anxious. **12 caytisned**, incarcerated (lit. captured; see note). **13 Straunge**, Weirdness (quasi-personified); **there me shulde be**, where I should be. **14 Neverthelater**, Nevertheless. **16 brennende**, burning; **bewent**, departed; **atwene**, between. **17 suffre**, permit. **18 wyl of**, while (see note). **19 dede**, dying. **20 traveyle**, suffering; **here**, hear. **22 sterve**, die. **24 God wote**, God knows.

myne hert breaketh nygh asonder. Howe shulde the grounde without kyndly noriture bringen forthe any frutes? Howe shulde a shippe withouten a sterne in the great see be governed? Howe shulde I withouten my blysse, my herte, my desyre, my joye, my goodnesse endure in this contrarious prison, that thynke every hour in the day an hundred wynter? Wel may nowe Eve sayne to me, "Adam, in sorowe fallen from welth, driven arte thou out of paradise, with sweate thy sustenaunce to beswynke." Depe in this pynynge pytte with wo I lygge ystocked, with chaynes lynked of care and of tene. It is so hye from thens I lye and the commune erth, there ne is cable in no lande maked, that myght stretche to me to drawe me into blysse, ne steyers to stey on is none, so that without recover endlesse here to endure I wotte wel I purveyde. O, where arte thou nowe, frenshyppe, that somtyme with laughande chere madest bothe face and countenaunce to me wardes? Truely nowe arte thou went out of towne, but ever me thynketh he weareth his olde clothes and that the soule in the whiche the lyfe of frendshyppe was in is drawen out from his other spyrites. Nowe than farewel frendshyp, and farewel felawes.

---

myne hert breaketh nygh a sonder/ **<326ra><326rb>**howe shulde the grou*n*de without kyndly noriture bringen forthe any frutes? Howe shulde a shippe withouten a sterne in the great see be gouerned? Howe shulde I withouten my blysse/ my herte/ my desyre/ my ioye/ my goodnesse/ endure in this contrarious prison/ that thynke euery hour in the day an hundred wynter? Wel may nowe Eue sayne to me Adam/ in sorowe fallen from welth/ driuen arte thou out of paradise/ with sweate thy sustenaunce to be swynke. Depe in this pynynge pytte with wo I lygge ystocked/ with chaynes lynked of care *and* of tene. It is so hye from thens I lye and the co*m*mune erth/ there ne is cable in no lande maked/ that myght stretche to me to drawe me in to blysse/ ne steyers to stey on is none/ so that without recouer endlesse here to endure I wotte wel I purueyde. O/ where arte thou nowe frenshyppe/ that so*m*tyme with laughande chere/ madest bothe face and countenau*n*ce to me wardes? truely nowe arte thou went out of towne/ but euer me thynketh he weareth his olde clothes/ *and* that th*e* soule in the whiche the lyfe of frendshyppe was in/ is drawen out from his other spyrites. Nowe than farewel frendshyp/ and farewel felawes/

25 noriture, nurture. **26 sterne**, rudder. **29 welth**, wealth, abundance. **30 beswynke**, work for. **31 pynynge**, (causing) suffering; **ystocked**, imprisoned in stocks; **tene**, sorrow. **32 hye from thens**, i.e., so vast a distance between where. **33 steyers**, stairs. **34 recover**, rescue; **purveyde**, am destined. **35 chere**, look. **35–36 to me wardes**, towards me.

Me thynketh ye al han taken your leave; no force of you al at ones. But lady of love ye wote what I mene, yet thinke on thy servaunt, that for thy love spylleth; al thynges have I forsake to folowen thyn hestes. Rewarde me with a thought, though ye do naught els. Remembraunce of love lythe so sore under my brest that other thought cometh not in my mynde but gladnesse to thynke on your goodnesse and your mery chere, ferdness and sorowe to thynke on your wreche and your daunger from whiche Christe me save. My great joye it is to have in meditacion the bounties, the vertues, the nobley in you printed; sorowe and hel comen at ones to suppose that I be veyned. Thus with care sorowe and tene am I shapte, myn ende with dethe to make. Nowe good goodly thynke on this. O wretched foole that I am fallen in to so lowe: the heate of my brennyng tene hath me al defased. How shulde ye, lady, sette prise on so foule fylthe? My connynge is thynne, my wytte is exiled. Lyke to a foole naturel am I comparysoned. Trewly, lady, but your mercy the more were, I wote wel al my labour were in ydel; your mercy than passeth right. God graunt that proposycion to be verifyed in me, so that by

---

me thynketh ye al han taken your leaue: no force of you al at ones. But lady of loue ye wote what I mene/ yet thinke on thy seruaunt/ that for thy loue spylleth/ al thynges haue I forsake to folowen thyn hestes: rewarde me with a thought/ though ye do naught els. Remembraunce of loue lythe so sore vnder my brest/ that other thought cometh not in my mynde/ but gladnesse to thynke on your goodnesse and your mery chere/ frendes and sorowe to thynke on your wreche and your daunger/ from whiche Christe me saue. My great ioye it is to haue in meditacion the bounties/ the vertues/ the nobley in you printed: sorowe and hel comen at ones/ to suppose that I be veyned. Thus with care/ sorowe/ and tene am I shapte myn ende with dethe to make. Nowe good goodly thynke on this. O wretched foole that I am fallen in to so lowe/ the heate of my brennyng tene hath me al defased: how shulde ye lady sette prise on so foule fylthe? My connynge is thynne/ my wytte is exiled/ **<326rb><326va>**lyke to a foole naturel am I comparysoned. Trewly lady but your mercy the more were/ I wote wel al my labour were in ydel: your mercy than passeth right. God graunt that proposycion to be verifyed in me/ so that by

39 no force of, it's no matter regarding. **40 wote**, know; **spylleth**, dies. **41 hestes**, commands. **43 ferdness**, fearfulness. **44 wreche**, vengeance; **daunger**, haughtiness. **45 nobley**, nobleness. **46 veyned**, abandoned (see note). **47 tene**, grief; **shapte**, destined. **48 brennyng**, burning. **49 defased**, defaced; **sette prise**, value, esteem; **connynge**, understanding.

truste of good hope I mowe come to the haven of ease. And sythe it is impossyble the colours of your qualyties to chaunge, and, forsothe, I wote wel wemme ne spotte maye not abyde there so noble vertue haboundeth, so that the defasyng to you is verily unymagynable, as countenaunce of goodnesse with encresynge vertue is so in you knytte to abyde by necessary maner; yet, if the revers might fal, which is ayenst kynde, I wot wel myn herte ne shulde therfore naught flytte by the leste poynt of gemetrye, so sadly is it sonded that away from your servyce in love maye he not departe. O love, whan shal I ben pleased? O charyté, whan shal I ben eased? O good goodly, whan shal the dyce turne? O ful of vertue, do the chaunce of comforte upwarde to fal. O love, whan wolt thou thynke on thy servaunt? I can no more but here, outcaste of al welfare, abyde the daye of my dethe, or els to se the syght that might al my wellynge sorowes voyde and of the flodde make an ebbe. These diseases mowen wel by duresse of sorowe make my lyfe to unbodye and so for to dye; but certes ye lady in a ful perfectyon of love ben so knytte with my soule that dethe may not thilke knotte unbynde ne departe,

---

truste of good hope/ I mowe come to the hauen of ease/ and sythe it is impossyble/ the colours of your qualyties to chaunge: and forsothe I wote wel wemme ne spotte maye not abyde/ there so noble vertue haboundeth/ so that the defasyng to you is verily ymagynable/ as countenaunce of goodnesse with encresynge vertue/ is so in you knytte to abyde by necessary maner/ yet if the reuers might fal/ which is ayenst kynde/ I wol wel myn herte ne shulde therfore naught flytte by the leste poynt of gemetrye/ so sadly is it sonded/ that away from your seruyce in loue maye he not departe. O loue/ whan shal I ben pleased? O charyte/ whan shal I ben eased? O good goodly/ whan shal the dyce turne? O ful of vertue do the chaunce of comforte vpwarde to fal. O loue/ whan wolt thou thynke on thy seruaunt? I can no more but here out caste of al welfare/ abyde the daye of my dethe/ or els to se the syght that might al my wellynge sorowes voyde/ and of the flodde make an ebbe. These diseases mowen wel by duresse of sorowe/ make my lyfe to vnbodye/ and so for to dye: but certes ye lady in a ful perfectyon of loue ben so knytte with my soule/ that dethe may not thilke knotte vnbynde ne departe/

54 wemme, stain. **55 there**, where; **haboundeth**, abounds. **58 wot**, know; **flytte**, be moved, prove flighty; **gemetrye**, measurement. **59 sadly**, solemnly, committedly; **sonded**, ordained, fixed (see note). **62 can**, know, am capable. **64 mowen**, may; **duresse**, duration and duress. **66 departe**, part in twain.

so that ye and my soule togyther endelesse in blysse shulde dwel, and there shal my soule at the ful ben eased that he may have your presence to shewe th'entent of his desyres. Ah, dere God, that shal be a great joye. Nowe erthely goddesse take regarde of thy servant, though I be feble, for thou arte wonte to prayse them better that wolde conne serve in love, al be he ful mener than kynges or princes that wol not have that vertue in mynde. Nowe precious Margaryte that with thy noble vertue haste drawen me into love first, me wenynge therof to have blisse, as galle and aloes are so moche spronge, that savour of swetnesse may I not ataste. Alas, that your benigne eyen in whiche that mercy semeth to have al his noriture nyl, by no waye, tourne the clerenesse of mercy to mewardes. Alas, that your brennande vertues shynyng amonges al folke and enlumynynge al other people by habundaunce of encreasing sheweth to me but smoke and no light. These thynges to thinke in myn herte maketh every day wepyng in myn eyen to renne. These lyggen on my backe so sore that importable burthen me semeth on my backe to be charged; it maketh me backwarde to meve whan my steppes

---

so that ye and my soule togyther is endelesse/ in blysse shulde dwel/ and there shal my soule at the ful ben eased/ that he may haue your presence to shewe thentent of his desyres: Ah dere god/ that shal be a great ioye. Nowe erthely goddesse take regarde of thy seruant/ though I be feble/ for thou arte wonte to prayse them better/ that wolde conne serue in loue/ al be he ful mener than kynges or princes/ that wol not haue that vertue in mynde. Nowe precious Margaryte/ that with thy noble vertue haste drawen me in to loue first/ me wenynge therof to haue blisse/ as galle and aloes are so moche spronge/ that sauour of swetnesse may I not ataste. Alas that your benigne eyen/ in whiche that mercy semeth to haue al his nori**<326va><326vb>**ture/ nyl by no waye tourne the clerenesse of mercy to mewardes. Alas that your brennande vertues/ shynyng amomges al folke/ and enlumynynge al other people by habundau*n*ce of encreasing/ sheweth to me but smoke and no light. These thynges to thinke in myn herte maketh euery day wepyng in myn eyen to renne. These lyggen on my backe so sore/ that importable burthen me semeth on my backe to be charged/ it maketh me backwarde to meue/ whan my steppes

68 th'entent, the purpose. **70–71 wolde conne**, would like to be able to. **71 mener**, meaner, lower in status. **73 wenynge**, expecting; **as galle and aloes**, i.e., since bitter substances. **75 noriture nyl**, nurture will not. **76 brennande**, burning. **79 renne**, run; **lyggen**, lie; **importable burthen**, unsupportable burden. **80 meve**, move, go.

by comune course even forthe pretende. These thynges also on right syde and lyft have me so envolved with care that wanhope of helpe is throughout me ronne. Trewly, I leve that gracelesse is my fortune whiche that ever sheweth it mewardes by a cloudy disease, al redy to make stormes of tene, and the blysful syde halte styl awayward, and wol it not suffre to mewardes to turne; no force, yet wol I not ben conquered.

O, alas that your nobley so moche among al other creatures commended by flowynge streme by al maner vertues, but ther ben wonderful. I not whiche that let the flode to come in to my soule; wherfore, purely mated with sorowe thorough sought, myselfe I crye on your goodnesse to have pyté on this caytife that in the inrest degré of sorowe and disease is lefte, and, without your goodly wyl, from any helpe and recovery. These sorowes maye I not sustene but if my sorowe shulde be tolde and to youwardes shewed; although moche space is bytwene us twayne, yet me thynketh that by suche joleynynge wordes my disease gynneth ebbe. Trewly me thynketh that the sowne of my lamentacious

---

by comune course euen forthe pretende: These thynges also on right syde and lyft/ haue me so enuolued with care/ that wanhope of helpe is throughout me ronne/ trewly and leue that gracelesse is my fortune/ whiche that euer sheweth it mewardes by a cloudy disease/ al redy to make stormes of tene/ and the blysful syde halte styl awayward/ and wol it not suffre to mewardes to turne: no force/ yet wol I not ben co*n*quered.

O/ alas that your nobley so moche among al other creatures co*m*mended by folowynge streme by al maner vertues/ but ther ben wo*n*derful/ I not whiche that let the flode to come in to my soule/ wherfore purely mated with sorowe thorough sought/ my selfe I crye on your goodnesse to haue pyte on this caytife/ that in the inrest degre of sorowe and disease is lefte/ *and* without your goodly wyl from any helpe and recouery. These sorowes maye I not sustene/ but if my sorowe shulde be tolde and to you wardes shewed/ although moche space is bytwene vs twayne/ yet me thynketh that by suche ioleynynge wordes/ my disease gynneth ebbe. Trewly me thynketh that the sowne of my lamentacious

81 even forthe, straight on (or forward); **lyft**, left. **82 wanhope**, despair; **ronne**, run. **83 leve**, believe. **84 tene**, sorrow; **halte styl awayward**, holds still in the opposite direction. **85 no force**, no matter. **86 nobley**, nobleness. **87 but ther ben**, unless there be something; **not**, do not know. **88 purely**, completely; **mated . . . thorough sought**, penetrated. **89 caytife**, prisoner, wretch; **inrest**, most inward. **92 joleynynge**, encouraging, cheering (see note). **93 gynneth**, begins [to]; **ebbe**, decrease; **sowne**, sound.

wepyng is right nowe flowe into your presence, and there cryeth after mercy and grace, to which thing me semeth thee lyst none answere to yeve, but with a deynous chere ye commaunden it to avoyde. But God forbyd that any worde shuld of you springe to have so lytel routh. Pardé, pyté and mercy in every Margarite is closed by kynde amonges many other vertues by qualites of comforte. But comfort is to me right naught worthe withouten mercy and pyté of you alone, whiche thynges hastely God me graunt for his mercy.

Chapter II

Rehersynge these thynges and many other without tyme or moment of rest me semed for anguysshe of disease that altogyder I was ravysshed, I can not tel howe; but holy al my passyons and felynges weren loste as it semed for the tyme and sodainly a maner of drede light in me al at ones. Nought suche feare as folke have of an enemy that were myghty and wolde hem greve or done hem disease. For I trowe this is wel knowe

---

wepyng/ is right nowe flowe in to your presence/ *and* there cryeth after mercy *and* grace/ to which thing me semeth the lyst none answere to yeue/ but with a deynous chere ye co*m*mau*n*den it to auoyde/ but god forbyd that any worde shuld of you springe to haue so lytel routh. Parde pyte *and* mercy in euery Margarite is closed by kynde amo*n*ges many other vertues/ by qualites of comforte/ but comfort is to me right naught worthe/ withouten mercy and pyte of you alone/ whiche thynges hastely god me grau*n*t for his mercy.**<326vb>**

<327ra>REhersynge these thynges and many other/ without tyme or moment of rest me semed for anguysshe of disease/ that al togyder I was rauysshed/ I can not tel howe/ but holy al my passyons and felynges weren loste/ as it semed for the tyme/ and sodainly a maner of drede light in me al at ones/ nought suche feare as folke haue of an enemy that were myghty/ and wolde hem greue or done hem disease: For I trowe this is wel knowe

95 yeve, give; **deynous**, disdainful. **96 chere**, aspect; **avoyde**, go away. **97 springe**, be rumored about; **routh**, pity; **Pardé**, Indeed. **98 kynde**, nature. **98–99 right naught worthe**, worth nothing. **101–02 me semed**, it seemed to me. **104 drede**, dread; **light**, lit. **105 wolde hem greve**, would aggrieve; **done hem**, cause them.

to many persones that otherwhyle, if a man be in his soveraignes presence, a maner of ferdenesse crepeth in his herte not for harme but of goodly subjection, namely as men reden that aungels ben aferde of our savyour in heven. And pardé, there ne is ne maye no passyon of disease be, but it is to meane that angels ben adradde not by ferdnes of drede, sythen they ben perfytely blyssed as affection of wonderfulnesse and by servyce of obedyence; suche ferde also han these lovers in presence of their loves and subjectes aforne their soveraynes. Right so with ferdenesse myn herte was caught. And, I sodainly astonyed, there entred into the place there I was lodged a lady, the semelyest and moste goodly to my syght that ever toforne apered to any creature, and trewly in the blustrynge of her looke she yave gladnesse and comforte sodaynely to al my wyttes, and ryght so she dothe to every wyght that cometh in her presence. And for she was so goodly (as me thought) myne herte beganne somdele to be enbolded and wexte a lytel hardy to speke, but yet with a quakynge voyce as I durste, I salved her and enquired what she was, and why she, so worthy to syght, dayned to entre into so foule a dongeon, and

---

to many persones/ that otherwhyle if a man be in his soueraignes presence/ a maner of ferdenesse crepeth in his herte/ not for harme/ but of goodly subiection: namely as men reden that aungels ben aferde of our sauyour in heuen. And parde there ne is/ ne maye no passyon of disease be/ but it is to meane that angels ben adradde/ not by frendes of drede/ sythen they ben perfytely blyssed/ as affection of wonderfulnesse *and* by seruyce of obedyence/ suche ferde also han these louers in presence of their loues/ and subiectes aforne their soueraynes: Right so with ferdenesse myn herte was caught. And I sodainly astonyed/ there entred in to the place there I was lodged a lady/ the semelyest and moste goodly to my syght/ that euer to forne apered to any creature/ and trewly in the blustrynge of her looke/ she yaue gladnesse and comforte sodaynely to al my wyttes/ and ryght so she dothe to euery wyght that cometh in her presence. And for she was so goodly (as me thought) myne herte beganne somdele to be enbolded/ and wexte a lytel hardy to speke/ but yet with a quakynge voyce/ as I durste/ I salued her/ and enquired what she was/ and why she so worthy to syght/ dayned to entre in to so foule a dongeon/ and

107 ferdenesse, fear or awe. **108 pardé**, indeed. **109 adradde**, full of dread. **110 blyssed**, blessed. **113 astonyed**, astonished; **semelyest**, most comely. **114 blustrynge**, sense *blowing* as in heraldic blason. **115 yave**, gave. **116 wyght**, person. **117 somdele**, somewhat; **wexte**, grew. **118 durste**, dared; **salved**, greeted. **119 dayned**, condescended.

namely a prisone without leave of my kepers. For certes, althoughe the vertue of dedes of mercy stretchen to vysyten the poore prisoners, and hem after that faculties ben had to comforte, me semed that I was so ferre fallen into myserye and wretched hyd caytifnesse, that me shulde no precyous thynge neyghe; and also, that for my sorowe every wyght shulde ben heavy and wysshe my recovery. But whan this lady had somdele apperceyved as wel by my wordes as by my chere what thought besyed me within, with a good womanly countenaunce she sayde these wordes:

"O my nory, wenyst thou that my maner be to foryet my frendes or my servauntes? Naye," quod she, "it is my ful entente to vysyte and comforte al my frenshippes and alyes as wel in tyme of perturbation as of moost propertye of blysse. In me shal unkyndnesse never be founden. And also, sithen I have so fewe especial trewe nowe in these dayes, wherfore I maye wel at more leysar come to hem that me deserven. And if my comynge maye in any thynge avayle, wete wel I wol come often."

"Nowe, good lady," quod I, "that art so fayre on to loke, reynynge honny by thy

---

namely a prisone/ without leaue of my kepers. For certes al thoughe the vertue of dedes of mercy stretchen to vysyten the poore prisoners/ and hem after that faculties ben had to comforte/ me semed that I was so ferre fallen in to myserye and wretched hyd caytifnesse/ that me shulde no precyous thynge neyghe: and also that for my sorowe euery wyght shulde ben**<327ra><327rb>**heauy/ and wysshe my recouery. But whan this lady had somdele apperceyued/ as wel by my wordes as by my chere/ what thought besyed me within/ with a good womanly countenaunce she sayde these wordes.

O my nory/ wenyst thou that my maner be/ to foryet my frendes or my seruauntes? naye (quod she) it is my ful entente to vysyte and comforte al my frenshippes and alyes/ as wel in tyme of perturbation/ as of moost propertye of blysse/ in me shal vnkyndnesse neuer be founden. And also sithen I haue so fewe especial trewe nowe in these dayes/ wherfore I maye wel at more leysar come to hem that me deseruen/ and if my comynge maye in any thynge auayle/ wete wel I wol come often.

Nowe good lady (quod I) that art so fayre on to loke/ reynynge honny by thy

121 after that faculties ben had, according as faculties are (i.e., as far as is possible under the circumstances). **123 caytifnesse**, captivity. **124 heavy**, depressed. **124–25 somdele apperceyved**, somewhat perceived. **125 besyed**, busied. **127 nory**, disciple (lit., one being nursed or nourished); **wenyst**, do you suppose; **foryet**, forget. **130 sithen**, since; **fewe especial trewe**, i.e., especially true friends. **131 leysar**, leisure. **133 reynynge honny**, raining honey.

wordes, blysse of paradise arn thy lokynges, joye and comforte are thy movynges. What is thy name? Howe is it that in you is so mokel werkynge vertues enpight, as me semeth, and in none other creature that ever sawe I with myne eyen?" "My disciple," quod she, "me wondreth of thy wordes and on thee that for a lytel disease haste foryeten my name: Woste thou not wel that I am Love, that first thee brought to thy servyce?" "O good lady," quod I, "is this worshyppe to thee or to thyne excellence for to come into so foule a place? Pardé, somtyme tho I was in prosperyté and with forayne goodes envolved, I had mokyl to done to drawe thee to myn hostel; and yet many wernynges thou madest er thou lyste fully to graunt thyne home to make at my dwellyng place; and nowe thou comest goodly by thyne owne vyse to comforte me with wordes, and so there thoroughe I gynne remembre on passed gladnesse. Trewly, lady, I ne wotte whether I shal say welcome or none sythen thy comyng wol as moche do me tene and sorowe as gladnesse and myrthe. Se why. For that me comforteth to thynke on passed gladnesse that me anoyeth efte to be in doynge. Thus thy comynge bothe gladdeth and teneth, and that is cause of moche sorowe: Lo, lady howe than I am comforted by your

---

wordes/ blysse of paradise arn thy lokynges/ ioye and comforte are thy mouynges. What is thy name? Howe is it that in you is so mokel werkynge vertues enpight/ as me semeth/ and in none other creature th*at* euer sawe I with myne eyen? My disciple (quod she) me wondreth of thy wordes and on the/ th*at* for a lytel disease haste foryeten my name: Woste thou not wel that I am Loue/ that first the brought to thy seruyce? O good lady (q*uo*d I) is this worshyppe to the or to thyne excellence for to come in to so foule a place? Parde somtyme tho I was in prosperyte/ and with forayne goodes enuolued/ I had mokyl to done to drawe the to myn hostel/ and yet many wernynges thou madest er thou lyste fully to graunt/ thyne home to make at my dwellyng place: *and* nowe thou comest goodly by thyne owne vyse/ to comforte me with wordes/ and so there thoroughe I gynne remembre on passed gladnesse. Trewly lady I ne wotte whether I shal say welcome or none/ sythen thy comyng wol as moche do me tene and sorowe/ as gladnesse and myrthe: se why. For that me comforteth to thynke on passed gladnesse/ that me anoyeth efte to be in doynge. Thus thy comynge bothe gladdeth and teneth/ and that is cause of moche sorowe: Lo lady/ howe**<327rb><327va>**than I am comforted by your

135 mokel, many; **enpight**, established. **140 forayne**, alien, i.e., not natural to human kind. **141 mokyl**, much; **wernynges**, warnings. **142 lyste**, were pleased. **143 vyse**, counsel. **144 gynne**, begin; **ne wotte**, do not know. **145 tene**, grief. **148 teneth**, grieves.

commynge?" And with that I gan in teeres to distylle and tenderly wepe. "Nowe certes," quod Love, "I se wel, and that me overthynketh, that wytte in thee fayleth and arte in poynte to dote."

"Trewly," quod I, "that have ye maked and that ever wol I rue." "Wottest thou not wel," quod she, "that every shepeherde ought by reson to seke his sperkelande shepe that arne ronne into wyldernesse amonge busshes and peryls and hem to their pasture ayen bringe and take on hem privy besy cure of kepyng? And tho the unconnynge shepe scattred wolde ben loste rennyng to wyldernesse and to desertes drawe, or els wolden put hem selfe to the swalowyng wolfe, yet shal the shepeherde by busynesse and travayle so put him forthe that he shal not let hem be loste by no waye. A good shepeherde putteth rather hys lyfe to ben loste for his shepe. But for thou shalte not wene me beyng of werse condycion, trewly, for everych of my folke, and for al tho that to mewarde be knyt in any condycion, I wol rather dye than suffre hem throughe errour to ben spylte. For me lyste and it me lyketh of al myne a shepherdesse to be

---

co*m*mynge/ and with that I gan in teeres to distylle/ and tenderly wepe. Nowe certes (quod Loue) I se wel (and that me ouerthynketh) that wytte in the fayleth/ and arte in poynte to dote.

Trewly (quod I) that haue ye maked/ and that euer wol I rue. Wottest thou not wel (quod she) that euery shepeherde ought by reson to seke his sperkelande shepe that arne ronne in to wyldernesse/ amonge busshes and peryls/ and hem to their pasture ayen bringe/ and take on hem priuy besy cure of kepyng? and tho the vnconnyngc shepe scattred wolde ben loste/ rennyng to wyldernesse/ and to desertes drawe/ or els wolden put hem selfe to the swalowyng wolfe/ yet shal the shepeherde by busynesse and trauayle so put him forthe/ that he shal not let hem be loste by no waye. A good shepeherde putteth rather hys lyfe to ben loste for his shepe. But for thou shalte not wene me beyng of werse condycion/ trewly for euerych of my folke/ and for al tho that to mewarde be knyt in any condycion/ I wol rather dye than suffre hem throughe errour to ben spylte. For me lyste/ and it me lyketh/ of al myne a shepherdesse to be

149 gan, began, or, did; **certes**, certainly. **150 me overthynketh**, I regret. **151 dote**, be insane. **152 maked**, caused, made; **rue**, regret; **Wottest**, Know. **153 sperkelande**, scattered. **154 ronne**, run. **155 ayen bringe**, bring back; **privy**, intimate, special; **cure**, care; **unconnynge**, unknowing. **156 rennyng**, running; **drawe**, drawn. **158 put him forthe**, exert himself. **159 for**, in order that. **160 wene**, suspect; **everych**, everyone; **tho**, those. **162 spylte**, lost, destroyed; **me lyste**, it pleases me; **me lyketh**, I like.

cleped. Wost thou not wel I fayled never wight but he me refused and wolde neglygently go with unkyndenesse? And yet, pardé, have I many such holpe and releved, and they have ofte me begyled; but ever at the ende, it discendeth in their owne neckes. Haste thou not radde howe kynde I was to Paris, Priamus sonne of Troy? How Jason me falsed, for al his false behest? Howe Sesars swonke, I lefte it for no tene tyl he was troned in my blysse for his servyce? What," quod she, "most of al maked I not a lovedaye bytwene God and mankynde, and chese a mayde to be nompere to put the quarel at ende? Lo, howe I have travayled to have thanke on al sydes, and yet lyst me not to rest and I might fynde on whome I shulde werche. But trewly myn owne disciple bycause I have thee founde at al assayes in thy wyl to be redy myn hestes to have folowed and haste ben trewe to that Margaryte perle that ones I thee shewed and she alwaye ayenwarde hath made but daungerous chere, I am come in propre person to put thee out of errours and make thee gladde by wayes of reason, so that sorow ne disease

---

cleped. Wost thou not wel I fayled neuer wight/ but he me refused/ *and* wolde neglygently go with vnkyndenesse? And yet parde haue I many such holpe and releued/ and they haue ofte me begyled/ but euer at the ende it discendeth in their owne neckes. Haste thou not radde howe kynde I was to Paris/ Priamus so*n*ne of Troy? How Jason me falsed for al his false behest? Howe Sesars sonke/ I lefte it for no tene tyl he was troned in my blysse for his seruyce. What (q*uo*d she) most of al/ maked I not a louedaye bytwene god and mankynde/ and chese a mayde to be nompere/ to put the quarel at ende? Lo/ howe I haue trauayled to haue thanke on al sydes/ *and* yet lyst me not to rest/ *and* I miȝt fynde on home I shulde werche. But trewly myn owne disciple/ bycause I haue the founde at al assayes in thy wyl to be redy myn hestes to haue folowed/ *and* haste ben trewe to that Margaryte perle/ that ones I the shewed/ and she alwaye ayenwarde hath made but daunge**<327va><327vb>**rous chere/ I am come in propre person to put the out of errours/ and make the gladde by wayes of reason/ so that sorow ne disease

163 cleped, called; **Wost**, Know; **wight**, creature. **164 pardé**, indeed; **holpe**, helped; **releved**, relieved. **165 begyled**, deceived. **166 radde**, read. **167 falsed**, betrayed; **behest**, promise; **swonke**, pomp (see note); **tene**, sorrow. **168 troned**, enthroned. **169 lovedaye**, day of accord; **chese**, chose; **nompere**, umpire. **170 lyst me not**, it does not please me. **171 and I**, if I; **werche**, work. **172 assayes**, attempts; **redy**, ready. **173 ones**, once. **174 ayenwarde**, in return; **daungerous chere**, disdainful demeanor; **in propre person**, in my own person.

shal no more hereafter thee amaistry. Wherthrough I hope thou shalte lyghtly come to the grace that thou longe haste desyred of thylke jewel. Haste thou not herde many ensamples howe I have comforted and releved the scholers of my lore? Who hath worthyed kynges in the felde? Who hath honoured ladyes in boure by a perpetuel myrrour of their truthe in my servyce? Who hath caused worthy folke to voyde vyce and shame? Who hath holde cyties and realmes in prosperyté? If thee lyste cleape ayen thyn olde remembraunce, thou coudest every poynte of this declare in especial and say that I thy maystresse have be cause, causyng these thynges and many mo other." "Nowe, iwys, madame," quod I, "al these thynges I knowe wel my selfe and that thyn excellence passeth the understandyng of us beestes, and that no mannes wytte erthely may comprehende thy vertues." "Wel than," quod she, "for I se thee in disease and sorowe I wote wel thou arte one of myn nories. I maye not suffre thee so to make sorowe thyn owne selfe to shende; but I myselfe come to be thy fere, thyne hevy charge to make to seme the lesse. For wo is him that is alone; and

---

shal no more hereafter the amaistry. Wherthrough I hope thou shalte lyghtly come to the grace/ that thou longe haste desyred/ of thylke iewel. Haste thou not herde many ensamples/ howe I haue comforted and releued the scholers of my lore? Who hath worthyed kynges in the felde? Who hath honoured ladyes in boure by a perpetuel myrrour of their truthe in my seruyce? Who hath caused worthy folke to voyde vyce and shame? Who hath holde cyties and realmes in prosperyte? If the lyste cleape ayen thyn olde remembraunce/ thou coudest euery poynte of this declare in especial/ and say that I thy maystresse haue be cause/ causyng these thynges and many mo other. Nowe iwys madame (quod I) al these thynges I knowe wel my selfe/ and that thyn excellence passeth the vnderstandyng of vs beestes/ and that no mannes wytte erthely may comprehende thy vertues. Wel than (quod she) for I se the in disease and sorowe/ I wote wel thou arte one of myn nories/ I maye not suffre the so to make sorowe/ thyn owne selfe to shende: but I my selfe come to be thy fere/ thyne heuy charge to make to seme the lesse/ for wo is him that is a lone: And

176 thee amaistry, overcome you. **177 thylke**, that same. **178 ensamples**, examples. **179 worthyed**, caused to become worthy; **felde**, (battle)field; **boure**, bower, bedchamber. **180 voyde**, avoid. **181 cyties,** cities; **the lyste**, it pleases you. **182 cleape ayen**, recall; **coudest**, could. **183 be**, been. **184 iwys**, certainly. **185 beestes**, beasts. **186 for I se the**, since I see you. **187 wote**, know; **nories**, disciples. **188 shende**, ruin. **189 fere**, companion; **charge**, burden.

to the sorye, to ben moned by a sorouful wight it is great gladnesse. Right so, with my sycke frendes I am sicke, and with sorie I can not els but sorowe make tyl whan I have hem releved in suche wyse that gladnesse in a maner of counterpaysyng shal restore as mokyl in joye as the passed hevynesse byforne dyd in tene. And also," quod she, "whan any of my servauntes ben alone in solytary place, I have yet ever besyed me to be with hem in comforte of their hertes, and taught hem to make songes of playnte and of blysse, and to endyten letters of rethorike in queynt understondynges, and to bethynke hem in what wyse they might best their ladyes in good servyce please, and also to lerne maner in countenaunce in wordes and in bearyng, and to ben meke and lowly to every wight, his name and fame to encrease, and to yeve gret yeftes and large, that his renome maye springen. But thee therof have I excused, for thy losse and thy great costages wherthroughe thou arte nedy arne nothinge to me unknowen, but I hope to God somtyme it shal ben amended, as thus as I sayd. In norture have I taught al myne and in curtesye

---

to the sorye to ben moned by a sorouful wight it is great gladnesse. Right so with my sycke frendes I am sicke/ and with sorie I can not els but sorowe make/ tyl whan I haue hem releued/ in suche wyse that gladnesse in a maner of counterpaysyng shal restore as mokyl in ioye as the passed heuynesse byforne dyd in tene. And also (q*uo*d she) whan any of my seruauntes ben a lone in solytary place/ I haue yet euer besyed me to be with hem/ in comforte of their hertes/ and taught hem to make songes of playnte and of blysse/ and to endyten letters of rethorike in queynt vnderstondynges/ *and* to bethynke hem in what wyse they might best their ladyes in good seruyce please/ and also to lerne maner in cou*n*tenau*n*ce in wordes/ *and* in bearyng/ *and* to ben meke and lowly to euery wight/ his name *and* fame to encrease/ and to yeue gret yeftes *and* large/ th*at* his**<327vb><328ra>**renome maye springen/ but the therof haue I excused for thy losse and thy great costages/ wherthroughe thou arte nedy/ arne nothinge to me vnknowen/ but I hope to god somtyme it shal ben amended/ as thus as I sayd. In norture haue I taught al myne/ and in curtesye

190 the sorye, the sorrowful person; **moned**, commiserated with; **wight**, person. **191 sorie**, the sorrowful. **192 hem**, them; **counterpaysyng**, counterbalancing. **193 mokyl**, much; **passed hevynesse**, recent depression; **tene**, sorrow. **194 besyed me**, busied myself. **195 hertes**, hearts; **playnte**, complaints. **196 endyten**, compose; **queynt**, ornate, involved. **197 lerne**, learn. **198 maner**, comportment; **meke**, meek. **199 yeve**, give; **yeftes**, gifts; **that**, so that; **renome**, renown. **200 springen**, spring up; **the**, you; **costages**, costs. **201 nedy arne**, needy are. **202 norture**, nurture.

made hem expert their ladyes hertes to wynne, and if any wolde ben deynous or proude, or be envyous or of wretches acqueyntaunce, hastelyche have I suche voyded out of my schole. For al vyces trewly I hate; vertues and worthynesse in al my power I avaunce. "Ah, worthy creature," quod I, "and by juste cause the name of Goddesse dignely ye mowe beare. In thee lythe the grace thorough whiche any creature in this worlde hath any goodnesse. Trewly, al maner of blysse and preciousnesse in vertue out of thee springen and wellen as brokes and ryvers proceden from their springes, and like as al waters by kynde drawen to the see, so al kyndely thynges thresten by ful appetyte of desyre to drawe after thy steppes and to thy presence aproche as to their kyndely perfection: howe dare than beestes in this worlde aught forfete ayenst thy devyne purveyaunce? Also, lady, ye knowen al the privy thoughtes: in hertes no counsayle maye ben hydde from your knowyng. Wherfore I wote wel, lady, that ye knowe your selfe that I in my conscience am and have ben wyllynge to your servyce, al coude I never do as I shulde, yet, forsothe, fayned I never to love otherwyse than was in myn

---

made hem expert their ladyes hertes to wynne/ and if any wolde endeynous or proude or be enuyous/ or of wretches acqueyntaunce/ hastelyche haue I suche voyded out of my schole: for al vyces trewly I hate: vertues and worthynesse in al my power I auaunce. Ah worthy creature (quod I) and by iuste cause the name of goddesse dignely ye mowe beare: In the lythe the grace thorough whiche any creature in this worlde hath any goodnesse/ trewly al maner of blysse and preciousnesse in vertue out of the springen/ and wellen/ as brokes and ryuers proceden from their springes/ and like as al waters by kynde drawen to the see/ so al kyndely thynges thresten by ful appetyte of desyre to drawe after thy steppes/ and to thy presence aproche/ as to their kyndely perfection: howe dare than beestes in this worlde aught forfete ayenst thy deuyne purueyaunce? Also lady ye knowen al the priuy thoughtes/ in hertes no counsayle maye ben hydde from your knowyng. Wherfore I wote wel lady that ye knowe your selfe that I in my conscie*n*ce am and haue ben wyllynge to your seruyce/ al coude I neuer do as I shulde/ yet forsothe fayned I neuer to loue otherwyse than was in myn

203 deynous, disdainful. **204 wretches**, wretches'; **hastelyche**, hastily. **206 avaunce**, advance. **207 dignely**, worthily; **the lythe**, you lie. **209 the**, you; **wellen**, wells up; **brokes**, brooks. **210 by kynde**, naturally; **thresten**, thrust. **211 kyndely**, natural, innate. **212 beestes**, beasts; **forfete**, forfeit, transgress. **212–13 devyne purveyaunce**, divine providence. **214 wote**, know. **215 al**, although. **216 fayned**, pretended.

herte; and if I coude have made chere to one and ythought another as many other doone aldaye afore myn eyen, I trowe it wolde not me have vayled." "Certes," quod she, "haddest thou so done, I wolde not nowe have thee here vysited." "Ye wete wel, lady, eke," quod I, "that I have not playde raket nettyl in docke out and with the wethercocke waved, and trewly there ye me sette by acorde of my conscience I wolde not flye tyl ye and reason by aperte strength maden myn herte to tourne." "In good faythe," quod she, "I have knowe thee ever of tho condycions, and sythen thou woldest (in as moch as in thee was) a made me privy of thy counsayle and juge of thy conscience, though I forsoke it in tho dayes tyl I saw better my tyme, wolde never God that I shuld nowe fayle, but ever I wol be redy wytnessyng thy sothe in what place that ever I shal ayenst al tho that wol the contrary susteyne. And for as moche as to me is naught unknowen ne hyd of thy privy hert but al hast thou tho thynges made to me open at the ful, that hath caused my comynge into this prison to voyde the webbes of thyne eyen to make thee clerely to se the errours thou hast ben in. And bycause that men ben of dyvers condycions,

---

herte: and if I coude haue made chere to one/ and ythought another/ as many other doone aldaye afore myn eyen/ I trowe it wolde not me haue vayled. Certes (quod she) haddest thou so done/ I wolde not nowe haue the here vysited. Ye wete wel lady eke (quod I) that I haue not playde raket/ nettyl in/ docke out/ and with the wethercocke waued/ and trewly there ye me sette/ by acorde of my conscie*n*ce/ I wolde not flye/ tyl ye and reason by aperte strength maden/ myn herte to tourne./ In good faythe (quod she) I haue knowe the euer of tho condycions/ and sythen thou woldest (in as moch as in the was) a made me priuy of thy counsayle/ and iuge of thy conscie*n*ce/ though I for**<328ra><328rb>**soke it in tho dayes/ tyl I saw better my tyme/ wolde neuer god that I shuld nowe fayle/ but euer I wol be redy wytnessyng thy sothe/ in what place that euer I shal/ ayenst al tho that wol the contrary susteyne: And for as moche as to me is naught vnknowen ne hyd of thy priuy hert/ but al hast thou tho thynges made to me open at the ful/ that hath caused my comynge in to this prison to voyde the webbes of thyne eyen/ to make the clerely to se the errours thou hast ben in/ and bycause that men ben of dyuers condycions/

217 made chere to, played the sycophant to. **218 aldaye**, continually; **trowe**, believe; **vayled**, availed; **Certes**, Certainly. **219 wete**, know. **220 eke**, also; **raket**, a game of racquets; **nettyl in docke out**, i.e., have not been inconstant. **221 waved**, vacillated; **sette**, placed, positioned. **222 aperte**, open. **223 tho**, those; **sythen**, since; **moch**, much. **224 a**, have. **226 sothe**, truth, fidelity, truthfulness; **ayenst**, against. **229 voyde**, cast off.

some a dradde to saye a sothe, and some for a sothe anone redy to fyght, and also that I maye not myselfe ben in place to withsay thilke men that of thee speken otherwyse than the sothe, I wol, and I charge thee, in vertue of obedyence that thou to me owest, to writen my wordes and sette hem in writynges that they mowe as my witnessynge ben noted amonge the people. For bookes written neyther dreden ne shamen ne stryve conne, but onely shewen the entente of the writer and yeve remembraunce to the herer; and if any wol in thy presence saye any thynge to tho writers, loke boldely: truste on Mars to answere at the ful. For certes, I shal hym enfourme of al the trouthe in thy love with thy conscience, so that of his helpe thou shalte not varye at thy nede. I trowe the strongest and the beste that maye be founde wol not transvers thy wordes, wherof than woldest thou drede.

Chapter III

Gretly was I tho gladed of these wordes, and, as who sayth, wexen somdele light in herte, both for the auctorité of witnesse, and also for sykernesse of helpe of the forsayd

---

some a dradde to saye a sothe/ and some for a sothe anone redy to fyght/ and also that I maye not my selfe ben in place to withsay thilke men that of the speken/ otherwyse than the sothe/ I wol and I charge the in vertue of obedyence/ that thou to me owest/ to writen my wordes/ and sette hem in writynges that they mowe as my witnessynge ben noted amonge the people. For bookes written neyther dreden ne shamen/ ne stryue conne/ but onely shewen the entente of the writer/ and yeue remembraunce to the herer: and if any wol in thy presence saye any thynge to tho writers/ loke boldely/ truste on Mars to answere at the ful. For certes I shal hym enfourme of al the trouthe in thy loue/ with thy conscience/ so that of his helpe thou shalte not varye at thy nede. I trowe the strongest and the beste that maye be founde/ wol not transuers thy wordes/ wherof than woldest thou drede.

GRetly was I tho gladed of these word*es*/ and as who sayth wexen somdele light in herte/ both for the auctorite of witnesse/ and also for sykernesse of helpe of the forsayd

231 a dradde, have fear; **sothe**, truth. **232 withsay thilke**, contradict those. **233 I wol**, I desire. **234 mowe**, may. **235 dreden**, dread. **235–36 stryve conne**, are able to contend. **236 yeve**, give. **237 wol**, will. **239 trowe**, believe. **240 transvers**, cross. **241 drede**, have dread. **242 tho**, then; **wexen somdele**, grown somewhat. **243 sykernesse**, certainty.

beheste. And sayd: "Trewly, lady, nowe am I wel gladded through comforte of your wordes. Be it nowe lykynge unto your nobley to shewe whiche folke diffame your servauntes sythe your servyce ought above al other thynges to ben commended." "Yet," quod she, "I se wel thy soule is not al out of the amased cloude. Thee were better to here thyng that thee myght light out of thyn hevy charge and after knowyng of thyn owne helpe than to styrre swete wordes and such resons to here. For in a thoughtful soule (and namely suche one as thou arte) wol not yet suche thynges synken. Come of, therfore, and let me sene thy hevy charge that I may the lyghtlyer for thy comforte purvey.

"Nowe, certes, lady," quod I, "the moste comforte I myght have were utterly to wete me be sure in herte of that Margaryte I serve, and so I thinke to don with al mightes whyle my lyfe dureth." "Than," quod she, "mayste thou therafter in suche wyse that mysplesaunce ne entre?" "In good fayth," quod I, "there shal no misplesaunce be caused through trespace on my syde." "And I do thee to weten," quod she, "I set never yet

---

beheste/ and sayd. Trewly lady nowe am I wel gladded through comforte of your wordes: be it nowe lykynge vnto your nobley to shewe whiche folke diffame your seruauntes/ sythe your seruyce ought aboue al other thynges to ben co*m*mended. Yet (quod she) I se wel thy soule is not al out of the amased cloude: the were better to here thyng that the myght light out of thyn heuy charge/ and after knowyng of thyn owne helpe/ than to styrre swete wor**<328rb><328va>**des/ and such resons to here: for in a thoughtful soule (and namely suche one as thou arte) wol not yet suche thynges synken. Come of therfore and let me sene thy heuy charge/ that I may the lyghtlyer for thy comforte puruey.

Nowe certes lady (quod I) the moste comforte I myght haue/ were vtterly to wete me be sure in herte of that Margaryte I serue/ and so I thinke to don with al mightes whyle my lyfe dureth. Than (q*uo*d she) mayste thou therafter/ in suche wyse that mysplesaunce ne entre? In good fayth (quod I) there shal no misplesauce be caused through trespace on my syde. And I do the to weten (quod she) I set neuer yet

245 nobley, nobleness. **246 sythe**, since. **247 amased**, confused, confusing. **248 myght light out of**, relieve of. **248–49 after knowyng of thyn owne helpe**, [be] conducive to knowing how. **249 styrre**, utter. **250 Come of**, Come on. **251 purvey**, provide. **252 certes**, certainly; **wete**, to know. **253 me**, myself. **254 dureth**, lasts. **255 mysplesaunce**, grievance, aggravation. **256 weten**, know.

person to serve in no place (but if he caused the contrary in defautes and trespaces) that he ne spedde of his servyce." "Myn owne erthly lady," quod I tho, "and yet remembre to your worthynesse howe long sythen by many revolvyng of yeres in tyme whan Octobre his leave gynneth take and Novembre sheweth hym to syght whan bernes ben ful of goodes as is the nutte on every halke, and than good londe tyllers gynne shape for the erthe with great travayle to bringe forthe more corne to mannes sustenaunce ayenst the nexte yeres folowyng. In suche tyme of plentie he that hath an home and is wyse lyste not to wander mervayles to seche, but he be constrayned or excited. Oft the lothe thyng is doone by excytacion of other mannes opynyon whiche wolden fayne have myn abydynge take in herte of luste to travayle, and se the wyndyng of the erthe in that tyme of wynter — by woodes that large stretes werne in, by smale pathes that swyne and hogges hadden made as lanes with ladels their maste to seche. I walked thynkynge alone a wonder great whyle, and the great beestes that the woode haunten and adorneth al maner forestes and heerdes gone to wylde. Than, er I was ware, I neyghed to a see

---

person to serue in no place (but if he caused the co*n*trary in defautes and trespaces) that he ne spedde of his seruyce. Myn owne erthly lady (quod I tho) and yet remembre to your worthynesse howe long sythen by many reuoluyng of yeres/ in tyme whan Octobre his leaue gynneth take/ *and* Nouembre sheweth hym to syght/ whan bernes ben ful of goodes as is the nutte on euery halke/ and than good londe tyllers gynne shape for the erthe/ with great trauayle to bringe forthe more corne to mannes sustenaunce/ ayenst the nexte yeres folowyng. In suche tyme of plentie/ he that hath an home/ and is wyse/ lyste not to wander meruayles to seche/ but he be constrayned or excited: oft the lothe thyng is doone by excytacion of other mannes opynyon/ whiche wolden fayne haue myn abydynge/ take in herte of luste to trauayle and se the wyndyng of the erthe in that tyme of wynter/ by woodes that large stretes werne in/ by smale pathes that swyne and hogges hadden made/ as lanes with ladels their maste to seche/ I walked thynkynge alone a wonder great whyle/ and the great beestes that the woode haunten and adorneth al maner forestes/ and heerdes gone to wylde: than er I was ware I neyghed to a see

257 but if, unless. **258 ne spedde**, did not profit. **259 sythen**, since. **260 bernes**, barns. **261 halke**, cavity, i.e., shell; **londe tyllers**, farmers (land-tillers); **shape for**, till, cultivate. **264 mervayles**, marvels; **seche**, seek; **lothe**, unattractive (see note). **266 of luste**, desire; **wyndyng**, pathways, circumstances. **267 stretes**, roadways. **268 ladels**, acorns (see note); **maste**, food. **270 heerdes gone**, herds [were] gone; **neyghed**, approached, drew nigh.

banke and, for ferde of the beestes, 'shypcrafte,' I cryde. For lady, I trowe ye wete wel yourselfe nothyng is werse than the beestes that shulden ben tame, if they catche her wyldenesse and gynne ayen waxe ramage. Thus, forsothe, was I aferde and to shyppe me hyed. Than were there ynowe to lache myn handes and drawe me to shyppe of whiche many I knewe wel the names. Syght was the first, Lust was a nother, Thought was the thirde, and Wyl eke was there a mayster: these broughten me within borde of this shyppe of traveyle. So whan the sayle was sprad and this shyppe gan to move the wynde and water gan for to ryse and overthwartly to turne the welken; the wawes semeden as they kyste togyder, but often under colour of kyssynge is mokel olde hate prively closed and kepte. The storme so straungely and in a devouring maner gan so faste us assayle that I supposed the date of my deth shulde have made there his gynnyng. Nowe up, nowe downe, nowe under the wawe, and nowe aboven was my shyppe a great whyle. And so by mokel duresse of wethers and of stormes and with great avowyng

---

banke/ and for ferde of the beestes shypcrafte I cryde: For lady I trowe ye wete wel your selfe nothyng is werse than the beestes that shulden ben tame/ if they catche her wyldenesse/ and gynne ayen waxe ramage: thus forsothe was I a ferde/ and to shyppe me hyed. Than were there ynowe to lache myn**<328va><328vb>**handes and drawe me to shyppe/ of whiche many I knewe wel the names. Syght was the first/ lust was a nother/ thought was the thirde/ and wyl eke was there a myster: these broughten me within borde of this shyppe of traueyle. So whan the sayle was sprad and this shyppe gan to moue/ the wynde and water gan for to ryse/ and ouerthwartly to turne the welken/ the wawes semeden as they kyste togyder/ but often vnder colour of kyssynge is mokel olde hate priuely closed and kepte. The storme so straungely and in a deuouring maner gan so faste vs assayle/ that I supposed the date of my deth shulde haue made there his gynnyng/ nowe vp nowe downe/ nowe vnder the wawe and nowe abouen was my shyppe a great whyle. And so by mokel duresse of wethers *and* of stormes/ and with great auowyng

271 ferde, fear; **beestes**, beasts'; **'shypcrafte,'** "Ship ahoy!" "All aboard!" "To sea!"; **trowe**, believe; **wete**, know. **272 catche her**, revert to their. **273 gynne**, begin; **ayen**, again; **waxe ramage**, grow wild; **aferde**, afraid. **274 me hyed**, hastened myself; **ynowe**, enough; **lache**, seize. **276 mayster**, master. **277 gan to**, began to (or, simply, did). **278 overthwartly**, upside-down; **welken**, sky. **278–79 wawes semeden**, waves seemed. **279 kyste**, kissed; **mokel**, much. **280 prively**, secretly. **281 date**, day. **283 wethers**, [harsh] weather; **avowyng**, promising (i.e., if I survive).

pylgrimages, I was driven to an yle where utterly I wende first to have be rescowed, but trewly, as the first gynnyng, it semed me so peryllous the haven to catche that but thorowe grace I had ben comforted of lyfe I was ful dispayred. Trewly, lady, if ye remembre a right, of al maner thynges yourselfe came hastely to sene us see driven and to weten what we weren. But first ye were deynous of chere, after whiche ye gonne better alyght, and ever, as me thought, ye lyved in great drede of disease — it semed so by your chere. And whan I was certifyed of your name, the lenger I loked in you the more I you goodly dradde and ever myn herte on you opened the more, and so in a lytel tyme my shyppe was out of mynde. But, lady, as ye me lad I was ware bothe of beestes and of fysshes a great nombre throngyng togyder: amonge whiche a muskel in a blewe shel had enclosed a Margaryte perle, the moste precious and best that ever to forne came in my syght, and ye tolden your selfe that ylke jewel in his kynde was so good and so vertuous that her better shulde I never fynde al sought I therafter to the worldes ende. And with that I helde my peace a great whyle; and ever sythen I have me bethought

---

pylgrimages I was driuen to an yle/ where vtterly I wende first to haue be rescowed/ but trewly as the first gynnyng/ it semed me so peryllous the hauen to catche/ that but thorowe grace I had ben comforted/ of lyfe I was ful dispayred. Trewly lady if ye remembre a right of al maner thynges/ your selfe came hastely to sene vs see driuen/ and to weten what we weren: but first ye were deynous of chere/ after whiche ye gonne better alyght/ *and* euer as me thought ye lyued in great drede of disease/ it semed so by your chere. and whan I was certifyed of your name/ the lenger I loked in you/ the more I you goodly dradde/ and euer myn herte on you opened the more/ and so in a lytel tyme my shyppe was out of mynde. But lady as ye me lad I was ware bothe of beestes and of fysshes a great nombre throngyng togyder: amonge whiche a muskel in a blewe shel had enclosed a Margaryte perle/ the moste precious and best that euer to forne came in my syght/ and ye tolden your selfe that ylke iewel in his kynde was so good and so vertuous/ that her better shulde I neuer fynde/ al sought I therafter to the worldes ende/ and with that I helde my peace a great whyle: and euer sythen I haue me bethought

284 yle, isle; **wende**, expected; **rescowed**, rescued. **285 the haven to catche**, to reach the haven. **286 thorowe**, through; **dispayred**, despaired. **288 weten**, know; **deynous**, disdainful; **chere**, demeanour. **289 alyght**, soften your countenance; **drede**, dread; **disease**, discomfiting. **290 lenger**, longer. **291 dradde**, feared. **292 lad**, led; **ware**, aware. **293 muskel**, mussel; **blewe**, blue. **294 to forne**, heretofore. **295 ylke**, same; **his**, its. **296 al**, even though. **297 sythen**, since.

on the man that sought the precious Margarytes, and whan he had founden one to his lykyng he solde al his good to bye that jewel. Iwys, thought I, and yet so I thynke, nowe have I founden the jewel that myne herte desyreth, wherto shulde I seche further? Trewly nowe wol I stynte and on this Margaryte I sette me for ever. Nowe than also, sythen I wyste wel it was your wyl that I shulde so suche a servyce me take, and so to desyre that thing of whiche I never have blisse, there lyveth none but he hath disease. Your might than that brought me to suche servyce that to me is cause of sorowe and of joye, I wonder of your worde that ye sayne to bringen men in to joye, and, pardé, ye wete wel that defaut ne trespace may not reasonably ben put to me wardes as ferre as my conscience knoweth. But of my disease me lyst now a whyle to speke and to enforme you in what maner of blysse ye have me thronge. For truly I wene that al gladnesse al joye and al myrthe is beshet under locke and the keye throwe in suche place that it may not be founde; my brennyng wo hath altred al my hewe. Whan I shulde slepe, I walowe and I thynke and me disporte. Thus combred I seme that al folke had

---

on the man that sought the precious Margarytes/ and whan he had founden one to his lykyng/ he solde al his good to bye that**<328vb><329ra>**iewel: Iwys thought I and yet so I thynke/ nowe haue I founden the iewel/ that myne herte desyreth/ wherto shulde I seche further/ trewly nowe wol I stynte/ and on this Margaryte I sette me for euer. Nowe than also sythen I wyste wel it was your wyl that I shulde so suche a seruyce me take/ and so to desyre that thing/ of whiche I neuer haue blisse/ there lyueth none/ but he hath disease: your might than that brought me to suche seruyce/ that to me is cause of sorowe and of ioye/ I wo*n*der of your worde that ye sayne/ to bringen men in to ioye/ and parde ye wete wel that defaut ne trespace may not reasonably ben put to me wardes/ as ferre as my conscience knoweth: But of my disease me lyst now a whyle to speke/ *and* to enforme you in what maner of blysse ye haue me thronge. For truly I wene that al gladnesse/ al ioye/ and al myrthe is beshet vnder locke/ and the keye throwe in suche place that it may not be founde: my brennyng wo hath altred al my hewe. Whan I shulde slepe/ I walowe *and* I thynke/ and me disporte. Thus combred/ I seme that al folke had

299 bye, buy; **Iwys**, Indeed. **300 seche**, seek. **301 stynte**, cease. **302 sythen**, since; **wyste**, know. **305 sayne**, say; **pardé**, indeed. **306 wete**, know. **307 me lyst**, it pleases me. **308 thronge**, thrust; **wene**, expect. **309 beshet**, shut. **310 brennyng**, burning; **hewe**, color, complexion. **311 me disporte**, preoccupy myself, fret; **combred**, encumbered; **I seme**, it seems to me.

me mased. Also, lady, myne desyre hath longe dured some speking to have, or els at the lest have ben enmoysed with syght, and for wantynge of these thinges my mouthe wolde, and he durst, pleyne right sore sythen yvels for my goodnesse arne manyfolde to me yolden. I wonder, lady, trewly, save evermore your reverence, howe ye mowe for shame suche thynges suffre on your servaunt to be so multyplied. Wherfore, knelyng with a lowe herte I pray you to rue on this caytife that of nothyng now may serve. Good lady, if ye lyste, nowe your helpe to me shewe that am of your privyest servantes at al assayes in this tyme and under your wynges of protection. No helpe to me wardes is shapen: howe shal than straungers in any wyse after socoure loke, whan I that am so privy yet of helpe I do fayle? Further maye I not but thus in this prison abyde: what bondes and chaynes me holden, lady, ye se wel yourselfe? A renyant forjuged hath not halfe the care. But thus syghyng and sobbyng I wayle here alone, and nere it for comforte of your presence, right here wolde I sterve. And yet a lytel am I gladed that so goodly

---

me mased. Also lady myne/ desyre hath longe dured/ some speking to haue/ or els at th*e* lest haue ben enmoysed with syght: and for wantynge of these thinges/ my mouthe wolde *and* he durst/ pleyne right sore/ sythen yuels for my goodnesse arne manyfolde to me yolden. I wonder lady trewly/ saue euermore your reuere*n*ce/ howe ye mowe for shame suche thynges suffre on your seruaunt to be so multyplied: Wherfore knelyng with a lowe herte I pray you to rue on this caytife/ that of nothyng now may serue. Good lady if ye lyste nowe your helpe to me shewe/ that am of your priuyest seruantes at al assayes in this tyme/ and vnder your wynges of protection. No helpe to me wardes is shapen/ howe shal than straungers in any wyse after socoure loke/ whan I that am so priuy/ yet of helpe I do fayle? Further maye I not/ but thus in this prison abyde: what bondes and chaynes me holden/ lady ye se wel your selfe? A renyant foriuged hath not halfe the care. But thus syghyng and sobbyng I wayle here alone/ and nere it for comforte of your presence/ right here wolde I sterue. And**<329ra><329rb>**yet a lytel am I gladed/ that so goodly

312 mased, amazed; **dured**, lasted; **speking**, speaking; **els**, else. **313 lest**, least; **enmoysed**, comforted. **314 and he durst**, if it dared; **pleyne**, complain; **sythen**, since. **315 yolden**, exchanged; **save**, saving; **mowe**, may. **317 rue**, take pity; **caytife**, prisoner, wretch; **of nothyng**, for nought. **318 if ye lyste**, if it pleases you. **319 assayes**, attempts. **320 loke**, look. **322 renyant**, heretic; **forjuged**, condemned. **323 wayle**, wail; **nere**, were not. **324 sterve**, die.

suche grace and none hap have I hente graciously to fynde the precious Margarite that, al other lefte, men shulde bye if they shulde therfore sel al her substaunce. Wo is me that so many let games and purpose brekers ben maked wayters, suche prisoners as I am evermore to overloke and to hynder, and for suche lettours it is harde any suche jewel to wynne. Is this, lady, an honour to thy deytie? Me thynketh by right suche people shulde have no maistrye ne ben overlokers over none of thy servauntes. Trewly, were it leful unto you to al the Goddes wolde I playne that ye rule your devyne purveyaunce amonges your servantes nothyng as ye shulde. Also, lady, my moeble is insuffysaunt to countervayle the price of this jewel, or els to make th'eschange. Eke no wight is worthy suche perles to weare but kynges or princes or els their peres. This jewel for vertue wold adorne and make fayre al a realme; the nobley of vertue is so moche that her goodnesse overal is commended. Who is it that wolde not wayle but he might suche rychesse have at his wyl? The vertue therof out of this prison may me delyver and naught els. And if I be not ther thorowe holpen, I se myselfe withouten recovery: Although

---

suche grace and none hap haue I hente/ graciously to fynde the precious Margarite/ that al other lefte men shulde bye/ if they shulde therfore sel al her substaunce. Wo is me that so many let games and purpose brekers ben maked wayters/ suche prisoners as I am euermore to ouerloke and to hynder/ and for suche lettours it is harde any suche iewel to wynne. Is this lady an honour to thy deytie? me thynketh by right/ suche people shulde haue no maistrye/ ne ben ouerlokers ouer none of thy seruauntes. Trewly were it leful vnto you/ to al the goddes wolde I playne/ that ye rule your deuyne purueyaunce amonges your seruantes nothyng as ye shulde. Also lady my moeble is insuffysaunt to cou*n*teruayle the price of this iewel/ or els to make theschange: eke no wight is worthy suche perles to weare/ but kynges or pri*n*ces/ or els their peres: this iewel for vertue wold adorne *and* make fayre al a realme/ the nobley of vertue is so moche th*at* her goodnesse oueral is co*m*mended. Who is it that wolde not wayle but he might suche rychesse haue at his wyl/ the vertue therof out of this prison may me delyuer/ *and* naught els. And if I be not ther thorowe holpen/ I se my selfe withouten recouery: Although

325 hap, fortune (i.e., it's grace, not luck). **326 bye**, buy; **if**, even if; **her**, their. **327 let games**, hinderers; **purpose brekers**, liars; **wayters**, watchmen. **328 lettours**, hinderers. **330 maistrye**, mastery. **331 leful**, lawful; **playne**, complain. **332 moeble**, movables, wealth. **334 peres**, peers. **335 nobley**, nobleness. **336 wayle**, wail. **338 ther thorowe holpen**, thereby helped.

I might hence voyde, yet wolde I not. I wolde abyde the daye that destenye hath me ordeyned, whiche I suppose is without amendement. So sore is myn herte bounden that I maye thynken none other. Thus strayte, lady, hath sir Daunger laced me in stockes, I leve it be not your wyl; and for I se you taken so lytel hede as me thynketh and wol not maken by your might the vertue in mercy of the Margaryte on me for to stretche, so as ye mowe wel in case that you lyste, my blysse and my mirthe arne feld. Sicknesse and sorowe ben alwaye redy. The cope of tene is wounde aboute al my body that stondyng is me best; unneth maye I lygge for pure miseasy sorowe, and yet al this is lytel ynoughe to be the ernest sylver in forwarde of this bargayne; for treblefolde so mokel muste I suffer er tyme come of myn ease. For he is worthy no welthe that maye no wo suffer. And certes I am hevy to thynke on these thynges. But who shal yeve me water ynough to drinke lest myn eyen drie for rennyng stremes of teares? Who shal waylen with me myne owne happy hevynesse? Who shal counsaile me nowe in my lykyng tene, and in

---

I might he*n*ce voyde/ yet wolde I not/ I wolde abyde the daye that destenye hath me ordeyned/ whiche I suppose is without amendement/ so sore is myn herte bounden/ that I maye thynken none other. Thus strayte (lady) hath sir Daunger laced me in stockes/ I leue it be not your wyl: and for I se you taken so lytel hede/ as me thynketh/ and wol not maken by your might the vertue in mercy of th*e* Margaryte on me for to stretche/ so as ye mowe wel/ in case that you lyste: my blysse and my mirthe arne feld/ sicknesse and sorowc ben alwaye redy/ the cope of tene is wounde aboute al my body/ that stondyng is me best/ vnneth maye I lygge for pure miseasy sorowe/ and yet al this is lytel ynoughe to be the ernest syluer/ in forwarde of this bargayne/ for treble folde/ so mokel muste I suffer/ er tyme come of myn ease. For he is worthy no welthe/ that maye no wo suffer. And certes I am heuy to thynke on these thynges/ **<329rb>** **<329va>**but who shal yeue me water ynough to dri*n*ke/ lest myn eyen drie for rennyng stremes of teares? Who shal waylen with me myne owne happy heuynesse? who shal cou*n*saile me nowe in my lykyng tene/ and in

339 voyde, escape. **341 strayte**, straight; **sir Daunger**, Sir Haughtiness. **342 leve**, believe. **344 mowe**, may; **you lyste**, it pleases you; **feld**, felled, brought down. **345 cope**, cope, garment. **345–46 stondyng is me best**, it is easiest for me to stand. **346 unneth**, hardly; **lygge**, lie; **miseasy**, uncomfortable. **347 ernest sylver**, pledge-money; **forwarde**, contract; **mokel**, much. **349 yeve**, give. **350 rennyng**, running; **waylen**, bewail. **351 lykyng tene**, pleasant sorrow.

my goodly harse? I not. For ever the more I brenne the more I coveyte; the more that I sorow the more thrist I in gladnesse. Who shal than yeve me a contraryous drinke to stanche the thurste of my blysful bytternesse? Lo, thus I brenne and I drenche. I shyver and I sweate. To this reversed yvel was never yet ordeyned salve: for soth, al lyches ben unconnyng save the Margaryte alone any suche remedye to purvey.

Chapter IV

And with these wordes I brast out to wepe that every teere of myne eyen for greatnesse semed they boren out the bal of my syght and that al the water had ben out ronne. Than thought me that love gan a lytel to heavy for miscomfort of my chere and gan soberly and in easy maner speke, wel avysinge what she sayd. Comenly the wyse speken easyly and softe for many skylles: One is their wordes are the better byleved; and also, in easy speakynge, avysement men may catche what to put forthe and what to holden in. And also the auctorité of easy wordes is the more, and eke they yeven the more understandynge

---

my goodly harse? I not. For euer the more I brenne/ the more I coueyte: the more that I sorow/ the more thrist I in gladnesse. Who shal than yeue me a contraryous drinke/ to stanche the thurste of my blysful bytternesse? Lo thus I brenne and I drenche/ I shyuer and I sweate/ to this reuersed yuel was neuer yet ordeyned salue/ for soth al lyches ben vnconnyng/ saue the Margaryte alone/ any suche remedye to puruey.

AND with these wordes I brast out to wepe/ that euery teere of myne eyen for greatnesse semed they boren out the bal of my syght/ and that al the water had ben out ronne. Than thought me/ that loue gan a lytel to heauy for miscomfort of my chere/ and gan soberly and in easy maner speke/ wel auysinge what she sayd. Comenly the wyse speken easyly and softe for many skylles: One is/ their wordes are the better byleued/ and also in easy speakynge/ auysement men may catche/ what to put forthe/ and what to holden in. And also the auctorite of easy wordes is the more/ and eke they yeuen the more vnderstandynge

352 harse, harshness (see note); **not**, know not; **brenne**, burn. **353 thrist**, thirst; **yeve**, give. **354 stanche**, staunch, stop; **drenche**, drown. **355 reversed yvel**, paradoxical evil (i.e., seeming evil); **lyches**, physicians. **356 unconnyng**, ignorant, unable. **357 brast**, burst. **358 bal**, eyeball. **359 thought me**, it seemed to me; **heavy**, to become depressed. **360 avysinge**, considering. **361 skylles**, reasons. **362 avysement**, advice, suggestions. **363 eke**, also; **yeven**, give.

to other intencion of the mater. Right so this ladye easely and in a softe maner gan say these wordes:

"Mervayle," quod she, "great it is that by no maner of semblaunt as ferre as I can espye thou lyst not to have any recour, but ever thou playnest and sorowest, and wayes of remedye, for folysshe wylfulnesse, thee lyste not to seche. But enquyre of thy next frendes, that is, thyne inwytte and me, that have ben thy maystresse and the recour and fyne of thy disease: for of disease is gladnesse and joy, with a ful vessel so helded that it quencheth the felynge of the firste tenes. But thou that were wonte not onely these thynges remembre in thyne herte, but also fooles therof to enfourmen in adnullynge of their errours and distroyeng of their derke opynions, and in comforte of their seare thoughtes, now canst thou not ben comforte of thyn owne soule in thynkyng of these thynges. O where haste thou be so longe commensal that hast so mykel eeten of the potages of foryetfulnesse and dronken so of ignorance that the olde soukyng whiche

---

to other intencion of the mater. Right so this ladye easely and in a softe maner gan say these wordes.

Meruayle (quod she) great it is/ that by no maner of semblaunt/ as ferre as I can espye/ thou lyst not to haue any recour/ but euer thou playnest and sorowest/ *and* wayes of remedye for folysshe wylfulnesse the lyste not to seche: but enquyre of thy next frendes/ that is thyne inwytte/ and me that haue ben thy maystresse and the recour and fyne of thy disease/ or of disease is gladnesse and ioy/ with a ful nessel so helded/ that it quencheth the felynge of the firste tenes. But thou that were wonte not onely these thynges remembre in thyne herte/ but also fooles therof to enfourmen/ in adnullynge of their errours/ and distroyeng of their derke opynions/ and in comforte of their seare thoughtes: now canst thou not ben comforte of thyn owne soule/ in thyn**<329va>** **<329vb>**kyng of these thynges. O where haste thou be so longe co*m*mensal/ that hast so mykel eeten of the potages of foryetfulnesse/ and dronken so of ignorance/ that the olde soukyng whiche

366 Mervayle, Marvellous; **semblaunt**, appearance. **367 thou lyst**, you care; **recour**, succour; **playnest**, complain. **368 thee lyste**, you care; **next**, close. **369 inwytte**, conscience. **370 fyne**, end; **for of**, for out of; **is**; comes; **helded**, yielded (obs. sp.). **371 felynge**, feeling; **tenes**, sorrows. **372 enfourmen**, inform; **adnullynge**, annulling. **373 seare**, dry, depressing. **375 commensal**, a companion of the dining table; **mykel**, much. **376 potages**, foods; **soukyng**, sucking, nursing.

thou haddest of me arne amaystred and lorn fro al maner of knowyng? O this is a worthy person to helpe other that can not counsayle him selfe." And with these wordes for pure and stronge shame I woxe al reed.

And she than seyng me so astonyed by dyvers stoundes, sodainly (whiche thynge kynde hateth) gan deliciously me comforte with sugred wordes, puttyng me in ful hope that I shulde the Margarite getten if I folowed her hestes, and gan with a fayre clothe to wypen the teares that hyngen on my chekes. And than sayd I in this wyse: "Nowe, wel of wysedom and of al welthe, withouten thee may nothyng ben lerned. Thou bearest the keyes of al privy thinges. In vayne travayle men to catche any stedshyp, but if ye, lady, first the locke unshet, ye, lady, lerne us the wayes and the by pathes to heven; ye, lady, maken al the hevenly bodyes goodly and benignely to done her course that governen us beestes here on erthe. Ye armen your servauntes ayenst al debates with imperciable harneys; ye setten in her hertes insuperable blode of hardynesse; ye leaden hem to the parfyte good. Yet al thynge desyreth ye wern no man of helpe that wele done your lore.

---

thou haddest of me/ arne a maystred and lorn fro al maner of knowyng? O this is a worthy person to helpe other/ that can not counsayle him selfe. And with these wordes for pure and stronge shame I woxe al reed.

And she than seyng me so astonyed by dyuers stoundes/ sodainly (whiche thynge kynde hateth) gan deliciously me comforte with sugred wordes/ puttyng me in ful hope that I shulde the Margarite getten/ if I folowed her hestes/ and gan with a fayre clothe to wypen the teares that hyngen on my chekes: and than sayd I in this wyse. Nowe wel of wysedom and of al welthe/ withouten the may nothyng ben lerned/ thou bearest the keyes of al priuy thinges. In vayne trauayle men to catche any stedshyp/ but if ye lady first the locke vnshet/ ye lady lerne vs the wayes and the by pathes to heuen: ye lady maken al the heuenly bodyes goodly and benignely to done her course/ that gouernen vs beestes here on erthe. ye armen your seruauntes ayenst al debates/ with imperciable harneys/ ye setten in her hertes insuperable blode of hardynesse/ ye leaden hem to the parfyte good. Yet al thynge desyreth/ ye wern no man of helpe th*at* wele done your lore/

377 amaystred, overcome; **lorn**, lost. **379 woxe**, grew; **reed**, red. **380 astonyed**, astonished; **dyvers stoundes**, diverse times, turns; **sodainly**, suddenly. **381 kynde**, nature. **382 hestes**, orders. **383 hyngen**, hung. **385 stedshyp**, stability; **but if**, unless. **386 unshet**, unlock; **lerne**, teach; **heven**, heaven. **387 done**, follow (lit., "do"). **388 beestes**, beasts. **388–89 imperciable harneys**, impenetrable armor. **389 hardynesse**, courage and endurance. **390 wern**, deny (lit., warn).

Graunt me nowe a lytel of your grace al my sorowes to cease." "Myne owne servaunt," quod she, "trewly thou syttest nye myne herte, and thy badde chere gan sorily me greve. But amonge thy playnyng wordes me thought thou allegest thynges to be lettyng of thyne helpynge and thy grace to hynder, wherthroughe me thynketh that wanhope is crope thorough thyn hert. God forbyd that nyse unthrifty thought shulde come in thy mynde thy wyttes to trouble, sythen every thyng in comyng is contyngent. Wherfore make no more thy proposycion by an impossyble. But nowe I praye thee reherse me ayen tho thynges that thy mistrust causen, and thylke thynges I thynke by reason to distroyen and put ful hope in thyn herte. "What understondest thou there," quod she, "by that thou saydest many lette games are thyn overlokers. And also by that thy moeble is insuffysant. I not what thou therof meanest."

"Trewly," quod I, "by the first I say that janglers evermore arne spekynge rather of yvel than of good, for every age of man rather enclyneth to wickednesse than any goodnesse to avaunce. Also false wordes spryngen so wyde by the steeryng of false

---

graunt me nowe a lytel of your grace/ al my sorowes to cease. Myne owne seruaunt (q*uo*d she) trewly thou syttest nye myne herte/ *and* thy badde chere gan sorily me greue: but amonge thy playnyng wordes me thought thou allegest thynges to be lettyng of thyne helpynge/ and thy grace to hynder/ wherthroughe me thynketh that wa*n*hope is crope thorough thyn hert: God forbyd that nyse vnthrifty thought shulde come in thy mynde thy wyttes to trouble/ sythen euery thyng in comyng is contyngent/ wherfore make no more thy proposycion by an impossyble. But nowe I praye the reherse me ayen tho thynges/ that thy mistrust causen/ and thylke thynges I thynke by reason to distroyen/ *and* put ful hope in thyn herte. What vnderstondest thou there (quod she) by that thou saydest/ many lette games are thyn**<329vb><330ra>**ouerlokers. And also by that thy moeble is insuffysant/ I not what thou therof meanest.

Trewly (q*uo*d I) by the first/ I say that ianglers euermore arne spekynge rather of yuel than of good/ for euery age of man rather enclyneth to wickednesse/ than any goodnesse to auaunce. Also false wordes spryngen so wyde/ by the steeryng of false

392 nye, near; **badde chere**, depressed demeanor; **sorily**, sorely. **393 playnyng**, complaining; **allegest**, alleged; **lettyng**, hindering. **394 wanhope**, despair. **395 is crope**, has crept; **nyse**, foolish; **unthrifty**, unprofitable. **398 thylke**, those same. **400 lette games**, hinderers; **overlokers**, jailors. **401 moeble**, moveables, wealth; **not**, do not know. **402 janglers**, tattletales. **404 avaunce**, advance; **steeryng**, steering, leading.

lyeng tonges that fame als swiftely flyeth to her eares and sayth many wicked tales, and as soone shal falsenesse ben leved as truthe, for al his gret sothnesse. Now by that other," quod I, "me thynketh thilke jewel so precious that to no suche wretche as I am wolde vertue therof extende and also I am to feble in worldly joyes any suche jewel to countrevayle. For suche people that worldly joyes han at her wyl ben sette at the highest degree and most in reverence ben accepted. For false wenyng maketh felycité therin to be supposed, but suche caytives as I am evermore ben hyndred." "Certes," quod she, "take good hede and I shal by reason to thee shewen that al these thynges mowe nat let thy purpose by the leest poynt that any wight coude pricke.

Chapter V

"Remembrest nat," quod she, "ensample is one of the strongest maner as for to preve a mannes purpose. Than if I nowe, by ensample, enduce thee to any proposytion, is it nat proved by strength?" "Yes, forsothe," quod I. "Wel," quod she, "raddest thou never

---

lyeng tonges/ that fame als swiftely flyeth to her eares/ *and* sayth many wicked tales/ and as soone shal falsenesse ben leued as truthe/ for al his gret sothnesse. Now by that other (q*uo*d I) me thynketh thilke iewel so precious/ that to uo suche wretche as I am/ wolde vertue therof extende/ *and* also I am to feble in worldly ioyes/ any suche iewel to countreuayle. For suche people that worldly ioyes han at her wyl/ ben sette at the highest degree/ and most in reuerence ben accepted/ for false wenyng maketh felycite therin to be supposed: but suche caytiues as I am euermore ben hyndred. Certes (q*uo*d she) take good hede *and* I shal by reason to the shewen/ th*at* al these thynges mowe nat let thy purpose/ by the leest poynt that any wight coude pricke.

REmembrest nat (q*uo*d she) ensample is one of the strongest maner/ as for to preue a ma*n*nes purpose. Than if I nowe by ensample enduce the to any proposytion/ is it nat proued by strength? Yes forsothe (q*uo*d I) Wel (q*uo*d she) raddest thou neuer

405 her, their. **406 leved**, believed; **for**, despite; **sothnesse**, truthfulness. **407 thilke**, that same. **409 countrevayle**, to be equal in worth to; to match in value. **410 most**, must; **wenyng**, assumption. **411 caytives**, wretches, prisoners; **Certes**, Certainly. **412 mowe**, may; **let**, hinder. **413 leest**, least; **wight**, person; **pricke**, isolate to emphasize. **414 ensample**, example; **preve**, prove. **416 raddest**, read.

howe Paris of Troye and Heleyne loved togyder, and yet had they not entrecomuned of speche? Also Acrisyus shette Dane his doughter in a tour for suertie that no wight shulde of her have no maistry in my servyce; and yet Jupiter, by signes without any speche, had al his purpose ayenst her fathers wyl. And many suche mo have ben knytte in trouthe, and yet spake they never togyder, for that is a thyng enclosed under secretnesse of pryvité why twey persons entremellen hertes after a sight. The power in knowyng of such thynges so preven shal nat al utterly be yeven to you beestes, for many thynges in suche precious maters ben reserved to jugement of devyne purveyaunce. For among lyveng people, by mannes consyderacion moun they nat be determyned. Wherfore I saye al the envy, al the janglynge that welny people upon my servauntes maken efte, is rather cause of esployte than of any hyndringe." "Why than," quod I, "suffre ye such wrong and moun whan ye lyst lightly al such yvels abate? Me semeth to you it is a great unworship." "O," quod she, "holde nowe thy peace. I have founden to many that han ben to me unkynde, that trewly I wol suffre every wight in that wyse to have disease;

---

howe Paris of Troye and Heleyne loued togyder/ and yet had they not entrecomuned of speche? Also Acrisyus shette Dane his doughter in a tour/ for suertie that no wight shulde of her haue no maistry in my seruyce/ and yet Jupiter by signes without any speche had al his purpose ayenst her fathers wyl. And many suche mo haue ben knytte in trouthe and yet spake they neuer togyder/ for that is a thyng enclosed vnder secretnesse of pryuite/ why twey p*er*sons entremellen hertes after a sight. The power in knowyng of such thynges so preuen/ shal nat al vtterly be yeuen to you beestes/ for many thynges in suche precious maters/ ben res*er*ued to iugement of deuyne purueyaunce/ for amo*n*g lyueng people/ by ma*n*nes co*n*syderacion moun they nat be determyned. Wherfore I saye/ al**<330ra><330rb>**the enuy/ al the ianglynge/ that welny people vpon my seruau*n*tes maken efte/ is rather cause of esployte/ than of any hyndringe. Why than (q*uo*d I) suffre ye such wrong/ and moun whan ye lyst/ lightly al such yuels abate/ me semeth to you it is a great vnworship. O (q*uo*d she) holde nowe thy peace/ I haue founden to many that han ben to me vnkynde/ that trewly I wol suffre euery wight in that wyse to haue disease/

417 entrecomuned, communicated. **418 tour**, tower. **419 maistry**, mastery. **422 twey**, two; **entremellen**, intermix. **423 preven**, prove; **yeven**, given. **424 devyne**, divine. **426 janglynge**, tattle-telling; **welny**, nearly all? willful? villainous? see note; **efte**, often. **427 esployte**, advantage and success. **428 and moun**, if [you] may; **ye lyst**, it pleases you. **429 unworship**, disgrace. **430 disease**, frustration, illness, anxiety.

and who that contynueth to the ende wel and trewly, hem wol I helpen and as for one of myne into blysse to wende. As marcial doyng in Grece. Who was ycrowned by God? Nat the strongest, but he that rathest come and lengest abode and contynued in the journey and spared nat to traveyle as long as the play lest. But thilke person that profred him nowe to my servyce, therin is a while and anon voydeth and redy to another and so nowe one he thynketh and nowe another and into water entreth and anon respireth. Such one lyst me nat into perfyte blysse of my servyce bringe. A tree ofte set in dyvers places wol nat by kynde endure to bringe forth frutes. Loke nowe, I pray thee, howe myne olde servauntes of tyme passed contynued in her servyce, and folowe thou after their steppes, and than myght thou not fayle in case thou worche in this wyse." "Certes," quod I, "it is nothyng lych this worlde to tyme passed; eke this countré hath one maner, and another countré hath another. And so may nat a man alwaye put to his eye the salve that he healed with his hele. For this is sothe: betwixe two thynges lyche, ofte dyversité is required."

"Nowe," quod she, "that is sothe: dyversité of nation, dyversité of lawe, as was

---

and who that contynueth to the ende wel and trewly/ hem wol I helpen/ *and* as for one of myne in to blysse to wende/ as marcial doyng in Grece. Who was ycrowned/ by god nat the stro*n*gest/ but he that rathest come and lengest abode *and* contynued in the iourney/ and spared nat to traueyle as long as th*e* play lest. But thilke person th*at* profred him nowe to my seruyce therin is a while/ *and* anon voydeth and redy to another/ *and* so nowe one he thynketh *and* nowe another/ and in to water entreth and anon respireth/ such one lyst me nat in to p*er*fyte blysse of my seruyce bringe. A tree ofte set in dyuers places wol nat by kynde endure to bri*n*ge forth frutes. Loke nowe I pray the/ howe myne olde seruauntes of tyme passed contynued in her seruyce/ *and* folowe thou after their steppes/ and than myght thou not fayle/ in case thou worche in this wyse. Certes (q*uo*d I) it is nothyng lych/ this worlde to tyme passed/ eke this countre hath one maner/ and another countre hath another. And so may nat a man alwaye put to his eye the salue that he healed with his hele. For this is sothe/ betwixe two thynges lyche/ ofte dyuersite is required.

Nowe (q*uo*d she) that is sothe/ dyuersite of nation/ dyuersite of lawe/ as was

432 wende, go; **marcial**, martial. **433 rathest**, soonest. **434 lest**, lasted; **thilke**, that same. **435 voydeth**, quits. **436 respireth**, breathes again. **437 lyst me**, it pleases me. **438 kynde**, nature; **Loke**, Look. **440 worche**, work. **441 lych**, like. **443 hele**, heel (foot); **sothe**, truth.

maked by many reasons, for that dyversyté cometh in by the contrarious malyce of wicked people that han envyous hertes ayenst other. But, trewly, my lawe to my servauntes ever hath ben in general, whiche may nat fayle. For right as mannes lawes that is ordayned by many determinations may nat be knowe for good or badde tyl assay of the people han proved it and to what ende it draweth, and than it sheweth the necessité therof, or els the impossibilyté, right so the lawe of my servauntes so wel hath ben proved in general that hytherto hath it not fayled.

"Wyste thou not wel that al the lawe of kynde is my lawe and by God ordayned and stablisshed to dure by kynde reasoun, wherfore al lawe by mannes wytte purveyde ought to be underputte to lawe of kynde, whiche yet hath be commune to every kyndely creature that my statutes and my lawe that ben kyndely arne general to al peoples? Olde doynges and by many turnynges of yeres used, and with the peoples maner proved, mowen nat so lightly ben defased, but newe doynges, contrariauntes suche olde, often causen diseases and breaken many purposes. Yet saye I nat therfore that ayen newe mischefe men shulde nat ordaynen a newe remedye, but alwaye looke it contrary not

---

maked by many reasons/ for that dyuersyte cometh in by th*e* contrarious malyce of wicked people/ th*at* han enuyous hertes aye*n*st other. But trewly my lawe to my seruauntes euer hath ben in general/ whiche may nat fayle/ for right as mannes lawes/ that is ordayned by many determinatio*ns*/ may nat be knowe for good or badde/ tyl assay of the people han p*ro*ued it/ *and* to what ende it draweth/ *and* than it sheweth the necessite therof/ or els the impossibilyte. Right so the lawe of my seruauntes so wel hath ben p*ro*ued in general/ that hytherto hath it not fayled.**<330rb><330va>**

Wyste thou not wel that al the lawe of kynde is my lawe/ and by god ordayned *and* stablisshed to dure by kynde reasoun/ wherfore al lawe by mannes wytte purueyde/ ought to be vnderputte to lawe of kynde/ whiche yet hath be co*m*mune to euery kyndely creature/ that my statutes and my lawe that ben kyndely/ arne general to al peoples. Olde doynges/ and by many turnynges of yeres vsed/ and with the peoples maner proued/ mowen nat so lightly ben defased/ but newe doynges contrariauntes suche olde/ often causen diseases and breaken many purposes. Yet saye I nat therfore/ that ayen newe mischefe/ men shulde nat ordaynen a newe remedye/ but alwaye looke it contrary not

449 assay, experience. **453 Wyste**, Know; **kynde**, nature. **454 dure**, endure. **455 underputte**, subject; **kyndely**, natural. **457 proved**, validated. **458 mowen**, may; **defased**, defaced; **contrariauntes**, contrary [to]. **460 contrary**, contradict.

the olde no ferther than the malyce stretcheth. Than foloweth it — the olde doynges in love han ben unyversal — as for most exployte forthe used. Wherfore I wol not yet that of my lawes nothynge be adnulled. But thanne to thy purpose, suche jangelers and lokers and wayters of games, if thee thynke in aught they mowe dere, yet love wel alwaye and sette hem at naught, and lette thy porte ben lowe in every wightes presence, and redy in thyne herte to maynteyne that thou hast begonne, and a lytel thee fayne with mekenesse in wordes; and thus with sleyght shalt thou surmount and dequace the yvel in their hertes. And wysdome yet is to seme flye otherwhyle there a man wol fyght. Thus with suche thynges the tonges of yvel shal ben stylled, els fully to graunt thy ful meanynge, for sothe, ever was and ever it shalbe that myn enemyes ben aferde to truste to any fightynge. And therfore have thou no cowardes herte in my servyce, no more than somtyme thou haddest in the contrarye, for if thou drede suche jangleres thy viage to make, understande wel, that he that dredeth any rayne to sowe his cornes he shal have thin bernes. Also he that is aferde of his clothes, let him daunce naked. Who

---

the olde/ no ferther than the malyce stretcheth. Than foloweth/ it the olde doynges in loue han ben vnyuersal/ as for most exployte forthe vsed: wherfore I wol not yet that of my lawes nothynge be adnulled. But thanne to thy purpose/ suche iangelers and lokers/ and wayters of games/ if the thynke in aught they mowe dere/ yet loue wel alwaye/ and sette hem at naught/ and lette thy porte ben lowe in euery wightes presence/ and redy in thyne herte to maynteyne that thou hast begonne/ and a lytel the fayne with mekenesse in wordes/ and thus with sleyght shalt thou surmount and dequace the yuel in their hertes. And wysdome yet is to seme flye otherwhyle there a man wol fyght. Thus with suche thynges/ the tonges of yuel shal ben stylled: els fully to graunt thy ful meanynge/ for sothe euer was and euer it shalbe/ that myn enemyes ben aferde to truste to any fightynge: and therfore haue thou no cowardes herte in my seruyce/ no more than somtyme thou haddest in the contrarye/ for if thou drede suche iangleres thy viage to make: vnderstande wel that he that dredeth any rayne to sowe his cornes/ he shal haue than bernes. also he th*at* is aferde of his clothes/ let him dau*n*ce naked. Who

463 jangelers, tattle-tellers. **464 wayters**, hinderers; **dere**, do harm. **465 porte**, comportment; **wightes**, person's. **466 the fayne**, pretend. **467 sleyght**, sleight; **dequace**, quash. **468 flye**, [to] fly; **otherwhyle**, at times. **472 jangleres**, tattle-tellers. **473 viage**, journey; **rayne**, rain; **cornes**, grains of corn. **474 bernes**, barns.

nothyng undertaketh and namely in my servyce nothyng acheveth. After great stormes the wether is often mery and smothe. After moche clatering, there is mokyl rownyng; thus after jangling wordes cometh 'huyssthe,' 'peace,' and 'be styl.'" "O good lady," quod I than, "se nowe howe seven yere passed and more have I graffed and groubed a vyne, and with al the wayes that I coude I sought to a fed me of the grape. But frute have I none founde. Also I have this seven yere served Laban to a wedded Rachel his doughter, but blere eyed Lya is brought to my bedde whiche alway engendreth my tene and is ful of chyldren in trybulacion and in care. And although the clippynges and kyssynges of Rachel shulde seme to me swete, yet is she so barayne that gladnesse ne joye by no way wol springe so that I may wepe with Rachel. I may not ben counsayled with solace sythen issue of myn hertely desyre is fayled. Nowe than I pray that to me sone fredom and grace in this eyght yere: this eighteth mowe to me bothe be kynrest and masseday after the seven werkedays of travayle to folowe the Christen lawe; and, whatever ye do els, that thilke Margaryte be holden so, lady, in your privy chambre that she in this case

---

nothyng vndertaketh/ *and* namely in my seruyce/ nothyng acheueth. After great stormes th*e* wether is often mery *and* smothe. After moche clatering/ there is mokyl rownyng: thus after iangling wordes cometh huysshte/ peace/ *and* be styl. O good lady (q*uo*d I than) se**<330va><330vb>**nowe howe seuen yere passed *and* more/ haue I graffed and groubed a vyne/ and with al the wayes that I coude I sought to a fed me of the grape/ but frute haue I none founde. also I haue this seuen yere serued Laban to a wedded Rachel his doughter/ but blere eyed Lya is brought to my bedde/ whiche alway engendreth my tene/ and is ful of chyldren in trybulacion *and* in care: and although the clippynges and kyssynges of Rachel shulde seme to me swete/ yet is she so barayne/ that gladnesse ne ioye by no way wol springe/ so that I may wepe with Rachel/ I may not ben counsayled with solace/ sythen issue of myn hertely desyre is fayled. Nowe than I pray that to me sone fredom and grace/ in this eyght yere/ this eighteth mowe to me bothe be kynrest and masseday after the seuen werkedays of trauayle/ to folowe the christen lawe: and what euer ye do els/ that thilke Margaryte be holden so lady in your priuy chambre/ that she in this case

476 clatering, loud talk; **rownyng**, whispering. **478 graffed**, dug; **groubed**, dug around the roots of a plant. **479 a fed**, have fed. **481 blere eyed**, bleary-eyed; **tene**, sorrow. **482 clippynges**, hugs. **483 swete**, sweet; **barayne**, barren. **485 sythen**, since; **sone**, soon [come] (see note). **486 eyght**, eighth, a date of completion (octave); **kynrest**, kingdom; **masseday**, feast-day. **488 thilke**, that same.

to none other person be commytted." "Loke than," quod she, "thou persever in my servyce in whiche I have thee grounded that thilke skorne in thyn enemyes mowe this on thy person be not sothed: lo this man began to edefye, but, for his foundement is bad, to the ende may he it not bringe. For mekenesse in countenaunce with a manly hert in dedes and in longe contynuaunce is the conysance of my lyvery to al my retynue delyvered. What wenyst thou that me lyst avaunce suche persons as loven the first syttynges at feestes, the highest stoles in churches and in hal, loutynges of peoples in markettes and fayres, unstedfaste to byde in one place any whyle togyder wenyng his owne wyt more excellent than other, scornyng al maner devyse but his own. Nay, nay, God wot these shul nothing parten of my blysse. Truly, my maner here toforne hath ben worshyp with my blysse lyons in the felde and lambes in chambre, egles at assaute and maydens in halle, foxes in counsayle styl in their dedes, and their protection is graunted redy to ben a bridge, and their baner is arered like wolves in the felde. Thus by these wayes shul men ben avaunced; ensample of David that from kepyng of shepe was

---

to none other person be co*m*mytted. Loke than (quod she) in this case to none other person be co*m*mytted: Loke than (q*uo*d she) thou perseuer in my seruyce/ in whiche I haue the grou*n*ded/ that thilke skorne in thyn enemyes mowe this on thy person be not sothed: lo this ma*n* began to edefye/ but for his foundeme*n*t is bad/ to the ende may he it not bringe. For mekenesse in cou*n*tenaunce/ with a manly hert in dedes/ and in longe co*n*tynuaunce/ is the conysance of my lyuery/ to al my retynue delyuered. What wenyst thou th*at* me lyst auaunce suche persons as louen the first syttynges at feestes/ the highest stoles in churches *and* in hal/ loutynges of peoples in markettes and fayres/ vnstedfaste to byde in one place any whyle togyder/ wenyng his owne wyt more excellent than other/ scornyng al maner deuyse but his own: Nay nay god wot/ these shul nothing p*ar*ten of my blysse. Truly my maner here toforne hath ben/ worshyp with my blysse/ Lyons in the felde/ and lambes in chambre/ Egles at assaute *and* maydens in halle/ foxes in counsayle/ styl in their dedes/ *and* their protection is grau*n*ted redy to ben a bridge/ *and* their baner is arered like wolues in the felde. Thus by these wayes shul men ben auaunced: ensa*m*ple of Dauid th*at* from kepyng**<330vb><331ra>**of shepe/ was

490 mowe, may. **491 sothed**, proved true; **edefye**, build; **for**, since; **foundement**, foundation. **493 conysance**, badge; **lyvery**, livery, uniform. **494 wenyst**, suppose; **me lyst**, it pleases me; **avaunce**, advance. **495 feestes**, feasts; **stoles**, stools, chairs; **loutynges**, bowings. **496 byde**, abide; **wenyng**, supposing. **498 parten of**, share in. **500 styl**, secretive, politic. **501 arered**, raised.

drawen up into the order of kyngly governaunce, and Jupiter, from a bole, to ben Europes fere, and Julius Cesar from the lowest degré in Rome to be mayster of al erthly princes, and Eneas from hel to be king of the countré there Rome is nowe stondyng. And so to thee I say, thy grace by beryng therafter may set thee in suche plyght that no janglyng may greve the lest tucke of thy hemmes, that their jangles is not to counte at a cresse in thy disavauntage."

Chapter VI

"Ever," quod she, "hath the people in this worlde desyred to have had great name in worthynesse and hated foule to beare any fame, and that is one of the objections thou alegest to be ayen thyne hertely desyre." "Ye, forsothe," quod I, "and that so comenly the people wol lye and bringe aboute suche enfamé." "Nowe," quod she, "if men with leasynges put on thee enfamé, wenest thyselfe therby ben enpeyred? That wenyng is wronge, se why: for as moche as they lyen thy meryte encreaseth and make thee ben more worthy to hem that knowen of thee the soth; by what thyng thou art apeyred, that

---

drawen vp in to the order of kyngly gouernau*n*ce/ and Jupiter from a bole to ben Europes fere/ and Julius Cesar from the lowest degre in Rome/ to be mayster of al erthly pri*n*ces/ and Eneas from hel/ to be king of the countre there Rome is nowe stondyng. And so to the I say/ thy grace by beryng therafter/ may set the in suche plyght/ that no ianglyng may greue the lest tucke of thy he*m*mes/ that are their ianghes/ is not to counte at a cresse in thy disauauntage.

EVer (quod she) hath the people in this worlde desyred to haue had great name in worthynesse/ and hated foule to beare any fame/ and that is one of the obiections thou alegest to be ayen thyne hertely desyre. ye forsothe (q*uo*d I) and that so comenly the people wol lye/ *and* bringe aboute suche enfame. Nowe (q*uo*d she) if men with leasynges put on the enfame/ wenest thy selfe therby ben enpeyred? That wenyng is wronge/ se why: for as moche as they lyen thy meryte encreaseth/ and make the ben more worthy to hem that knowen of th*e* the soth/ by what thyng thou art apeyred/ th*at*

503 bole, bull. **504 fere**, mate. **506 beryng therafter**, comporting [yourself] accordingly. **507 janglyng**, tattle-telling; **greve**, grieve; **jangles**, jangling. **507–08 at a cresse**, worth a bladeof cress. **510 fame**, reputation. **511 ayen**, against. **513 leasynges**, lies; **enfamé**, infamy; **wenest**, suppose; **enpeyred**, damaged; **wenyng**, assumption. **515 soth**, truth; **apeyred**, damaged.

in so mokyl thou arte encreased of thy beloved frendes. And sothly a wounde of thy frende to thee lasse harme, ye sir, and better than a false kyssyng in disceyvable glosyng of thyne enemye; above that than to be wel with thy frende maketh suche enfamé. *Ergo*, thou art encresed and not apeyred." "Lady," quod I, "somtyme yet if a man be in disease th'estymacion of the envyous people ne loketh nothyng to desertes of men ne to the merytes of their doynges, but only to the aventure of fortune, and therafter they yeven their sentence. And some loken the voluntary wyl in his herte and therafter telleth his jugement, not takyng hede to reason ne to the qualité of the doyng, as thus: If a man be ryche and fulfylde with worldly welfulnesse, some commenden it and sayne it is so lente by juste cause. And he that hath adversyté they sayne he is weaked and hath deserved thilke anoye. The contrarye of these thinges some men holden also and sayne that to the ryche prosperyté is purvayed into his confusyon, and upon this mater many autorites of many and great-wytted clerkes they alegen. And some men sayn though al good estymacion forsaken folk that han adversyté, yet is it meryte and encrease of his

---

in so mokyl thou arte encreased of thy beloued frendes: and sothly a wounde of thy frende to the lasse harme/ ye sir/ and better than a false kyssyng in disceyuable glosyng of thyne enemye/ aboue that than to be wel with thy fre*n*de maketh suche enfame. Ergo thou art encresed and not apeyred. Lady (q*uo*d I) somtyme yet if a man be in disease/ thestymacion of the enuyous people ne loketh nothyng to desertes of men/ ne to the merytes of their doynges/ but only to the auenture of fortune/ and therafter they yeuen their sentence: and some loken the voluntary wyl in his herte/ and therafter telleth his iugement/ not takyng hede to reason ne to the qualite of the doyng/ as thus. If a man be ryche and fulfylde with worldly welfulnesse/ some co*mm*enden it/ and sayne it is so lente by iuste cause: and he that hath aduersyte/ they sayne he is weaked/ and hath deserued thilke anoye. The contrarye of these thinges some men holden also/ and sayne that to the ryche prosperyte is puruayed in to his confusyon/ and vpon this mater/ many au**<331ra><331rb>**torites of many and great wytted clerkes they alegen. And some men sayn/ though al good estymacion forsaken folk that han aduersyte/ yet is it meryte and encrease of his

516 mokyl, much; **sothly**, truly; **of**, by, from. **517 glosyng**, flattering. **518 maketh**, renders [void] (see note). **519** ***Ergo***, Therefore; **apeyred**, damaged. **520 loketh . . . to**, considers. **521 aventure**, fortuitous event. **522 yeven**, give; **loken**, consider. **524 welfulnesse**, prosperity. **525 weaked**, wicked. **526 thilke anoye**, that same misfortune, distress. **528 alegen**, allege.

blysse, so that these purposes arne so wonderful in understandyng that trewly for myn adversyté nowe, I not howe the sentence of the indifferent people wyl jugen my fame." "Therfore," quod she, "if any wyght shulde yeve a trewe sentence on suche maters, the cause of the disease maist thou se wel. Understande therupon after what ende it draweth, that is to sayne good or badde, so ought it to have his fame by goodnesse or enfamé by badnesse. For every reasonable person and namely of a wyse man, his wytte ought not without reason to forne herde sodainly in a mater to juge. After the sawes of the wise, thou shalt not juge ne deme toforne thou knowe." "Lady," quod I, "ye remembre wel that in moste laude and praysyng of certayne sayntes in holy churche is to rehersen their convercion from badde into good, and that is so rehersed as by a perpetual myrrour of remembraunce in worshyppynge of tho sayntes and good ensample to other misdoers in amendement. Howe turned the Romayne Zedeoreys fro the Romaynes to be with Hanybal ayenst his kynde nacion; and afterwardes him semyng the Romayns to be at the next degré of confusyon turned to his olde alyes, by whose wytte after was Hanybal discomfyted. Wherfore, to enfourme you, lady, the maner why I meane, se nowe. In

---

blysse/ so that these purposes arne so wonderful in vnderstandyng/ that trewly for myn aduersyte nowe I not howe the sentence of the indifferent people wyl iugen my fame. Therfore (quod she) if any wyght shulde yeue a trewe sentence on suche maters/ the cause of the disease maist thou se wel/ vnderstande thervpon after what ende it draweth/ that is to sayne good or badde/ so ought it to haue his fame/ or by goodnesse enfame by badnesse: for euery reasonable person/ *and* namely of a wyse man/ his wytte ought not without reason to forne herde/ sodainly in a mater to iuge. After the sawes of the wise/ thou shalt not iuge ne deme toforne thou knowe. Lady (quod I) ye remembre wel that in moste laude and praysyng of certayne sayntes in holy churche/ is to rehersen their conuercion from badde in to good/ *and* that is so rehersed/ as by a perpetual myrrour of remembraunce in worshyppynge of tho sayntes/ and good ensample to other misdoers in amendement. Howe turned the romayne zedeoreys fro the romaynes/ to be with Hanybal ayenst his kynde nacion: and afterwardes him semyng the romayns to be at the next degre of confusyon/ turned to his olde alyes/ by whose wytte after was Hanybal discomfyted. Wherfore to enfourme you lady the maner why I meane/ se nowe in

531 not, know not. **532 yeve**, give. **535 enfamé**, infamy. **536 sawes**, wise sayings. **537 toforne**, before. **538 laude**, praise or glorification. **542 kynde**, native; **him semyng**, it seeming to him. **543 alyes**, allies. **544 discomfyted**, frustrated; **maner why**, reasons.

my youth I was drawe to ben assentaunt and, in my mightes, helpyng to certayn conjuracions and other great maters of ruling of cytezins, and thilke thynges ben my drawers in, and exitours to tho maters werne so paynted and coloured that, at the prime face, me semed them noble and glorious to al the people. I than, wenyng mykel meryte have deserved in furtheryng and mayntenaunce of tho thynges, besyed and laboured with al my dyligence in werkynge of thylke maters to the ende. And trewly, lady, to tel you the sothe, me rought lytel of any hate of the mighty senatours in thilke cyté, ne of comunes malyce, for two skylles: One was I had comforte to ben in suche plyte that bothe profyte were to me and to my frendes. Another was for commen profyte in comynaltie is not but peace and tranquylité with just governaunce proceden from thylke profyte, sythen by counsayle of myne inwytte me thought the firste paynted thynges malyce and yvel meanynge, withouten any good avaylyng to any people, and of tyrannye purposed. And so for pure sorowe and of my medlynge and badde infame that I was in ronne,

---

my youth I was drawe to ben assentaunt and in my mightes helpyng to certayn co*n*iuracions/ and other great maters of ruling of cytezins/ and thilke thynges ben my drawers in/ *and* exitours to tho maters werne so paynted and coloured/ that at the prime face/ me semed them noble and glorious to al the people: I than wenyng mykel meryte haue deserued in furtheryng and mayntenaunce of tho thynges/ besyed and laboured with al my dyligence/ in werkynge of thylke maters to the ende. And trewly lady to tel you the sothe/ me rought lytel of any hate of the mighty senatours in thilke cyte/ ne of comunes malyce/ for two skylles: One was I had comforte to ben in**<331rb><331va>** suche plyte/ that bothe profyte were to me and to my frendes. Another was for co*m*men profyte in comynaltie is not but peace and tranquylite/ with iust gouernaunce proceden from thylke profyte/ sythen by counsayle of myne inwytte/ me thought the firste paynted thynges/ malyce and yvel meanynge/ withouten any good auaylyng to any people: and of tyrannye purposed/ and so for pure sorowe and of my medlynge and badde infame that I was in ronne/

545 assentaunt, assenting. **547 drawers in**, inducers or seducers; **exitours**, agitators. **547–48 prime face**, i.e., *prima facie*. **548 wenyng mykel**, assuming much. **549 besyed**, busied [myself]. **550 thylke**, those same. **551 me rought**, I myself cared. **552 comunes**, commons'; **skylles**, reasons. **553 for**, because. **555 inwytte**, intuition. **557 medlynge**, meddling; **in ronne**, run into.

tho teeres lasshed out of myne eyen were thus awaye wasshe; than the under hydde malyce and the rancoure of purposynge envye, fornecaste and ymagyned in distruction of mokyl people, shewed so openly that had I ben blynde with myne hondes al the circumstaunce I might wel have feled.

Nowe than tho persones that suche thynges have caste to redresse for wrathe of my first medlynge shopen me to dwel in this pynande prison tyl Lachases my threde no lenger wolde twyne. And ever I was sought if me lyste to have grace of my lyfe and frenesse of that prison, I shulde openly confesse howe peace myght ben endused to enden al the firste rancours. It was fully supposed my knowyng to be ful in tho maters. Than, lady, I thought that every man that by any waye of right rightfully done, maye helpe any comune helpe to ben saved — whiche thynge to kepe above al thynges I am holde to mayntayne; and namely in distroyeng of a wrong, al shulde I therthrough enpeche myn owne fere if he were gylty and to do misdede assentaunt. And mayster ne frende maye nought avayle to the soule of him that in falsnesse deyeth, and also that I

---

tho teeres lasshed out of myne eyen/ were thus awaye wasshe/ than the vnder hydde malyce and the rancoure of purposynge enuye fornecaste and ymagyned/ in distruction of mokyl people/ shewed so openly/ that had I ben blynde/ with myne hondes al the circumstaunce I might wel haue feled.

Nowe than tho persones that suche thynges haue caste to redresse/ for wrathe of my first medlynge/ shopen me to dwel in this pynande prison/ tyl Lachases my threde no lenger wolde twyne. And euer I was sought/ if me lyste to haue grace of my lyfe/ and frenesse of that prison/ I shulde openly confesse howe peace myght ben endused to enden al the firste rancours. It was fully supposed my knowyng to be ful in tho maters. Than lady I thought that euery man that by any waye of right/ rightfully done/ maye helpe any comune helpe to ben saued/ whiche thynge to kepe aboue al thynges I am holde to mayntayne/ and namely in distroyeng of a wrong/ al shulde I therthrough enpeche myn owne fere/ if he were gylty/ and to do misdede assentaunt. And mayster ne frende maye nought auayle to the soule of him that in falsnesse deyeth/ and also that I

558 tho teeres, those tears [that] (see note). **559 fornecaste**, forecast. **560 of mokyl**, by many. **561 feled**, felt. **562 caste**, planned. **563 shopen me**, caused me; **pynande**, grievous; **threde**, thread. **564 twyne**, weave; **me lyste**, it pleased me. **565 frenesse of**, freedom from; **endused**, induced, brought about. **566 ful**, complete. **570 enpeche**, impeach; **fere**, friend or companion; **assentaunt**, assenting. **571 frende**, friend; **deyeth**, dies.

nere desyred wrathe of the people ne indignacion of the worthy, for nothynge that ever I wrought or dyd in any doyng myselfe els but in the mayntenaunce of these foresayd errours and in hydynge of the privytees therof. And that al the peoples hertes holdynge on the errours syde weren blynde and of elde so ferforthe begyled that debate and stryfe they maynteyned and in distruction on that othersyde, by whiche cause the peace, that moste in comunaltie shulde be desyred, was in poynte to be broken and adnulled. Also the cytie of London, that is to me so dere and swete, in whiche I was forthe growen; and more kyndely love have I to that place than to any other in erthe, as every kyndely creature hath ful appetyte to that place of his kyndly engendrure, and to wylne reste and peace in that stede to abyde: thylke peace shulde thus there have ben broken — and of al wyse it is commended and desyred. For knowe thynge it is, al men that desyren to comen to the perfyte peace everlastyng must the peace by God commended bothe mayntayne and kepe. This peace by angels voyce was confyrmed, our God entrynge in this worlde. This as for His Testament He left to al His frendes whanne He retourned to

---

nere desyred wrathe of the people/ ne indignacion of the worthy/ for nothynge that euer I wrought or dyd/ in any doyng my selfe els/ but in the mayntenaunce of these foresayd errours/ and in hydynge of the priuytees therof. And that al the peoples hertes holdynge on the errours syde/ weren blynde and of elde so ferforthe begyled/ that debate and stryfe they maynteyned/ and in distruction on that othersyde/ by whiche cause the peace/ that moste in comunaltie shulde be desyred/ was in poynte to be broken and ad**<331va><331vb>**nulled. Also the cytie of London/ that is to me so dere and swete/ in whiche I was forthe growen/ and more kyndely loue haue I to that place than to any other in erthe/ as euery kyndely creature hath ful appetyte to that place of his kyndly engendrure/ and to wylne reste and peace in that stede to abyde: thylke peace shulde thus there haue ben broken/ and of al wyse it is co*m*mended and desyred. For knowe thynge it is/ al men that desyren to comen to the perfyte peace euerlastyng/ must the peace by god co*m*mended/ bothe mayntayne and kepe. This peace by angels voyce was confyrmed/ our god entrynge in this worlde. This as for his Testame*n*t he left to al his fre*n*des/ whanne he retourned to

572 nere, never. **575 elde**, old age; **ferforthe**, far. **577 adnulled**, nullified. **578 cytie of London**, city of London [was nullified]. **579 kyndely**, natural; **kyndely**, native. **580 engendrure**, begetting; **wylne**, wish, desire. **581 stede**, place; **thylke**, that same. **582 knowe**, known. **584 entrynge**, entering.

the place from whence He came: this His Apostel amonesteth to holden, without whiche man perfytely may have none insyght. Also this God by His comyng made not peace alone betwene hevenly and erthly bodyes, but also amonge us on erthe so He peace confyrmed, that in one heed of love one body we shulde perfourme. Also I remembre me wel howe the name of Athenes was rather after the god of peace than of batayle, shewynge that peace moste is necessarye to comunalties and cytes. I than so styred by al these wayes toforne nempned, declared certayne poyntes in this wyse. Firste that thilke persones that hadden me drawen to their purposes and, me not wetyng the privy entent of their meanynge, drawen also the feoble-wytted people, that have none insyght of gubernatyfe prudence, to clamure and to crye on maters that they styred; and under poyntes for comune avauntage they enbolded the passyfe to take in the actyves doynge, and also styred innocentes of connyng to crye after thynges whiche," quod they, "may not stande but we ben executours of tho maters, and auctorité of execucion by comen election to us be delyvered. And that muste entre by strength of your mayntenaunce, for we, out of suche degree put, oppressyon of these olde hyndrers shal agayne surmounten

---

the place from whence he came: this his Apostel amonesteth to holden/ without whiche man perfytely may haue none insyght. Also this god by his comyng/ made not peace alone betwene heuenly and erthly bodyes/ but also amonge vs on erthe/ so he peace confyrmed/ that in one heed of loue/ one body we shulde perfourme. Also I re*m*embre me wel howe the name of Athenes was rather after the god of peace than of batayle/ shewynge that peace moste is necessarye to comunalties and cytes. I than so styred by al these wayes toforne nempned/ declared certayne poyntes in this wyse. Firste that thilke persones that hadden me drawen to their purposes/ and me not wetyng the priuy entent of their meanynge/ drawen also the feoble wytted people/ that haue none insyght of gubernatyfe prudence/ to clamure and to crye on maters that they styred/ and vnder poyntes for comune auauntage/ they enbolded the passyfe to take in the actyues doynge/ and also styred innocentes of connyng to crye after thynges/ whiche (quod they) may not stande but we ben executours of tho maters/ and auctorite of execucion by comen election to vs be delyuered/ and that muste entre by strength of your mayntenaunce/ for we out of suche degree put/ oppressyon of these olde hyndrers shal agayne surmounten

586 amonesteth, admonishes. **589 heed**, head; **one body**, [as] one body. **591 styred**, steered. **592 nempned**, named. **593 thilke**, those same; **wetyng**, knowing. **595 gubernatyfe**, governmental; **clamure**, clamor. **597 styred**, directed; **connyng**, knowledge, shrewdness. **598 comen**, common. **600 hyndrers**, hinderers.

and putten you in such subjection that in endelesse wo ye shul complayne. The governementes," quod they, "of your cyté, lefte in the handes of torcencious cytezyns, shal bringe in pestylence and distruction to you, good men; and therfore let us have the comune admynistracion to abate suche yvels. Also," quod they, "it is worthy the good to commende and the gylty desertes to chastice. There ben cytezens many, forferde of execucion that shal be doone, for extorcions by hem commytted ben evermore ayenst these purposes and al other good menynges. Never-the-latter, lady, trewly the meanynge under these wordes was fully to have apeched the mighty senatoures whiche hadden heavy herte for the misgovernaunce that they seen. And so, lady, whan it fel that free election by great clamour of moche people for great disease of misgovernaunce so fervently stoden in her election that they hem submytted to every maner face, rather than have suffred the maner and the rule of the hated governours, not withstandynge that in the contrary helden moche comune meyny that have no consyderacion but onely to voluntary lustes withouten reason. But than thylke governour so forsaken, faynynge toforne his undoynge for misrule in his tyme, shope to have letted thilke electyon and

---

and putten you in such subiection/ that i*n* endelesse wo ye shul complayne. The gouernementes (q*uo*d they) of your cyte lefte in the handes of tor**<331vb><332ra>**cencious cytezyns shal bringe in pestylence and distruction to you good men/ and therfore let vs haue the comune admynistracion to abate suche yuels. Also (quod they) it is worthy the good to co*m*mende/ and the gylty desertes to chastice. There ben cytezens many for ferde of execucion that shal be doone/ for extorcions by hem commytted/ ben euermore ayenst these purposes/ and al other good menynges. Neuer the latter lady/ trewly the meanynge vnder these wordes/ was fully to haue apeched the mighty senatoures/ whiche hadden heauy herte for the misgouernaunce that they seen. And so lady whan it fel that free election/ by great clamour of moche people/ for great disease of misgouernaunce so feruently stoden in her election/ that they hem submytted to euery maner face/ rather than haue suffred the maner and the rule of the hated gouernours/ not withstandynge that in the contrary helden moche comune meyny that haue no consyderacion/ but onely to voluntary lustes/ withouten reason. But than thylke gouernour so forsaken/ faynynge to forne his vndoynge for misrule in his tyme/ shope to haue letted thilke electyon/ and

602 torcencious, extortionate. **605 chastice**, chastise, punish; **forferde**, afraid. **607 menynges**, motives; **Never-the-latter**, Nevertheless. **608 apeched**, impeached. **611 stoden**, stood. **613 meyny**, groups. **614 voluntary**, willful; **faynynge**, pretending. **615 shope**, arranged; **letted**, prevented.

have made anewe himselfe to have ben chosen, and under that mokyl rore have arered. These thynges, lady, knowen amonge the princes and made open to the people, draweth in amendement that every degree shal ben ordayned to stande there as he shulde, and that of errours comyng herafter men may lightly tofornehande purvaye remedye, in this wyse peace and rest to be furthered and holde. Of the whiche thynges, lady, thylke persones broughten in answere toforne their moste soverayne juge, not coarted by paynynge dures openly knowlegeden, and asked therof grace, so that apertely it preveth my wordes ben sothe without forgynge of leasynges.

But nowe it greveth me to remembre these dyvers sentences in janglynge of these shepy people. Certes me thynketh they oughten to maken joye that a sothe maye be knowe. For my trouthe and my conscience ben wytnesse to me bothe that this knowynge sothe have I sayde, for no harme ne malyce of tho persones but onely for trouthe of my sacrament in my leigeaunce by whiche I was charged on my kynges behalfe. But se ye not nowe, lady, how the felonous thoughtes of this people and covyns of wicked men

---

haue made a newe him selfe to haue ben chosen/ and vnder th*at* mokyl rore haue arered. These thynges lady knowen amonge the princes/ and made open to the people/ draweth in amendement/ that euery degree shal ben ordayned to stande there as he shulde/ and that of errours comyng herafter/ men may lightly to forne hande puruaye remedye/ in this wyse peace and rest to be furthered and holde. Of the whiche thynges lady/ thylke persones broughten in answere to forne their moste souerayne iuge/ not coarted by paynynge dures/ openly knowlegeden/ and asked therof grace/ so that apertely it preueth my wordes ben sothe/ without forgynge of leasynges.

But nowe it greueth me to remembre these dyuers sentences/ in ianglynge of these shepy people: certes me thynketh they oughten to maken ioye that a sothe maye be knowe. For my trouthe and my conscience ben wytnesse to me bothe/ that this knowynge sothe haue**<332ra><332rb>**I sayde for no harme ne malyce of tho persones/ but onely for trouthe of my sacrament in my leigeaunce/ by whiche I was charged on my kynges behalfe. But se ye not nowe lady/ how the felonous thoughtes of this people/ and couyns of wicked men/

616 mokyl rore, great outcry, roar; **arered**, raised up. **618 degree**, [member of a] social rank. **619 tofornehande**, beforehand. **621 toforne**, before; **coarted**, coerced. **622 paynynge dures**, painful duress; **apertely**, openly; **preveth**, proves. **623 leasynges**, lies. **624 greveth**, grieves; **dyvers**, various; **janglynge**, chattering. **625 shepy**, sheep-like. **627 sothe**, truth. **628 leigeaunce**, allegiance. **629 covyns**, bands.

conspyren ayen my sothfast trouth? Se ye not every wight that to these erronyous opinyons were assentaunt and helpes to the noyse and knewen al these thynges better than I my selven apparaylen to fynden newe frendes and cleapen me false and studyen howe they mowen in her mouthes werse plyte nempne? O God, what maye this be that thylke folke whiche that in tyme of my mayntenaunce and whan my might avayled to stretch to the forsayd maters, tho me commended and yave me name of trouth in so manyfolde maners that it was nyghe in every wightes eere there as any of thilke people weren; and, on the other syde, thilke company somtyme passed yevynge me name of badde loos. Nowe bothe tho peoples turned the good into badde and badde into good, whiche thyng is wonder, that they knowynge me sayng but sothe arne nowe tempted to reply her olde praysynges, and knowen me wel in al doynges to ben trewe, and sayne openly that I false have sayd many thynges. And they aleged nothynge me to ben false or untrewe, save thilke mater knowleged by the parties hemselfe. And, God wote, other mater is none. Ye also, lady, knowe these thynges for trewe: I avaunte not

---

conspyren ayen my sothfast trouth. Se ye not euery wiȝt that to these erronyous opinyo*n*s were assentaunt and helpes to the noyse/ and knewen al these thynges better than I my seluen/ apparaylen to fynden newe frendes/ and cleapen me false/ and studyen howe they mowen in her mouthes werse plyte nempne. O god what maye this be/ that thylke folke whiche that in tyme of my mayntenau*n*ce/ and whan my might auayled to stretch to th*e* forsayd maters/ tho me co*m*mended/ and yaue me name of trouth/ in so manyfolde maners that it was nyghe in euery wightes eere/ there as any of thilke people weren: and on the other syde/ thilke company somtyme passed/ yeuynge me name of badde loos. Nowe bothe tho peoples turned the good in to badde/ and badde in to good/ whiche thyng is wonder/ that they knowynge me sayng but sothe/ arne nowe tempted to reply her olde praysynges/ and knowen me wel in al doynges to ben trewe/ and sayne openly that I false haue sayd many thynges. And they aleged nothynge me to ben false or vntrewe/ saue thilke mater knowleged by the parties hem selfe: and god wote other mater is none. Ye also lady knowe these thynges for trewe/ I auaunte not

630 wight, person. **631 assentaunt**, assenting. **632 apparaylen**, make preparations; **cleapen**, call. **633 mowen**, may; **plyte nempne**, conditions name. **634 thylke**, that same. **635 tho**, then; **yave**, gave. **636 nyghe**, near; **wightes eere**, person's ear. **637 yevynge**, giving. **638 loos**, reputation. **639 sothe**, truth. **640 reply her**, retract their. **641 aleged**, alleged. **642 thilke**, that same; **hemselfe**, themselves. **643 wote**, knows; **avaunte**, boast.

in praysyng of myselfe, therby shulde I lese the precious secré of my conscience. But ye se wel that false opinyon of the people for my trouthe in tellyng out of false conspyred maters; and after the jugement of these clerkes I shulde not hyde the sothe of no maner person, mayster ne other. Wherfore I wolde not drede were it put in the consyderacion of trewe and of wyse. And for comers hereafter shullen fully out of denwere al the sothe knowe of these thinges in acte, but as they werne I have put it in scripture, in perpetuel remembraunce of true meanynge. For trewly, lady, me semeth that I ought to beare the name of trouthe that for the love of rightwysnesse have thus me submytten. But nowe than the false fame which that clerkes sayn flyeth as faste as dothe the fame of trouthe shal so wyde sprede tyl it be brought to the jewel that I of meane, and so shal I ben hyndred withouten any measure of trouthe."

Chapter VII

Than gan Love sadly me beholde and sayd in a chaunged voyce, lower than she had spoken in any tyme: "Fayne wolde I," quod she, "that thou were holpen, but haste thou

---

in praysyng of my selfe/ therby shulde I lese the precious secre of my conscience. But ye se wel that false opinyon of the people for my trouthe/ in tellyng out of false conspyred maters/ and after the iugement of these clerkes/ I shulde not hyde the sothe of no maner person/ mayster ne other/ Wherfore I wolde not drede/ were it put in the consyderacion of trewe and of wyse. And for comers hereafter shullen fully out of denwere/ al the sothe knowe of these thinges in acte/ but as they werne I haue put it in scripture/ in perpetuel remembraunce of true meanynge. For trewly lady me semeth/ that I ought to beare the name of trouthe/ that for**<332rb><332va>**the loue of rightwysnesse haue thus me submytten: But nowe than the false fame which that clerkes sayn flyeth as faste as dothe the fame of trouthe/ shal so wyde sprede/ tyl it be brought to the iewel that I of meane/ and so shal I ben hyndred withouten any measure of trouthe.

THan gan Loue sadly me beholde/ and sayd in a chau*n*ged voyce/ lower than she had spoken in any tyme. Fayne wolde I (q*uo*d she) that thou were holpen/ but haste thou

644 lese, lose; **secré**, secrecy or intimacy. **646 sothe**, truth. **647 mayster**, master. **648 comers**, those living; **denwere**, danger (see note). **649 werne**, were. **652 flyeth**, flies. **655 sadly**, sombrely. **656 holpen**, helped.

sayd any thynge whiche thou myght not proven?" "Pardé," quod I, "the persones every thyng as I have sayd han knowleged hemselfe." "Yea," quod she, "but what if they hadden nayed? Howe woldest thou have maynteyned it?" "Sothely," quod I, "it is wel wyste bothe amongest the greatest and other of the realme that I profered my body so largely into provynge of tho thynges, that Mars shulde have juged the ende. But for sothnesse of my wordes they durste not to thylke juge truste." "Nowe certes," quod she, "above al fames in this worlde the name of marcial doynges moste pleasen to ladyes of my lore, but sythen thou were redy, and thyne adversaryes in thy presence refused thilke doyng, thy fame ought to be so borne as if in dede it had take to the ende. And therfore every wight that any droppe of reason hath and hereth of thee infame for these thynges hath this answere to saye: 'trewly thou saydest, for thyne adversaryes thy wordes affirmed.' And if thou haddest lyed, yet are they discomfyted, the prise leaned on thy syde, so that fame shal holde down infamé: he shal bringe upon none halfe.

"What greveth thee thyne enemye to sayne their owne shame as thus: 'We arne

---

sayd any thynge whiche thou myght not prouen? Parde (quod I) the persones/ euery thyng as I haue sayd/ han knowleged hem selfe. Yea (q*uo*d she) but what if they hadden nayed/ howe woldest thou haue maynteyned it. Sothely (quod I) it is wel wyste bothe amongest the greatest/ and other of the realme/ th*at* I profered my body so largely in to prouynge of tho thynges/ that Mars shulde haue iuged the ende: but for sothnesse of my wordes they durste not to thylke iuge truste. Nowe certes (quod she) aboue al fames in this worlde/ the name of marcial doynges moste pleasen to ladyes of my lore/ but sythen thou were redy/ and thyne aduersaryes in thy presence refused thilke doyng/ thy fame ought to be so borne/ as if in dede it had take to the ende. And therfore euery wight that any droppe of reason hath/ and hereth of the infame/ for these thynges hath this answere to saye: trewly thou saydest for thyne aduersaryes thy wordes affirmed. And if thou haddest lyed/ yet are they discomfyted/ the prise leaned on thy syde/ so that fame shal holde down infame/ he shal bringe vpon none halfe.

What greueth the thyne enemye to sayne their owne shame/ as thus: We arne

657 Pardé, Indeed. **658 knowleged hemselfe**, acknowledged [it] themselves. **659** nayed, said no. **662 sothnesse**, truthfulness; **durste**, dared; **thylke**, that. **623 marcial**, martial; **pleasen to**, please. **664 sythen**, since. **665 dede**, deed; **take**, endurance. **666 wight**, person. **668 prise**, honor, prize; **leaned**, left. **669 he**, i.e., infamy; **none**, no. **670 greveth**, grieves.

discomfyted, and yet our quarel is trewe?' Shal not the loos of thy frendes ayenward dequace thilke enfamé and saye they graunted a sothe without a stroke or fighting? Many men in bataile ben discomfyted and overcome in a rightful quarel that is Goddes privy jugement in heven; but yet although the partie be yolden he may with wordes saye his quarel is trewe and to yelde him in the contrarye, for drede of dethe he is compelled; and he that graunteth and no stroke hath feled, he maye not crepe away in this wyse by none excusacion. Indifferent folke wyl say, 'ye, who is trewe, who is false, himselfe knowlegeth tho thinges.' Thus in every syde fame sheweth to thee good and no badde."

"But yet," quod I, "some wyl say I ne shulde for no dethe have discovered my maysters, and so by unkyndnesse they wol knette infamé to pursue me aboute. Thus enemyes of wyl in manyfolde maner wol seche privy serpentynes queyntyses to quenche and distroye by venym of many besynesses the light of truthe to make hertes to murmure ayenst my persone to have me in hayne withouten any cause." "Nowe," quod she, "here me a fewe wordes, and thou shalte fully ben answerde I trowe. Me thynketh," quod she,

---

discomfyted/ and yet our quarel is trewe. Shal not the loos of thy frendes ayenward dequace thilke enfame/ and saye they graunted a sothe without a stroke or fighti*ng*. Many men in bataile ben discomfyted and ouercome in a right ful quarel/ that is goddes priuy iugement in heuen: but yet although the partie be yolden/ he may with wordes saye his quarel is trewe/ and to yelde him in the contrarye for drede of**<332va> <332vb>** dethe/ he is compelled:/ and he that graunteth and no stroke hath feled/ he maye not crepe away in this wyse/ by none excusacion. Indifferent folke wyl say/ ye who is trewe/ who is false/ him selfe knowlegeth tho thi*n*ges. Thus in euery syde fame sheweth to the good and no badde. But yet (q*uo*d I) some wyl say I ne shulde for no dethe haue discouered my maystresse/ and so by vnkyndnesse they wol knette infame to pursue me aboute: thus enemyes of wyl in manyfolde maner wol seche priuy serpentynes queyntyses/ to quenche and distroye by venym of many besynesses the light of truthe/ to make hertes to murmure ayenst my persone/ to haue me in hayne withouten any cause. Nowe (quod she) here me a fewe wordes/ and thou shalte fully ben answerde I trowe. Me thynketh (quod she)

671 loos, praise; **ayenward**, to the contrary. **672 dequace**, quash; **thilke**, that same. **673 bataile**, battle. **674 yolden**, yielded. **676 feled**, felt; **wyse**, manner. **678 knowlegeth**, acknowledges. **680 knette**, knit (as in a net). **681 queyntyses**, contrivances. **683 hayne**, hatred; **here me**, listen to.

"right nowe by thy wordes that sacrament of swearyng, that is to say, chargyng by othe, was one of the causes to make thee discover the malicious ymaginatyons tofore nempned. Every othe, by knyttynge of copulation, muste have these lawes, that is trewe jugement and rightwysenesse, in whiche thynge, if any of these lacke, the othe is ytourned into the name of perjury. Than to make a trewe serment, most nedes these thynges folowe, for ofte tymes a man, to saye sothe, but jugement and justyce folowe, he is forsworne: ensample of Herodes for holdynge of his serment was dampned.

"Also, to saye truthe rightfullyche but in jugement otherwhile is forboden by that al sothes be nat to sayne. Therfore in jugement in truthe and rightwisenesse is every creature bounden up payne of perjury, ful knowyng to make tho it were of his owne persone for drede of synne. After that worde, 'better is it to dey than lyve false,' and al wolde perverted people false reporte make, in unkyndnesse in that entent thy fame to reyse, whan lyght of truthe in these maters is forthe sprongen and openly publysshed among commens, than shal nat suche derke enfamé dare appere, for pure shame of his

---

right nowe by thy wordes/ that sacrament of swearyng/ th*at* is to say/ chargyng by othe was one of the causes to make th*e* discouer the malicious ymaginatyons tofore nempned/ euery othe by knyttynge of copulation muste haue these lawes/ That is trewe iugement *and* rightwysenesse/ in whiche thynge if any of these lacke/ the othe is ytourned in to the name of periury: than to make a trewe serment/ most nedes these thynges folowe/ for ofte tymes a man to saye sothe/ but iugement and iustyce folowe he is forsworne: ensample of Herodes for holdynge of his serment was dampned.

Also to saye truthe rightfullyche but in iugement otherwhile is forboden/ by that al sothes be nat to sayne. Therfore in iugement in truthe and rightwisenesse is euery creature bounden vp payne of periury ful knowyng to make/ tho it were of his owne persone for drede of synne/ after that worde better is it to dey than lyue false/ and al wolde peruerted people false reporte make in vnkyndnesse/ in that entent thy fame to reyse/ whan lyght of truthe in these maters is forthe sprongen/ and openly publysshed among co*m*mens/ than shal nat suche derke enfame dare appere for pure shame of his

685 chargyng, charging (with responsibility). **687 nempned**, named. **689 serment**, oath. **690 but**, unless. **691 forsworne**, perjured; **holdynge**, maintaining; **dampned**, damned. **692 otherwhile**, at times, occasionally; **forboden**, forbidden; **by that**, because. **694 up**, upon; **knowyng**, acknowledgment; **of**, pertained to. **695 dey**, die; **al**, although. **697 reyse**, raise. **698 commens**, the commons; **derke**, dark.

falsnesse, as some men ther ben that their owne enfamé can none otherwyse voide or els excuse, but be hyndringe of other mennes fame, which that by non other cause cleapen other men false. But for with their owne falsnesse mowen they nat ben avaunsed or els by false sklaundrynge wordes other men shendyn, their owne trewe sklaunder to make seme the lasse, for if such men wolden their eyen of their conscience revolven, shulden sene the same sentence they legen on other springe out of their sydes with so many braunches it were impossyble to nombre. To whiche, therfore, maye it be sayd in that thynge this man thou demest, therin thy selfe thou condempnest. But," quod she, "understande nat by these wordes that thou wene me saye thee to be worthy sclaunder, for any mater tofore written truely I wolde wytnesse the contrary. But I saye that the beames of sclaundryng wordes may nat be done awaye tyl the daye of dome. For howe shulde it nat yet amonges so great plentie of people ben many shrewes, sithen whan no mo but eight persons in Noes shippe were closed, yet one was a shrewe and skorned his father. These thynges," quod she, "I trowe shewen that false fame is nat to drede ne of wyse persons to accepte and namely nat of thy Margarite, whose wysedom here-

---

falsnesse/ as some me*n* ther ben th*at* their owne enfame can none otherwyse voide or els excuse/ but be hyndringe of other men**<332vb><333ra>**nes fame/ which that by non other cause/ cleapen other men false/ but for with their owne falsnesse mowen they nat ben auaunsed/ or els by false sklaundynge wordes/ other men shendyn/ their owne trewe sklaunder/ to make seme the lasse/ for if such men wolden their eyen of their conscience reuoluen/ shulden sene the same sentence they legen on other/ springe out of their sydes/ with so many braunches it were impossyble to nombre. To whiche therfore maye it be sayd in that thynge/ this man thou demest/ therin thy selfe thou co*n*dempnest. But (quod she) vndersta*n*de nat by these wordes/ that thou wene me saye the to be worthy sclaunder/ for any mater tofore written/ truely I wolde wytnesse the contrary/ but I saye that the beames of sclaundryng wordes/ may nat be done awaye tyl the daye of dome. For howe shulde it nat yet amonges so great plentie of people ben many shrewes/ sithen whan no mo but eight persons in Noes shippe were closed/ yet one was a shrewe and skorned his father. These thynges (quod she) I trowe/ shewen that false fame is nat to drede/ ne of wyse persons to accepte/ and namely nat of thy Margarite/ whose wysedom here

700 be, by. **701 cleapen**, call; **mowen**, may. **702 sklaundrynge**, slandering (see line 709); **shendyn**, destroy. **704 shulden**, [they] should; **legen**, lay. **706 demest**, judge. **707 wene**, suppose. **708 tofore**, heretofore. **709 beames**, trumpets. **711 skorned**, scorned, ridiculed. **712 trowe**, believe.

after I thynke to declare, wherfore, I wotte wel, suche thynge shal nat her asterte; than of unkyndnesse thyne othe hath thee excused at the fulle. But nowe if thou woldest nat greve me lyst a fewe thynges to shewe." "Say on," quod I, "what ye wol. I trowe ye meane but trouthe and my profyte in tyme comynge." "Trewly," quod she, "that is sothe, so thou con wel kepe these wordes and, in the inrest secré chambre of thyne herte, so faste hem close that they never flytte than shalte thou fynde hem avaylyng. Loke nowe what people haste thou served, whiche of hem al in tyme of thyne exile ever thee refresshed by the valewe of the leste coyned plate that walketh in money. Who was sorye or made any rewth for thy disease? If they hadden getten their purpose, of thy misaventure sette they nat an hawe. Lo, whan thou were enprisonned howe faste they hyed in helpe of thy delyveraunce. I wene of thy dethe they yeve but lyte. They loked after nothynge but after their owne lustes. And if thou lyste say the sothe, al that meyny that in this brigge thee broughten lokeden rather after thyne helpes than thee to have releved.

---

after I thynke to declare/ wherfore I wotte wel suche thynge shal nat her asterte/ than of vnkyndnesse thyne othe hath the excused at the fulle. But nowe if thou woldest nat greue/ me lyst a fewe thynges to shewe. Say on (quod I) what ye wol/ I trowe ye meane but trouthe/ and my profyte in tyme comynge. Trewly (quod she) that is sothe/ so thou con wel kepe these wordes/ and in the inrest secre chambre of thyne herte/ so faste hem close that they neuer flytte/ than shalte thou fynde hem auaylyng. Loke nowe what people haste thou serued/ whiche of hem al in tyme of thyne exile euer the refresshed/ by the valewe of the leste coyned plate that walketh in money. Who was sorye or made any rewth for thy disease? if they hadden getten their purpose of thy misauenture sette they nat an hawe. Lo whan thou were enprisonned/ howe faste they hyed in helpe of thy delyueraunce. I wene of thy dethe they yeue but lyte: They loked after no**<333ra><333rb>**thynge/ but after their owne lustes. And if thou lyste say the sothe/ al that meyny that in this brigge the broughten/ lokeden rather after thyne helpes/ than the to haue releued.

714 wotte, know; **her asterte**, make her move or go away. **715 othe**, oath. **715–16 if thou woldest nat greve**, if you wouldn't mind. **716 trowe**, believe. **718 inrest**, innermost. **719 flytte**, fly away. **721 walketh**, circulates. **722 rewth**, pity; **getten**, got. **723 hawe**, trifle. **724 hyed**, hastened; **wene**, suppose; **yeve but lyte**, cared but a little. **725 lyste**, are pleased. **726 meyny**, troop; **brigge**, trouble; **lokeden . . . after**, had regard to; **helpes**, [the] help [you could give them].

Owen nat yet some of hem money for his commens? Paydest nat thou for some of her dispences tyl they were tourned out of Selande? Who yave thee ever ought for any rydynge thou madest? Yet, pardye, some of hem token money for thy chambre and putte tho pens in his purse, unwetynge of the renter.

Lo for which a company thou medlest that neyther thee ne themselfe myghten helpe; of unkyndnesse nowe they beare the name that thou supposest of hem for to have. What myght thou more have done than thou dyddest, but if thou woldest in a false quarel have been a stynkynge martyr? I wene thou fleddest as longe as thou myght their pryvité to counsayle whiche thynge thou helest lenger than thou shuldest. And thilke that ought thee money no penny wolde paye; they wende thy returne hadde ben an impossyble. Howe might thou better have hem proved but thus in thy nedy diseases? Nowe haste thou ensaumple for whom thou shalte meddle: trewly, this lore is worthe many goodes.

Owen nat yet some of hem money for his co*mm*ens? Paydest nat thou for some of her dispences/ tyl they were tourned out of Selande? Who yaue the euer ought for any rydynge thou madest? yet pardye some of hem token money for thy chambre/ and putte tho pens in his purse vnwetynge of the renter.

Lo for which a company thou medlest/ that neyther the ne them selfe myghten helpe of vnkyndnesse/ nowe they beare the name th*at* thou supposest of hem for to haue. What myght thou more haue done than thou dyddest/ but if thou woldest in a false quarel haue been a stynkynge martyr? I wene thou fleddest as longe as thou myght/ their pryuite to counsayle/ whiche thynge thou helest lenger than thou shuldest. And thilke th*at* ought the money no penny wolde paye/ they wende thy returne hadde ben an impossyble. Howe might thou better haue hem proued/ but thus in thy nedy diseases? Nowe haste thou ensaumple for whom thou shalte meddle: trewly this lore is worthe many goodes.

728 commens, provisions. **729 dispences**, expenses. **730 rydynge**, journeys; **pardye**, indeed. **731 unwetynge**, unconscious (i.e., indifferent); **renter**, proprietor. **732 medlest**, were busy. **733 of**, because of. **734 but if**, unless. **735 wene**, assume. **736 helest**, held (see note). **737 ought**, owed; **wende**, assumed. **738 hem proved**, proven them [for what they are]. **739 meddle**, get involved.

Chapter VIII

Efte gan Love to sterne me these wordes: "thynke on my speche, for trewly hereafter it wol do thee lykynge, and howesoever thou se Fortune shape her wheele to tourne, this meditation by no waye revolve. For certes, Fortune sheweth her fayrest whan she thynketh to begyle. And as me thought heretoforne thou saydest thy loos in love (for thy rightwysenesse ought to be raysed) shulde be alowed in tyme comynge. Thou myght in love so thee have that loos and fame shul so ben raysed that to thy frendes comforte, and sorowe to thyne enemys, endlesse shul endure.

But if thou were the one shepe amonges the hundred were loste in deserte and out of the way hadde erred and nowe to the flocke arte restoored, the shepeheerd hath in thee no joye and thou ayen to the forrest tourne. But that right as the sorowe and anguysshe was great in tyme of thyne outwaye goynge, ryght so joye and gladnesse shal be doubled to sene thee converted, and nat as Lothes wyfe ayen lokynge, but in hoole counsayle with the shepe folowynge, and with them grasse and herbes gadre. Neverthelater,"

OFte gan Loue to sterne me these wordes/ thynke on my speche/ for trewly here after it wol do the lykynge/ and howe so euer thou se Fortune shape her wheele to tourne/ this meditation by no waye reuolue. For certes Fortune sheweth her fayrest/ whan she thynketh to begyle. And as me thought here toforne thou saydest thy loos in loue/ for thy rightwysenesse ought to be raysed/ shulde be a lowed in tyme comynge. Thou myght in loue so the haue/ that loos and fame shul so ben raysed/ that to thy frendes co*m*forte/ and sorowe to thyne enemys endlesse shul endure.

But if thou were th*e* one shepe amonges the hundred were loste in deserte/ and out of the way hadde erred/ and nowe to the flocke arte restoored/ the shepeheerd hath in the no ioye/ and thou ayen to the forrest tourne. But that right as the sorowe and anguysshe was great in tyme of thyne out waye goynge/ ryght so**<333rb><333va>**ioye and gladnesse shal be doubled to sene the conuerted/ and nat as Lothes wyfe ayen lokynge/ but hoole counsayle with the shepe folowynge/ and with them grasse and herbes gadre. Neuer the later

740 Efte, Again; **sterne**, guide. **742 meditation . . . revolve**, essay [shall] in no way shift ground. **743 loos**, praise. **744 raysed**, elevated; **alowed**, lowered. **749 and thou**, if you. **750 outwaye goynge**, i.e., being lost. **751 Lothes**, Lot's; **ayen lokynge**, looking back; **hoole**, entire. **752 gadre**, gather; **Neverthelater**, Nevertheless.

quod she, "I saye nat these thynges for no wantrust that I have in supposynge of thee otherwyse thanne I shulde. For trewly, I wotte wel that nowe thou arte sette in suche a purpose out of whiche thee lyste nat to parte. But I saye it for many men there bene that to knowynge of other mennes doynges setten al their cure and lightly desyren the badde to clatter rather than the good and have no wyl their owne maner to amende. They also hate of olde rancoure lightly haven, and there that suche thynge abydeth sodaynly in their mouthes procedeth the habundaunce of the herte and wordes as stones out throwe. Wherfore my counsayle is ever more openly and apertely in what place thou sytte countreplete th'errours and meanynges in as ferre as thou hem wystyst false and leave for no wyght to make hem be knowe in every bodyes eare. And be alwaye pacient and use Jacobes wordes whatsoever menne of thee clappen, 'I shal sustayne my ladyes wrathe whiche I have deserved, so longe as my Margarite hath rightwysed my cause.' And certes," quod she, "I wytnesse myselfe if thou thus converted sorowest in good meanynge in thyne herte, wolte from al vanyté parfitely departe, in consolatyoun of al

---

(quod she) I saye nat these thynges for no wantrust that I haue in supposynge of the otherwyse thanne I shulde/ For trewly I wotte wel/ that nowe thou arte sette in suche a purpose/ out of whiche the lyste nat to parte. But I saye it/ for many men there bene/ that to knowynge of other me*n*nes doynges setten al their cure/ and lightly desyren the badde to clatter rather than the good/ and haue no wyl their owne maner to amende. They also hate of olde rancoure lightly hauen/ and there that suche thynge abydeth/ sodaynly in their mouthes procedeth the habundaunce of the herte/ and wordes as stones/ stones out throwe. Wherfore my cou*n*sayle is euer more openly and apertely/ in what place thou sytte/ countreplete therrours and meanynges/ in as ferre as thou hem wystyst false/ and leaue for no wyght to make hem be knowe in euery bodyes eare/ and be alwaye pacient and vse Jacobes wordes/ what so euer menne of the clappen/ I shal sustayne my ladyes wrathe whiche I haue deserued/ so longe as my Margarite hath rightwysed my cause. And certes (quod she) I wytnesse my selfe/ if thou thus conuerted sorowest in good meanynge in thyne herte/ wolte from al vanyte parfitely departe/ in consolatyoun of al

753 wantrust, despair. **755 thee lyste**, it pleases you. **756 cure**, care, attention; **lightly**, easily. **760 apertely**, overtly. **761 countreplete**, rebut; **wystyst**, know. **762 leave**, leave off; **wyght**, person. **763 clappen**, call out. **764 rightwysed**, justified. **765 certes**, certainly. **765–66 in good meanynge**, sincerely.

good pleasaunce of that, Margaryte whiche that thou desyrest after wyl of thyn herte, in a maner of a mothers pyté, shul fully accepte thee into grace. For ryght as thou rentest clothes in open syghte, so openly to sowe hem at his worshippe withouten reprofe commended. Also, right as thou were ensample of mochefolde errour, right so thou must be ensample of manyfolde correctioun, so good savour to forgoyng al errour distroyeng causeth dilygent love with many playted praysynges to folowe, and than shal al the fyrste errours make the folowynge worshyppes to seme hugely encreased. Blacke and white sette togyder every for other more semeth, and so dothe every thynges contrary in kynde. But infamé that gothe alwaye tofore and praysynge worshippe by any cause folowynge after maketh to ryse the ylke honour in double of welth, and that quencheth the spotte of the fyrst enfamé. Why wenyste, I saye, these thinges in hyndringe of thy name? Naye, nay, God wotte, but for pure encreasyng worshyp thy rightwysenesse to commende, and thy trouthe to seme the more. Wost nat wel thyselfe that thou in fourme of making passeth nat Adam that ete of the apple? Thou passeth nat the

---

good pleasaunce of that Margaryte/ whiche that thou desyrest after wyl of thyne hert/ in a maner of a mothers pyte/ shul fully accepte the in to grace. For ryght as thou re*n*test clothes in open syghte/ so openly to sowe hem at his worshippe withouten reprofe commended. Also right as thou were ensample of moche folde errour/ right so thou must be ensample of manyfolde correctioun/ so good sauour to forgoyng al errour distroyeng causeth dilygent loue/ with many playted praysynges to folowe/ and than shal al the fyrste errours make the folowynge worshyppes to seme hugely encreased/ blacke and white sette togyder/ euery for other more semeth/ and so**<333va>** **<333vb>**dothe euery thynges contrary in kynde. But infame that gothe alwaye tofore/ and praysynge worshippe by any cause folowynge after/ maketh to ryse the ylke honour in double of welth/ and that quencheth the spotte of the fyrst enfame. Why wenyste I saye these thi*n*ges/ in hyndringe of thy name? Naye nay god wotte/ but for pure encreasyng worshyp thy rightwysenesse to co*m*mende/ *and* thy trouthe to seme the more. Wost nat wel thy selfe/ that thou in fourme of making passeth nat Adam that ete of the apple. Thou passeth nat the

768 shul, [she] shall. **769 rentest**, tear; **sowe**, mend. **770 commended**, [is] commended (see note); **mochefolde**, manyfold. **771 forgoyng**, abandonment. **772 playted**, ornate, intricate. **774 thynges**, thing's. **776 ylke**, same; **in double of**, doubled in. **777 wenyste**, suppose you. **778 wotte**, knows. **779 Wost**, Know.

stedfastnesse of Noe, that eatynge of the grape become dronke. Thou passyst nat the chastyté of Lothe, that lay by his doughter. Eke the nobley of Abraham, whom God reproved by his pride. Also Davydes mekenesse, whiche for a woman made Urye be slawe. What also Hector of Troye in whome no defaute myght be founde, yet is he reproved that he ne hadde with manhode nat suffred the warre begon, ne Paris to have went into Grece, by whom ganne al the sorowe. For trewly hym lacketh no venym of pryvé consentyng whiche that openly leaveth a wronge to withsay. Lo eke an olde proverbe amonges many other: 'He that is stylle, semeth as he graunted.'

"Nowe by these ensamples thou myght fully understonde that these thynges ben wrytte to your lernyng and in rightwysenesse of tho persones, as thus: To every wight his defaute commytted made goodnesse afterwardes done be the more in reverence and in open shewyng. For ensample, is it nat song in holy churche, 'Lo, howe necessary was Adams synne.' Davyd the kyng gate Salomon the kyng of her that was Uryes wyfe. Truly, for reprofe is none of these thynges writte. Right so, tho I reherce thy before dede I repreve thee never the more, ne for no vyllany of thee are they rehersed but

---

stedfastnesse of Noe/ that eatynge of the grape become dronke. Thou passyst nat the chastyte of Lothe/ that lay by his doughter. Eke the nobley of Abraham/ whom god reproued by his pride. Also Dauydes mekenesse/ whiche for a woman made Vrye be slawe. What also Hector of Troye/ in whome no defaute myght be founde/ yet is he reproued that he ne hadde with manhode nat suffred the warre begon/ ne Paris to haue went in to Grece/ by whom ganne al the sorowe: for trewly hym lacketh no venym of pryue consentyng/ whiche that openly leaueth a wronge to withsay.

Lo eke an olde prouerbe amonges many other/ he that is stylle semeth as he graunted.

Nowe by these ensamples/ thou myght fully vnderstonde/ that these thynges ben wrytte to your lernyng/ and in rightwysenesse of tho persones/ as thus: To euery wight his defaute co*m*mytted/ made goodnesse afterwardes done/ be the more in reuere*n*ce and in open shewyng/ for ensa*m*ple is it nat song in holy churche. Lo howe necessary was Adams synne/ Dauyd the kyng gate Salomon the kyng/ of her that was Vryes wyfe. Truly for reprofe is none of these thynges writte: Right so tho I reherce thy before dede/ I repreue the neuer the more/ ne for no vyllany of the are they rehersed/ but

782 by, with (intercourse). **784 slawe**, slain. **786 lacketh**, is lacking to. **787 leaveth**, evades [lit., leaves]; **withsay**, contradict. **788 as he graunted**, as if he had assented (i.e., silence is consent). **793 gate**, begat. **795 before dede**, early deeds.

for worshippe, so thou contynewe wel hereafter, and for profyte of thy selfe I rede thou on hem thynke."

Than sayde I right thus. "Lady of unyté and accorde, envy and wrathe lurken there thou comest in place, ye weten wel yourselve, and so done many other, that whyle I admynystred the offyce of commen doynge, as in rulyng of the stablysshmentes amonges the people I defouled never my conscyence for no maner dede, but ever by wytte and by counsayle of the wysest the maters weren drawen to their right endes. And thus trewly for you, lady, I have desyred suche cure, and certes in your servyce was I nat ydel as ferre as suche doynge of my cure stretcheth."

"That is a thyng," quod she, "that may drawe many hertes of noble and voice of commune into; glory and fame is nat but wretched and fyckle. Alas, that mankynde coveyteth in so leude a wyse to be rewarded of any good dede, sithe glorie of fame in this worlde is nat but hyndrynge of glorye in tyme commynge. And certes," quod she, "yet at the hardest suche fame into heven is nat the erthe but a centre to the cercle of heven. A pricke is wonder lytel in respecte of al the cercle, and yet in al this pricke may

---

for worshippe/ so thou contynewe wel here after/ and for profyte of thy selfe/ I rede thou on hem thynke.

Than sayde I right thus. Lady of vnyte and accorde/ enuy and wrathe lurken there thou comest in place/ ye weten wel your selue and so done many other/ that whyle I admy**<333vb><334ra>**nystred the offyce of co*m*men doynge/ as in rulyng of the stablysshmentes amonges the people/ I defouled neuer my conscyence for no maner dede/ but euer by wytte and by counsayle of the wysest/ the maters weren drawen to their right endes. And thus trewly for you lady I haue desyred suche cure/ and certes in your seruyce was I nat ydel/ as ferre as suche doynge of my cure stretcheth. That is a thyng (quod she) that may drawe many hertes of noble/ and voice of co*m*mune in to glory/ and fame is nat but wretched and fyckle.

Alas that ma*n*kynde coueyteth in so leude a wyse/ to be rewarded of any good dede/ sithe glorie of fame in this worlde/ is nat but hyndrynge of glorye in tyme co*m*mynge. And certes (quod she) yet at the hardest suche fame in to heuen/ is nat the erthe but a centre to the cercle of heuen. A pricke is wonder lytel in respecte of al the cercle/ and yet in al this pricke may

796 rede, counsel. **799 weten**, know. **804 ydel**, idle. **805 noble**, nobility. **806 commune**, common-folk. **807 leude**, ignorant; **sithe**, since. **810 pricke**, point.

no name be borne in maner of peersyng, for many obstacles, as waters and wyldernesse and straunge langages; and nat onely names of men ben stylled and holden out of knowlegynge by these obstacles, but also cytees and realmes of prosperité ben letted to be knowe and their reason hyndred so that they mowe nat ben parfitely in mennes proper understandynge. Howe shulde than the name of a synguler Londenoys passe the gloryous name of London, whiche by many it is commended, and by many it is lacked, and in many mo places in erthe nat knowen than knowen? For in many countrees lytel is London in knowyng or in spech, and yet among one maner of people may nat such fame in goodnes come, for as many as praysen commenly as many lacken. Fye than on such maner fame. Slepe and suffre him that knoweth prevyté of hertes to dele suche fame in thylke place there nothynge ayenst a sothe shal neyther speke ne dare apere by attourney ne by other maner. Howe many great named and many great in worthynesse losed han be tofore this tyme that nowe out of memorie are slydden and clenely forgeten for defaute of writynges? And yet scriptures for great elde so ben

---

no name be borne in maner of peersyng for many obstacles/ as waters and wyldernesse/ and straunge langages/ and nat onely names of men ben stylled and holden out of knowlegynge by these obstacles/ but also cytees and realmes of prosperite ben letted to be knowe/ and their reason hyndred/ so that they mowe nat ben parfitely in mennes proper vnderstandynge. Howe shulde than the name of a synguler londenoys passe the gloryous name of London/ whiche by many it is commended/ and by many it is lacked/ and in many mo places in erthe nat knowen/ than knowen: for in many countrees lytel is London in knowyng or in spech/ *and* yet among one maner of people may nat such fame in goodnes co*m*e/ for as many as praysen co*m*menly as many lacken. Fye tha*n* on such maner fame/ slepe *and* suffre him th*at* knoweth p*re*uyte of hert*es*/ to dele suche fame/ in thylke place there nothynge ayenst a sothe shal neyther speke ne dare apere/ by attourney ne by other maner. Howe many great named and many great in worthynesse losed/ han be tofore this tyme/ that nowe out of memorie are slydden and clenely for geten/ for defaute of writynges/ and yet scriptures for great elde so ben

811 peersyng, piercing; **for**, on account of. **813 letted**, prevented. **815 Londenoys**, Londoner. **817 lacked**, found fault with. **819 lacken**, detract. **820 Slepe**, Relax; **dele**, deal. **821 thylke**, that same; **sothe**, truth. **822 apere**, appear. **823 losed**, praised. **824 clenely**, completely; **elde**, age.

defased that no perpetualté maye in hem ben juged. But if thou wolte make comparisoun to ever, what joye mayst thou have in erthly name? It is a fayre lykenesse, a pees or one grayne of wheate to a thousande shippes ful of corne charged.

"What nombre is betwene the one and thother? And yet mowe bothe they be nombred, and ende in rekenynge have. But trewly, al that may be nombred is nothyng to recken as to thilke that maye nat be nombred. For ofte thynges ended is made comparison, as one lytel another great, but in thynges to have an ende and another no ende, suche comparisoun may nat be founden. Wherfore in heven to ben losed with God hath none ende, but endlesse endureth, and thou canste nothynge done aright, but thou desyre the rumoure therof be healed and in every wightes eare, and that dureth but a pricke in respecte of the other. And so thou sekest rewarde of folkes smale wordes and of vayne praysynges. Trewly, therin thou lesest the guerdon of vertue, and lesest the grettest valoure of consyence, and uphap thy renome everlastyng. Therfore, boldely renome of fame of the erthe shulde be hated, and fame after deth shulde be desyred, for werkes of

---

defased/ that no perpetualte maye in hem ben iuged. But if thou**<334ra><334rb>**wolte make comparisoun to euer/ what ioye mayst thou haue in erthly name/ it is a fayre lykenesse/ a pees or one grayne of wheate/ to a thousande shippes ful of corne charged.

What nombre is betwene the one and thother/ and yet mowe bothe they be nombred/ *and* ende in rekenynge haue. But trewly al that may be nombred/ is nothyng to recken/ as to thilke that maye nat be nombred/ for ofte thynges ended is made comparison/ as one lytel/ another great/ but in thynges to haue an ende/ *and* another no ende/ suche comparisoun may nat be founden. Wherfore in heuen to ben losed with god hath none ende/ but endlesse endureth/ and thou canste nothynge done aright/ but thou desyre the rumoure therof be healed and in euery wightes eare/ *and* that dureth but a pricke/ in respecte of the other. And so thou sekest rewarde of folkes smale wordes/ and of vayne praysynges. Trewly therin thou lesest the guerdon of vertue/ and lesest the grettest valoure of consyence/ and vphap thy renome euerlastyng. Therfore boldely renome of fame of the erthe shulde behated/ and fame after deth shulde be desyred/ of werkes of

825 defased, defaced. **826 pees**, piece. **827 grayne**, grain; **charged**, laden. **828 mowe**, may. **829 ende**, a termination. **830 thynges ended**, things with definite limits. **832 losed**, praised. **834 healed**, sown or broadcast, or perhaps praised (see note); **wightes**, person's. **836 lesest**, lose; **guerdon**, reward. **837 uphap**, perhaps; **renome**, renown.

vertue asketh guerdonyng, and the soule causeth al vertue. Than the soule delyvered out of prisone of erthe is most worthy suche guerdone among to have in the everlastynge fame, and nat the body that causeth al mannes yvels.

Chapter IX

Of twey thynges arte thou answered as me thynketh," quod Love, "and if any thynge be in doute in thy soule, shewe it forth thyne ignoraunce to clere and leave it for no shame." "Certes," quod I, "there ne is no body in this worlde that aught coude saye by reason ayenst any of your skylles, as I leve, and by my wytte nowe fele I wel that yvel spekers or bearers of enfame may lytel greve or lette my purpose, but rather by suche thynge my quarel to be forthered." "Yea," quod she, "and it is proved also that the ilke jewel in my kepynge shal nat there thorowe be steered of the lest moment that myght be ymagyned." "That is soth," quod I. "Wel," quod she, "than leneth there to declare that thy insuffysance is no maner letting, as thus: for that she is so worthy thou shuldest not clymbe so highe, for thy moebles and thyne estate arne voyded; thou thynkest fallen in

---

vertue asketh guerdonyng/ and the soule causeth al vertue. Than the soule delyuered out of prisone of erthe/ is most worthy suche guerdone among to haue in the euerlastynge fame/ and nat the body that causeth al mannes yuels.

OF twey thynges arte thou answered as me thynketh (quod Loue) and if any thynge be in doute in thy soule/ shewe it forth thyne ignoraunce to clere/ and leaue it for no shame. Certes (quod I) there ne is no body in this worlde/ that aught coude saye by reason ayenst any of your skylles/ as I leue/ and by my wytte nowe fele I wel/ that yuel spekers or bearers of enfame/ may lytel greue or lette my purpose/ but rather by suche thynge my quarel to be forthered. Yea (q*uo*d she) and it is proued also/ that the ilke iewel in my kepynge shal nat there thorowe be steered/ of the lest moment th*at* myght be ymagyned. That is soth (q*uo*d I) Wel (q*uo*d she) than leneth there/ to declare th*at* thy insuffysance is no maner letting**<334rb><334va>**as thus/ for that she is so worthy thou shuldest not clymbe so highe/ for thy moebles and thyne estate arne voyded/ thou thynkest fallen in

839 guerdonyng, rewarding. **842 twey**, two. **845 skylles**, arguments; **leve**, believe. **846 greve**, frustrate; **lette**, hinder. **848 steered**, manipulated; **lest**, least. **849 leneth**, incline, turn. **850 letting**, hindrance. **851 moebles**, wealth; **thynkest**, think [yourself].

suche myserie that gladnesse of thy pursute wol nat on thee discende." "Certes," quod I, "that is sothe: right suche thought is in myne hert, for commenly it is spoken, and for an olde proverbe it is leged: 'He that heweth to hye, with chyppes he maye lese his syght.' Wherfore I have ben about in al that ever I myght to studye wayes of remedye by one syde or by another." "Nowe," quod she, "God forbede ere thou seke any other doynges but suche as I have lerned thee in our restynge whyles, and suche herbes as ben planted in oure gardyns. Thou shalte wel understande that above man is but one God alone." "Howe," quod I, "han men toforne this tyme trusted in writtes and chauntementes and in helpes of spirites that dwellen in the ayre, and therby they han getten their desyres, whereas first for al his manly power, he daunced behynde?"

"O," quod she, "fye on suche maters. For trewly that is sacrilege, and that shal have no sort with any of my servauntes. In myne eyen shal suche thynge nat be loked after. Howe often is it commaunded by these passed wyse that to one God shal men serve and nat to goddes? And who that lyste to have myne helpes shal aske none helpe of foule spirites. Alas, is nat man maked semblable to God? Wost thou nat wel that al vertue of

---

suche myserie/ that gladnesse of thy pursute wol nat on the discende. Certes (quod I) that is sothe: right suche thought is in myne hert/ for co*mm*enly it is spoken/ *and* for an olde prouerbe it is leged: He that heweth to hye/ with chyppes he maye lese his syght. Wherfore I haue ben about in al that euer I myght/ to studye wayes of remedye by one syde or by another. Nowe (quod she) god forbede are thou seke any other doynges/ but suche as I haue lerned the in our restynge whyles/ and suche herbes as ben planted in oure gardyns. Thou shalte wel vnderst*a*n*de*/ that aboue man is but one god alone. Howe (q*uo*d I)han men to forne this tyme trusted in writtes and chauntementes/ and in helpes of spirites that dwellen in the ayre/ and therby they han getten their desyres/ where as first for al his manly power he daunced behynde.

O (quod she) fye on suche maters/ for trewly that is sacrilege/ and that shal haue no sort with any of my seruau*n*tes/ in myne eyen shal suche thynge nat be loked after. Howe often is it co*mm*aunded by these passed wyse/ that to one god shal men serue/ and nat to goddes?

And who that lyste to haue myne helpes/ shal aske none helpe of foule spirites. Alas/ is nat man maked semblable to god? wost thou nat wel that al vertue of

854 leged, alleged; **heweth**, chops, hews; **hye**, high. **856 seke**, seek. **857 lerned**, taught. **859 chauntementes**, enchantments. **861 daunced behynde**, failed, lagged. **863 sort**, relationship. **865 lyste**, desire. **866 semblable**, similar; **Wost**, Know.

lyvelych werkynge by Goddes purveyaunce is underputte to resonable creature in erthe? Is nat every thynge a thishalfe god, made buxome to mannes contemplation, understandynge in heven and in erthe, and in helle? Hath not manne beynge with stones, soule of wexyng with trees and herbes? Hath he nat soule of felynge, with beestes, fysshes, and foules? And he hath soule of reason and understandyng with aungels, so that in him is knytte al maner of lyvenges by a reasonable proporcioun. Also man is made of al the foure elementes. Al unyversytee is rekened in him alone. He hath under God pryncipalité above al thynges. Nowe is his soule here, nowe a thousande myle hence; nowe ferre, nowe nygh, nowe hye, nowe lowe, as ferre in a momente as in mountenaunce of tenne wynter, and al this is in mannes governaunce and disposytion. Than sheweth it that men ben lyche unto goddes, and chyldren of moost heyght. But nowe sythen al thynges underputte to the wyl of reasonable creatures, God forbede any man to wynne that lordshippe and aske helpe of anythynge lower than himselfe, and than namely of foule thynges innominable. Now than why shuldest thou wene to love to highe, sythen

---

lyuelych werkynge by goddes purueyaunce is vnderputte to resonable creature in erthe/ is nat euery thynge a thishalfe god? made buxome to ma*n*nes co*n*templation/ understandynge in heuen and in erthe/ and in helle. Hath not manne beynge with stones/ soule of wexyng with trees and herbes. Hath he nat soule of felynge/ with beestes/ fysshes/ and foules/ and he hath soule of reason and vnderstandyng with aungels/ so that in him is knytte al maner of lyuenges by a reasonable proporcioun. Also man is made of al the foure elementes. Al vnyuersytee is rekened in him alone: he hath vnder god pryncipalite aboue al thynges. Nowe is his soule here/ nowe a thousande myle hence/ nowe ferre nowe nygh/ nowe hye nowe lowe/ **<334va><334vb>**as ferre in a momente/ as in mountenaunce of tenne wynter/ and al this is in mannes gouernaunce and disposytion. Than sheweth it/ that men ben lyche vnto goddes/ and chyldren of moost heyght. But nowe sythen al thynges vnderputte to the wyl of reasonable creatures/ god forbede any man to wynne that lordshippe/ and aske helpe of any thynge lower than him selfe/ *and* than namely of foule thyng*es* innominable. Now tha*n* why shuldest thou wene to loue to highe/ sythen

867 lyvelych, vital; **purveyaunce**, providence; **underputte**, ordained. **868 a thishalfe god**, i.e., made here below; **buxome**, obedient. **870 wexyng**, growth. **873 unyversytee**, universality or universal nature. **875 mountenaunce**, extent. **877 lyche**, like; **heyght**, stature (moral sense); **sythen**, since. **878 underputte**, [are] subjected. **880 innominable**, unnameable; **wene**, assume.

nothynge is thee above but God alone? Trewly, I wote wel that thylke jewel is in a maner evyn in lyne of degree there thou arte thyselve and nought above save thus. Aungel upon angel, manne upon manne, and devyl upon devyl han a maner of soveraygntie and that shal cease at the daye of dome. And so I say, thoughe thou be putte to serve the ylke jewel durynge thy lyfe, yet is that no servage of underputtynge, but a maner of travaylyng plesaunce to conquere and gette that thou haste not. I sette nowe the hard-est: in my service nowe thou deydest for sorowe of wantynge in thy desyres; trewly, al hevenly bodyes with one voyce shul come and make melody in thy comynge and saye, 'Welcome, our fere, and worthy to entre into Jupyters joye, for thou with myght haste overcome dethe. Thou woldest never flytte out of thy servyce, and we al shul nowe pray to the goddes, rowe by rowe, to make thilk Margarite that no routh had in this persone, but unkyndely without comforte lette thee deye shal besette herselfe in suche wyse that in erthe, for parte of vengeaunce, shal she no joye have in loves servyce. And whan she is deed, than shal her soule ben brought up into thy presence, and whyder thou wylte chese thilke soule shal ben commytted.' Or els after thy dethe, anone al the

---

nothynge is the aboue but god alone. Trewly I wote wel/ that thylke iewel is in a maner euyn in lyne of degree there thou arte thy selue/ and nought aboue/ saue thus. Aungel vpon angel/ manne vpon manne/ and deuyl vpon deuyl/ han a maner of soueraygntie/ and that shal cease at the daye of dome: and so I say/ thoughe thou be putte to serue the ylke iewel durynge thy lyfe/ yet is that no seruage of vnderputtynge/ but a maner of trauaylyng plesaunce/ to conquere and gette that thou haste not. I sette nowe the hard-est/ in my seruice nowe thou deydest for sorowe of wantynge in thy desyres: trewly al heuenly bodyes with one voyce shul come and make melody in thy comynge/ and saye welcome our fere/ and worthy to entre in to Jupyters ioye/ for thou with myght haste ouercome dethe/ thou woldest neuer flytte out of thy seruyce/ and we al shul nowe pray to the goddes rowe by rowe to make thilk Margarite th*at* no routh had in this persone/ but vnkyndely without comforte lette the deye/ shal besette her selfe in suche wyse/ that in erthe for parte of vengeaunce/ shal she no ioye haue in loues seruyce/ and whan she is deed/ than shal her soule ben brought vp in to thy presence/ and whyder thou wylte chese/ thilke soule shal ben commytted. Or els after thy dethe anone al the

881 wote, know; **thylke**, that same. **882 lyne of degree**, i.e., rank. **884 dome**, judgment. **886 travaylyng**, laboring; **sette**, pose [as a proposition]. **887 deydest**, died. **889 fere**, mate, companion. **890 flytte**, fly. **891 routh**, pity. **895 chese**, choose.

foresayd hevenly bodyes by one accorde shal benommen from thylke perle al the vertues that firste her were taken. For she hath hem forfeyted by that on thee, my servaunt, in thy lyve she wolde not suffre to worche al vertues withdrawen by might of the hygh bodyes. Why than shuldest thou wene so any more? And if the lyste to loke upon the lawe of kynde and with order whiche to me was ordayned, sothely none age none overtournynge tyme but hytherto had no tyme ne power to chaunge the weddyng, ne the knotte to unbynde of two hertes thorowe one assent, in my presence, togyther accorden to enduren tyl dethe hem departe. What, trowest thou every ydeot wotte the menynge and the privy entent of these thynges? They wene, forsothe, that suche accorde may not be, but the rose of maydenhede be plucked. Do waye, do waye. They knowe nothyng of this; for consente of two hertes alone maketh the fastenynge of the knotte. Neyther lawe of kynde ne mannes lawe determyneth neyther the age ne the qualyté of persones, but onely accorde bytwene thylke twaye. And trewly after tyme that suche accorde by their consent in hert is ensealed and put in my tresorye amonges my privy

---

foresayd heuenly bodyes by one accorde/ shal beno*m*men from thylke perle/ al the vertues that firste her were taken/ for she hath hem forfeyted/ by that on the my seruaunt in thy lyue she wolde not suffre to worche al vertues withdrawen/ by might of the hygh bodyes: Why than shuldest thou wene so any more. And if the lyste to loke vpon the lawe**<334vb><335ra>**of kynde/ and with order whiche to me was ordayned/ sothely none age/ none ouertournynge tyme/ but hytherto had no tyme ne power to chaunge the weddyng/ ne the knotte to vnbynde of two hertes thorowe one assent in my presence/ togyther accorden to enduren tyl dethe hem departe. What trowest thou euery ydeot wotte the menynge and the priuy entent of these thynges? they wene forsothe that suche accorde may not be/ but the rose of maydenhede be plucked/ do waye do waye/ they knowe nothyng of this: for consente of two hertes alone/ maketh the fastenynge of the knotte/ neyther lawe of kynde ne mannes lawe/ determyneth neyther the age ne the qualyte of persones/ but onely accorde bytwene thylke twaye. And trewly after tyme that suche accorde by their consent in hert/ is ensealed and put in my tresorye amonges my priuy

896 benommen, take, remove; **thylke**, that same. **897 by that**, because. **899 wene**, assume, suspect; **lyste**, it please. **900 sothely**, truly. **902 thorowe**, through. **903 trowest**, believe; **ydeot wotte**, idiot knows. **904 wene**, assume. **908 thylke twaye**, those two. **909 ensealed**, sealed.

thynges: than gynneth the name of spousayle, and although they breaken forwarde bothe, yet suche mater ensealed is kepte in remembrance forever. And se nowe that spouses have the name anon after accorde, though the rose be not take. The aungel bade Joseph take Marye his spouse and to Egypte wende. Lo, she was cleped spouse, and yet toforne ne after neyther of hem bothe mente no flesshly luste knowe. Wherfore the wordes of trouthe acorden that my servauntes shulden forsake bothe father and mother and be adherande to his spouse, and they two in unyté of one flesshe shulden accorde. And this wyse two that werne firste in a lytel maner disacordaunt, hygher that one and lower that other, ben made evenlyche in gree to stonde. But nowe to enfourme thee that ye ben lyche to goddes, these clerkes sayne and in determynacion shewen that thre thynges haven the names of goddes ben cleaped: that is to sayn, man, dyvel, and ymages, but yet is there but one God of whom al goodnesse, al grace, and al vertue cometh, and He is lovyng and trewe and everlastyng and pryme cause of al beyng thynges. But men ben goddes lovynge and trewe, but not everlastyng, and that is by

---

thynges: than gynneth the name of spousayle/ and although they breaken forwarde bothe/ yet suche mater ensealed is kepte in remembrance for euer. And se nowe that spouses haue the name anon after accorde/ though the rose be not take. The aungel bade Joseph take Marye his spouse/ and to Egypte wende: Lo she was cleped spouse/ and yet toforne ne after neyther of hem bothe mente no flesshly luste knowe/ wherfore the wordes of trouthe acorden/ that my seruauntes shulden forsake bothe father and mother/ and be adherande to his spouse/ and they two in vnyte of one flesshe shulden accorde. And this wyse two that werne firste in a lytel maner disacordaunt/ hygher that one and lower that other/ ben made euenlyche in gree to stonde. But nowe to enfourme the that ye ben lyche to goddes/ these clerkes sayne/ and in determynacion shewen/ that thre thynges hauen th*e* names of goddes ben cleaped/ that is to sayn: man/ dyuel/ and ymages/ but yet is there but one god/ of whom al goodnesse/ al grace/ and al vertue cometh/ and he his louyng *and* trewe/ and euerlastyng/ and pryme cause of al beyng thynges: but men ben goddes/ louynge and trewe/ but not euerlastyng/ and that is by

910 spousayle, marriage; **forwarde**, contract. **913 wende**, go; **cleped**, called. **914 mente no flesshly luste**, did not intend to partake of any fleshly pleasure. **916 adherande**, adhering. **917 this wyse**, [in] this way. **918 in gree**, reconciled, in agreement. **919 lyche**, like. **920 cleaped**, called. **922 pryme**, first.

adopcyoun of the everlastynge God. Dyvels ben goddes styrrynge by a maner of lyveng, but neyther ben they trewe ne everlastynge, and their name of godlyheed they han by usurpacion, as the prophete saythe: 'Al goddes of gentyles, that is to say, paynyms, are dyvels.' But ymages ben goddes by nuncupacion, and they ben neyther lyvynge, ne trewe, ne everlastynge: After these wordes they cleapen goddes ymages wrought with mennes handes. But nowe reasonable creature that by adopcion alone arte to the great God everlastynge, and therby thou arte god cleped: lette thy Fathers maners so entre thy wyttes that thou myght folowe in as moche as longeth to thee thy Fathers worshyppe, so that in nothynge thy kynde from His wyl declyne ne from His nobley perverte. In this wyse if thou werche, thou arte above al other thynges save God alone, and so say no more thyn herte to serve in to hye a place.

Chapter X

"Fully have I nowe declared thyn estate to be good, so thou folow therafter and that the abjection first be thee aleged in worthynesse of thy Margaryte shal not thee lette, as

---

adopcyoun of the euerlastynge god. Dyuels ben goddes/ styrrynge by a maner of lyueng/ **<335ra><335rb>**but neyther ben they trewe ne euerlastynge/ and their name of godlyheed thy han by vsurpacion/ as the prophete saythe: Al goddes of gentyles/ that is to say paynyms/ are dyuels. But ymages ben goddes by nuncupacion/ and they ben neyther lyuynge ne trewe/ ne euerlastynge: After these wordes they cleapen goddes ymages wrought with mennes handes. But nowe reasonable creature/ that by adopcion alone arte to the great god euerlastynge/ and therby thou arte god cleped: lette thy fathers maners so entre thy wyttes/ that thou myght folowe/ in as moche as longeth to the thy fathers worshyppe/ so that in nothynge thy kynde from his wyl declyne/ ne from his nobley peruerte. In this wyse if thou werche/ thou arte aboue al other thynges saue god alone/ and so say no more thyn herte to serue in to hye a place.

FULly haue I nowe declared thyn estate to be good/ so thou folow therafter/ and that the abiection first be the aleged in worthynesse of thy Margaryte shal not the lette/ as

926 paynyms, pagans. **927 nuncupacion**, nomenclature, act of naming. **928 cleapen**, call. **931 longeth**, belongs. **932 kynde**, nature; **nobley**, nobility. **933 werche**, work. **934 to**, too; **hye**, high. **936 be thee aleged**, alleged by you; **lette**, hinder.

it shal forther thee and encrease thee. It is nowe to declare the last objection in nothing may greve."

"Yes, certes," quod I, "bothe greve and let muste it nedes. The contrarye maye not ben proved, and se nowe why. Whyle I was glorious in worldly welfulnesse and had suche goodes in welth as maken men ryche, tho was I drawe into companyes that loos, prise, and name yeven. Tho louteden blasours, tho curreyden glosours, tho welcomeden flatterers, tho worshypped thylke that nowe deynen nat to loke. Every wight in such erthly wele habundant is holde noble, precious, benigne, and wyse to do what he shal in any degree that men hym set, albeit that the sothe be in the contrarye of al tho thynges. But he that can ne never so wel him behave and hath vertue habundaunt in manyfolde maners, and be nat welthed with suche erthly goodes, is holde for a foole and sayd his wytte is but sotted. Lo, how false for aver is holde trewe. Lo, howe trewe is cleaped false for wantyng of goodes. Also, lady, dignytees of office maken men mykel comended, as thus: he is so good, were he out, his pere shulde men not fynde. Trewly I trowe of

---

it shal forther the/ and encrease the/ it is nowe to declare/ th*e* last obiection in nothing may greue.

Yes certes (q*uo*d I) bothe greue and let muste it nedes/ the contrarye maye not ben proued/ and se nowe why. Whyle I was glorious in worldly welfulnesse/ and had suche goodes in welth as maken men ryche/ tho was I drawe in to companyes that loos/ prise/ and name yeuen: tho louteden blasours/ tho curreyden glosours/ tho welcomeden flatterers/ tho worshypped thylke/ that nowe deynen nat to loke. Euery wight in such erthly wele habundant/ is holde noble/ precious/ benigne/ and wyse to do what he shal/ in any degree that men hym set/ al be it that the sothe be in the contrarye of al tho thynges: But he that can/ ne neuer so wel him behaue/ and hath vertue habunda*un*t in manyfolde maners/ *and* be nat welthed with suche erthly goodes/ is holde for a foole/ and sayd his wytte is but sotted. Lo how false for auer is holde trewe. Lo howe trewe is cleaped false for wantyng of goodes. Also lady/ dignytees of office maken men mykel comended as thus: he is so good/ were he out his pere**<335rb><335va>**shulde men not fynde. Trewly I trowe of

937 forther, further. **938 greve**, grieve. **941 loos**, renown. **942 prise**, praise; **yeven**, give; **louteden**, flattered; **blasours**, flatterers, or "trumpeters"; **curreyden**, curried favor; **glosours**, flatterers. **943 thylke**, those very ones; **deynen**, deign; **wight**, person. **944 wele**, fortune. **947 welthed**, wealthy. **948 sotted**, besotted; **aver**, payment; **cleaped**, called. **949 wantyng**, lack; **mykel**, much. **950 out**, out [of office]; **pere**, peer; **trowe**, believe.

some suche that are so praysed, were they out ones, another shulde make him so be knowe he shulde of no wyse no more ben loked after: but onely fooles, wel I wotte, desyren suche new thynges. Wherfore I wonder that thilke governour out of whome alone the causes proceden that governen al thynges whiche that hath ordeyned this worlde in werkes of the kyndely bodyes so be governed, not with unstedfast or happyous thyng, but with rules of reason whiche shewen the course of certayne thynges: why suffreth he suche slydyng chaunges that misturnen suche noble thynges as ben we men that arne a fayre parsel of the erthe and holden the upperest degré under God, of benigne thinges, as ye sayden right nowe yourselfe — shulde never man have ben set in so worthy a place but if his degré were ordayned noble. Alas, thou that knyttest the purveyaunce of al thynges, why lokest thou not to amenden these defautes? I se shrewes that han wicked maners sytten in chayres of domes lambes to punysshen there wolves shulden ben punisshed. Lo, vertue shynende naturelly for povertie lurketh and is hydde under cloude. But the moone false, forsworne as I knowe myselfe for aver and yeftes, hath usurped to shyne by day light with peynture of other mens praysinges: and trewly

---

some suche that are so praysed/ were they out ones/ another shulde make him so be knowe/ he shulde of no wyse no more ben loked after: but onely fooles wel I wotte/ desyren suche new thynges. Wherfore I wonder that thilke gouernour/ out of whome alone the causes proceden/ that gouernen al thynges/ whiche that hath ordeyned this worlde in werkes of the kyndely bodyes so be gouerned/ not with vnstedfast or happyous thyng/ but with rules of reason/ whiche shewen the course of certayne thynges: why suffreth he suche slydyng chaunges/ that misturnen suche noble thynges as ben we men/ that arne a fayre parsel of the erthe/ and holden the vpperest degre vnder god of benigne thinges/ as ye sayden right nowe your selfe/ shulde neuer man haue ben set in so worthy a place/ but if his degre were ordayned noble. Alas/ thou that knyttest the purueyaunce of al thynges/ why lokest thou not to amenden these defautes: I se shrewes that han wicked maners/ sytten in chayres of domes/ lambes to punysshen/ there wolues shulden ben punisshed. Lo vertue shynende naturelly/ for pouertie lurketh and is hydde vnder cloude: but the moone false forsworne/ as I knowe my selfe/ for auer *and* yeftes hath vsurped to shyne by day light/ with peynture of other mens praysinges: and trewly

952 wotte, know. **953 thilke**, that same. **955 kyndely**, natural; **happyous**, fortuitous. **957 slydyng**, variable. **960 but if**, unless. **962 chayres of domes**, judges' seats. **963 shynende**, shining. **964 aver**, payment; **yeftes**, gifts. **965 peynture**, painting.

thilke forged lyght fouly shulde fade were the trouth away of colours feyned. Thus is nyght turned into daye and daye into night, wynter into sommer, and sommer into wynter, not in dede but in miscleapyng of folyche people."

"Now," quod she, "what wenest thou of these thinges? How felest thou in thyn hert, by what governaunce that this cometh aboute?"

"Certes," quod I, "that wotte I never but if it be that Fortune hath graunt from above to lede the ende of man as her lyketh." "Ah, nowe I se," quod she, "th'entent of thy meanyng. Lo, bycause thy worldly goodes ben fullyche dispent, thou berafte out of dignité of office in whiche thou madest the gatherynge of thilke goodes, and yet dyddest in that office by counsaile of wyse any thing were ended, and true were unto hem whose profyte thou shuldest loke, and seest nowe many that in thilke hervest made of thee mokel and nowe, for glosing of other, deyneth thee nought to forther, but enhaunsen false shrewes by wytnessynge of trouthe, these thynges greveth thyn herte to sene thyselfe thus abated. And than fraylté of mankynde ne setteth but lytel by the lesers of

---

thilke forged ly3t fouly shulde fade/ were the trouth away of colours feyned. Thus is nyght turned in to daye/ and daye in to night/ wynter in to so*mm*er/ and so*mm*er in to wynter/ not in dede/ but in miscleapyng of folyche people.

Now (quod she) what wenest thou of these thinges? how felest thou in thyn hert/ by what gouernaunce that this cometh aboute?

Certes (q*uo*d I) that wotte I neüer/ but if it be that fortune hath graunt from aboue/ to lede the ende of man as her lyketh. Ah nowe I se (quod she) thentent of thy meanyng: Lo bycause thy worldly goodes ben fullyche dispent/ thou berafte out of dignite of office/ in whiche thou madest the gatherynge of thilke goodes/ and yet dyddest in that office by counsaile of wyse/ any thing were ended: and true were vnto hem/ whose profyte thou shuldest**<335va><335vb>**loke/ and seest nowe many that in thilke heruest made of the mokel/ and nowe for glosing of other/ deyneth the nought to forther/ but enhaunsen false shrewes/ by wytnessynge of trouthe./ These thynges greueth thyn herte to sene thy selfe thus abated/ and than fraylte of mankynde ne setteth but lytel by the lesers of

968 miscleapyng, misnaming; **folyche**, foolish. **969 wenest**, suppose. **971 wotte**, know. **972 lede**, lead. **973 dispent**, spent; **berafte out of**, deprived of, booted from, expelled. **976 loke**, look [after]. **977 mokel**, much; **glosing**, lying, coloring the truth; **deyneth**, deign. **978 greveth**, grieve. **979 abated**, lessened, reduced in status; **lesers**, losers.

suche rychesse, have he never so moche vertue. And so thou wenest of thy jewel to renne in dispyte and not ben accepted into grace. Al this shal thee nothing hynder. Nowe," quod she, "first thou woste wel thou lostest nothyng that ever mightest thou chalenge for thyn owne. Whan nature brought thee forthe come thou not naked out of thy mothers wombe? Thou haddest no rychesse, and whan thou shalt entre into the ende of every flesshly body, what shalt thou have with thee than? So every rychesse thou haste in tyme of thy lyvynge nys but lente. Thou might therin chalenge no propertie. And se nowe, everything that is a mannes owne he may do therwith what him lyketh, to yeve or to kepe. But richesse thou playnest from thee lost, if thy might had stretched so ferforth, fayne thou woldest have hem kept, multyplied with mo other. And so ayenst thy wyl ben they departed from the — wherfore they were never thyn. And if thou laudest and joyest any wight, for he is stuffed with suche maner richesse, thou arte in that beleve begiled, for thou wenest thilke joye to be selynesse or els ease and he that hath loste suche happes to ben unsely." "Ye forsoth," quod I. "Wel," quod she, "than wol I

---

suche rychesse/ haue he neuer so moche vertue/ and so thou wenest of thy iewel to renne in dispyte/ and not ben accepted in to grace: Al this shal the nothing hynder. Nowe (q*uo*d she) first thou woste wel thou lostest nothyng that euer mightest thou chalenge for thyn owne: Whan nature brought the forthe/ come thou not naked out of thy mothers wombe? thou haddest no rychesse/ and whan thou shalt entre in to the ende of euery flesshly body/ what shalt thou haue with the than? So euery rychesse thou haste in tyme of thy lyuynge/ nys but lente/ thou might therin chalenge no propertie. And se nowe euery thing that is a mannes owne/ he may do therwith what him lyketh/ to yeue or to kepe: but richesse thou playnest from the lost/ if thy might had stretched so ferforth/ fayne thou woldest haue hem kept multyplied with mo other: and so ayenst thy wyl ben they dep*ar*ted from the/ wherfore they were neuer thyn. And if thou laudest *and* ioyest any wight/ for he is stuffed with suche maner richesse/ th*ou* arte in that beleue begiled/ for thou wenest thilke ioye to be selynesse or els ease/ *and* he that hath loste suche happes to ben vnsely. Ye forsoth (q*uo*d I). Wel (q*uo*d she) than wol I

980 wenest, assume. **981 renne**, collapse, run out of control. **982 woste**, know; **chalenge**, claim. **986 nys**, it is not; **chalenge**, claim. **987 yeve**, give. **988 playnest**, complain. **991 laudest**, praise; **joyest**, glorify; **for**, since. **992 beleve**, belief, conviction; **wenest**, assume; **selynesse**, fortune. **993 happes**, circumstances; **unsely**, miserable, unfortunate.

prove that unsely in that wise is to preise, and so the t'other is, the contrary, to be lacked." "Howe so?" quod I. "For Unsely," quod she, "begyleth nat but sheweth th'entent of her workyng. *Et e contra.* Selynesse begyleth, for in prosperité she maketh a jape in blyndnesse; that is, she wyndeth him to make sorowe whan she withdraweth. Wolte thou nat," quod she, "preise him better that sheweth to thee his herte, tho it be with bytande wordes and dispitous than him that gloseth and thinketh in their absence to do thee many harmes?" "Certes," quod I, "the one is to commende and the other to lacke and dispice." "A ha," quod she, "right so Ease while he lasteth, gloseth and flatereth, and lightly voydeth whan she most plesauntly sheweth, and ever in her absence she is aboute to do thee tene and sorowe in herte. But Unsely albeit with bytande chere, sheweth what she is, and so doth not that other, wherfore Unsely dothe not begyle. Selynesse disceyveth; Unsely put awaye doute. That one maketh men blynde; that other openeth their eyen in shewynge of wretchydnesse. The one is ful of drede to lese that is not his owne; that other is sobre and maketh men discharged of mokel hevynesse in burthen.

proue that vnsely in that wise is to preise/ *and* so the tother is the co*n*trary to be lacked. Howe so (q*uo*d I) For vnsely (q*uo*d she) begyleth nat/ but sheweth thentent of her workyng. Et eco*n*tra. Selynesse begyleth/ for in prosperite she maketh a iape in blyndnesse/ that is she wyndeth him to make sorowe whan she withdraweth. Wolte thou nat (q*uo*d she) preise him better that sheweth to the his herte/ tho it be with bytande wordes *and* dispitous/ tha*n* him that gloseth *and* thi*n*keth in their absence to do the many harmes Certes (q*uo*d I) the one is to co*m*mende/ *and* the other to lacke *and* dispice. A ha (q*uo*d she) right so ease while he lasteth/ gloseth *and* flatereth/ *and* liȝtly voydeth whan she most plesau*n*tly sheweth/ **<335vb><336ra>**and euer in her absence she is aboute to do the tene and sorowe in herte: but vnsely al be it with bytande chere/ sheweth what she is/ and so doth not that other/ wherfore vnsely dothe not begyle. Selynesse disceyueth: vnsely put awaye doute. That one maketh men blynde/ that other openeth their eyen in shewynge of wretchydnesse. The one is ful of drede to lese that is not his owne: that other is sobre and maketh men discharged of mokel heuynesse in burthen.

994 to preise, to [be] praised; **the contrary**, on the other hand. **995 lacked**, blamed; **Unsely**, Misery, Misfortune, Infelicity. **996 *Et e contra***, As for the contrary; **Selynesse**, Fortune; **jape**, joke, jest. **997 wyndeth**, winds (as about "her little finger"). **999 bytande**, biting; **dispitous**, spiteful; **gloseth**, flatters. **1000 commende**, praise; **lacke**, blame. **1001 dispice**, despise. **1002 voydeth**, departs. **1003 do thee tene**, cause you grief; **bytande**, biting. **1006 lese**, lose. **1007 mokel**, much.

The one draweth a man from very good, the other haleth hym to vertue by the hookes of thoughtes. And wenyst thou nat that thy disease hath done thee mokel more to wynne than ever yet thou lostest, and more than ever the contrary made thee wynne? Is nat a great good to thy thynking for to knowe the hertes of thy sothfast frendes? Pardy, they ben proved to the ful, and the trewe have discevered from the false. Trewly, at the goynge of the ylke brotel joye ther yede no more awaye than the ylke that was nat thyne proper. He was never from that lyghtly departed. Thyne owne good, therfore, leaveth it stylle with thee. Nowe good," quod she, "for howe moche woldest thou somtyme have bought this verry knowyng of thy frendes from the flatterynge flyes that thee glosed whan thou thought thyselfe sely. But thou that playnest of losse in rychesse hast founden the most dereworthy thynge. That thou cleapest unsely hath made thee moche thynge to wynnen. And also, for conclusyoun, of al he is frende that nowe leaveth nat his hert from thyne helpes. And if that Margarite denyeth nowe nat to suffre her vertues shyne to thee wardes with spreadynge beames as farre or farther than if thou were sely

---

The one draweth a man from very good/ the other haleth hym to vertue by the hookes of thoughtes. And wenyst thou nat that thy disease hath done the mokel more to wynne/ than euer yet thou lostest? and more than euer the contrary made the wynne. Is nat a great good to thy thynking/ for to knowe the hertes of thy sothfast frendes. Pardy they ben proued to the ful/ and the trewe haue disceuered from the false. Trewly at the goynge of the ylke brotel ioye/ ther yede no more awaye/ than the ylke that was nat thyne proper: he was neuer from that lyghtly departed/ thyne owne good therfore leaueth it stylle with the. Nowe good (quod she) for howe moche woldest thou somtyme haue bought/ this verry knowyng of thy frendes/ from the flatterynge flyes that the glosed/ whan thou thought thy selfe sely. But thou that playnest of losse in rychesse/ hast founden the most dere worthy thynge that thou cleapest vnsely/ hath made the moche thynge to wynnen. And also for conclusyoun of al/ he is frende that nowe leaueth nat his hert from thyne helpes. And if that Margarite denyeth nowe nat to suffre her vertues shyne to the wardes/ with spreadynge beames/ as farre or farther than if thou were sely

1008 haleth, hauls. **1009 wenyst**, suppose. **1011 sothfast**, trustworthy; **Pardy**, Indeed. **1012 discevered**, separated. **1013 ylke**, same; **brotel**, changeable; **yede**, went. **1014 leaveth**, believe. **1016 flatterynge flyes**, grovelling courtiers, parasites, flatterers; **glosed**, deceived. **1017 sely**, fortunate; **playnest**, complain. **1018 dereworthy**, valuable; **cleapest**, call; **unsely**, unfortunate, miserable. **1019 leaveth**, withdraws. **1020 denyeth**, deigns (see note).

in worldly joye; trewly I saye nat els but she is somdele to blame."

"Ah, peace," quod I, "and speke no more of this. Myne herte breaketh nowe thou touchest any suche wordes." "A, wel," quod she, "thanne lette us syngen: thou herest no more of these thynges at this tyme."

Thus endeth the firste booke of the *Testament of Love*, and herafter foloweth the seconde.

---

in worldly ioye: trewly I saye nat els but she is somdele to blame.

Ah/ peace (quod I) and speke no more of this/ myne herte breaketh/ nowe thou touchest any suche wordes. A wel (quod she) thanne lette vs syngen/ thou herest no more of these thynges at this tyme.

Thus endeth the firste booke of the Testament of Loue/ and herafter foloweth the seconde.**<336ra>**

1022 somdele, somewhat.

The Testament of Love

Book 2

Chapter I

Very welth may not be founden in al this worlde, and that is wel sene: Lo, howe in my mooste comforte as I wende and moost supposed to have hadde ful answere of my contrary thoughtes sodaynly it was vanysshed. And al the workes of man faren in the same wyse, whan folke wenen best her entent for to have and wylles to perfourme, anone, chaungyng of the lyft syde to the ryght halve tourneth it so clene into another kynde that never shal it come to the fyrst plyte in doynge.

Of this wrongful steeryng so soone otherwysed out of knowynge, but for my purpose was at my begynnynge and so dureth yet, if God of His grace tyme wol me graunt, I thynke to perfourme this worke as I have begonne in love, after as my thynne wytte with inspyracion of Hym that hyldeth al grace wol suffre. Grevously God wotte have I suffred

---

<336rb>VEry welth may not be founden in al this worlde/ and that is wel sene: Lo howe in my mooste comforte/ as I wende and moost supposed to haue hadde ful answere of my contrary thoughtes/ sodaynly it was vanysshed. And al the workes of man faren in the same wyse/ whan folke wenen best her entent for to haue/ and wylles to perfourme/ anone chaungyng of the lyft syde to the ryght halue/ tourneth it so clene in to another kynde/ th*at* neuer shal it come to the fyrst plyte in doynge.

O this wrongful steeryng so soone otherwysed out of knowynge/ but for my purpose was at my begynnynge/ and so dureth yet/ if god of his grace tyme wol me graunt/ I thynke to perfourme this worke as I haue begonne/ in loue/ after as my thynne wytte/ with inspyracion of hym that hyldeth al grace wol suffre. Greuously god wotte haue I suffred

1 sene, seen. **2 wende**, expected. **4 wenen**, assume; **her**, their. **5 lyft**, left. **6 plyte**, condition. **7 steeryng**, governance; **otherwysed**, altered. **8 dureth**, lasts. **10 hyldeth**, pours out; **wotte**, knows.

a great throwe that the Romayne emperour whiche in unyté of love shulde acorde and every with other in cause of other to avaunce, and namely sythe this empyre to be corrected of so many sectes in heresie of faith, of servyce, of rule in loves relygion. Trewly, al were it but to shende erronyous opinyons, I maye it no lenger suffre. For many menne there ben that sayne love to ben in gravel and sande that with see ebbynge and flowynge woweth as riches that sodaynly vanissheth. And some sayn that love shulde be in wyndy blastes that stoundmele turneth as a phane and glorie of renome whiche after lustes of the varyaunt people is areysed or stylled.

Many also wenen that in the sonne and the moone and other sterres love shulde ben founden, for amonge al other planettes moste soverainly they shynen as dignytees in reverence of estates rather than good han and occupyen. Ful many also there ben that in okes and in huge postes supposen love to ben grounded, as in strength and in might whiche mowen not helpen their owne wretchydnesse whan they gynne to fal. But suche dyversyté of sectes ayenst the rightful byleve of love these errours ben forthe

---

a great throwe that the romayne emperour/ whiche in vnyte of loue shulde acorde and euery with other in cause of other to auaunce/ and namely sythe this empyre to be corrected of so many sectes in heresie/ of faith/ of seruyce/ o rule in loues relygion. Trewly al were it but to shende erronyous opinyons/ I maye it no lenger suffre: for many menne there ben that sayne loue to ben in grauel and sande/ that with see ebbynge and flowynge woweth/ as riches that sodaynly vanissheth. And some sayn that loue shulde be in wyndy blastes/ that stoundmele turneth as a phane/ and glorie of renome/ whiche after lustes of the varyaunt people is areysed or stylled.

Many also wenen that in the sonne and the moone/ and other sterres/ loue shulde ben fou*n*den/ for amonge al other planettes moste souerainly they shynen/ as dignytees in reuerence of estates rather than good han and occupyen. Ful many also there ben that in okes and in huge postes supposen loue to ben grou*n*ded/ as in strength *and* in might/ whiche mowen not helpen their owne wretchydnesse/ whan they gynne to fal. But suche dyuersyte of**<336rb><336va>**sectes ayenst the rightful byleue of loue/ these errours ben forthe

11 throwe, mischance, fall. **12 sythe**, since. **14 al**, although; **shende**, destroy. **16 woweth**, weave. **17 stoundmele**, sometimes; **phane**, weathervane; **renome**, renown. **18 varyaunt**, changeable; **areysed**, raised. **19 wenen**, assume. **22 okes**, oaks. **23 mowen**, may. **24 byleve**, faith, belief.

spredde that loves servantes in trewe rule and stedfaste faythe in no place darne apere. Thus irrecuperable joy is went, and anoy endlesse is entred. For no man aright reproveth suche errours, but confyrmen their wordes and sayn that badde is noble good, and goodnesse is badde: to which folke the prophete byddeth wo without ende.

Also manye tonges of great false techynges in gylynge maner, principally in my tymes not onely with wordes but also with armes, loves servauntes and professe in his relygion of trewe rule pursewen to confounden and to distroyen. And for as moche as holy fathers that our christen fayth aproved and strenghthed to the Jewes as to men resonable and of divynité lerned proved thilke faythe with resones and with auctorites of the Olde Testament and of the newe her pertynacie to distroy. But to paynyms that for beestes and houndes were holde to put hem out of their errour was myracles of God shewed. These thynges were fygured by comynge of th'angel to the shepeherdes and by the sterre to paynyms kynges, as who saythe: angel resonable to resonable creature and sterre of myracle to people bestyal (not lerned) werne sent to enforme. But I, lovers clerke, in al my connyng and with al my mightes, trewly I have no suche grace in vertue

---

spredde/ that loues seruantes in trewe rule and stedfaste faythe/ in no place darne apere: Thus irrecuperable ioy is went/ and anoy endlesse is entred. for no man aright reproueth suche errours/ but confyrmen their wordes/ and sayn that badde is noble good/ and goodnesse is badde: to which folke the prophete byddeth/ Wo without ende.

Also manye tonges of great false techynges in gylynge maner/ principally in my tymes/ not onely with wordes/ but also with armes/ loues seruauntes and professe in his relygion of trewe rule/ pursewen to confounden and to distroyen./ And for as moche as holy fathers/ that our christen fayth aproued and strenghthed to the iewes/ as to men resonable/ and of diuynite lerned/ proued thilke faythe with resones/ and with auctorites of the olde testament *and* of the newe/ her pertynacie to distroy: But to paynyms/ that for beestes and houndes were holde/ to put hem out of their errour/ was myracles of god shewed. These thynges were fygured by comynge of thangel to the shepeherdes/ and by the sterre to paynyms kynges/ as who saythe: angel resonable to resonable creature/ and sterre of myracle to people bestyal not lerned/ werne sent to enforme. But I louers clerke in al my connyng and with al my mightes/ trewly I haue no suche grace in vertue

25 darne apere, dare appear. **26 went**, departed; **anoy**, frustration. **29 gylynge**, beguiling. **31 pursewen**, pursue. **33 thilke**, that same. **34 pertynacie**, obstinacy; **paynyms**, pagans, heathens. **37 sterre**, star. **38 werne**, were. **39 connyng**, wit.

of myracles ne for no discomfyte falsheedes suffyseth not auctorytes alone sythen that suche heretykes and maintaynours of falsytes. Wherfore I wotte wel, sythen that they ben men and reason is approved in hem, the clowde of erroure hath her reason bewonde probable resons whiche that catchende wytte rightfully may not withsytte. By my travaylynge studye I have ordeyned hem with that auctorité misglosed by mannes reason to graunt shal be enduced.

Nowe gynneth my penne to quake to thinken on the sentences of the envyous people whiche alwaye ben redy, bothe ryder and goer, to skorne and to jape this leude booke, and me for rancoure and hate in their hertes they shullen so dispyse, that althoughe my booke be leude, yet shal it ben more leude holden and by wicked wordes in many maner apayred. Certes, me thynketh the sowne of their badde speche right nowe is ful bothe myne eeres. O good precious Margaryte, myne herte shulde wepe if I wyste ye token hede of suche maner speche, but trewly I wotte wel in that your wysdome shal not

---

of myracles/ ne for no discomfyte falsheedes/ suffyseth not auctorytes alone sythen that suche heretykes and maintaynours of falsytes. wherfore I wotte wel sythen that they ben men/ and reason is approued in hem/ the clowde of erroure hath her reason bewonde probable resons/ whiche that catchende wytte rightfully may not with sytte. By my trauaylynge studye I haue ordeyned hem/ with that auctorite misglosed by mannes reason/ to graunt shal be enduced.

Nowe gynneth my penne to quake/ to thinken on the sentences of the enuyous people/ whiche alwaye ben redy/ bothe ryder and goer to skorne and to iape this leude booke/ and me for rancoure and hate in their hertes they shullen so dispyse/ that althoughe my booke**<336va><336vb>**be leude/ yet shal it ben more leude holden/ and by wicked wordes in many maner apayred. Certes me thynketh the sowne of their badde speche/ right nowe is ful bothe myne eeres. O good precious Margaryte/ myne herte shulde wepe if/ I wyste ye token hede of suche maner speche/ but trewly I wotte wel in that your wysdome shal not

40 sythen that, because of. **41 wotte**, know; **sythen**, since. **43 catchende**, apprehending; **withsytte**, resist. **44 travaylynge**, laboring; **misglosed**, wrongly glossed. **47 ryder**, horseback-rider, i.e., wealthy; **goer**, pedestrian, i.e., poor; **leude**, rude, unlearned. **48 me**, people; **shullen**, shall. **50 apayred**, denigrated (lit., damaged); **sowne**, sound. **51 eeres**, ears; **wyste**, knew. **52 hede**, heed.

asterte. For of God, maker of kynde, wytnesse I toke that for none envy ne yvel have I drawe this mater togyder, but only for goodnesse to maintayn, and errours in falsetees to distroy. Wherfore (as I sayd) with reason I thynke thylke forsayd errours to distroye and dequace.

These reasons and suche other if they enduce men in loves servyce trewe to beleve of parfyte blysse, yet to ful faithe in credence of deserte fully mowe they nat suffyse, sithen faith hath no meryte of mede whan mannes reason sheweth experyence in doyng. For utterly no reason the parfyte blysse of love by no waye maye make to be comprehended. Lo, what is a persel of lovers joye? Parfyte science in good servyce of their desyre to comprehende in bodily doynge the lykynge of the soule, not as by a glasse to have contemplacion of tyme comynge, but thilke first ymagyned and thought after face to face in beholdyng. What herte, what reason, what understandynge can make his heven to be feled and knowe without assaye in doynge? Certes, none, sythen thanne of love cometh suche fruite in blysse, and love in hymselfe is the most amonge other vertues, as clerkes sayne: "The sede of suche springynge in al places, in al

---

asterte. For of god maker of kynde wytnesse I toke/ that for none enuy ne yuel haue I drawe this mater togyder/ but only for goodnesse to maintayn/ and errours in falsetees to distroy. Wherfore (as I sayd) with reason I thynke/ thylke forsayd errours to distroye and dequace.

These reasons and suche other/ if they enduce men in loues seruyce/ trewe to beleue of parfyte blysse/ yet to ful faithe in credence of deserte/ fully mowe they nat suffyse/ sithen faith hath no meryte of mede/ whan mannes reason sheweth experyence in doyng. For vtterly no reason the parfyte blysse of loue by no waye maye make to be comprehended. Lo what is a persel of louers ioye/ parfyte science in good seruyce/ of their desyre to comprehende in bodily doynge the lykynge of the soule/ not as by a glasse to haue contemplacion of tyme comynge/ but thilke first ymagyned and thought/ after face to face in beholdyng: what herte/ what reason/ what vnderstandynge can make his heuen to be feled and knowe without assaye in doynge? certes none. Sythen thanne of loue cometh suche fruite in blysse/ and loue in hym selfe is the most amonge other vertues/ as clerkes sayne: The sede of suche springynge in al places/ in al

53 asterte, start [involving itself]. **56 dequace**, quash. **57 trewe**, truly. **58 mowe**, may. **59 sithen**, since; **mede**, reward. **61 persel**, part. **63 thilke**, that same. **65 feled**, felt; **assaye**, experience. **67 sede**, seed.

countreys, in al worldes shulde ben sowe."

But o, welawaye, thilke sede is forsake and mowen not ben suffred the londe tyllers to set a werke without medlynge of cockle: badde wedes whiche somtyme stonken hath caught the name of love amonge ydiotes and badde meanynge people. Neverthe-later, yet howe so it be that menne cleape thilke thynge preciousest in kynde with many eke names that other thynges that the soule yeven the ylke noble name it sheweth wel that in a maner men have a great lykynge in worshyppynge of thilke name. Wherfore this worke have I writte, and to thee, tytled of loves name, I have it avowed in a maner of sacrifyse, that whereever it be radde it mowe in meryte by the excellence of thilke name the more wexe in authorité and worshyppe of takynge in hede, and to what entent it was ordayned the inseeres mowen ben moved. Every thynge to whom is owande occasyon done as for his ende, Aristotle supposeth that the actes of every thynge ben in a maner his fynal cause. A fynal cause is noblerer, or els even as noble, as thilke thynge that is fynally to thilke ende, wherfore accion of thynge everlastyng is demed to be

---

countreys/ in al worldes shulde ben sowe.

But o welawaye thilke sede is forsake/ and mowen not ben suffred the londe tyllers to set a werke/ without medlynge of cockle/ badde wedes whiche somtyme stonken/ hath caught the name of loue amonge ydiotes and badde meanynge people. Neuer the later/ yet howe so it be that menne cleape thilke kynge preciousest in kynde/ with many eke names/ that other thynges that the soule yeuen the ylke noble name/ it sheweth wel that in a maner men haue a great lykynge in worshyppynge**<336vb><337ra>**of thilke name/ wherfore this worke have I writte/ and to the tytled of loues name/ I haue it auowed in a maner of sacrifyse/ that where euer it be radde/ it mowe in meryte by the excellence of thilke name the more wexe in authorite and worshyppe of takynge in hede/ and to what entent it was ordayned/ the inseeres mowen ben moued: Euery thynge to whom is owande occasyon done as for his ende/ Aristotle supposeth that the actes of euery thynge ben in a maner his fynal cause. A fynal cause is noblerer or els euen as noble as thilke thynge that is fynally to thilke ende/ wherfore accion of thynge euerlastyng/ is demed to be

68 sowe, sown. **69 welawaye**, alas; **thilke**, that same; **mowen**, may. **70 medlynge**, mixing; **cockle**, weeds; **stonken**, stank. **72 cleape**, call; **kynde**, nature. **73 eke names**, nickname; **yeven**, gives. **75 tytled of**, entitled with; **avowed**, dedicated. **76 radde**, read; **mowe**, may. **77 wexe**, grow. **78 inseeres**, lookers into, readers. **78–79 owande occasyon**, owing cause.

eternal and not temporal sythen it is his fynal cause. Ryght so the actes of my boke *Love,* and love is noble. Wherfore, though my boke be leude, the cause with whiche I am stered and for whom I ought it done, noble forsothe ben bothe. But bycause that in connynge I am yonge and canne yet but crepe, this leude A B C have I sette into lernyng. For I can not passen the tellyng of thre as yet. And if God wyl, in shorte tyme I shal amende this leudnesse in joynynge syllables, whiche thynge for dulnesse of wytte I maye not in thre letters declare. For trewly I saye the goodnesse of my Margaryte perle wolde yeve mater in endityng to many clerkes. Certes, her mercy is more to me swetter than any lyvynges, wherfore my lyppes mowen not suffyse in spekyng of her ful laude and worshyppe as they shulde. But who is that in knowyng of the orders of heven and putteth his resones in the erthe? I forsothe maye not with blere eyen the shynyng sonne of vertue in bright whele of this Margaryte beholde; therfore, as yet I maye her not discryve in vertue as I wolde. In tyme comynge, in another tretyse, thorowe Goddes grace, this sonne in clerenesse of vertue to be knowe, and howe she enlumyneth al this day I thynke to declare.

---

eternal/ and not temporal/ sythen it is his fynal cause: Ryght so the actes of my boke Loue/ and loue is noble/ wherfore though my boke be leude/ the cause with whiche I am stered/ *and* for whom I ought it done/ noble forsothe ben bothe. But bycause that in connynge I am yonge/ and canne yet but crepe/ this leude A/ b/ c/ haue I sette in to lernyng/ for I can not passen the tellyng of thre as yet: and if god wyl in shorte tyme I shal amende this leudnesse in ioynynge syllables/ whiche thynge for dulnesse of wytte I maye not in thre letters declare. For trewly I saye the goodnesse of my Margaryte perle wolde yeue mater in endityng to many clerkes: certes her mercy is more to me swetter than any lyuynges/ wherfore my lyppes mowen not suffyse in spekyng of her ful laude and worshyppe as they shulde. But who is that in knowyng of the orders of heuen/ *and* putteth his resones in the erthe: I forsothe maye not with blere eyen/ th*e* shynyng so*n*ne of vertue in bright whele of this Margaryte beholde/ therfore as yet I maye her not discryue in vertue as I wolde. In tyme comynge in another tretyse thorowe goddes grace/ this sonne in clerenesse of vertue to be knowe/ and howe she enlumyneth al this day/ I thynke to declare.

83 leude, unlearned. **84 stered**, guided. **85 connynge**, intelligence. **85 crepe**, creep. **89 yeve**, give; **endityng**, composing. **90 swetter**, sweeter; **mowen**, may. **91 laude**, praise. **92 blere eyen**, cloudy eyes. **93 whele**, wheel. **94 discryve**, describe. **95 thorowe**, through; **be knowe**, acknowledge.

Chapter II

In this meane whyle this comfortable lady ganne synge a wonder mater of enditynge in Latyn. But trewly the noble colours in rethorik wyse knytte were so craftely that my connyng wol not stretche to remembre; but the sentence I trowe somdele have I in mynde. Certes, they were wonder swete of sowne, and they were touched al in lamentacion wyse and by no werbles of myrthe. Lo, thus ganne she synge in Latyn, as I may constrewe it in our Englysshe tonge:

"Alas, that these hevenly bodyes their lyght and course shewen as nature yave hem in commaundement at the gynnyng of the first age, but these thynges in free choyce of reson han none understondynge. But man that ought to passe al thynge of doynge of right course in kynde overwhelmed sothnesse by wrongful tytle and hath drawen the sterre of envye to gon by his syde, that the clyps of me that shulde be his shynande sonne so ofte is sey that it wened thilke errour thorowe hem come in shulde ben myn owne defaute. Trewly therfore, I have me withdrawe and made my dwellynge out of

---

IN this meane whyle this comfortable lady ganne synge/ a wonder mater of enditynge in latyn/ but trewly the noble colours in rethorik wyse knytte were so craftely/ that my connyng wol not stretche to remem**<337ra><337rb>**bre/ but the sentence I trowe somdele haue I in mynde. Certes they were wonder swete of sowne/ and they were touched al in lamentacion wyse/ and by no werbles of myrthe: Lo thus ganne she synge in latyn/ as I may constrewe it in our englysshe tonge.

Alas that these heuenly bodyes their lyght and course shewen/ as nature yaue hem in co*m*maundement at the gynnyng of the first age/ but these thynges in free choyce of reson han none vnderstondynge: but man that ought to passe al thynge of doynge/ of right course in kynde/ ouer whelmed sothnesse by wrongful tytle/ and hath drawen the sterre of enuye to gon by his syde/ that the clyps of me that shulde be his shynande sonne/ so ofte is sey that it wened thilke errour thorowe hem come in/ shulde ben myn owne defaute. Trewly therfore I haue me withdrawe/ and made my dwellynge out of

97 enditynge, composing. **98 in rhetorik wyse**, rhetorically. **99 connyng**, understanding; **trowe**, trust; **somdele**, somewhat. **100 swete**, sweet; **sowne**, sound. **101 werbles**, warbling. **103 yave**, gave. **106 sothnesse**, truthfulness; **tytle**, title. **107 sterre**, star; **clyps**, eclipse. **108 sey**, seen; **wened**, assumed; **thilke**, that same.

lande in an yle by myselfe in the occian closed, and yet sayne there many they have me harberowed, but God wote they faylen. These thynges me greven to thynke, and namely on passed gladnesse that in this worlde was wonte me disporte of hyghe and lowe. And nowe it is fayled. They that wolden maystries me have in thilke stoundes, in heven on hyghe above Saturnes sphere in seasonable tyme were they lodged, but now come queynte counsaylours that in no house wol suffre me sojourne, wherof is pyté; and yet sayne some that they me have in celler with wyne shet, in gernere there corne is layde covered with whete, in sacke sowed with wolle, in purse with money faste knytte, amonge pannes mouled in a wyche, in presse amonge clothes layde with ryche pelure arayed, in stable amonge horse and other beestes, as hogges, shepe, and nete, and in other many wyse. But thou maker of lyght (in wynking of thyn eye the sonne is queynt) woste right wel that I in trewe name was never thus herberowed.

"Somtyme toforn the sonne in the seventh partie was smyten, I bare both crosse and mytre to yeve it where I wolde. With me the pope went a fote, and I tho was wor-

---

lande in an yle by my selfe/ in the occian closed/ and yet sayne there many they haue me harberowed/ but god wote they faylen. These thynges me greuen to thynke/ and namely on passed gladnesse/ that in this worlde was wonte me disporte of hyghe and lowe/ and nowe it is fayled: they that wolden maystries me haue in thilke stoundes. In heuen on hyghe aboue Saturnes sphere/ in seasonable tyme were they lodged/ but now come queynte counsaylours that in no house wol suffre me soiourne/ wherof is pyte: and yet sayne some that they me haue in celler with wyne/ shed in gernere there corne is layde/ couered with whete/ in sacke sowed with wolle/ in purse with money faste knytte/ amonge pannes mouled in a wyche/ in presse amonge clothes layde with ryche pelure arayed/ in stable amonge horse *and* other beestes/ as hogges/ shepe/ and nete/ and in other many wyse. But thou maker of lyght/ (in wynking of thyn eye the sonne is queynt) woste right wel that I in trewe name was neuer thus herberowed.

Somtyme toforn the sonne in th*e* seuenth partie was smyten/ I bare both crosse *and* mytre/ to yeue it where I wolde. With me th*e* pope went a fote/ *and* I tho was wor-

110 yle, island. **111 harberowed**, harbored; **wote**, knows; **greven**, grieve. **112 disporte**, please. **116 celler**, cellar; **gernere**, granary. **117 wolle**, wool. **118 pannes**, pans or cloths; **mouled**, put away; **wyche**, chest; **pelure**, fur. **119 nete**, cattle. **120 queynt**, quenched. **121 woste**, know; **herberowed**, harbored. **122 partie was smyten**, part declined, or suffered eclipse; **bare**, bore. **123 yeve**, give; **a fote**, on foot.

shyped of al holy church. Kynges baden me their crownes holden. The law was set as it shuld: tofore the juge as wel the poore durste shewe his grefe as the ryche, for al his money. I defended tho taylages and was redy for the poore to pay. I made great feestes in my tyme and noble songes and maryed damoselles of gentyl feture withouten golde or other rychesse. Poore clerkes for wytte of schole I sette in churches and made suche persones to preache: and tho was servyce in holy churche honest and devoute in plesaunce bothe of God and of the people. But nowe the leude for symonye is avaunced and shendeth al holy churche. Nowe is stewarde for his achates, nowe is courtyour for his debates, nowe is eschetoure for his wronges, nowe is losel for his songes personer, and provendre alone with whiche manye thrifty shulde encrease. And yet is this shrewe behynde; free herte is forsake, and losengeour is take. Lo, it acordeth, for suche there ben that voluntarye lustes haunten in courte with rybaudye that tyl mydnight and more wol playe and wake, but in the churche at matyns he is behynde, for yvel disposycion

---

shyped of al holy church/ Kynges baden me their crownes holden. The law was set as it shuld: tofore th*e* iuge as wel th*e***<337rb><337va>**poore durste shewe his grefe as the ryche/ for al his money. I defended tho taylages and was redy for the poore to pay. I made great feestes in my tyme/ and noble songes/ and maryed damoselles of gentyl feture/ withouten golde or other rychesse. Poore clerkes for wytte of schole/ I sette in churches/ and made suche persones to preache: and tho was seruyce in holy churche honest and deuoute/ in plesaunce bothe of god and of the people. But nowe the leude for symonye is auaunced/ and shendeth al holy churche. Nowe is stewarde for his achates/ nowe it courtyour for his debates/ nowe is eschetoure for his wronges/ nowe is losel for his songes/ personer and prouendre alone/ with whiche manye thrifty shulde encrease. And yet is this shrewe behynde/ free herte is forsake/ and losengeour is take. Lo it acordeth/ for suche there ben that voluntarye lustes haunten in courte with rybaudye/ that tyl mydnight and more wol playe and wake/ but in the churche at matyns he is behynde/ for yuel disposycion

125 durste, dared; **grefe**, grievance. **126 taylages**, taxes. **127 feture**, features. **128 wytte of schole**, because of their intelligence. **130 leude**, unlearned; **symonye**, simony (i.e., sale of Church offices). **131 shendeth**, destroys; **achates**, purchases. **132 eschetoure**, collector of escheats (a kind of forfeiture); **losel**, flatterer; **personer**, partner. **133 provendre**, provisions. **134 losengeour**, flatterer; **it acordeth**, it's consistent. **135 voluntarye**, voluntarily.

of his stomake; therfore, he shulde eate beane breed, and so dyd his syre his estate ther with to strenghthen. His auter is broke and lowe lythe in poynte to gone to the erthe, but his horse muste ben easy and hye to beare him over great waters. His chalyce poore, but he hath ryche cuppes. No towayle but a shete there God shal ben handled. And on his meate borde there shal ben borde clothes and towelles many payre. At masse serveth but a clergyon; fyve squiers in hal. Poore chaunsel, open holes in every syde, beddes of sylke with tapytes goyng al aboute his chambre. Poore masse boke and leude chapelayne and broken surplyce with many an hole, good houndes and many to hunte after harte and hare to fede in their feestes. Of poore men have they great care, for they ever crave and nothynge offren: they wolden have hem dolven. But amonge legystres there dare I not come: my doynge, they sayne, maken hem nedy. They ne wolde for nothyng have me in town, for than were tort and forthe nought worthe an hawe about and pleasen no men but thilk grevous and torcious ben in might and in doyng. These thynges toforne

---

of his stomake: therfore he shulde eate beane breed/ and so dyd his syre/ his estate ther with to strenghthen. His auter is broke/ and lowe lythe in poynte to gone to the erthe/ but his horse muste ben easy and hye to beare him ouer great waters. His chalyce poore/ but he hath ryche cuppes. No towayle but a shete there god shal ben handled. And on his meate borde there shal ben borde clothes and towelles many payre. At masse serueth but a clergyon: fyue squiers in hal. Poore chaunsel/ open holes in euery syde: beddes of sylke with tapytes goyng al aboute his chambre. Poore masse boke and leude chapelayne/ and broken surplyce with many an hole: good houndes and many/ to hunte after harte and hare/ to fede in their feestes. Of poore men haue they great care/ for they euer craue and nothynge offren/ they wolden haue hem doluen. But amonge legystres there dare I not come/ my doynge they sayne maken hem nedy/ they ne wolde for nothyng haue me in town/ for than were tort and forthe nought worthe an hawe about and pleasen no men/ but thilk greuous and torcious ben in might and in doyng: these**<337va><337vb>**thynges to forne

137 beane breed, bread made with bean meal. **138 auter**, altar; **lythe**, lies. **140 towayle**, towel; **God**, i.e., species of the sacrament. **141 meate borde**, table for eating meat, etc. **142 clergyon**, young cleric; **chaunsel**, chancel (part of church where sacrament is celebrated). **143 tapytes**, tapestries; **leude**, ignorant. **144 surplyce**, a priest's vestment. **146 dolven**, buried; **legystres**, lawyers. **148 tort**, law torts; **hawe**, worthless plant. **149 thilk**, the same; **torcious**, injurious [men].

sayd mowe wel, if men lyste, ryme. Trewly, they acorde nothynge. And for as moch as al thynges by me shulden of right ben governed, I am sorye to se that governaunce fayleth as thus: to sene smale and lowe governe the hye and bodies above. Certes, that polesye is naught. It is forbode by them that of governaunce treaten and enformen. And right as beestly wytte shulde ben subjecte to reason, so erthly power in itselfe the lower shulde ben subject to the hygher. What is worth thy body but it be governed with thy soule? Right so lytel or naught is worthe erthely power, but if reignatyfe prudence in heedes governe the smale, to whiche heedes the smale owen to obey and suffre in their governaunce. But soverainnesse ayenwarde shulde thynke in this wyse: 'I am servaunt of these creatures to me delyvered, not lorde, but defendour; not mayster, but enfourmer; not possessoure, but in possessyon; and to hem lyche a tree in whiche sparowes shullen stelen her byrdes to norisshe and forthe bring under suretie ayenst al raveynous foules and beestes, and not to be tyraunt themselfe.' And than the smale, in reste and quyete, by the heedes wel disposed, owen for their soveraynes helth and prosperyté to pray, and in other doynges in maintenaunce therof performe withouten other admynistracion

---

sayd mowe wel if men lyste ryme/ trewly they acorde nothynge. And for as moch as al thynges by me shulden of right ben gouerned/ I am sorye to se that gouernaunce fayleth/ as thus: to sene smale and lowe gouerne the hye/ and bodies aboue. Certes th*at* polesye is naught/ it is forbode by them that of gouernaunce treaten *and* enformen. And right as beestly wytte shulde ben subiecte to reason/ so erthly power in it selfe/ the lower shulde ben subiect to th*e* hygher. What is worth thy body/ but it be gouerned with thy soule? right so lytel or naught is worthe erthely power/ but if reignatyfe prudence in heedes gouerne the smale/ to whiche heedes the smale owen to obey/ and suffre in their gouernau*n*ce. But souerainnesse ayenwarde shulde thynke in this wyse: I am seruaunt of these creatures to me delyuered/ not lorde but defendour/ not mayster but enfourmer/ not possessoure but in possessyon/ and to hem lyche a tree in whiche sparowes shullen stelen/ her byrdes to norisshe and forthe bring vnder suretie ayenst al raueynous foules and beestes/ and not to be tyraunt them selfe. And than the smale in reste and quyete/ by the heedes wel disposed/ owen for their soueraynes helth and prosperyte to pray/ and in other doynges/ in maintenaunce therof performe/ withouten other admynistracion

150 mowe, may; **lyste**, please; **acorde nothynge**, are congruous not at all. **153 forbode**, forbidden; **treaten**, treat. **156 reignatyfe**, governing. **157 heedes**, tops, i.e., rulers; **owen**, ought. **158 ayenwarde**, on the other hand. **160 lyche**, like; **shullen**, shall. **161 stelen**, steal, hide themselves. **162 And**, And [if].

in rule of any maner governaunce. And they wyt have in hem and grace to come to suche thynges, yet shulde they cease tyl their heedes them cleped, although profyte and pleasaunce shulde folowe. But trewly, other governaunce ne other medlynge ought they not to clayme, ne the heedes on hem to put. Trewly, amonges cosynage dare I not come but if rychesse be my meane; sothly, she and other bodily goodes maketh nigh cosinage ther never propynquité ne alyaunce in lyve was ne shuld have be, nere it for her medling maners, wherfore kindly am I not ther leged. Povert of kynred is behynde, rychesse suffreth him to passe: truly, he saith he com never of Japhetes childre. Wherof I am sory that Japhetes children for povert in no linage ben rekened, and Caynes children for riches be maked Japhetes heires. Alas, this is a wonder chaunge bytwene tho two Noes chyldren, sythen that of Japhetes ofspring comeden knightes and of Cayn discended the lyne of servage to his brothers childre. Lo, howe gentyllesse and servage as cosyns bothe discended out of two bretherne of one body. Wherfore I saye in sothnesse that gentylesse in kynrede maken not gentyl lynage in successyon without deserte of a mans

---

in rule of any maner gouernaunce. And they wyt haue in hem/ and grace to come to suche thynges/ yet shulde they cease tyl their heedes them cleped/ although profyte and pleasaunce shulde folowe. But trewly other gouernaunce ne other medlynge ought they not to clayme/ ne th*e* heedes on hem to put. Trewly amonges cosynage dare I not come/ but if rychesse be my meane/ sothly she *and* other bodily goodes maketh nigh cosinage/ ther neuer propynquite ne alyaunce in lyue was/ ne shuld haue be/ nere it for her medli*ng* maners/ wherfore kindly am I not ther leged. Pouert of kynred is behynde/ rychesse suffreth him to passe: truly he saith he com neuer of Japhetes childre. Wherof I am sory th*at* Japhetes childre*n* for pouert/ i*n* no linage ben rekened/ *and* Caynes children for riches be maked Japhetes heires. Alas this is a wonder chaunge bytwene tho**<337vb><338ra>**two Noes chyldren sythen that of Japhetes ofspring comeden knightes/ *and* of Cayn discended the lyne of seruage to his brothers childre. Lo howe gentyllesse and seruage as cosyns/ bothe discended out of two bretherne of one body: Wherfore I saye in sothnesse/ that gentylesse in in kynrede maken not gentyl lynage in successyon/ without deserte of a mans

166 cleped, called. **168 cosynage**, friends and relatives. **169 but if**, unless; **sothly**, truly. **170 ther**, where; **nere it for**, were it not for. **171 kindly**, by nature; **leged**, lodged; **behynde**, i.e., lacking in kin. **173 Caynes**, i.e., Ham's (see note). **176 servage**, slavery. **177 sothnesse**, truth. **178 gentylesse**, gentility; **in kynrede**, by birth.

own selfe. Where is nowe the lyne of Alysaundre the noble or els of Hector of Troye? Who is discended of right bloode of lyne fro king Artour? Pardé, sir Perdicas whom that kynge Alysandre made to ben his heire in Grece was of no kynges bloode — his dame was a tombystere. Of what kynred ben the gentyles in our dayes? I trow therfore if any good be in gentylesse, it is only that it semeth a maner of necessyté be input to gentylmen that they shulden not varyen fro the vertues of their auncestres. Certes, al maner lynage of men ben evenliche in byrth, for one father, maker of al goodnes, enformed hem al, and al mortal folke of one sede arne greyned. Wherto avaunt men of her lynage in cosynage or in elde fathers? Loke now the gynnyng and to God, maker of mans person; there is no clerke ne no worthy in gentilesse; and he that norissheth his corare with vyces and unresonable lustes and leaveth the kynde course to whiche ende him brought forthe his byrthe, trewly, he is ungentyl and amonge clerkes may ben nempned. And therfore he that wol ben gentyl he mote daunten his flesshe fro vyces that causen ungentylnesse and leave also reignes of wicked lustes and drawe to him

---

own selfe. Where is nowe the lyne of Alysaundre the noble/ or els of Hector of Troye? Who is discended of right bloode of lyne fro king Artour? Parde sir Perdicas/ whom that kynge Alys*a*ndre made to ben his heire in Grece/ was of no kynges bloode/ his dame was a tombystere. Of what kynred ben the gentyles in our dayes: I trow therfore if any good be in gentylesse/ it is only that it semeth a maner of necessyte be input to gentylmen/ that they shulden not varyen fro the vertues of their auncestres. Certes al maner lynage of men ben euenliche in byrth/ for one father maker of al goodnes enformed hem al/ *and* al mortal folke of one sede arne greyned. Wherto auau*n*t men of her lynage/ in cosynage or in elde fathers. Loke now the gynnyng/ and to god maker of mans person/ there is no clerke ne no worthy in gentilesse: and he that norissheth his corare with vyces *and* vnresonable lustes/ and leaueth the kynde course/ to whiche ende him brought forthe his byrthe/ trewly he is vngentyl/ and amonge clerkes may ben nempned. And therfore he that wol ben gentyl/ he mote daunten his flesshe fro vyces th*at* causen vngentylnesse/ and leaue also reignes of wicked lustes/ and drawe to him

180 Pardé, Indeed. **182 tombystere**, a female tumbler; **gentyles**, people of gentle birth; **trow**, believe. **185 evenliche**, equal. **186 sede**, seed; **greyned**, sprung; **Wherto**, Why; **avaunt**, boast. **187 cosynage**, friends and relatives; **elde fathers**, elders; **Loke**, Consider. **189 corare**, heart, spirit; **leaveth**, abandons; **kynde**, natural. **191 nempned**, counted, named; **mote**, must; **daunten**, control. **192 leave**, abandon; **reignes**, rule.

vertue, that in al places gentylnesse gentylmen maketh. And so speke I, in feminyne gendre in general, of tho persones at the reverence of one whom every wight honoureth, for her bountie and her noblesse ymade her to God so dere that His moder she became, and she me hath had so great in worshyp that I nyl for nothyng in open declare that in any thynge ayenst her secte maye so wene. For al vertue and al worthynesse of plesaunce in hem haboundeth. And although I wolde any thing speke, trewly, I can not. I may fynde in yvel of hem no maner mater."

Chapter III

Right with these wordes she stynte of that lamentable melodye, and I ganne with a lyvely herte to praye if that it were lykyng unto her noble grace, she wolde her deyne to declare me the mater that firste was begonne in whiche she lefte and stynte to speke beforne she gan to synge.

"O," quod she, "this is no newe thynge to me to sene you menne desyren after mater whiche your selfe caused to voyde."

---

vertue/ that in al places gentylnesse gentylmen maketh. And so speke I in feminyne gendre in general/ of tho persones at the reuerence of one/ whom euery wight honoureth/ for her bountie and her noblesse ymade her to god so dere/ that his moder she became/ and she me hath had so great in worshyp/ that I nyl for nothyng in open declare/ that in any thynge ayenst her secte maye so wene: for al vertue and al worthynesse of plesaunce in hem haboundeth. And although I wolde any thing speke/ trewly I can not/ I may fynde in yuel of hem no maner mater.**<338ra>**

<338rb>RIght with these wordes she stynte of that lamentable melodye/ and I ganne with a lyuely herte to praye/ if that it were lykyng vnto her noble grace/ she wolde her deyne to declare me the mater that firste was begonne/ in whiche she lefte and stynte to speke beforne she gan to synge.

O (quod she) this is no newe thynge to me/ to sene you menne desyren after mater/ whiche your selfe caused to voyde.

194 wight, person. **196 nyl**, will not. **197 secte**, sect, following; **wene**, make assumptions or allegations (see note). **198 haboundeth**, abounds. **199 yvel**, evil. **200 stynte**, ceased. **201 deyne**, condescend. **204 sene**, see. **205 voyde**, disappear.

"Ah good lady," quod I, "in whom victorie of strength is proved above al other thynge after the jugement of Esdram whose lordshyp al lignes: who is that right as emperour hem commaundeth whether thilke ben not women in whose lykenesse to me ye aperen? For right as man halte the principalté of al thyng under his beynge in the masculyne gender, and no mo genders ben there but masculyn and femenyne, al the remenaunt ben no gendres but of grace in facultie of grammer, right so in the femenyne the women holden the upperest degree of al thynges under thilke gendre conteyned. Who bringeth forthe kynges whiche that ben lordes of see and of erthe? And al peoples of women ben borne: they norysshe hem that graffen vynes, they maken men comforte in their gladde cheres. Her sorowe is dethe to mannes herte. Without women the beyng of men were impossyble. They conne with their swetnesse the crewel herte ravysshe and make it meke buxome and benigne without vyolence mevynge. In beautie of their eyen or els of other maner fetures is al mens desyres, ye, more than in golde, precious stones, eyther any rychesse. And in this degree, lady, yourselfe many hertes of men have so bounden that parfyte blysse in womankynde to ben men wenen and in nothynge

---

Ah good lady (q*uo*d I) in whom victorie of strength is proued aboue al other thynge/ after the iugement of Esdram/ whose lordshyp al lignes: who is that right as emperour hem com*m*aundeth/ whether thilke ben not women/ in whose lykenesse to me ye aperen. For right as man halte the principalte of al thyng vnder his beynge/ in the masculyne gender/ and no mo genders ben there but masculyn and femenyne/ al the remenaunt ben no gendres but of grace/ in facultie of grammer. Right so in the femenyne/ the women holden the vpperest degree of al thynges vnder thilke gendre conteyned. Who bringeth forthe kynges/ whiche that ben lordes of see and of erthe/ and al peoples of women ben borne: they norysshe hem that graffen vynes/ they maken men comforte in their gladde cheres. Her sorowe is dethe to mannes herte. Without women the beyng of men were impossyble. They conne with their swetnesse the crewel herte rauysshe and make it meke/ buxome/ and benigne/ without vyolence meuynge. In beautie of their eyen/ or els of other maner fetures is al mens desyres/ ye more than in golde/ precious stones/ eyther any rychesse. And in this degree lady your selfe many hertes of men haue so bounden/ that parfyte blysse in womankynde to ben men wenen/ and in nothynge

207 lignes, rules. **208 thilke**, those same. **209 aperen**, appear; **halte**, holds. **210 mo**, more. **212 upperest**, highest; **thilke**, that same. **214 norysshe**, nourish; **graffen**, dig, cultivate. **216 conne**, can; **crewel**, cruel. **217 meke**, meek; buxome, obedient; **mevynge**, moving. **219 eyther**, or. **220 wenen**, suppose.

els. Also, lady, the goodnesse, the vertue of women by properté of discrecion, is so wel knowen by lytelnesse of malyce that desyre to a good asker by no waye conne they warne. And ye thanne that wol not passe the kynde werchynge of your sectes by general discrecion, I wotte wel ye wol so enclyne to my prayere that grace of my requeste shal fully ben graunted."

"Certes," quod she, "thus for the more parte fareth al mankynde to praye and to crye after womans grace and fayne many fantasies to make hertes enclyne to your desyres, and whan these sely women for freelté of their kynde beleven your wordes and wenen al be gospel the promise of your behestes, than graunt they to you their hertes and fulfyllen your lustes wherthrough their lyberté in maystreshyp that they toforne had is thralled and so maked soverayn and to be prayed that first was servaunt and voice of prayer used. Anon as fylled is your lust, many of you be so trewe that lytel hede take ye of suche kyndnesse, but with traysoun anon ye thynke hem begyle, and let lyght of that thyng whiche firste ye maked to you wonders dere, so what thing to women it is to love

---

els. Also lady the goodnesse/ the vertue of women/ by properte of discrecion/ is so wel knowen/ by lytelnesse of malyce/ that desyre to a good asker by no waye conne they warne: and ye thanne that wol not passe the kynde werchynge of your sectes by general discrecion/ I wotte wel ye wol so enclyne to my prayere/ that grace of my requeste shal**<338rb><338va>**fully ben graunted. Certes (q*uo*d she) thus for the more parte fareth al mankynde to praye/ and to crye after womans grace/ and fayne many f*an*tasies to make hertes enclyne to your desyres: *and* whan these sely women for freelte of their kynde beleuen your wordes/ and wenen al be gospel the promise of your behestes/ than graunt they to you their hertes/ and fulfyllen your lustes/ wherthrough their lyberte in maystreshyp that they toforne had is thralled/ *and* so maked souerayn and to be prayed/ th*at* first was seruaunt/ *and* voice of prayer vsed.

Anon as fylled is your lust/ many of you be so trewe/ that lytel hede take ye of suche kyndnesse/ but with traysoun anon ye thynke hem begyle/ *and* let lyght of that thyng whiche firste ye maked to you wonders dere/ so what thing to women it is to love

221 properté, characteristic. **222 good**, polite. **223 warne**, deny; **werchynge**, working. **224 wotte**, know. **226 fareth**, fares. **227 fayne**, pretend. **228 sely**, innocent; **freelté**, frailty; **beleven**, believe. **229 gospel**, i.e., the "gospel" truth; **behestes**, proffers. **230 lustes**, desires; **maystreshyp**, mastery; **toforne**, before. **231 thralled**, enslaved. **232 hede**, heed. **233 traysoun**, betrayal; **let lyght**, make light. **234 wonders**, wondrously; **dere**, valuable.

any wight er she hym wel knowe and have him proved in many halfe. For every glyttryng thyng is nat golde, and under colour of fayre speche many vices may be hyd and conseled. Therfore, I rede no wyght to trust on you to rathe. Mens chere and her speche right gyleful is ful ofte. Wherfore, without good assay it is nat worthe on many of you to truste. Trewly, it is right kyndely to every man that thynketh women betraye and shewen outwarde al goodnesse tyl he have his wyl performed. Lo, the birde is begyled with the mery voice of the foulers whistel. Whan a woman is closed in your nette, than wol ye causes fynden and beare unkyndenesse her unhande, or falseté upon her putte, your owne malycious trayson with suche thynge to excuse. Lo, than han women none other wreche in vengeaunce but blober and wepe tyl hem lyst stynt and sorily her mishap complayne, and is put into wenyng that al men ben so untrewe. Howe often have men chaunged her loves in a lytel while or els for faylyng their wyl in their places hem sette. For frenship shal be one, and fame with another him lyste for to have,

---

any wight er she hym wel knowe/ *and* haue him p*ro*ued in many halfe/ for euery glyttryng thyng is nat golde/ *and* vnder colour of fayre speche many vices may be hyd *and* conseled. Therfore I rede no wyght to trust on you to rathe/ mens chere *and* her speche right gyleful is ful ofte/ Wherfore without good assay/ it is nat worthe on many on you to truste: Trewly it is right kyndely to euery man that thynketh women betraye/ *and* shewen outwarde al goodnesse/ tyl he haue his wyl p*er*formed. Lo the birde is begyled with the mery voice of the foulers whistel. Whan a woman is closed in your nette/ than wol ye causes fynden/ *and* beare vnkyndenesse her vnh*an*de/ or falsete vpon her putte/ your owne malycious trayson with suche thynge to excuse. Lo than han women none other wreche in ve*n*geaunce/ but bloder *and* wepe tyl hem lyst stynt/ *and* sorily her mishap co*m*playne/ *and* is put in to wenyng that al men ben so vntrewe. Howe often haue men chaunged her loues in a lytel while/ or els for faylyng their wyl in their places hem sette: for frenship shal be one/ *and* fame with another him lyste for to haue/

235 wight, person; **in many halfe**, i.e., in many ways. **237 conseled**, concealed; **rede**, counsel; **to rathe**, too soon; **chere**, demeanor; **her**, their. **238 gyleful**, deceitful; **assay**, experiment. **239 kyndely**, natural. **241 foulers**, bird-catcher's; **whistel**, whistle. **242 beare . . . unhande**, accuse of. **243 trayson**, betrayal. **244 wreche**, retribution; **blober**, blubber; **wepe**, weep; **hem lyst stynt**, [it] pleases them to stop. **245 her**, their; **complayne**, lament; **wenyng**, understanding. **246 faylyng**, i.e., not getting. **247 lyste**, desire.

and a thirde for delyte, or els were he lost bothe in packe and in clothes. Is this faire? Nay, God wot. I may nat tel by thousande partes the wronges in trechery of suche false people, for make they never so good a bonde, al sette ye at a myte whan your hert tourneth. And they that wenen for sorowe of you dey, the pité of your false herte is flowe out of towne. Alas, therfore that ever any woman wolde take any wyght in her grace tyl she knowe at the ful on whom she might at al assayes trust. Women con no more crafte in queynt knowynge to understande the false disceyvable conjectementes of mannes begilynges. Lo, howe it fareth: though ye men gronen and cryen certes, it is but disceyt and that preveth wel by th'endes in your werkynge. Howe many women have ben lorne and with shame foule shent by longe lastynge tyme whiche thorowe mennes gyle have ben disceyved? Ever their fame shal dure and their dedes radde and songe in many londes that they han done, recoveren shal they never, but alway ben demed lightly in suche plyte ayen shulde they fal, of whiche slaunders and tenes ye false

---

and a thirde for delyte/ or els were he lost bothe in packe *and* in clothes: Is this faire/ nay god wot? I may nat tel by thousande partes/ the wro*n*ges in trechery of suche false people/ for make they neuer so good a bo*n*de/ al sette ye at a myte whan your hert tourneth: And they that wenen for**<338va><338vb>**sorowe of you dey/ the pite of your false herte is flowe out of towne. Alas therfore/ th*at* euer any woman wolde take any wyght in her grace/ tyl she knowe at the ful on whom she might at al assayes trust. Wome*n* con no more crafte in queynt knowynge/ to vnderstande the false disceyuable coniectementes of mannes begilynges. Lo howe it fareth/ though ye men gronen and cryen certes it is but disceyt/ and that preueth wel by thendes in your werkynge. Howe many women haue ben lorne/ and with shame foule shent by longe lastynge tyme/ whiche thorowe mennes gyle haue ben disceyued? euer their fame shal dure/ and their dedes radde and songe in many londes/ that they han done recoueren shal they neuer but alway ben demed lightly/ in suche plyte a yen shulde they fal/ of whiche slaunders and tenes ye false

248 packe, bundle, suitcase. **249 wot**, knows. **250 they**, i.e., women; **ye**, i.e., men; **myte**, trifle. **251 wenen**, expect. **252 flowe**, flown; **wyght**, person. **253 assayes**, experiences; **con**, can, know. **254 queynt**, curious; **conjectementes**, pretenses. **255 gronen**, groan. **256 disceyt**, deceit; **preveth**, proves; **werkynge**, working. **257 lorne**, lost; **shent**, ruined, destroyed; **thorowe**, through. **258 gyle**, guile; **dure**, last; **radde**, read. **260 demed**, judged; **lightly**, as light; **plyte**, plight; **tenes**, sorrows.

men and wicked ben the verey causes. On you by right ought these shames and these reproves al holy discende. Thus arne ye al nyghe untrewe, for al your fayre speche your herte is ful fyckel. What cause han ye women to dispyse? Better fruite than they ben, ne swetter spyces to your behove, mowe ye not fynde as farre as worldly bodyes stretchen. Loke to their formynge at the makyng of their persones by God in joye of paradyce, for goodnesse of mans propre body were they maked after the sawes of the Byble, rehersyng Goddes wordes in this wyse: 'It is good to mankynde that we make to him an helper.' Lo, in paradyse for your helpe was this tree graffed out of whiche al lynage of man discendeth. If a man be noble frute, of noble frute it is sprongen: the blysse of paradyse to mennes sory hertes yet in this tree abydeth. O noble helpes ben these trees, and gentyl jewel to ben worshypped of every good creature. He that hem anoyeth dothe his owne shame. It is a comfortable perle ayenst al tenes. Every company is myrthed by their present beyng. Trewly, I wyst never vertue but a woman were therof the rote. What is heven the worse though Sarazins on it lyen? Is your faythe untrewe thoughe rennogates maken theron leasynges? If the fyre doth any wight brenne,

---

men and wicked ben the verey causes/ on you by right ought these shames and these reproues al holy discende. Thus arne ye al nyghe vntrewe/ for al your fayre speche your herte is ful fyckel. What cause han ye women to dispyse? better fruite than they ben/ ne swetter spyces to your behoue mowe ye not fynde/ as farre as worldly bodyes stretchen. Loke to their formynge at the makyng of their persones by god in ioye of paradyce/ for goodnesse of mans propre body were they maked/ after the sawes of the byble/ rehersyng goddes wordes in this wyse: It is good to mankynde that we make to him an helper. Lo in paradyse for your helpe was this tree graffed/ out of whiche al lynage of man discendeth: if a man be noble frute/ of noble frute it is sprongen: the blysse of paradyse to mennes sory hertes/ yet in this tree abydeth. O noble helpes ben these trees/ and gentyl iewel to ben worshypped of euery good creature: he that hem anoyeth dothe his owne shame/ it is a comfortable perle ayenst al tenes. Euery company is myrthed by their present beyng. Trewly I wyst neuer vertue/ but a woman were therof th*e* rote. What is heuen the worse though Sarazins on it lyen? Is your faythe vntrewe thoughe rennogates maken theron leasynges. If the fyre doth any wight brenne/

261 verey, true. **262 al nyghe**, nearly all. **264 swetter**, sweeter; **behove**, needs; **mowe**, may. **265 Loke to**, Consider. **266 sawes**, teachings. **268 graffed**, planted. **272 perle**, pearl; **tenes**, sorrows. **273 wyst**, knew. **274 rote**, root; **lyen**, lie, blaspheme. **275 rennogates**, recreants; **leasynges**, lies; **brenne**, burn.

blame his owne wytte that put himselfe so farre in the heate. Is not fyre gentyllest and moste element comfortable amonges al other? Fyre is chefe werker in fortherynge sustenaunce to mankynde. Shal fyre ben blamed for it brende a foole naturelly by his own stulty wytte in sterynge? Ah, wicked folkes, for your propre malyce and shreudnesse of your selfe: ye blame and dispyse the precioust thyng of your kynde, and whiche thynges amonge other moste ye desyren. Trewly, Nero and his children ben shrewes that dispysen so their dames. The wickednesse and gylyng of men in disclaundring of thilke that moste hath hem gladed and pleased were impossyble to write or to nempne. Neverthelater yet I say, he that knoweth a way may it lightly passe. Eke an herbe proved may safely to smertande sores ben layde: So I say in him that is proved is nothyng suche yvels to gesse. But these thynges have I rehersed to warne you women al at ones that to lyghtly, without good assaye, ye assenten not to mannes speche. The sonne in the daylyght is to knowen from the moone that shyneth in the nyght. Nowe to thee thyselfe," quod she, "as I have ofte sayd I knowe wel thyne herte. Thou arte none of al the tofore nempned people, for I knowe wel the contynuaunce of thy servyce that never

---

blame his owne wytte that put him**<338vb><339ra>**selfe so farre in the heate. Is not fyre gentyllest and moste element comfortable amonges al other? fyre is chefe werker in fortherynge sustenaunce to mankynde: shal fyre ben blamed for it brende a foole naturelly/ by his own stulty wytte in sterynge. Ah wicked folkes/ for your propre malyce/ and shreudnesse of your selfe: ye blame and dispyse the precioust thyng of your kynde/ and whiche thynges amonge other moste ye desyren. Trewly Nero and his children ben shrewes/ that dispysen so their dames. The wickednesse and gylyng of men/ in disclau*n*dring of thilke that moste hath hem gladed and pleased/ were impossyble to write or to nempne. Neuer the later yet I say he that knoweth a way/ may it lightly passe: eke an herbe proued may safely to smertande sores ben layde: So I say/ in him that is proued is nothyng suche yuels to gesse. But these thynges haue I rehersed to warne you women al at ones/ that to lyghtly without good assaye ye assenten not to mannes speche. The sonne in the day lyght/ is to knowen from the moone that shyneth in the nyght. Nowe to the thy selfe (quod she) as I haue ofte sayd/ I knowe wel thyne herte/ thou arte none of al the tofore nempned people/ for I knowe wel the contynuaunce of thy seruyce/ that neuer

277 werker, worker; **fortherynge**, furthering. **279 stulty**, stupid; **sterynge**, guiding [himself]. **282 gylyng**, deceiving. **283 thilke**, those same (i.e., women); **nempne**, name. **284 proved**, tested. **285 smertande**, hurting. **286 gesse**, guess. **290 tofore nempned**, aforementioned.

sythen I set thee a werke myght thy Margaryte for plesaunce, frendeshyp, ne fayrehede of none other, be in poynte moved from thyne herte, wherfore into myne housholde hastely I wol that thou entre and al the parfyte privyté of my werkyng make it be knowe in thy understondyng as one of my privy famyliers. Thou desyrest," quod she, "fayne to here of tho thynges there I lefte." "Ye forsothe," quod I, "that were to me a great blysse." "Nowe," quod she, "for thou shalt not wene that womans condycions for fayre speche suche thyng belongeth."

Chapter IV

"[T]hou shalte," quod she, "understonde first amonge al other thynges that al the cure of my servyce to me in the parfyte blysse in doyng is desyred in every mannes herte, be he never so moche a wretche. But every man travayleth by dyvers studye and seke thylke blysse by dyvers wayes. But al the endes are knyt in selynesse of desyre in the parfyte blysse that is suche joye whan men it have gotten there lyveth no thynge more to ben coveyted. But howe that desyre of suche perfection in my servyce be kyndely

---

sythen I set the a werke/ myght thy Margaryte for plesaunce/ frendeshyp/ ne fayrehede of none other/ be in poynte moued from thyne herte/ wherfore in to myne housholde hastely I wol that thou entre/ and al the parfyte priuyte of my werkyng make it be knowe in thy vnderstondyng/ as one of my priuy famyliers. Thou desyrest (q*uo*d she) fayne to here of tho thynges there I lefte. Ye forsothe (q*uo*d I) that were to me a great blysse. Nowe (q*uo*d she) for thou shalt not wene that womans condycions for fayre speche suche thyng belongeth.

[T]Hou shalte (q*uo*d she) vnderstonde first amonge al other thynges/ that al the cure of my seruyce to me in the parfyte blysse in doyng is desyred in euery mannes herte/ be he neuer so moche a wretche/ but euery man trauayleth by dyuers studye/ and seke thylke blysse by dyuers wayes/ but al the endes are**<339ra><339rb>**knyt in selynesse of desyre in the p*ar*fyte blysse/ that is suche ioye/ whan men it haue gotten/ there lyueth no thynge more to ben coueyted: But howe that desyre of suche perfection in my seruyce be kyndely

291 sythen, since; **fayrehede**, beauty. **295 here**, hear; **lefte**, left [off]. **296 wene**, suppose. **298 cure**, care. **301 selynesse**, felicity. **302 lyveth**, remains. **303 howe**, however.

set in lovers hertes, yet her erronyous opinyons misturne it by falsenesse of wenyng. And although mennes understandyng be misturned to knowe whiche shuld ben the way unto my person and whyther it abydeth; yet wote they there is a love in every wight weneth by that thyng that he coveyteth moste, he shulde come to thilke love, and that is parfyte blysse of my servauntes, but than fulle blysse maye not be, and there lacke any thynge of that blysse in any syde. Eke it foloweth than that he that must have ful blysse lacke no blysse in love on no syde."

"Therfore lady," quod I tho, "thylke blysse I have desyred and sohte toforne this myselfe by wayes of riches of dignité of power and of renome, wenyng me in tho thinges had ben thilke blysse, but ayenst the heere it turneth. Whan I supposed beste thilke blysse have get and come to the ful purpose of your servyce, sodaynly was I hyndred and throwen so fer abacke that me thynketh an inpossyble to come there I lefte." "I wot wel," quod she, "and therfore hast thou fayled, for thou wentest not by the hye way: a lytel misgoyng in the gynnyng causeth mykyl errour in the ende, wherfore of thilke blysse thou fayledest, for havyng of rychesse, ne non of the other thynges

---

set in louers hertes/ yet her erronyous opinyons misturne it by falsenesse of wenyng. And although mennes vnderstandyng be misturned/ to knowe whiche shuld ben the way vnto my person/ and whyther it abydeth: yet wote they there is a loue in euery wight/ weneth by that thyng that he coueyteth moste/ he shulde come to thilke loue/ and that is parfyte blysse of my seruauntes/ but than fulle blysse maye not be/ and there lacke any thynge of that blysse in any syde. Eke it foloweth than/ that he that must haue ful blysse/ lacke no blysse in loue on no syde.

Therfore lady (quod I tho) thylke blysse I haue desyred/ and sothe toforne this my selfe by wayes of riches/ of dignite/ of power/ and of renome/ wenyng me in tho thrages had ben thilke blysse/ but ayenst the heere it turneth. Whan I supposed beste thilke blysse haue get and come to the ful purpose of your seruyce/ sodaynly was I hyndred/ and throwen so fer abacke/ th*a*t me thynketh an inpossyble to come there I lefte. I wol wel (q*uo*d she) and therfore hast thou fayled/ for thou wentest not by the hye way: a lytel misgoyng in the gynnyng causeth mykyl errour in the ende/ wherfore of thilke blysse thou fayledest for hauyng of rychesse/ ne non of the other thyng*e*s

304 her, their; **wenyng**, assumption. **306 wote**, know; **wight**, person. **307 weneth**, assumes; **thilke**, that same. **308 and**, if. **312 wenyng**, assuming. **313 heere**, hair (i.e., it goes against the grain). **316 wot**, know. **317 gynnyng**, beginning; **mykyl**, much.

thou nempnedest mowen nat make suche parfite blisse in love as I shal shewe. Therfore they be nat worthy to thilke blysse, and yet somwhat must ben cause and way to thilke blysse. *Ergo*, there is some suche thing and some way, but it is lytel in usage and that is nat openly iknowe. But what felest in thyne hert of the service in whiche by me thou art entred? Wenest aught thy selfe yet be in the hye way to my blisse? I shal so shewe it to thee thou shalte nat con saye the contrary."

"Good lady," quod I, "altho I suppose it in my herte, yet wolde I here thyn wordes howe ye meanen in this mater." Quod she, "That I shal with my good wyl. Thilke blysse desyred, some deale ye knowen, altho it be nat parfitly, for kyndly entention ledeth you therto, but in thre maner lyvenges is al suche wayes shewed. Every wight in this world, to have this blisse, one of thilke thre wayes of lyves must procede, whiche after opynions of great clerkes arne by names cleaped resonable, manlych, and bestiallich. Resonablich is vertuous; manlych is worldlich; bestialliche is lustes and delytable, nothynge restrayned by bridel of reason. Al that joyeth and yeveth gladnesse to the hert, and it be ayenst reason, is lykened to bestial lyveng whiche thynge foloweth lustes and

---

thou ne*m*pnedest/ mowen nat make suche pa*r*fite blisse i*n* loue as I shal shewe. Therfore they be nat worthy to thilke blysse/ *and* yet somwhat must be*n* cause and way to thilke blysse: Ergo there is some suche thing *and* some way/ but it is lytel i*n* vsage and that is nat openly iknowe. But what felest in thyne hert of th*e* seruice/ in whiche by me thou art entred: Wenest aught thy selfe yet be in the hye way to my blisse? I shal so shewe it to the/ thou shalte nat con saye the contrary.

Good lady (q*uo*d I) altho I suppose it in my herte/ yet wolde I here thyn wordes/ howe ye meanen in this mater. (Q*uo*d she) that I shal with my good wyl. Thilke blysse desyred/ so*m*e deale ye knowen/ altho it be nat parfitly/ for kyndly entention ledeth you therto/ but in thre**<339rb><339va>**maner lyuenges is al suche wayes shewed. Euery wight in this world to haue this blisse one of thilke thre wayes of lyues must p*ro*cede/ whiche after opynions of great clerkes arne by names cleaped/ bestiallich/ resonablich is vertuous: manlych is worldlich/ bestialliche is lustes *and* delytable/ nothynge restrayned by bridel of reason/ al that ioyeth *and* yeueth gladnesse to the hert/ and it be ayenst reason/ is lykened to bestial lyueng/ whiche thynge foloweth lustes *and*

319 nempnedest, named; **mowen**, may. **322 felest**, feel [you]. **323 Wenest**, Assume [you]. **324 con**, know how to. **327 kyndly**, natural. **328 wight**, person. **330 cleaped**, called. **332 yeveth**, gives. **333 and it**, if it.

delytes; wherfore in suche thinge maye nat that precious blysse that is maister of al vertues abyde. Your fathers toforne you have cleped such lusty lyvenges after the flessh passions of desyre, which are innominable tofore God and man both. Than after determination of suche wyse we accorden that suche passions of desyre shul nat be nempned, but holden for absolute from al other lyvenges and provynges, and so lyveth in to lyvenges, manlich and resonable, to declare the maters begonne. But to make thee fully have understandyng in manlich lyvenges, whiche is holden worldlich in these thynges so that ignorance be made no letter, I wol," quod she, "nempne these forsayd wayes be names and conclusions. First riches, dignité, renome, and power shul in this worke be cleaped bodily goodes, for in hem hath ben a gret throw mannes trust of selynesse in love: as in riches, suffisance to have maintayned that was begon by worldly catel; in dignité, honour, and reverence of hem that werne underput by maistry therby to obey; in renome, glorie of peoples praysyng after lustes in their hert, without hede takyng to qualité and maner of doing; and in power, by trouth of lordships mayntenaunce thyng to procede forth in doyng. In al whiche thynges a longe tyme

---

delytes/ wherfore in suche thi*n*ge maye nat that p*re*cious blysse that is maister of al vertues abyde. your fathers toforne you haue cleped such lusty lyuenges after th*e* flessh passions of desyre/ which are innominable to fore god *and* ma*n* both. Tha*n* after determination of suche wyse/ we accorden that suche passio*n*s of desyre shul nat be nempned/ but holden for absolute from al other lyue*n*ges *and* prouynges/ and so lyueth in to lyuenges/ manlich *and* resonable to declare the maters begonne. But to make the fully haue vndersta*n*dyng in ma*n*lich lyuenges/ whiche is holden worldlich in these thynges/ so that ignorance be made no letter. I wol (q*uo*d she) ne*m*pne these forsayd wayes be names *and* co*n*clusions. First riches/ dignite/ renome/ *and* power/ shul in this worke be cleaped bodily goodes/ for in he*m* hath ben a gret throw ma*n*nes trust of selynesse in loue/ as in riches/ suffisance to haue maintayned that was begon by worldly catel/ in dignite/ honour *and* reuerence of hem that werne vnderput by maistry therby to obey. In renome glorie of peoples praysyng/ after lustes in their hert/ without hede takyng to qualite *and* maner of doing/ and in power/ by trouth of lordships mayntenaunce thyng to p*ro*cede forth in doyng. In al whiche thynges a longe tyme

335 cleped, called. **336 innominable**, unnameable. **338 nempned**, named. **339 lyveth in to**, remain in two. **341 letter**, hindrance. **343 cleaped**, called; **throw**, while. **344 selynesse**, felicity; **suffisance**, an adequate amount. **345 catel**, chattels, belongings.

mannes coveytise in commune hath ben greatly grounded to come to the blysse of my service, but trewly they were begyled, and for the principal muste nedes fayle, and in helping mowe nat availe. Se why: for holdest him not poore that is nedy?" "Yes, pardé," quod I. "And him for dishonored that moche folke deyne nat to reverence?" "That is soth," quod I. "And what him that his mightes faylen and mowe nat helpen?" "Certes," quod I, "me semeth of al men he shulde be holden a wretch." "And wenest nat," quod she, "that he that is lytel in renome but rather is out of the praysynges of mo men than a fewe be nat in shame?" "For soth," quod I, "it is shame and villany to him that coveyteth renome, that more folk nat prayse in name than preise." "Soth," quod she, "thou sayst soth, but al these thinges are folowed of suche maner doynge and wenden in riches suffisaunce; in power, might; in dignyté, worship; and in renome, glorie, wherfore they discended into disceyvable wenyng, and in that service disceite is folowed. And thus in general thou and al suche other that so worchen faylen of my blysse that ye long han desyred, wherfore truly, in lyfe of reason is the hye way to this blysse, as I

---

man*n*es coueytise in com*m*une hath ben greatly grounded/ to co*m*e to the blysse of my seruice/ but trewly they were begyled/ *and* for the principal muste nedes fayle *and* in helping mowe nat auaile. Se why/ for holdest him not poore th*at* is nedy? Yes parde (q*uo*d I) And him for dishonored that moche folke deyne nat to reuere*n*ce. That is soth (q*uo*d I). *and* what him th*at* his mightes faylen *and* mowe nat helpen. Certes (q*uo*d I) me semeth of al me*n* he shulde be holden a wretch. And wenest nat**<339va>** **<339vb>**(q*uo*d she) that he that is lytel in reno*me*/ but rather is out of the praysynges of mo men than a fewe be nat in shame? For soth (q*uo*d I) it is shame *and* villany to him that coueyteth renome/ that more folk nat prayse in name than preise Soth (q*uo*d she) thou sayst soth/ but al these thi*n*ges are folowed of suche maner doynge/ and wenden in riches suffisau*n*ce/ in power might/ in dignyte worship/ *and* in renome glorie/ wherfore they disce*n*ded in to disceyuable wenyng/ *and* in that seruice disceite is folowed. And thus in general/ thou *and* al suche other that so worchen faylen of my blysse that ye long han desyred/ wherfore truly i*n* lyfe of reason is the hye way to this blysse/ as I

351 mowe, may; **holdest**, consider [you]. **352 deyne**, deign. **353 what**, what [of]; **mowe**, may; **Certes**, Certainly. **354 holden**, considered; **wenest**, suppose [you]. **355 renome**, renown. **357 Soth**, True. **358 are folowed of**, are consequences of. **359 wenden**, assume. **360 wenyng**, assumptions. **361 worchen**, work.

thynke more openly to declare herafter. Neverthelater, yet in a lytel to comforte thy herte in shewyng of what waye thou arte entred thyselfe, and that thy Margarite may knowe thee set in the hye way, I wol enforme thee in this wise. Thou hast fayled of thy first purpose, bicause thou wentest wronge and leftest the hye waye on thy right syde, as thus: thou lokedest on worldly lyveng, and that thyng thee begyled, and lightly therfore as a lytel assay thou songedest, but whan I turned thy purpose and shewed thee a parte of the hye waye, tho thou abode therin, and no dethe ne ferdnesse of non enemy might thee out of thilk way reve. But ever one in thyne hert, to come to the ilke blysse, whan thou were arested and fyrste tyme enprisoned, thou were loth to chaunge thy way, for in thy hert thou wendest to have ben there thou shuldest; and for I had routhe to sene thee myscaried, and wyst wel thyne ablenesse my servyce to forther and encrease, I come myselfe without other mean to visyt thy person in comforte of thy hert. And pardy in my commyng thou were greatly gladed, after whiche tyme no disease, no care, no tene might move me out of thy hert. And yet am I gladde and greatly enpited howe contynually

---

thynke more openly to declare herafter. Neuer the later/ yet in a lytel to co*m*forte thy herte/ in shewyng of what waye thou arte entred thy selfe/ *and* that thy Margarite may knowe the set in the hye way/ I wol enforme the in this wise. Thou hast fayled of thy first purpose/ bicause thou wentest wro*n*ge and leftest the hye waye on thy right syde/ as thus/ thou lokedest on worldly lyueng *and* that thyng the begyled/ *and* lightly therfore as a lytel assay thou songedest/ but whan I turned thy purpose/ *and* shewed the a parte of thc hye waye tho thou abode therin/ and no dethe ne ferdnesse of non enemy might th*e* out of thilk way reue/ but euer one in thyne hert/ to come to the ilke blysse whan thou were arested and fyrste tyme enprisoned/ thou were loth to chau*n*ge thy way/ for in thy hert thou wendest to haue ben there thou shuldest/ *and* for I had routhe to sene the myscaried/ *and* wyst wel thyne ablenesse my seruyce to forther *and* encrease/ I come my selfe without other mean to visyt thy person/ in co*m*forte of thy hert: *and* p*ar*dy in my com*m*yng th*o*u were greatly gladed/ after whiche tyme/ no disease/ no care/ no tene/ miȝt moue me out of thy hert And yet am I gladde *and* greatly enpited/ howe contynually

364 entred, entered into. **365 knowe thee set in**, know you [to be] set upon; **hye**, high. **368 as a lytel assay**, as if for a short trial; **songedest**, dreamed. **369 tho**, then. **370 thilk**, that same; **reve**, steal; **one**, at one; **ilke**, that very. **372 wendest**, assumed. **373 forther**, further, promote. **374 mean**, intercessor, intermediary; **pardy**, indeed. **375 tene**, sorrow. **376 enpited**, made compassionate, moved to feel pity.

thou haddest me in mynde with good avysement of thy conscience whan thy kyng and his princes by huge wordes and great loked after variaunce in thy speche. And ever thou were redy for my sake in plesaunce of the Margarite peerle and many mo other thy body to oblyge into Marces doyng, if any contraried thy sawes. Stedfast way maketh stedfast hert, with good hope in the ende. Trewly, I wot that thou it wel knowe, for I se thee so set and not chaungynge herte haddest in my servyce, and I made thou haddest grace of thy kynge, in foryevenesse of mykel misdede. To the gracious kyng arte thou mykel holden, of whose grace and goodnesse somtyme herafter I thinke thee enforme whan I shew the grounde where as moral vertue groweth. Who brought thee to werke? Who brought this grace aboute? Who made thy hert hardy? Trewly it was I, for haddest thou of me fayled, than of this purpose haddest thou never taken in this wyse. And therfore I say thou might wel truste to come to thy blysse, sythen thy gynnynge hath ben harde, but ever graciously after thy hertes desyre hath proceded. Sylver fyned with many heates men knowen for trew, and safely men may trust to the alay in werkynge.

---

thou haddest me in mynde/ with good auysement of thy conscience/ whan thy kyng *and* his princes by huge wordes *and* great/ loked after variaunce in thy speche/ *and* euer thou were redy for my sake in plesaunce of th*e* Margarite peerle/ and many mo other/ thy body to oblyge in to Marces doyng/ if any contraried thy sawes/ stedfast way maketh stedfast hert/ **<339vb><340ra>**with good hope in the ende. Trewly I wol that thou it wel knowe/ for I se the so set and not chaungynge herte haddest in my seruyce/ and I made thou haddest grace of thy kynge/ in foryeuenesse of mykel misdede: to th*e* gracious kyng arte thou mykel holden/ of whose grace *and* goodnesse somtyme herafter I thinke the enforme/ whan I shew the grounde where as moral vertue groweth. Who brought the to werke? Who brought this grace aboute? Who made thy hert hardy? Trewly it was I/ for haddest thou of me fayled/ than of this purpose had neuer taken in this wyse. And therfore I say thou might wel truste to come to thy blysse/ sythen thy gynnynge hath ben harde but euer graciously after thy hertes desyre hath proceded. Syluer fyned with many heates men knowen for trew/ and safely men may trust to the alay in werkynge.

380 oblyge in, commit to; **Marces doyng**, i.e., battle; **contraried**, opposed; **sawes**, sayings. **381 wot**, know. **383 foryevenesse**, forgiveness; **mykel**, much, great. **385 werke**, work. **388 sythen**, since. **389 fyned**, refined. **390 heates**, firings; **alay**, alloy.

This disease hath proved what waye hence forwarde thou thynkest to holde." "Nowe in good fayth lady," quod I tho, "I am nowe in. Me semeth it is the hye way and the ryght." "Ye forsothe," quod she, "and nowe I wol disprove thy first wayes, by whiche many men wenen to gette thilke blysse. But for as moche as every herte that hath caught ful love is tyed with queynt knyttynges, thou shalt understande that love and thilke foresayd blysse toforne declared in this provynges shal hote the knot in the hert." "Wel," quod I, "this inpossession I wol wel understande." "Nowe also," quod she, "for the knotte in the herte muste ben from one to another, and I knowe thy desyre, I wol thou understande these maters to ben sayd of thyselfe in disprovyng of thy first servyce, and in strengthynge of thilke that thou haste undertake to thy Margaryte perle." "A Goddes halfe," quod I, "ryght wel I fele that al this case is possyble and trewe, and therfore I admyt it al togyther." "Understanden wel," quod she, "these termes, and loke no contradyction thou graunt."

"If God wol," quod I, "of al these thynges wol I not fayle, and if I graunt contradyction, I shulde graunte an impossyble and that were a foule inconvenyence for whiche

---

This diseases hath proued what waye hence forwarde thou thynkest to holde. Nowe in good fayth lady (quod I tho) I am nowe in/ me semeth it is the hye way and the ryght. Ye forsothe (quod she) and nowe I wol disproue thy first wayes/ by whiche many men wenen to gette thilke blysse. But for as moche as euery herte that hath caught ful loue/ is tyed with queynt knyttynges/ thou shalt vnderstande that loue and thilke foresayd blysse toforne declared in this prouynges/ shal hote the knot in the hert. Wel (q*uo*d I) this inpossession I wol wel vnderstande. Nowe also (q*uo*d she) for the knotte in the herte muste ben from one to an other/ and I knowe thy desyre: I wol thou vnderstande these maters to ben sayd of thy selfe in disprouyng of thy first seruyce/ and in stre*n*gthynge of thilke that thou haste vndertake to thy Margaryte perle. A goddes halfe (q*uo*d I) ryght wel I fele that al this case is possyble and trewe/ and therfore I admytted al togyther. Vnderstanden wel (quod she) these termes/ and loke no contradyction thou graunt.

If god wol (q*uo*d I) of al these thynges wol I not fayle/ and if I graunt contradyction/ I shulde graunte an impossyble/ and that were a foule inconuenye*n*ce/ for whiche

394 wenen, suppose. **395 tyed**, tied; **queynt**, curious. **396 thilke**, that same; **hote**, be called. **397 inpossession** (imposition), instituting a name (see note); **for**, since. **398 and** if. **400 thilke**, that other. **401 halfe**, part, half (i.e., in God's name); **fele**, feel. **402 loke**, see.

thynges, ladye, iwys herafter I thinke me to kepe."

Chapter V

"Wel," quod she, "thou knowest that every thynge is a cause wherthroughe any thyng hath beyng that is cleped 'caused.' Than if richesse causen knot in herte, thilke rychesse arne cause of thilke precious thynge beyng. But after the sentence of Aristotle, every cause is more in dignyté than his thynge caused. Wherthrough it foloweth rychesse to ben more in dignyté than thilke knot. But rychesses arne kyndely naughty, badde, and nedy, and thilke knotte is thynge kyndely good, moste praysed and desyred. *Ergo*, thynge naughty, badde, and nedy in kyndely understandynge is more worthy than thynge kyndely good moste desyred and praysed. The consequence is false: nedes, the antecedent mote ben of the same condycion. But that rychesses ben bad, naughty, and nedy that wol I prove, wherfore they mowe cause no suche thyng that is so glorious and good: The more richesse thou haste, the more nede hast thou of helpe hem to kepe. *Ergo*, thou nedest in rychesse whiche nede thou shuldest not have if thou hem wantest. Than muste rychesse ben nedy, that in their havyng maken thee nedy to helpes, in suretie

---

thynges ladye iwys herafter I thinke me to kepe.**<340ra>**
<340rb>WEl (q*uo*d she) thou knowest that euery thynge is a cause wherthroughe any thyng hath beyng/ that is cleped caused/ than if richesse causen knot in herte/ thilke rychesse arne cause of thilke precious thynge beyng: but after the sente*n*ce of Aristotle/ euery cause is more in dignyte than his thynge caused/ wherthrough it foloweth rychesse to ben more in dignyte tha*n* thilke knot/ but rychesses arne kyndely naughty/ badde/ and nedy/ and thilke knotte is thynge kyndely good/ moste praysed and desyred: Ergo thynge naughty/ badde/ and nedy/ in kyndely vnderstandynge is more worthy than thynge kyndely good/ moste desyred and praysed: the consequence is false/ nedes the antecedent mote ben of the same condycion. But that rychesses ben bad/ naughty/ and nedy/ that wol I proue/ wherfore they mowe cause no suche thyng/ that is so glorious and good: The more richesse thou haste/ the more nede hast thou of helpe hem to kepe. Ergo thou nedest in rychesse/ whiche nede thou shuldest not haue if thou hem wantest. Than muste rychesse ben nedy/ that in their hauyng maken th*e* nedy to helpes in suretie

408 cleped, called. **411 kyndely**, naturally; **naughty**, nothing, vain. **412 *Ergo***, Therefore. **414 nedes**, needs be (i.e., therefore). **415 mote**, must. **416 mowe**, may. **418 wantest**, lack.

thy rychesse to kepen wherthrough foloweth rychesse to ben nedy. Everything causynge yvels is badde and naughty; but rychesse in one causen misease in another they mowen not evenly stretchen al about. Wherof cometh plee, debate, thefte, begylinges but rychesse to wynne whiche thynges ben badde, and by richesse arne caused: *Ergo*, thylke rychesse ben badde, whiche badnesse and nede ben knyt into rychesse by a maner of kyndely propertie, and every cause and caused accorden, so that it foloweth thilke richesse to have the same accordaunce with badnesse and nede that their cause asketh. Also, every thynge hath his beyng by his cause. Than if the cause be distroyed, the beyng of caused is vanysshed. And so if rychesse causen love, and rychesse weren distroyed, the love shulde vanysshe. But thylke knotte, and it be trewe, may not vanysshe for no goyng of no rychesse. Ergo, rychesse is no cause of the knot. And many men, as I sayd, setten the cause of the knotte in rychesse. Thilke knytten the rychesse and nothynge the yvel. Thilke persons, whatever they ben, wenen that ryches is most worthy to be had, and that make they the cause; and so wene they thilke ryches be better than the person. Commenly, suche asken rather after the quantyté than after the qualyté,

---

thy rychesse to kepen/ wherthrough foloweth rychesse to ben nedy. Euery thing causynge yuels is badde *and* naughty: but rychesse in one causen misease/ in another they mowen not euenly stretchen al about. Wherof cometh plee/ debate/ thefte/ begylinges/ but rychesse to wynne/ whiche thynges ben badde/ and by richesse arne caused: Ergo thylke rychesse ben badde/ whiche badnesse and nede ben knyt in to rychesse by a maner of kyndely propertie/ and euery cause and caused accorden/ so that it foloweth thilke richesse to haue the same accordaunce with badnesse and nede/ that their cause asketh. Also euery thynge hath his beyng by his cause/ than if th*e* cause be distroyed/ the beyng of caused is vanysshed: And so if rychesse causen loue/ and rychesse weren distroyed/ the loue shulde vanysshe/ but thylke knotte and it be trewe may not vanysshe for no goyng of no rychesse: Ergo rychesse is no cause of the knot. And many men as I sayd/ setten the cause of the knotte in rychesse/ thilke knytten the rychesse/ and nothynge the yuel:**<340rb><340va>** thilke persons what euer they ben/ wenen that ryches is most worthy to be had/ *and* that make they the cause: *and* so wene they thilke ryches be better than the person. Com*m*enly suche asken rather after the quantyte that after the qualyte/

421 mowen, may. **422 plee**, lawsuits; **but**, only. **424 kyndely**, natural. **425 and**, if. **429 and**, if. **430 goyng**, i.e., departing. **431 knytten**, make the knot of. **432 wenen**, assume. **433 wene**, suppose.

and suche wenen as wel by hemselfe as by other that conjunction of his lyfe and of his soule is no more precious but in as mykel as he hath of rychesse. Alas, howe maye he holden suche thynges precious or noble that neyther han lyfe ne soule ne ordynaunce of werchynge lymmes. Suche rychesse ben more worthy whan they ben in gatheryng; in departing gynneth his love of other mens praysyng. And avaryce gatheryng maketh be hated, and nedy to many out helpes. And whan leveth the possessyon of such goodes, and they gynne vanyssh, than entreth sorowe and tene in their hertes. O, badde and strayte ben thilke that at their departynge maketh men teneful and sory, and in the gatheryng of hem make men nedy. Moche folke at ones mowen not togyder moche therof have. A good gest gladdeth his hoste and al his meyny, but he is a badde gest that maketh his hoste nedy and to be aferde of his gestes goyng." "Certes," quod I, "me wondreth therfore that the comune opinyon is thus: 'He is worthe no more than that he hath in catel.'" "O," quod she, "Loke thou be not of that opynion, for if golde or money or other maner of riches shynen in thy sight, whose is that? Nat thyn. And tho they

and suche wenen as wel by hem selfe as by other/ that coniunction of his lyfe and of his soule is no more precious/ but in as mykel as he hath of rychesse. Alas howe maye he holden suche thynges precious or noble/ that neyther han lyfe ne soule/ ne ordynaunce of werchynge lymmes: suche ben more worthy whan they ben in gatheryng/ in departing gynneth his loue of other mens praysyng. And auaryce gatheryng maketh be hated and nedy to many out helpes: and whan leueth the possessyon of such goodes/ and they gynne vanyssh/ than entreth sorowe and tene in their hertes. O badde *and* strayte ben thilke that at their departynge maketh men teneful and sory/ and in the gatheryng of hem make men nedy:/ Moche folke at ones mowen not togyder moche therof haue. A good gest gladdeth his hoste and al his meyny/ but he is a badde gest that maketh his hoste nedy/ *and* to be aferde of his gestes goyng. Certes (q*uo*d I) me wondreth therfore that the comune opinyon is thus: He is worthe no more than that he hath in catel. O (q*uo*d she) loke thou be not of that opynion/ for if golde or money/ or other maner of riches shynen in thy sight/ Whose is that? nat thyn: *and* tho they

436 mykel, much. **437 ordynaunce**, organic order. **438 werchynge**, working, living; **lymmes**, limbs; **ben**, are; **gatheryng**, accumulation. **439 gynneth**, begins. **440 nedy**, beholden; **out helpes**, external aids; **leveth**, departs. **441 tene**, grief. **442 strayte**, miserly, pinched; **teneful**, sorrowful. **443 mowen**, may. **444 gest**, guest; **meyny**, entourage. **447 catel**, wealth, possessions.

have a lytel beautie, they be nothyng in comparison of our kynde. And therfore, ye shulde nat set your worthynesse in thyng lower than yourselfe, for the riches, the fairnesse, the worthynesse of thilke goodes, if ther be any suche preciousnesse in hem, are nat thyne. Thou madest hem so never; from other they come to thee, and to other they shul from thee. Wherfore enbracest thou other wightes goodes as tho they were thyn? Kynde hath drawe hem by hemselfe. It is sothe the goodes of the erth ben ordayned in your fode and norisshynge, but if thou wolte holde thee apayde with that suffiseth to thy kynde thou shalt nat be in daunger of no suche riches; to kynde suffiseth lytel thing who that taketh hede. And if thou wolt algates with superfluité of riches be a throted, thou shalt hastelych be anoyed or els yvel at ease. And fairnesse of feldes ne of habytations, ne multytude of meyné, maye nat be rekened as riches that are thyn owne. For if they be badde, it is great sclaunder and villany to the ocupyer. And if they be good or faire, the mater of the workeman that hem made is to prayse. Howe shulde otherwyse bountie be compted for thyne? Thilke goodnesse and fairnesse be proper to

---

haue a lytel beautie/ they be nothyng in co*m*parison of our kynde/ *and* therfore ye shulde nat set your worthynesse in thyng lower than your selfe/ for the riches/ the fairnesse/ the worthynesse of thilke goodes/ if ther be any suche preciousnesse in hem are nat thyne/ thou madest hem so neuer/ from other they come to the/ *and* to other they shul from the: wherfore enbracest thou other wightes good*es* as tho they were thyn? kynde hath drawe hem by hem selfe. It is sothe the goodes of the erth ben ordayned in your fode *and* norisshynge/ but if thou wolte holde the apayde with that suffiseth to thy kynde/ thou shalt nat be in dau*n*ger of no suche riches/ to kynde suffiseth lytel thi*n*g who that taketh hede. And if thou wolt algates with sup*er*fluite of riches be a throted/ thou**<340va><340vb>**shalt hastelych be anoyed/ or els yuel at ease. And fairnesse of feldes ne of habytations/ ne multytude of meyne/ maye nat be rekened as riches that are thyn owne/ for if they be badde it is great sclaunder *and* villany to the ocupyer/ and if they be good or faire/ the mater of the workeman that hem made is to prayse. Howe shulde otherwyse bountie be co*m*pted for thyne/ thilke goodnesse *and* fairnesse be p*ro*per to

451 thilke, those same. **453 shul**, shall go; **wightes**, person's. **454 Kynde**, Nature; **drawe hem**, created them. **455 apayde**, satisfied. **457 algates**, anyway; **a throted**, gorged. **458 hastelych**, quickly; **feldes**, fields. **459 meyné**, entourage. **462 compted**, counted; **Thilke**, That same.

tho thinges hemselfe. Than if they be nat thyne, sorow nat whan they wende, ne glad thee nat in pompe and in pride whan thou hem hast. For their bountie and their beautes cometh out of their owne kynde and nat of thyne owne person. As faire ben they in their not havyng as whan thou haste hem. They be nat faire for thou haste hem, but thou haste geten hem for the fairnesse of themselfe. And there the vaylance of men is demed in richesse outforth, wenen me to have no proper good in themselfe, but seche it in straunge thinges. Trewly the condytion of good wenyng is in thee mistourned to wene your noblesse be not in yourselfe, but in the goodes and beautie of other thynges. Pardy, the beestes that han but felyng soules have suffisaunce in their owne selfe; and ye, that ben lyke to God, seken encrease of suffisaunce from so excellent a kynde of so lowe thynges. Ye do great wrong to Him that you made lordes over al erthly thynges, and ye put your worthynesse under the nombre of the fete of lower thynges and foule. Whan ye juge thilke riches to be your worthynesse than put ye your selfe by estimacion under thilke foule thynges, and than leve ye the knowyng of yourselfe, so be ye viler than any dombe beest that cometh of shrewde vice. Right so thilke persons that loven

---

tho thi*n*ges hem selfe/ than if they be nat thyne sorow nat whan they wende/ ne glad the nat in po*m*pe and i*n* pride whan thou hem hast/ for their bou*n*tie and their beautes cometh out of their owne kynde/ *and* nat of thyne owne p*er*son: as faire ben they in their not hauyng as whan thou haste hem/ they be nat faire for thou haste hem/ but thou haste geten hem for the fairnesse of them selfe. *and* there the vaylance of men is demed in richesse outforth/ wenen me to haue no proper good in them selfe/ but seche it in straunge thinges. Trewly the co*n*dytion of good wenyng is in th*e* mistourned/ to wene your noblesse be not in your selfe/ but in the goodes *and* beautie of other thynges. Pardy the beestes that han but felyng soules/ haue suffisaunce in their owne selfe: *and* ye that ben lyke to god/ seken encrease of suffisaunce from so excellent a kynde of so lowe thynges/ ye do great wrong to him that you made lordes ouer al erthly thynges/ *and* ye put your worthynesse vnder the no*m*bre of the fete of lower thynges *and* foule/ whan ye iuge thilke riches to be your worthynesse/ than put ye your selfe by estimacion vnder thilke foule thynges/ *and* than leue ye the knowyng of your selfe/ so be ye viler than any dombe beest/ that cometh of shrewde vice. Right so thilke persons that louen

463 wende, depart. **467 vaylance**, value, worth. **468 outforth**, externally; **wenen**, suppose; **me**, men. **469 wenyng**, assumption. **471 Pardy,** Indeed. **472 seken**, seek. **474 nombre**, number. **476 leve**, abandon. **477 shrewde**, corrupt.

non yvel for dereworthynesse of the persone, but for straunge goodes, and saith the adornement in the knot lyth in such thing his errour is perilous and shreude, and he wrieth moche venym with moche welth, and that knot maye nat be good whan he hath it getten.

"Certes, thus hath riches with flyckering sight anoyed many; and often whan there is a throweout shrewe he coyneth al the golde, al the precious stones that mowen be founden, to have in his bandon. He weneth no wight be worthy to have suche thynges but he alone. Howe manye haste thou knowe nowe in late tyme that in their rychesse supposed suffysance have folowed, and nowe it is al fayled." "Ye lady," quod I, "that is for misse medlyng, and otherwyse governed thilke rychesse than they shulde." "Ye," quod she tho, "had not the floode greatly areysed and throwe to hemwarde both gravel and sande, he had made no medlynge. And right as see yeveth floode, so draweth see ebbe and pulleth ayen under wawe al the firste out throw, but if good pyles of noble governaunce in love in wel meanynge maner ben sadly grounded, the whiche

---

non yuel for dereworthynesse of the persone/ but for strau*n*ge goodes/ *and* saith the adornement in the knot lyth in such thing/ his errour is perilous *and* shreude/ and he wrieth moche venym with moche welth/ *and* that knot maye nat be good whan he hath it getten.

Certes thus hath riches with flyckering sight anoyed many: *and* often whan there is a throwe out shrewe/ he coyneth al the golde/ al the precious stones that mowen be founden to haue in his bandon/ he weneth no wight be worthy to haue suche thynges but he alone. Howe ma**<340vb><341ra>**nye haste thou knowe nowe in late tyme/ that in their rychesse supposed suffysance haue folowed/ *and* nowe it is al fayled. Ye lady (q*uo*d I) that is for misse medlyng and otherwyse gouerned thilke rychesse than they shulde. Ye (q*uo*d she tho) had not the floode greatly areysed/ and throwe to hemwarde both grauel and sande/ he had made no medlynge. And right as see yeueth floode/ so draweth see ebbe and pulleth ayen vnder wawe al the firste out throw/ but if good pyles of noble gouernau*n*ce in loue/ in wel meanynge maner/ ben sadly grounded/ to whiche

479 lyth, lies. **480 wrieth**, conceals. **483 throweout**, thorough. **484 mowen**, may; **bandon**, control; **weneth**, supposes; **wight**, person. **488 areysed**, risen. **489 yeveth**, gives. **490 ayen**, again; **wawe**, waves; **out throw**, what had been sent out at first; **but if**, unless; **pyles**, foundation, stakes, pilings. **491 sadly**, stably.

holde thilke gravel as for a whyle, that ayen lightly mowe not it turne. And if the pyles ben trewe, the gravel and sande wol abyde. And certes, ful warnyng in love shalte thou never thorowe hem get ne cover that lightly with an ebbe, er thou beware it, wol ayen meve. In rychesse many men have had tenes and diseases whiche they shulde not have had if therof they had fayled. Thorowe whiche nowe declared partely it is shewed that for rychesse shulde the knotte in herte neyther ben caused in one ne in other. Trewly, knotte maye ben knytte, and I trowe more stedfast in love though rychesse fayled. And els in rychesse is the knotte and not in herte. And than suche a knotte is false whan the see ebbeth and withdraweth the gravel, that such rychesse voydeth, thilke knotte wol unknytte. Wherfore no trust, no way, no cause, no parfyte beyng is in rychesse of no suche knotte; therfore another way muste we have."

Chapter VI

"Honour in dignyté is wened to yeven a ful knot." "Ye certes," quod I, "and of that opinyon ben many, for they sayne dignyté with honour and reverence causen hertes to

---

holde thilke grauel as for a whyle/ that ayen lightly mowe not it turne: and if the pyles ben trewe/ the grauel and sande wol abyde. And certes ful warnyng in loue shalte thou neuer thorowe hem get ne couer/ that lightly with an ebbe er thou beware it wol ayen meue. In rychesse many men haue had tenes and diseases/ whiche they shulde not haue had/ if therof they had fayled. Thorowe whiche nowe declared partely it is shewed/ that for rychesse shulde the knotte in herte neyther ben caused in one ne in other: trewly knotte maye ben knytte/ and I trowe more stedfast in loue though rychesse fayled/ and els in rychesse is the knotte *and* not in herte. And than suche a knotte is false/ whan the see ebbeth and withdraweth the grauel/ that such rychesse voydeth/ thilke knotte wol vnknytte. Wherfore no trust/ no way/ no cause/ no parfyte beyng is in rychesse of no suche knotte/ therfore another way muste we haue.

HOnour in dignyte is wened to yeuen a ful knot. Ye certes (q*uo*d I) and of that opinyon ben many/ for they sayne dignyte/ with honour/ and reuerence causen hertes to

492 mowe, may. **493 warnyng**, advance warning. **494 thorowe**, through; **cover**, recover. **495 meve**, move; **tenes**, sorrows. **497 in one ne in other**, in one person or another. **498 trowe**, believe. **501 unknytte**, unravel. **503 wened**, assumed; **yeven**, give.

encheynen and so abled to be knytte togyther for the excellence in soveraynté of such degrees."

"Nowe," quod she, "if dignyté, honour, and reverence causen thilke knotte in herte, this knot is good and profytable. For every cause of a cause is cause of thyng caused. Than thus good thynges and profytable ben by dignyté honour and reverence caused. *Ergo*, they accorden and dignytes ben good with reverences and honour, but contraryes mowen not accorden. Wherfore by reason there shulde no dignytee no reverence none honour acorde with shrewes, but that is false. They have ben cause to shrewes in many shreudnes, for with hem they accorden. *Ergo*, from begynnyng to argue ayenwarde tyl it come to the laste conclusyon, they are not cause of the knot. Lo, al day at eye arne shrewes not in reverence, in honour, and in dignyté? Yes, forsothe, rather than the good. Than foloweth it that shrewes rather than good shul ben cause of this knot. But of this contrarie of al lovers is byleved and for a sothe openly determyned to holde."

"Nowe," quod I, "fayne wolde I here howe suche dignytees acorden with shrewes."

---

encheynen/ and so abled to be knytte togyther/ for th*e* excellence in soueraynte of such degrees.

Nowe (q*uo*d she) if dignyte/ honour/ and reuerence causen thilke knotte in herte/ this knot is good and profytable. For euery cause of a cause/ is cause of thyng caused: Than thus/ good thynges and profytable ben by dignyte/ honour/ and reuerence caused. Ergo they accorden/ and dignytes ben good with reuerences and honour/ but contraryes mowen not**<341ra><341rb>**accorden: Wherfore by reason there shulde no dignytee/ no reuerence/ none honour acorde with shrewes/ but that is false: they haue ben cause to shrewes in many shreudnes/ for with hem they accorden. Ergo from begynnyng to argue ayenwarde tyl it come to the laste conclusyon/ they are not cause of the knot. Lo al day at eye/ arne shrewes not in reuerence/ in honour/ and in dignyte? yes forsothe/ rather than the good. Than foloweth it that shrewes rather than good shul ben cause of this knot. But of this contrarie of al louers is byleued/ and for a sothe openly determyned to holde.

Nowe (quod I) fayne wolde I here/ howe suche dignytees acorden with shrewes.

505 encheynen, bind themselves to each other. **510 *Ergo***, Therefore. **511 mowen**, may. **513 shreudnes**, misdeeds. **515 at eye**, visibly. **516 of**, by. **518 to holde**, to be held.

"O," quod she, "that wol I shewe in manyfolde wise." "Ye wene," quod she, "that dignytes of offyce here in your cyté is as the sonne; it shyneth bright withouten any cloude, whiche thynge, whan they comen in the handes of malycious tyrauntes, there cometh moche harme and more grevaunce therof than of the wylde fyre though it brende al a strete. Certes, in dignyté of offyce the werkes of the occupyer shewen the malyce and the badnesse in the person. With shrewes they maken manyfolde harmes, and moche people shamen. Howe often han rancours for malyce of the governour shulde ben mainteyned? Hath not than suche dignytees caused debate, rumours, and yvels? Yes, God wote, but suche thynges have ben trusted to make mens understandyng enclyne to many queynte thynges. Thou wottest wel what I meane." "Ye," quod I, "therfore, as dignyté suche thynge in tene ywrought, so ayenwarde the substaunce in dignité chaunged, relyed to bring ayen good plyte in doyng." "Do way, do way," quod she, "if it so betyde, but that is selde that suche dignyté is betake in a good mannes governaunce. What thynge is to recken in the dignytees goodnesse? Pardé, the bountie

---

O (q*uo*d she) that wol I shewe in manyfolde wise.Ye wene (q*uo*d she) that dignytes of offyce here in your cyte is as the sonne/ it shyneth bright withouten any cloude: whiche thynge whan they comen in the handes of malycious tyrauntes/ there cometh moche harme/ *and* more greuau*n*ce therof/ than of th*e* wylde fyre/ though it brende al a strete. Certes in dignyte of offyce/ the werkes of the occupyer shewen the malyce and the badnesse in the person/ with shrewes they maken manyfolde harmes/ and moche people shamen. Howe often han rancours for malyce of the gouernour shulde ben mainteyned? Hath not than suche dignytees caused debate/ rumours/ and yuels? yes god wote/ by suche thynges haue ben trusted to make mens vnderstandyng enclyne to many queynte thynges. Thou wottest wel what I meane. Ye (q*uo*d I) therfore as dignyte suche thynge in tene ywrought/ so ayenwarde the substaunce in dignite chau*n*ged/ relyed to bring ayen good plyte in doyng. Do way/ do way (q*uo*d she) if it so betyde/ but that is selde/ that suche dignyte is betake in a good mannes gouernaunce. What thynge is to recken in the dignytees goodnesse? parde the bountie

520 wene, suppose. **524 brende**, burned; **strete**, street; **werkes**, works. **528 wote**, knows. **529 queynte**, weird; **wottest**, know. **530 tene**, sorrow. **531 relyed**, it (i.e., dignity) is rallied, re-grouped; **plyte**, plight, circumstance. **532 selde**, seldom; **betake**, entrusted to. **533 Pardé**, Indeed.

and goodnesse is hers that usen it in good governaunce, and therfore cometh it that honoure and reverence shulde ben done to dignyté bycause of encreasynge vertue in the occupyer, and not to the ruler bycause of soverayntie in dignité. Sythen dignité may no vertue cause who is worthy worshyp for suche goodnesse? Not dignyté, but person that maketh goodnesse in dignyté to shyne." "This is wonder thyng," quod I, "for me thynketh as the person in dignité is worthy honour for goodnesse, so tho a person for badnesse magré hath deserved, yet the dignité leneth to be commended." "Let be," quod she, "thou errest right foule. Dignité with badnesse is helper to performe the felonous doyng. Pardy, were it kyndly good or any properté of kyndly vertue hadden in hemselfe, shrewes shulde hem never have; with hem shulde they never accorde. Water and fire that ben contrarious mowen nat togider ben assembled. Kynde wol nat suffre such contraries to joyn. And sithen at eye by experience in doyng we sene that shrewes have hem more often than good menne, syker mayste thou be that kyndly good in suche thynges is nat appropred. Pardy, were they kyndly good, as wel one as other shulden evenlych in vertue of governaunce ben worthe. But one fayleth in goodnesse, an-

---

and goodnesse is hers/ that vsen it in good gouernaunce/ and therfore cometh it that honoure and reuerence shulde ben done to dignyte/ bycause of encreasynge vertue in the occupyer/ and not to the ruler/ bycause of souerayntie in dignite. Sythen dignite may no vertue cause/ who is worthy worshyp for suche goodnesse?**<341rb><341va>**not dignyte/ but person th*at* maketh goodnesse in dignyte to shyne. This is wonder thyng (q*uo*d I) for me thynketh/ as the person in dignite is worthy honour for goodnesse/ so tho a person for badnesse magre hath deserued/ yet the dignite leneth to be co*m*mended. Let be (q*uo*d she) thou errest right foule/ dignite with badnesse is helper to p*er*forme the felonous doyng: pardy were it kyndly good or any properte of kyndly vertue hadden in hem selfe/ shrewes shulde hem neuer haue/ with hem shulde they neuer accorde. water *and* fire that ben contrarious mowen nat togider ben assembled/ kynde wol nat suffre such co*n*traries to ioyn. *and* sithen at eye by experie*n*ce in doyng/ we sene that shrewes haue hem more often than good menne/ syker mayste thou be/ that kyndly good in suche thyng*es* is nat appropred. Pardy were they kyndly good/ as wel one as other shulden eue*n*lych in vertue of gouernau*n*ce ben worthe: but one fayleth in goodnesse an-

534 hers, theirs. **536 Sythen**, Since. **540 magré**, disdain; **leneth**, inclines. **542 Pardy**, Indeed. **544 mowen**, may; **Kynde**, Nature. **545 at eye**, evidently. **546 syker**, certain. **547 appropred**, proper, appropriate; **kyndly**, naturally. **548 evenlych**, equally.

other dothe the contrary; and so it sheweth kyndly goodnesse in dignyté nat be grounded. And this same reason," quod she, "may be made in general on al the bodily goodes, for they comen ofte to throwe out shrewes. After this, he is strong that hath might to have great burthyns, and he is lyght and swifte that hath soverainté in ronnyng to passe other. Right so he is a shrewe on whom shreude thynges and badde han most werchynge. And right as philosophy maketh philosophers, and my service maketh lovers, right so if dignytes weren good or vertuous, they shulde maken shrewes good, and turne her malyce, and make hem be vertuous, but that do they nat as it is proved, but causen rancour and debate. *Ergo*, they be nat good but utterly badde. Had Nero never ben Emperour, shulde never his dame have be slayn to maken open the privyté of his engendrure. Herodes, for his dignyté slewe many children. The dignité of kyng John wolde have distroyed al Englande. Therfore mokel wysedom and goodnesse both nedeth in a person the malice in dignité slyly to bridel, and with a good bytte of arest to withdrawe, in case it wolde praunce otherwise than it shulde. Trewly, ye yeve to dignites

---

other dothe the co*n*trary/ *and* so it sheweth kyndly goodnesse in dignyte nat be grou*n*ded. And this same reason (q*uo*d she) may be made in general on al the bodily goodes/ for they comen ofte to throwe out shrewes. After this he is strong that hath miȝt to haue great burthyns/ *and* he is lyght *and* swifte that hath souerainte in ro*n*nyng to passe other right so he is a shrewe on whom shreude thynges *and* badde han most werchynge. *And* right as philosophy maketh philosophers/ *and* my seruice maketh louers: Right so if dignytes weren good or vertuous/ they shulde maken shrewes good/ *and* turne her malyce *and* make hem be vertuous/ but that do they nat/ as it is p*ro*ued/ but causen ra*n*cour *and* debate. ergo they be nat good but vtterly badde. Had Nero neuer ben Emperour/ shulde neuer his dame haue be slayn/ to maken open the priuyte of his enge*n*drure. Herodes for his dignyte slewe many children. The dignite of kyng John wolde haue distroyed al Engla*n*de. Therfore mokel wysedom *and* goodnesse both/ nedeth in a person/ the malice in dignite slyly to bridel/ *and* with a good bytte of arest to withdrawe/ in case it wolde prau*n*ce otherwise than it shulde: trewly ye yeue to dignites

551 throwe out, thorough. **552 burthyns**, burdens. **553 shreude**, wicked; **werchynge**, effect. **555 her**, their. **557** ***Ergo***, Therefore. **558 dame**, mother; **privyté**, private part (i.e., womb). **559 engendrure**, birth. **560 mokel**, much. **561 slyly**, dexterously; **bytte**, bit; **arest**, halting. **562 yeve**, give.

wrongful names in your clepyng. They shulde hete nat dignité, but moustre of badnesse and mayntenour of shrewes. Pardy, shyne the sonne never so bright, and it bring forthe no heate ne sesonably the herbes out bringe of the erthe, but suffre frostes and colde and the erthe barayne to lygge by tyme of his compas in cyrcute about, ye wolde wonder, and dispreyse that son. If the mone be at ful and sheweth no lyght, but derke and dymme to your syght appereth, and make distruction of the waters, wol ye nat suppose it be under cloude or in clips? And that some prevy thing unknowen to your wittes is cause of suche contrarious doynge? Than, if clerkes that han ful insyght and knowyng of suche impedimentes enforme you of the sothe, very idiottes ye ben but if ye yeven credence to thilk clerkes wordes. And yet it doth me tene to sene many wretches rejoycen in such maner planettes. Trewly, lytel con they on philosophy or els on my lore that any desyre haven suche lyghtynge planettes in that wyse any more to shewe." "Good lady," quod I, "tel ye me howe ye mean in these thynges." "Lo," quod she, "the dignites of your cyté, sonne and mone, nothyng in kynde shew their shynyng

---

wro*n*gful names i*n* your clepyng. They shulde hete nat dignite/ but moustre of bad**<341va><341vb>**nesse *and* mayntenour of shrewes. Pardy shyne the sonne neuer so bright/ *and* it bring forthe no heate/ ne sesonably the herbes out bringe of th*e* erthe/ but suffre frostes *and* colde/ *and* the erthe barayne to lygge by tyme of his compas in cyrcute about/ ye wolde wonder *and* dispreyse that son. If the Mone be at ful *and* sheweth no lyȝt but derke *and* dymme to your syght appereth/ *and* make distruction of th*e* waters/ wol ye nat suppose it be vnder cloude or in clips? *and* that some preuy thing vnknowen to your wittes/ is cause of suche co*n*trarious doynge. Than if clerkes that han ful insyght *and* knowyng of suche impedimentes enforme you of the sothe/ very idiottes ye ben/ but if ye yeuen crede*n*ce to thilk clerkes word*es*. *And* yet it doth me tene/ to sene many wretches reioycen in such maner planettes. Trewly lytel con they on philosophy or els on my lore/ th*at* any desyre hauen suche lyghtynge planettes in that wyse any more to shewe. Good lady (q*uo*d I) tel ye me howe ye mean in these thynges. Lo (q*uo*d she) the dignites of yo*ur* cyte/ Sonne *and* Mone/ nothyng in kynde shew their shynyng

563 clepyng, calling, naming; **hete**, be called; **moustre**, display. **566 barayne**, barren; **lygge**, lie. **569 clips**, eclipse; **prevy**, secret. **571 but if**, unless. **572 yeven**, give; **thilk**, those same; **tene**, sorrow. **573 con they on**, understand. **574 suche lyghtynge**, i.e., (ill-) shining.

as they shulde. For the sonne made no brennyng hete in love, but freesed envye in mennes hertes for feblenesse of shynyng hete. And the moone was about under an olde cloude, the lyvenges by waters to distroye."

"Lady," quod I, "it is supposed they had shyned as they shulde." "Ye," quod she, "but nowe it is proved at the ful their beauté in kyndly shynyng fayled wherfore dignyté of hym selven hath no beautie in fairnesse ne dryveth nat awaye vices, but encreaseth and so be they no cause of the knotte. Now se in good trouth: holde ye nat such sonnes worthy of no reverence and dignites worthy of no worshyp, that maketh men to do the more harmes?" "I not," quod I. "No," quod she, "and thou se a wyse good man for his goodnesse and wysenesse wolte thou nat do him worship? Therof he is worthy." "That is good skil," quod I, "it is dewe to suche both reverence and worship to have." "Than," quod she, "a shrewe for his shreudnesse, altho he be put forthe toforne other for ferde, yet is he worthy for shrewdnesse to be unworshipped. Of reverence no parte is he worthy to have, to contrarious doyng belongeth. And that is good skyl, for right as he besmyteth the dignites, thilke same thyng ayenwarde him smyteth, or else shulde

---

as they shulde. For the Sonne made no bre*nn*yng hete in loue/ but freesed enuye in me*nn*es hertes for feblenesse of shynyng hete: *and* the Moone was about vnder an olde cloude/ the lyuenges by waters to distroye.

Lady (q*uo*d I) it is supposed they had shyned as they shulde. ye (q*uo*d she) but nowe it is proued at the ful their beaute in kyndly shynyng fayled/ wherfore dignyte of hym seluen hath no beautie in fairnesse/ ne dryueth nat awaye vices but encreaseth/ *and* so be they no cause of the knotte. Now se in good trouth/ holde ye nat such sonnes worthy of no reuerence *and* dignites/ worthy of no worshyp/ th*at* maketh men to do the more harmes? I not (q*uo*d I) No (q*uo*d she) *and* thou se a wyse good man/ for his goodnesse *and* wysenesse wolte thou nat do him worship? Therof he is worthy. That is good skil (q*uo*d I) it is dewe to suche/ both reuere*n*ce and worship to haue. Than (q*uo*d she) a shrewe for his shreudnesse/ altho he be put forthe toforne other for ferde/ yet is he worthy for shrewdnesse to be vnworshipped: of reuerence no p*ar*te is he worthy to haue/ to co*n*trarious doyng belongeth *and* that is good skyl. for right as he be**<341vb>** **<342ra>**smyteth the dignites/ thilke same thyng ayenwarde him smyteth/ or else shulde

577 brennyng, burning; **hete**, heat; **freesed**, frozen. **581 kyndly**, natural. **585 not**, do not know. **587 skil**, reasoning; **dewe**, due. **588 shreudnesse**, shrewishness; **ferde**, fear, intimidation. **591 besmyteth**, harms; **thilke**, that.

smyte. And over this thou woste wel," quod she, "that fyre in every place heateth where it be, and water maketh wete. Why? For kyndely werkyng is so yput in hem to do suche thynges. For every kyndely in werkyng sheweth his kynde. But though a wight had ben mayre of your cytie many wynter togyder and come in a straunge place there he were not knowen he shulde for his dignyté have no reverence. Than neyther worshyppe ne reverence is kyndely propre in no dignité sythen they shulden don their kynde in suche doynge if any were. And if reverence ne worshyppe kyndely be not set in dignytees, and they more therin ben shewed than goodnesse for that in dignyté is shewed, but it proveth that goodnesse kyndely in hem is not grounded. Iwys, neyther worshyppe, ne reverence, ne goodnesse in dignyté done none offyce of kynde. For they have none suche propertie in nature of doynge but by false opinyon of the people. Lo, howe somtyme thilke that in your cytie werne in dignyté noble, if thou lyste hem nempne, they ben nowe overturned bothe in worshyp, in name, and in reverence. Wherfore such dignites have no kyndly werchyng of worshyppe and of reverence, ne that hath no worthynesse on itselfe. Nowe it ryseth and nowe it vanissheth, after the

smyte. And ouer this thou woste wel (quod she) that fyre in euery place heateth where it be/ and water maketh wete: Why? for kyndely werkyng is so yput in hem to do suche thynges: for euery kyndely in werkyng sheweth his kynde. But though a wight had ben mayre of your cytie many wynter togyder/ and come in a strau*n*ge place there he were not knowen/ he shulde for his dignyte haue no reuerence. Than neyther worshyppe ne reuerence is kyndely propre in no dignite/ sythen they shulden don their kynde/ in suche doynge if any were. And if reuerence ne worshyppe kyndely be not set in dignytees/ and they more therin ben shewed than goodnesse/ for that in dignyte is shewed but it proueth that goodnesse kyndely in hem is not grounded. Iwys neyther worshyppe ne reuerence ne goodnesse in dignyte/ done none offyce of kynde/ for they haue none suche propertie in nature of doynge/ but by false opinyon of the people. Lo howe somtyme thilke that in your cytie werne in dignyte noble/ if thou lyste hem nempne/ they ben nowe ouerturned/ bothe in worshyp/ in name/ and in reuere*n*ce: wherfore such dignites haue no kyndly werchyng of worshyppe and of reuerence/ he that hath no worthynesse on it selfe. nowe it ryseth and nowe it vanissheth after the

593 kyndely, natural. **595 mayre**, mayor. **600 Iwys**, Certainly. **603 lyste**, were pleased. **604 nempne**, name.

varyaunt opinyon in false hertes of unstable people. Wherfore, if thou desyre the knotte of this jewel, or els if thou woldest suppose she shulde sette the knotte on thee for suche maner dignyté, than thou wenest beautie or goodnesse of thilke somwhat encreaseth the goodnesse or vertue in the body: But dignyté of hemselfe ben not good, ne yeven reverence ne worshyppe by their owne kynde. Howe shulde they than yeve to any other a thynge, that by no waye mowe they have hemselfe? It is sene in dignyté of the emperour and of many mo other that they mowe not of hem selve kepe their worshyppe ne their reverence, that in a lytel whyle it is nowe up and nowe downe by unstedfaste hertes of the people. What bountie mowe they yeve that with cloude lightly leaveth his shynynge? Certes, to the occupier is mokel appeyred, sythen suche doynge dothe villanye to him that maye it not mayntayne. Wherfore thilke waye to the knotte is croked. And if any desyre to come to the knot he must leave this waye on his lefte syde, or els shal he never come there."

---

varyaunt opinyon in false hertes of vnstable people. Wherfore if thou desyre the knotte of this iewel/ or els if thou woldest suppose she shulde sette the knotte on the for suche maner dignyte/ than thou wenest beautie or goodnesse of thilke somwhat encreaseth the goodnesse or vertue in the body: But dignyte of hem selfe ben not good/ ne yeuen reuerence ne worshyppe by their owne kynde/ howe shulde they than yeue to any other a thynge/ that by no waye mowe they haue hem selfe? It is sene in dignyte of the emperour and of many mo other/ that they mowe not of hem selue kepe their worshyppe ne their reuerence/ that that in a lytel whyle it is nowe vp *and* nowe downe/ by vnstedfaste hertes of the people. What bou*n*tie mowe they yeue that with cloude light**<342ra>** **<342rb>**ly leaueth his shynynge? Certes to the occupier is mokel appeyred/ sythen suche doynge dothe villanye to him that maye it not mayntayne/ wherfore thilke waye to the knotte is croked: and if any desyre to come to the knot/ he must leaue this waye on his lefte syde/ or els shal he neuer come there.

609 wenest, suppose; **thilke**, that same. **610 yeven**, give. **612 mowe**, may; **sene**, seen. **615 cloude**, i.e., when it turns cloudy; **leaveth**, quits. **616 mokel**, much; **appeyred**, worsened. **617 croked**, crooked. **618 leave**, leave.

Chapter VII

"Avayleth aught," quod she, "power of might in mayntenaunce of worthy to come to this knot?" "Pardé," quod I, "ye, for hertes ben ravysshed from suche maner thinges." "Certes," quod she, "though a fooles herte is with thyng ravysshed, yet therfore is no general cause of the powers ne of a syker parfyte herte to be loked after. Was not Nero the moste shrewe one of thilke that men rede, and yet had he power to make senatours, justyces, and princes of many landes? Was not that great power?" "Yes, certes," quod I. "Wel," quod she, "yet might he not helpe himselfe out of disease whan he gan fal. Howe many ensamples canste thou remembre of kynges great and noble, and huge power holden and yet they might not kepe hemselve from wretchydnesse? Howe wretched was kyng Henry Curtmantyl er he deyde? He had not so moche as to cover with his membres, and yet was he one of the greatest kynges of al the Normandes ofspring and moste possessyon had. O, a noble thynge and clere is power that is not founden myghty to kepe himselfe. Nowe, trewly, a great fole is he that for suche thyng wolde sette the knotte in thyne herte. Also, power of realmes is not thylke greatest power amonges the

---

AVayleth aught (quod she) power of might in mayntenaunce of worthy to come to this knot. Parde (quod I) ye/ for hertes ben rauysshed from suche maner thinges. Certes (quod she) though a fooles herte is with thyng rauysshed/ yet therfore is no general cause of th*e* powers/ ne of a syker parfyte herte to be loked after. Was not Nero the moste shrewe one of thilke that men rede/ and yet had he power to make senatours iustyces/ and princes of many landes? Was not that great power? Yes certes (quod I) Wel (q*uo*d she) yet might he not helpe him selfe out of disease/ whan he gan fal. Howe many ensamples canste thou remembre of kynges great and noble/ and huge power holden/ and yet they might not kepe hem selue from wretchydnesse. Howe wretched was kyng Henry Curtmantyl er he deyde? he had not so moche as to couer with his membres: and yet was he one of the greatest kynges of al the Normandes ofspring/ and moste possessyon had. O/ a noble thynge and clere is power/ that is not founden myghty to kepe him selfe. Nowe trewly a great fole is he/ that for suche thyng wolde sette the knotte in thyne herte. Also power of realmes is not thylke greatest power amonges the

620 Avayleth, Helps; **worthy**, a distinguished person. **621 Pardé**, Indeed; **from**, by. **623 syker**, secure. **624 one of thilke**, i.e., among those.

worldly powers reckened? And if suche powers han wretchydnesse in hemselfe, it foloweth other powers of febler condycion to ben wretched and than that wretchydnesse shulde be cause of suche a knotte. But every wyght that hath reason wote wel that wretchydnesse by no way may ben cause of none suche knotte; wherfore, suche power is no cause. That powers have wretchydnesse in hemselfe may right lyghtly ben preved. If power lacke on any syde on that syde is no power, but no power is wretchydnesse. For al be it so the power of emperours or kynges or els of their realmes (whiche is the power of the prince) stretchen wyde and brode, yet besydes is ther mokel folke of whiche he hath no commaundement ne lordshyppe; and there as lacketh his power his nonpower entreth, whereunder springeth that maketh hem wretches. No power is wretchydnesse and nothing els. But in this maner hath kynges more porcion of wretchydnesse than of power. Trewly, suche powers ben unmighty, for ever they ben in drede howe thilke power from lesyng may be keped of sorow; so drede sorily prickes ever in their hertes: litel is the power whiche careth and ferdeth it selfe to mayntayne. Unmighty is that wretchydnesse whiche is entred by the ferdful wenynge

---

worldly powers reckened? And if suche powers han wretchydnesse in hem selfe/ it foloweth other powers of febler condycion to ben wretched/ and than that wretchydnesse shulde be cause of suche a knotte. But euery wyght that hath reason wote wel that wretchydnesse by no way may ben cause of none suche knotte/ wherfore suche power is no cause. That powers haue wretchydnesse in hem selfe/ may right lyghtly ben preued. If power lacke on any syde/ on that**<342rb><342va>**syde is no power/ but no power is wretchydnesse: for al be it so the power of emperours or kynges/ or els of their realmes (whiche is the power of the prince) stretchen wyde and brode/ yet besydes is ther mokel folke of whiche he hath no co*m*maundement ne lordshyppe/ and there as lacketh his power/ his nonpower entreth/ where vnder springeth that maketh hem wretches. No power is wretchydnesse/ and nothing els: but in this maner hath kynges more porcion of wretchydnesse than of power. Trewly suche powers ben vnmighty/ for euer they ben in drede howe thilke power fro*m* lesyng may be keped of sorow/ so drede sorily prickes euer i*n* their hertes: litel is th*e* power whiche careth and ferdeth it selfe to mayntayne. Unmighty is that wretchydnesse whiche is entred by the ferdful wenynge

634 hemselfe, themselves. **641 brode**, broad. **642 mokel**, much, many. **646 drede**, dread; **lesyng**, being lost; **keped of**, kept [on account] of. **647 ferdeth**, fears. **648 ferdful**, fearful; **wenynge**, assumption.

of the wretche himselfe, and knot ymaked by wretchydnesse is betwene wretches; and wretches al thyng bewaylen. Wherfore the knot shulde be bewayled, and there is no suche parfyte blysse that we supposed at the gynnyng. *Ergo*, power in nothyng shulde cause suche knottes. Wretchydnesse is a kyndely propertie in suche power as by way of drede whiche they mowe not eschewe ne by no way lyve in sykernesse. For thou woste wel," quod she, "he is nought mighty that wolde done that he may not done ne perfourme." "Therfore," quod I, "these kynges and lordes that han suffysaunce at the ful of men and other thynges mowen wel ben holden mighty. Their comaundementes ben done, it is nevermore denyed." "Foole," quod she, "or he wotte himselfe mighty or wotte it not. For he is nought mighty that is blynde of his might and wote it not." "That is sothe," quod I. "Than if he wot it, he must nedes ben a dradde to lesen it. He that wotte of his might is in doute that he mote nedes lese, and so leadeth him drede to ben unmighty. And if he retche not to lese, lytel is that worthe that of the lesyng reason retcheth nothyng. And if it were mighty in power or in strength, the lesyng shulde ben withset; and whan it cometh to the lesyng he may it not withsytte. *Ergo* thilke might is

---

of the wretche him selfe: and knot ymaked by wretchydnesse is betwene wretches/ and wretches al thyng bewaylen: wherfore the knot shulde be bewayled/ and there is no suche parfyte blysse that we supposed at th*e* gynnyng. Ergo power in nothyng shulde cause suche knottes. Wretchydnesse is a kyndely propertie in suche power/ as by way of drede/ whiche they mowe not eschewe ne by no way lyue in sykernesse. For thou woste wel (quod she) he is nought mighty that wolde done that he may not done ne perfourme. Therfore (quod I) these kynges and lordes that han suffysaunce at the ful of men and other thynges/ mowen wel ben holden mighty: their comaundementes ben done/ it is neuermore denyed. Foole (q*uo*d she) or he wotte him selfe mighty or wotte it not: for he is nought mighty/ that is blynde of his might and wote it not. That is sothe (q*uo*d I) Than if he wot it/ he must nedes ben a dradde to lesen it. He that wotte of his might is in doute that he mote nedes lese/ and so leadeth him drede to ben vnmighty. And if he retche not to lese/ lytel is that worthe that of the lesyng reason retcheth nothyng: and if it were miȝty in power or in strength/ th*e* lesyng shulde ben withset/ and whan it cometh to the lesyng he may it not withsytte. Ergo thilke might is

651 *Ergo*, Therefore. **653 sykernesse**, certainty. **656 mowen**, may. **657 wotte**, knows. **659 lesen**, lose. **660 leadeth him drede**, dread leads him. **661 retche**, cares; **lese**, lose. **663 withset**, resisted.

leude and naughty. Such mightes arne ilyke to postes and pyllers that upright stonden and great might han to beare many charges; and if they croke on any syde, lytel thynge maketh hem overthrowe." "This is a good ensample," quod I, "to pyllers and postes that I have sene overthrowed myselfe, and hadden they ben underput with any helpes they had not so lightly fal." "Than holdest thou him mighty that hath many men armed and many servauntes and ever he is adradde of hem in his herte, and, for he gasteth hem somtyme, he mote the more feare have. Comenly he that other agasteth other in him ayenwarde werchen the same, and thus warnisshed mote he be and of warnysshe the hour drede. Lytel is that might and right leude who so taketh hede." "Than semeth it," quod I, "that suche famulers aboute kynges and great lordes shulde great might have. Althoughe a sypher in augrym have no might in signifycacion of it selve, yet he yeveth power in signifycacion to other and these clepe I the helpes to a poste to kepe him from fallyng." "Certes," quod she, "thilke skylles ben leude. Why? but if the shorers be wel grounded, the helpes shullen slyden and suffre the charge to fal; her myght lytel

---

leude and naughty. Such mightes arne ilyke to postes and pyllers that vpright stonden/ **<342va><342vb>**and great might han to beare many charges/ and if they croke on any syde/ lytel thynge maketh hem ouerthrowe. This is a good ensample (quod I) to pyllers and postes that I haue sene ouerthrowed my selfe/ and hadden they ben vnderput with any helpes/ they had not so lightly fal. Than holdest thou him mighty that hath many men armed and many seruauntes/ and euer he is adradde of hem in his herte/ and for he gasteth hem/ somtyme he mote the more feare haue. Comenly he that other agasteth/ other in him ayenwarde werchen the same: and thus warnisshed mote he be/ and of warnysshe the hour drede: Lytel is that might *and* right leude/ who so taketh hede. Than semeth it (quod I) that suche famulers aboute kynges and great lordes/ shulde great might haue. Althoughe a sypher in augrym haue no might in signifycacion of it selue/ yet he yeueth power in signifycacion to other/ and these clepe I the helpes to a poste to kepe him from fallyng. Certes (quod she) thilke skylles ben leude. Why? but if the shorers be wel grounded/ the helpes shullen slyden and suffre the charge to fal/ her myght lytel

664 leude, infirm. **665 croke**, lean, bend. **669 adradde**, afraid; **gasteth**, is aghast of. **670 feare**, fear. **671 werchen**, work, do; **warnisshed**, guarded; **mote**, must; **warnysshe**, guarding. **673 famulers**, familiars. **674 sypher**, zero; **augrym**, mathematics, arithmetic. **675 yeveth**, gives; **clepe**, call. **676 Certes**, Certainly; **thilke**, those same; **skylles**, reasonings; **leude**, uninformed; **but if**, unless; **shorers**, foundations. **677 charge**, weight; **her**, their.

avayleth." "And so me thynketh," quod I, "that a poste alone stonding upright upon a basse may lenger in great burthen endure than croken pylers for al their helpes, and her grounde be not syker." "That is soth," quod she, "for as the blynde in bearyng of the lame gynne stomble, bothe shulde fal, right so suche pyllers so envyroned with helpes in fallyng of the grounde fayleth al togyther. Howe ofte than suche famulers in their moste pride of prosperyté ben sodainly overthrowen. Thou haste knowe many in a moment so ferre overthrowe that cover might they never. Whan the hevynesse of such faylyng cometh by case of fortune, they mowe it not eschue; and might and power, if ther were any, shulde of strength such thinges voyde and weyve, and so it is not. Lo, than whiche thing is this power that tho men han it they ben agast, and in no tyme of ful having be they syker. And if they wold weyve drede, as they mow not, litel is in worthynes. Fye therfore on so naughty thing any knot to cause. Lo, in adversité thilk ben his foes that glosed and semed frendes in welth. Thus arn his famyliers his foes and his enemyes; and nothyng is werse ne more mighty for to anoy than is a famylier enemye, and these thynges may they not weyve. So trewly, their might is not worthe a

---

auayleth. And so me thynketh (quod I) that a poste alone stonding vpright vpon a basse/ may lenger in graet burthen endure/ than croken pylers for al their helpes/ and her grou*n*de be not syker. That is soth (q*uo*d she) for as the blynde in bearyng of the lame gynne stomble/ bothe shulde fal right/ so suche pyllers so enuyroned with helpes in fallyng of the grounde/ fayleth al togyther/ howe ofte than suche famulers in their moste pride of prosperyte ben sodainly ouerthrowen. Thou haste knowe many in a mome*n*t so ferre ouerthrowe/ that couer might they neuer/ Whan the heuynesse of such faylyng cometh by case of fortune/ they mowe it not eschue: and might and power/ if ther were any/ shulde of stre*n*gth such thinges voyde and weyue/ *and* so it is not. Lo than whiche thing is this power/ th*at* tho men han it they ben agast/ *and* in no tyme of ful haui*n*g be they syker: *and* if they wold weyue drede/ as they mow not/ litel is in worthynes. Fye therfore on so naughty thing any knot to cause. Lo i*n* aduersite/ thilk ben his foes th*at* glosed *and* semed frendes i*n* welth: thus arn**<342vb><343ra>**his famyliers his foes and his enemyes: and nothyng is werse ne more mighty for to anoy than is a famylier enemye/ and these thynges may they not weyue: so trewly their might is not worthe a

679 croken, crooked, wobbly; **and**, if. **680 syker**, sure. **682 than**, then; **famulers**, familiars. **684 ferre**, far; **cover**, recover. **685 mowe**, may. **686 voyde**, avoid; **weyve**, avert. **688 mow**, may. **689 naughty**, full of nothing; **thilk**, those. **690 glosed**, flattered. **692 weyve**, put aside, avert.

cresse. And over al thynge he that maye not withdrawe the bridel of his flesshly lustes and his wretched complayntes (nowe thynke on thy selfe) trewly he is not mighty. I can sene no waye that lythe to the knotte. Thilke people than that setten their hertes upon suche mightes and powers often ben begyled. Pardé he is not mighty that may do any thyng that another maye doone hym the selve and that men have as great power over him as he over other. A justyce that demeth men ayenwarde hath ben often demed. Buserus slewe his gestes, and he was slayne of Hercules his geste. Hugest betraysshed many men and of Collo was he betrayed. He that with swerde smyteth, with swerde shal be smytten."

Than gan I to studyen a whyle on these thinges and made a countenaunce with my hande in maner to ben huyshte. "Nowe let sene," quod she, "me thynketh somwhat there is within thy soule that troubleth thy understandyng. Saye on what it is." Quod I tho, "Me thynketh that although a man by power have suche might over me as I have over other that disproveth no myght in my person, but yet may I have power and myght neverthelater." "Se nowe," quod she, "thyne owne leudenesse. He is mighty that maye

---

cresse. And ouer al thynge/ he that maye not withdrawe the bridel of his flesshly lustes and his wretched complayntes (nowe thynke on thy selfe) trewly he is not mighty: I can sene no waye that lythe to the knotte. Thilke people than that setten their hertes vpon suche mightes and powers/ often ben begyled. Parde he is not mighty that may do any thyng/ that another maye doone hym the selue/ and that men haue as great power ouer him as he ouer other. A iustyce that demeth men/ ayenwarde hath ben often demed. Buserus slewe his gestes/ and he was slayne of Hercules his geste. Hugest betraysshed many men/ and of Collo was he betrayed. He that with swerde smyteth/ with swerde shal be smytten. Than gan I to studyen a whyle on these thinges/ and made a countenaunce with my hande in maner to ben huyshte. Nowe let sene (q*uo*d she) me thynketh somwhat there is within thy soule/ that troubleth thy vnderstandyng/ saye on what it is. (Quod I tho) me thynketh that although a man by power haue suche might ouer me/ as I haue ouer other/ that disproueth no myght in my person/ but yet may I haue power and myght neuer the later. Se nowe (quod she) thyne owne leudenesse: He is mighty that maye

693 cresse, trifle (lit., crease). **695 lythe to**, lies in [the direction of]. **696 Pardé**, Indeed. **697 the selve**, the same [thing, to him]. **698 demeth**, judges. **699 gestes**, guests. **703 huyshte**, hushed. **707 neverthelater**, nevertheless; **leudenesse**, ignorance; **maye**, may [do what he will].

without wretchydnesse, and he is unmyghty that may it not withsytte. But than he, that might over thee, and he wol put on thee wretchydnesse thou might it not withsytte. *Ergo*, thou seest thyselfe what foloweth. But nowe," quod she, "woldest thou not skorne, and thou se a flye han power to done harme to another flye and thilke have no myght ne ayenturnyng him selfe to defende." "Yes certes," quod I. "Who is a frayler thyng," quod she, "than the fleshly body of a man over whiche have oftentyme flyes and yet lasse thyng than a flye mokel might in grevaunce and anoyeng withouten any withsyttynge, for al thilke mannes mightes. And sythen thou seest thyne flesshly body in kyndely power fayle, howe shulde than the accydent of a thynge ben in more suretė of beynge than substancial? Wherfore, thilke thynges that we clepe power is but accident to the flesshly body, and so they may not have that suretie in might whiche wanteth in the substancial body. Why there is no waye to the knotte that loketh aright after the hye waye, as he shulde.

Chapter VIII

Verily, it is proved that rychesse dignyté and power ben not trewe waye to the knotte

---

without wretchydnesse/ and he is vnmyghty that may it not withsytte: but than he that might ouer the/ and he wol put on the wretchydnesse/ thou might it not withsytte. Ergo thou seest thy selfe what foloweth. But nowe (quod she) woldest thou not skorne and thou se a flye han power to done harme to an other flye/ *and* thilke haue no myght ne ayenturnyng him selfe to defende. Yes certes (quod I) Who is a frayler thyng (quod she) than the fleshly body of a man/ ouer whiche haue oftentyme flyes/ and yet lasse thyng than a flye/ mokel might in greuaunce and anoyeng withouten any withsyttynge/ for al thilke mannes mightes. And sythen thou seest thyne flesshly body in kyndely power fayle/ howe shulde than the**<343ra><343rb>**accydent of a thynge ben in more surete of beynge than substancial: Wherfore thilke thynges that we clepe power/ is but accident to the flesshly body/ and so they may not haue that suretie in might/ whiche wanteth in the substancial body. Why there is no waye to the knotte/ that loketh aright after the hye waye as he shulde.

VErily it is proued that rychesse/ dignyte/ and power/ ben not trewe waye to the knotte/

708 withsytte, resist. **709 and he wol**, if he will; ***Ergo***, Therefore. **712 ayenturnyng**, wheeling about; **frayler**, frailer. **714 mokel**, much; **withsyttynge**, resistance. **716 suretė**, security.

but as rathe by suche thynges the knotte to be unbounde. Wherfore on these thynges I rede no wight truste to gette any good knotte. But what shul we saye of renome in the peoples mouthes? Shulde that ben any cause? What supposest thou in thyn herte?"

"Certes," quod I, "yes, I trowe, for your slye resons I dare not safely it saye." "Than," quod she, "wol I preve that shrewes as rathe shul ben in the knotte as the good, and that were ayenst kynde." "Fayne," quod I, "wolde I that here. Me thinketh wonder howe renome shuld as wel knytte a shrewe as a good person. Renome in every degré hath avaunced, yet wyst I never the contrarye. Shulde than renome accorde with a shrewe? It maye not synke in my stomake tyl I here more." "Nowe," quod she, "have I not sayd alwayes that shrewes shul not have the knotte?" "What nedeth," quod I, "to reherse that any more? I wotte wel every wight by kyndely reason shrewes in knyttyng wol eschewe." "Than," quod she, "the good ought thilke knotte to have." "Howe els," quod I. "It were great harme," quod she, "that the good were weyved and put out of espoire of the knotte, if he it desyred." "O," quod I, "alas, on suche thing to thinke I

---

but as rathe by suche thynges the knotte to be vnbounde: Wherfore on these thynges I rede no wight truste/ to gette any good knotte. But what shul we saye of renome in the peoples mouthes/ shulde that ben any cause: what supposest thou in thyn herte?

Certes (quod I) yes I trowe/ for your slye resons I dare not safely it saye. Than (quod she) wol I preue that shrewes as rathe shul ben in the knotte as the good/ and that were ayenst kynde. Fayne (quod I) wolde I that here/ me thinketh wonder howe renome shuld as wel knytte a shrewe as a good person: renome in euery degre hath auaunced/ yet wyst I neuer the contrarye: shulde than renome accorde with a shrewe? it maye not synke in my stomake tyl I here more. Nowe (quod she) haue I not sayd alwayes/ th*a*t shrewes shul not haue the knotte. What nedeth (quod I) to reherse that any more/ I wotte wel euery wight by kyndely reason/ shrewes in knyttyng wol eschewe. Than (q*uo*d she) the good ought thilke knotte to haue. Howe els (quod I) It were great harme (quod she) that the good were weyued and put out of espoire of the knotte/ if he it desyred. O (q*uo*d I) alas/ on suche thing to thinke I

722 rathe, soon. **723 rede**, advise; **wight**, person; **renome**, renown. **725 trowe**, believe; **for**, because of. **727 Fayne**, Gladly; **here**, hear. **729 wyst**, knew. **732 wotte**, know; **knyttyng**, determining what the knot will be. **733 thilke**, that same. **734 weyved**, deflected. **735 espoire**, hope.

wene that heven wepeth to se such wronges here ben suffred on erthe. The good ought it to have and no wight els." "The goodnesse," quod she, "of a person may not ben knowe outforth but by renome of the knowers. Wherfore he must be renomed of goodnesse to come to the knot." "So must it be," quod I, "or els al lost that we carpen." "Sothly," quod she, "that were great harme, but if a good man myght have his desyres in servyce of thilke knot and a shrewe to be veyned, and they ben not knowen in general but by lackyng and praysing and in renome. And so by the consequence it foloweth a shrewe to ben praysed and knyt, and a good to be forsake and unknyt." "Ah," quod I tho, "have ye, lady, ben here abouten. Yet wolde I se by grace of our argumentes better declared howe good and bad do acorden by lacking and praysyng. Me thynketh it ayenst kynde." "Nay," quod she, "and that shalt thou se as yerne. These elementes han contraryous qualyties in kynde by whiche they mowe not acorde no more than good and badde; and in qualytees they acorde so that contraries by qualyté acorden by qualyté. Is not erthe drie and water that is next and bytwene th'erthe is wete? Drie and wete ben

---

wene that heuen wepeth to se such wronges here ben suffred on erthe: the good ought it to haue and no wight els. The goodnesse (q*uo*d she) of a person may not ben knowe outforth/ but by renome of th*e* knowers/ wherfore he must be renomed of goodnesse to come to th*e* knot. So must it be (q*uo*d I) or els al lost that we carpen. Sothly (q*uo*d she) th*at* were great harme/ but if a good man myght haue his desyres in seruyce of thilke knot/ *and* a shrewe to be veyned/ *and* they ben not knowen in general but**<343rb><343va>**by lackyng and praysing and in renome/ and so by the consequence it foloweth/ a shrewe to ben praysed and knyt/ *and* a good to be forsake and vnknyt. Ah (q*uo*d I tho) haue ye lady ben here abouten/ yet wolde I se by grace of our argumentes better declared/ howe good *and* bad do acorden by lacking and praysyng/ me thynketh it ayenst kynde. Nay (q*uo*d she) and that shalt thou se as yerne: these elementes han co*n*traryous qualyties in kynde/ by whiche they mowe not acorde no more than good *and* badde: and in qualytees they acorde/ so that co*n*traries by qualyte/ acorden by qualyte. Is not erthe drie/ and water th*at* is next and bytwene therthe is wete: drie and wete ben

736 wene, assume. **738 outforth**, externally. **739 carpen**, speak of. **741 veyned**, in vain, shown to be false (feigned). **742 lackyng**, blaming. **743 knyt**, associated with the knot. **744 tho**, then; **here abouten**, busy with this subject. **745 lacking**, blaming. **746 as yerne**, quickly. **747 mowe**, may.

contrarie and mowen not acorde, and yet this discordaunce is bounde to acorde by cloudes, for bothe elementes ben colde. Right so the eyre that is next the water is wete, and eke it is hotte. This eyre by his hete contraryeth water that is colde, but thilke contrariousty is oned by moysture, for bothe be they moyst. Also the fyre that is next the eyre and it encloseth al about is drie, wherthrough it contraryeth eyre that is wete; and in hete they acorde, for bothe they ben hote. Thus by these acordaunces discordantes ben joyned, and in a maner of acordaunce they acorden by connection that is knyttyng togyther. Of that accorde cometh a maner of melodye that is right noble. Right so good and bad arne contrarie in doynges by lacking and praysyng: good is bothe lacked and praysed of some and badde is bothe lacked and praysed of some. Wherfore their contraryoustie acorde bothe by lackyng and praysing. Than foloweth it, though good be never so mokel praysed, oweth more to ben knyt than the badde; or els bad for the renome that he hath must be taken as wel as the good, and that oweth not." "No, forsothe," quod I. "Wel," quod she, "than is renome no waye to the knot. Lo, foole," quod she, "howe clerkes writen of suche glorie of renome. 'O glorie, glorie, thou arte

---

contrarie *and* mowen not acorde/ and yet this discordaunce is bou*n*de to acorde by cloudes/ for bothe elementes ben colde. Right so the eyre that is next the water is wete/ *and* eke it is hotte. This eyre by his hete contraryeth water that is colde/ but thilke co*n*trariousty is oned my moysture/ for bothe be they moyst. Also the fyre that is next the erth/ and it encloseth al about/ is drie: wherthrough it contraryeth erthe th*a*t is wete: and in hete they acorde for bothe they ben hote. Thus by these acordaunces/ discordantes ben ioyned and in a maner of acordaunce they acorden by connection/ that is knyttyng togyther: of that accorde cometh a maner of melodye that is right noble. Right so good and bad arne contrarie in doynges/ by lacking and praysyng: good is bothe lacked and praysed of some/ and badde is bothe lacked and praysed of some: wherfore their contraryoustie acorde bothe by lackyng and praysing. Than foloweth it/ though good be neuer so mokel praysed/ oweth more to ben knyt than the badde: or els bad for the renome that he hath/ must be taken as wel as th*e* good/ and that oweth not. No forsothe (quod I) Wel (q*uo*d she) than is renome no waye to the knot: Lo foole (q*uo*d she) howe clerkes writen of suche glorie of renome. O glorie/ glorie/ thou arte

752 eke, also. **753 oned**, reconciled. **754 eyre**, air (see note). **758 lacking**, blaming. **761 mokel**, much; **knyt**, associated with the knot. **762 oweth not**, ought not [be]. **764 writen**, write.

none other thynge to thousandes of folke but a great sweller of eeres.' Many one hath had ful great renome by false opinyon of varyaunt people. And what is fouler than folke wrongfully to ben praysed or by malyce of the people gyltlesse lacked? Nedes shame foloweth therof to hem that with wrong prayseth, and also to the desertes praysed and vylanye and reprofe of hym that disclaundreth.

"Good chylde," quod she, "what echeth suche renome to the conscience of a wyse man that loketh and measureth his goodnesse not by slevelesse wordes of the people but by sothfastnesse of conscience? By God, nothyng. And if it be fayre a mans name be eched by moche folkes praysing and fouler thyng that mo folke not praysen. I sayd to thee a lytel herebeforne that no folke in straunge countreyes nought praysen; suche renome may not comen to their eeres bycause of unknowyng and other obstacles as I sayde: wherfore more folke not praysen, and that is right foule to him that renome desyreth, to wete, lesse folke praisen than renome enhaunce. I trowe the thanke of a people is naught worthe in remembraunce to take, ne it procedeth of no wyse jugement. Never is it stedfast pardurable. It is veyne and fleyng, with wynde wasteth and encreaseth.

---

none other thynge to thousandes of folke/ but a great sweller of eeres. Many one hath had ful great renome by false opinyon of varyaunt people: And what is fouler than folke wrongfully to ben praysed/ or by malyce of th*e* people gyltlesse lacked? nedes shame**<343va><343vb>**foloweth therof to hem that with wrong prayseth/ and also to the desertes praysed/ and vylanye and reprofe of hym that disclaundreth.

Good chylde (quod she) what echeth suche renome to the conscience of a wyse man/ that loketh and measureth his goodnesse/ not by sleuelesse wordes of th*e* people/ but by sothfastnesse of conscience: by god nothyng. And if it be fayre a mans name be eched by moche folkes praysing/ and fouler thyng that mo folke not praysen. I sayd to the a lytel here beforne/ that no folke in straunge countreyes nought praysen/ suche renome may not comen to their eeres/ bycause of vnknowyng/ and other obstacles/ as I sayde: wherfore more folke not praysen/ and that is right foule to him that renome desyreth/ to wete lesse folke praisen than renome enhaunce. I trowe the thanke of a people is naught worthe in remembraunce to take/ ne it procedeth of no wyse iugement/ neuer is it stedfast pardurable: It is veyne and fleyng/ with wynde wasteth and encreaseth.

765 eeres, ears. **767 lacked**, [to be] blamed; **Nedes**, [It] needs [be that]. **770 echeth**, adds. **771 slevelesse**, trifling. **773 eched**, increased. **777 wete**, know; **trowe**, believe. **779 fleyng**, fleeting.

Trewly, suche glorie ought to be hated. If gentyllesse be a clere thynge renome and glorie to enhaunce, as in reckenyng of thy lynage, than is gentylesse of thy kynne; for why it semeth that gentylesse of thy kynne is but praysynge and renome that come of thyne auncestres desertes: and if so be that praysyng and renome of their desertes make their clere gentyllesse, than mote they nedes ben gentyl for their gentyl dedes and not thou. For of thyselfe cometh not such maner gentylesse praysynge of thy desertes. Than gentyllesse of thyne auncesters, that forayne is to thee, maketh thee not gentyl, but ungentyl and reproved, and if thou contynuest not their gentylesse. And therfore a wyse man ones sayde: 'Better is it thy kynne to ben by thee gentyled than thou to glorifye of thy kynnes gentylesse and haste no deserte therof thyselfe.'

"Howe passynge is the beautie of flesshly bodyes? More flyttynge than movable floures of sommer. And if thyne eyen weren as good as the lynx, that maye sene thorowe many stone walles bothe fayre and foule in their entrayles of no maner hewe shulde apere to thy syght that were a foule syght. Than is fayrnesse by feblesse of eyen, but of no kynde. Wherfore thilke shulde be no way to the knot. Whan thilke is went the

---

Trewly suche glorie ought to be hated. If gentyllesse be a clere thynge/ renome and glorie to enhau*n*ce/ as in reckenyng of thy lynage/ than is gentylesse of thy kynne/ for why it semeth that gentylesse of thy kynne/ is but praysynge and renome that come of thyne auncestres desertes: and if so be that praysyng and renome of their desertes make their clere gentyllesse/ than mote they nedes ben gentyl for their gentyl dedes/ and not thou: for of thy selfe cometh not such maner gentylesse/ praysynge of thy desertes. Than gentyllesse of thyne auncesters that forayne is to the/ maketh the not gentyl/ but vngentyl and reproued/ and if thou contynuest not their gentylesse. And therfore a wyse man ones sayde: Better is it thy kynne to ben by the gentyled/ than thou to glorifye of thy kynnes gentylesse/ and haste no deserte therof thy selfe.

Howe passynge is the beautie of flesshly bodyes? more flyttynge than mouable floures of so*m*mer. And if thyne eyen weren as good as the Lynx/ that maye sene thorowe many stone walles/ bothe fayre and foule in their entrayles/ of no maner hewe shulde apere to thy syght/ that were a foule syght. Than is**<343vb><344ra>**fayrnesse by feblesse of eyen/ but of no kynde/ wherfore thilke shulde be no way to the knot: Whan thilke is went the

781 lynage, lineage. **781–82 for why**, whence, wherefore. **784 mote**, must. **787 and**, if. **788 gentyled**, rendered gentle (noble). **794 went**, gone.

knotte wendeth after. Lo, nowe at al proves none of al these thynges mowe parfytly ben in understandyng to ben waye to the duryng blysse of the knotte. But nowe, to conclusyon of these maters herkeneth these wordes. Very sommer is knowe from the wynter: in shorter cours draweth the dayes of Decembre than in the moneth of June. The springes of Maye faden and falowen in Octobre. These thinges ben not unbounden from their olde kynde. They have not loste her werke of their propre estate. Men of voluntarious wyl withsytte that hevens governeth. Other thynges suffren thynges paciently to werche. Man, in what estate he be, yet wolde he ben chaunged. Thus by queynt thynges blysse is desyred, and the fruite that cometh of these springes nys but anguys and bytter. Although it be a whyle swete, it maye not be with holde, hastely they departe: thus al daye fayleth thynges that fooles wende. Right thus haste thou fayled in thy first wenyng. He that thynketh to sayle and drawe after the course of the sterre *de polo antartico* shal he never come northwarde to the contrarye sterre of *polus articus*; of whiche thynges if thou take kepe, thy first out-waye-goynge prison and exile may be cleped. The grounde

---

knotte wendeth after. Lo nowe at al proues/ none of al these thynges mowe parfytly ben in vnderstandyng/ to ben waye to the duryng blysse of the knotte. But nowe to conclusyon of these maters/ herkeneth these wordes. Very so*m*mer is knowe from the wynter: in shorter cours draweth the dayes of Decembre/ than in the moneth of June: The springes of Maye faden and folowen in Octobre. These thinges ben not vnbounden from their olde kynde/ they haue not loste her werke of their propre estate. Men of voluntarious wyl/ withsytte that heuens gouerneth. Other thynges suffren thynges paciently to werche: Man in what estate he be yet wolde he ben chaunged. Thus by queynt thynges blysse is desyred/ and the fruite that cometh of these springes/ nys but anguys and bytter/ al though it be a whyle swete/ it maye not be with holde/ hastely they departe: thus al daye fayleth thynges that fooles wende. Right thus haste thou fayled in thy first wenyng. He that thynketh to sayle/ and drawe after the course of the sterre/ de polo autartico/ shal he neuer come northwarde to the contrarye sterre of polus articus: of whiche thynges if thou take kepe/ thy first out waye goynge/ prison and exile may be cleped. The grounde

795 wendeth, goes; **mowe**, may. **796 duryng**, enduring. **797 Very**, True. **799 falowen**, [lie] fallow. **801 withsytte**, resist; **werche**, work. **802 what**, whatsoever; **queynt**, curious, weird. **803 anguys**, excruciating. **804 with holde**, maintained. **805 wenyng**, assumption. **808 kepe**, heed; **out-waye-goynge**, journey, wandering; **cleped**, called.

falsed underneth and so hast thou fayled. No wyght, I wene, blameth him that stynteth in mysgoyng and secheth redy way of his blisse. Nowe me thynketh," quod she, "that it suffiseth in my shewyng the wayes by dignetè rychesse renome and power if thou loke clerely arn no ways to the knotte."

Chapter IX

"Every argument, lady," quod I tho, "that ye han maked in these forenempned maters, me thynketh hem in my ful wytte conceyved; shal I no more, if God wyl, in the contrarye be begyled. But fayne wolde I, and it were your wyl, blysse of the knotte to me were declared. I might fele the better howe my herte myght assente to pursue the ende in servyce as he hath begonne." "O," quod she, "there is a melodye in heven whiche clerkes clepen 'armony,' but that is not in brekynge of voyce, but it is a maner swete thing of kyndely werchyng that causeth joye out of nombre to recken, and that is joyned by reason and by wysdome in a quantyté of proporcion of knyttyng. God made al thyng in reason, and in wytte of proporcion of melody we mowe not suffyse to

---

falsed vnderneth/ and so hast thou fayled. No wyght I wene blameth him that stynteth in mysgoyng/ and secheth redy way of his blisse. Nowe me thynketh (quod she) that it suffiseth in my shewyng the wayes/ by dignete/ rychesse/ renome/ and power/ if thou loke clerely arn no ways to the knotte.

EVery argume*n*t lady (quod I tho) that ye han maked in these fore nempned maters/ me thynketh hem in my ful wytte conceyued/ shal I no more if god wyl in the contrarye be begyled: But fayne wolde I and it were your wyl/ blysse of the knotte to me were declared/ I might fele the better howe**<344ra><344rb>**my herte myght assente to pursue the ende in seruyce as he hath begonne. O (quod she) there is a melodye in heuen/ whiche clerkes clepen armony/ but that is not in brekynge of voyce/ but it is a maner swete thing of kyndely werchyng/ that causeth ioye out of nombre/ to recken/ and that is ioyned by reason and by wysdome/ in a quantyte of proporcion of knyttyng. God made al thyng in reason and in wytte of proporcion of melody/ we mowe not suffyse to

809 wyght, person; **wene**, assume; **stynteth**, ceases. **810 secheth**, seeks. **813 forenempned**, aforementioned. **815 fayne**, gladly. **818 brekynge**, uttering. **819 werchyng**, working. **821 mowe**, may.

shewe. It is written by great clerkes and wise that in erthly thynges lightly by studye and by travayle the knowynge may be getten. But of suche hevenly melody mokel travayle wol bringe out in knowyng right lytel. Swetenesse of this paradyse hath you ravisshed. It semeth ye slepten, rested from al other diseases, so kyndely is your hertes therin ygrounded. Blysse of two hertes in ful love knytte may not aright ben ymagyned. Ever is their contemplacion in ful of thoughty studye to plesaunce, mater in bringynge, comforte everyche to other. And, therfore, of erthly thinges mokel mater lightly cometh in your lerning. Knowledge of understonding that is nyghe after eye but not so nyghe the covetyse of knyttynge in your hertes. More soveraine desyre hath every wight in lytel herynge of hevenly connynge than of mokel materyal purposes in erthe. Right so it is in propertie of my servauntes that they ben more affyched in sterynge of lytel thynge in his desyre than of mokel other mater lasse in his conscience. This blysse is a maner of sowne delycious in a queynte voyce touched and no dynne of notes. There is none impressyon of breakynge laboure. I canne it not otherwyse nempne

---

shewe. It is written by great clerkes and wise/ that in erthly thynges lightly by studye and by trauayle/ the knowynge may be getten: but of suche heuenly melody/ mokel trauayle wol bringe out in knowyng right lytel. Swetenesse of this paradyse hath you rauisshed/ it semeth ye slepten/ rested from al other diseases/ so kyndely is your hertes therin ygrounded. Blysse of two hertes in ful loue knytte/ may not aright ben ymagyned: euer is their co*n*templacion i*n* ful of thoughty studye to plesaunce/ mater in bringynge/ comforte eueryche to other. And therfore of erthly thinges/ mokel mater lightly cometh in your lerning. Knowledge of vnderstondi*n*g that is nyghe after eye/ but not so nyghe the couetyse of knyttynge in your hertes: More soueraine desyre hath euery wight in lytel herynge of heuenly connynge/ than of mokel materyal purposes in erthe. Right so it is in propertie of my seruauntes/ that they ben more affyched in sterynge of lytel thynge in his desyre/ than of mokel other mater/ lasse in his conscience. This blysse is a maner of sowne delycious/ in a queynte voyce touched/ and no dynne of notes: there is none impressyon of breakynge laboure. I canne it not otherwyse nempne/

823 mokel, much. **829 nyghe after eye**, based on experience, desire. **830 covetyse**, desire. **831 wight**, person; **herynge**, hearing; **mokel**, many. **832 affyched**, fixed; **sterynge**, steering, governing. **833 lasse**, less. **834 queynte**, curious. **835 breakynge**, articulatory; **nempne**, name.

for wantynge of privy wordes, but paradyse terrestre ful of delycious melody, withouten travayle in sown, perpetual servyce in ful joye coveyted to endure. Onely kynde maketh hertes in understonding so to slepe that otherwyse may it nat be nempned, ne in other maner names for lykyng swetnesse can I nat it declare. Al sugre and hony, al mynstralsy and melody ben but soote and galle in comparison, by no maner proporcion to reken in respecte of this blysful joye. This armony, this melody, this perdurable joye may nat be in doynge, but betwene hevens and elementes or twey kyndly hertes ful knyt in trouth of naturel understondyng, withouten wenynge and disceit as hevens and planettes, whiche thynges contynually for kyndly accordaunces foryeteth al contrarious mevynges that into passyve diseases may sowne. Evermore it thyrsteth after more werkyng. These thynges in proporcion be so wel joyned that it undoth al thyng whiche into badnesse by any way may be accompted." "Certes," quod I, "this is a thyng precious and noble. Alas, that falsnesse ever or wantrust shulde ever be maynteyned this joye to voyde. Alas, that ever any wretch shulde thorowe wrath or envy janglynge dare make

---

for wantynge of priuy wordes/ but paradyse terrestre ful of delycious melody/ withouten trauayle in sown/ p*er*petual seruyce in ful ioye coueyted to endure. Onely kynde maketh hertes in vnderstondi*ng* so to slepe/ that otherwyse may it nat be ne*m*pned/ ne i*n* other maner names for lykyng swetnesse can I nat it declare/ al sugre *and* hony/ al mynstralsy *and* melody ben but soote and galle in co*m*parison by no maner p*ro*porcion to reken/ **<344rb><344va>**in respecte of this blysful ioye. This armony this melody/ this p*er*durable ioye may nat be in doynge/ but betwene heuens *and* elementes/ or twey kyndly hertes/ ful knyt in trouth of naturel vndersto*n*dyng/ withouten wenynge and disceit/ as heuens *and* planettes/ whiche thynges co*n*tynually for kyndly accordau*n*ces/ foryeteth al contrarious meuynges/ that in to passyue diseases may sowne/ euermore it thyrsteth after more werkyng. These thynges in proporcion be so wel ioyned/ that it vndoth al thyng/ whiche in to badnesse by any way may be acco*m*pted. Certes (q*uo*d I) this is a thyng p*re*cious and noble. Alas that falsnesse euer or wantrust shulde euer be maynteyned/ this ioye to voyde. Alas that euer any wretch shulde thorowe wrath or enuy/ ianglynge dare make

836 privy, appropriate. **840 reken**, reckon. **842 twey**, two. **843 wenynge**, presumption. **844 foryeteth**, forget. **845 passyve**, listless, unresponsive; **sowne**, lead. **847 accompted**, accounted; **Certes**, Certainly. **848 wantrust**, despair. **849 voyde**, [render] void; **thorowe**, through; **janglynge**, complaint.

to shove this melody so farre a backe that openly dare it nat ben used. Trewly, wretches ben fulfylled with envy and wrathe and no wight els. Flebring and tales in such wretches dare appere openly in every wightes eare, with ful mouth so charged, mokel malyce moved many innocentes to shende — God wolde their soule therwith were strangled. Lo, trouth in this blysse is hyd and overal under covert him hydeth. He dare nat come a place for waytynge of shrewes. Commenly badnesse goodnesse amaistreth; with myselfe and my soule this joye wolde I bye if the goodnesse were as moche as the nobley in melody." "O," quod she, "what goodnesse may be acompted more in this material worlde? Truly, non. That shalt thou understonde. Is nat every thing good that is contrariant and distroyeng yvel?" "Howe els," quod I. "Envy, wrathe, and falsnesse ben general," quod she, "and that wot every man beyng in his ryght mynde. The knotte the whiche we have in this blysse is contraryaunt and distroyeth such maner yvels. *Ergo*, it is good. What hath caused any wight to don any good dede? Fynde me any good, but if this knotte be the chefe cause. Nedes mote it be good that causeth so many good dedes.

---

to shoue this melody so farre a backe/ that ope*n*ly dare it nat ben vsed: trewly wretches ben fulfylled with enuy *and* wrathe/ and no wight els. Flebring *and* tales in such wretches dare appere openly in euery wightes eare/ with ful mouth so charged/ mokel malyce moued many innoct*en*es to shende/ god wolde their soule therwith were stra*n*gled. Lo/ trouth in this blysse is hyd and oueral vnder couert him hydeth: He dare nat come a place for waytynge of shrewes.

Co*mm*enly badnesse/ goodnesse amaistreth/ wi*th* my selfe *and* my soule this ioye wolde I bye/ if the goodnesse were as moche as the nobley in melody. O (q*uo*d she) what goodnesse may be aco*m*pted more i*n* this material worlde/ truly non that shalt thou vndersto*n*de. Is nat euery thi*n*g good that is co*n*trariant and distroyeng yuel? Howe els (q*uo*d I) Enuy/ wrathe *and* falsnesse ben general (q*uo*d she) *and* that wot euery man beyng in his ryght mynde/ the knotte the whiche we haue in this blysse/ is contraryaunt and distroyeth such maner yuels. Ergo it is good. What hath caused any wight to don any good dede? Fynde me any good/ but if this knotte be the chefe cause: Nedes mote it be good/ that causeth so many good dedes.

850 a backe, backward. **851 wight**, person; **Flebring**, Chattering. **852 mokel**, much. **853 shende**, destroy. **855 waytynge**, ambush; **amaistreth**, overcomes. **856 bye**, buy; **nobley**, nobleness. **857 acompted**, accounted. **860 wot**, knows. **861 *Ergo***, Therefore. **863 Nedes mote**, Needs must.

Every cause is more and worthyer than thynge caused, and in that mores possessyon al thinges lesse ben compted. As the king is more than his people and hath in possessyon al his realme after. Right so the knot is more than al other goodes. Thou myght recken al thynges lasse and that to hym longeth oweth into his mores cause of worshyp and of wyl do turne. It is els rebel and out of his mores defendyng to voyde. Right so of every goodnesse into the knot and into the cause of his worshyp oweth to tourne. And trewly every thyng that hath beyng profytably is good, but nothyng hath to ben more profytably than this knot. Kynges it maintayneth and hem their powers to mayntayne: It maketh mysse to ben amended with good governaunce in doyng. It closeth hertes so togyder that rancour is out thresten. Who that it lengest kepeth, lengest is gladed." "I trowe," quod I, "heretykes and mysse meanyng people hence forwarde wol maintayne this knotte, for therthorough shul they ben maintayned and utterly wol turne and leave their olde yvel understandyng, and knytte this goodnesse and profer so ferre in servyce that name of servauntes myght they have. Their jangles shal cease. Me thynketh hem lacketh

---

Euery cause is more and worthyer than thynge caused/ and in that mores possessyon/ al thinges lesse ben compted. As the king is more than his people and hath in possessyon al his realme after: Right so the knot is more than al other goo**<344va><344vb>**des/ thou myght recken al thynges lasse/ and that to hym longeth oweth in to his mores cause of worshyp and of wyl do turne/ it is els rebel and out of his mores defendyng to voyde. Right so of euery goodnesse in to the knot and in to the cause of his worshyp oweth to tourne. And trewly euery thyng that hath beyng profytably is good/ but nothyng hath to ben more profytably than this knot: kynges it maintayneth/ and hem their powers to mayntayne: It maketh mysse to ben amended with good gouernaunce in doyng. It closeth hertes so togyder/ that ra*n*cour is out thresten. Who that it lengest kepeth/ lengest is gladed. I trowe (q*uo*d I) heretykes and mysse meanyng people hence forwarde wol maintayne this knotte/ for therthorough shul they ben maintayned/ and vtterly wol turne and leaue their olde yuel vnderstandyng/ *and* knytte this goodnesse/ and profer so ferre in seruyce/ that name of seruauntes myght they haue. Their iangles shal cease/ me thynketh hem lacketh

864 mores, superior's. **865 compted**, counted. **867 longeth**, belongs; **mores**, supervisor's. **872 mysse**, error, misdeed. **873 out thresten**, thrust out; **lengest**, longest; **trowe**, believe. **874 mysse meanyng**, error-prone. **875 leave**, leave. **876 ferre**, far. **877 jangles**, absurdities.

mater nowe to alege." "Certes," quod Love, "if they of good wil thus turned, as thou sayst, wolen trewly perfourme, yet shul they be abled party of this blysse to have. And they wol not, yet shul my servauntes the werre wel susteyne in myn helpe of maintenaunce to the ende. And they for their good travayle shullen in rewarde so ben meded, that endelesse joye, body and soule togyther, in this shullen abyden. There is ever action of blysse withouten possyble corrupcion; there is action perpetuel in werke without travayle; there is everlastyng passyfe withouten any of labour. Contynuel plyte, without ceasynge, coveyted to endure. No tonge may tel ne hert may thinke the leest poynte of this blysse."

"God bring me thyder," quod I than. "Contynueth wel," quod she, "to the ende, and thou might not fayle than, for though thou spede not here, yet shal the passyon of thy martred lyfe ben written and radde toforne the great Jupyter, that god is of routhe, an hygh in the holownesse of heven, there he sytte in his trone: and ever thou shalt forwarde ben holden amonge al these hevyns for a knyght that mightest with no penaunce ben discomfyted. He is a very martyr that lyvyngly goynge is gnawen to

---

mater nowe to alege. Certes (quod Loue) if they of good wil thus turned as thou sayst wolen trewly perfourme/ yet shul they be abled party of this blysse to haue: and they wol not/ yet shul my seruau*n*tes the werre wel susteyne in myn helpe of maintenaunce to the ende. And they for their good trauayle shullen in rewarde so ben meded/ that endelesse ioye body and soule togyther in this shullen abyden/ there is euer action of blysse withouten possyblc corrupcion/ there is action p*er*petuel in werke without trauayle/ there is euerlastyng passyfe/ withouten any of labour: contynuel plyte without ceasynge coueyted to endure.

No tonge may tel ne hert may thinke the leest poynte of this blysse. God bring me thyder (q*uo*d I than) Contynueth wel (q*uo*d she) to the ende/ *and* thou might not fayle than/ for though thou spede not here/ yet shal the passyon of thy martred lyfe ben written and radde toforne the great Jupyter that god is of routhe/ an hygh in the holownesse of heuen/ there he sytte in his trone: and euer thou shalt forwarde ben holden amonge al these heuyns for a knyght/ that mightest with no penaunce ben discomfyted. He is a very martyr that lyuyngly go**<344vb><345ra>**ynge is gnawen to

878 alege, allege, adduce. **879 wolen**, will. **880 werre**, war. **882 meded**, satisfied; **shullen**, shall. **884 plyte**, condition. **885 leest**, least. **888 spede**, prosper. **889 martred**, martyred; **radde**, read; **routhe**, pity. **890 holownesse**, cavity; **trone**, throne. **892 penaunce**, pain; **lyvyngly**, still alive.

the bones." "Certes," quod I, "these ben good wordes of comforte; a lytel myne herte is rejoyced in a mery wyse." "Ye," quod she, "and he that is in heven felyth more joye than whan he firste herde therof speke." "So it is," quod I, "but wyst I the sothe that after disease comforte wolde folowe with blysse, so as ye have often declared, I wolde wel suffre this passyon with the better chere, but my thoughtful sorowe is endelesse to thinke howe I am cast out of a welfare, and yet dayneth not this yvel none herte none hede to mewarde throwe which thynges wolde greatly me by wayes of comforte disporte to weten in myselfe a lytel with other me ben ymoned; and my sorowes peysen not in her balaunce the weyght of a peese. Slynges of her daunger so hevyly peysen, they drawe my causes so hye, that in her eyen they semen but lyght and right lytel."

"O, for," quod she, "heven with skyes that foule cloudes maken and darke wethers with gret tempestes and huge, maketh the mery dayes with softe shynyng sonnes. Also the yere with draweth floures and beautie of herbes and of erth. The same yeres maketh springes and jolyté in Vere so to renovel with peynted coloures, that erthe semeth as gay

---

the bones. Certes (q*uo*d I) these ben good wordes of co*m*forte/ a lytel myne herte is reioyced in a mery wyse. Ye (q*uo*d she) and he that is in heuen felyth more ioye/ than whan he firste herde therof speke. So it is (q*uo*d I) but wyst I the sothe/ that after disease comforte wolde folowe with blysse/ so as ye haue often declared/ I wolde wel suffre this passyon with the better chere/ but my thoughtful sorowe is endelesse/ to thinke howe I am cast out of a welfare/ *and* yet dayneth not this yuel none herte none hede to mewarde throwe/ which thynges wolde greatly me by wayes of comforte disporte/ to weten in my selfe a lytel with other me ben ymoned: and my sorowes peysen not in her balaunce the weyght of a peese: Slynges of her daunger so heuyly peysen/ they drawe my causes so hye/ that in her eyen they semen but lyght and right lytel.

O/ for (q*uo*d she) heuen with skyes that foule cloudes maken and darke wethers/ with gret tempestes and huge/ maketh the mery dayes with softe shynyng sonnes. Also the yere with draweth floures and beautie of herbes and of erth. The same yeres maketh springes and iolyte in Vere so to renouel with peynted coloures/ that erthe semeth as gay

894 felyth, feels. **895 wyst**, knew. **898 dayneth**, deigns. **898–99 none . . . none hede**, neither heart nor head. **899 to mewarde**, toward me; **throwe**, cast; **disporte**, refresh. **900 weten**, know; **with . . . ymoned**, that by others I am lamented; **peysen**, weigh. **901 her**, their; **peese**, pea; **daunger**, peril. **902 hye**, high. **903 wethers**, storms. **905 yere**, year. **906 Vere**, Summer; **renovel**, renew.

as heven. Sees that blasteth and with wawes throweth shyppes, of whiche the lyvyng creatures for great peryl for hem dreden. Right so the same sees maketh smothe waters and golden saylyng and comforteth hem with noble haven that firste were so ferde. Hast thou not," quod she, "lerned in thy youth, that Jupyter hath in his warderobe bothe garmentes of joye and of sorowe? What wost thou howe soone he wol turne of thee the garment of care, and clothe thee in blysse? Pardé, it is not ferre fro thee. Lo, an olde proverbe aleged by many wyse: 'Whan bale is greatest than is bote a nye bore.' Wherof wylte thou dismaye? Hope wel and serve wel, and that shal thee save, with thy good byleve."

"Ye, ye," quod I, "yet se I not by reason howe this blysse is comyng — I wote it is contyngent. It may fal on other." "O," quod she, "I have mokel to done to clere thyne understandyng and voyde these errours out of thy mynde. I wol prove it by reason thy wo may not alway enduren. Every thyng kyndely," quod she, "is governed and ruled by the hevenly bodyes, whiche haven ful werchynge here on erthe, and after course of these bodyes, al course of your doynges here ben governed and ruled by kynde.

---

as heuen. Sees that blasteth and with wawes throweth shyppes/ of whiche the lyuyng creatures for great peryl for hem dreden: right so th*e* same sees maketh smothe waters and golden saylyng/ and comforteth hem with noble hauen that firste were so ferde. Hast thou not (q*uo*d she) lerned in thy youth/ that Jupyter hath in his warderobe bothe garmentes of ioye and of sorowe? What wost thou howe soone he wol turne of the th*e* garment of care/ *and* clothe the in blysse? parde it is not ferre fro the. Lo an olde pronerbe aleged by many wyse: Whan bale is greatest/ than is bote a nye bore. Wherof wylte thou dismaye? hope wel and serue wel/ and that shal the saue/ with thy good byleue.

Ye/ ye (quod I) yet se I not by reason howe this blysse is comyng/ I wote it is contynge*nt*/ it may fal on other. O (q*uo*d she) I haue mokel to done to clere thyne vnderstandyng and voyde these errours out of thy mynde/ I wol proue it by reason thy wo may not alway en**<345ra><345rb>**duren. Euery thyng kyndely (q*uo*d she) is gouerned *and* ruled by the heuenly bodyes/ whiche hauen ful werchynge here on erthe/ and after course of these bodyes/ al course of your doynges here ben gouerned and ruled by kynde.

907 wawes, waves. **909 ferde**, afraid. **911 wost**, know. **912 Pardé**, indeed; **ferre**, far. **913 aleged**, alleged, adduced; **bale**, harm; **bote**, remedy; **nye bore**, neighbor. **915 wote**, know. **918 kyndely**, natural. **919 werchynge**, working.

"Thou wost wel by cours of planettes al your dayes proceden, and to everich of synguler houres be enterchaunged stondmele about, by submytted worchyng naturally to suffre, of whiche changes cometh these transitory tymes that maketh revolvyng of your yeres thus stondmele. Every hath ful might of worchynge, tyl al seven han had her cours about. Of which worchynges and possessyon of houres the dayes of the weke have take her names after denomination in these seven planettes. Lo, your Sonday gynneth at the first hour afternoon on the Saturday, in whiche hour is than the sonne in ful might of worchyng, of whom Sonday taketh his name. Next him foloweth Venus and after Mercurius, and than the Moone, so than Saturnus after whom Jovis, and than Mars, and ayen than the Sonne, and so forth, be twenty-four houres togider, in whiche hour gynnyng in the seconde day stante the Moone, as maister for that tyme to rule, of whom Monday taketh his name. And this course foloweth of al other dayes generally in doyng. This course of nature of these bodyes chaungyng stynten at a certayne terme, lymytted by their first kynde. And of hem al governementes in this elemented worlde proceden, as in springes, constellacions, engendrures, and al that folowen kynde and reson. Wherfore the course that foloweth sorowe and joy, kyndely moten entrechangen

---

Thou wost wel by cours of planettes al yo*ur* dayes proceden/ *and* to euerich of synguler houres be enterchau*n*ged stondmele about/ by submytted worchyng naturally to suffre/ of whiche changes cometh these tra*n*sitory tymes that maketh reuoluyng of your yeres thus stondmele/ euery hath ful might of worchynge/ tyl al seuen han had her cours about. Of which worchynges *and* possessyon of houres/ th*e* dayes of the weke haue take her names/ after denomination i*n* these seuen planettes. Lo your so*n*day gynneth at th*e* first hour afternoon on the saturday/ in whiche hour is than the sonne in ful might of worchyng/ of whom *s*onday taketh his name. Next him foloweth Venus/ *and* after Mercurius/ *and* than the Moone/ so than Saturnus/ after who*m* Jouis/ *and* than Mars and ayen tha*n* the Sonne/ *and* so forth be . xxiiii. houres togider/ in whiche hour gynnyng in th*e* seconde day stante the Moone/ as maister for that tyme to rule/ of whom mo*n*day taketh his name/ and this course foloweth of al other dayes generally in doyng. This course of nature of these bodyes chaungyng/ stynten at a certayne terme/ lymytted by their first kynde/ and of hem al gouernementes in this elemented worlde proceden/ as in springes/ constellacions/ engendrures/ *and* al that folowen kynde and reson/ wherfore the course that foloweth sorowe and ioy/ kyndely moten entrechangen

924 stondmele, at regular intervals. **930 be**, by. **933 stynten**, ceases. **936 moten**, must.

their tymes, so that alway on wele as alway on wo may not endure. Thus seest thou appertly thy sorowe into wele mote ben chaunged; wherfore in suche case to better syde evermore enclyne thou shuldest. Trewly, next the ende of sorowe anon entreth joy. By maner of necessyté it wol ne may non other betyde, and so thy contingence is disproved. If thou holde this opinion any more, thy wyt is right leude. Wherfore in ful conclusyon of al this, thilke Margaryte thou desyrest hath ben to thee dere in thy herte, and for her hast thou suffred many thoughtful diseases, herafter shal be cause of mokel myrth and joye, and loke howe glad canste thou ben, and cease al thy passed hevynesse with manyfolde joyes. And than wol I as blythly here thee speken thy myrthes in joy as I nowe have yherde thy sorowes and thy complayntes. And if I mowe in aught thy joye encrease, by my trouthe, on my syde shal nat be leaved for no maner traveyle that I with al my myghtes right blythly wol helpe, and ever ben redy you bothe to plese. And than thanked I that lady with al goodly maner that I worthely coude, and trewly I was greatly rejoysed in myne hert of her fayre behestes, and proferd me to be slawe, in al that she me wolde ordeyne, while my lyfe lested.

---

their tymes/ so that alway on wele as alway on wo may not endure. Thus seest thou appertly thy sorowe in to wele mote ben chaunged/ wherfore in suche case to better syde euermore enclyne thou shuldest. Trewly next the ende of sorowe anon entreth ioy/ by maner of necessyte it wol ne may non other betyde/ and so thy contygence is disproued: if thou holde this opinion any more/ thy wyt is right leude. Wherfore in ful conclusyon of al this/ thilke Margaryte thou desyrest/ hath ben to the dere in thy herte/ and for her hast thou suffred many thoughtful diseases/ herafter shal be cause**<345rb><345va>**of mokel myrth and ioye/ and loke howe glad canste thou ben/ and cease al thy passed heuynesse with manyfolde ioyes. And than wol I as blythly here the speken thy myrthes in ioy/ as I nowe haue yherde thy sorowes and thy complayntes. And if I mowe in aught thy ioye encrease/ by my trouthe on my syde shal nat be leaued for no maner traueyle/ that I with al my myghtes right blythly wol helpe/ and euer ben redy you bothe to plese. And tha*n* thanked I that lady with al goodly maner th*at* I worthely coude/ and trewly I was greatly reioysed in myne hert/ of her fayre behestes/ *and* proferd me to be slawe in al that she me wolde ordeyne while my lyfe lested.

937 wele, prosperity. **938 appertly**, openly; **mote**, must. **940 betyde**, fall out. **941 leude**, uninformed. **942 dere**, dear, precious. **943 mokel**, much. **947 leaved**, left out. **950 slawe**, [ready to be] slain. **951 lested**, lasted.

Chapter X

"Me thynketh," quod I, "that ye have right wel declared, that way to the knot shuld not ben in none of these disprovynge thynges, and nowe order of our purpose this asketh, that ye shulde me shewe if any way be thyther, and whiche thilke way shulde ben, so that openly maye be sey the verry hye waye in ful confusyoun of these other thynges."

"Thou shalt," quod she, "understande that one of thre lyves (as I fyrst sayd) every creature of mankynde is sprongen, and so forth procedeth. These lyves ben thorowe names departed in thre maner of kyndes, as bestiallyche, manlyche, and resonablyche, of whiche two ben used by flesshely body, and the thirde by his soule. Bestial among resonables is forboden in every lawe and every secte, bothe in Christen and other, for every wight dispyseth hem that lyveth by lustes and delytes, as him that is thral and bounden servaunt to thynges right foule. Suche ben compted werse than men; he shal nat in their degré ben rekened ne for suche one alowed. Heritykes, sayne they, chosen lyfe bestial, that voluptuously lyven, so that (as I first sayde to thee) in manly and resonable lyvenges, our mater was to declare. But manly lyfe in lyveng after flesshe or els flesshly

---

ME thynketh (q*uo*d I) that ye haue right wel declared/ that way to th*e* knot shuld not ben in none of these disprouynge thynges/ and nowe order of our purpose this asketh/ that ye shulde me shewe if any way be thyther/ and whiche thilke way shulde ben/ so that openly maye be sey/ the verry hye waye in ful confusyoun of these other thynges.

Thou shalt (quod she) vnderstande/ that one of thre lyues (as I fyrst sayd) euery creature of mankynde is sprongen/ and so forth procedeth. These lyues ben thorowe names departed in thre maner of kyndes/ as bestiallyche/ manlyche/ and resonablyche/ of whiche two ben vsed by flesshely body/ and the thirde by his soule. Bestial among resonables is forboden in euery lawe and euery secte/ bothe in christen and other/ for euery wight dispyseth hem that lyueth by lustes and delytes/ as him that is thral and bounden seruaunt to thynges right foule/ suche ben compted werse than men/ he shal nat in their degre ben rekened/ ne for suche one alowed. Heritykes sayne they/ chosen lyfe bestial/ that voluptuously lyuen/ so that (as I first sayde to the) in manly and resonable lyueng*es/* our mater was to declare/ but manly lyfe in lyueng after flesshe or els flesshly

955 sey, seen. **957 sprongen**, sprung. **961 wight**, person. **962 compted**, accounted.

wayes to chese may nat blysse in this knotte be conquered, as by reason it is proved. Wherfore by resonable lyfe he must nedes it have, sithe a way is to this knotte, but nat by the firste tway lyves, wherfore nedes mote it ben to the thirde. And for to lyve in flesshe but nat after flessh is more resonablich than man lyche rekened by clerkes. Therfore howe this waye cometh in I wol it blythely declare.

"Se nowe," quod she, "that these bodily goodes of manliche lyvenges yelden soroufully stoundes and smertande houres. Whoso wele remembre him to their endes, in their worchinges they ben thoughtful and sorie. Right as a bee that hath hadde his hony anone at his flyght begynneth to stynge; so thilke bodily goodes at the laste mote awaye, and than stynge they at her goynge, wherthrough entreth and clene voydeth al blisse of this knot."

"Forsothe," quod I, "me thynketh I am wel served in shewyng of these wordes. Although I hadde lytel in respecte amonge other great and worthy, yet had I a faire parcel as me thought for the tyme in forthering of my sustenauce whiche, while it dured, I thought me havynge mokel hony to myne estate. I had richesse suffisauntly to weyve nede; I had dignité to be reverenced in worship. Power me thought that I had to

---

wayes to chese/ may nat blysse in this knotte be co*n*quered/ as by reason it is proued. Wherfore by resonable lyfe he must nedes it haue/ sithe away is to this knotte/ but nat by the firste tway lyues/ wherfore nedes mote it ben to the thirde/ and for to lyue in flesshe but**<345va><345vb>**nat after flessh/ is more resonablich tha*n* man lyche rekened by clerkes. Therfore howe this waye cometh in/ I wol it blythely declare.

Se nowe (quod she) that these bodily goodes of manliche lyuenges/ yelden soroufully stoundes and smerta*n*de houres/ Who so wele remembre him to their endes/ in their worchi*n*ges they ben thoughtful and sorie. Right as a bee that hath hadde his hony/ anone at his flyght begynneth to stynge: So thilke bodily goodes at the laste mote awaye/ and than stynge they at her goynge/ wherthrough entreth and clene voydeth al blisse of this knot.

Forsothe (quod I) me thynketh I am wel serued/ in shewyng of these wordes. although I hadde lytel in respecte amonge other great and worthy/ yet had I a faire parcel/ as me thought for the tyme/ in forthering of my sustenauce/ whiche while it dured/ I thought me hauynge mokel hony to myne estate. I had richesse suffisauntly to weyue nede/ I had dignite to be reuerenced in worship. Power me thought that I had to

968 mote, must. **971 yelden**, yield. **972 stoundes**, times; **smertande**, smarting. **974 mote**, must. **980 mokel**, much. **981 weyve**, forestall.

kepe fro myne enemyes and me semed to shyne in glorie of renome as manhode asketh in meane. For no wight in myne admynistration coude non yvels ne trechery by sothe cause on me putte. Lady, yourselve weten wel that of tho confederacies maked by my soverayns I nas but a servaunt, and yet mokel meane folke wol fully ayenst reason thilke maters maynteyne, in whiche mayntenaunce glorien themselfe; and as often ye haven sayde therof ought nothynge in yvel to be layde to mewardes, sythen as repentaunt I am tourned, and no more I thynke, neither tho thynges ne none suche other to sustene but utterly distroye without medlynge maner in al my mightes. Howe am I nowe caste out of al swetnesse of blysse and myschevously stongen my passed joy? Sorοufully muste I bewayle and lyve as a wretche.

Every of tho joyes is tourned into his contrary: For richesse nowe have I poverté, for dignité, nowe am I enprisoned. Instede of power, wretchednesse I suffre, and for glorye of renome I am nowe dispised and foulych hated. Thus hath farn fortune, that sodaynly am I overthrowen and out of al welth dispoyled. Trewly, me thynketh this way in entre is right harde. God graunt me better grace er it be al passed. The other way,

---

kepe fro myne enemyes and me semed to shyne in glorie of renome as manhode asketh in meane/ for no wight in myne admynistration coude non yuels ne trechery by sothe cause on me putte. Lady your selue weten wel/ that of tho confederacies maked by my souerayns I nas but a seruaunt/ and yet mokel meane folke wol fully ayenst reason thilke maters maynteyne/ in whiche mayntenaunce glorien them selfe/ and as often ye hauen sayde/ therof ought nothynge in yuel to be layde to mewardes/ sythen as repe*n*taunt I am tourned/ and no more I thynke/ neither tho thynges ne none suche other to sustene/ but vtterly distroye without medlynge maner/ in al my mightes. Howe am I nowe caste out of al swetnesse of blysse/ and myscheuously stongen my passed ioy? souroufully muste I bewayle/ and lyue as a wretche.

Euery of tho ioyes is tourned in to his contrary: For richesse nowe haue I pouerte/ for dignite nowe am I enprisoned/ in stede of power wretchednesse I suffre/ and for glorye of renome I am nowe dispised/ and foulych hated: thus hath farn fortune/ that sodaynly am I ouerthrowen/ *and* out of al welth dispoyled.**<345vb><346ra>**trewly me thynketh this way in entre is right harde/ god graunt me better grace er it be al passed/ the other way

982 renome, renown. **983 in meane**, in moderation; **wight**, person. **984 weten**, know. **985 mokel**, many. **987 sythen**, since. **992 his**, its. **994 farn**, fared.

ladye, me thought right swete." "Nowe certes," quod Love, "me lyst for to chide. What ayleth thy darke dulnesse? Wol it nat in clerenesse ben sharped? Have I nat by many reasons to the shewed suche bodily goodes faylen to yeve blysse, their might so ferforthe wol nat stretche? Shame," quod she, "it is to say thou lyest in thy wordes. Thou ne hast wyst but right fewe that these bodily goodes had al atones. Commenly they dwellen nat togider. He that plenté hath in riches, of his kynne is ashamed; another of lynage right noble and wel knowe; but povert him handleth, he were lever unknowe. Another hath these, but renome of peoples praysyng may he nat have. Overal he is hated and defamed of thynges right foule. Another is faire and semely, but dignité him fayleth, and he that hath dignyté is croked or lame or els misshapen and fouly dispysed. Thus partable these goodes dwellen commenly; in one houshold ben they but sylde. Lo, howe reetched is your truste on thyng that wol nat accorde. Me thinketh thou clepest thilke plyte thou were in selynesse of fortune, and thou sayest for that the selynesse is departed, thou arte a wretch. Than foloweth this upon thy wordes: every soule resonable of man may nat dye, and if dethe endeth selynesse and maketh wretches, as nedes of

---

ladye me thought right swete. Nowe certes (q*uo*d Loue) me lyst for to chide. What ayleth thy darke dulnesse? wol it nat in clerenesse ben sharped. Haue I nat by many reasons to the shewed suche bodily goodes faylen to yeue blysse/ their might so ferforthe wol nat stretche? Shame (q*uo*d she it is to say) thou lyest in thy word*es*. Thou ne hast wyst but right fewe/ that these bodily goodes had al atones/ co*m*menly they dwellen nat togider. He that plente hath in riches/ of his kynne is a shamed: another of lynage right noble *and* wel knowe/ but pouert him ha*n*dleth he were leuer vnknowe. Another hath these/ but reno*m*e of peoples praysyng may he nat haue/ oueral he is hated *and* defamed of thynges right foule. Another is faire *and* semely but dignite him fayleth: *and* he that hath dignyte is croked or lame/ or els misshapen *and* fouly dispysed. thus p*ar*table these goodes dwellen/ com*m*enly i*n* one houshold ben they but sylde. Lo howe reetched is your truste/ on thyng that wol nat accorde. Me thi*n*keth thou clepest thilke plyte thou were in selynesse of fortune/ *and* thou sayest for that th*e* selynesse is dep*ar*ted/ thou arte a wretch. Than foloweth this vpon thy wordes/ euery soule resonable of man/ may nat dye/ *and* if dethe endeth selynesse *and* maketh wretches/ as nedes of

997 me lyst, it pleases me. **999 yeve**, give. **1000 ferforthe**, far. **1001 wyst**, known; **atones**, at once. **1003 lynage**, lineage; **were lever**, would rather [be]. **1007 partable**, not whole; **houshold**, i.e., place; **sylde**, seldom. **1009 plyte**, condition; **selynesse**, felicity. **1011 selynesse**, happiness; **as nedes**, necessarily.

fortune maketh it an ende. Than soules after dethe of the body in wretchednesse shulde lyven. But we knowe many that han geten the blysse of heven after their dethe. Howe than may this lyfe maken men blysful, that whan it passeth it yeveth no wretchednesse, and many tymes blysse, if in this lyfe he con lyve as he shulde? And wolte thou acompt with fortune, that nowe at the first she hath done thee tene and sorowe. If thou loke to the maner of al glad thynges and sorouful, thou mayst nat nay it, that yet, and namely nowe, thou standest in noble plyte in a good ginnyng with good forth goyng herafter. And if thou wene to be a wretch, for such welth is passed, why than art thou nat wel fortunate for badde thynges and anguys wretchednesse ben passed? Art thou nowe come first in to the hostry of this lyfe, or else the both of this worlde? Art thou nowe a sodayne gest into this wretched exile? Wenest there be any thynge in this erthe stable? Is nat thy first arest passed that brought thee in mortal sorowe? Ben these nat mortal thynges agon with ignorance of beestial wyt and hast receyved reason in knowyng of vertue? What comforte is in thy hert? The knowinge sykerly in my servyce be grounded. And woste thou nat wel as I said that deth maketh ende of al fortune? What than?

---

fortune maketh it an ende/ Than soules after dethe of th*e* body in wretchednesse shulde lyuen But we knowe many that han geten th*e* blysse of heuen after their dethe. Howe th*an* may this lyfe maken men blysful/ that whan it passeth it yeueth no wretchednesse/ and many tymes blysse/ if in this lyfe he con lyue as he shulde. And wolte thou aco*m*pt with fortune/ th*at* nowe at he first she hath done the tene *and* sorowe: if th*ou* loke to the maner of al glad thynges *and* sorouful/ thou mayst nat nay it that yet/ *and* namely nowe thou sta*n*dest in noble plyte in a good gi*n*nyng/ with good forth goyng herafter. And if thou wene to be a wretch for such welth is passed/ why than art thou nat wel fortunate for badde thynges *and* anguys wretchednesse be*n* passed? Art thou nowe come first in to the hostry of this lyfe/ or else the both of this worlde/ art**<346ra><346rb>**thou nowe a sodayne gest in to this wretched exile? Wenest there be any thynge in this erthe stable? Is nat thy first arest passed/ th*at* brouȝt the in mortal sorowe? Ben these nat mortal thynges agon with ignorance of beestial wyt and hast receyued reason in knowyng of vertue? What co*m*forte is in thy hert? the know*in*ge sykerly in my seruyce be grou*n*ded. And woste thou nat wel as I said/ that deth maketh ende of al fortune? What than/

1014 yeveth, gives. **1015 acompt**, present a bill to. **1016 tene**, grief. **1018 plyte**, condition. **1019 wene**, imagine [yourself]. **1020 anguys**, anxious. **1021 hostry**, hostelry. **1022 sodayne**, sudden; **gest**, guest; **Wenest**, Do you believe. **1024 hast**, i.e., you have. **1025 sykerly**, certainly.

Standest thou in noble plyte, lytel hede or reckyng to take, if thou let fortune passe dying, or els that she fly whan her lyst, now by thy lyve? Pardy, a man hath nothyng so lefe as his lyfe, and for to holde that he doth al his cure and dilygent traveyle. Than say I thou art blysful and fortunat sely, if thou knowe thy goodes that thou hast yet be loved whiche nothynge may doute, that they ne ben more worthy than thy lyfe?" "What is that," quod I. "Good contemplation," quod she, "of wel doing in vertue in tyme comyng, bothe in plesaunce of me and of thy Margarit peerl. Hastely thyn hert in ful blysse with her shalbe eased. Therfore, dismay thee nat. Fortune in hate grevously ayenst thy bodily person, ne yet to gret tempest hath she nat sent to thee, sithen the holdyng cables and ankers of thy lyfe holden by knyttyng so faste that thou discomforte thee nought of tyme that is now, ne dispayre thee not of tyme to come, but yeven thee comforte in hope of wel doyng and of gettyng agayne the double of thy lesyng with encreasyng love of thy Margarite perle therto. For this hyderto thou hast had al her ful daunger, and so thou myght amende al that is mysse, and al defautes that somtyme thou dyddest, and that now in al thy tyme to that ilke Margaryte in ful servyce of my lore thyne herte hath

---

sta*n*dest thou in noble plyte lytel hede or rcekyng to take/ if thou let fortune passe dyng/ or els that she fly wha*n* her lyst/ now by thy lyue. Pardy a man hath nothyng so lefe as his lyfe/ *and* for to holde that he doth al his cure *and* dilygent traueyle. Than say I thou art blysful *and* fortunat sely/ if thou knowe thy goodes that thou hast yet be loued whiche nothynge may doute/ that they ne ben more worthy than thy lyfe? What is that (q*uo*d I) Good conte*m*plation (q*uo*d she) of wel doing in vertue in tyme comyng/ bothe in plesaunce of me *and* of thy Margarit peerle: Hastely thyn hert in ful blysse with her shalbe eased. Therfore dismay the nat/ fortune i*n* hate greuously ayenst thy bodily p*er*son/ ne yet to gret tempest hath she nat sent to the/ sithen the holdyng cables *and* ankers of thy lyfe/ holden by knyttyng so faste/ that thou discomforte the nought of tyme that is now/ ne dispayre the not of tyme to come/ but yeuen the comforte in hope of wel doyng/ and of gettyng agayne the double of thy lesyng/ with encreasyng loue of thy Margarite perle therto. For this hyderto thou hast had al her ful dauuger/ and so thou myght amende al that is mysse/ and al defautes that somtyme thou dyddest/ and that now in al thy tyme to that ilke Margaryte in ful seruyce of my lore thyne herte hath

1027 plyte, condition; **reckyng**, caring. **1028 Pardy**, Indeed. **1029 lefe**, desirable (precious). **1030 sely**, felicitous. **1035 to**, too. **1037 yeven**, give. **1038 lesyng**, [what you] lost. **1039 daunger**, resistance. **1040 defautes**, trespasses. **1041 ilke**, same.

contynued, wherfore she ought moche the rather enclyne fro her daungerous sete. These thynges ben yet knyt by the holdyng anker in thy lyve, and holden mote they. Lo God, I pray al these thynges at ful ben performed. For whyle this anker holdeth I hope thou shalte safely escape, and whyle thy trewe meanyng servyce aboute bringe, in dispyte of al false meaners, that thee of newe haten; for in this trewe servyce thou arte nowe entred."

"Certayn," quod I, "amonge thynges I asked a question, whiche was the way to the knot. Trewly, lady, howe so it be I tempt you with questions and answers in spekyng of my first service, I am nowe in ful purpose in the pricke of the hert, that thilke service was an enprisonment and alway bad and naughty, in no maner to be desyred. Ne that in gettyng of the knot may it nothyng aveyle. A wyse gentyl hert loketh after vertue and none other bodily joyes alone. And bycause to forne this in tho wayes I was sette, I wote wel myselfe I have erred and of the blysse fayled, and so out of my way hugely have I ron." "Certes," quod she, "that is sothe, and there thou hast myswent, eschewe the pathe from hens forwarde, I rede. Wonder I trewly why the mortal folke of this worlde

---

contynued/ wherfore she ought moche the rather enclyne fro her daungerous sete. These thynges ben yet knyt by the holdyng anker in thy lyue/ and holden mote they: Lo god I pray al these thynges at ful ben performed. For whyle this anker holdeth I hope thou shalte safely escape/ *and* whyle thy trewe meanyng seruyce aboute bringe/ in dispyte of al false meaners/ that the of newe haten/ for this trewe seruyce thou arte nowe entred.**<346rb>**

<346va>CErtayn (q*uo*d I) amonge thynges I asked a question/ whiche was the way to the knot. Trewly lady howe so it be/ I tempt you with questions *and* answers/ in spekyng of my first seruice/ I am nowe in ful purpose in the pricke of th*e* hert/ that thilke seruice was an enprisonment/ *and* alway bad *and* naughty in no maner to be desyred. Ne that in gettyng of the knot/ may it nothyng aueyle. a wyse gentyl hert loketh after vertue/ *and* none other bodily ioyes alone. And bycause to forne this/ in tho wayes I was sette/ I wote wel my selfe I haue erred/ *and* of the blysse fayled/ *and* so out of my way hugely haue I ron. Certes (q*uo*d she) that is sothe/ *and* there thou hast myswent/ eschewe th*e* pathe from hens forwarde I rede. Wonder I trewly why the mortal folke of this worlde

1042 daungerous sete, i.e., her haughty position. **1043 mote**, must. **1046 meaners**, i.e., people who mean ill. **1048 Certayn**, See note on questionable chapter division at this point. **1053 to forne**, before. **1055 Certes**, Certainly. **1056 rede**, counsel.

seche these wayes outforth, and it is proved in yourselfe. Lo, howe ye ben confounded with errour and folly. The knowing of very cause and way is goodnesse and vertue. Is there any thynge to thee more precious than thyselfe? Thou shalt have in thy power that thou woldest never lese and that in no way may be taken fro thee, and thilke thyng is that is cause of this knot. And if dethe mowe it nat reve more than an erthly creature, thilke thynge than abydeth with thyselfe soule. And so our conclusion to make suche a knot thus getten, abydeth with this thynge and with the soule, as long as they last. A soule dieth never. Vertu and goodnesse evermore with the soule endureth, and this knot is perfite blysse. Than this soule in this blysse endlesse shal enduren. Thus shul hertes of a trewe knot ben eased; thus shul their soules ben pleased; thus perpetually in joye shul they synge." "In good trouth," quod I, "here is a good beginnyng, yeve us more of this way." Quod she, "I said to thee nat longe sithen, that resonable lyfe was one of thre thynges and it was proved to the soule.

Chapter XI

Every soule of reason hath two thynges of steryng lyfe, one in vertue and another in

---

seche these wayes outforth/ *and* it is p*ro*ued i*n* your selfe. Lo howe ye ben confouded with errour and folly. The knowing of very cause *and* way is goodnesse *and* vertue. Is there any thynge to the more precious than thy selfe? Thou shalt haue i*n* thy power/ that thou woldest neuer lese and that in no way may be taken fro the/ and thilke thyng is that is cause of this knot. And if dethe mowe it nat reue more than an erthly creature/ thilke thynge than abydeth with thy selfe soule. *and* so our conclusion to make suche a knot thus getten/ abydeth with this thynge and with th*e* soule/ as long as they last. a soule dieth neuer/ vertu *and* goodnesse euermore with the soule endureth/ *and* this knot is p*er*fite blysse. Than this soule in this blysse endlesse shal enduren. Thus shul hertes of a trewe knot ben eased: thus shul their soules ben pleased: thus perpetually in ioye shul they synge. In good trouth (q*uo*d I) here is a good begi*n*nyng/ yeue vs more of this way. (Q*uo*d she) I said to the nat longe sithen/ that resonable lyfe was one of thre thynges/ *and* it was proued to the soule.

EVERY soule of reason hath two thynges of steryng lyfe/ one in vertue *and* another in

1057 outforth, externally. **1060 lese**, lose; **thilke**, that very. **1061 mowe**, may; **reve**, take away. **1067 yeve**, give. **1068 sithen**, since. **1070 steryng**, guiding.

the bodily workynge. And whan the soule is the maister over the body, than is a man maister of himselfe. And a man to be a maister over himselfe lyveth in vertue and in goodnesse. And as reson of vertue techeth, so the soule and the body worching vertue togider lyven resonable lyfe, whiche clerkes clepen felycité in lyveng. And therin is the hye way to this knot. These olde philosophers, that hadden no knowing of divine grace of kyndly reason alone, wenden that of pure nature, withouten any helpe of grace, me might have yshoned th'other lyvenges. Resonably have I lyved; and for I thynke herafter, if God wol (and I have space) thilke grace after my leude knowyng declare, I leave it as at this tyme. But, as I said, he that outforth loketh after the wayes of this knot, connyng with whiche he shulde knowe the way inforth, slepeth for the tyme. Wherfore, he that wol this way knowe must leave the lokyng after false wayes outforth, and open the eyen of his conscience and unclose his herte. Seest nat he that hath trust in the bodily lyfe is so besy bodily woundes to anoynt, in keping from smert (for al out may they nat be healed), that of woundes in his true understanding he taketh no hede. The knowing evenforth slepeth so harde, but anon as in knowing a wake than gynneth the prevy

---

the bodily workynge: *and* whan the soule is the maister ouer the body/ than is a man maister of himselfe: *And* a man to be a maister ouer him selfe/ lyueth in vertue *and* in goodnesse/ *and* as reson of vertue techeth. so the soule *and* the body worchi*ng* v*er*tue togider lyuen resonable lyfe/ whiche cler**<346va><346vb>**kes clepen felycite i*n* lyueng/ *and* therin is the hye way to this knot. these olde philosophers that hadden no knowing of diuine grace of kyndly reason alone/ wenden that of pure nature/ withouten any helpe of grace/ me might haue yshoned thother lyuenges/ resonably haue I lyued: *and* for I thynke herafter/ if god wol (*and* I haue space) thilke grace after my leude knowyng declare: I leaue it as at this tyme. But (as I said) he that outforth loketh after the wayes of this knot/ connyng with whiche he shulde knowe th*e* way inforth slepeth for the tyme/ wherfore he that wol this way knowe/ must leaue the lokyng after false wayes outforth/ *and* open the eyen of his conscience *and* vnclose his herte. Seest nat he that hath trust in the bodily lyfe is so besy bodily woundes to anoynt in keping from smert (for al out may they nat be healed) that of woundes in his true vndersta*n*ding he taketh no hede/ the knowing euenforth slepeth so harde/ but anon as i*n* knowing a wake/ than gynneth the preuy

1076 wenden, assumed; **me**, men. **1078 leude**, uninformed. **1079 outforth**, externally; **connyng**, intelligence. **1083 smert**, pain. **1085 evenforth**, equally.

medicines for healyng of his trewe entent, inwardes lightly healeth conscience if it be wel handled. Than must nedes these wayes come out of the soule by steryng lyfe of the body, and els maye no man come to perfyte blysse of this knotte. And thus by this waye he shal come to the knotte and to the perfyte selynesse that he wende have had in bodily goodes outforth?" "Ye," quod I "shal he have both knot, riches, power, dignité, and renome in this maner waye?" "Ye," quod she, "that shal I shewe thee. Is he nat riche that hath suffisaunce, and hath the power that no man may amaistrien? Is nat great dignité to have worshyp and reverence? And hath he nat glorie of renome whose name perpetual is duryng, and out of nombre in comparation?" "These be thynges that men wenen to getten outforth," quod I. "Ye," quod she, "they that loken after a thynge that nought is, therof, in al ne in partie, longe mowe they gapen after." "That is sothe," quod I. "Therfore," quod she, "they that sechen golde in grene trees and wene to gader precious stones amonge vynes, and layne her nettes in mountayns to fysshe, and thinken to hunt in depe sees after hart and hynde, and sechen in erth thilke thynges that surmounteth heven — what may I of hem say? but folysshe ignoraunce mysledeth wandring

---

medicines for healyng of his trewe entent/ inward*es* lightly healeth co*n*science if it be wel handled. Than must nedes these wayes come out of th*e* soule by steryng lyfe of the body/ *and* els maye no man come to p*er*fyte blysse of this knotte: *and* thus by this waye he shal come to the knotte/ and to the p*er*fyte selynesse that he wende haue had in bodily goodes outforth? Ye (q*uo*d I) shal he haue both knot/ riches/ power/ dignite/ *and* renome in this maner waye? Ye (q*uo*d she) th*at* shal I shewe the. Is he nat riche that hath suffisau*n*ce/ *and* hath the power that no man may amaistrien? Is nat great dignite to haue worshyp and reuerence? *and* hath he nat glorie of renome whose name p*er*-petual is duryng/ *and* out of no*m*bre in co*m*paration? These be thynges that men wenen to getten outforth (q*uo*d I). Ye (q*uo*d she) they that loken after a thynge that nought is therof in al ne in p*ar*tie/ longe mowe they gapen after: That is sothe (q*uo*d I): therfore (q*uo*d she) they that sechen golde in grene trees/ *and* wene to gader precious stones amonge vynes/ and layne her nettes in mountayns to fysshe/ and thinken to hunt *in* depe sees after hart *and* hynde/ and sechen in erth thilke thynges that surmou*n*teth heuen/ What may I of hem say? but fo**<346vb><347ra>**lysshe ignoraunce mysledeth wandring

1087 steryng, guiding. **1089 selynesse**, felicity; **wende**, expected [to]. **1091 renome**, renown. **1092 amaistrien**, overcome, master. **1094 duryng**, enduring. **1095 wenen**, expect. **1096 partie**, part; **mowe**, may. **1097 sechen**, seek; **wene**, think.

wretches by uncouth wayes that shulden be forleten, and maketh hem blynde fro the right pathe of trewe way that shulde ben used. Therfore, in general, errour in mankynde departeth thilke goodes by mysse sechyng, whiche he shulde have hole and he sought by reason. Thus goth he begyled of that he sought. In his hode men have blowe a jape." "Nowe," quod I, "if a man be vertuous and al in vertue lyveth, howe hath he al these thynges?" "That shal I proven," quod she. "What power hath any man to let another of lyveng in vertue? For prisonment or any other disese, if he take it paciently, discomfiteth he nat. The tyrant over his soule no power maye have. Than hath that man so tourmented suche power, that he nyl be discomfit. Ne overcome may he nat ben, sithen pacience in his soule overcometh and is nat overcomen. Suche thyng that may nat be a maistred, he hath nede to nothing, for he hath suffisaunce ynowe to helpe himselfe. And thilke thyng that thus hath power and suffysance, and no tyrant may it reve, and hath dignité to sette at nought al thynges, here it is a great dignité that deth may a maistry. Wherfore, thilke power and suffisaunce so enclosed with dignité by al reson renome must have. This is thilke riches with suffisance ye shulde loke after: this

---

wretches by vncouth wayes that shulden be forleten/ *and* maketh hem blynde fro the right pathe of trewe way that shulde ben vsed. Therfore in general errour in ma*n*kynde/ dep*ar*teth thilke goodes by mysse sechyng/ whiche he shulde haue hole *and* he sought by reason. Thus goth he begyled of that he sought/ in his hode men haue blowe a iape. Nowe (q*uo*d I) if a man be vertuous *and* al in vertue lyueth/ howe hath he al these thynges? That shal I prouen (q*uo*d she) What power hath any man to let another of lyueng in vertue? for priso*n*ment or any other disese/ he take it pacie*n*tly/ disco*m*fiteth he nat/ the tyrant ouer his soule no power maye haue? Than hath that man so tourme*n*ted suche power/ th*at* he nyl be disco*m*fit/ ne ouercome may he nat ben/ sithen pacie*n*ce i*n* his soule ouercometh/ and as nat ouercomen. Suche thyng th*at* may nat be a maistred/ he hath nede to nothing/ for he hath suffisa*un*ce ynowe to helpe him selfe. And thilke thyng that thus hath power *and* suffysance/ *and* no tyrant may it reue/ *and* hath dignite to sette at nought al thynges/ here it is a great dignite that deth may a maistry. Wherfore thilke power suffisaunce so enclosed with dignite/ by al reson renome must haue. This is thilke riches with suffisa*n*ce ye shulde loke after: this

1101 forleten, abandoned. **1103 and he**, if he. **1104 hode**, hood. **1104–05 blowe a jape**, i.e., made a mockery of him, he is deceived. **1106 let**, hinder. **1111 ynowe**, enough. **1112 thilke**, that same. **1113 reve**, take it away; **deth**, death. **1114 a maistry**, have mastery. **1115 renome**, renown.

is thilke worshipful dignité ye shulde coveyt; this is thilke power of myght, in whiche ye shulde truste. This is the ilke renome of glorie that endlesse endureth, and al nys but substaunce in vertuous lyveng." "Certes," quod I, "al this is sothe, and so I se wel that vertue with ful gripe encloseth al these thynges. Wherfore, in sothe I may saye by my trouth, vertue of my Margarite brought me first in to your service, to have knyttyng with that jewel, nat sodayn longynges ne folkes smale wordes, but onely our conversation togider. And than I seinge th'entent of her trewe menyng with florisshing vertue of pacience that she used nothynge in yvel to quyte the wicked leasynges that false tonges ofte in her have layde, I have sey it myselfe, goodly foryevenesse hath spronge out of her hert. Unité and accorde above al other thinges she desyreth in a good meke maner, and suffereth many wicked tales.

"Trewly, lady, to you it were a gret worship that suche thynges by due chastysment were amended." "Ye," quod she, "I have thee excused. Al suche thynges as yet mowe nat be redressed: thy Margarites vertue I commende wel the more that paciently suche anoyes suffreth. David kyng was meke and suffred mokel hate and many yvel speches.

---

is thilke worshipful dignite ye shulde coueyt: this is thilke power of myght/ in whiche ye shulde truste: this is the ilke renome of glorie that endlesse endureth/ *and* al nys but substaunce in vertuous lyueng. Certes (q*uo*d I) al this is sothe/ *and* so I se wel that vertue with ful gripe encloseth al these thynges. Wherfore in sothe I may saye/ by my trouth/ vertue of my Margarite brouȝt me first in to your seruice/ to haue knyttyng with that iewel/ nat sodayn longynges ne folkes smale wordes/ but onely our co*n*uersation togider: *and* than I sei*n*ge thentent of her trewe menyng with florisshi*n*g vertue of pacience/ that she vsed nothynge in yuel/ to quyte the wicked leasynges that false to*n*ges ofte in her haue layde/ I haue sey it my selfe/ goodly foryeuenesse hath spronge out of her hert/ unite *and* accorde aboue al other thi*n*ges she desyreth in a good meke maner/ and suffereth many wicked tales.**<347ra>**

<347rb>TRewly lady to you it were a gret worship/ that suche thynges by due chastysment were ame*n*ded. Ye (q*uo*d she) I haue the excused/ al suche thynges as yet mowe nat be redressed: thy Margarites vertue I commende wel the more that paciently suche anoyes suffreth. Dauid kyng was meke *and* suffred mokel hate *and* many yuel speches:

1119 gripe, grip. **1121 sodayn**, sudden. **1123 quyte**, requite; **leasynges**, lies. **1124 sey**, seen. **1128 mowe**, may. **1130 meke**, meek; **mokel**, much.

No dispite ne shame that his enemys him deden might nat move pacience out of his herte, but ever in one plyte mercy he used. Werfore God Himselfe toke rewarde to the thynges and theron suche punysshment let fal. Trewly, by reason it ought be ensample of drede to al maner peoples myrth. A man vengeable in wrath no governance in punisshment ought to have. Plato had a cause his servant to scoure, and yet cleped he his neighbour to performe the doynge; himselfe wolde nat, lest wrath had him a maistred, and so myght he have layde on to moche. Evermore grounded vertue sheweth th'entent fro within. And trewly I wotte wel for her goodnesse and vertue thou hast desyred my service to her plesance wel the more and thyselfe therto fully haste profered." "Good lady," quod I, "is vertue the hye waye to this knot that long we have yhandled?" "Ye for soth," quod she, "and without vertue goodly this knot may nat be goten." "Ah, nowe I se," quod I, "howe vertu in me fayleth, and I as a seer tre without burjonyng or frute alwaye welke, and so I stonde in dispeyre of this noble knot for vertue in me hath no maner workynge. A wydewhere aboute have I traveyled." "Peace," quod she, "of thy first way thy traveyle is in ydel, and as touchynge the seconde way, I se wel thy

---

no dispite ne shame that his enemys him deden/ might nat moue pacie*n*ce out of his herte/ but euer in one plyte mercy he vsed. Werfore god him selfe toke rewarde to the thynges/ *and* theron suche punysshment let fal. Trewly by reason it ought be ensa*m*ple of drede to al maner peoples myrth A man ve*n*geable in wrath no gouernance in punisshment ought to haue. Plato had a cause his seruant to scoure/ *and* yet cleped he his neig*h*bour to p*er*forme the doynge/ him selfe wolde nat/ lest wrath had him a maistred/ *and* so myȝt he haue layde on to moche: euermore grou*n*ded vertue sheweth thentent fro within. *And* trewly I wotte wel for her goodnesse *and* vertue/ thou hast desyred my seruice to her plesance wel the more/ *and* thy selfe therto fully haste profered. Good lady (q*uo*d I) is vertue the hye waye to this knot/ that long we haue yhandled? ye for soth (q*uo*d she) and without vertue goodly this knot may nat be goten. Ah nowe I se (quod I) howe vertu in me fayleth/ *and* I as a seer tre without burionyng or frute alwaye welke/ *and* so I stonde in dispeyre of this noble knot/ for vertue in me hath no maner workynge. A wydewhere aboute haue I traueyled. Peace (q*uo*d she) of thy first way thy traueyle is in ydel/ *and* as touchynge the seconde way/ I se wel thy

1131 deden, did. **1132 plyte**, in one, i.e., in the same condition. **1135 cleped**, called. **1137 Evermore grounded**, Well-founded. **1138 wotte**, know. **1142 seer**, dry, barren; **burjonyng**, blooming. **1143 welke**, withered. **1144 A wydewhere aboute**, A great region all about.

meanyng. Thou woldest conclude me if thou coudest bycause I brought thee to service, and every of my servantes I helpe to come to this blysse, as I sayd here beforne. And thou saydest thyselfe thou mightest nat be holpen as thou wenyst, bycause that vertue in thee fayleth. And this blysse perfitly without vertue maye nat be goten, thou wenest of these wordes contradiction to folowe. Pardé, at the hardest I have no servant but he be vertuous in dede and thought. I brought thee in my service, yet arte thou nat my servant. But I say thou might so werche in vertue herafter that than shalt thou be my servaunt, and as for my servant acompted. For habyte maketh no monke, ne wearynge of gylte spurres maketh no knyght. Neverthelater in conforte of thyne herte, yet wol I otherwyse answere." "Certes, lady," quod I tho, "so ye must nedes, or els I had nyghe caught suche a cordiacle for sorowe, I wotte it wel I shulde it never have recovered. And therfore nowe I praye to enforme me in this, or els I holde me without recoverye. I may nat long endure tyl this lesson be lerned and of this myschefe the remedy knowen." "Nowe," quod she, "be nat wrothe, for there is no man on lyve that maye come to a precious thyng longe coveyted but he somtyme suffre teneful diseases, and wenyst

---

meanyng. Thou woldest co*n*clude me if th*ou* coudest/ bycause I brought the to seruice/ and euery of my seruantes I helpe to come to this blysse/ as I sayd here beforne: *and* thou saydest thy selfe/ thou mightest nat be holpen as thou wenyst/ bycause that vertue in the fayleth. *and* this blysse p*er*fitly without vertue maye nat be goten/ thou wenest of these wordes co*n*tradiction to folowe. Parde/ at the hardest I haue no seruant but he be vertuous in dede *and* thought. I brought the in my seruice/ yet arte thou nat my seruant: but I say/ thou might so werche in vertue herafter that than shalt thou be my**<347rb>** **<347va>**seruaunt/ and as for my seruant acompted. For habyte maketh no monke/ ne wearynge of gylte spurres maketh no knyght. Neuer the later/ in conforte of thyne herte/ yet wol I otherwyse answere. Certes lady (q*uo*d I tho) so ye must nedes/ or els I had nyghe caught suche a cordiacle for sorowe/ I wotte it wel I shulde it neuer haue recouered. And therfore nowe I praye to enforme me in this/ or els I holde me without recoueryе. I may nat long endure tyl this lesson be lerned/ and of this myschefe the remedy knowen. Nowe (quod she) be nat wrothe/ for there is no man on lyue that maye come to a precious thyng longe coueyted/ but he somtyme suffre teneful diseases/ and wenyst

1146 conclude, confute. **1148 holpen**, helped; **wenyst**, assume. **1149 And**, If. **1150 Pardé**, Indeed. **1152 werche**, work. **1153 habyte**, the habit [a garment]. **1155 Certes**, Certainly. **1156 cordiacle**, heart attack, or failure; **wotte**, know. **1160 teneful**, sorrowful.

thy selfe to ben unlyche to al other? That maye nat ben. And with the more sorowe that a thynge is getten, the more he hath joye the ilke thyng afterwardes to kepe, as it fareth by chyldren in schole, that for lernynge arne beaten whan their lesson they foryetten. Commenly, after a good disciplynyng with a yerde, they kepe right wel doctryne of their schole."

Chapter XII

Right with these wordes on this lady I threwe up myne eyen to se her countenaunce and her chere, and she, aperceyvyng this fantasye in myne herte, gan her semblaunt goodly on me caste and sayde in this wyse.

"It is wel knowe, bothe to reason and experience in doynge every actyve worcheth on his passyve, and whan they ben togider actyve and passyve ben ycleaped by these philosophers. If fyre be in place chafynge thynge able to be chafed or hete and thilke thynges ben sette in suche a distaunce that the one may werche, the other shal suffre. Thilke Margarite thou desyrest is ful of vertue and able to be actyve in goodnesse. But every herbe sheweth his vertue outforthe from within. The sonne yeveth lyght that

---

thy selfe ben vnlyche to al other? that maye nat ben: And with the more sorowe that a thynge is getten/ the more he hath ioye/ the ilke thyng afterwardes to kepe/ as it fareth by chyldren in schole that for lernynge arne beaten/ whan their lesson they foryetten/ co*m*menly after a good disciplynyng with a yerde/ they kepe right wel doctryne of their schole.

RIght with these wordes/ on this lady I threwe vp myne eyen to se her countenaunce and her chere/ and she ap*er*ceyuyng this fantasye in myne herte/ gan her semblaunt goodly on me caste/ and sayde in this wyse.

It is wel knowe/ bothe to Reason and experience in doynge/ euery actyue worcheth on his passyue/ and whan they ben togider/ actyue and passyue ben ycleaped by these philosophers/ if fyre be in place chafynge thynge able to be chafed or hete/ and thilke thynges ben sette in suche a distaunce that the one may werche/ the other shal suffre. Thilke Margarite thou desyrest is ful of vertue/ and able to be actyue in goodnesse:/ but euery herbe sheweth his vertue outforthe from within/ the sonne yeueth lyght that

1161 unlyche, unlike. **1162 ilke**, same. **1164 yerde**, branch, rod. **1167 chere**, looks. **1169 worcheth**, works. **1170 ycleaped**, called. **1174 outforthe**, externally.

thynges may be sey. Every fyre heteth thilke thyng that it neighed and it be able to be hete. Vertue of this Margarite outforth wercheth, and nothynge is more able to suffre worching or worke catche of the actyfe, but passyfe of the same actyfe, and no passyfe to vertues of this Margaryte, but thee, in al my donet can I fynde. So that her vertue muste nedes on thee werche in what place ever thou be, within distaunce of her worthynesse, as her very passyfe thou arte closed. But vertue may thee nothynge profyte, but thy desyre be perfourmed and al thy sorowes ceased. *Ergo*, through werchynge of her vertue thou shalte easely ben holpen and driven out of al care, and welcome to this longe by thee desyred." "Lady," quod I, "this is a good lesson in gynnyng of my joye. But wete ye wel, forsothe, thoughe I suppose she have moche vertue, I wolde my spousayle were proved, and than maye I lyve out of doute and rejoyce me greatly in thynkyng of tho vertues so shewed." "I herde thee say," quod she, "at my begynnyng whan I receyved thee firste for to serve, that thy jewel thilke Margaryte thou desyrest was closed in a muskle with a blewe shel." "Ye, forsothe," quod I, "so I sayd, and so it is." "Wel," quod she, "everything kyndly sheweth it selfe: this jewel, closed in a blewe shel, by

---

thynges may be sey. Euery fyre heteth thilke thyng that it neighed and it be able to be hete/ vertue of this Margarite outforth wrethe/ and nothynge is more able to suffre worching or worke catche of the actyfe/ but passyfe of the same actyfe/ and no**<347va>** **<347vb>**passyfe to vertues of this Margaryte/ but the in al my donet can I fynde/ so that her vertue muste nedes on the werche/ in what place euer thou be within distaunce of her worthynesse/ as her very passyfe thou arte closed: but vertue may the nothynge profyte/ but thy desyre be perfourmed and al thy sorowes ceased. Ergo through werchynge of her vertue thou shalte easely ben holpen and driuen out of al care/ and welcome to this longe by the desyred. Lady (quod I) this is a good lesson in gynnyng of my ioye: but wete ye wel forsothe/ thoughe I suppose she haue moche vertue/ I wolde my spousayle were proued/ and than maye I lyue out of doute/ and reioyce me greatly in thynkyng of tho vertues so shewed. I herde the say (quod she) at my begynnyng whan I receyued the firste for to serue that thy iewel/ thilke Margaryte thou desyrest/ was closed in a muskle with a blewe shel. Ye forsothe (quod I) so I sayd/ and so it is. Wel (quod she) euery thing kyndly sheweth it selfe: this iewel closed in a blewe shel/

1175 it neighed and, is near it if. **1178 donet**, book of principles, first things. **1181 *Ergo***, Therefore. **1182 holpen**, helped. **1183 gynnyng**, [the] beginning. **1184 wete**, know; **spousayle**, marriage. **1188 muskle**, mussel; **blewe**, blue. **1189 kyndly**, naturally.

excellence of coloures sheweth vertue from within, and so every wight shulde rather loke to the propre vertue of thynges than to his forayne goodes. If a thyng be engendred of good mater, comenly and for the more parte, it foloweth, after the congelement, vertue of the first mater, and it be not corrupt with vyces, to procede with encrease of good vertues: eke right so it fareth of badde. Trewly, great excellence in vertue of lynage, for the more parte, discendeth by kynde to the successyon in vertues to folowe. Wherfore I saye, the colours of every Margarit sheweth from within the fynesse in vertue. Kyndely heven, whan mery wether is a lofte, apereth in mannes eye of coloure in blewe, stedfastnesse in peace betokenyng within and without. Margaryte is engendred by hevenly dewe and sheweth in itselfe by fynenesse of coloure whether the engendrure were maked on morowe or on eve: thus sayth kynde of this perle. This precious Margaryte that thou servest sheweth itselfe discended by nobley of vertue from this hevenlych dewe, norisshed and congeled in mekenesse, that mother is of al vertues, and by werkes that men sene withouten, the signyfication of the coloures ben shewed, mercy and pytie in the herte, with peace to al other. And al this is yclosed in a muskle, who so

---

excellence of coloures sheweth vertue from within/ and so euery wight shulde rather loke to the propre vertue of thynges/ than to his forayne goodes. If a thyng be engendred of good mater/ comenly and for the more parte it foloweth after the congelement vertue of the first mater/ and it be not corrupt with vyces/ to procede with encrease of good vertues: eke right so it fareth of badde. Trewly great excellence in vertue of lynage/ for the more parte discendeth by kynde to the successyon in vertues to folowe. Wherfore I saye/ the colours of euery Margarit sheweth from within the fynesse in vertue. Kyndely heuen whan mery wether is a lofte/ apereth in mannes eye of coloure in blewe/ stedfastnesse in peace betokenyng within and without: Margaryte is engendred by heuenly dewe/ and sheweth in it selfe by fynenesse of coloure/ whether the engendrure were maked on morowe or on eue: thus sayth kynde of this perle. This precious Margaryte that thou seruest sheweth it selfe discended by nobley of vertue from this heuenlych dewe/ norisshed and congeled in mekenesse/ that mother is of al vertues/ and by**<347vb>** **<348ra>**werkes that men sene withouten the signyfication of the coloures/ ben shewed mercy and pytie in the herte with peace to al other/ and al this is yclosed in a muskle/ who so

1191 forayne, foreign, alien. **1192 congelement**, congealing. **1193 and it be**, providing that it be. **1194 eke**, also. **1195 lynage**, lineage. **1201 nobley**, nobility.

redily these vertues loken. Al thyng that hath soule is reduced into good by meane thynges as thus: Into God man is reduced by soules resonable, and so forthe beestes or bodyes that mowe not moven after place ben reduced into manne by beestes meve that movyn from place to place. So that thilke bodyes that han felynge soules and move not from places holden the lowest degree of soulynge thynges in felynge, and suche ben reduced into man by meanes. So, it foloweth, the muskle, as mother of al vertues, halte the place of mekenesse, to his lowest degree discendeth downe of heven, and there, by a maner of virgyne engendrure, arne these Margarytes engendred and afterwarde congeled. Made not mekenesse so lowe the hye heven to enclose and catche out therof so noble a dewe, that after congelement a Margaryte, with endelesse vertue and everlastyng joy, was with ful vessel of grace yeven to every creature that goodly wolde it receyve?" "Certes," quod I, "these thynges ben right noble. I have er this herde these same sawes." "Than," quod she, "thou woste wel these thynges ben sothe?" "Ye, forsothe," quod I, "at the ful." "Nowe," quod she, "that this Margaryte is ful of vertue it is wel proved, wherfore some grace some mercy amonge other vertues, I wotte ryght

---

redily these vertues loken. Al thyng that hath soule is reduced in to good by meane thynges/ as thus: In to god man is reduced by soules resonable/ and so forthe beestes or bodyes that mowe not mouen/ after place ben reduced in to manne/ by beestes meue that mouyn from place to place: so that thilke bodyes that han felynge soules/ and moue not from places/ holden the lowest degree of soulynge thynges in felynge/ and suche ben reduced in to man by meanes. So it foloweth/ the muskle as mother of al vertues/ halte the place of mekenesse to his lowest degree discendeth downe of heuen/ and there by a maner of virgyne engendrure arne these Margarytes engendred/ and afterwarde congeled. Made not mekenesse so lowe the hye heuen to enclose *and* catche out therof so noble a dewe/ that after congelement a Margaryte with endelesse vertue and euerlastyng ioy was with ful vessel of grace yeuen to euery creature/ that goodly wolde it receyue. Certes (quod I) these thynges ben right noble/ I haue er this herde these same sawes. Than (quod she) thou woste wel these thynges ben sothe? ye forsothe (q*uo*d I) at the ful. Nowe (quod she) that this Margaryte is ful of vertue it is wel proued/ wherfore some grace/ some mercy amonge other vertues/ I wotte ryght

1205 loken, considers; **meane**, mediatory. **1207 meve**, means (see note). **1209 soulynge**, entities endowed with souls. **1215 yeven**, given. **1217 sawes**, sayings.

wel, on thee shal discende?" "Ye," quod I, "yet wolde I have better declared vertues in this Margaryte kyndely to ben grounded." "That shal I shew thee," quod she, "and thou woldest it lerne?" "Lerne?" quod I, "what nedeth suche wordes? Wete ye nat wel, lady, yourselfe that al my cure, al my dyligence, and al my might have turned by your counsayle in plesaunce of that perle? Al my thought and al my studye, with your helpe, desyreth in worshyppe thilke jewel to encrease al my travayle and al my besynesse in your servyce, this Margaryte to gladde in somehalve. Me were leaver her honour, her pleasaunce, and her good chere thorowe me for to be mayntayned and kepte, and I of suche thynge in her lykynge to be cause, than al the welthe of bodyly goodes ye coude recken. And wolde never God, but I put myselfe in great jeoperdye of al that I wolde, that is nowe no more but my lyfe alone, rather than I shulde suffre thylke jewel in any poynte ben blemisshed as ferre as I may suffre and with my mightes stretche." "Suche thyng," quod she, "maye mokel further thy grace, and thee in my servyce avaunce. But nowe," quod Love, "wylte thou graunte me thilke Margaryte to ben good?" "O good God," quod I, "why tempte ye me and tene with suche maner speche? I wolde graunt that

---

wel on the shal discende? ye (quod I) yet wolde I haue better declared vertues in this Margaryte/ kyndely to ben grounded. That shal I shew the (q*uo*d she) and thou woldest it lerne? Lerne (quod I) what nedeth suche wordes: Wete ye nat wel lady your selfe that al my cure/ al my dyligence/ and al my might haue turned by your counsayle/ in plesaunce of that perle/ al my thought and al my studye/ with your helpe desyreth/ in worshyppe thilke iewel to encrease al my trauayle and al my besynesse in your seruyce/ this Margaryte to gladde in somehalue: me were leauer her honour/ her pleasaunce/ and her good chere thorowe me for to be mayntayned and kepte/ and I of suche**<348ra>** **<348rb>**thynge in her lykynge to be cause/ than al the welthe of bodyly goodes ye coude recken. And wolde neuer god/ but I put my selfe in great ieoperdye of al that I wolde/ that is nowe no more but my lyfe alone/ rather than I shulde suffre thylke iewel in any poynte ben blemisshed/ as ferre as I may suffre/ and with my mightes stretche. Suche thyng (q*uo*d she) maye mokel further thy grace/ and the in my seruyce auaunce. But nowe (quod Loue) wylte thou graunte me thilke Margaryte to ben good? O good good (q*uo*d I) why tempte ye me and tene with suche maner speche: I wolde graunt that/

1222 Wete, Know. **1226 Me were leaver**, I would prefer. **1229 wolde**, wield (see note). **1231 ferre**, far. **1232 mokel**, much. **1234 tene**, trouble [me].

thoughe I shulde anone dye and by my trouthe fyght in the quarel if any wight wolde coutreplede. It is so moche the lyghter," quod Love, "to prove our entent."

"Ye," quod I, "but yet wolde I here howe ye wolde prove that she were good by reasonable skyl, that it mowe not ben denyed. For althoughe I knowe, and so dothe many other, manyfolde goodnesse and vertue in this Margaryte ben printed, yet some men there ben that no goodnesse speken. And wherever your wordes ben herde and your reasons ben shewed, suche yvel spekers, lady, by auctorité of your excellence shullen be stopped and ashamed. And more, they that han none acquayntaunce in her persone, yet mowe they knowe her vertues and ben the more enfourmed in what wyse they mowe sette their hertes whan hem lyste into your servyce any entré make. For trewly, al this to begynne, I wote wel myselfe that thilke jewel is so precious perle, as a womanly woman in her kynde, in whome of goodnesse of vertue and also of answerynge shappe of lymmes and fetures so wel in al poyntes acordyng, nothynge fayleth. I leve that kynde her made with great studye, for kynde in her person nothyng hath foryet, and that is wel sene. In every good wyghtes herte she hath grace of commendyng and

---

thoughe I shulde anone dye/ and by my trouthe fyght in the quarel/ if any wight wolde coutreplede. It is so moche the lyghter (quod Loue) to proue our entent.

Ye (quod I) but yet wolde I here howe ye wolde proue that she were good by reasonable skyl/ that it mowe not ben denyed/ for althoughe I knowe and so dothe many other/ manyfolde goodnesse and vertue in this Margaryte ben printed/ yet some men there ben that no goodnesse speken: and wher euer your wordes ben herde and your reasons ben shewed/ suche yuel spekers lady by auctorite of your excellence/ shullen be stopped and ashamed. And more they that han none acquayntaunce in her persone/ yet mowe they knowe her vertues/ and ben the more enfourmed in what wyse they mowe sette their hertes/ whan hem lyste in to your seruyce any entre make: for trewly al this to begynne/ I wote wel my selfe that thilke iewel is so precious perle/ as a womanly woman in her kynde/ in whome of goodnesse/ of vertue/ and also of answerynge/ shappe of lymmes/ and fetures so wel in al poyntes acordyng/ nothynge fayleth: I leue that kynde her made with great studye/ for kynde in her person nothyng hath foryet/ and that is wel sene. In euery good wyghtes herte she hath grace of co*m*mendyng and

1235 wight, person. **1236 coutreplede**, contradict; **lyghter**, easier. **1238 mowe**, may. **1242 shullen**, shall; **han**, have. **1244 hem lyste**, it pleases them. **1245 wote**, know. **1246 kynde**, nature. **1247 lymmes**, limbs; **leve**, believe. **1249 wyghtes**, person's.

of vertuous praysyng. Alas, that ever kynde made her deedly, save onely in that I wot wel that Nature in fourmynge of her in nothynge hath erred."

Chapter XIII

"Certes," quod Love, "thou haste wel begonne and I aske thee this questyon: Is not, in general, every thynge good?" "I not," quod I. "No," quod she, "saw not God every thynge that he made and werne right good?" "Than is wonder," quod I, "howe yvel thynges comen a place, sythen that al thynges weren right good." "Thus," quod she, "I wol declare everyche qualyté and every action and every thyng that hath any maner of beynge, it is of God, and God it made, of Whom is al goodnesse and al beyng. Of Him is no badnesse. Badde to be is naught; good to be is somwhat, and therfore good and beyng is one in understandyng." "Howe may this be?" quod I, "for often han shrewes me assailed, and mokel badnesse therin have I founden, and so me semeth bad to be somwhat in kynde." "Thou shalt," quod she, "understande that suche maner badnesse whiche is used to purifye wronge doers is somwhat, and God it made and beyng hath. And that is good. Other badnesse no beyng hath utterly. It is in the negatyve of somwhat,

---

of vertuous praysyng. Alas that euer kynde made her deedly/ saue onely in that I wot wel/ that Nature in fourmynge of her in no thynge hath erred.**<348rb>**
<348va>CErtes (quod Loue) thou haste wel begonne/ and I aske the this questyon: Is not in general euery thynge good? I not (quod I) No (quod she) saue not god euery thynge that he made/ and werne right good. Than is wonder (q*uo*d I) howe yuel thynges comen a place/ sythen that al thynges weren right good. Thus (q*uo*d she) I wol declare eueryche qualyte and euery action/ and euery thyng that hath any maner of beynge it is of god/ and god it made/ of whom is al goodnesse *and* al beyng/ of him is no badnesse: badde to be is naught: good to be is somwhat/ and therfore good and beyng is one in vnderstandyng. Howe may this be (quod I) for often han shrewes me assailed/ and mokel badnesse therin haue I founden/ and so me semeth bad to be somwhat in kynde. Thou shalt (q*uo*d she) vnderstande th*at* suche maner badnesse/ whiche is vsed to purifye wronge doers is somwhat/ and god it made and beyng hath/ and that is good: other badnesse no beyng hath vtterly/ it is in the negatyue of somwhat/

1250 deedly, mortal. **1252 Certes**, Certainly. **1253 not**, don't know. **1255 sythen**, since. **1260 mokel**, much. **1261 somwhat**, something.

and that is naught and nothyng beyng. The parties essencial of beyng arne sayd in double wyse, as that it is, and these parties ben founde in every creature. For al thyng, a this halfe the first beyng, is beyng through partycipacion, takyng partie of beyng, so that in every creature is difference bytwene beynge and of him through whom it is and his own beyng. Right as every good is a maner of beyng, so is it good thorowe beyng, for it is naught other to be. And every thyng though it be good is not of himselfe good, but it is good by that it is ordynable to the great goodnesse. This dualyte after clerkes determission is founden in every creature, be it never so syngle of onhed." "Ye," quod I, "but there as it is ysayde that God saw everythynge of his makyng, and were right good, as yourselfe sayd to me not longe tyme sythen, I aske whether every creature is ysayde good throughe goodnesse unfourmed eyther els fourmed, and afterwarde if it be accepte utterly good?" "I shal say thee," quod she, "these great passed clerkes han devyded good into good beyng alone, and that is nothynge but good. For nothynge is good in that wyse but God. Also in good by partycipacion, and that is ycleped good, for farre fette and representatyve of goodly goodnesse, and after this manyfolde good is

---

and that is naught/ and nothyng beyng. The parties essencial of beyng arne sayd in double wyse/ as that it is/ and these parties ben fou*n*de in euery creature/ for al thyng a this halfe the first beyng is beyng through partycipacion/ takyng partie of beyng/ so that euery creature is difference bytwene beynge and of him through whom it is and his own beyng: right as euery good is a maner of beyng/ so is it good thorowe beyng/ for it is naught other to be: and euery thyng though it be good is not of him selfe good/ but it is good by that it is ordynable to the great goodnesse. This dualyte after clerkes determission is founden in euery creature/ be it neuer so syngle of onhed. ye (q*uo*d I) but there as it is ysayde that god saue euerythynge of his makyng/ and were right good/ as your selfe sayd to me not longe tyme sythen. I aske whether euery creature is ysayde good/ throughe goodnesse vnfourmed eyther els fourmed/ and afterwarde if it be accepte vtterly good? I shal say the (quod she) these great passed clerkes han deuyded good in to good beyng alone/ and that is nothynge but good/ for nothynge is good in that wyse but**<348va><348vb>**god. Also in good by partycipacion/ and that is ycleped good/ for farre fette and representatyue of goodly goodnesse/ and after this manyfolde good is

1266 a this halfe, on this side (i.e., here below). **1270 by**, by [virtue of the fact that]. **1271 onhed**, unity. **1273 sythen**, since, ago. **1274 eyther els**, or else. **1277 ycleped**, called. **1277–78 for farre fette**, i.e., at a distance (metaphorically).

sayd, that is to saye, good in kynde and good in gendre, and good of grace, and good of joy. Of good in kynde Austen saythe, 'al that ben ben good.' But peraunter thou woldest wete whether of hemselfe it be good or els of anothers goodnesse, for naturel goodnesse of every substaunce is nothing els than his substancial beyng, whiche is ycleaped goodnesse after comparyson that he hath to his first goodnesse, so as it is inductatife by meanes into the first goodnesse. Boece sheweth this thynge at the ful that this name 'good' is, in general, name in kynde, as it is comparysoned generally to his principal ende, whiche is God, knotte of al goodnesse. Every creature cryeth 'God us made,' and so they han ful apeted to thilke God by affection suche as to hem longeth. And in this wyse al thynges ben good of the gret God, whiche is good alone." "This wonder thyng," quod I, "howe ye have by many reasons proved my first waye to be errour and misgoyng, and cause of badnesse and feble menynge in the grounde ye aleged to be roted. Whence is it that suche badnesse hath springes, sythen al thynges thus in general ben good, and badnesse hath no beyng, as ye have declared? I wene, if al thynges ben good, I might than with the first way in that good have ended, and so by

---

sayd/ that is to saye/ good in kynde and good in gendre/ and good of grace/ and good of ioy. Of good in kynde Austen saythe/ al that ben ben good: But peraunter thou woldest wete whether of hem selfe it be good/ or els of anothers goodnesse/ for naturel goodnesse of euery substaunce is nothing els than his substancial beyng/ whiche is ycleaped goodnesse/ after comparyson that he hath to his first goodnesse/ so as it is inductatife by meanes i*n* to the first goodnesse. Boece sheweth this thynge at the ful/ that this name good is in general name in kynde/ as it is co*m*parysoned generally to his principal ende/ whiche is god knotte of al goodnesse. Euery creature cryeth god vs made/ and so they han ful apeted to thilke god by affection/ suche as to hem longeth: and in this wyse al thynges ben good of th*e* gret god/ whiche is good alone. This wonder thyng (quod I) howe ye haue by many reasons proued my first waye to be errour and misgoyng/ and cause of baddesse and feble menynge in the grounde ye aleged to be roted: whence is it that suche baddesse hath springes/ sythen al thynges thus in general ben good/ and badnesse hath no beyng/ as ye haue declared: I wene if al thynges ben good/ I might than with the first way in that good haue ended/ and so by

1279 gendre, type. **1280 Austen**, St. Augustine. **1281 wete**, know. **1287 apeted**, appetite, expressed their desire for him; **longeth**, belongs. **1291 aleged**, alleged; **roted**, rooted. **1292 wene**, think.

goodnesse have comen to blysse in your servyce desyred." "Al thyng," quod she, "is good by beyng in partycipacion out of the firste goodnesse, whiche goodnesse is corrupte by badnesse and badde-meanyng maners. God hath in good thynges that they ben good by beyng, and not in yvel, for there is absence of rightful love. For badnesse is nothynge but onely yvel wyl of the user and through giftes of the doer wherfore at the gynnyng of the worlde every thyng by himselfe was good, and in unyversal they werne right good. An eye or a hande is fayrer and betterer in a body sette in his kyndely place than from the body discevered. Everythyng in his kyndly place being kyndly good dothe werche, and out of that place voyded it dissolveth and is defouled himselve. Our noble God, in glyterande wyse, by armony this worlde ordeyned as in purtreytures storied with colours medled, in whiche blacke and other derke coloures commenden the golden and the asured paynture. Every putte in kyndely place, one besyde another, more for other glytereth: ryght so lytle fayre maketh right fayre more glorious, and right so of goodnesse and of other thynges in vertue. Wherfore, other badde and not so good perles as this Margaryte that we han of this matier yeven by the ayre lytel

---

goodnesse haue comen to blysse in your seruyce desyred. Al thyng (quod she) is good by beyng in partycipacion out of the firste goodnesse/ whiche goodnesse is corrupte by badnesse/ and badde meanyng maners: god hath in good thynges that they ben good by beyng/ and not in yuel/ for there is absence of rightful loue/ for badnesse is nothynge but onely yuel wyl of the vser/ and through giftes of the doer/ wherfore at the gynnyng of the worlde/ euery thyng by him selfe was good/ and in vnyuersal they werne right good. An eye or a hande is fayrer and betterer in a body sette in his kyndely place/ than from the body disceuered. Euery thyng in his kyndly place being kyndly good dothe werche/ and out of that place voyded/ **<348vb><349ra>**it dissolueth and is defouled him selue. Our noble god in glyterande wyse by armony this worlde ordeyned/ as in purtreytures storied with colours medled/ in whiche blacke and other derke coloures com*m*enden the golden and the asured paynture/ euery putte in kyndely place one besyde another/ more for other glytereth: ryght so lytle fayre maketh right fayre more glorious/ and right so of goodnesse and of other thynges in vertue. Wherfore other badde/ and not so good perles as this Margaryte that we han of this matier/ yeuen by the ayre lytel

1300 kyndely, natural. **1304 commenden**, commend [by setting off]. **1305 asured**, painted or enameled with azure (lapis lazuli). **1308 yeven**, given.

goodnesse and lytel vertue, ryght mokel goodnesse and vertue in thy Margaryte to ben proved in shynynge wyse to be founde and shewed. Howe shulde ever goodnesse of peace have ben knowe but if unpeace somtyme reigne and mokel yvel wrothe? Howe shulde mercy ben proved and no trespeace were by due justifycacion to be punysshed? Therfore grace and goodnesse of a wight is founde the sorouful hertes in good meanynge to endure ben comforted; unyté and acorde bytwene hertes knytte in joye to abyde. What, wenest thou I rejoyce or els accompte hym amonge my servauntes that pleaseth Pallas in undoynge of Mercurye, albeit that to Pallas he be knytte by tytle of lawe, not accordyng to reasonable conscience, and Mercurie in doynge have grace to ben suffered. Or els hym that weneth the moone for fayrenesse of the eve sterre? Lo, otherwhyle by nyghtes, lyght of the moone greatly comforteth in derke thoughtes and blynde. Understandyng of love yeveth great gladnesse. Whoso lyste not byleve whan a sothe tale is shewed adewe and a deblys his name is entred. Wyse folke and worthy in gentyllesse, bothe of vertue and of lyvynge, yeven ful credence in sothnesse of love with a good hert, thereas good evydence or experyence in doynge sheweth not the

---

goodnesse and lytel vertue/ ryght mokel goodnesse and vertue in thy Margaryte to ben proued/ in shynynge wyse to be founde and shewed. Howe shulde euer goodnesse of peace haue ben knowe/ but if vnpeace somtyme reigne/ and mokel yuel wrothe? Howe shulde mercy ben proued and no trespeace were/ by due iustifycacion to be punysshed? Therfore grace *and* goodnesse of a wight is founde/ the sorouful hertes in good meanynge to endure/ ben comforted/ vnyte and acorde bytwene hertes knytte in ioye to abyde. What wenest thou I reioyce or els accompte hym amonge my seruauntes that pleaseth Pallas/ in vndoynge of Mercurye/ al be it that to Pallas he be knytte by tytle of lawe/ not accordyng to reasonable conscience: and Mercurie in doynge haue grace to ben suffered: or els hym that weneth the moone for fayrenesse of the eue sterre. Lo otherwhyle by nyghtes lyght of the moone/ greatly comforteth in derke thoughtes and blynde. Vnderstandyng of loue yeueth great gladnesse: Who so lyste not byleue whan a sothe tale is shewed/ adewe and a deblys his name is entred. Wyse folke and worthy in gentyllesse bothe of vertue and of lyuynge/ yeuen ful credence in sothnesse of loue with a good hert/ there as good euydence or experyence in doynge sheweth not the

1309 mokel, much. **1315 wenest**, suppose; **accompte**, account. **1320 yeveth**, gives; **lyste**, pleases; **sothe**, true. **1321 adewe**, God; **deblys**, devil. **1322 yeven**, give.

contrarye. Thus mightest thou have ful prefe in thy Margarytes goodnesse, by commendement of other jewels badnesse and yvelnesse in doyng. Stoundemele diseases yeveth several houres in joye."

"Nowe by my trouthe," quod I, "this is wel declared that my Margaryte is good, for sythen other ben good, and she passeth manye other in goodnesse and vertue, wherthroughe by maner necessarye she muste be good. And goodnesse of this Margaryte is no thynge els but vertue, wherfore she is vertuous. And if there fayled any vertue in any syde, there were lacke of vertue. Badde nothynge els is, ne may be, but lacke and wante of good and goodnesse, and so shulde she have that same lacke, that is to saye, badde, and that maye not be, for she is good, and that is good, methynketh al good. And so by consequence, me semeth vertuous and no lacke of vertue to have. But the sonne is not knowe but he shyne, ne vertuous herbes but they have her kynde werchynge ne vertue, but it stretche in goodnesse or profyte to another, is no vertue. Than, by al wayes of reason, sythen mercy and pytie ben moste commended amonge other vertues, and they myght never ben shewed refresshement of helpe and of comforte, but nowe

---

contrarye. Thus mightest thou haue ful prefe in thy Margarytes goodnesse/ by co*m*mendement of other iewels badnesse/ and yuelnesse in doyng. Stoundemele diseases yeueth seueral houres in ioye.

Nowe by my trouthe (quod I) this is wel**<349ra><349rb>**declared that my Margaryte is good/ for sythen other ben good/ and she passeth manye other in goodnesse and vertue/ wherthroughe by maner necessarye she muste be good: and goodnesse of this Margaryte is no thynge els but vertue/ wherfore she is vertuous/ and if there fayled any vertue in any syde/ there were lacke of vertue: badde nothynge els is ne may be/ but lacke and wante of good and goodnesse/ and so shulde she haue that same lacke/ that is to saye badde/ and that maye not be for she is good and that is good methynketh al good: and so by consequence me semeth vertuous and no lacke of vertue to haue. But the sonne is not knowe but he shyne/ ne vertuous herbes but they haue her kynde werchynge/ ne vertue but it stretche in goodnesse or profyte to another/ is no vertue. Than by al wayes of reason/ sythen mercy and pytie ben moste commended amonge other vertues/ and they myght neuer ben shewed refresshement of helpe and of comforte/ but nowe

1324 prefe, proof. **1325 Stoundemele**, Sometimes. **1328 sythen**, since. **1335 but**, unless; **kynde werchynge**, natural function. **1337 sythen**, since. **1338 shewed**, shown.

at my moste nede and that is the kynde werkynge of these vertues; trewly, I wene I shal not varye from these helpes.

Fyre, and if he yeve none heate, for fyre is not demed. The sonne, but he shyne, for sonne is not accompted. Water, but it wete, the name shal ben chaunged. Vertue but it werche of goodnesse dothe it fayle, and into his contrarye the name shal ben reversed. And these ben impossyble, wherfore the contradictorie that is necessarye, nedes muste I leve."

"Certes," quod she, "in thy person and out of thy mouthe these wordes lyen wel to ben said and in thyne understandyng to be leved as in entent of this Margaryte alone. And here nowe my speche in conclusyon of these wordes.

Chapter XIV

"In these thinges," quod she, "that me lyst nowe to shewe openly, shal be founde the mater of thy sicknesse, and what shal ben the medicyn that may be thy sorowes lysse and comfort, as wel thee as al other that amysse have erred and out of the way walked,

---

at my moste nede/ and that is the kynde werkynge of these vertues: trewly I wene I shal not varye from these helpes.

Fyre and if he yeue none heate/ for fyre is not demed. The sonne but he shyne/ for sonne is not accompted. Water but it wete/ the name shal ben chaunged. Vertue but it werche /of goodnesse dothe it fayle/ and in to his contrarye the name shal ben reuersed/ and these ben impossyble: wherfore the contradictorie that is necessarye/ nedes muste I leue.

Certes (quod she) in thy person and out of thy mouthe these wordes lyen wel to ben said/ and in thyne vnderstandyng to be leued/ as in entent of this Margaryte alone: and here nowe my speche in conclusyon of chese wordes.

IN these thinges (quod she) that me lyst nowe to shewe openly/ shal be founde the mater of thy sicknesse/ *and* what shal ben the medicyn th*at* may be thy sorowes lysse *and* com*f*ort/ **<349rb><349va>**as wel the as al other that amysse haue erred/ and out of the way walked/

1339 wene, know. **1341 yeve**, give; **demed**, held, judged. **1342 accompted**, accounted; **but it wete**, unless it be wet. **1345 leve**, believe. **1346 lyen wel**, are appropriate. **1349 me lyst**, it pleases me. **1350 lysse**, relief.

so that any drope of good wyl in amendement ben dwelled in their hertes. Proverbes of Salomon openly teacheth howe somtyme an innocent walkyd by the way in blyndnesse of a derke night, whom mette a woman (if it be lefely to saye) as a strumpet arayed redily purveyed in turnynge of thoughtes with veyne janglynges, and of rest inpacient, by dissymulacion of my termes, sayeng in this wyse: 'Come and be we dronken of our swete pappes; use we coveytous collynges.' And thus drawen was this innocent as an oxe to the larder." "Lady," quod I, "to me this is a queynte thynge to understonde. I praye you, of this parable declare me the entent." "This innocent," quod she, "is a scholer lernynge of my lore in sechyng of my blysse, in whiche thynge the daye of his thought turnyng enclyneth into eve, and the sonne, of very lyght faylinge, maketh derke nyght in his connynge. Thus in derknesse of many doutes he walketh, and for blyndenesse of understandynge, he ne wote in what waye he is in. Forsothe, suche one may lightly ben begyled. To whome came love fayned, not clothed of my lyvery, but unleful lustye habyte, with softe speche and mery, and with fayre honyed wordes heretykes and misse-menynge people skleren and wymplen their errours. Austen

---

so that any drope of good wyl in amendement ben dwelled in their hertes. Prouerbes of Salomon openly teacheth/ howe somtyme an innocent walkyd by th*e* way in blyndnesse of a derke night/ whom mette a woman (if it be lefely to saye) as a strumpet arayed/ redily purueyed in turnynge of thoughtes with veyne ianglynges/ and of rest inpacient by dissymulacion of my termes/ sayeng in this wyse: Come and be we dronken of our swete pappes/ vse we coueytous collynges. And thus drawen was this innocent/ as an oxe to the larder. Lady (q*uo*d I) to me this is a queynte thynge to vnderstonde: I praye you of this parable declare me the entent. This innocent (quod she) is a scholer lernynge of my lore/ in sechyng of my blysse/ in whiche thynge the daye of his thought turnyng enclyneth in to eue/ and the sonne of very lyght faylinge/ maketh derke nyght in his connynge. Thus in derknesse of many doutes he walketh/ and for blyndenesse of vnderstandynge/ he ne wote in what waye he is in: forsothe suche one may lightly ben begyled. To whome came loue fayned/ not clothed of my lyuery/ but vnleful lustye habyte/ with softe speche and mery/ and with fayre honyed wordes heretykes and misse menynge people skleren and wymplen their errours. Austen

1354 lefely, permissible. **1357 collynges**, embraces. **1358 queynte**, curious, difficult. **1360 sechyng**, seeking. **1362 connynge**, understanding. **1363 wote**, knows. **1364 lightly**, easily. **1365 unleful**, inappropriate. **1366 skleren**, veil; **wymplen**, conceal.

wytnesseth of an heretyke that, in his first begynnynge, he was a man right experte in resones and swete in his wordes, and the werkes miscorden. Thus fareth fayned love in her firste werchynges. Thou knowest these thynges for trewe. Thou haste hem proved by experience, somtyme in doyng to thyne owne person, in whiche thyng thou hast founde mater of mokel disease. Was not fayned love redily purveyed, thy wyttes to catche and tourne thy good thoughtes? Trewly, she hath wounded the conscience of many with florisshynge of mokel janglyng wordes, and goodworthe thanked I it for no glose. I am gladde of my prudence thou haste so manly her veyned. To me arte thou moche holden that in thy kynde course of good meanyng I returne thy mynde. I trowe ne had I shewed thee thy Margaryte, thou haddest never returned. Of first in good parfyte joye was ever fayned love impacient, as the water of Syloe whiche evermore floweth with stylnesse and privy noyse tyl it come nyghe the brinke, and than gynneth it so out of measure to bolne with novelleries of chaungyng stormes that in course of every rennyng it is in poynte to spyl al his circuite of bankes. Thus fayned love prively

---

wytnesseth of an heretyke that in his first begynnynge he was a man right experte in resones/ and swete in his wordes/ and the werkes miscorden. Thus fareth fayned loue in her firste werchynges: thou knowest these thynges for trewe/ thou haste hem proued by experience. Somtyme in doyng to thyne owne person/ in whiche thyng thou hast founde mater of mokel disease/ Was not fayned loue redily purueyed thy wyttes to catche and tourne thy good thoughtes? trewly she hath wounded the conscience of many with florisshynge of mokel ianglyng wordes: and goodworthe thanked I it for no glose/ I am gladde of my prudence thou haste so manly her veyned. To me arte thou moche holden/ that in thy kynde course of good meanyng I returne thy mynde: I trowe ne had I shewed**<349va><349vb>**the thy Margaryte/ thou haddest neuer returned./ Of first in good parfyte ioye was euer fayned loue impacie*nt*/ as the water of Syloe/ whiche euermore floweth with stylnesse and priuy noyse/ tyl it come nyghe the brinke/ and than gynneth it so out of measure to bolne/ with nouelleries of chaungyng stormes/ that in course of euery rennyng it is in poynte to spyl al his circuite of cankes. Thus fayned loue priuely

1371 mokel, much. **1373 mokel**, many. **1374 glose**, and without any sugaring over, I called it of good worth; **veyned**, turned away. **1375 trowe**, trust. **1379 bolne**, boil, swell; **novelleries**, variableness.

at the fullest of his flowynge newe stormes debate to arayse. And albeit that Mercurius often with hole understandynge knowen suche peryllous maters, yet Veneriens so lusty ben and so leude in their wyttes that in suche thynges right lytel or naught don they fele, and writen and cryen to their felawes: 'here is blysse here is joye,' and thus into one same errour mokel folke they drawen. 'Come,' they sayne and 'be we dronken of our pappes,' that ben fallas and lyeng glose, of whiche mowe they not souke mylke of helthe, but deedly venym and poyson corrupcion of sorowe. Mylke of fallas is venym of disceyte: Mylke of lyeng glose is venym of corrupcion. Lo, what thynge cometh out of these pappes: 'Use we coveyted collynges, desyre we and meddle we false wordes with sote, and sote with false.' Trewly this is the sorynesse of fayned love. Nedes of these surfettes sicknesse must folowe. Thus, as an oxe to thy langoring deth were thou drawen. The sote of the smoke hath thee al defased. Ever the deper thou somtyme wadest, the soner thou it founde. If it had thee kylled, it had be lytel wonder. But on that other syde, my trewe servaunt not faynen ne disceyve conne. Sothly, their doynge is

---

at the fullest of his flowynge/ newe stormes debate to arayse. And al be it that Mercurius often with hole vnderstandynge knowen suche peryllous maters/ yet Veneriens so lusty ben and so leude in their wyttes/ that in suche thynges right lytel or naught don they fele and writen and cryen to their felawes: here is blysse/ here is ioye/ and thus in to one same errour/ mokel folke they drawen. Come they sayne/ and be we dronken of our pappes/ that ben fallas and lyeng glose/ of whiche mowe they not souke mylke of helthe/ but deedly venym and poyson corrupcion of sorowe. Mylke of fallas/ is venym of disceyte: Mylke of lyeng glose is venym of corrupcion. Lo what thynge cometh out of these pappes: vse we coueyted collynges/ desyre we and meddle we false wordes with sote/ and sote with false/ trewly this is the sorynesse of fayned loue/ nedes of these surfettes sicknesse must folowe. Thus as an oxe to thy langoring deth were thou drawen/ the sote of the smoke hath the al defased. Euer the deper thou somtyme wadest the soner thou it founde: if it had the kylled it had be lytel wonder. But on that other syde my trewe seruaunt not faynen ne disceyue conne/ sothly their doynge is

1381 Mercurius, i.e., servants of Mercury. **1382 Veneriens**, i.e., servants of Venus. **1383 leude**, ignorant. **1385 mokel**, many. **1386 pappes**, breasts; **fallas**, deceitful; **mowe**, may; **souke**, suck. **1387 fallas**, fallacy. **1389 collynges**, embraces. **1390 sote**, sweet; **Nedes**, Necessarily. **1391 surfettes**, surfeits. **1392 sote**, soot; **deper**, deeper. **1393 soner**, sooner. **1394 faynen**, pretend; **conne**, can, know how to.

open, my foundement endureth, be the burthen never so great. Ever in one it lasteth. It yeveth lyfe and blysful goodnesse in the laste endes, though the gynnynges ben sharpe. Thus of two contraries, contrarye ben the effectes. And so thylke Margaryte thou servest shal sene thee, by her servyce out of peryllous trybulacion delyvered, bycause of her servyce into newe disease fallen, by hope of amendement in the laste ende, with joye to be gladded. Wherfore, of kynde pure, her mercy with grace of good helpe shal she graunt, and els I shal her so strayne that with pyté shal she ben amaystred. Remembre in thyne herte howe horrybly somtyme to thyne Margaryte thou trespasest, and in a great wyse ayenst her thou forfeytest. Clepe ayen thy mynde, and knowe thyne owne gyltes. What goodnesse, what bountie with mokel folowyng pyté founde thou in that tyme? Were thou not goodly accepted into grace? By my pluckynge was she to foryevenesse enclyned. And after I her styred to drawe thee to house, and yet wendest thou utterly for ever have ben refused. But wel thou wost sythen that I in suche sharpe disease might so greatly avayle what thynkest in thy wyt? Howe ferre maye my wytte

---

open/ my foundement endureth/ be the burthen neuer so great/ euer in one it lasteth: it yeueth lyfe and blysful goodnesse in the laste endes/ though the gynnynges ben sharpe. Thus of two contraries/ contrarye ben the effectes. And so thylke Margaryte thou seruest shal sene the by her seruyce out of peryllous trybulacion delyuered/ bycause of her seruyce in to newe disease fallen/ by hope of amendement in the laste ende/ with ioye to be gladded/ wherfore of kynde pure/ her mercy with grace of good helpe shal she**<349vb><350ra>**grau*n*t/ and els I shal her so strayne/ that with pyte shal she ben amaystred. Remembre in thyne herte howe horrybly somtyme to thyne Margaryte thou trespasest/ and in a great wyse ayenst her thou forfeytest: clepe ayen thy mynde/ and knowe thyne owne gyltes. What goodnesse/ what bountie/ with mokel folowyng pyte founde thou in that tyme? Were thou not goodly accepted in to grace? by my pluckynge was she to foryeuenesse enclyned. And after I her styred to drawe the to house/ and yet wendest thou vtterly for euer haue ben refused. But wel thou wost/ sythen that I in suche sharpe disease might so greatly auayle/ what thynkest in thy wyt? howe ferre maye my wytte

1396 yeveth, gives. **1397 thylke**, that very. **1401 amaystred**, mastered. **1403 forfeytest**, transgressed; **Clepe**, Call. **1404 mokel**, much. **1406 styred**, steered; **wendest**, assumed. **1407 wost**, know; **sythen**, since.

stretche? And thou lache not on thy syde, I wol make the knotte: Certes, in thy good beryng I wol acorde with the psauter. I have founde David in my servyce true, and with holy oyle of peace and of rest longe by him desyred, utterly he shal be anoynted. Truste wel to me, and I wol thee not fayle. The leavyng of the first way with good herte of contynuance that I se in thee grounded, this purpose to parfourme, draweth me by maner of costrainyng that nedes must I ben thyne helper. Although myrthe a whyle be taryed, it shal come at suche season that thy thought shal ben joyed. And wolde never God, sythen thyne herte to my reasones arne assented and openly haste confessed thyne amysse-goynge and nowe cryest after mercy, but if mercy folowed. Thy blysse shal ben redy, iwys thou ne wost how sone. Now be a good chylde I rede. The kynde of vertues in thy Margaryte rehersed by strength of me in thy person shul werche. Comforte thee in this, for thou mayst not miscary."

And these wordes sayde, she streyght her on length and rested a whyle.

Thus endeth the seconde booke, and here after foloweth the thirde boke.

---

stretche? and thou lache not on thy syde I wol make the knotte: Certes in thy good beryng I wol acorde with the psauter. I haue foude Dauid in my seruyce true/ and with holy oyle of peace and of rest longe by him desyred/ vtterly he shal be anoynted. Truste wel to me/ and I wol the not fayle. The leanyng of the first way with good herte of contynuance/ that I se in the grounded/ this purpose to parfourme/ draweth me by maner of costrainyng/ that nedes must I ben thyne helper: although myrthe a whyle be taryed/ it shal come at suche season/ that thy thought shal ben ioyed. And wolde neuer god/ sythen thyne herte to my reasones arne assented/ and openly haste confessed thyne amysse goynge/ and nowe cryest after mercy/ but if mercy folowed: thy blysse shal ben redy iwys/ thou ne wost how sone. Now be a good chylde I rede. The kynde of vertues in thy Margaryte rehersed/ by strength of me in thy person shul werche. Comforte the in this/ for thou mayst not miscary.

And these wordes sayde/ she streyght her on length and rested a whyle.

Thus endeth the seconde booke/ and here after foloweth the thirde boke.**<350ra>**

1409 lache not, are not negligent. **1410 psauter**, Psalter. **1412 leavyng**, leaving. **1415 taryed**, delayed. **1416 sythen**, since. **1418 iwys**, indeed; **sone**, soon; **rede**, advise. **1421 streyght her on length**, reclined.

The Testament of Love

Book 3

Chapter I

Of nombre, sayne these clerkes, that it is naturel somme of discrete thynges, as in tellynge one, two, thre, and so forth, but amonge al nombres thre is determyned for moste certayne. Wherfore in nombre certayne this werke of my besy leudenesse I thynke to ende and parfourme. Ensample by this worlde in thre tymes is devyded: of whiche the firste is cleped Deviacion, that is to say, goyng out of trewe way; and al that tho dyeden, in hel were they punisshed for a mans synne, tyl grace and mercy fette hem thence, and there ended the firste tyme. The seconde tyme lasteth from the commyng of merciable grace untyl the ende of transytorie tyme, in whiche is shewed the true way in fordoynge of the badde, and that is ycleped tyme of Grace. And that thynge is not yeven by deserte of yeldynge one benefyte for another, but onely through goodnesse of the yever of grace in thilke tyme. Whoso can wel understande is shapen to be saved in

---

<350rb>OF nombre sayne these clerkes that it is naturel so*m*me of discrete thynges/ as in tellynge one/ two/ thre and so forth: but amonge al nombres thre is determyned for moste certayne. Wherfore in nombre certayne this/ werke of my besy leudenesse I thynke to ende and parfourme. Ensample by this worlde in thre tymes is deuyded: of whiche the firste is cleped Demacion/ that is to say/ goyng out of trewe way/ and al that tho dyeden/ in hel were they punisshed for a mans synne/ tyl grace *and* mercy fette hem thence/ and there ended the firste tyme. The seconde tyme lasteth from the co*m*myng of merciable grace/ vntyl the ende of transytorie tyme/ in whiche is shewed the true way in fordoynge of the badde/ and that is ycleped tyme of grace: and that thynge is not yeuen by deserte of yeldynge one benefyte for another/ but onely through goodnesse of the yeuer of grace in thilke tyme. Who so can wel vnderstande/ is shapen to be saued in

3 leudenesse, ignorance, lack of learning. **4 in**, into. **6 dyeden**, died; **fette**, fetched. **9 ycleped**, called. **10 yeven**, given. **11 yever**, giver; **thilke**, that same; **shapen**, shaped.

souled blysse. The thirde tyme shal gyn whan transytorie thynges of worldes han made their ende, and that shal ben in Joye, glorie, and rest, both body and soule, that wel han deserved in the tyme of grace. And thus in that heven togyther shul they dwel perpetuelly without any ymaginatyfe yvel in any halve. These tymes are fygured by tho thre dayes that our God was closed in erthe, and in the thirde arose shewyng our resurrection to joye and blysse of tho that it deserven by his merciable grace. So this leude boke in thre maters accordaunt to tho tymes lightly by a good inseer maye ben understonde as in the firste, erroure of mysse goynge is shewed with sorowful pyne punysshed that cryed after mercy. In the seconde, is grace in good waye proved, whiche is faylinge without deserte, thylke first mysse amendynge in correction of tho erroures and even waye to bringe with comforte of welfare in to amendement wexynge. And in the thirde, joye and blysse graunted to hym that wel canne deserve it and hath savour of understandynge in the tyme of grace. Thus in joye of my thirde boke shal the mater be tyl it ende. But special cause I have in my hert to make this processe of a Margarit peerle that is so precious a gemme, whit, clere and lytel, of whiche stones or jewel the tonges of us

---

souled blysse. The thirde tyme shal gyn whan tra*n*sytorie thynges of worldes han made their ende and that shal ben in ioye/ glorie/ and rest/ both body and soule/ that wel han deserued in the tyme of grace. And thus in that heuen togyther shul they dwel perpetuelly without any ymaginatyfe yuel in any halue. These tymes are fygured by tho thre dayes that our god was closed in erthe/ and in the thirde arose shewyng our resurrection/ to ioye and blysse of tho that it deseruen/ hy his merciable grace. So this leude boke in thre maters accordaunt to tho tymes/ lightly by a good inseer maye ben vnderstonde/ as in the firste erroure of mysse goynge is shewed/ with sorowful pyne punysshed is cryed after mercy. In the seconde is grace in good waye proued/ whiche is faylinge without deserte/ thylke first mysse amendynge in correction of tho erroures and euen waye to bringe/ with comforte of welfare in to amendement wexynge. And in the thirde ioye and blysse graunted to hym that wel canne deserue it/ and hath sauour of vnderstandynge in the tyme of grace. Thus in ioye of my thirde boke shal the mater be tyl it**<350rb>** **<350va>**ende. But special cause I haue in my hert to make this processe of a Margarit peerle/ that is so precious a ge*m*me with clere *and* lytel/ of whiche stones or iewel/ the tonges of vs

12 souled blysse, bliss appropriate to the soul. **15 in any halve**, on any side; **tho**, those. **17 leude**, uninformed. **18 inseer**, investigator. **19 pyne**, pain. **22 wexynge**, growing.

Englissh people tourneth the right names and clepeth hem "Margery perles." Thus varyeth our speche from many other langages, for trewly, Latyn, Frenche, and many mo other langages cleapeth hem Margery perles the name Margarites or Margarite perles; wherfore in that denomynacion I wol me acorde to other mens tonges in that name clepyng. These clerkes that treaten of kyndes and studyen out the propertie there of thynges sayne the Margarite is a lytel whyte perle, throughout holowe and rounde and vertuous, and, on the see sydes in the more Britayne, in muskle shelles, of the hevenly dewe the best ben engendred; in whiche by experience ben founde thre fayre vertues. One is, it yeveth comforte to the felyng spyrites in bodily persones of reason. Another is good: it is profytable helthe ayenst passyons of sorie mens hertes. And the thirde, it is nedeful and noble in staunchyng of bloode, there els to moche wolde out ren. To whiche perle and vertues me lyst to liken at this tyme Philosophie with her thre speces, that is, natural and moral and resonable, of whiche thynges hereth what sayne these great clerkes. Philosophie is knowyng of devynly and manly thinges joyned with studye of good lyvyng, and this stante in two thynges: that is connynge and opinyon. Connynge is

---

Englissh people tourneth the riȝt names/ *and* clepeth hem Margery perles: thus varyeth our speche fro*m* many other langages. For trewly latyn/ frenche/ and many mo other langages cleapeth hem Margery perles/ the name Margarites or Margarite perles: wherfore in that denomynacion I wol me acorde to other mens tonges/ in that name clepyng. These clerkes that treaten of kyndes/ *and* studyen out the propertie there of thynges/ sayne the Margarite is a lytel whyte perle/ throughout holowe and rounde/ and vertuous/ and on the see sydes in the more Britayne in muskle shelles of th*e* heuenly dewe the best ben engendred: in whiche by experience ben founde thre fayre vertues. One is/ it yeueth comforte to the felyng spyrites in bodily persones of reason. Another is good/ it is profytable helthe ayenst passyons of sorie mens hertes. And the thirde it is nedeful and noble in staunchyng of bloode/ there els to moche wolde out ren. To whiche perle and vertues me lyst to liken at this tyme Philosophie with her thre speces/ that is natural and moral/ and resonable: of whiche thynges hereth what sayne these great clerkes. Philosophie is knowyng of deuynly *and* manly thinges ioyned with studye of good lyuyng/ and this stante in two thynges/ that is connynge and opinyon: connynge is

27 clepeth hem, call them. **33 more Britayne**, Great Britain. **35 felyng**, animal; **Another**, A second. **37 to**, too; **ren**, run. **38 me lyst**, it pleases me; **liken**, compare; **speces**, species, branches. **41 connynge**, understanding.

whan a thyng by certayne reson is conceyved. But wretches and fooles and leude men, many wyl conceyve a thyng and mayntayne it as for sothe, though reson be in the contrarye, wherfore connynge is a straunger. Opinyon is whyle a thyng is in non certayne and hydde from mens very knowlegyng, and by no parfyte reason fully declared as thus: if the sonne be so mokel as men wenen, or els if it be more than the erthe. For in sothnesse the certayn quantyté of that planet is unknowen to erthly dwellers, and yet by opinyon of some men it is holden for more than mydle erth. The first spece of philosophie is naturel, whiche in kyndely thynges treten and sheweth causes of heven and strength of kyndely course, as by arsmetrike, geometry, musyke, and by astronomye techeth wayes and course of hevens, of planetes, and of sterres aboute heven and erthe and other elementes. The seconde spece is moral, whiche in order of lyvyng maners techeth, and by reson proveth vertues of soule moste worthy in our lyveng; whiche ben prudence, justyce, temperaunce, and strength. Prudence is goodly wysdome in knowyng of thynges. Strength voydeth al adversitees alyche even. Temperaunce distroyeth beestyal lyveng with easy bearyng. And justyce rightfully jugeth,

---

whan a thyng by certayne reson is co*n*ceyued. But wretches and fooles and leude men/ many wyl conceyue a thyng and mayntayne it as for sothe/ though reson be in the contrarye/ wherfore connynge is a straunger. Opinyon is whyle a thyng is in non certayne/ and hydde from mens very knowlegyng/ and by no parfyte reason fully declared/ as thus: if the sonne be so mokel as men wenen/ or els if it be more than the erthe. For in sothnesse the certayn quantyte of that planet is vnknowen to erthly dwellers/ and yet by opinyon of some men it is holden for more than mydle erth The first spece of philosophie is naturel/ whiche in kyndely thynges treten/ and sheweth causes of heuen/ and**<350va><350vb>**strength of kyndely course: as by arsmetrike/ geometry/ musyke/ *and* by astronomye/ techeth wayes and course of heuens/ of planetes/ and of sterres aboute heuen and erthe/ and other eleme*n*tes. The seconde spece is moral/ whiche in order of lyuyng maners techeth/ and by reson proueth vertues of soule moste worthy in our lyueng/ whiche ben prudence/ iustyce/ temperaunce/ and strength. Prudence is goodly wysdome in knowyng of thynges. Strength voydeth al aduersitees alyche euen. Temperaunce distroyeth beestyal lyueng/ with easy bearyng. And iustyce rightfully iugeth/

42 leude, ignorant. **46 mokel**, great; **wenen**, assume; **more**, greater. **48 mydle erth**, middle-earth. **49 spece**, type, species; **kyndely**, natural. **55 alyche**, alike, equally. **56 easy bearyng**, easy bearing, (i.e., moderation).

and jugyng departeth to every wight that is his owne. The thirde spece turneth into reason of understandyng al thynges to be sayd soth and discussed, and that in two thynges is devyded. One is arte, another is rethorike, in whiche two al lawes of mans reason ben grounded, or els maintayned. And for this booke is al of love and therafter beareth his name, and phylosophie and lawe muste hereto acorden by their clergyal discripcions — as phylosophie for love of wisdome is declared, lawe for mainteynaunce of peace is holden — and these with love must nedes acorden, therfore of hem in this place have I touched. Ordre of homly thinges and honest maner of lyvynge in vertue with right ful jugement in causes and profitable administration in commynalties of realmes and cytes by evenhed profitably to raigne nat by singuler avauntage, ne by privé envy, ne by soleyn purpose in covetise of worship or of goodes, ben disposed in open rule shewed by love, philosophy, and lawe, and yet love toforn al other. Wherfore as susterne in unité they accorden, and one ende — that is peace and rest — they causen norisshinge, and in the joye maynteynen to endure.

Nowe than, as I have declared: my boke acordeth with discription of thre thynges,

---

and iugyng departeth to euery wight that is his owne. The thirde spece turneth in to reason of vnderstandyng/ al thynges to be sayd soth and discussed/ *and* that in two thynges is deuyded: one is arte/ another is rethorike/ in whiche two al lawes of mans reason ben grounded or els maintayned. And for this booke is al of loue/ and therafter beareth his name/ and phylosophie and lawe muste here to acorden by their clergyal discripcions: as phylosophie for loue of wisdome is declared: Lawe for mainteynaunce of peace is holden/ and these with loue must nedes acorden/ therfore of hem in this place haue I touched. Ordre of homly thinges *and* honest maner of lyuynge in vertue/ with right ful iugem*en*t in causes and p*ro*fitable administration in co*m*mynalties of realmes *and* cytes/ by euenhed profitably to raigne/ nat by singuler auau*n*tage ne by priue enuy/ ne by soleyn purpose in couetise of worship or of goodes/ ben disposed in open rule shewed/ by loue philosophy/ *and* lawe/ *and* yet loue toforn al other. Wherfore as susterne in vnite they accorden *and* one ende that is peace *and* rest/ they causen norisshinge/ *and* in the ioye maynteynen to endure.

Nowe than/ as I haue declared: my boke acordeth with discription of thre thynges/

57 wight, person; **that**, that [which]. **61 clergyal**, clerical, learned. **67 privé**, private, secret; **soleyn**, sullen, anti-social.

and the Margarit in vertue is lykened to Philosophy, with her thre speces. In whiche maters ever twey ben acordaunt with bodily reason, and the thirde with the soule. But in conclusyon of my boke and of this Margarite peerle in knyttynge togider, lawe by thre sondrie maners shal be lykened; that is to saye, lawe, right, and custome, whiche I wol declare. Al that is lawe cometh of Goddes ordynance by kyndly worchyng, and thilke thynges ordayned by mannes wyttes arn ycleped right, which is ordayned by many maners and in constitution written. But custome is a thyng that is accepted for right or for lawe, there as lawe and right faylen, and there is no difference whether it come of scripture or of reason. Wherfore it sheweth that lawe is kyndly governaunce. Right cometh out of mannes probable reson; and custome is of commen usage by length of tyme used, and custome nat writte is usage; and if it be writte, constitutyon it is ywritten and ycleped. But lawe of kynde is commen to every nation, as conjunction of man and woman in love, succession of children in heritance, restitution of thyng by strength taken or lent, and this lawe among al other halte the soveraynest gree in worship, whiche lawe began at the begynnyng of reasonable creature. It varyed yet never

---

and the Margarit in vertue is lykened to philosophy/ with her thre speces. In whiche maters euer twey ben acordaunt with bodily reason/ *and* the thirde with the soule: But in co*n*clusyon of my boke *and* of this Margarite peerle in knyttynge togider lawe by thre sondrie maners shalbe lykened/ that is to saye/ lawe/ right/ *and* custome/ whiche I wol declare: al that is lawe cometh**<350vb><351ra>**of goddes ordynance by kyndly worchyng/ *and* thilke thynges ordayned by man*n*es wytt*es* arn ycleped right/ which is ordayned by many maners *and* in co*n*stitution written: but custome is a thyng that is accepted for right or for lawe/ there as lawe *and* right faylen/ *and* there is no difference/ whether it come of scripture or of reason. Wherfore it sheweth that lawe is kyndly gouernaunce: Right cometh out of man*n*es p*ro*bable reson: *and* custome is of com*m*en vsage by length of tyme vsed/ *and* custome nat writte is vsage/ *and* if it be writte co*n*stitutyon it is ywritten *and* ycleped: But lawe of kynde is co*m*men to euery nation/ as co*n*iunction of man and woman in loue/ succession of children in herit*an*ce restitution of thyng by strentgh taken or lent/ and this lawe among al other halte the soueraynest gree in worship/ Whiche lawe began at the begynnyng of reasonable creature/ it varyed yet neuer

73 twey, two. **76 kyndly worchyng**, natural operation. **77 ycleped**, called. **82 writte**, written. **85 gree**, degree.

for no chaungyng of tyme. Cause, forsothe, in ordaynyng of lawe was to constrayne mens hardynesse into peace, and withdrawing his yvel wyl, and turnyng malyce into goodnesse, and that innocence sykerly withouten teneful anoye amonge shrewes safely might inhabyte by protection of safe-conducte, so that the shrewes, harme for harme, by bridle of ferdenesse shulden restrayne. But, forsothe, in kyndely lawe nothynge is commended but such as Goddes wyl hath confyrmed, ne nothyng denyed but contraryoustie of Goddes wyl in heven. Eke, than al lawes or custome or els constitucion by usage or writyng that contraryen lawe of kynde utterly ben repugnaunt and adversarye to our Goddes wyl of heven. Trewly, lawe of kynde for Goddes own lusty wyl is verily to maintayne, under which lawe (and unworthy) bothe professe and reguler arne obedyencer and bounden to this Margarite perle as by knotte of loves statutes and stablysshment in kynde whiche that goodly maye not ben withsetten. Lo, under this bonde am I constrayned to abyde, and man under lyveng lawe ruled; by that lawe oweth after desertes to ben rewarded by payn or by mede, but if mercy weyve the payne. So than be parte reasonfully may be sey that mercy bothe right and lawe

---

for no chaungyng of tyme: cause forsothe in ordaynyng of lawe/ was to constrayne mens hardynesse in to peace/ and withdrawing his yuel wyl/ and turnyng malyce in to goodnesse/ and that innocence sykerly withouten teneful anoye amonge shrewes safely might inhabyte by protection of safe-conducte/ so that the shrewes harme for harme by bridle of ferdenesse shulden restrayne. But forsothe in kyndely lawe nothynge is co*m*mended/ but such as goddes wyl hath confyrmed/ ne nothyng denyed but co*n*traryoustie of goddes wyl in heuen: eke than al lawes or custome/ or els co*n*stitucion by vsage or writyng that co*n*traryen lawe of kynde/ vtterly ben repugnaunt and aduersarye to our goddes wyl of heuen. Trewly lawe of kynde for goddes own lusty wyl is verily to maintayne/ under which lawe (*and* vnworthy) bothe professe and reguler arne obedyencer and bounden to this Margarite perle/ as by knotte of loues statutes and stablysshment in kynde/ whiche that goodly maye not ben withsetten. Lo vnder this bonde am I constrayned to abyde/ and man vnder lyueng lawe ruled: by that lawe oweth after desertes to ben rewarded by payn or by mede/ but if mercy weyue the payne: so than be parte/ reasonfully may be sey/ that mercy bothe right and lawe

89 teneful, painful. **91 ferdenesse**, fear. **93 Eke**, Also. **96 professe**, religious; **reguler**, lay (not having "professed" vows). **98 withsetten**, resisted. **100 after**, according to; **mede**, wealth; **but if**, unless; **weyve**, waive. **101 sey**, seen.

passeth. Th'entent of al these maters is, at the lest clere understanding, to weten at th'ende of this thirde boke. Ful knowing thorowe Goddes grace I thynke to make neverthelater yet, if these thynges han a good; and a sleight inseer, whiche that can souke hony of the harde stone, oyle of the drye rocke, may lyghtly fele nobley of mater in my leude ymagination closed. But for my boke shal be of joye (as I said) and I so ferre set fro thilke place fro whens gladnesse shulde come, my corde is to short to let my boket ought catch of that water, and fewe men be abouten my corde to eche, and many in ful purpose ben redy it shorter to make and to enclose th'entré, that my boket of joye nothing shulde catch, but empty returne, my careful sorowes to encrese. And if I dye for payne, that were gladnesse at their hertes. Good Lorde sende me water into the cop of these mountayns, and I shal drynke therof my thurstes to stanch, and sey, "these be comfortable welles; in to helth of goodnesse of my saviour am I holpen." And yet I saye more: the house of joye to me is nat opened. How dare my sorouful goost than in any mater of gladnesse thynken to trete? For ever sobbynges and complayntes be redy refrete in his meditations, as werbles in manyfold stoundes commyng about I

---

passeth/ thentent**<351ra><351rb>**of al these maters is the lest clere vnderstanding/ to weten at thende of this thirde boke ful knowing thorowe goddes grace/ I thynke to make neuerthelater/ yet if these thynges han a good and a sleight inseer/ whiche that can souke hony of the harde stone/ oyle of the drye rocke/ may lyghtly fele nobley of mater i*n* my leude ymagination closed. But for my boke shal be of ioye (as I said) *and* I so ferre set fro thilke place/ fro whens gladnesse shulde come my corde is to short to let my boket ouȝt catch of that water/ *and* fewe men be abouten my corde to eche/ *and* many in ful purpose ben redy it shorter to make/ *and* to enclose thentre/ that my boket of ioye nothing shulde catch/ but empty returne/ my careful sorowes to encrese. *and* if I dye for payne/ that were gladnesse at their hertes. Good lorde sende me water into the cop of these mountayns/ *and* I shal drynke therof/ my thurstes to sta*n*ch: *and* sey these be co*m*fortable welles in to helth of goodnesse of my sauiour am I holpen. And yet I saye more/ the house of ioye to me is nat opened. How dare my sorouful goost than in any mater of gladnesse thynken to trete? for euer sobbynges *and* complayntes be redy refrete in his meditatio*ns*/ as werbles in manyfold stou*n*des co*m*myng about I

102 passeth, surpasses; **weten**, know. **104 sleight**, penetrating (see note); **inseer**, insightful viewer, reader. **105 fele**, feel; **nobley**, nobility. **106 leude**, uneducated. **108 eche**, lengthen. **109 th'entré**, entrance-way. **112 cop**, summit; **stanch**, slake, staunch. **113 holpen**, helped. **114 goost**, spirit. **116 refrete**, refrain; **werbles**, warblings; **stoundes**, times.

not than. And therfore, what maner of joye coude I endite? But yet at dore shal I knocke if the key of David wolde the locke unshyt, and He bring me in, whiche that childrens tonges both openeth and closeth, whose spirite where He wel worcheth departyng goodly as Him lyketh.

Nowe to Goddes laude and reverence, profite of the reders, amendement of maners of the herers, encresyng of worship among loves servauntes, relevyng of my hert into grace of my jewel, and frenship plesance of this peerle, I am stered in this makyng and for nothyng els. And if any good thyng to mennes lyking in this scripture be founde, thanketh the Maister of grace, whiche that of that good and al other is authour and principal doer. And if any thing be insufficient or els myslyking, wyte that the leudnesse of myne unable connyng, for body in disese anoyeth the understanding in soule. A disesely habitation letteth the wyttes in many thinges and namely in sorowe. The custome, neverthelater, of love be long tyme of service in termes I thinke to pursue, whiche ben lyvely to yeve understandyng in other thynges. But nowe to enform thee of this Margarites goodnesse I may her nat halfe preyse. Wherfore nat she for my boke, but

---

not than. And therfore what maner of ioye coude endite/ but yet at dore shal I knocke/ if the key of Dauid wolde the locke vnshyt/ *and* he bring me in/ whiche that childrens to*n*ges both openeth *and* closeth. Whose spirite/ where he wel worcheth/ departyng goodly as him lyketh.

Nowe to goddes laude *and* reuerence/ p*ro*fite of the reders/ ame*n*dement of maners of th*e* herers encresyng of worship among loues seruauntes/ releuyng of my hert in to grace of my iewel/ *and* frenship plesance of this peerle. I am stered in this makyng/ *and* for nothyng els: *and* if any good thyng to me*n*nes lyking in this scripture be founde/ thanketh the maister of grace/ whiche th*at* of that good *and* al other is authour/ *and* principal doer. And if any thing be insufficie*n*t or els myslyking/ with that th*at* the leudnesse of myne vnable co*n*nyng/ for body in disese anoyeth the vndersta*n*ding in soule. A disesely habitation letteth th*e* wyttes many thinges/ *and* namely in sorowe. The custome neuer the later of**<351rb><351va>**loue be long tyme of seruice in termes I thi*n*ke to pursue/ whiche ben lyuely to yeue vndersta*n*dyng in other thynges. But nowe to enform the of this Margarites goodnesse/ I may her nat halfe preyse. Wherfore nat she for my boke/ but

117 not than, don't know when; **endite**, compose. **118 unshyt**, open. **121 reders**, readers. **123 stered**, directed. **126 wyte**, blame that [on]; **leudnesse**, ignorance. **127 connyng**, understanding. **128 letteth**, hinders. **130 yeve**, give. **131 preyse**, praise.

this boke for her is worthy to be commended, tho my boke be leude; right as thinges nat for places, but places for thynges, ought to be desyred and praysed.

Chapter II

"Nowe," quod Love, "trewly thy wordes I have wel understonde. Certes, me thynketh hem right good, and me wondreth why thou so lightly passest in the lawe." "Sothly," quod I, "my wyt is leude and I am right blynde, and that mater depe. Howe shulde I than have waded? Lightly might I have drenched and spilte ther my selfe." "Yea," quod she, "I shal helpe thee to swym. For right as lawe punyssheth brekers of preceptes and the contrary doers of the written constitutions, right so ayenwarde lawe rewardeth and yeveth mede to hem that lawe strengthen. By one lawe this rebel is punisshed and this innocent is meded; the shrewe is enprisoned and this rightful is corowned. The same lawe that joyneth by wedlocke without forsakyng, the same lawe yeveth lybel of departicion bycause of devorse both demed and declared." "Ye, ye," quod I, "I fynde in no lawe to mede and rewarde in goodnes the gyltie of desertes." "Fole," quod she, "gyltie converted in your lawe mykel merite deserveth. Also Paulyn of Rome was

---

this boke for her is worthy to be co*m*mended/ tho my boke be leude: right as thy*n*ges nat for places/ but places for thinges ought to be desyred and praysed.

NOwe (q*uo*d Loue) trewly thy wordes I haue wel vnderst*on*de. Certes me thynketh hem right good/ *and* me wo*n*dreth why thou so lightly passest in the lawe. Sothly (q*uo*d I) my wyt is leude *and* I am right blynde *and* that mater depe/ howe shulde I than haue waded/ lightly miȝt I haue drenched *and* spilte ther my selfe. Yea (q*uo*d she) I shal helpe th*e* to swym. For riȝt as lawe punyssheth brekers of preceptes/ *and* the co*n*trary doers of the written constitutions: right so aye*n*warde/ lawe rewardeth *and* yeueth mede to he*m* that lawe strengthen. By one lawe this rebel is punisshed *and* this innocet is meded/ th*e* shrewe is enprisoned *and* this riȝtful is corowned. The same lawe that ioyneth by wedlocke without forsakyng/ the same lawe yeueth lybel of dep*ar*ticion bycause of deuorse both demed *and* declared. Ye ye (q*uo*d I) I fynde in no lawe tomede and rewarde in goodnes/ th*e* gyltie of desertes. Fole (q*uo*d she) gyltie co*n*uerted i*n* your lawe/ mykel merite deserueth. Also Pauly of Rome was

137 drenched, drowned; **spilte**, slain. **140 yeveth**, gives; **mede**, meed, wealth. **141 meded**, rewarded. **144 Fole**, Fool. **145 mykel**, much.

crowned that by him the maynteyners of Pompeus weren knowen and distroyed; and yet toforne was this Paulyn chefe of Pompeus counsaile. This lawe in Rome hath yet his name of mesuring in mede the bewrayeng of the conspiracy. Ordayned by tho senatours, the dethe of Julyus Cesar is acompted into Catons right wisnesse, for ever in trouth florissheth his name amonge the knowers of treason. Perdicas was crowned in the heritage of Alexander the great for tellynge of a prevy hate that kynge Porrus to Alexander hadde. Wherfore every wight, by reason of lawe after his rightwysenesse apertely, his mede may chalenge; and so thou that maynteynest lawe of kynde and therfore disease hast suffred in the lawe rewarde is worthy to be rewarded and ordayned, and apartly thy mede might thou chalenge." "Certes," quod I, "this have I wel lerned, and ever hensforward I shal drawe me therafter in onehed of wyl to abide, this lawe bothe mayntene and kepe, and so hope I best entre into your grace wel deservynge into worship of a wight without nedeful compulsion ought medefully to be rewarded." "Truly," quod Love, "that is sothe, and tho by constitution good service into profite and avauntage stretch, utterly many men it demen to have more desert of mede than

---

crowned/ th*at* by him the maynteyners of Pompeus weren knowen *and* distroyed: *and* yet to forne was this Paulyn chefe of Po*m*peus cou*n*saile. This lawe in Rome hath yet his name of mesuring in mede/ the bewrayeng of the co*n*spiracy/ ordayned by tho senatours the dethe. Julyus Cesar is aco*m*pted in to Catons right wisnesse/ for euer in trouth florissheth his name amonge the knowers of reason. Perdicas was crowned in the heritage of Alexa*n*der the great/ for tellynge of a preuy hate that kynge Porrus to Alexander hadde. Wherfore euery wight by reason of lawe after his rightwysenesse apertely his mede may chalenge: *and* so thou that maynteynest lawe of kynde/ *and* therfore disease hast suffred in th*e* lawe/ rewarde is worthy to be rewarded *and* ordayned/ *and* apartly thy**<351va><351vb>**mede might thou chalenge. Certes (q*uo*d I) this haue I wel lerned/ *and* euer hensforward I shal drawe me therafter in onehed of wyl to abide this lawe bothe mayntene *and* kepe/ *and* so hope I best entre in to your grace/ wel deseruynge in to worship of a wight/ without nedefnl compulsion/ ought medefully to be rewarded. Truly (q*uo*d Loue) that is sothe/ *and* tho by constitution good seruice in to p*ro*fite *and* auautage stretch/ vtterly many men it demen to haue more desert of mede/ than

148 mede, reward. **151 prevy**, secret. **153 apertely**, openly. **155 apartly**, openly; **chalenge**, claim. **156 onehed**, singleness.

good wyl nat compelled." "Se now," quod I, "howe may men holden of this the contrary. And what is good service? Of you wolde I here this question declared." "I shal say thee," quod she, "in a fewe wordes: resonable workynges in plesaunce and profite of thy soverayne."

"Howe shulde I this performe?" quod I. "Right wel," quod she, "and here me nowe a lytel. It is hardely," quod she, "to understande that right as mater by due overchaungynges foloweth his perfection and his forme, right so every man by rightful werkynges ought to folowe the leful desyres in his hert and se toforn to what ende he deserveth. For many tymes he that loketh nat after th'endes, but utterly therof is unknowen, befalleth often many yvels to done, wherthrough er he be ware, shamefully he is confounded. Th'ende ther of neden to be before loked. To every desirer of suche foresight in good service, thre thynges specially nedeth to be rulers in his workes. First, that he do good; next that he do by electyon in his owne hert; and the thirde, that he do godly withouten any surquedry in thoughtes. That your werkes shulden be good, in servyce or in any other actes, authorites many may be aleged; neverthelater, by reason thus maye it be

---

good wyl nat co*m*pelled. Se now (q*uo*d I) howe may men holden of this the contrary. And what is good seruice? of you wolde I here this question declared. I shal say the (q*uo*d she) in a fewe wordes/ resonable workynges in plesaunce *and* profite of thy souerayne.

Howe shulde I this p*er*forme (q*uo*d I) Riȝt wel (q*uo*d she) *and* here me nowe a lytel. It is hardely (q*uo*d she to vndersta*n*de) that right as mater by due ouerchau*n*gynges foloweth his p*er*fection *and* his forme: Right so euery man by riȝtful werkynges ought to folowe the leful desyres i*n* his hert/ *and* se toforn to what ende he deserueth/ for many tymes he that loketh nat after the*n*des/ but vtterly therof is vnknowen/ befalleth often many yuels to done wherthrough er he be ware/ shamefully he is confou*n*ded/ thende ther of neden to be before loked to euery desirer of suche foresight i*n* good seruice thre thynges specially nedeth to be rulers in his workes. First that he do good/ next th*at* he do by electyon i*n* his owne hert/ *and* the thirde that he do godly withouten any surquedry in thoughtes. That yo*ur* werkes shulden be good in seruyce or in any other actes/ authorites many may be aleged neuerthelater/ by reason thus maye it be

168 leful, lawful; **toforn**, before. **169 unknowen**, ignorant of. **170 ware**, aware. **171 loked**, considered. **174 surquedry**, pride.

shewed. Al your werkes be cleped seconde and moven in vertue of the Firste Wercher, whiche in good workes wrought you to procede, and right so your werkes moven into vertue of the laste ende; and right in the first workynge were nat, no man shulde in the seconde werche. Right so, but ye feled to what ende, and seen their goodnes closed, ye shuld no more recche what ye wrought; but the gynnyng gan with good, and there shal it cease in the last ende, if it be wel consydred. Wherfore the myddle, if other wayes it drawe than accordant to the endes, there stynteth the course of good, and another maner course entreth. And so it is a partie by himselve, and every parte be nat accordant to his al, is foule and ought to be eschewed. Wherfore every thinge that is wrought and be nat good is nat accordant to th'endes of his al hole. It is foule and ought to be withdrawe. Thus the persons that neither don good ne harme shamen foule their makyng: Wherfore without workyng of good actes in good service may no man ben accepted. Truely, the ilke that han might to do good and done it nat, the crowne of worship shal be take from hem, and with shame shul they be anulled. And so to make one werke acordant with his endes, every good servaunt, by reason of consequence,

---

shewed. Al your werkes be cleped seconde/ *and* mouen in vertue of the firste wercher/ whiche in good workes wrought you to procede/ *and* right so your werkes mouen i*n* to vertue of the laste ende/ *and* right in the first workynge were nat/ no man shulde in the seco*n*de werche. Right so but ye feled to what ende *and* seen their goodnes closed/ ye shuld no more recth what ye wrouȝt but the gynnyng gan with good/ *and* there shal it cease in the last ende/ if it be wel consydred. Wherfore the myddle/ if other wayes it drawe than accordant to the endes/ there stynteth the**<351vb><352ra>**course of good/ *and* another maner course entreth/ *and* so it is a p*ar*tie by him selue/ *and* euery p*ar*te be nat accordant to his al/ is foule *and* ought to be eschewed. wherfore euery thi*n*ge th*at* is wrouȝt and be nat good/ is nat accordant to thendes of his al hole/ it is foule/ *and* ought to be withdrawe. Thus the p*er*sons that neither don good ne harme/ shamen foule their makyng: Wherfore without workyng of good actes in good seruice/ may no man ben accepted. Truely the ilke that han might to do good *and* done it nat/ th*e* crowne of worship shal be take from hem/ *and* with shame shul they be anulled. *and* so to make one werke acordant wi*th* his endes/ euery good seruaunt by reason of consequence

176 cleped, called; **First Wercher**, Prime Mover. **179 feled**, felt. **182 stynteth**, stops. **183 be nat**, that is not. **184 al**, all, whole. **188 ilke**, same.

muste do good nedes. Certes, it suffiseth nat alone to do good, but goodly withal folowe. The thanke of goodnesse els in nought he deserveth. For right as al your being come from the greatest good in whom al goodnesse is closed, right so your endes ben directe to the same good. Aristotel determyneth that ende and good ben one and convertible in understanding, and he that in wyl doth away good, and he that loketh nat to th'ende, loketh nat to good. But he that doth good and doth nat goodly and draweth away the direction of th'ende nat goodly, must nedes be bad. Lo, badde is nothing els but absence or negatyfe of good, as derkenesse is absence or negatyve of lyght. Than he that doth nat goodly directeth thilke good in to th'ende of badde. So muste thyng nat good folowe; eke, badnesse to suche folke ofte foloweth. Thus contrariaunt workers of th'ende that is good ben worthy the contrary of th'ende that is good to have." "How," quod I, "may any good dede be done but if goodly it helpe?" "Yes," quod Love, "the devyl dothe many good dedes, but goodly he leveth behynde. For ever badly and in disceyvable wyse he worketh, wherfore the contrary of th'ende him foloweth. And do he never so many good dedes bicause goodly is away, his goodnes is nat rekened. Lo, than, tho a man do good, but he do goodly, th'ende in goodnesse wol nat folowe, and

---

muste do good nedes. Certes it suffiseth nat alone to do good/ but goodly withal folowe/ the tha*n*ke of goodnesse els in nought he deserueth: For riȝt as al your being come from the greatest good in whom al goodnesse is closed. Right so yo*ur* endes ben directe to the same good. Aristotel determyneth that ende *and* good ben one/ and co*n*uertible in vndersta*n*ding/ and he that in wyl doth away good/ *and* he that loketh nat to the*n*de loketh nat to good/ but he that doth good and doth nat goodly/ draweth away the direction of thende nat goodly/ must nedes be bad. Lo badde is nothing els/ but absence or negatyfe of good/ as derkenesse is absence or negatyue of lyght. Than he that doth goodly/ directeth thilke good in to thende of badde: So muste thyng nat good folowe/ eke badnesse to suche folke ofte foloweth. Thus co*n*trariaunt workers of thende that is good/ ben worthy the co*n*trary of thende that is good to haue. How (q*uo*d I) may any good dede be done/ but if goodly it helpe. Yes (q*uo*d Loue) the deuyl dothe many good dedes/ but goodly he leueth be hynde/ for euen badly *and* in disceyuable wyse he worketh/ Wherfore the co*n*trary of thende him foloweth. And do he neuer so many good dedes/ bicause goodly is away/ his goodnes is nat rekened. Lo than tho a man do good/ but he do goodly thende in goodnesse wol nat folowe/ *and*

196 goodly, with a good motive. **203 leveth**, leaves.

thus in good service both good dede and goodly done musten joyne togider and that it be done with free choise in hert; and els deserveth he nat the merite in goodnes — that wol I prove. For if thou do anythyng good by chaunce or by happe, in what thyng art thou therof worthy to be commended? For nothing by reason of that turneth into thy praysing ne lackyng. Lo, thilke thing done by hap by thy wyl is nat caused, and therby shulde I thanke or lacke deserve? And sythen that fayleth th'ende which that wel shulde, rewarde must neds faile. Clerkes sayn no man but wyllynge is blessed; a good dede that he hath done is nat done of free choice wyllyng, without whiche blyssednesse may nat folowe. *Ergo*, neither thanke of goodnesse ne service in that is contrary of the good ende, so than to good service longeth good dede goodly don thorowe fre choice in hert." "Truely," quod I, "this have I wel understande." "Wel," quod she, "every thyng thus done sufficiently by lawe that is cleped justice may after-rewarde claym. For lawe and justice was ordayned in this wise suche desertes in goodnesse after quantité in doynge by mede to rewarde; and of necessyté of suche justyce, that is to say, rightwysenesse, was free choice in deservyng of wel or of yvel graunted to resonable creatures. Every man hath

---

thus in good seruice both good dede *and* goodly done musten ioyne togider/ *and* that it be done with free choise in hert: *and* els deserueth he nat th*e* merite in goodnes/ that wol I proue. for if thou**<352ra><352rb>**do any thyng good by chau*n*ce or by happe/ in what thyng art thou therof worthy to be eommen*d*ed? for nothing by reason of that turneth in to thy praysing ne lackyng. Lo thilke thi*n*g done by hap by thy wyl is nat caused/ *and* therby shulde I thanke or lacke deserue: *and* sythen that fayleth/ thende which that wel shulde rewarde/ must neds faile. clerkes sayn/ no man but wyllynge is blessed a good dede th*at* he hath done is nat done of free choice wyllyng/ without whiche blyssednesse may nat folowe. Ergo neither tha*n*ke of goodnesse ne seruice i*n* that is co*n*trary of the good ende/ so than to good s*er*uice lo*n*geth good dede goodly don/ thorowe fre choice i*n* hert. Truely (q*uo*d I) this haue I wel vnderstande. Wel (q*uo*d she) euery thyng thus done sufficie*n*tly by lawe/ that is cleped iustice/ after rewarde claym. For lawe *and* iustice was ordayned in this wise/ suche desertes in goodnesse after quantite in doynge/ by mede to rewardc/ *and* of necessyte of suche iustyce/ th*at* is to say/ riȝtwysenesse was free choice in des*er*uyng of wel or of yuel grau*n*ted to resonable creatures. Euery man hath

207 done, doing. **211 lackyng**, blame. **212 sythen**, since. **215** ***Ergo***, Therefore. **216 longeth**, belongs. **218 after-rewarde claym**, may claim a reward.

free arbitrement to chose good or yvel to performe." "Nowe," quod I tho, "if I by my good wyl deserve this Margarit perle and am nat therto compelled, and have free choice to do what me lyketh, she is than holden as me thynketh to rewarde th'entent of my good wyl." "Goddes forbode els," quod Love, "no wight meaneth otherwise, I trowe. Free wyl of good hert after-mede deserveth." "Hath every man," quod I, "fre choice by necessary maner of wyl in every of his doynges that him lyketh by Goddes proper purvyaunce? I wolde se that wel declared to my leude understanding, for 'necessary' and 'necessyté' ben wordes of mokel entention, closyng (as to saye) 'so mote it be nedes,' and 'otherwyse may it nat betyde.'" "This shalt thou lern," quod she, "so thou take hede in my speche. If it were nat in mannes owne lyberté of fre wyl to do good or bad, but to the one teyed by bonde of Goddes preordynaunce, than do he never so wel it were by nedeful compulcion of thilk bonde and nat by fre choice, wherby nothyng he desyreth; and, do he never so yvel, it were nat man for to wyte, but onelych to him that suche thyng ordayned him to done. Wherfore he ne ought for bad be punished ne for no good dede be rewarded, but of necessité of rightwisnesse was therfore fre choice of

---

free arbitreme*n*t to chose good or yuel to p*er*forme. Nowe (q*uo*d I tho) if I by my good wyl deserue this Margarit p*er*le and am nat therto/ co*m*pelled *and* haue free choice to do what me lyketh: She is than holden as me thynketh to rewarde thentent of my good wyl. Goddes forbode els (q*uo*d Loue) no wiȝt meaneth otherwise I trowe/ free wyl of good hert after mede deserueth. Hath euery man (q*uo*d I) fre choice by necessary maner of wyl i*n* euery of his doynges/ that him lyketh by goddes proper puruyau*n*ce. I wolde se that wel declared to my leude vndersta*n*ding/ for necessary *and* necessyte ben wordes of mokel ente*n*tion/ closyng (as to saye) so mote it be nedes/ *and* otherwyse may it nat betyde. This shalt thou lern (q*uo*d she) so thou take hede in my speche. If it were nat in ma*n*nes owne lyberte of fre wyl to do good or bad/ but to the one teyed by bonde of goddes preordynau*n*ce: Than do he neuer so wel it were by nedeful co*m*pulcion of thilk bo*n*de and nat by fre choice/ wherby nothyng he desyreth/ *and* do he neuer so yuel it were nat man for to wyte/ but onelych to him th*at* suche thyng ordayned him to done. Wherfore he ne ought**<352rb><352va>**for bad be punished/ ne for no good dede be rewarded/ but of necessite of riȝtwisnesse was therfore fre choice of

222 arbitrement, will. **225 trowe**, believe. **226 after-mede**, reward. **227 him lyketh**, pleases him. **228 leude**, uninformed. **229 mokel**, great; **closyng**, including. **230 betyde**, happen. **232 teyed**, tied. **234 wyte**, blame; **onelych**, only.

arbitrement put in mans proper disposition. Truely, if it were otherwise, it contraried Goddes charité that badnesse and goodnesse rewardeth after desert of payn or of mede." "Me thynketh this wonder," quod I, "for God by necessité forwote al thynges comyng, and so mote it nedes be; and thilke thinges that ben don be our fre choice comen nothing of necessité but onely be wyl. Howe may this stonde togyther? And so me thynketh truely that fre choyce fully repugneth Goddes forwetyng. Trewly, lady, me semeth they mowe nat stande togyther."

Chapter III

Than gan Love nygh me nere and with a noble countenance of visage and lymmes dressed her nigh my sytting place. "Take forth," quod she, "thy pen and redily write these wordes, for if God wol I shal hem so enforme to thee that thy leudnesse which I have understand in that mater shal openly be clered, and thy sight in ful loking therin amended. First, if thou thynke that Goddes prescience repugne lyberté of arbetry of arbitrement, it is impossible that they shulde accorde in onheed of sothe to understonding." "Ye," quod I, "forsothe, so I it conceyve." "Wel," quod she, "if thilke

---

arbitreme*n*t put in mans proper disposition: truely if it were otherwise it co*n*traried goddes charite/ th*at* badnesse *and* goodnesse rewardeth after desert of payn or of mede. Me thynketh this wo*n*der (q*uo*d I) for god by necessite forwote al thynges comyng/ and so mote it nedes be: *and* thilke thi*n*ges that ben don be our fre choice comen nothi*n*g of necessite but onely be wyl: Howe may this stonde togyther? and so me thynketh truely/ that fre choyce fully repugneth goddes forwetyng. Trewly lady me semeth they mowe nat stande togyther.

THAN gan loue nygh me nere/ *and* with a noble countenance of visage *and* lymmes/ dressed her nigh my sytting place. Take forth (q*uo*d she) thy pen *and* redily write these wordes/ for if god wol/ I shal hem so enforme to the/ th*at* thy leudnesse which I haue vndersta*n*d in that mater/ shal openly be clered/ *and* thy sight in ful loking therin ame*n*ded. First if thou thynke that goddes prescie*n*ce repugne lyberte of arbetry of arbitrement/ it is impossible that they shulde accorde in onheed of sothe to vndersto*n*ding. Ye (q*uo*d I) forsothe so I it co*n*ceyue. Wel (q*uo*d she) if thilke

238 mede, reward. **239 forwote**, foreknows. **242 forwetyng**, foreknowledge. **244 nygh me nere**, draw nearer to me. **249 arbitrement**, free will; **onheed**, unity.

impossible were away, the repugnaunce that semeth to be therin were utterly removed." "Shewe me the absence of that impossibilyté," quod I. "So," quod she, "I shal. Nowe I suppose that they mowe stande togider: prescience of God whom foloweth necessité of thinges commyng and lyberté of arbitrement thorowe whiche thou belevest many thinges to be without necessité." "Bothe these proporcions be sothe," quod I, "and wel mowe stande togider wherfore this case as possyble I admyt." "Truely," quod she, "and this case is impossible." "Howe so," quod I. "For herof," quod she, "foloweth and wexeth another impossyble." "Prove me that," quod I. "That I shal," quod she, "for somthing is commyng without necessyté, and God wot that toforn, for al thing commyng He before wot, and that He beforn wot of necessyté is commyng; as He beforne wot be the case. By necessary maner than or els thorowe necessité is somthyng to be without necessité and wheder to every wight that hath good understanding is seen these thynges to be repugnaunt: Prescience of God, whiche that foloweth necessyté, and lyberté of arbytrement, fro whiche is removed necessyté, for truely, it is necessary that God have forwetyng of thing withouten any necessité commynge." "Ye,"

---

impossible were away/ the repuguau*n*ce that semeth to be therin/ were vtterly remoued. Shewe me the absence of that impossibilyte (q*uo*d I) So (q*uo*d she I shal). Nowe I suppose that they mowe sta*n*de togider/ p*re*science of god who*m* foloweth necessite of thi*n*ges co*m*myng and lyberte of arbitreme*nt*/ thorowe whiche th*ou* beleuest many thi*n*ges to be without necessite. Bothe these p*ro*porcions be sothe (q*uo*d I) *and* wel mowe sta*n*de togider/ wherfore this case as possyble I admyt. Truely (q*uo*d she) *and* this case is impossible. Howe so (q*uo*d I) For herof (q*uo*d she foloweth *and* wexeth another i*m*possyble. Proue me that (q*uo*d I). that I shal (q*uo*d she) for so*m*thing is co*mm*yng without necessyte/ *an*d god wot that toforn/ for al thi*n*g co*m*myng he before wot/ and that he beforne wot of necessyte is co*m*myng: as he beforn wot be the case by necessary maner than/ or els thorowe necessite is so*m*thyng to be**<352va><352vb>**without necessite/ *and* whedto to euery wiȝt th*at* hath good vnderstanding/ is seen these thynges to be repugnaunt. Prescie*n*ce of god/ whiche that foloweth necessyte *and* lyberte of arbytrement/ fro whiche is remoued necessyte/ for truely it is necessary that god haue forwetyng of thi*n*g withouten any necessite co*m*mynge. Ye

253 mowe stande togider, may obtain at the same time. **258 wexeth**, grows. **259 wot**, knows. **262 wheder**, whether. **265 forwetyng**, foreknowledge.

quod I, "but yet remeve ye nat away fro myne understandyng the necessyté folowyng Goddes beforewetyng, as thus: God beforne wote me in service of love to be bounden to this Margarite perle, and therfore by necessité thus to love am I bounde, and if I nat had loved, thorowe necessyté had I ben kepte from al love dedes." "Certes," quod Love, "bicause this mater is good and necessary to declare, I thynke herein wel to abyde and not lyghtly to passe. Thou shalte not," quod she, "say al onely, 'God beforne wote me to be a lover or no lover,' but thus: 'God beforne wote me to be a lover without necessyté.' And so it foloweth, whether thou love or not love every of hem is and shal be. But nowe thou seest the impossibylité of the case, and the possibylité of thilke that thou wendest had been impossyble, wherfore the repugnaunce is adnulled." "Ye," quod I, "and yet do ye not a waye the strength of necessyté whan it is said, through necessyté it is me in love to abyde, or not to love without necessyté, for God beforne wote it. This maner of necessyté, forsothe, semeth to some men into coaction, that is to sayne, constraynyng, or else prohibycion, that is defendynge, wherfore necessyté is me to love of wyl. I understande me to be constrayned by some privy strength to the wyl of lovynge, and if no love, to be defended from the wyl of lovynge, and so thorowe

---

(q*uo*d I) but yet remeue ye nat away fro myne vnderstandyng/ the necessyte folowyng goddes be forewetyng/ as thus. God beforne wote me in seruice of loue to be bounden to this Margarite p*er*le/ *and* therfore by necessite thus to loue am I bounde/ *and* if I nat had loued/ thorowe necessyte had I ben kepte from al loue dedes. Certes (q*uo*d Loue) bicause this mater is good *and* necessary to declare/ I thynke here in wel to abyde and not lyghtly to passe. Thou shalte not (quod she) say al onely god beforne wote me to be a louer or no louer/ but thus: god beforne wote me to be a louer without necessyte. And so it foloweth whether thou loue or not loue/ euery of hem is and shal be. But nowe thou seest the impossibylite of the case/ and the possibylite of thilke that thou wendest had been impossyble/ wherfore the repugnau*n*ce is adnulled. ye (quod I) and yet do ye not a waye the strength of necessyte whan it is said/ though necessyte it is me in loue to abyde/ or not to loue without necessyte for god beforne wote it. This maner of necessyte forsothe semeth to some men in to coaction/ that is to sayne/ constraynyng or else prohibycion that is defendynge/ wherfore necessyte is me to loue of wyl. I vnderstande me to be constrayned by some priuy strength to the wyl of louynge/ and if no loue to be defended from the wyl of louynge/ and so thorowe

274 thilke, that one. **275 wendest**, assumed. **277 wote**, knows. **278 coaction**, compulsion. **279 defendynge**, preventing, forbidding. **281 defended**, prevented.

necessyté me semeth to love, for I love; or els not to love, if I not love, wherthrough neyther thanke ne maugre in tho thynges maye I deserve."

"Nowe," quod she, "thou shalte wel understande that often we sayne thynge thorowe necessyté to be that by no strength to be neyther is coarted ne constrayned, and throughe necessyté not to be that with no defendynge is removed. For we sayne it is thorowe necessyté God to be immortal, nought deedlyche, and it is necessyté God to be rightful, but not that any strength of violente maner constrayneth him to be immortal, or defendeth him to be unrightful, for nothing may make him dedly or unrightful. Right so, if I say thorowe necessyté is thee to be a lover or els none, onely thorowe wyl as God beforne wete, it is nat to understonde that anythyng defendeth or forbit thee thy wyl, whiche shal nat be, or els constrayneth it to be whiche shal be. That same thynge, forsoth, God before wot, whiche He beforn seeth, anythyng commende of onely wyl, that wyl neyther is constrayned ne defended thorowe any other thing. And so thorowe lyberté of arbitrement it is do that is done of wyl. And trewly, my good childe, if these thynges be

---

necessyte me semeth to loue/ for I loue/ or els not to loue/ if I not loue/ wherthrough neyther tha*n*ke ne maugre in tho thynges maye I deserue.

Nowe (quod she) thou shalte wel vnderstande that often we sayne thynge thorowe necessyte to be that by no strength to be neyther is coarted ne constrayned/ and throughe necessyte not to be/ that with no defendynge is remoued/ for we sayne it is thorowe necessyte god to be immortal nought deedlyche/ and it is necessyte god to be rightful/ but not**<352vb><353ra>**that any stre*n*gth of violente maner co*n*strayneth him to be immortal/ or defendeth him to be vnrightful/ for nothi*n*g may make him dedly or vnrightful. Right so if I say thorowe necessyte is th*e* to be a louer or els none/ onely thorowe wyl/ as god beforne wete/ It is nat to vndersto*n*de that any thyng defe*n*deth or forbit/ the thy wyl/ whiche shal nat be/ or els co*n*strayneth it to be whiche shalbe: that same thynge forsoth god before wot/ whiche he beforn seeth any thyng co*m*mende of onely wyl/ th*at* wyl neyther is co*n*strayned ne defe*n*ded thorowe any other thing. *and* so thorowe lyberte of arbitreme*n*t it is do/ that is done of wyl. And trewly my good childe/ if these thynges be

282 for I love, because I love. **283 maugre**, displeasure, spite (i.e., something contrary to my desires). **285 coarted**, compelled. **287 deedlyche**, deadly (i.e., mortal). **288 defendeth**, prohibits. **291 wete**, knew. **293 wot**, knows. **294 defended**, hindered. **295 arbitrement**, choice.

wel understond, I wene that non inconvenyent shalt thou fynde betwene Goddes forwetyng and lyberté of arbitrement, wherfore I wot wel they may stande togider. Also farthermore, who that understandyng of prescience properlych consydreth, thorowe the same wyse that any thyng be afore wyst is said, for to be commyng it is pronounced, there is nothing toforn wist but thing commyng. Foreweting is but of trouth; dout may nat be wyst: wherfore whan I sey that God toforn wote anythyng, thorowe necessyté is thilke thyng to be commyng. Al is one if I sey if it shal be, but this necessyté neither constrayneth ne defendeth anythyng to be or nat to be. Therfore, sothly, if love is put to be, it is said of necessyté to be; or els for it is put nat to be, it is affirmed nat to be of necessyté, nat for that necessité constrayneth or defendeth love to be or nat to be. For whan I say if love shal be of necessité it shal be, here foloweth necessyté, the thyng toforne put. It is as moch to say as if it were thus pronounced 'that thyng shal be.' None other thyng signifyeth this necessyté but onely thus, that shal be may nat togider be and nat be. Evenlych also it is soth, love was, and is, and shal be nat of necessyté. And nede is to have be al that was, and nedeful is to be al that is, and commyng to al

---

wel vndersto*n*d I wene that non inco*n*uenyent shalt thou fynde betwene goddes forwetyng *and* lyberte of arbitreme*nt*/ wherfore I wot wel they may sta*n*de togider. Also farthermore/ who that vndersta*n*dyng of prescie*n*ce prop*er*lych co*n*sydreth/ thorowe the same wyse that any thyng be afore wyst/ is said for to be co*m*myng it is pro*n*ounced/ there is nothing toforn wist/ but thi*n*g co*m*myng/ foreweti*n*g is but of trouth dout may nat be wyst: wherfore whan I sey that god toforn wote any thyng/ thorowe necessyte is thilke thyng to be co*m*myng/ al is one if I sey/ if it shalbe/ but this necessyte neither co*n*strayneth ne defe*n*deth any thyng to be or nat to be. Therfore sothly if loue is put to be/ it is said of necessyte to be/ or els for it is put nat to be/ it is affirmed nat to be of necessyte: nat for th*at* necessite co*n*strayneth or defendeth loue to be or nat to be. For whan I say/ if loue shal be of necessite it shal be/ here foloweth necessyte. the thyng toforne put/ it is as moch to say/ as if it were thus p*r*onou*n*ced/ that thyng shalbe: None other thyng signifyeth this necessyte but onely thus/ that shalbe may nat togider be *and* nat be. Eue*n*lych also it is soth/ loue was *and* is/ *and* shalbe/ nat of necessyte/ *and* nede is to haue be al that was/ *and* nedeful is to be al that is/ *and* co*m*myng to al

296 wene, assume. **297 forwetyng**, foreknowing. **299 wyst**, known. **303 defendeth**, hinders. **305 for that**, because. **308 that**, that which.

that shal be. And it is nat the same to saye, love to be passed, and love passed to be passed; or love present to be present, and love to be present; or els love to be commynge, and love commynge to be commyng: dyversité in settyng of wordes maketh dyversité in understandynge, altho in the same sentence they accorden of signification, right as it is nat al one, love swete to be swete, and love to be swete. For moch love is bytter and sorouful er hertes ben eased, and yet it gladeth thilke sorouful hert on suche love to thynke." "Forsothe," quod I, "outherwhile I have had mokel blysse in hert of love that stoundmele hath me sorily anoyed. And certes, lady, for I se myselfe thus knit with this Margarite peerle as by bonde of your servyce and of no lyberté of wyl, my hert wyl nowe nat acorde this servyce to love. I can demyn in myselfe non otherwise, but thorowe necessité am I constrayned in this service to abyde. But alas. Than if I thorowe nedeful compulsioun maugre me be withholde, lytel thanke for al my great traveil have I than deserved." "Nowe," quod this lady, "I saye as I sayde: me lyketh this mater to declare at the ful, and why. For many men have had dyvers fantasyes and reasons, both on one syde therof and in the other. Of whiche right sone, I trowe, if thou wolt

---

that shalbe: *and* it is nat the same to saye/ loue to be passed/ and loue passed to be passed/ or loue present to be present/ and loue to be present/ or els loue to be commynge/ and loue commynge to be co*m*myng: dyuersite in settyng of wordes/ maketh dyuersite in vndersta*n*dynge/ **<353ra><353rb>**altho in the same sente*n*ce they accorden of signification/ right as it is nat al one: loue swete to be swete/ *and* loue to be swete: for moch loue is bytter *and* sorouful er hertes ben eased/ *and* yet it gladeth thilke sorouful hert on suche loue to thynke. Forsothe (q*uo*d I) outherwhile I haue had mokel blysse in hert of loue/ th*at* stou*n*dmele hath me sorily anoyed: *and* certes lady/ for I se my selfe thus knit with this Margarite peerle as by bonde of your seruyce/ *and* of no lyberte of wyl/ my hert wyl nowe nat acorde this seruyce to loue. I can demyn in my selfe non otherwise/ but thorowe necessite am I co*n*strayned in this seruice to abyde. But alas than/ if I thorowe nedeful co*m*pulsioun maugre me be with holde/ lytel tha*n*ke for al my great traueil haue I than deserued. Nowe (q*uo*d this lady) I saye as I sayde: Me lyketh this mater to declare at the ful/ *and* why: for many men haue had dyuers fantasyes *and* reasons/ both on one syde therof *and* in the other. Of whiche riȝt sone I trowe if thou wolt

315 swete, sweet. **316 er**, before. **317 mokel**, much. **318 stoundmele**, sometimes. **320 demyn**, judge. **322 maugre me**, in spite of myself.

understonde, thou shalte con yeve the sentence to the partie more probable by reason and in soth knowing, by that I have of this mater maked an ende." "Certes," quod I, "of these thynges longe have I had great luste to be lerned, for yet I wene Goddes wyl and His prescience acordeth with my service in lovynge of this precious Margarite perle, after whom ever in my hert with thurstyng desire weete, I do brenne. Unwastyng I langour and fade, and the day of my desteny in dethe or in joye I unbyde, but yet in th'ende I am comforted be my supposaile in blysse and in joye to determyne after my desyres." "That thyng," quod Love, "hastely to thee neigh, God graunt of His grace and mercy, and this shal be my prayer, tyl thou be lykende in herte at thyne owne wyl. But nowe to enforme thee in this mater," quod this lady, "thou wost where I lefte; that was love to be swete, and love swete to be swete, is nat al one for to say. For a tree is nat alway by necessité white. Somtyme, er it were white, it myght have be nat white, and after tyme it is white it maye be nat white. But a whyte tree evermore nedeful is to be white, for neither toforn ne after it was white myght it be togider white and nat white.

---

vndersto*n*de/ thou shalte con yeue the sente*n*ce/ to the p*ar*tie more probable by reason/ *and* in soth knowing/ by that I haue of this mater maked an ende. Certes (q*uo*d I) of these thynges longe haue I had great luste to be lerned/ for yet I wene goddes wyl *and* his prescie*n*ce acordeth with my seruice/ in louynge of this p*re*cious Margarite perle. After whom euer in my hert with thurstyng desire weete I do brenne: vnwastyng I la*n*gour *and* fade/ and the day of my desteny in dethe or in ioye I vnbyde/ but yet in thende I am comforted be my supposaile in blysse/ *and* in ioye to determyne after my desyres. That thyng (q*uo*d Loue) hastely to the neigh/ god grau*n*t of his grace *and* mercy/ and this shalbe my prayer tyl thou be lykende in herte at thyne owne wyl. But nowe to enforme the in this mater (q*uo*d this lady) thou wost where I lefte/ that was loue to be swete and loue swete to be swete/ is nat al one for to say: for a tree is nat alway by necessite white so*m*tyme er it were white/ it myght haue be nat white: *and* after tyme it is white/ it maye be nat white: But a whyte tree euermore nedeful is to be white: for neither toforn ne after it was white/ myght it be togider white *and* nat white.

326 con, be able to; **yeve**, give. **327 by that**, by the time that. **328 luste**, desire; **lerned**, taught; **wene**, suppose. **330 weete**, wet; **brenne**, burn. **331 unbyde**, await. **332 supposaile**, expectation; **to determyne after**, to be predetermined according to, or to be foretold by. **333 neigh**, draw nigh. **335 wost**, know. **336 al one for to say**, one and the same thing.

Also love, by necessyté, is nat present as nowe in thee, for er it were present it myght have be that it shulde nowe nat have be. And yet it maye be that it shal nat be present, but thy love present, whiche to her, Margarite, thee hath bounde, nedeful is to be present. Trewly, some doyng of action nat by necessyté is commynge, for toforn it be it may be that it shal nat be commynge. Thyng, forsoth, commyng nedeful is to be comming, for it may nat be that commyng shal nat be commyng. And right as I have sayd of present and of future tymes, the same sentence in sothnesse is of the preterit, that is to say, tyme passed, for thyng passed must nedes be passed. And er it were, it might have nat be, wherfore it shulde nat have passed. Right so whan love comming is said of love that is to come, nedeful is to be that is said; for thing commyng never is nat commynge, and so ofte the same thynge we sayn of the same, as whan we sayne, 'every man is a man,' or 'every lover is a lover,' so muste it be nedes. In no waye may he be man and no man togider. And if it be nat by necessité, that is to say nedeful, al thyng commyng to be commyng, than somthyng commyng is nat commynge, and that is impossible. Right as these termes 'nedeful,' 'necessité,' and 'necessary' betoken and signify thyng nedes to be, and it may nat otherwise be, right as this terme 'impossible'

Also loue by necessyte is nat present as nowe**<353rb><353va>**in the/ for er it were present it myght haue be that it shulde nowe nat haue be/ *and* yet it maye be that it shal nat be present: but thy loue present whiche to her Margarite the hath boude/ nedeful is to be present. Trewly some doyng of action nat by necessyte is co*m*mynge ferre toforn it be/ it may be that it shal nat be co*m*mynge: thyng forsoth co*m*myng nedeful is to be co*m*ming/ for it may nat be that co*m*myng shal nat be co*m*myng. *And* right as I haue sayd of present and of future tymes/ the same sente*n*ce in sothnesse is of the preterit/ th*at* is to say tyme passed for thyng passed must nedes be passed/ *and* er it were it might haue nat be/ wherfore it nat haue passed. Right so whan loue co*m*ming is said of loue that is to come/ nedeful is to be that is said/ for thing co*m*myng neuer is nat co*m*mynge/ *and* so ofte the same thynge we sayn of the same/ as whan we sayne euery man is a man/ or euery louer is a louer/ so muste it be nedes/ in no waye may he be man *and* no man togider. And if it be nat by necessite/ that is to say/ nedeful al thyng co*m*myng to be co*m*myng/ than somthyng co*m*myng is nat co*m*mynge/ and that is impossible/ right as these termes nedeful/ necessite/ *and* necessary betoken and signify thyng nedes to be/ *and* it may nat otherwise be. Right these termes impossible

349 that, that which. **354 Right**, Just.

signifieth that thyng is nat and by no way may it be, than thorowe pert necessité al thyng commyng is commyng, but that is by necessité foloweth with nothyng to be constrayned. Lo, whan that commyng is said of thynge nat alway thyng thorowe necessité is, altho it be commyng. For if I say 'tomorowe love is commyng in this Margarites hert,' nat therfore thorow necessité shal the ilke love be. Yet it may be that it shal nat be, altho it were commyng. Neverthelater, somtyme it is soth that somthyng be of necessité that is sayd to come: as if I say tomorowe by commynge the risynge of the sonne. If therfore with necessité I pronounce commyng of thyng to come, in this maner love tomorne commynge in thyne Margarite to thee-warde, by necessité is commynge, or els the risyng of the sonne tomorne commynge through necessité is commynge. Love, sothely, whiche may nat be of necessyté alone folowynge, thorowe necessyté commyng it is made certayne. For futur of future is said; that is to sayn, commyng of commynge is said; as if to morowe commyng is thorow necessité, commynge it is. Arisyng of the sonne thorowe two necessités in commyng, it is to understande that one is to forgoing necessité, whiche maketh thyng to be; therfore it shal be, for nedeful is that it be. Another is folowyng necessité whiche nothyng

---

signifieth/ that thyng is nat *and* by no way may it be/ than thorowe pert necessite/ al thyng co*m*myng is commyng/ but that is by necessite/ foloweth with nothyng to be co*n*strayned. lo whan that commyng is said of thynge/ nat alway thyng thorowe necessite/ is altho it be co*m*myng. For if I say to morowe loue is co*m*myng i*n* this Margarit*es* hert/ nat therfore thorow necessite shal the ilke loue be/ yet it may be that it shal nat be/ altho it were co*m*myng. Neuerthelater/ so*m*tyme it is soth that somthyng be of necessite/ that is sayd to come: as if I say to morowe by commynge the risynge of the sonne. If therfore with necessite I pronounce co*m*myng of thyng to come/ in this maner loue to morne co*m*mynge in thyne Margarite to the warde by necessite is co*m*mynge/ or els the risyng of the sonne to morne co*m*mynge/ through necessite is commynge. Loue sothely/ whiche may nat be of necessyte alone folowynge/ thorowe necessyte**<353va><353vb>**co*m*myng it is made certayne. For futur of future is said/ that is to sayn co*m*myng of co*m*mynge is said: as if to morowe co*m*myng is thorow necessite co*m*mynge it is. Arisyng of the sonne thorowe two necessites in co*m*myng/ it is to vndersta*n*de/ that one is to forgoing necessite/ whiche maketh thyng to be/ therfore it shalbe/ for nedeful is that it be. Another is folowyng necessite/ whiche nothyng

356 pert, open. **364 to thee-warde**, toward you.

constrayneth to be, and so by necessyté it is to come. Why? For it is to come. Nowe than whan we sayn that God beforn wot thyng commyng, nedeful is to be commyng, yet therfore make we nat in certayne evermore, thynge to be thorowe necessité commynge. Sothly, thyng commyng maye nat be nat commyng by no way, for it is the same sentence of understandyng; as if we say thus: If God beforn wot anythyng, nedeful is that to be commyng. But yet therfore foloweth nat the prescience of God thyng thorowe necessité to be commyng. For altho God toforn wote al thinges commyng, yet nat therfore He beforn wot every thyng commyng thorowe necessité. Some thinges He beforn wot commyng of fre wyl out of resonable creature." "Certes," quod I, "these termes 'nede' and 'necessité' have a queynt maner of understandyng. They wolden dullen many mennes wyttes." "Therfore," quod she, "I wol hem openly declare and more clerely than I have toforn er I departe hense."

Chapter IV

"Here of this mater," quod she, "thou shalte understande that right as it is nat nedeful God to wylne that He wyl, no more in many thynges is nat nedeful a man to wylne that

---

co*n*strayneth to be/ and so by necessyte it is to come/ why: for it is to come. Nowe than/ whan we sayn/ that god beforn wot thyng co*m*myng nedeful is to be co*m*myng/ yet therfore make we nat in certayne/ euermore thynge to be thorowe necessite commynge. Sothly thyng co*m*myng maye nat be nat co*m*myng by no way/ for it is the same sentence of vndersta*n*dyng: as if we say thus. If god beforn wot any thyng/ nedeful is that to be co*m*myng. But yet therfore foloweth nat th*e* prescie*n*ce of god/ thyng thorowe necessite to be co*m*myng: for al tho god toforn wote al thi*n*ges co*m*myng/ yet nat therfore he beforn wot euery thyng co*m*myng thorowe necessite. So*m*e thi*n*ges he beforn wot co*m*myng of fre wyl out of resonable creature. Certes (q*uo*d I) these termes/ nede *and* necessite/ haue a queynt maner of vndersta*n*dyng/ they wolden dullen many me*n*nes wyttes. Therfore (q*uo*d she) I wol hem openly declare/ *and* more clerely than I haue toforn er I departe hense.

HERE of this mater (q*uo*d she) thou shalte vndersta*n*de/ that right as it is nat nedeful god to wylne that he wyl/ no more in many thynges is nat nedeful a man to wylne that

372 For, Because. **373 wot**, knows. **381 queynt**, curious, difficult.

he wol. And ever right as nedeful is to be what that God wol, right so to be it is nedeful that man wol in tho thynges whiche that God hath put into mannes subjection of wyllynge: as if a man wol love that he love; and if he ne wol love, that he love nat; and of suche other thynges in mannes disposition. For why nowe than, that God wol may nat be whan He wol the wyl of man thorowe no necessyté to be constrayned or els defended for to wylne, and he wol th'effecte to folow the wyl, than is it nedeful wyl of man to be fre, and also to be that he wol. In this maner it is soth that thorowe necessité is mannes werke in lovyng that he wol do, altho he wol it not with necessyté." Quod I than, "Howe stante it in love of thilke wyl, sythen men loven willyng of free choyce in herte? Wherfore, if it be thorowe necessyté I praye you lady of an answere this questyon to assoyle." "I wol," quod she, "answere thee blyvely. Right as men wyl not thorowe necessyté, right so is not love of wyl thorowe necessyté, ne thorowe necessyté wrought thilke same wyl. For if he wolde it not with good wyl, it shulde nat have ben wrought, although that he dothe, it is nedeful to be doone. But if a man do synne, it is nothyng els

---

he wol. And euer right as nedeful is to be what that god wol/ right so to be it is nedeful that man wol in tho thynges/ whiche that god hath put in to mannes subiection of wyllynge: as if a ma*n* wol loue/ that he loue: *and* if he ne wol loue/ that he loue nat/ *and* of suche other thynges in ma*n*nes disposition. For why/ nowe than that god wol may nat be/ whan he wol the wyl of man thorowe no necessyte to be co*n*strayned or els defended for to wylne/ *and* he wol theffecte to folow the wyl/ than is it nedeful wyl of man to be fre/ *and* also to be that he wol. In this maner it is soth/ that thorowe necessite is ma*n*nes werke in louyng/ that he wol do altho he wol**<353vb><354ra>**it not with necessyte. (Quod I than) howe stante it in loue of thilke wyl/ sythen men louen willyng of free choyce in herte. wherfore if it be thorowe necessyte/ I praye you lady of an answere this questyon to assoyle. I wol (q*uo*d she) answere the blyuely: Right as men wyl not thorowe necessyte/ right so is not loue of wyl thorowe necessyte/ ne thorowe necessyte wrought thilke same wyl: for if he wolde it not with good wyl/ it shulde nat haue ben wrought/ although that he dothe it is nedeful to be doone. But if a man do synne it is nothyng els

390 defended, hindered. **392 that he wol**, that [which] the will wants. **394 sythen**, since; **willyng**, willingly. **396 assoyle**, solve; **thee blyvely**, you happily. **397 is not love of wyl thorowe necessyté**, there is no love in the will through necessity. **397–98 wrought thilke same wyl**, did that same will operate. **398 with good wyl**, willingly. **399 that**, that which.

but to wyl that he shulde not. Right so synne of wyl is not to be maner necessary done, no more than wyl is necessarye. Neverthelater, this is sothe: if a man wol synne, it is necessarye him to synne, but through thilke necessyté nothyng is constrayned ne defended in the wyl, right so thilke thynge that fre wyl wol and maye, and not may not wylne. And nedeful is that to wylne he maye not wylne, but thilke to wylne nedeful is; for impossyble to him it is one thyng and the same to wylne he may not wylne. But thilk to wylne nedeful is; for impossyble to him it is one thyng and the same to wylne and not to wylne. The werke, forsothe, of wyl to whome it is yeve that it be that he hath in wyl, and that he wol not, voluntarie or spontanye it is, for by spontanye wyl it is do, that is to saye, with good wyl not constrayned: than by wyl not constrayned it is constrayned to be, and that is it may not togyther be. If this necessyté maketh lybertie of wyl whiche that, aforne they weren, they might have ben eschewed and shonned. God than, whiche that knoweth al truthe, and nothynge but truthe, al these thynges as they arne spontanye or necessarie seeth; and as he seeth, so they ben. And so with these thynges wel consydred it is open at the ful that without al maner repugnaunce God beforne wote al maner thynges ben done by fre wyl whiche, aforne they weren, might have ben

---

but to wyl/ that he shulde not: right so synne of wyl is not to be maner necessary done/ no more than wyl is necessarye. Neuer the later this is sothe/ if a man wol synne/ it is necessarye him to synne/ but though thilke necessyte nothyng is constrayned ne defended in the wyl/ right so thilke thynge that frewyl wol and maye/ and not may/ not wylne/ and nedeful is that to wylne he mayc not wylne/ but thilke to wylne nedeful is/ for impossyble to him it is one thyng/ and the same to wylne he may not wylne/ but thilk to wylne nedeful is: for impossyble to him it is one thyng/ and the same to wylne and not to wylne. The werke forsothe of wyl/ to whome it is yeue that it be that he hath in wyl/ and that he wol not/ volu*n*tarie of spontanye it is/ for by spontanye wyl it is do/ that is to saye with good wyl not constrayned: than by wyl not constrayned it is constrayned to be/ and that is it may not togyther be. If this necessyte maketh lybertie of wyl/ whiche that aforne they weren they might haue ben eschewed *and* shonned: God than/ whiche th*at* knoweth al truthe/ and nothynge but truthe/ al these thynges as they arne spontanye or necessarie syght/ and as he seeth so they ben: and so with these thynges wel consydred it is open at the ful/ that without al maner repugnaunce/ god beforne wote al maner thynges ben done by frewyl/ whiche aforne they weren might haue ben

402–03 defended, blocked, prohibited. **407 yeve**, given.

never they shulde be. And yet ben they thorowe a maner necessyté from fre wyl discendeth.

"Hereby maye," quod she, "lightly ben knowe that not al thinges to be is of necessyté, though God have hem in His prescience. For somthynges to be is of lybertie of wyl. And to make thee to have ful knowynge of Goddes beforne-wetyng, here me," quod she, "what I shal say." "Blythly lady," quod I, "me lyst this mater entyrely to understande." "Thou shalte," quod she, "understande that in heven is Goddes beynge; although He be over al by power, yet there is abydinge of devyne persone, in whiche heven is everlastynge presence, withouten any movable tyme. There is nothyng preterit, ne passed; there is nothyng future, ne commyng, but al thynges togider in that place ben present everlastyng, without any mevyng. Wherfore, to God al thynge is as nowe; and though a thynge be nat in kyndly nature of thynges, as yet, and if it shulde be herafter, yet evermore we shul saye, 'God it maketh be tyme present and nowe, for no future ne preterit in hym may be founde.' Wherfore His wetyng and His before-wetyng is al one in understandyng. Than if wetyng and before-wetyng of God putteth in necessité to al thynges whiche He

---

neuer they shulde be/ and yet ben they thorowe a maner necessyte from frewyl discendeth.

Hereby maye (quod she) lightly ben knowe that not al thi*n*ges to be is of necessyte/ though**<354ra><354rb>**god haue hem in his prescience/ for somthynges to be is of lybertie of wyl: and to make the to haue ful knowynge of goddes beforne wetyng/ here me (quod she) what I shal say. Blythly lady (quod I) me lyst this mater entyrely to vnderstande. Thou shalte (q*uo*d she) vnderstande/ that in heuen is goddes beynge/ although he be ouer al by power/ yet there is abydinge of deuyne persone/ in whiche heuen is euerlastynge presence/ withouten any mouable tyme there/**<354rb line 11><358va line 25>**is nothyng preterit ne passed there is nothyng future ne co*m*myng/ but al thynges togider in that place ben present euerlastyng without any meuyng/ wherfore to god al thynge is as nowe: *and* though a thynge be nat in kyndly nature of thynges as yet/ and if it shulde be herafter/ yet euermore we shul saye god it maketh be tyme present/ *and* nowe for no future ne preterit in hym may be founde. Wherfore his wetyng *and* his before wetyng/ is al one in vndersta*n*dyng. Than if wetyng *and* before wetyng of god putteth in necessite to al thynges whiche he

424 presence, i.e., present. **426 mevyng**, moving. **429 wetyng**, knowing; **before-wetyng**, foreknowledge.

wot or before-wot, ne thyng after eternyté or els after any tyme He wol or dothe of lyberté, but al of necessyté, whiche thyng if thou wene it be ayenst reason, nat thorowe necessyté to be or nat to be, al thinge that God wot or before-wot to be or nat to be, and yet nothynge defendeth anythynge to be wyst or to be before-wist of Him in our wylles or our doynges to be done, or els commynge to be for free arbitrement. Whan thou haste these declarations wel understande, than shalt thou fynde it resonable at prove and that many thinges be nat thorowe necessyté, but thorowe lyberté of wyl, save necessyté of free wyl, as I tofore said, and, as me thynketh, al utterly declared." "Me thynketh lady," quod I, "so I shulde you nat displease and evermore your reverence to kepe that these thynges contraryen in any understandyng, for ye sayne, somtyme is thorowe lyberté of wyl and also thorowe necessité. Of this have I yet no savour, without better declaration." "What wonder," quod she, "is there in these thynges, sithen al day thou shalte se at thyne eye in many thynges receyven in hemselfe revers, thorow dyvers reasons, as thus: I pray thee," quod she, "which thinges ben more revers than 'comen' and 'gone?' For if I bydde thee 'come to me,' and thou come, after, whan I

---

wot or before wot ne thyng after eternyte/ or els after any tyme he wol or dothe of lyberte but al of necessyte/ whiche thyng if thou wene it be ayenst reason nat thorowe necessyte to be or nat to be/ al thi*n*ge that god wot or before wot/ to be or nat to be/ *and* yet nothynge defendeth any thynge to be wyst or to be before wist of hi*m* in our wylles or our doynges to be done/ or els co*m*mynge to be for free arbitrement. Whan thou haste these declarations wel vndersta*n*de/ than shalt thou fynde it resonable at proue/ *and* that many thi*n***<358va><358vb>**ges be nat thorowe necessyte/ but thorowe lyberte of wyl/ saue necessyte of free wyl/ as I tofore said: *and* as me thynketh al vtterly declared. Me thynketh lady (q*uo*d I) so I shulde you nat displease/ *and* euermore your reuere*n*ce to kepe/ that these thynges co*n*traryen in any vndersta*n*dyng/ for ye sayne somtyme is thorowe lyberte of wyl *and* also thorowe necessite. Of this haue I yet no sauour/ without better declaration. What wonder (q*uo*d she) is there in these thynges/ sithen al day thou shalte se at thyne eye/ in many thynges receyuen in hem selfe reuers/ thorow dyuers reasons/ as thus. I pray the (q*uo*d she) which thi*n*ges ben more reuers tha*n* comen *and* gone: For if I bydde the come to me/ and thou come/ after whan I

432 wene, think. **435 arbitrement**, deciding. **441 savour**, understanding. **442 sithen**, since. **443 revers**, opposite.

bydde thee 'go' and thou go, thou reversest fro thy first commyng." "That is soth," quod I. "And yet," quod she, "in thy first alone by dyvers reasone was ful reversynge to understande." "As howe," quod I. "That shal I shewe thee," quod she, "by ensample of thynges that have kyndly movyng. Is there any thyng that meveth more kyndly than doth the hevens eye whiche I clepe the sonne." "Sothly," quod I, "me semeth it most kyndly to move." "Thou sayest soth," quod she. "Than if thou loke to the sonne in what parte he be under heven evermore he heigheth him in movyng fro thilke place, and higheth mevyng towarde the ilke same place; to thylke place from whiche he gothe, he heigheth commynge, and without any ceasynge to that place he neigheth, from whiche he is chaunged and withdrawe. But nowe in these thynges after dyversité of reason, revers in one thinge may be sey without repugnaunce. Wherfore in the same wyse, without any repugnaunce, by my reasons tofore maked, al is one to beleve, somthyng to be thorowe necessyté comminge for it is commyng, and yet with no necessité constrayned to be comming but with necessité that cometh out of free wyl, as I have sayd." Tho lyst me a lytel to speke and gan stynt my penne of my writyng and

---

bydde the go *and* thou go/ thou reuersest fro thy first co*m*myng. That is soth (q*uo*d I) *and* yet (q*uo*d she) in thy first alone by dyuers reasone was ful reuersynge to vndersta*n*de. As howe (q*uo*d I) That shal I shewe the (q*uo*d she) by ensa*m*ple of thynges that haue kyndly mouyng. Is there any thyng th*at* meueth more kyndly than doth the heuens eye whiche I clepe the sonne. Sothly (q*uo*d I) me semeth it most kyndly to moue. Thou sayest soth (q*uo*d she) Than if thou loke to the sonne/ in what parte he be vnder heuen/ euermore he heigheth him in mouyng fro thilke place/ and higheth meuyng towarde the ilke same place/ to thylke place from whiche he gothe he heigheth co*m*mynge/ and without any ceasynge to that place he neigheth from whiche he is chau*n*ged *and* withdrawe. But nowe in these thynges after dyuersite of reason/ reuers in one thinge may be sey without repugnaunce. Wherfore in the same wyse/ without any repugnaunce by my reasons tofore maked/ al is one to beleue/ somthyng to be thorowe necessyte co*m*minge for it is co*m*myng/ *and* yet with no necessite co*n*strayned to be co*m*ming/ but with necessite that cometh out of free wyl/ as I haue sayd. Tho lyst me a lytel to speke/ *and* gan stynt my penne of my writyng/ *and*

446 bydde thee, order you. **447 alone**, movement (OF *aloigner*). See note. **449 kyndly movyng**, natural development. **450 clepe**, call. **452 what part**, whatever part. **454 heigheth**, hastens. **460 Tho lyst**, Then [it] pleased; **stynt**, stop.

sayd in this wyse: "Trewly, lady, as me thynketh, I can allege authoritees gret that contrarien your sayenges. Job saith of mannes person, 'thou hast putte his terme, whiche thou might not passe.' Than saye I that no man may shorte ne length the day ordayned of his dying, altho somtyme to us it semeth some man to do a thynge of free wyl, wher-thorowe his dethe he henteth." "Naye, forsothe," quod she, "it is nothing ayenst my sayeng; for God is nat begiled, ne He seeth nothing wheder it shal come of lyberté or els of necessyté, yet it is sayd to be ordayned at God immovable whiche at man or it be done may be chaunged. Suche thyng also is that Poule the apostel saithe of hem that tofore werne purposed to be sayntes, as thus: whiche that God before wyst and hath predestyned conformes of ymages of his Sonne that He shulde ben the firste begeten, that is to saye, here amonges many brethern. And whom He hath predestyned hem He hath cleped, and whom he hath cleped hem he hath justifyed and whom he hath justifyed hem he hath magnifyed. This purpose after whiche they ben cleped payntes or holy in the everlasting present wher is neither tyme passed ne tyme commynge, but ever it is onely present, and nowe as mokel a moment as sevyn thousande wynter. And

---

sayd in this wyse. Trewly lady as me thynketh/ I can allege authoritees gret that co*n*trarien your sayenges. Job saith of mannes person/ thou hast putte his terme/ whiche thou might not passe. Than saye I that no man may shorte ne length the day or**<358vb>** **<359ra>**dayned of his doyng/ altho somtyme to vs it semeth some man to do a thynge of free wyl/ wherthorowe his dethe he henteth. Naye forsothe (q*uo*d she) it is nothing ayenst my sayeng for god is nat begiled/ ne he seeth nothing wheder it shal come of lyberte or els of necessyte/ yet it is sayd to be ordayned at god immouable/ whiche at man or it be done may be chau*n*ged. Suche thyng also is that Poule the apostel saithe of hem that tofore werne purposed to be sayntes/ as thus/ whiche that god before wyst/ *and* hath predestyned/ co*n*formes of ymages of his sonne/ that he shulde ben the firste begeten/ that is to saye/ here amonges many brethern/ *and* whom he hath predestyned/ hem he hath cleped/ and whom he hath cleped/ hem he hath iustifyed/ *and* whom he hath iustifyed/ hem he hath magnifyed. This purpose after whiche they ben cleped sayntes or holy in the euerlasting present/ wheris neither tyme passed ne tyme co*m*mynge/ but euer it is onely present/ *and* nowe as mokel a mome*n*t as seuyn thousande wynter/ *and*

465 henteth, takes (seizes). **468 or**, before. **469 purposed**, chosen; **wyst**, knew. **472 cleped**, called. **475 mokel**, much.

so ayenwarde withouten any mevyng is nothyng lych temporel presence for thinge that there is ever present. Yet amonges you men, er it be in your presence, it is movable thorowe lyberté of arbytrement. And right as in the everlastyng present no maner thyng was, ne shal be, but onely is, and nowe here in your temporel tyme, somthyng was and is and shal be, but movynge stoundes, and in this is no maner repugnaunce, right so in the everlastynge presence nothyng may be chaunged; and in your temporel tyme otherwhile it is proved movable by lyberté of wyl or it be do withouten any inconvenyence therof to folowe. In your temporel tyme is no suche presence as in the t'other, for your present is done whan passed and to come gynnen entre, whiche tymes here amonges you everych easely foloweth other. But the presence everlastyng dureth in onehed withouten any ymaginable chaungyng, and ever is present and nowe. Trewly, the course of the planettes and overwhelmynges of the sonne in dayes and nightes with a newe gynnyng of his circute after it is ended, that is to sayn, one yere to folowe another — these maken your transitory tymes with chaungynge of lyves and mutation of people. But right as your temporel presence coveyteth every place, and al thinges in

---

so ayenwarde withouten any meuyng is nothyng lych te*m*porel presence/ for thi*n*ge that there is euer present. Yet amo*n*ges you men er it be in your presence it is mouable thorowe lyberte of arbytrement. And right as in the euerlastyng present no maner thyng was ne shalbe/ but onely is/ *and* nowe here in your te*m*porel tyme/ somthyng was *and* is/ *and* shalbe/ but mouynge stoundes/ *and* in this is no maner repugnaunce. Right so in the euerlastynge presence nothyng may be chau*n*ged: *and* in your te*m*porel tyme otherwhile it is p*ro*ued mouable by lyberte of wyl or it be do/ withouten any inco*n*uenyence therof to folowe. In your temporel tyme is no suche presence as in the tother/ for your present is done/ whan passed *and* to come gynnen entre/ whiche tymes here amo*n*ges you euerych easely foloweth other/ but the prese*n*ce euerlastyng dureth in onehed/ withouten any ymaginable chau*n*gyng/ *and* euer is present and nowe. Trewly the course of the planettes *and* ouerwhelmynges of the sonne in dayes *and* nightes/ with a newe gynnyng of his circute after it is ended/ that is to sayn/ one yere to folowe another. These maken your tra*n*sitory tymes with chau*n*gynge of lyues *and* mutation of peo<**359ra**> <**359rb**>ple. But right as your te*m*porel presence coueyteth euery place/ *and* al thinges in

476 mevyng, moving; **lych**, like. **480 stoundes**, times. **482 or**, before. **485 dureth**, endures. **486 onehed**, unity.

every of your tymes be contayned, and as nowe both sey and wist to Goddes very knowynge." "Than," quod I, "me wondreth why Poule spake these wordes by voice of signification in tyme passed that God His sayntes before-wist hath predestined, hath cleped, hath justifyed, and hath magnified. Me thynketh He shulde have sayde tho wordes in tyme present and that had ben more accordaunt to the everlastyng present than to have spoke in preterit voice of passed understandyng."

"O," quod Love, "by these wordes I se wel thou hast lytel understandyng of the everlastyng presence, or els of my before spoken wordes, for never a thing of tho thou hast nempned was tofore other or after other, but al atones evenlych at the God ben, and al togider in the everlastyng present be nowe to understandyng. The eternal presence, as I sayd, hath inclose togider in one al tymes in which close and one al thynges that ben in dyvers tymes and in dyvers places temporel, without posteriorité or priorité ben closed therin perpetual nowe and maked to dwel in present sight. But there thou sayest that Poule shulde have spoke thilke forsaid sentence be tyme present, and that most shulde have ben acordaunt to the everlastynge presence, why gabbest thou to thy

---

euery of your tymes be co*n*tayned/ *and* as nowe both sey *and* wist to goddes very knowynge. Than (q*uo*d I) me wondreth why Poule spake these wordes/ by voice of signification i*n* tyme passed/ that god his sayntes before wist/ hath predestined/ hath cleped/ hath iustifyed/ *and* hath magnified: Me thynketh he shulde haue sayde tho wordes in tymc present/ *and* that had ben more accordaunt to the euerlastyng present/ than to haue spoke in preterit voice of passed vnderstandyng.

O (q*uo*d Loue) by these wordes I se wel thou hast lytel vndersta*n*dyng of the euerlastyng p*re*sence/ or els of my before spoken wordes/ for neuer a thing of tho thou hast ne*m*pned was tofore other or after other/ but al atones eue*n*lych at the god ben/ *and* al togider in the euerlastyng present be nowe to vndersta*n*dyng/ the eternal presence/ as I sayd/ hath inclose togider i*n* one/ al tymes/ in which close *and* one al thynges that ben in dyuers tymes *and* in dyuers places temporel without posteriorite or priorite be*n* closed therin p*er*petual nowe/ *and* maked to dwel in present sight. But there thou sayest that Poule shulde haue spoke thilke forsaid sentence be tyme present/ *and* that most shulde haue ben acordaunt to the euerlastynge presence/ why gabbest thou to thy

491 sey, seen; **wist**, known. **499 nempned**, named; **evenlych**, equally. **501 close and one**, are closed and united. **504 thilke**, that same. **505 gabbest**, chatter.

wordes? Sothly, I say, Poule moved the wordes by signification of tyme passed to shewe fully that thilk wordes were nat put for temporel signification, for at thilk tyme were nat thilke seintes temporallych borne whiche that Poule pronounced God have tofore knowe and have cleped than magnified, wherthorowe it may wel be know that Poule used tho wordes of passed signification for nede and lacke of a worde in mannes bodily spech be tokenynge the everlastyng presence. And therfore in wordes moste semelyche in lykenesse to everlastyng presence he toke his sentence, for thynges that here beforne ben passed utterly be immovable, ilyke to the everlasting presence. As thilke that ben there never mowe not ben present, so thynges of tyme passed ne mowe in no wyse not ben passed. But al thinges in your temporal presence that passen in a lytel while shullen ben not present. So than in that, it is more symilytude to the everlastyng presence signification of tyme passed than of tyme temporal present, and so more in accordaunce. In this maner, what thynge of these that ben done thorowe fre arbitrement, or els as necessary, holy writte pronounceth. After eternyté he speketh, in whiche presence is everlastyng sothe and nothyng but sothe immovable, nat after tyme in whiche

---

wordes? Sothly I say Poule moued th*e* wordes by signification of tyme passed/ to shewe fully that thilk wordes were nat put for te*m*porel signification/ for al thilk tyme were nat thilke sente*n*ce te*m*porallych borne/ whiche that Poule pronounced god haue tofore knowe/ *and* haue cleped than magnified/ wherthorowe it may wel be know that Poule vsed tho wordes of passed signification/ for nede *and* lacke of a worde in ma*n*nes bodily spech be tokenynge the euerlastyng presence. And therfore worde is moste semelyche in lykenesse to euerlastyng presence/ he toke his sentence for thynges that here beforne ben passed/ vtterly be immouable/ ilyke to th*e* euerlasting prese*n*ce. As thilke that ben there neuer mowe not ben present/ so thynges of tyme passed ne mowe in no wyse not ben passed: but al thi*n*ges in your temporal presence that passen in a lytel while/ shullen ben not present. So than in that it is**<359rb><359va>**more symilytude to the euerlastyng presence/ signification of tyme passed/ than of tyme temporal present/ *and* so more in accordaunce. In this maner what thynge of these that ben done thorowe fre arbitrement/ or els as necessary/ holy writte pronou*n*ceth/ after eternyte he speketh/ in whiche prese*n*ce is euerlastyng sothe and nothyng but sothe immouable/ nat after tyme/ in whiche

506 moved, uttered. **514 mowe,** may. **519 he,** i.e., Holy Scripture.

naught alway ben your wylles and your actes. And right as while they be nat it is nat nedeful hem to be, so ofte it is nat nedeful that somtyme they shulde be." "As how," quod I, "for yet must I be lerned by some ensample." "Of love," quod she, "wol I nowe ensample make, sithen I knowe the heed knotte in that yelke. Lo, somtyme thou wrytest nat, ne arte than in no wyl to write. And right as while thou writest nat or els wolt nat write, it is nat nedeful thee to write or els wylne to write. And for to make thee knowe utterly that thynges ben otherwise in the everlastyng presence than in temporal tyme, se nowe my good childe; for somthyng is in the everlastynge presence, than in temporal tyme it was nat; in eternyté, tyme in eterne presence shal it nat be. Than no reason defendeth that somthynge ne may be in tyme temporal movyng that in eterne is immovable. Forsothe, it is no more contrary ne revers for to be movable in tyme temporel, and, immovable in eternyté, than nat to be in any tyme and to be alway in eternité and have to be or els to come in tyme temporel, and nat have be ne nought commyng to be in eternyté. Yet neverthelater, I say nat somthyng to be never in tyme temporel that ever is in eternyté, but al onely in somtyme nat to be; for I saye nat thy love to morne in no tyme to be, but today alone I deny ne it to be, and yet, neverthelater it is alwaye in eternyté."

---

naught alway ben your wylles *and* your actes. *and* right as while they be nat/ it is nat nedeful hem to be: so ofte it is nat nedeful that somtyme they shulde be. As how (quod I) for yet must I be lerned by some ensample. Of loue (quod she) wol I nowe ensample make/ sithen I knowe the heed knotte in that yelke. Lo/ somtyme thou wrytest no arte/ ne arte than in no wyl to write. *and* right as while th*ou* writest nat/ or els wolt nat write/ it is nat nedeful the to write/ or els wylne to write. And for to make th*e* knowe vtterly/ that thynges ben otherwise in the euerlastyng presence/ than in temporal tyme: se nowe my good childe/ for somthyng is in the euerlastynge presence/ than in temporal tyme/ it was nat in eternyte tyme/ in eterne presence shal it nat be. Than no reason defendeth/ that so*m*thynge ne may be in tyme temporal mouyng/ that in eterne is immouable. Forsothe it is no more contrary ne reuers for to be mouable in tyme temporel/ and mouable in eternyte/ than nat to be in any tyme/ and to be alway in eternite and haue to be or els to come in tyme temporel *and* nat haue be ne nought co*m*myng to be in eternyte. Yet neuer the later/ I say nat somthyng to be neuer in tyme temporel/ that euer is eternyte/ but al onely in somtyme nat to be for I saye nat thy loue to morne in no tyme to be/ but to day alone I deny ne it to be/ and yet neuer the later it is alwaye in eternyte.

524 sithen, since; **yelke**, yoke. **530 defendeth**, prohibits (forbids).

"A so," quod I, "it semeth to me that commyng thyng or els passed here in your temporal tyme to be in eternité ever nowe and present oweth nat to be denied; and yet foloweth nat thylke thynge that was or els shal be, in no maner therto ben passed or els commyng: than utterly shul we deny, for there without ceasyng it is, in his present maner." "O," quod she, "myne own disciple nowe gynnest thou be able to have the name of my servaunt. Thy wytte is clered; away is nowe errour of cloude in unconnyng, awaye is blyndnesse of love, awaye is thoughtful study of medlyng maners. Hastely shalte thou entre into the joye of me that am thyne owne maistres. Thou haste," quod she, "in a fewe wordes wel and clerely concluded mokel of my mater. And right as there is no revers ne contrarioustie in tho thynges, right so withouten any repugnaunce, it is sayd somthyng to be movable in tyme temporel afore it be that in eternyté dwelleth immovable, nat afore it be or after that it is, but without cessyng. For right naught is there after tyme; that same is there everlastynge that temporallyche somtyme nys, and toforne it be it maye not be, as I have sayd." "Nowe sothly," quod I, "this have I wel understande, so that nowe me thynketh that prescience of God and fre arbytrement

---

A so (quod I) it semeth to me that co*m*myng thyng or els passed here in your te*m*poral tyme to be/ in eternite euer nowe and present oweth nat to be demed/ and yet foloweth nat thylke thynge/ that was or els shal be/ in no maner therto ben passed/ or els co*m*myng: than vtterly shul we deny/ for there without ceasyng/ it is in his present maner. O (quod she) myne own disciple/ nowe gynnest thou able to haue**<359va>** **<359vb>**the name of my seruaunt. Thy wytte is clered/ away is nowe errour of cloude in vnconnyng/ awaye is blyndnesse of loue/ awaye is thoughtful study/ of medlyng maners hastely shalte thou entre in to the ioye of me/ that am thyne owne maistres. Thou haste (quod she) in a fewe wordes/ wel and clerely concluded mokel of my mater. And right as there is no reuers ne contrarioustie in tho thynges/ right so withouten any repugnau*n*ce/ it is sayd somthyng to be mouable in tyme temporel/ *and* for it be/ that in eternyte dwelleth immouable nat afore it be or after that it is/ but without cessyng/for right naught is there after tyme/ that same is there euerlastynge/ that te*m*porallyche somtyme nys/ and toforne it be it maye not be/ as I haue sayd. Nowe sothly (q*uo*d I) this haue I wel vndersta*n*de/ so that nowe me thynketh that prescience of god and fre arbytreme*n*t

538 denied, judged. **542 unconnyng**, ignorance. **545 mokel**, much. **549 nys**, is not.

withouten any repugnaunce acorden, and that maketh the strength of eternyté whiche encloseth by presence duryng al tymes and al thinges that ben, han ben, and shul ben in any tyme. I wolde nowe," quod I, "a lytel understande sythen that God al thyng thus beforne wot, whether thilke wetynge be of tho thynges, or els thilke thynges ben to ben of Goddes wetyng, and so of God nothynge is: and if every thyng be thorowe Goddes wetyng and therof take His beyng, than shulde God be maker and auctour of badde werkes, and so He shulde not ryghtfully punysshe yvel doynges of mankynde." Quod Love, "I shal tel thee this lesson to lerne: myne owne trewe servaunt the noble philosophical poete in Englissh whiche evermore hym besyeth and travayleth right sore my name to encrease, wherfore al that wyllen me good owe to do him worshyp and reverence bothe, trewly, his better ne his pere in schole of my rules coude I never fynde; he," quod she, "in a treatise that he made of my servant Troylus, hath this mater touched, and at the ful this questyon assoyled. Certaynly his noble sayenges can I not amende: In goodnes of gentyl manlyche speche without any maner of nycité of starieres ymagynacion

---

withouten any repugnaunce acorden/ and th*at* maketh the strength of eternyte/ whiche encloseth by presence duryng al tymes/ and al thinges that ben/ han ben/ and shul ben in any tyme. I wolde nowe (q*uo*d I) a lytel vnderstande sythen that al thyng thus beforne wot/ whether thilke wetynge be of tho thynges/ or els thilke thynges ben to ben of goddes wetyng/ and so of god nothynge is: and if euery thyng be thorowe goddes wetyng/ and therof take his beyng/ than shulde god be maker and auctour of badde werkes/ and so he shulde not ryghtfully punysshe yuel doynges of mankynde. (Q*uo*d Loue) I shal tel the/ this lesson to lerne myne owne trewe seruaunt/ the noble philosophical poete/ in Englissh/ whiche euermore hym besyeth and trauayleth right sore my name to encrease/ wherfore al that wyllen me good/ owe to do him worshyp *and* reuerence bothe/ trewly his better ne his pere in schole of my rules coude I neuer fynde: He (q*uo*d she) in a treatise th*at* he made of my seruant Troylus/ hath this mater touched/ and at the ful this questyon assoyled. Certaynly his noble sayenges can I not amende: In goodnes of gentyl manlyche speche/ without any maner of nycite of starieres ymagynacion

553 presence duryng, enduring present. **555 of tho thynges**, by means of those things; **ben to ben**, i.e., possess being. **556 of Goddes wetyng**, by His knowledge. **559–60 the noble philosophical poete**, i.e., Chaucer. **562 pere**, peer; **schole**, school. **564 assoyled**, solved. **565 starieres**, fabler's.

in wytte and in good reason of sentence he passeth al other makers. In the *Boke of Troylus* the answere to thy questyon mayste thou lerne. Neverthelater, yet may lightly thyne understandynge somdele ben lerned if thou have knowyng of these to fornsayd thinges. With that thou have understandyng of two the laste chapiters of this seconde boke, that is to say good to be somthyng and bad to want al maner beyng, for badde is nothing els but absence of good, and that God in good maketh that good dedes ben good, in yvel he maketh that they ben but naught that they ben bad; for to nothyng is badnesse to be." "I have," quod I tho, "ynough knowyng therin. Me nedeth of other thinges to here, that is to saye, howe I shal come to my blysse so longe desyred."

Chapter V

"In this mater toforn declared," quod Love, "I have wel shewed that every man hath fre arbytrement of thinges in his power to do or undo what him lyketh. Out of this grounde muste come the spire that by processe of tyme shal in greatnesse sprede to have braunches and blosmes of waxyng frute in grace, of whiche the taste and the savour is endelesse blysse in joy ever to onbyde."

---

in wytte and in good reason of sentence he passeth al other makers. In the boke of Troylus/ the answere**<359vb><360ra>**to thy questyon mayste/ thou lerne/ neuer the later yet may lightly thyne vnderstandynge somdele ben lerned/ if thou haue knowyng of these to fornsayd thinges/ with that thou haue vnderstandyng of two the laste chapiters of this seconde boke/ th*at* is to say/ good to be somthyng/ and bad to want al maner beyng/ for badde is nothing els but absence of good/ and that god in good/ maketh that good dedes ben good/ in yuel he maketh th*at* they ben but nauȝt/ that they ben bad: for to nothyng is badnesse to be. I haue (q*uo*d I tho) ynough knowyng therin/ me nedeth of other thinges to here/ that is to saye/ howe I shal come to my blysse so longe desyred. **IN** this mater toforn declared (q*uo*d loue) I haue wel shewed/ that euery ma*n* hath fre arbytrement of thinges in his power to do or vndo what him lyketh. Out of this grou*n*de muste come the spire/ that by processe of tyme shal in greatnesse sprede/ to haue braunches *and* blosmes of waxyng frute in grace/ of whiche the taste and the sauour is endelesse blysse in ioy euer to onbyde.

568 somdele, somewhat. **571 that God**, just as God. **577 spire**, shoot, sprout. **579 onbyde**, abide.

"Nowe lady," quod I, "that tree to set fayne wolde I lerne." "So thou shalt," quod she, er thou departe hence. The first thing thou muste set thy werke on grounde syker and good accordaunt to thy springes. For if thou desyre grapes thou goest not to the hasel; ne for to fetchen roses thou sekest not on okes; and if thou shalt have honysoukels thou leavest the frute of the soure docke. Wherfore, if thou desyre this blysse in parfite joy, thou must set thy purpose there vertue foloweth and not to loke after the bodily goodes, as I said whan thou were writyng in thy seconde booke. And for thou haste set thyselfe in so noble a place and utterly lowed in thyn herte the misgoyng of thy first purpose, this setling is the esyer to spring and the more lighter thy soule in grace to be lyssed. And, trewly, thy desyre that is to say thy wyl algates mote ben stedfast in this mater without any chaungynge, for if it be stedfast no man maye it voyde." "Yes, parde," quod I, "my wyl maye ben turned by frendes and disease of manace and thretnyng in lesynge of my lyfe and of my lymmes and in many otherwyse that nowe cometh not to mynde. And also it mote ofte ben out of thought, for no remembraunce may holde one thyng contynuelly in herte be it never so lusty desyred."

Nowe lady (q*uo*d I) that tree to set fayne wolde I lerne. So thou shalt (q*uo*d she) er thou departe hence. The first thing thou muste set thy werke on grou*n*de syker and good/ accordaunt to thy springes. For if thou desyre grapes/ thou goest not to the hasel/ ne for to fetchen roses/ thou sekest not on okes: and if thou shalt haue hony soukels/ thou leauest the frute of the soure docke. Wherfore if thou desyre this blysse i*n* parfite ioy/ thou must set thy purpose there vertue foloweth/ and not to loke after th*e* bodily goodes/ as I said whan thou were writyng in thy seconde booke. And for thou haste set thy selfe in so noble a place/ and vtterly lowed in thyn herte the misgoyng of thy first purpose/ this setteles is the esyer to spring/ and the more lighter thy soule in grace to be lyssed. And trewly thy desyre/ that is to say thy wyl/ algates mote ben stedfast in this mater without any chaungynge/ for if it be stedfast/ no man maye it voyde. yes parde (q*uo*d I) my wyl maye ben turned by frendes/ and disease of manace *and* thretnyng in lesynge of my lyfe and of my lymmes/ and in many other**<360ra><360rb>**wyse/ that nowe cometh not to mynde. And also it mote ofte ben out of thought/ for no remembraunce may holde one thyng contynuelly in herte/ be it neuer so lusty desyred.

582 springes, shoots. **584 soure docke**, sorrel. **587 lowed**, admitted. **588 setling**, a slip taken from a tree and planted. **589 lyssed**, healed, relieved; **mote**, must. **591 manace**, menace. **592 lesynge**, losing. **594 lusty**, eagerly.

"Nowe se," quod she, "hou thy wyl shal folowe thy frewil to be grounded contynuelly to abyde. It is thy fre wyl that thou lovest and haste loved and yet shal loven this Margaryte perle, and in thy wyl thou thinkest to holde it. Than is thy wyl knyt in love, not to chaunge for no newe lust besyde: this wyl teacheth thyn herte from al maner varyeng. But than although thou be thretened in dethe or els in otherwyse, yet is it in thyn arbytrement to chose thy love to voyde or els to holde: And thilke arbytrement is in a maner a jugement bytwene desyre and thy herte. And if thou deme to love thy good wyl fayleth, than arte thou worthy no blysse that good wyl shulde deserve. And if thou chose contynuaunce in thy good servyce, than thy good wyl abydeth; nedes blysse folowyng of thy goodwyl must come by strength of thilke jugement. For thy first wyl that taught thyn herte to abyde and halte it from th'eschaunge, with thy reson is accorded. Trewly, this maner of wyl thus shal abyde; impossible it were to turne if thy hert be trewe, and if every man dyligently the menynges of his wyl consyder, he shal wel understande that good wyl knyt with reason but in a false herte never is voyded. For power and might of kepyng this good wyl is thorowe lyberté of arbytrement in hert,

---

Nowe se (q*uo*d she) thou thy wyl shal folowe/ thy frewil to be grou*n*ded co*n*tynuelly to abyde: It is thy frewyl that thou louest and haste loued/ and yet shal louen this Margaryte perle/ and in thy wyl thou thinkest to holde it. Than is thy wyl knyt in loue/ not to chaunge for no newe lust besyde: this wyl teacheth thyn herte from al maner varyeng. But than although thou be thretened in dethe or els in otherwyse/ yet is it in thyn arbytrement to chose/ thy loue to voyde or els to holde: And thilke arbytrement is in a maner a iugement bytwene desyre and thy herte. And if thou deme to loue thy good wyl fayleth/ than arte thou worthy no blysse that good wyl shulde deserue: and if thou chose contynuaunce in thy good seruyce/ than thy good wyl abydeth/ nedes blysse folowyng of thy goodwyl must come by stre*n*gth of thilke iugement: for thy first wyl th*at* taught thyn herte to abyde/ *and* halte it from theschau*n*ge with thy reson is accorded. Trewly this maner of wyl thus shal abyde/ impossible it were to turne if thy hert be trewe/ and if euery man dyligently the menynges of his wyl consyder/ he shal wel vnderstande that good wyl knyt with reason/ but in a false herte neuer is voyded: for power *and* might of kepyng this goodwyl is thorowe lyberte of arbytreme*n*t in hert/

596 thy fre wyl, of thy free will. **598 lust**, delight. **601 deme**, judge. **603 nedes**, necessarily. **608 but**, except.

but goodwil to kepe may not fayle. Eke, than if it fayle it sheweth it selfe that good wyl in kepyng is not there. And thus false wyl that putteth out the good anone constrayneth the herte to accorde in lovynge of thy goodwyl and this acordaunce bytwene false wyl and thyn herte in falsyté ben lykened togyther. Yet a lytel wol I say thee in good wyl thy good wylles to rayse and strength. Take hede to me," quod she, "howe thy wylles thou shalt understande. Right as ye han in your body dyvers membres and fyve sondrie wyttes, everyche aparte to his owne doyng whiche thynges as instrumentes ye usen as your handes aparte to handle, fete to go, tonge to speke, eye to se, right so the soule hath in him certayne sterynges and strengthes whiche he useth as instrumentes to his certayne doynges. Reason is in the soule which he useth thinges to knowe and to prove, and wyl whiche he useth to wylne; and yet is neyther wyl ne reason al the soule, but everych of hem is a thing by himself in the soule. And right as everich hath thus singuler instrumentes by hemselfe they han as wel dyvers aptes and dyvers maner usinges and thilke aptes mowen in wyl ben cleped affections. Affection is an instrument of willynge in his apetytes. Wherfore mokel folke sayn if a resonable creatures soule anythinge

---

but goodwil to kepe may not fayle. Eke than if it fayle/ it sheweth it selfe that goodwyl in kepyng is not there. And thus false wyl that putteth out the good/ anone constrayneth the herte to accorde in louynge of thy goodwyl/ and this acordaunce bytwene false wyl *and* thyn herte/ in falsyte ben lykened togyther. yet a lytel wol I say the/ in good wyl thy goodwylles to rayse *and* strength. Take hede to me (q*uo*d she) howe thy wylles thou shalt vnderstande. Right as ye han in your body dyuers membres/ and fyue sondrie wyttes/ eueryche aparte to his owne doyng/ whiche thynges as instrume*n*tes ye vsen/ as your handes aparte to handle/ fete to go/ tonge to speke/ eye to se: Right so th*e* soule hath in him certayne sterynges and**<360rb><360va>**strengthes whiche he vseth as instrume*n*tes to his certayne doynges. Reason is in the soule/ which he vseth thinges to knowe *and* to proue/ *and* wyl whiche he vseth to wylne: *and* yet is neyther wyl ne reason al th*e* soule/ but euerych of hem is a thing by him self in th*e* soule. And right as euerich hath thus singuler instrume*n*tes by he*m*selfe/ they han as wel dyuers aptes *and* dyuers maner vsinges/ *and* thilke aptes mowen in wyl ben cleped affectio*n*s. Affection is an instrume*n*t of willynge in his apetytes. Wherfore mokel folke sayn/ if a resonable creatures soule any thinge

616 aparte, appropriate, open; **his**, its. **619 which**, by which. **623 aptes**, aptitudes.

ferventIy wylneth, affectuously he wylneth. And thus may wyl by terme of equivocas in thre wayes ben understande: One is instrument of willing; another is affection of this instrument; and the third is use that setteth it a werke. Instrument of willyng is thilke strength of the soule which that constrayneth to wylne, right as reason is instrument of resons which ye usen whan ye loken. Affection of this instrument is a thyng by whiche ye be drawe desyrously any thyng to wylne in coveytous maner, albeit for the tyme out of your mynde, as if it come in your thought thilke thyng to remembre anon ye ben willyng thilke to done or els to have. And thus is instrument wyl — and affection is wyl also — to wylne thynge as I sayd, as for to wylne helth whan wyl nothing theron thinketh, for anon as it cometh to memorie it is in wyl, and so is affection to wylne slepe whan it is out of mynde; but anon as it is remembred wyl wylneth slepe whan his tyme cometh of the doynge. For affection of wyl never accordeth to sicknesse ne alway to wake. Right so in a true lovers affection of willyng, instrument is to wylne truthe in his servyce, and this affection alway abydeth, although he be slepyng or thretned or els not theron thinkyng; but anon as it cometh to mynde, anon he is stedfast in that wyl to abyde. Use of this instrument, forsothe, is another thing by himselfe, and that have ye

---

feruen*t*ly wylneth/ affectuously he wylneth/ *and* thus may wyl by terme of equiuocas in thre wayes ben vndersta*n*de: One is instrume*n*t of willing/ another is affection of this instrume*n*t: *and* the third is vse/ th*at* setteth it a werke Instrume*n*t of willyng is thilke stre*n*gth of the soule/ which th*at* co*n*strayneth to wylne/ right as reason is instrument of resons/ which ye vsen whan ye loken. Affection of this instrume*n*t is a thyng/ by whiche ye be drawe desyrously any thyng to wylne in coueytous maner/ al be it for the tyme out of your mynde: as if it come in your thought thilke thyng to remembre/ anon ye ben willyng thilke to done or els to haue. And thus is instrument wyl/ *and* affection is wyl also/ to wylne thynge as I sayd: as for to wylne helth/ whan wyl nothi*n*g theron thinketh/ for anon as it cometh to memorie it is in wyl/ and so is affection to wylne slepe whan it is out of mynde/ but anon as it is remembred wyl wylneth slepe/ whan his tyme cometh of th*e* doynge. For affection of wyl neuer accordeth to sicknesse/ ne alway to wake. Right so in a true louers affection of willyng instrument/ is to wylne truthe in his seruyce/ and this affectio*n* alway abydeth/ although he be slepyng or thretned/ or els not theron thinkyng/ but anon as it cometh to mynde/ anon he is stedfast in that wyl to abyde. Vse of this instrument forsothe is another thing by himselfe/ *and* that haue ye

625 equivocas, equivocation. **627 a**, to.

not but whan ye be doyng in wylled thing by affecte or instrument of wyl purposed or desyred. And this maner of usage in my servyce wisely nedeth to be ruled from wayters with envye closed, from spekers ful of jangeling wordes, from proude folk and hautayn that lambes and innocentes bothe scornen and dispysen. Thus in doyng varieth the actes of willynge everich from other, and yet ben they cleped wyl, and the name of wyl utterly owen they to have, as instrument of wyl is wyl whan ye turne into purpose of any thing to don, be it to syt or to stande or any such thing els. This instrument may ben had, although affect and usage be left out of doyng, right as ye have sight and reson, and yet alway use ye ne ought to loke thynges with resonnyng to prove. And so is instrument of wyl wyl, and yet varyeth he from effecte and using bothe. Affection of wyl also for wyl is cleped, but it varyeth from instrument in this maner wise by that name lyche whan it cometh in to mynde anon right it is in wyllynge desyred; and the negatyfe therof with wyllyng nyl not acorde. This is closed in herte, thoughe usage and instrument slepe. This slepeth whan instrument and us waken: and of suche maner affection, trewly, some man hath more and some man lesse. Certes trewe lovers wenen ever

---

not but whan ye be doyng in wylled thing by affecte or instrume*n*t of wyl pursosed or desyred/ *and* this maner of vsage in my seruyce wisely nedeth to be ruled fro*m* wayters w*ith* enuye closed/ from spekers ful of ia*n*geling word*es*/ from proude folk *and* hautayn/ that lambes *and* innoce*n*tes bothe scornen *and* dispysen.**<360va><360vb>**Thus in doyng varicth the actes of willynge euerich from other/ *and* yet ben they cleped wyl/ *and* the name of wyl vtterly owen they to haue/ as instrume*n*t of wyl is wyl/ whan ye turne in to purpose of any thing to don/ be it to syt or to sta*n*de/ or any such thi*ng* els. This instrume*n*t may ben had/ although affect *and* vsage be left out of doyng/ right as ye haue sight *and* reson/ *and* yet alway vse ye **<360vb line 9><356va line 5>**ne ought to loke thynges with resonnyng to p*ro*ue/ and so is instrume*n*t of wyl/ wyl: and yet varyeth he from effecte *and* vsing bothe. Affection of wyl also for wyl is cleped/ but it varyeth from instrument in this maner wise/ by that name/ lyche whan it cometh in to mynde anon right it is in wyllynge desyred/ and the negatyfe therof with wyllyng nyl not acorde: this is closed in herte/ thoughe vsage and instrument slepe. This slepeth whan instrume*n*t and vs waken: and of suche maner affection trewly some man hath more and some man lesse. Certes trewe louers wenen euer

642 ruled from, restricted from; **wayters,** inhibitors, interferers. **643–44 hautayn that,** haughty who. **645 cleped**, called. **653 nyl**, will not. **654 us**, use. **655 wenen**, think.

therof to lytel to have. False lovers in lytel wenen have right mokel: Lo, instrument of wyl in false and trewe bothe evenlyche is proporcioned, but affection is more in some place than in some, bycause of the goodnesse that foloweth, and that I thynke herafter to declare. Use of this instrument is wyl, but it taketh his name whan wylned thyng is in doyng. But utterly grace to catche in thy blysse desyred to ben rewarded, thou muste have than affection of wyl at the ful and use whan his tyme asketh wysely to ben governed. Sothly, my discyple, without fervent affection of wil may no man ben saved. This affection of good servyce in good love may not ben grounded without fervent desyre to the thyng in wyl coveyted. But he that never retcheth to have or not to have affection of wyl in that hath no restyng place. Why? For whan thing cometh to mynde and it be not taken in hede to comyn or not come, therfore in that place affection fayleth; and for thilke affection is so lytel thorow whiche in goodnesse he shulde come to his grace, the lytelnesse wyl it not suffre to avayle by no way in to his helpes: Certes, grace and reason thilke affection foloweth. This affection with reason knytte dureth in everyche trewe herte and evermore is encreasyng; no ferdnesse no strength maye it

---

therof to lytel to haue. False louers in lytel wenen haue right mokel: Lo instrument of wyl in false and trewe bothe euen lyche is proporcioned/ but affection is more in some place than in some/ bycause of the goodnesse th*at* foloweth/ and that I thynke herafter to declare. Vse of this instrume*nt* is wyl/ but it taketh his name whan wylned thyng is in doyng. but vtterly grace to catche in thy blysse/ desyred to ben rewarded/ Thou muste haue than affection of wyl at the ful/ and vse whan his tyme asketh wysely to ben gouerned. Sothly my discyple without feruent affection of wil may no man ben saued: this affection of good seruyce in good loue/ may not ben grounded/ without feruent desyre to the thyng in wyl coueyted. But he that neuer retcheth to haue or not to haue/ affection of wyl in that hath no restyng place. Why? for whan thing cometh to mynde and it be not taken in hede to comyn or not come/ therfore in that place affection fayleth: and for thilke affection is so lytel/ thorow whiche in goodnesse he shulde come to his grace/ the lytelnesse wyl it not suffre to auayle by no way in to his helpes: Certes grace and reason thilke affection foloweth. This affection with reason knytte/ dureth in eueryche trewe herte/ and euermore is encreasyng/ no ferdnesse/ no strength maye it

656 mokel, much. **661 his**, its. **664 retcheth**, cares. **667 for**, since. **669 dureth**, endures. **670 ferdnesse no**, fear nor.

remove whyle truthe in herte abydeth. Sothly, whan falsheed gynneth entre truthe draweth away — grace and joy both; but than thilke falsheed that trouth hath thus voyded hath unknyt the bonde of understandyng reason bytwene wyl and the herte. And whoso that bonde undothe and unknytteth wyl to be in other purpose than to the first accorde knytteth him with contrarye of reason, and that is unreason. Lo, than wyl and unreson bringeth a man from the blisse of grace, which thyng of pure kynde every man ought to shonne and to eschewe, and to the knot of wyl and reason confyrme. Me thynketh," quod she, "by thy studyent lokes thou wenest in these wordes me to contrarien from other sayenges here toforne in other place as whan thou were somtyme in affection of wyl to thinges that nowe han brought thee in disease, whiche I have thee counsayled to voyde, and thyn herte discover. And there I made thy wyl to ben chaunged, whiche now thou wenest I argue to witholde and to kepe. Shortly I say the revers in these wordes may not ben founde, for though dronkennesse be forboden men shul not alway ben drinklesse. I trowe right, for thou thy wyl out of reason shulde not tourne, thy wyl in one reason shulde not unbyde. I say thy wyl in thy first purpose with unreason was

---

remoue whyle truthe in herte abydeth. Sothly whan falsheed gynneth entre/ truthe draweth away/ grace and ioy both:**<356va><356vb>**but than thilke falsheed that trouth hath thus voyded/ hath vnknyt the bonde of vnderstandyng reason/ bytwene wyl and the herte. And who so that bonde vndothe/ and vnknytteth wyl to be in other purpose than to the first accorde/ knytteth him with contrarye of reason/ and that is vnreason. Lo/ than wyl and vnreson bringeth a man from the blisse of grace/ which thyng of pure kynde/ euery man ought to shonne *and* to eschewe/ and to the knot of wyl and reason confyrme. Me thynketh (q*uo*d she) by thy study*en*t lokes/ thou wenest in these wordes me to co*n*trarien/ from other sayenges here toforne in other place/ as whan thou were so*m*tyme in affection of wyl/ to thinges that nowe han brought the in disease/ whiche I haue the counsayled to voyde/ and thyn herte discouer/ and there I made thy wyl to ben chaunged/ whiche now thou wenest I argue to witholde and to kepe. Shortly I say th*e* reuers in these wordes may not ben fou*n*de: for though dronke*n*nesse be forboden/ men shul not alway ben drinklesse. I trowe right for thou thy wyl out of reason shulde not tourne/ thy wyl in one reason shulde not vnbyde/ I say thy wyl in thy first purpose with vnreason was

671 falsheed, falsehood. **672 both**, as well. **677 shonne**, shun. **678 wenest**, suppose. **684 trowe**, believe; **thou**, though. **685 unbyde**, abide.

closed: Constrewe forthe of the remenante what thee good lyketh. Trewly, that wyl and reson shulde be knyt togyder was fre wyl of reason; after tyme thyne herte is assentaunt to them bothe. Thou might not chaunge but if thou from rule of reason varye, in whiche variaunce to come to thilke blysse desyred contrariously thou werchest; and nothyng may knowe wyl and reason but love alone. Than if thou voide love than wevest the bonde that knytteth, and so nedes or els right lightly that other gone a sondre, wherfore thou seest apertly that love holdeth this knot and amaystreth hem to be bounde. These thinges as a ringe in cyrcuit of wrethe ben knyt in thy soule without departyng." "A, let be, let be," quod I, "it nedeth not of this no rehersayle to make; my soule is yet in parfyte blysse in thynking of that knotte."

Chapter VI

"Nowe trewly, lady, I have my grounde wel understonde, but what thynge is thilke spire that into a tree shulde wexe? Expowne me that thing what ye therof meane." "That shal I," quod she, "blithly and take good hede to the wordes I thee rede. Contynuaunce

---

closed: Constrewe forthe of the remenante what the good lyketh. Trewly that wyl *and* reson shulde be knyt togyder was fre wyl of reason/ after tyme thyne herte is assentaunt to them bothe/ thou might not chau*n*ge/ but if thou from rule of reason varye/ in whiche variaunce to come to thilke blysse desyred/ co*n*trariously thou werchest: and nothyng may knowe wyl *and* reason but loue alone. Than if thou voide loue/ than weuest the bonde that knytteth/ and so nedes or els right lightly/ that other gone a sondre/ wherfore thou seest apertly that loue holdeth this knot/ and amaystreth hem to be bounde. These thinges/ as a ringe in cyrcuit of wrethe ben knyt in thy soule without departyng. A let be/ let be (q*uo*d I) it nedeth not of this no rehersayle to make/ my soule is yet in parfyte blysse/ in thynking of that knotte.

NOwe trewly lady I haue my grou*n*de wel vnderstonde/ but what thynge is thilke spire that in to a tree shulde wexe: ex**<356vb><357ra>**powne me that thing/ what ye therof meane. That shal I (q*uo*d she) blithly/ and take good hede to the wordes I the rede. Contynuaunce

687 assentaunt, assenting. **689 werchest**, work. **692 apertly**, plainly, openly; **amaystreth**, masters. **693 wrethe**, wreath. **697 wexe**, grow; **Expowne**, Explain. **698 rede**, counsel.

in thy good servyce by longe processe of tyme in ful hope abydyng, without any chaunge to wylne in thyne herte: this is the spire whiche if it be wel kept and governed shal so hugely springe tyl the fruite of grace is plentuously out sprongen. For althoughe thy wyl be good, yet may not therfore thilk blysse desyred hastely on thee discenden — it must abyde his sesonable tyme. And so by processe of growyng with thy good traveyle it shal into more and more wexe, tyl it be founde so mighty that wyndes of yvel speche ne scornes of envy make nat the traveyle overthrowe ne frostes of mystrust ne hayles of jelousy right lytel myght have in harmynge of suche springes. Every yonge setlyng lightly with smale stormes is apeyred, but whan it is woxen somdele in gretnesse than han great blastes and wethers but lytel might any disavantage to them for to werche." "Myne owne soverayne lady," quod I, "and welth of myne hert and it were lykyng unto your noble grace therthrough nat to be displeased, I suppose ye erren. Nowe ye maken jelousy envy and distourbour to hem that ben your servauntes. I have lerned ofte toforne this tyme that in every lovers hert great plentie of jelousies greves ben sowe, wherfore

---

in thy good seruyce/ by longe processe of tyme in ful hope abydyng/ without any chaunge to wylne in thyne herte: this is the spire/ whiche if it be wel kept and gouerned/ shal so hugely springe/ tyl the fruite of grace is plentuously out sprongen: for al thoughe thy wyl be good/ yet may not therfore thi*lk* blysse desyred hastely on the disce*n*den/ it must abyde his sesonable tyme. *and* so by p*ro*cesse of growyng/ with thy good traueyle/ it shal in to more *and* more wexe/ tyl it be foundc so mighty/ that wyndes of yuel speche/ ne scornes of enuy/ make nat the traueyle ouerthrowe/ ne frostes of mystrust/ ne hayles of ielousy right lytel myght haue in harmynge of suche springes. Euery yonge setlyng lightly with smale stormes is a peyred/ but whan it is woxen somdele in gretnesse/ than han great blastes *and* wethers but lytel might/ any disauantage to them for to werche. Myne owne souerayne lady (q*uo*d I) and welth of myne hert/ and it were lykyng vnto your noble grace/ therthrough nat to be displeased/ I suppose ye erren/ nowe ye maken ielousy enuy/ *and* distourbour to hem that ben your seruauntes. I haue lerned ofte toforne this tyme/ that in euery louers hert/ great ple*n*tie of ielousies greues ben sowe/ wherfore

706 springes, shoots; **setlyng**, plant. **707 apeyred**, damaged; **woxen**, grown; **somdele**, somewhat. **708 wethers**, storms; **werche**, cause. **709 and it**, if it. **712 greves**, griefs; **sowe**, sown.

me thynketh ye ne ought in no maner accompte thilke thynge among these other welked wyners and venomous serpentes, as envy, mystrust, and yvel speche." "O fole," quod she, "mystrust with foly, with yvel wil medled, engendreth that welked padde. Truely if they were distroyed jelousy undone were for ever, and yet some maner of jelousy I wot wel is ever redy in al the hertes of my trewe servauntes as thus: to be jelous over him selfe lest he be cause of his own disease. This jelousy in ful thought ever shulde be kept for ferdnesse to lese his love by miskepyng thorowe his owne doyng in leudnesse, or els thus: Lest she that thou servest so fervently is beset there her better lyketh, that of al thy good service she compteth nat a cresse. These jelousies in herte for acceptable qualytees ben demed. These oughten every trewe lover by kynde evermore haven in his mynde tyl fully the grace and blysse of my service be on him discended at wyl. And he that than jelousy catcheth, or els by wenyng of his owne folysshe wylfulnesse mystrusteth, truely with fantasy of venyme he is foule begyled. Yvel wyl hath grounded thilke mater of sorowe in his leude soule, and yet nat for than to every wight shuld me

---

me thynketh ye ne ought in no maner accompte/ thilke thynge among these other welked wyners and venomous serpe*n*tes/ as enuy/ mystrust/ *and* yuel speche. O fole (q*uo*d she) mystrust with foly with yuel wil medled/ enge*n*dreth that welked padde. Truely if they were distroyed ielousy vndone were for euer/ *and* yet some maner of ielousy I wot wel is euer redy in al the hertes of my trewe seruau*n*tes/ as thus: to be ielous ouer hi*m* selfe/ lest he be cause of his own disease. This ielousy in ful thouȝt euer shulde be kept for ferdnesse to lese his loue by miskepyng/ thorowe his owne doyng in leudnesse/ or els thus: Lest she that thou seruest so feruently is beset there her better lyketh/ that of al thy good seruice she compteth nat a cresse. These ielousies in herte for acceptable qualytees ben demed: these oughten euery trewe lo**<357ra><357rb>**uer by kyndly/ euermore hauen in his mynde/ tyl fully the grace *and* blysse of my seruice be on him disce*n*ded at wyl. *and* he that than ielousy catcheth/ or els by wenyng of his owne folysshe wylfulnesse mystrusteth/ truely with fantasy of venyme/ he is foule begyled. Yuelwyl hath grounded thilke mater of sorowe in his leude soule/ *and* yet nat for than to euery wight shuld me

713 accompte, account. **713–14 welked wyners**, swollen vipers (see note). **714 as**, such as. **715 medled**, mixed; **welked padde**, swollen toad, frog. **716 wot**, know. **719 ferdnesse**, fear; **leudnesse**, ignorance. **721 compteth**, account; **cresse**, trifle, sprig of watercress. **722 demed**, judged. **724 wenyng**, supposing. **726 leude**, ignorant; **nat for than**, nevertheless; **me**, men.

nat trust ne every wight fully mysbeleve: the meane of these thynges owen to be used. Sothly, withouten causeful evydence, mistrust in jelousy shulde nat be wened in no wyse person commenly; suche leude wickednesse shulde me nat fynde. He that is wise and with yvel wil nat be acomered can abyde wel his tyme tyl grace and blisse of his service folowyng have him so mokel eased as his abidynge toforehande hath him diseased." "Certes lady," quod I tho, "of som thyng me wondreth sythen thilke blysse so precious is and kyndly good and wel is and worthy in kynde whan it is medled with love and reason as ye toforn have declared. Why, anon as hye one is sprong, why springeth nat the t'other? And anone as the one cometh, why receyveth nat the other? For every thynge that is out of his kyndly place by ful appetite ever cometh thiderwarde kyndely to drawe, and his kyndly beyng therto him constrayneth. And the kindly stede of this blysse is in suche wyl medled to unbyde and nedes in that it shulde have his kyndly beyng. Wherfore, me thinketh, anon as that wyl to be shewed and kydde him profreth, thilke blysse shulde him hye thilk wyl to receyve, or els kynde of goodnesse worchen

---

nat trust/ ne euery wight fully mysbeleue/ the meane of these thynges owen to be vsed. Sothly withouten causeful euydece/ mistrust in ielousy shulde nat be wened in no wyse person co*m*menly/ suche leude wickednesse shulde me nat fynde. He that is wise *and* with yuel wil nat be acomered/ can abyde wel his tyme/ tyl grace *and* blisse of his seruice folowyng/ haue hi*m* so mokel eased/ as his abidynge toforehande hath hi*m* diseased. Certes lady (q*uo*d I tho) of no thyng me wo*n*dreth/ sythen thilke blysse so precious is *and* kyndly good/ *and* wel is *and* worthy in kynde/ whan it is medled with loue *and* reason/ as ye toforn haue declared. Why/ anon as hye one is sprong/ why springeth nat the tother? *and* anone as the one cometh/ why receyueth nat the other? For euery thynge that is out of his kyndly place/ by ful appetite/ euer cometh thiderwarde kyndely to drawe/ *and* his kyndly beyng therto him co*n*strayneth. *and* the ki*n*dly stede of this blysse/ is in suche wyl medled to vnbyde/ *and* nedes in that it shulde haue his kyndly beyng. Wherfore me thinketh anon as that wyl to be shewed *and* kydde him profreth/ thilke blysse shulde hi*m* hye thilk wyl to receyue/ orels kynde of goodnesse worchen

727 wight, person; **owen**, ought. **728 wened**, construed. **730 wil nat be acomered**, desires not to be encumbered. **731 mokel**, much. **732 sythen**, since. **733 medled**, mixed. **736 kyndly**, natural. **737 stede**, place. **738 unbyde**, abide. **739 kydde**, made known. **740 hye**, hasten.

nat in hem as they shulde. Lo be the sonne never so ferre ever it hath his kynde werching in erthe. Great weight on hye onlofte caried stynteth never tyl it come to his restyng place. Waters to the seewarde ever ben they drawing; thing that is lyght blithly wyl nat synke but ever ascendeth and upward draweth. Thus kynde in every thyng his kyndly course and his beynge place sheweth. Wherfore be kinde on this good wil anon as it were spronge this blysse shulde thereon discende, her kynde wolde they dwelleden togider and so have ye sayde yourselfe." "Certes," quod she, "thyne hert sytteth wonder sore this blysse for to have; thyne hert is sore agreved that it tarieth so longe, and if thou durstest as me thynketh by thyne wordes this blysse woldest thou blame. But yet I saye thilke blysse is kyndly good and his kyndely place in that wyl to unbyde. Neverthelater, their commyng togider after kyndes ordynaunce nat sodaynly maye betyde; it muste abyde tyme, as kynde yeveth him leave, for if a man as this wyl medled gonne hym shewe and thilke blysse in haste folowed, so lyghtly commynge shulde lyghtly cause going: longe tyme of thurstyng causeth drinke to be the more delycious whan it is atasted." "Howe is it," quod I than, "that so many blysses se I al daye at myne

---

nat in he*m* as they shulde. Lo/ be the sonne neuer so ferre/ euer it hath his kynde werching in erthe: great weiȝt on hye onlofte caried/ stynteth neuer tyl it co*me* to this restyng place. Waters to the see warde euer ben they drawing/ thi*n*g that is lyght blithly wyl nat synke/ but euer asce*n*deth *and* vpward draweth. Thus kynde i*n* euery thyng his kyndly course/ *and* his beynge place sheweth: Wherfore be ki*n*de on this good wil/ anon as it were spronge/ this blysse shulde thereon disce*n*de/ her kynde wolde they dwelleden togider/ *and* so haue ye sayde your selfe. Certes (q*uo*d she) thyne hert sytteth wo*n*der sore this blysse for to haue/ thyne hert is sore agreued th*at* it tarieth so lo*n*ge/ **<357rb>** **<357va>**and if thou durstest/ as me thynketh by thyne wordes/ this blysse woldest thou blame. But yet I saye/ thilke blysse is kyndly good/ and his kyndely place in that wyl to vnbyde. Neuer the later/ their co*m*myng togider after kyndes ordynaunce nat sodaynly maye betyde/ it muste abyde tyme/ as kynde yeueth him leaue for if a man/ as this wyl medled gonne hym shewe/ and thilke blysse in haste folowed/ so lyghtly co*m*mynge shulde lyghtly cause going/ longe tyme of thurstyng/ causeth drinke to be the more delycious whan it is atasted. Howe is it (quod I than) that so many blysses se I al daye at myne

742 hye, high; **onlofte**, aloft; **stynteth**, ceases; **his**, its. **746 her**, their. **749 durstest**, dared. **750 unbyde**, abide. **752 betyde**, happen; **yeveth**, gives.

eye in the firste moment of a syght with suche wyl accorde? Ye, and yet otherwhyle with wyl assenteth syngulerly by himselfe there reason fayleth. Traveyle was none; servyce had no tyme. This is a queynt maner thynge howe suche doynge cometh aboute." "O," quod she, "that is thus: the erthe kyndely after seasons and tymes of the yere bringeth forthe innumerable herbes and trees, bothe profytable and other; but suche as men might leave though they were nought in norisshynge to mannes kynde serven or els suche as tournen soone unto mennes confusyon in case that therof they ataste comen forthe out of the erthe by their owne kynde, withouten any mannes cure or any busynesse in traveyle. And the ylke herbes that to mennes lyvelode necessarily serven, without whiche goodly in this lyfe creatures mowen nat enduren, and most ben nourisshen to mankynde, without great traveyle, great tylthe, and longe abidynge tyme, comen nat out of the erthe, and yit with seede toforne ordayned suche herbes to make spring and forthe growe. Right so the parfyte blysse, that we have in meanynge of duryng tyme to abyde, may nat come so lyghtly, but with great traveyle and right besy tylth, and yet good seed to be sowe, for ofte the croppe fayleth of badde seede be it

---

eye/ in the firste moment of a syght with suche wyl accorde. ye/ and yet other whyle with wyl assenteth/ syngulerly by him selfe there reason fayleth/ traueyle was none/ seruyce had no tyme. This is a queynt maner thynge/ howe suche doynge cometh aboute. O (quod she) that is thus/ the erthe kyndely after seasons and tymes of the yere/ bringeth forthe innumerable herbes and trees bothe profytable and other/ but suche as men might leaue/ though they were nought in norisshynge to mannes kynde seruen/ or els suche as tournen soone vnto me*n*nes confusyon in case that therof they ataste/ comen forthe out of the erthe by their owne kynde/ withouten any mannes cure or any busynesse in traueyle: and the ylke herbes that to me*n*nes lyue lode necessarily seruen/ without whiche goodly in this lyfe creatures mowen nat enduren/ and most ben nourisshen to mankynde/ with out great traueyle/ great tylthe/ and longe abidynge tyme/ comen nat out of the erthe/ and it with seede toforne ordayned suche herbes to make spring and forthe growe. Right so the parfyte blysse/ that we haue in meanynge of duryng tyme to abyde may nat come so lyȝtly/ but with great traueyle *and* right besy tylth/ and yet good seed to be sowe/ for ofte th*e* croppe fayleth of badde seede/ be it

759 thus, so. **764 lyvelode**, livelihood. **765 mowen**, may. **766 tylthe**, tillage. **768 meanynge**, the meanwhile. **769 duryng tyme**, duration.

never so wel traveyled. And thilke blysse thou spoke of so lightly in commyng, trewly, is nat necessary ne abidynge. And but it the better be stamped and the venomous jeuse out wrongen it is lykely to enpoysonen al tho that therof tasten. Certes, right bytter ben the herbes that shewen first in the yere of her own kynde. Wel the more is the harvest that yeldeth many graynes, tho longe and sore it hath ben traveyled. What woldest thou demen if a man wold yeve thre quarters of nobles of golde — that were a precious gyft?" "Ye certes," quod I. "And what," quod she, "thre quarters ful of peerles?" "Certes," quod I, "that were a riche gifte." "And what," quod she, "of as mokel azure?" Quod I, "a precious gifte at ful." "Were nat," quod she, "a noble gifte of al these atones?" "In good faith," quod I, "for wantyng of Englyssh namyng of so noble a worde I can nat for preciousnesse yeve it a name." "Rightfully," quod she, "haste thou demed, and yet love knytte in vertue passeth al the golde in this erthe. Good wyl accordant to reason with no maner proporté may be countrevayled. Al the azure in the worlde is nat to accompte in respecte of reason. Love that with good wyl and reason accordeth with non erthly riches may nat ben amended. This yeft hast thou yeven, I know it myselfe, and thy Margarite thilke gift hath receyved, in whiche thynge to rewarde she hath her

---

neuer so wel traueyled. And thilke blysse thou spoke of so liȝtly in com*m*yng/ trewly is nat necessary ne abidynge: and but it the better be stamped/ *and* the venomous ieuse out wrongen/ it is lykely to enpoysonen al tho that therof tasten. Certes right bytter ben th*e* herbes that shewen first the yere of her own kynde. Wel the more is the**<357va><357vb>**haruest that yeldeth many graynes/ tho longe and sore it hath ben traueyled. What woldest thou demen if a man wold yeue thre quarters of nobles of golde/ that were a precious gyft? ye certes (q*uo*d I). And what (q*uo*d she) thre quarters ful of peerles? Certes (q*uo*d I) that were a riche gifte. And what (q*uo*d she) of as mokel azure? (Q*uo*d I) a precious gifte at ful. Were nat (q*uo*d she) a noble gifte of al these atones? In good faith (q*uo*d I) for wa*n*tyng of englyssh namyng of so noble a worde/ I can nat for p*re*ciousnesse yeue it a name. Rightfully (q*uo*d she) haste thou demed/ and yet loue knytte in vertue/ passeth al the golde in this erthe. Good wyl accordant to reason/ with no maner properte may be countreuayled/ al the azure i*n* the worlde is nat to acco*m*pte in respecte of reason/ loue that with good wyl *and* reason accordeth/ with non erthly riches may nat ben ame*n*ded. This yeft hast thou yeuen I know it my selfe and thy margarite thilke gift hath receyued/ i*n* whiche thynge to rewarde she hath her

772 jeuse, juice. **776 demen**, judge. **778 mokel**, much; **azure**, lapis lazuli. **779 atones**, at once. **781 yeve**, give. **783 countrevayled**, weighed. **784 accompte**, be reckoned. **785 yeft**, gift.

selfe bounde. But thy gifte, as I said, by no maner riches may be amended; wherfore with thynge that may nat be amended thou shalt of thy Margarites rightwisenesse be rewarded. Right suffred yet never but every good dede somtyme to be yolde. Al wolde thy Margarite with no rewarde thee quyte, right, that never more dieth, thy mede in merit wol purvey. Certes, such sodayne blisse as thou first nempnest ryght wil hem rewarde as thee wel is worthy, and though at thyn eye it semeth the rewarde the desert to passe, right can after sende suche bytternesse evenly it to rewarde. So that sodayne blysse by al wayes of reason in gret goodnesse may not ben acompted, but blisse long, both long it abideth and endlesse it wol last. Se why thy wyl is endelesse, for if thou lovedest ever thy wyl is ever ther t'abyde and nevermore to chaunge: evenhed of rewarde must ben don by right. Than muste nedes thy grace and this blysse endelesse in joy to unbyde. Evenlyche disese asketh evenlyche joy whiche hastely thou shalt have." "A," quod I, "it suffyseth not than alone good wyl be it never so wel with reson medled but if it be in good servyce longe travayled. And so through servyce shul men come to the joye, and this me thynketh shulde be the wexyng tre of which ye first meved."

---

selfe bou*n*de. But thy gifte as I said/ by no maner riches may be ameded/ wherfore with thynge that may nat be ame*n*ded/ th*ou* shalt of thy margarites riȝtwisenesse be rewarded. Right suffred yet neuer but euery good dede so*m*tyme to be yolde. al wolde thy Margarite with no rewarde the quyte/ Right that neuer more dieth thy mede in merit wol puruey. Certes such sodayne blisse as thou first ne*m*pnest/ ryȝt wil he*m* rewarde as th*e* wel is worthy/ and though at thyn eye it semeth the rewarde th*e* desert to passe/ riȝt can after sende suche bytternesse eue*n*ly it to rewarde: so th*at* sodayne blysse by alwayes of reason in gret goodnesse may not ben acompted/ but blisse long/ both long it abideth/ *and* endlesse it wol last. Se why thy wyl is endelesse/ for if thou louedest euer/ thy wyl is euer ther tabyde and neuermore to chau*n*ge: euenhed of rewarde must ben don by right: than muste nedes thy grace *and* this blysse endelesse in ioy to vnbyde. Euenlyche disese asketh euenlyche ioy/ whiche hastely thou shalt haue. A (q*uo*d I) it suffyseth not than alone good wyl/ be it neuer so wel w*ith* reson medled/ but if it be in good seruyce longe trauayled. And so through seruyce shul men come to the ioye/ *and* this me thynketh shulde be the wexyng tre of which ye first meued.**<357vb>**

789 Right, Justice; **yolde**, paid back. **790 quyte**, repay; **mede**, reward. **791 nempnest**, named. **794 acompted**, accounted, reckoned. **796 evenhed**, equity. **798 unbyde**, abide. **799 medled**, mixed. **801 wexyng**, growing; **meved**, moved, discoursed.

Chapter VII

"Very trouth," quod she, "hast thou nowe conceyved of these thinges in thyne hert; hastely shalt thou be able very joye and parfyte blysse to receyve. And nowe I wot wel thou desyrest to knowe the maner of braunches that out of the tree shulde spring." "Therof lady," quod I, "hertely I you pray. For than leve I wel that right soone after I shal atast of the frute that I so long have desyred." "Thou hast herde," quod she, "in what wyse this tre, toforn this have I declared, as in grounde and in stocke of wexyng. First the grounde shulde be thy fre wyl ful in thyne hert, and the stocke (as I sayde) shulde be contynuaunce in good service by long tyme in traveyle tyl it were in greatnesse right wel woxen. And whan this tree suche gretnesse hath caught as I have rehersed, the braunches than that the frute shulde forth bringe speche must they be nedes, in voice of prayer in complayning wise used." "Out, alas," quod I tho, "he is sorofully wounded that hydeth his speche and spareth his complayntes to make. What, shal I speke the care? But payne even lyke to hel sore hath me assayled, and so ferforth in payne me thronge that I leve my tre is seer and never shal it frute forth bring. Certes, he

---

<358ra>UEry trouth (q*uo*d she) hast thou nowe co*n*ceyued of these thi*n*ges in thyne hert hastely shalt thou be able very ioye *and* parfyte blysse to receyue. *and* nowe I wot wel thou desyrest to knowe the maner of braunches/ that out of the tree shulde spring. Therof lady (q*uo*d I) hertely I you pray: for than leue I wol/ that right soone after I shal atast of the frute that I so long haue desyred. Thou hast herde (q*uo*d she) in what wyse this tre toforn this haue I declared/ as in grou*n*de *and* in stocke of wexyng. First the grou*n*de shulde be thy frewyl ful in thyne hert/ *and* the stocke (as I sayde) shulde be co*n*tynuaunce in good seruice/ by long tyme in traueyle/ tyl it were in greatnesse right wel woxen. *and* whan this tree suche gretnesse hath caught/ as I haue rehersed: the brau*n*ches than that the frute shulde forth bringe/ speche must they be nedes in voice of prayer/ in co*m*play*n*ing wise vsed. Out alas (q*uo*d I tho) he is sorofully wou*n*ded that hydeth his speche *and* spareth his co*m*playntes to make/ What shal I speke th*e* care: but payne euen lyke to hel/ sore hath me assayled/ *and* so ferforth in payne me thronge/ that I leue my tre is seer/ *and* neuer shal it frute forth bring. Certes he

803 wot, know. **805 leve**, believe. **806 atast**, taste, eat. **807 wexyng**, growing. **810 woxen**, grown. **811 nedes**, necessarily. **814 ferforth**, far. **815 thronge**, thrust; **leve**, believe; **seer**, dry.

is greatly eased that dare his prevy mone discover to a true felowe that connyng hath and might wherthrough his pleint in any thynge may ben amended. And mokel more is he joyed that with herte of hardynesse dare complayne to his lady what cares that he suffreth by hope of mercy with grace to be avaunced. Truely, I saye for me sythe I came this Margarit to serve durst I never me discover of no maner disease, and wel the later hath myn herte hardyed suche thynges to done, for the great bounties and worthy refresshmentes that she of her grace goodly without any desert on my halve ofte hath me rekened; and nere her goodnesse the more with grace and with mercy medled, whiche passen al desertes, traveyls, and servynges that I in any degre might endite, I wolde wene I shulde be without recover in gettyng of this blysse for ever. Thus have I stylled my disease; thus have I covered my care, that I bren in sorouful anoy as gledes and coles wasten a fyre under deed asshen. Wel the hoter is the fyre that with asshen it is overleyn. Right longe this wo have I suffred." "Lo," quod Love, "howe thou farest. Me thynketh the palasy yvel hath acomered thy wittes; as faste as thou hiest forwarde,

---

is greatly eased/ th*at* dare his preuy mone discouer to a true felowe/ that co*n*nyng hath *and* might/ wherthrough his pleint in any thynge may ben ame*n*ded. *and* mokel more is he ioyed that with herte of hardynesse dare co*m*playne to his lady/ what cares that he suffreth/ by hope of mercy with grace to be auau*n*ced. Truely I saye for me/ sythe I came this Margarit to serue/ durst I neuer me discouer of no maner disease/ *and* wel the later hath myn herte hardyed suche thynges to done/ for the great bounties *and* worthy refressh-mentes that she of her grace goodly without any desert on my halue ofte hath me rekened/ and nere her goodnesse the more with grace *and* with mercy medled/ whiche passen al desertes/ traueyls/ and seruynges/ that I in any degre might endite/ I wolde wene I shulde be without recouer/ in gettyng of this blysse for euer. Thus haue I styled my disease/ thus haue I couered my care/ that I bren in sorouful anoy/ as gledes *and* coles wasten a fyre vnd*er* deed asshen. Wel the hoter is the fyre/ that with asshen it is**<358ra><358rb>**ouerleyn: right longe this wo haue I suffred. Lo (q*uo*d Loue) howe thou farest: me thynketh the palasy yuel hath acomered thy wittes/ as faste as thou hiest forwarde/

816 connyng, understanding. **817 mokel**, much. **821 hardyed**, [grown in] hardiness. **823 nere**, were not; **medled**, mixed. **824 endite**, write. **825 wene**, suppose; **recover**, recourse. **826 bren**, burn; **gledes**, sparks, burning brands. **829 palasy yvel**, palsy; **acomered**, encumbered.

anon sodaynly backwarde thou movest. Shal nat yet al thy leudnesse out of thy braynes? Dul ben thy skilful understandinges thy wyl hath thy wyt so a maistred. Wost thou nat wel," quod she, "but every tree in his sesonable tyme of burjonynge shewe his blomes fro within in signe of what frute shulde out of him spring, els the frute for that yere men halte delyvered be the grounde never so good? And though the stocke be mighty at the ful and the braunches seer and no burjons shewe, farwel the gardyner: he may pype with an yve lefe, his frute is fayled. Wherfore, thy braunches must burjonen in presence of thy lady if thou desyre any frute of thy ladies grace, but beware of thy lyfe that thou no wodelay use as in askyng of thynges that stretchen into shame, for tha myght thou nat spede by no way that I can espy. Vertue wol nat suffre villany out of himselfe to spring. Thy wordes may nat be queynt ne of subtel maner understandinge. Freel-witted people supposen in suche poesies to be begyled. In open understandinge must every worde be used. 'Voice without clere understandyng of sentence,' saith Aristotel, 'right nought printeth in hert.' Thy wordes than to abide in hert and clene in ful sentence of trewe menyng platly must thou shewe and ever be obedient her hestes and her wyls to

---

anon sodaynly backwarde thou mouest: Shal nat yet al thy leudnesse out of thy braynes? dul ben thy skilful vnderst*an*ding*es*/ thy wyl hath thy wyt so a maistred. Wost thou nat wel (q*uo*d she) but euery tree in his sesonable tyme of burionynge shewe his blomes fro within/ i*n* signe of what frute shulde out of him spring/ els th*e* frute for that yere men halte delyuered/ be the grounde neuer so good. *and* though the stocke be mighty at the ful/ *and* the braunches seer *and* no burions shewe/ farwel the gardyner he may pype with an yue lefe his frute is fayled. Wherfore thy brau*n*ches must burionen i*n* prese*n*ce of thy lady/ if thou desyre any frute of thy ladies grace/ but beware of thy lyfe/ that thou no wodelay vse/ as in askyng of thynges that stretchen in to shame/ for tha myght thou nat spede by no way that I can espy. Vertue wol nat suffre villany out of him selfe to spring. Thy wordes may nat be queynt ne of subtel maner vnderstandinge. Freelwitted people supposen in suche poesies to be begyled/ in open vnderst*an*dinge must euery worde be vsed. Voice without clere vnderst*an*dyng of sente*n*ce saith Aristotel/ right nouȝt pri*n*teth i*n* hert. Thy wordes tha*n* to abide in hert/ *and* clene in ful sente*n*ce of trewe menyng platly must thou shewe *and* euer be obedient/ her hestes *and* her wyls to

830 leudnesse, ignorance. **831 a**, have; **Wost**, Know. **832 burjonynge**, burgeoning. **834 delyvered**, destroyed. **835 seer**, dry; **burjons**, buds. **836 yve lefe**, ivy-leaf. **838 wodelay**, mad law or custom; **tha**, then. **839 spede**, prosper. **840 queynt**, curious, over-wrought; **Freel-witted**, Frail-witted. **843 printeth**, make an impression. **844 hestes**, commands.

performe and be thou set in suche a wyt to wete by a loke ever more what she meaneth. And he that lyst nat to speke but stylly his disease suffre, what wonder is it tho he come never to his blysse? Who that traveyleth unwist and coveyteth thyng unknowe, unwetyng he shal be quyted and with unknowe thyng rewarded." "Good lady," quod I than, "it hath ofte be sene that wethers and stormes so hugely have fal in burjonyng tyme and by perte duresse han beaten of the springes so clene, wherthrough the frute of thilke yere hath fayled. It is a great grace whan burjons han good wethers their frutes forthe to bringe. Alas, than after suche stormes howe harde is it to avoyde, tyl efte wedring and yeres han maked her circute cours al about er any frute be able to be tasted. He is shent for shame, that foule is rebuked of his speche. He that is in fyre brennyng sore smarteth for disease. Him thynketh ful long er the water come that shulde the fyre quenche. While men gone after a leche the body is buryed. Lo, howe semely this frute wexeth; me thynketh that of tho frutes maye no man ataste for pure bytternesse in savoure. In this wyse bothe frute and the tree wasten away togider though mokel besy occupation

---

p*er*forme/ and be thou set in suche a wyt to wete by a loke euer more what she meaneth. And he that lyst nat to speke/ but stylly his disease suffre: what wo*n*der is it tho he come neuer to his blysse? Who that traueyleth vnwist/ *and* coueyteth thyng vnknowe/ vnwetyng he shal be quyted/ *and* with vnknowe thyng rewarded. Good lady (q*uo*d I than) it hath ofte be sene/ that wethers *and* stormes so hugely haue fal in burionyng tyme/ *and* by perte duresse han beaten of the springes so clene/ wherthrough th*e* frute of thilke yere hath fayled. It is a great grace whan burions han good wethers/ their frutes forthe to bringe. Alas/ than after suche stormes howe harde is it to auoyde/ tyl efte wedring *and* yeres han maked her circute cours al about er any frute be**<358rb>** **<358va>**able to be tasted he is shent for shame/ th*at* foule is rebuked of his speche. He that is in fyre bre*n*nyng sore smarteth for disease. Him thynketh ful long er the water come/ that shulde th*e* fyre quenche. While men gone after a leche/ the body is buryed. Lo howe semely this frute wexeth/ me thynketh that of tho frutes maye no man ataste/ for pure bytternesse in sauoure. In this wyse bothe frute and the tree wasten away togider/ though mokel besy occupation

845 wete, know. **846 lyst**, [is] pleased; **stylly**, quietly, silently. **847 unwist**, unknown; **unwetyng**, unknowing. **848 quyted**, repaid. **850 perte**, open; **beaten of**, beaten back; **thilke**, that same. **852 efte**, again. **853 shent**, destroyed. **855 Him thynketh**, It seems to him. **856 leche**, physician; **wexeth**, grows. **858 mokel**, much.

have be spente to bringe it so ferforthe that it was able to spring. A lyte speche hath maked that al this labour is in ydel." "I not," quod she, "wherof it serveth thy questyon to assoyle. Me thynketh thee nowe duller in wittes than whan I with thee first mette. Although a man be leude, commenly for a foole he is nat demed but if he no good wol lerne. Sottes and foles lette lyghtly out of mynde the good that men teacheth hem. I sayd therfore, thy stocke must be stronge and in greatnesse wel herted; the tree is ful feble that at the firste dent falleth. And although frute fayleth one yere or two, yet shal suche a season come one tyme or other that shal bringe out frute. That, fole, have I not sayd toforn this? As tyme hurteth, right so ayenward tyme healeth and rewardeth, and a tree oft fayled is holde more in deyntie whan it frute forthe bringeth. A marchaunt that for ones lesynge in the see no more to aventure thynketh, he shal never with aventure come to rychesse. So ofte must men on the oke smyte tyl the happy dent have entred, whiche with the okes owne swaye maketh it to come al at ones. So ofte falleth the lethy water on the harde rocke tyl it have thorowe persed it. The even draught of the wyre drawer

---

haue be spente to bringe it so ferforthe/ that it was able to spring. A lyte speche hath maked that al this labour is in ydel. I not (q*uo*d she) wherof it serueth thy questyon to assoyle/ me thynketh the nowe duller i*n* wittes/ than whan I with the first mette/ although a man be leude/ co*m*menly for a foole he is nat demed/ but if he no good wol lerne/ sottes and foles lette lyghtly out of mynde/ the good that men teacheth hem. I sayd therfore thy stocke must be stronge/ *and* in greatnesse wel herted/ the tree is ful feble that at the firste dent falleth: and although frute fayleth one yere or two/ yet shal suche a season come one tyme or other/ that shal bringe out frute that**<358va line 25><354rb line 11>**fole haue I not sayd toforn this/ as tyme hurteth/ right so ayenward tyme healeth and rewardeth: and a tree oft fayled/ is holde more in deyntie whan it frute forthe bringeth. A marchaunt that for ones lesynge in the see no more to auenture thynketh/ he shal neuer with auenture come to rychesse: so ofte must men on the oke smyte tyl the happy dent haue entred/ whiche with the okes owne swaye maketh it to come al at ones. So ofte falleth the lethy water on the harde rocke/ tyl it haue thorowe persed it. The euen draught of the wyre drawer/

859 lyte, frivolous, irresponsible. **860 not**, do not know. **861 assoyle**, answer. **862 leude**, ignorant; **demed**, judged. **863 Sottes**, Idiots; **lette**, let. **864 herted**, hearted. **865 dent**, blow, i.e., stroke of the ax. **869 ones**, once; **lesynge**, [suffering a] loss. **870 oke**, oak. **871 lethy**, inducing Lethe-like results. **872 persed**, pierced; **wyre drawer**, one who draws metal into wire.

maketh the wyre to ben even and supple werchynge, and if he stynted in his draught the wyre breaketh a sonder. Every tre wel springeth whan it is wel grounded and not often removed." "What shal this frute be," quod I, "nowe it gynneth rype?" "Grace," quod she, "in parfyte joy to endure and therwith thou begon." "Grace," quod I, "me thynketh I shulde have a rewarde for my longe travayle?" "I shal tel thee," quod she, "retrybucion of thy good wylles to have of thy Margaryte perle, it beareth not the name of mede but onely of good grace, and that cometh not of thy deserte, but of thy Margarytes goodnesse and vertue alone." Quod I, "shulde al my longe travayle have no rewarde but thorowe grace and somtyme your selven sayd rightwysnesse evenlyche rewardeth to quyte one benefyte for another." "That is sothe," quod Love, "ever as I sayde as to him that dothe good whiche to done he were neyther holden ne yet constrayned." "That is sothe," quod I. "Trewly," quod she, "al that ever thou doest to thyne Margaryte perle of wyl, of love, and of reson thou owest to done it, yet is nothyng els but yeldyng of thy dette in quitynge of thy grace whiche she thee lent whan ye first mette." "I wene," quod I, "right lytle grace to me she delyvered. Certes it was harde grace; it hath nyghe me astrangled."

---

maketh the wyre to ben euen and supple werchynge/ and if he stynted in his draught/ the wyre breaketh a sonder. Euery tre wel springeth/ whan it is wel grou*n*ded and not often remoued. What shal this frute be (q*uo*d I) nowe it gynneth rype? Grace (quod she) in parfyte ioy to endure/ and therwith thou begon. Grace (quod I) me thynketh I shulde haue a rewarde for my longe trauayle? I shal tel the (quod she) retrybucion of thy good wylles to haue of thy Margaryte perle/ it beareth not the name of mede/ but onely of good grace/ and that cometh not of thy deserte but of thy Margarytes goodnesse/ and vertue alone. (Quod I) shulde al my longe trauayle haue no rewarde but thorowe grace/ and somtyme your seluen sayd/ rightwysnesse euenlyche rewardeth to quyte one benefyte for another. That is sothe (quod Loue) euer as I sayde/ as to him that dothe good/ whiche to done he were neyther holden ne yet constrayned. That is sothe (quod I). Trewly (quod she) al that euer thou doest to thyne Margaryte perle/ of wyl/ of loue/ and of reson thou owest to done**<354rb><354va>**it/ yet is nothyng els but yeldyng of thy dette in quitynge of thy grace/ whiche she the lent whan ye first mette. I wene (quod I) right lytle grace to me she delyuered. Certes it was harde grace/ it hath nyghe me astrangled.

878 mede, reward (usually monetary). **881 evenlyche**, equally; **quyte**, repay. **885 yeldyng**, yielding. **886 wene**, suppose. **887 nyghe**, nearly.

"That it was good grace I wot wel thou wylt it graunt er thou departe hence. If any man yeve to another wight to whom that he ought not and whiche that of himselfe nothynge maye have, a garnement or a cote, though he weare the cote or els thilke clothyng it is not to put to him that was naked the cause of his clothynge, but onely to him that was yever of the garnement. Wherfore I saye thou that were naked of love and of thyselfe non have mightest, it is not to put to thyne owne persone, sythen thy love came thorowe thy Margaryte perle. *Ergo*, she was yever of the love, althoughe thou it use, and there lent she thee grace thy servyce to begynne. She is worthy the thanke of this grace, for she was the yever. Al the thoughtes, besy doynges, and plesaunce in thy might and in thy wordes that thou canste devyse ben but right lytel in quitynge of thy dette, had she not ben, suche thing hadde not ben studyed. So al these maters kyndely drawen homewarde to this Margaryte perle, for from thence were they borowed: al is holy her to wyte the love that thou havest. And thus quytest thou thy dette, in that thou stedfastly servest. And kepe wel that love, I thee rede, that of her thou hast borowed, and use it in her servyce thy dette to quite, and than arte thou able right sone to have grace, wherfore

---

That it was good grace I wot wel thou wylt it graunt er thou departe hence. If any man yeue to another wight to whom that he ought not/ and whiche that of him selfe nothynge maye haue/ a garnement or a cote/ though he weare the cote or els thilke clothyng/ it is not to put to him that was naked the cause of his clothynge/ but onely to him that was yeuer of the garnement. Wherfore I saye/ thou that were naked of loue/ and of thy selfe non haue mightest/ it is not to put to thyne owne persone/ sythen thy loue came thorowe thy Margaryte perle. Ergo she was yeuer of the loue althoughe thou it vse/ and there lent she the grace thy seruyce to begynne. She is worthy the thanke of this grace/ for she was the yeuer. Al the thoughtes/ besy doynges/ and plesaunce in thy might and in thy wordes that thou canste deuyse/ ben but right lytel in quitynge of thy dette: had she not ben/ suche thing hadde not ben studyed. So al these maters kyndely drawen homewarde to this Margaryte perle/ for from thence were they borowed/ al is holy her to wyte the loue that thou hauest: and thus quytest thou thy dette/ in that thou stedfastly seruest. And kepe wel that loue I the rede/ that of her thou hast borowed/ and vse it in her seruyce thy dette to quite/ and than arte thou able right sone to haue grace/ wherfore

888 wot, know. **889 yeve**, give. **890 garnement**, garment; **cote**, coat. **892 yever**, giver. **893 sythen**, since. **894 *Ergo***, Therefore. **897 quitynge**, repayment. **899 wyte**, assign responsibility for. **901 rede**, counsel.

after mede in none halve maist thou loke. Thus thy gynnyng and endyng is but grace alone and in thy good deservynge thy dette thou aquitest. Without grace is nothyng worthe, what so ever thou werche. Thanke thy Margaryte of her great grace that hytherto thee hath gyded, and praye her of contynuaunce forthe in thy werkes herafter and that for no mishappe thy grace overthwartly tourne. Grace glorie and joye is comyng thorowe good folkes desertes, and by gettyng of grace therin shullen ende. And what is more glorie or more joye than wysdome and love in parfyte charité whiche God hath graunted to al tho that wel canne deserve." And with that this lady al at ones sterte in to myn hert: "here wol I onbyde," quod she, "for ever and never wol I gon hence and I wol kepe thee from medlynge while me lyste here onbyde: thyne entermetyng maners in to stedfastnesse shullen be chaunged."

Chapter VIII

Soberlyche tho threwe I up myn eyen and hugely tho was I astonyed of this sodayne adventure and fayne wolde I have lerned howe vertues shulden ben knowen, in whiche

---

after mede in none halue maist thou loke. Thus thy gynnyng and endyng is but grace alone/ and in thy good deseruynge thy dette thou aquitest: without grace is nothyng worthe what so euer thou werche. Thanke thy Margaryte of her great grace that hytherto the hath gyded/ and prayc her of contynuaunce forthe in thy werkes herafter/ and that for no mishappe thy grace ouerthwartly tourne. Grace/ glorie/ and ioye/ is comyng thorowe good folkes desertes/ and by gettyng of grace therin shullen ende. And what is more glorie or more ioye than wysdome and loue in parfyte charite/ whiche god hath grau*n***<354va><354vb>**ted to al tho that wel canne deserue. And with that this lady al at ones sterte in to myn hert: here wol I onbyde (quod she) for euer/ and neuer wol I gon hence/ and I wol kepe the from medlynge while me lyste here onbyde: thyne entermetyng maners in to stedfastnesse shullen be chaunged.

SOberlyche tho threwe I vp myn eyen/ and hugely tho was I astonyed of this sodayne aduenture/ and fayne wolde I haue lerned howe vertues shulden ben knowen/ in whiche

903 mede, reward; **in none halve**, nowhere. **905 werche**, work. **906 gyded**, guided. **907 overthwartly**, adversely. **910 tho**, those. **911 sterte**, moved; **onbyde**, abide. **912 me lyste**, it pleases me; **entermetyng**, variable, hence meddling. **914 tho**, then; **astonyed**, astonished.

thynges I hope to God hereafter she shal me enfourmen and namely sythen her restynge place is nowe so nyghe at my wyl. And anon al these thynges that this lady said I remembred me by myselfe and revolved the lyves of myne understondynge wyttes. Tho founde I fully al these maters parfytely there written: howe mysse rule by fayned love bothe realmes and cyties hath governed a great throwe; howe lightly me might the fautes espye; howe rules in love shulde ben used; howe somtyme with fayned love foule I was begyled; howe I shulde love have knowe; and howe I shal in love with my servyce procede. Also furthermore I founde of perdurable letters wonderly there graven these maters whiche I shal nempne. Certes, none age ne other thynge in erthe maye the leest syllable of this in no poynte deface, but clerely as the sonne in myne understandynge soule they shynen. This maye never out of my mynde howe I maye not my love kepe, but thorowe wyllynge in herte: Wylne to love maye I not, but I lovynge have. Love have I none but thorowe grace of this Margarite perle. It is no maner doute that wyl wol not love but for it is lovynge, as wyl wol not rightfully but for it is rightful itselve. Also, wyl is not lovynge, for he wol love, but he wol love for he is lovynge. It is al one to wyl to

---

thynges I hope to god here after she shal me enfourmen/ and namely sythen her restynge place is nowe so nyghe at my wyl: and anon al these thynges that this lady said/ I remembred me by my selfe/ and reuolued the lyues of myne vnderstondynge wyttes. Tho founde I fully al these maters parfytely there written/ howe mysse rule by fayned loue bothe realmes and cyties hath gouerned a great throwe. Howe lightly me might the fautes espye/ howe rules in loue shulde ben vsed/ howe somtyme with fayned loue foule I was begyled/ howe I shulde loue haue knowe/ and howe I shal in loue with my seruyce procede. Also furthermore I founde of perdurable letters wo*n*derly there grauen/ these maters whiche I shal nempne. Certes none age ne other thynge in erthe maye the leest syllable of this in no poynte deface/ but clerely as the sonne in myne vnderstandynge soule they shynen. This maye neuer out of my mynde/ howe I maye not my loue kepe/ but thorowe wyllynge in herte: Wylne to loue maye I not/ but I louynge haue. Loue haue I none but thorowe grace of this Margarite perle. It is no maner doute/ that wyl wol not loue but for it is louynge /as wyl wol not rightfully/ but for it is rightful it selue. Also wyl is not louynge for he wol loue/ but he wol loue for he is louynge: it is al one to wyl to

916 sythen, since. **920 throwe**, while; **me might**, one might. **924 nempne**, name. **929 but for**, except because; **wol**, desires.

be lovynge, and lovynges in possessyon to have. Right so wyl wol not love, for of love hath he no partie, and yet I denye not lovynge wyl wylne more love to have whiche that he hath, not whan he wolde more than he hath, but I saye he maye no love wylne if he no love have, through which thilke love he shuld wylne. But to have this lovyng wyl may no man of himselfe, but onely through grace toforne-goyng. Right so maye no man it kepe but by grace-folowynge. Consyder nowe every man aright, and let sene if that any wight of himselfe mowe this lovyng wel get, and he therof first nothynge have, for if it shulde of himselfe spring eyther it muste be wyllyng or not wyllyng. Wyllyng by himselfe may he it not have, sythen him fayleth the mater that shulde it forthe bring. The mater him fayleth. Why? He maye therof have no knowyng tyl whan grace put it in his herte. Thus willyng by himselfe may he it not have, and not wyllyng may he it not have. Pardé, every conseyt of every reasonable creature otherwyse wyl not graunt: Wyl in affyrmatife with not wyllyng by no way mowe acorde. And although this lovyng wol come in myn hert by frenesse of arbytrement, as in this booke fully is shewed, yet owe I not therfore as moche alowe my fre wyl as grace of that Margaryte to me leaned. For

---

be louynge/ and louynges in possessyon to haue. Right so wyl wol not loue/ for of loue hath he no partie/ *and* yet I denye not louynge wyl wylne more loue to haue/ whiche that he hath not whan he wolde more than he hath/ **<354vb><355ra>**but I saye he maye no loue wylne/ if he no loue haue/ through which thilke loue he shuld wylne: but to haue this louyng wyl may no man of him selfe/ but onely through grace toforne goyng: Right so maye no man it kepe/ but by grace folowynge. Consyder nowe euery man aright/ and let sene if th*at* any wight of him selfe mowe this louyng wel get/ and he therof first nothyge haue: for if it shulde of him selfe spring/ eyther it muste be wyllyng or not wyllyng. Wyllyng by him selfe may he it not haue/ sythen him fayleth the mater that shulde it forthe bring/ the mater him fayleth: Why? he maye therof haue no knowyng/ tyl whan grace put it in his herte. Thus willyng by him selfe may he it not haue/ and not wyllyng may he it not haue. Parde euery conseyt of euery reasonable creature otherwyse wyl not graunt: Wyl in affyrmatife with not wyllyng by no way mowe acorde. And although this louyng wol come in myn hert by frenesse of arbytrement/ as in this booke fully is shewed/ yet owe I not therfore as moche alowe my frewyl/ as grace of that Margaryte to me leaned/ for

931 for, if. **937 mowe**, may. **939 sythen**, since. **942 conseyt**, conception. **943 mowe**, may. **945 alowe**, applaud; **leaned**, loaned.

neyther might I without grace toforn-goyng and afterwarde-folowyng thilke grace get ne kepe, and lese shal I it never but if fre wyl it make as in wyllynge otherwyse than grace hath me graunted. For right as whan any person taketh wyllyng to be sobre and throweth that away, willyng to be dronke or els taketh wyl of drinkyng out of mesure, whiche thyng anon as it is done maketh thorowe his owne gylte by fre wyl that leseth his grace. In whiche thing, therfore, upon the nobley of grace I mote trusten, and my besy cure set thilke grace to kepe that my fre wyl otherwyse than by reason it shulde werche cause not my grace to voyde. For thus must I bothe loke to fre wyl and to grace. For right as naturel usage in engendring of children maye not ben without father ne also but with the mother, for neyther father ne mother in begettyng maye it lacke, right so grace and fre wyl accorden, and without hem bothe maye not lovynge wyl in no partie ben getten. But yet is not fre wyl in gettynge of that thyng so mokel thankeworthy as is grace, ne in the kepynge therof so moche thanke deserveth, and yet in gettynge and kepyng bothe done they accorde. Trewly, oftentyme grace fre wyl helpeth in fordoynge of contrarye thinges that to wyllynge love not accorden and strength wyl

---

neyther might I without grace to forn goyng/ and afterwarde folowyng/ thilke grace get ne kepe/ and lese shal I it neuer but if frewyl it make/ as in wyllynge otherwyse than grace hath me graunted. For right as whan any person taketh wyllyng to be sobre/ and throweth th*at* away/ willyng to be dronke/ or els taketh wyl of drinkyng out of mesure: whiche thyng anon as it is done/ maketh thorowe his owne gylte by frewyl that leseth his grace. In whiche thing therfore vpon the nobley of grace I mote trusten/ *and* my besy cure set thilke grace to kepe/ that my frewyl otherwyse than by reason it shulde werche/ cause not my grace to voyde: for thus must I bothe loke to frewyl and to grace. For right as naturel vsage in engendring of children maye not ben without father/ ne also but with the mother/ for neyther father ne mother in begettyng maye it lacke: right so grace and frewyl accorden/ and without hem bothe maye not louynge wyl in no partie ben getten. But yet is not frewyl in gettynge of that thyng so mokel tha*n*ke worthy as is grace/ ne in the ke**<355ra><355rb>**pynge therof/ so moche thanke deserueth/ and yet in gettynge and kepyng bothe done they accorde. Trew y often tyme gra e frewyl helpeth in fordoynge of contrarye thinges/ that to wyllynge loue not accorden/ and strength wyl

947 lese, lose; **it make**, cause it [to be so]. **953 werche**, work. **957 mokel**, much. **960 fordoynge**, destruction.

adversytees to withsytte, wherfore al togyther to grace oweth to ben accepted that my wulyng deserveth. Fre wyl to lovyng in this wyse is accorded. I remembre me wel howe al this booke (whoso hede taketh) consydereth al thynges to werchynges of mankynde evenly accordeth, as in turnyng of this worde 'love' into 'trouthe' or els 'rightwysnesse,' whether that it lyke. For what thyng that falleth to man in helpyng of free arbytrement, thilke rightwysnesse to take or els to kepe thorowe whiche a man shal be saved, of whiche thyng al this booke mencion hath maked in every poynte — therof grace oweth to be thanked. Wherfore, I saye every wight havynge this rightwysnesse rightful is, and yet therfore I fele not in my conscience that to al rightful is behoten the blysse everlastynge, but to hem that ben rightful withouten any unrightfulnesse. Some man after some degree maye rightfully ben accompted as chaste men in lyvyng, and yet ben they janglers and ful of envy pressed. To hem shal this blysse never ben delyvered. For right as very blisse is without al maner nede, right so to no man shal it be yeven but to the rightful, voyde from al maner unrightfulnesse founde, so no man to her blysse shal ben folowed but he be rightful and with unrightfulnesse

---

aduersytees to withsytte/ wherfore al togyther to grace oweth to ben accepted/ that my wulyng deserueth: Frewyl to louyng in this wyse is accorded. I remembre me wel howe al this booke (who so hede taketh) consydereth al thynges to werchynges of mankynde euenly accordeth/ as in turnyng of this worde loue in to trouthe/ or els rightwysnesse/ whether that it lyke. For what thyng that falleth to man in helpyng of free arbytrement/ thilke rightwysnesse to take or els to kepe/ thorowe whiche a man shal be saued/ of whiche thyng al this booke mencion hath maked/ in euery poynte therof grace oweth to be thanked. Wherfore I saye/ euery wight hauyuge this rightwysnesse rightful is/ and yet therfore I fele not in my conscience/ that to al rightful is behoten the blysse euerlastynge/ but to hem that ben rightful withouten any vnrightfulnesse. Some man after some degree maye rightfully ben accompted: as chaste men in lyuyng/ and yet ben they ianglers and ful of enuy pressed: to hem shal this blysse neuer ben delyuered. For right as very blisse is with out al maner nede/ riȝt so to no man shal it be yeuen but to the rightful/ voyde from al maner vnrightfulnesse founde/ so no man to her blysse shal ben folowed/ but he be rightful/ and with vnrightfulnesse

961 withsytte, resist. **963 werchynges**, workings. **966 thilke**, that same. **970 behoten**, promised. **971 accompted**, accounted. **974 yeven**, given.

not bounde and in that degree fully be knowe. This rightfulnesse, in as moche as in himselfe is, of none yvel is it cause, and of al maner goodnesse trewly it is mother. This helpeth the spyrit to withsytte the leude lustes of flesshly lykinge. This strengtheth and maintayneth the lawe of kynde, and if that otherwhyle me weneth harme of this precious thyng to folowe, therthorough is nothynge the cause — of somwhat els cometh it aboute who so taketh hede. By rightfulnesse, forsothe, werne many holy sayntes good savour in swetenesse to God almighty, but that to some folkes they weren savour of dethe into deedly ende. That come not of the sayntes rightwysnesse, but of other wycked mennes badnesse hath proceded. Trewly, the ilke wyl whiche that the Lady of Love me lerned 'affectyon of wyl' to nempne, whiche is in wyllyng of profytable thynges, yvel is it not but whan to flesshly lustes it consenteth ayenst reason of soule. But that this thynge more clerely be understand it is for to knowe whence and howe thylke wyl is so vycious and so redye yvel dedes to perfourme. Grace at the gynnynge ordeyned thilke wyl in goodnesse ever to have endured and never to badnesse have assented. Men shulde not byleve that God thilke wyl maked to be vycious. Our firste father as Adam

---

not bounde/ and in that degree fully be knowe. This rightfulnesse in as moche as in him selfe is/ of none yuel is it cause/ and of al maner goodnesse trewly it is mother. This helpeth the spyrit to withsytte the leude lustes of flesshly lykinge: This strengtheth and maintayneth the lawe of kynde/ and if that otherwhyle me weneth harme of this precious thyng to folowe/ therthorough is nothynge the cause/ of somwhat els cometh it aboute who so taketh hede. By rightfulnesse forsothe werne many holy sayntes good sauour i*n* swetenesse to god almighty but that to some folkes they weren sauour of dethe in to deedly ende/ that come not of the**<355rb><355va>**sayntes rightwysnesse/ but of other wycked mennes badnesse hath proceded. Trewly the ilke wyl/ whiche that the lady of loue me lerned/ affectyon of wyl to nempne/ whiche is in wyllyng of profytable thynges/ yuel is it not/ but whan to flesshly lustes it co*n*senteth/ ayenst reason of soule: But that this thynge more clerely be vndersta*n*d/ it is for to knowe/ whe*n*ce and howe thylke wyl is so vycious and so redye/ yuel dedes to perfourme. Grace at the gynnynge/ ordeyned thilke wyl in goodnesse euer to haue endured/ and neuer to badnesse haue assented: Men shulde not byleue/ that god thilke wyl maked to be vycious. Our firste father as Adam

978 withsytte, resist. **979 otherwhyle**, at other times; **me weneth**, I suppose. **981 werne**, were. **985 lerned**, taught; **nempne**, name. **990 byleve**, believe.

and Eve, for vycious appetytes and vycious wyl to suche appetytes consentynge, ben not on thynge in kynde; other thyng is done for the other. And howe this wyl fyrst into man first assented, I holde it profytable to shewe. But if the first condycion of reasonable creature wol be consydred and apertly loked, lightly the cause of suche wyl may be shewed. Intencion of God was that rightfully and blyssed shulde reasonable nature ben maked himselfe for to kepe, but neyther blysful ne rightful might it not be withouten wyl in them bothe. Wyl of rightfulnesse is thilke same rightfulnesse as here to forne is shewed. But wyl of blysse is not thilke blysse, for every man hath not thilke blysse in whom the wyl therof is abydynge. In this blysse after every understandynge is suffysaunce of covenable comodytees without any maner nede, whether it be blysse of aungels or els thilke that grace first in paradise suffred Adam to have. For al though angels blysse be more than Adams was in paradyse, yet maye it not be denyded that Adam in paradyse ne had suffysaunce of blysse. For ryght as great herte is without al maner of coldenesse and yet maye another herte more heate have, right so nothynge defended Adam in paradyse to ben blessed without al maner nede. Althoughe aungels

---

and Eue/ for vycious appetytes and vycious wyl to suche appetytes consentynge/ ben not on thynge in kynde/ other thyng is done for the other. And howe this wyl fyrst in to man first assented I holde it profytable to shewe: but if the first condycion of reasonable creature wol be consydred and apertly loked/ lightly the cause of suche wyl may be shewed. Intencion of god was that rightfully and blyssed shulde reasonable nature ben maked/ him selfe for to kepe/ but neyther blysful ne rightful might it not be/ withouten wyl in them bothe. Wyl of rightfulnesse is thilke same rightfulnesse/ as here to forne is shewed: but wyl of blysse is not thilke blysse/ for euery man hath not thilke blysse/ in whom the wyl therof is abydynge. In this blysse after euery vnderstandynge is suffysaunce of couenable comodytees without any maner nede/ whether it be blysse of aungels or els thilke/ that grace first in paradise suffred Adam to haue. For al though angels blysse be more than Adams was in paradyse/ yet maye it not be denyded/ that Adam in paradyse ne had suffysaunce of blysse: for ryght as great herte is without al maner of coldenesse/ and yet maye another herte more heate haue/ right so nothynge defended Adam in paradyse to ben blessed/ without al maner nede. Al thoughe aungels

992 on, one. **994 apertly**, openly. **1005 defended**, prevented; **without al maner nede**, without any kind of necessity.

blysse be moche more, forsothe it foloweth not lasse than another to have, therfore hym nedeth, but for to wante a thynge whiche that behoveth to ben had, that maye nede ben cleped and that was not in Adam at the first gynnyng. God and the Margaryte weten what I meane. Forsothe, where as is nede, there is wretchydnesse. God without cause toforngoyng made not reasonable creature wretched, for hym to understande and love had He firste maked. God made therfore man blyssed without al maner indygence. Togyther and at ones toke reasonable creature blysse, and wyl of blyssednesse, and wyl of rightfulnesse, whiche is rightfulnesse itselve, and lybertie of arbytrement, that is fre wyl with whiche thilke rightfulnesse may he kepe and lese. So and in that wyse God ordayned thylke two that wyl, whiche that instrument is cleaped, as here toforne mencion is maked, shulde use thilke rightfulnesse by teachyng of his soule to good maner of governaunce in thought and in wordes, and that it shulde use the blysse in obedyent maner, withouten any incommodyté. Blysse, forsothe, into mannes profyte and rightwysnesse into his worshyp God delyvered at ones. But rightfulnesse so was yeven

---

blysse be moche more/ forsothe it foloweth not lasse than another to haue therfore hym nedeth/ but for to wante a thynge whiche that behoueth to ben had/ that maye nede ben cleped/ and that**<355va><355vb>**was not in Adam at the first gynnyng. God and the Margaryte weten what I meane. Forsothe where as is nede/ there is wretchydnesse/ good without cause to forngoyng made not reasonable creature wretched/ for hym to vnderstande and loue had he firste maked. God made therfore man blyssed without al maner indygence/ togyther and at ones toke reasonable creature blysse/ and wyl of blyssednesse/ and wyl of rightfulnesse/ whiche is rightfulnesse it selue/ and lybertie of arbytrement/ that is fre wyl/ with whiche thilke rightfulnesse may he kepe and lese. So and in that wyse ordayned thylke two/ that wyl whiche that instrument is cleaped/ as here toforne mencion is maked/ shulde vse thilke rightfulnesse/ by teachyng of his soule to good maner of gouernaunce/ in thought and in wordes/ and that it shulde vse the blysse in obedyent maner/ withouten any inco*mm*odyte. Blysse forsothe in to mannes profyte/ and rightwysnesse in to his worshyp god delyuered at ones: but rightfulnesse so was yeuen

1007 hym nedeth, something is lacking in him. **1008 cleped**, called; **weten**, know. **1010 toforngoyng**, beforehand. **1014 lese**, lose. **1018 incommodyté**, inconvenience. **1019 yeven**, given.

that man might it lese, whiche if he not loste had not, but contynuelly have it kepte, he shulde have deserved the avauncement into the felowshyppe of angels; in whiche thyng, if he that loste, never by himselfe forwarde shulde he it mowe ayenwarde recover, and as wel the blysse that he was in, as aungels blysse that to himwardes was comyng, shulde be nome at ones, and he deprived of hem bothe. And thus fyl man unto lykenesse of unreasonable bestes, and with hem to corrupcion and unlusty apetytes was he under throwen. But yet wyl of blysse dwelleth, that by indygence of goodes whiche that he loste through great wretchydnesse by right shulde he ben punisshed. And thus for he weyved rightfulnesse, loste hath he his blysse, but fayle of his desyre in his owne comodyté may he not; and where comodytes to his reasonable nature whiche he hath loste may he not have, to false lustes whiche ben bestyal appetytes he is turned. Folye of unconnyng hath him begyled in wenyng that thilke ben the comoditees that owen to ben desyred. This affection of wyl by lyberté of arbitrement is enduced to wylne thus thing that he shulde not, and so is wyl not maked yvel but unrightful by absence of rightfulnesse, whiche thing by reason ever shulde he have. And frenesse of arbytrement

---

th*at* man might it lese/ whiche if he not loste had not/ but contynuelly haue it kepte/ he shulde haue deserued the auauncement in to the felowshyppe of angels/ in whiche thyng if he that loste/ neuer by him selfe forwarde shulde he it mowe ayenwarde recouer: and as wel the blysse that he was in/ as aungels blysse that to him wardes was comyng/ shulde be nome at ones/ and he depriued of hem bothe. And thus fyl man vn to lykenesse of vnreasonable bestes/ and with hem to corrupcion and vnlusty apetytes was he vnder throwen/ but yet wyl of blysse dwelleth/ that by indygence of goodes whiche that he loste through great wretchydnesse/ by right shulde he ben punisshed. And thus for he weyued rightfulnesse/ loste hath he his blysse: but fayle of his desyre in his owne comodyte may he not/ and were comodytes to his reasonable nature whiche he hath loste may he not haue. To false lustes/ whiche ben bestyal appetytes he is turned: folye of vnconnyng hath him be gyled/ in wenyng th*at* thilke ben the comoditees that owen to ben desyred. This affection of wyl by lyberte of arbitrement is enduced to wylne thus thing that he shulde not/ and so is**<355vb><356ra>**wyl not maked yuel but vnrightful/ by abse*n*ce of rightfulnesse/ whiche thing by reason euer shulde he haue. And frenesse of arbytrement

1020 lese, lose. **1022 mowe**, might. **1024 nome**, taken. **1025 unlusty**, undesirable. **1031 unconnyng**, ignorance; **wenyng**, assuming. **1034 frenesse of arbytrement**, freedom of choice.

may he not wylne whan he it not haveth, for whyle he it had thilke halpe it not to kepe, so that without grace may it not ben recovered. Wyl of commodyté, inasmoche as unrightful it is maked by wyllynge of yvel lustes, wyllyng of goodnesse may he not wylne: for wyl of instrument to affection of wyl is thralled, sythen that other thyng may it not wylne. For wyl of instrument to affection desyreth, and yet ben bothe they wyl cleped. For that instrument wol, through affection it wylneth, and affection desyreth thilke thyng wherto instrument him ledeth. And so fre wyl to unlusty affection ful servaunt is maked, for unrightfulnesse maye he not releve; and without rightfulnesse ful fredome may it never have. For kyndly lybertie of arbytrement without it veyne and ydel is, forsothe. Wherfore, yet I say as often have I sayd the same whan instrument of wyl loste hath rightfulnesse, in no maner but by grace may he ayen retourne rightfulnesse to wylne. For sythen nothyng but rightfulnesse alone shulde he wylne, what that ever he wylneth with out rightfulnesse unrightfully he it wylneth. These than unrightful appetytes and unthrifty lustes which the flesh desyreth in as mokel as they ben in kynde, ben they nat bad; but they ben unrightful and badde, for they ben in resonable

---

may he not wylne/ whan he it not haueth/ for whyle he it had/ thilke halpe it not to kepe: so that without grace may it not ben recouered. Wyl of co*m*modyte/ in as moche as vnrightful it is maked/ by wyllynge of yuel lustes/ wyllyng of goodnesse may he not wylne: for wyl of instrument to affection of wyl is thralled/ sythen that other thyng may it not wylne/ for wyl of instrument to affection desyreth/ *and* yet ben bothe they wyl cleped: for that instrument wol/ through affection it wylneth/ *and* affection desyreth thilke thyng wherto instrument him ledeth. And so frewyl to vnlusty affection ful seruaunt is maked/ for vnrightfulnesse maye he not releue/ *and* without rightfulnesse ful fredome may it neuer haue. For kyndly lybertie of arbytrement without it/ veyne and ydel is forsothe. Wherfore yet I say/ as often haue I sayd the same/ whan instrument of wyl loste hath rightfulnesse/ in no maner but by grace may he ayen retourne rightfulnesse to wylne. For sythen nothyng but rightfulnesse alone shulde he wylne/ what th*at* euer he wylneth with out rightfulnesse/ vnrightfully he it wylneth. These than vnrightful appetytes *and* vnthrifty lustes which the flyes desyreth/ in as mokel as they ben in kynde/ ben they nat bad/ but they ben vnrightful and badde/ for they ben in resonable

1035 halpe, helped. **1037 he**, i.e., will of commodity. **1038 thralled**, enslaved; **sythen**, since. **1040 cleped**, called. **1043 veyne**, vain. **1046 sythen**, since. **1048–49 in kynde**, natural.

creature, where as their beyng in no waye shulde ben suffred. In unreasonable beestes neyther ben they yvel ne unrightful for there is their kynde beyng.

Chapter IX

Knowen may it wel ben nowe of these thynges toforne declared that man hath not alway thilke rightfulnesse which by duté of right evermore haven he shulde, and by no way by himselfe may he it get ne kepe. And after he it hath, if he it lese, recover shal he it never without especial grace. Wherfore the comune sentence of the people in opinyon that every thynge after destenye is ruled false and wicked is to byleve. For thoughe predestynacion be as wel of good as of badde, sythen that it is sayde God badnesse made, whiche He never ne wrought, but for He suffreth hem to be maked as that He hardeth whan he naught missaythe, or ledde into temptacion whan He not delyvereth. Wherfore, it is none inconvenyent if in that maner be sayd God toforne have destenyed bothe badde and her badde werkes whan hem ne their yvel dedes neyther amendeth ne therto hem grace leneth. But specyallyche predestynacion of goodnesse alone is sayde

---

creature/ where as they beyng in no waye shulde ben suffred. In vnreasonable beestes neyther ben they yuel ne vnrightful/ for there is their kynde beyng.

KNowen may it wel ben nowe/ of these thynges toforne declared/ th*at* man hath not alway thilkc rightfulnesse/ which by dute of right euermore hauen he shulde/ and by no way by him selfe may he it get ne kepe/ *and* after he it hath if he it lese/ recouer shal he it neuer/ without especial grace: Wherfore the comune sentence of the people in opinyon/ that euery thynge after destenye is ruled/ false and wicked is to byleue: For thoughe predestynacion be as wel of good as of badde/ sythen that it is sayde god hadnest made/ whiche he neuer**<356ra><356rb>**ne wrought/ but for he suffreth hem to be maked/ as that he hardeth whan he naught missaythe/ or ledde in to temptacion whan he not delyuereth/ wherfore it is none inconuenyent if in that maner be sayd/ god toforne haue destenyed bothe badde/ and her badde werkes/ whan hem ne their yuel dedes neyther amendeth/ ne therto hem grace leueth. But specyallyche predestynacion of goodnesse alone/ is sayde

1054 lese, lose. **1057 sythen**, since. **1059 hardeth**, to make something difficult to interpret. **1061 amendeth**, i.e., He, God, amends. **1062 leneth**, loans.

by these great clerkes, for in Him God dothe that they ben, and that in goodnesse they werchen. But the negatyfe herof in badnesse is holden as the Lady of Love hath me lerned, whoso aright in this booke loketh. And utterly it is to weten that predestynacion properly in God may not ben demed no more than beforne-wetyng. For in the chapitre of Goddes beforne-wetyng as Love me rehersed al these maters apertely maye ben founden. Al thynges to God ben nowe togyther and in presence durynge. Trewly, presence and predestynacion in nothynge disacorden, wherfore as I was lerned howe Goddes before-wetyng and free choyce of wyl mowe stonden togyther, me thynketh the same reason me leadeth that destenye and fre wyl accorden so that neyther of hem bothe to other in nothing contraryeth. And reasonablyche may it not ben demyd as often as any thyng falleth, fre wyl werchyng, as if a man another man wrongfully anoyeth, wherfore he him sleeth, that it be constrayned to that ende as mokel folke cryeth and sayth: 'Lo, as it was destenyed of God toforne-know, so it is thorowe necessyté fal, and other wyse might it not betyde.' Trewly, neyther he that the wronge wrought ne he

---

by these great clerkes/ for in him god dothe that they ben/ and that in goodnesse they werchen. But the negatyfe herof in badnesse is holden/ as the lady of loue hath me lerned/ who so aright in this booke loketh. And vtterly it is to weten/ that predestynacion properly i*n* god may not ben demed/ no more than beforne wetyng. For in the chapitre of goddes beforne wetyng/ as Loue me rehersed/ al these maters apertely maye ben founden. Al thynges to god ben nowe togyther and in presence durynge. Trewly presence and predestynacion in nothynge disacorden/ wherfore as I was lerned howe goddes beforewetyng and free choyce of wyl mowe stonden togyther/ me thynketh the same reason me leadeth/ that destenye and frewyl accorden/ so that neyther of hem bothe to other in nothing contraryeth. And reasonablyche may it not ben demyd/ as often as any thyng falleth frewyl werchyng/ as if a man another man wrongfully anoyeth/ wherfore he him sleeth/ that it be constrayned to that ende/ as mokel folke cryeth and sayth: Lo/ as it was destenyed of god toforne know/ so it is thorowe necessyte fal/ and other wyse might it not betyde. Trewly neyther he that the wronge wrought/ ne he

1063 in Him, i.e., in goodness; **dothe that they ben**, causes them to be good. **1064 werchen**, work. **1065 lerned**, taught; **loketh**, looks; **weten**, know. **1066 demed**, judged; **beforne-wetyng**, foreknowledge. **1067 apertely**, openly. **1068 in presence durynge**, in the enduring present. **1070 mowe**, may. **1073 werchyng**, working. **1074 sleeth**, slays; **mokel**, many.

that himselfe venged, none of thilke thinges thorowe necessyté wrought. For if that with fre wyl there had it not wylled, neyther had wrought that he perfourmed. And so utterly grace that fre wyl in goodnesse bringeth and kepeth and fro badnesse it tourneth, in al thynge moste thanke deserveth. This grace maketh seyntes in vertue to abyde, wherfore in body and in soule in ful plentie of connynge after their good deservyng in the everlastynge joy, after the day of dome shul they endelesse dwel, and they shul ben lerned in that kyngdome with so mokel affecte of love and of grace that the leste joye shal of the greatest in glorie rejoyce and ben gladded as if he the same joye had. What wonder syth God is the greatest love and the grettest wisdom in hem shal he be, and they in God. Nowe than whan al false folke be ashamed which wenen al bestyalté and erthly thing be swetter and better to the body than hevenly is to the soule, this is the grace and the frute that I long have desyred: it dothe me good the savour to smel. Christ now to Thee I crye of mercy and of grace and graunt of Thy goodnes to every maner reder ful understandyng in this leude pamflet to have, and let no man wene other cause in this werke than is verily the soth. For envy is ever redy al innocentes to shende;

---

that him selfe venged/ none of thilke thinges thorowe necessyte wrought: for if that with frewyl there had it not wylled/ neyther had wrought that he perfourmed: and so vtterly grace that frewyl in goodnesse bringeth and kepeth/ and fro badnesse it tourneth/ in al thynge moste thanke deserueth. This grace maketh sente*n*ce in vertue to abyde/ wherfore in body and in soule in ful plentie of connynge after their good deseruyng in the euerlastynge ioy/ after the day of dome shul they endelesse dwel/ and they shul ben lerned in that kyngdome with**<356rb><356va>**so mokel affecte of loue and of grace/ that the leste ioye shal of the greatest in glorie reioyce and ben gladded/ as if he the same ioye had. What wonder syth god is th*e* greatest loue/ and the**<356va line 5><360vb line 9>**grettest wisdom in hem shal he be/ *and* they in god. Nowe than whan al false folke be ashamed/ which wenen al bestyalte *and* erthly thi*n*g be swetter *and* better to th*e* body/ than heue*n*ly is to th*e* soule: this is the grace *and* the frute that I long haue desyred/ it dothe me good th*e* sauour to smel. Christ now to th*e* I crye of mercy *and* of grace/ *and* grau*n*t of thy goodnes to euery maner reder ful vndersta*n*dyng in this leude pamflet to haue/ *and* let no man wene other cause in this werke/ than is verily th*e* soth: For enuy is euer redy al innoce*n*tes to shende/

1077 that, that one, the former. **1080 moste**, most. **1083 mokel,** great. **1086 wenen,** assume. **1087 swetter,** sweeter. **1090 reder**, reader; **leude**, ignorant; **wene**, suppose. **1091 werke**, work; **shende**, destroy.

wherfore, I wolde that good speche envy evermore hynder. But no man wene this werke be sufficiently maked, for Goddes werke passeth mans. No mans wyt to perfyt werke may by no way purvay th'ende. How shuld I than so leude aught wene of perfection any ende to get? Neverthelater, grace, glorie, and laude I yelde and put with worshipful reverences to the sothfast God in thre, with unité closed whiche that the hevy langour of my sicknesse hath turned into myrth of helth to recover. For right as I was sorowed thorow the gloton cloud of manyfolde sickly sorow, so mirth of ayen-comyng helth hath me gladed and gretly comforted. I beseche and pray, therfore, and I crye on Goddes gret pyté and on his mokel mercy that this present scorges of my flessh mow make medecyn and lechcraft of my inner mans helth, so that my passed trespas and tenes through wepyng of myn eyen ben wasshe, and I voyded from al maner disese, and no more to wepe. Herafter I now be kept thorowe Goddes grace, so that Goddes hande, which that merciably me hath scorged, herafter in good plite from thence merciably me kepe and defende. In this boke be many privy thinges wimpled and folde. Unneth shul leude men the plites unwinde, wherfore I pray to the Holygost He

---

wherfore I wolde that good speche enuy euermore hynder. But no man wene this werke be sufficie*n*tly maked/ for godd*es* werke passeth mans/ no mans wyt to p*er*fyt werke may by no way puruay thende: How shuld I than so leude/ aught wene of p*er*fection any ende to get? Neuer the later grace/ glorie/ *and* laude I yelde *and* put wi*th* worshipful reuere*n*ces to th*e* sothfast god i*n* thre/ with vnite closed whiche th*at* the heuy la*n*gour of my sicknesse hath turned in to myrth of helth to recouer: for riȝt as I was sorowed thorow th*e* gloton cloud of manyfolde sickly sorow/ so mirth ayen comyng helth hath me gladed *and* gretly co*m*forted. I beseche *and* pray therfore/ *and* I crye on goddes gret pyte *and* on his mokel mercy/ th*at* this present scorg*es* of my flessh mow make medecyn *and* lechcraft of my inner mans helth/ so th*at* my passed trespas *and* tenes/ through wepyng of myn eyen ben wasshe/ *and* I voyded from al maner disese/ *and* no more to wepe herafter/ I now be kept thorowe goddes grace: so th*at* goddes ha*n*de which th*at* merciably me hath scorged/ herafter in good plite fro*m* the*n*ce merciably me kepe *and* defe*n*de. In this boke be many priuy thi*nges* wi*m*pled *and* folde/ vnneth shul leude men th*e* plites vnwi*n*de/ wherfore I pray to th*e* holygost he

1095 yelde, yield. **1098 gloton**, villainous. **1100 mokel**, great. **1101 mow**, may. **1102 tenes**, pains, vexations. **1104 plite**, plight, condition. **1105 wimpled**, veiled. **1106 Unneth**, Scarcely; **leude**, ignorant; **plites**, folds.

lene of His oyntmentes mens wittes to clere, and for Goddes love no man wonder why or how this question come to my mynde, for my great lusty desyre was of this lady to ben enfourmed my leudenesse to amende. Certes, I knowe not other mennes wyttes what I shulde aske, or in answere what I shulde saye. I am so leude myselfe that mokel more lernynge yet me behoveth. I have made therfore as I coude, but not suffyciently as I wolde, and as mater yave me sentence, for my dul wytte is hyndred by stepmother of foryetyng and with cloude of unconnyng that stoppeth the lyght of my Margarite perle, wherfore it may not shyne on me as it shulde. I desyre not onely a good reder, but also I coveyte and pray a good booke amender in correction of wordes and of sentence. And onely this mede I coveyte for my travayle, that every inseer and herer of this leude fantasye devoute horisons and prayers to God the great juge yelden, and prayen for me in that wyse that in His dome my synnes mowe ben released and foryeven. He that prayeth for other, for himselfe travayleth. Also I praye that every man parfytly mowe knowe thorowe what intencion of herte this treatyse have I drawe. Howe was it that

---

lene of his oyntme*n*tes mens witt*es* to clere/ *and* for godd*es* loue no man wo*n*der why or how this question come to my mynde/ for my great lusty desyre was of**<360vb><361ra>**this lady to ben enfourmed/ my leudenesse to amende. Certes I knowe not other mennes wyttes what I shulde aske/ or in answere what I shulde saye/ I am so leude my selfe/ that mokel more lernynge yet me behoueth. I haue made therfore as I coude/ but not suffyciently as I wolde/ and as mater yaue me sentence/ for my dul wytte is hyndred by stepmother of foryetyng/ and with cloude of vnconnyng/ that stoppeth the lyght of my Margarite perle/ wherfore it may not shyne on me as it shulde. I desyre not onely a good reder/ but also I coueyte and pray a good booke amender/ in correction of wordes and of sentence: and onely this mede I coueyte for my trauayle/ that euery inseer and herer of this leude fantasye/ deuoute horisons and prayers to god the great iuge yelden/ and prayen for me/ in that wyse that in his dome my synnes mowe ben released *and* foryeuen: He that prayeth for other/ for him selfe trauayleth. Also I praye that euery man parfytly mowe knowe thorowe what intencion of herte this treatyse haue I drawe. Howe was it th*at*

1107 lene, loan. **1109 leudenesse**, ignorance. **1110 mokel**, much. **1112 yave**, gave. **1113 unconnyng**, ignorance. **1116 mede**, reward; **leude**, ignorant. **1117 horisons**, beseechings, prayers; **yelden**, yield. **1118 mowe**, may.

syghtful Manna in deserte to chyldren of Israel was spirytuel meate. Bodily also it was, for mennes bodies it norissheth. And yet neverthelater, Christ it signyfyed. Ryght so a jewel betokeneth a gemme and that is a stone vertuous or els a perle: Margarite a woman betokeneth grace, lernyng, or wisdom of God, or els holy church. If breed thorowe vertue is made holy flesshe, what is that our God saythe? It is the spyrite that yeveth lyfe; the flesshe of nothyng it profyteth. Flesshe is flesshly understandynge; flessh without grace and love naught is worth. The letter sleeth, the spyrit yeveth lyfelych understandyng. Charyté is love, and love is charyté. God graunt us al therin to be frended. And thus the *Testament of Love* is ended.

Thus endeth the *Testament of Love*

---

syghtful Ma*n*na in deserte to chyldren of Israel was spirytuel meate: bodily also it was/ for men*n*es bodies it norissheth. And yet neuer th*e* later Christ it signyfyed. Ryght so a iewel betokeneth a gemme/ and that is a stone vertuous/ or els a perle. Margarite a woman betokeneth grace/ lernyng/ or wisdom of god/ or els holy church. If breed thorowe vertue is made holy flesshe/ what is that our god saythe? It is the spyrite that yeueth lyfe/ the flesshe of nothyng it profyteth. Flesshe is flesshly vnderstandynge: flessh without grace *and* loue naught is worth. The letter sleeth/ the spyrit yeueth lyfelych vndersta*n*dyng. Charyte is loue/ and loue is charyte/ god graunt vs al therin to be frended. And thus the Testament of Loue is ended.

Thus endeth the Testament of Loue

1121 syghtful, visible; **meate**, food. **1122 Ryght so**, Just as. **1126 yeveth**, gives. **1129 frended**, befriended.

Notes

As readers will have already surmised from the Introduction to the edition as a whole, annotating *TL* is no easy task. This is a matter of great concern to me. There are about 800 annotations in the edition. On the one hand, we can argue that, of course, there should be no upper limit to the explanatory matter offered. On the other hand, however, realistically speaking, there has to be some limit. Knowing that practically there is an upper limit, I have endeavored to include information, wherever it is needed, *that will get the reader started*: from simple definitions to core bibliography and across a wide spectrum of information between, I have followed the guiding principle of helping readers know enough to decide when they need to know more.

All annotations originating with me are unmarked. All material originating with other editors and/or scholars is marked typically by their surnames (Skeat's surname refers, unless otherwise indicated, to his 1897 edition of *TL*). Regarding the work of Jellech, Leyerle, and Skeat, I should observe that material originating with them usually refers to their notes on a particular word, phrase, or moment in *TL* within the sequence of their textual notes. I am particularly grateful to Schaar for his closely reasoned emendations of corrupt passages.

Of Skeat's annotations, I have retained generally those that provide source and background information and have omitted those that are primarily his speculations. With the work of Jellech, Leyerle, and Schaar, I have exercised my judgment always on the principle of helping the reader get started.

Abbreviations: *Boece*: Chaucer's translation of the *Consolation of Philosophy*; *BD: Book of the Duchess; CA*: *Confessio Amantis*; *CT*: *Canterbury Tales*; *Conc.*: *De Concordia Praescientiae et Praedestinationis et Gratiae Dei cum Libero Arbitrio*; *Conf.*: *Confessions*; *Cons.*: *Consolation of Philosophy*; *EETS*: *Early English Text Society* (o.s., Original Series and e.s., Extra Series); *HF*: *House of Fame*; *MED*: *Middle English Dictionary*; *N&Q*: *Notes and Queries*; *OED*: *Oxford English Dictionary*; *PPl*: *Piers Plowman*; *PL*: *Patrologia Latina*; *Purg.*: *Purgatorio*; *T&C*: *Troilus and Criseyde*; *Th: Thynne; TL*: *The Testament of Love*

The Testament of Love

Prologue

2 *jestes*. According to Leyerle, *jestes* means "a form of composition distinct from that in *ryme* or prose" (p. 219).

by queynt knyttyng coloures. Skeat glosses as "curious fine phrases, that knit or join the words or verses together" (p. 451). The word *knytting* anticipates or even prefigures an entire complex of imagery of knots in *TL*; see the Introduction iii c (pp. 8–13) and below, Book 2, lines 98ff.

3–6 The reader should note the general similarity between Usk's situation and that of Boethius at the beginning of *Cons*. Usk makes extensive use of that work and of Chaucer's translation of it as well.

6 *inrest*. Skeat emends to *in[ne]rest*, thereby displacing one neologism with another.

20 *whiche*. Skeat emends to *[of] whiche*.

31 *necessaryes to catche*. Skeat: "to lay hold of necessary ideas. Throughout this treatise, we frequently find the verb placed *after* the substantive which it governs, or relegated to the end of the clause or sentence" (p. 451).

32 *Certes, the soveraynst*. Skeat emends to *Certes, [perfeccion is] the soveraynest*. The syntax of the sentence is certainly contorted, but emendation may not be necessary. The sense is: "Certainly, reasonable creatures have, or should have, the most sovereign thing of desire and the greatest, [that is], the full appetite of their perfection." For the general argument, see *Boece*, 3. pr. 10 and 11, where superlative fulfillment is represented by *suffisaunce*, as, e.g., in 3. pr. 11, line 25 (pp. 451–52).

39 *be*. Usk typically has *be* for *by*. Normally I will gloss this at the foot of the page, but not always.

42 *knowlegynge sothe*. Skeat emends to *knowleginge [of] sothe*, followed by Leyerle.

43–45 *Lo, David sayth . . . makynge*. Skeat, Schaar, Jellech, and Leyerle comment on the obscurity of this passage. Skeat makes no change in the text, but calls it hopelessly corrupt. He sees a possible reference to Ps. cxxxix. 14 (p. 452). But Jellech argues against that reference citing instead Psalm 91.4: *Quia delectasti me, Domine, in factura*, which Usk translates literally:

> The explanation which Usk provides [Jellech continues] would also seem to be a literal translation of some now lost commentary, but the English meaning is quite obscure. In the context of the first three verses of the psalm, the word *tune* would not be impossible; these are: *Bonum est confiteri Domino, et psallere nomine tuo, Altissime. / Ad annuntiandum mane misericordiam tuam, et veritatem tuam per noctem. / In decachordo psalterio, eum cantico in cithara* [It is good to give praise to the Lord: and to sing to thy name, O most High. To shew forth thy mercy in the morning, and thy truth in the night: Upon an instrument of ten strings, upon the psaltery: with a canticle upon the harp]. According to the *OED, tune*, from L. *tonus*, began to be differentiated from "tone" in the fourteenth century, and usually refers to the human voice. Still, the passage remains only partially intelligible and no reasonable emendation has suggested itself to me, so the passage has been left unchanged." (p. 132)

Jellech's hunch is probably a good one, except for the assumption that the commentary is "lost." I suspect it is the commentary of St. Augustine, who writes, e.g., (*Expositions* 4, p. 313) that

> . . . God teacheth us no other hymn but that of faith, hope, and charity: that our faith may be firm in Himself, as long as we do not see Him, believing in Him Whom we do not see, that we may rejoice when we see Him . . .

Augustine continues with this emphasis on the invisibility of God and the need for faith as the Christian waits for the day when s/he will see God: ". . . endure the present, hope for the future, love Whom he seeth not, that he may embrace Him when he seeth Him" (*Expositions* 4, p. 314). Usk, then, is probably recalling from memory (my speculation) a well-known interpretation of Psalm 91, which is also consonant with the famous Pauline dictum, "for the invisible things of him, from the creation of the world, are clearly seen, being understood by the things that are made" (Romans 1.20). Hence, my gloss for *tune*, "harmonious totality of composition," attempts to capture the sense of the whole creation as the song-like communication ("eum cantico in cithara") that brings us "the ful knowlegynge sothe." I think then, in sum, that although the English is corrupt, the sense is recuperable, and therefore I have not emended:

the gist of the passage is that the harmonious totality of the creation intimates for us the "unsene privytees" of God.

44 *tune, how God hath lent*. Schaar would emend to: *time, thou god hast sent.*

45 *Wherof Aristotle*. Skeat adduces *De Animalibus* 1.5. In this quite famous passage, Aristotle says, at one point, "For even in the study of animals unattractive to the senses, the nature that fashioned them offers immeasurable pleasures . . . to those who can learn the causes and are naturally lovers of wisdom" (pp. 17–18).

47 *consydred*. The passage implies for Skeat that, "the forms of natural things and their creation being considered, men should have a great natural love to the Workman that made them" (p. 452). Skeat imagines the term to be head of the next clause: *Considred, forsoth, the formes. . . .* But *the formes . . . and the shap* is simply an appositional phrase, the antecedent of *hem* (line 48). Such constructions are typical of Usk's prose; we can think of them as loose ablative absolutes; Leyerle (p. 316) also observes this phenomenon.

48 *me*. In Middle English *me* is commonly written for *men*. Skeat labels it "the unemphatic form of *man*, in the impersonal sense of 'one' or 'people' . . . . Strict grammar requires the form *him* for *hem* . . . as *me* is properly singular; but the use of *hem* is natural enough in this passage, as *me* really signifies created beings in general" (p. 452).

51 *of causes the propertyes*. Skeat emends to *of causes [of] the propertees*. But the repetition of *of* is unnecessary. The sense is that philosophers have left to us causes of the properties in the nature of things, where *of causes* is a kind of affixation. The source of the idea may be *Boece*, I. m. 2. 15ff., where Philosophy describes the healthy Boethius as one who not only appreciated the things of nature but also "was wont to seken the causes." The greatest expression of this idea in the Latin tradition is probably Virgil's: "Felix, qui potuit rerum cognoscere causas" (*Georgics* 2.490): "Happy is he who can discern the causes of things" (my translation). Leyerle speculates that the phrase *of causes the propertyes in natures of thynges* is a reference to *De Proprietatibus Rerum*, by Bartholomaeus Anglicus (p. 222).

56–57 *Stixe, the foule pytte of helle*. See *T&C* 4.1540. Jellech notes that Spenser pointed out ["Chaucer's Hell, A Study in Medieval Convention," *Speculum* 2 (1927), p. 181], that Chaucer's reference to Styx as the "pit of hell" is used as the part for the whole, and that there are many medieval references to hell pit (p. 134).

58–59 *the pryme causes of sterynge . . . for wantynge of desyre*. Jellech observes: "The primary causes governing the activity of loving, along with the suffering and unhappiness brought about by lack of fulfillment of the lover's desire. Usk generally uses the term 'steer' for 'control' or 'govern'" (p. 134).

61ff. Leyerle (pp. 222–24) proposes a source in Trevisa's translation of Higden's *Polychronicon* (which Usk certainly knew) and concludes: "wresting the sword from the hands of Hercules is a metaphor for direct use of texts written by *auctours*, that is by authoritative writers of the past" (p. 224).

62 *Gades a myle*. Gades marks the pillars of Hercules, located by medieval geographers at Cadiz. Skeat suggests that the reference may come from Guido delle Colonne (p. 452).

62–63 *he had power . . . might never wagge*. Skeat notes: "There seems to be some confusion here. It was King Arthur who drew the magic sword out of the stone . . . Alexander's task was to untie the Gordian knot" (p. 452). Jellech points out, however, that "neither the medieval English versions of the Alexander story nor the French *Roman de Alexander* contains the episode of the cutting of the Gordian knot. Cary, *The Medieval Alexander* . . . does not list the incident. What anecdote of Alexander Usk had in mind remains unexplained. Usk's point is that Alexander, or some hero, was unable to lift the spear: Arthur did succeed in withdrawing the sword from the rock" (p. 135).

64–66 *And that . . . conquere*? Skeat paraphrases: "and who says that, surpassing all wonders, he will be master of France by might, whereas even King Edward III could not conquer all of it" (p. 452). The allusion is to the Hundred Years' War between England and France over the English claim to the throne of France.

68 *the cloudy cloude of unconnynge*. Jellech questions a possible reference to the famous, anonymous mystical treatise of the fourteenth century, *The Cloud of Unknowing*: "[it] is not appropriate here because Dyonysius's theme is that the cloud of unknowing is a spiritual benefit, whereas Usk, following Boethius, uses the image of the cloud to refer to ignorance which prevents the viewer from understanding his true situation" (p. 135). I am less secure about this matter. I would prefer to leave open the possibility that there may be a connection between the two texts. I have as yet to explore the connection at any length, but in my opinion, there is a mystical tendency in Usk, underdeveloped I would admit, that may have led him to appropriate the phrase for his own uses. However, against my opinion and in support of Jellech's can be adduced such a passage as Book 1, lines 246–47.

72–73 *Envye forsothe commendeth . . . it never so trusty*. Jellech glosses: "Envy will not approve the plans of anyone he scorns, even if they are good."

73–74 *good workmen and worthy theyr hyer*. Usk paraphrases Luke 10.7.

73–78 *these noble repers . . . to the almesse*. This extended image relates perhaps to Chaucer's *Legend of Good Women*, F Prol. 73–77; it also recalls Dante's use of a similar image in *Convivio* 1.1.67–86. Perhaps it is part of an elaborate exegetical trope on reaping and glossing; see the essay by Martin.

81–82 *A slye servaunt . . . moche commended*. See Luke 16.1–8, the parable of the steward.

83 *Aristotle*. Skeat cites *Nicomachean Ethics* 1.7, here. In the Loeb translation, the possibly relevant passage reads

> and in this working out of details Time seems to be a good inventor or at all events coadjutor. This indeed is how advances in the arts have actually come about, since anyone can fill in the gaps. (1.7.17)

I can find no passage any closer in sense to Usk's statement than this. I can report, though, that this passage is also translated, quite closely, in Oresme's *Le Livre de éthiques d'Aristote* (c. 1370; p. 122), which may have been known in England in the 1380s (see Shoaf [1983], p. 244).

84 Leyerle comments here and elsewhere on the frequent absence of grammatical concord between subject and predicate in *TL* (pp. 226 *et alia*). I would emphasize, as does Leyerle, but more generally, that often Usk "feels" grammatically singular subjects as conceptually plural.

86 *Utterly, these thynges . . . to throwe to hogges*. Jellech (p. 138) sees a possible reference to Matthew 7.6:

> Nolite dare sanctum canibus neque mittatis margaritas vestras ante porcos, ne forte conculcent eas pedibus suis et conversi dirumpant vos. [Give not that which is holy to dogs; neither cast ye your pearls before swine, less perhaps they trample them under their feet, and turning upon you, they tear you.]

However, the connection between dreams and sacred or valuable objects is uncertain; no use is made of the reference to pearls in the biblical passage.

86–87 *It is lyfelyche meate for chyldren of trouthe*. Compare Boethius, *Cons*. I. p. 2. 3–6 (*Boece*, p. 399).

87 *and as they me betiden*. Schaar corrects *Th* and *Sk* as follows:

> Skeat is not satisfied with this passage, which seems to him to contain a gap: "this sudden transition to the mention of the author's pilgrimage suggests that a portion of the Prologue is missing here." This, however, hardly does justice to the paragraph. The author's pilgrimage into a wild and desolate landscape, ravaged by furious elements, is a symbol of deep melancholy, of an existence in grief and spiritual agony. . . . This wintry existence, however, as the whole treatise shows, is made endurable by the life-giving rays of Philosophy: the Consolation of Philosophy. *Lyflich mete*, in our passage, goes with both *for children of trouthe* and the *as*-clause: *these thinges*, then, are no empty dreams but vital nourishment for those who love truth and when they happened to me in a period of great spiritual need and distress. (pp. 8–9)

Leyerle also comments that "the incomplete syntax [between "and" and "as they me betiden"] indicates, as Skeat suggests, that some material is missing . . ." (p. 226) at this juncture.

The Testament of Love

Book 1

1 *Fortune*. There are six references to Fortune in Book 1, eight in Book 2, and none in Book 3. There are three references to *selynesse* ("felicity") in Book 1, seven to *unsely*, and two to *sely*; in Book 2, there are six references to *selynesse* and one to *sely*. The word does not occur in Book 3. Thus, if Fortune plays a less dominant role in *TL* than in *Cons*. (Jellech's argument, p. 140 and elsewhere), still it is not a negligible role. Moreover, it is noteworthy that in Boethius, Fortune is more prominent in *Cons.* Books 1 and 2 than it is in 3–5, which concern issues beyond Fortune's purview. If *TL* seeks more to define the "knot in the heart" than to complain against Fortune, Fortune is still recognized as an impediment to the "knot in the heart," if an impediment that, as in the case of Boethius, too, can and must be overcome.

6 *Certes, her absence is to me an hell.* Compare *T&C* 5.1396: "'For though to me youre absence is an helle.'"

6–7 *my sternyng*. Skeat emends to *sterving*, i.e., languishing (lit., dying). Leyerle argues that "the protest to Fortune in language implicitly referring to her wheel and the use of the verb *turne* at line [8] suggest that the correct reading is *mysternyng*, 'turning amiss' . . ." (p. 227).

8 *thyng*. Skeat suggests that *thyng* means "person," the sense being, "the person that cannot now embrace me when I wish for comfort" (p. 453).

12 *caytisned*. Skeat emends to *caitived*, observing "the correction of *caytisned* (with *f* for *s*) to *caytifued* (better spelt *caitived*) is obvious" (p. 453). Jellech and Leyerle agree.

wode. Skeat emends to *word*, needlessly.

18 *Margarite precious*. See Introduction iii c; and Appendix 1 below. Note that this is the first mention of the Margarite. Farmer (pp. 318–19) writes:

> Very popular in the later Middle Ages in England and elsewhere, Margaret probably never existed as a historical person, but only as a character in pious fiction. . . . At the

> end of her life, she promised, as the Sarum breviary relates: that those who write or read her "history" will receive an unfading crown in heaven, that those who invoke her on their death-beds will enjoy divine protection and escape from the devils, that those who dedicate churches or burn lights in her honour will obtain anything useful they pray for, and that pregnant women who invoke her will escape the dangers of childbirth, as will their infants. These apocryphal promises contributed powerfully to the spread of her cult. This can be traced back before the Norman Conquest in England, when the first of seven vernacular Lives were [*sic*] written. Well over 200 ancient English churches were dedicated to her, including fifty-eight in Norfolk. She was frequently depicted in wall paintings and stained-glass windows. . . .

18–19 *yet wyl of that . . . my luste to have*. Leyerle argues: "The single emendation of *wyl* to *[y]wy[s]* gives the sentence adequate coherence. The meaning is 'yet, indeed, my desire is to have nought else of that (comfort for me in sorrow) at this time'" (p. 228).

19 *dede*. Skeat emends to *d[r]ede*, needlessly.

20–21 *to here of a twynckelynge in your disease*. Skeat: "to hear of a small matter tending toward your discomfort."

25 *kyndly noriture*. Compare *T&C* 4.766–68 (emphasis added):

> "What is Crisyede worth, from Troilus?
> How sholde a plaunte or lyves creature
> Lyve withouten his *kynde noriture*?"

32 *It is so hye*. Skeat paraphrases: "Paradise is so far away from the place where I am lying and from the common earth, that no cable (let down from it) can reach me."

34 *I purveyde*. Skeat: *I [am] purveyed*, followed by Jellech and Leyerle.

36–37 *weareth his olde clothes*. Schaar (p. 32) observes:

> The reference to the *olde clothes* is puzzling, and there must be something wrong with the last sentence. It seems that the author has in mind a passage in Joshua (9. 5),

telling how the inhabitants of Gibeon, desiring a covenant with the Israelites, went to their camp in old garments and with dry bread *(callide cogitantes . . . induti veteribus vestimentis: panes quoque . . . duri erant)* in order to make them believe that they came from a far off country (otherwise no covenant would be possible). This act appears in the commentaries of some of the Fathers as a symbol of false spiritual friendship; those coming to the Church in their "old garments" are the people who do not seriously seek the Christian truth but are full of their old vices; who do not really want the friendship of God . . . those, in other words, who have outward friendship only and none in the heart. Hence, probably, Usk's reflection, about the false friend, that the soul of friendship is *Ydrawn out from his other spirits*. The passage should probably read: *But ever, me thinketh, he wereth his olde clothes, and that soule in the whiche the lyfe of frendship was in, is drawen out from his other spirites.*

37 *that the soule*. Schaar would emend to *that soule*.

43 *chere, ferdness*. Th: *chere/frendes*. Observing the placement of the vergule in Thynne, Skeat places a full stop after *chere* and emends *frendes* to *ferdnes*, observing: "*ferdnes* is obviously the right word, though misprinted *frendes*. It signifies 'fear,' and occurs again in lines [107] and [112]; besides, it is again misprinted as *frendes* in the same chapter, line [109]" (p. 453). Jellech and Leyerle follow Skeat's suggestion and emend to *ferdness*, as I do also.

46 *veyned*. Skeat: *weyved*, followed by Jellech and Leyerle.

51–52 *your mercy than passeth right*. Compare *T&C* 3.1282–88:

"Here may men seen that mercy passeth right;
Th'experience of that is felt in me,
That am unworthi to so swete a wight.

52 *God graunt that proposycion to be verifyed in me*. Jellech observes: "The *proposycion* is, that *your mercy than passeth right*. Note the scholastic terminology of *proposycion* and *verifyed*," and cites John Conley's note on neologisms (p. 146).

56 *unymagynable*. Th: *ymaginable*. Skeat's emendation, followed by Jellech and Leyerle.

58 *wot*. Th: *wol*. Skeat's emendation, followed by Jellech and Leyerle.

59 *sonded*. Skeat emends to *souded* ("fixed"), the n/u being a common compositor's error. Jellech and Leyerle follow him. But *sonded* occasionally occurs as the past participle of *senden*, in which case the sense might be "ordained" or "placed." (See MED *senden* [n. 7b]). Though Skeat is probably right, I have glossed the term "ordained," and not emended it.

59–60 *O love . . . O charyté*. Compare *T&C* 3.1254–60:

Than seyde he thus, "O Love, O Charite!
Thi moder ek, Citheria the swete,
After thiself next heried be she —
Venus mene I, the wel-willy planete! —
And next that, Imeneus, I the grete,
For nevere man was to yow goddes holde
As I, which ye han brought fro cares colde."

61 *do*. Skeat glosses as "cause" and reads, "cause the lucky throw of comfort to fall upward," alluding to dice-play (p. 454).

66 *knotte*. Here the knot is introduced, anticipating its extended development in Book 2; it is mentioned again in Book 1 at lines 902 and 906.

67 *endelesse in*. Th: *is endeless in*. Skeat emends to *in endeles blisse*. Jellech and Leyerle, also, as do I, omit *is*.

73 *as*. Skeat emends to *[ther]-as*; Leyerle emends to *a[la]s*.

76 *amonges*. Th: *amomges*.

82–83 *Trewly, I leve*. Th: *trewly and leve*. Skeat's emendation, followed by Jellech and Leyerle.

86 *O, alas that your nobley.* Leyerle proposes (p. 232): "'Oh, alas! that your noble quality — by continuing stream, by all manner of powers — so much commended among all other creatures, only there is wonderful' [i.e., 'among all other creatures']."

92 *joleynynge.* Skeat emends to *joleyiynge*, i.e., cheering, making joyous.

109 *ferdnes.* Th: *frendes*. Skeat's emendation, followed by Jellech and Leyerle.

110 *as affection.* According to Leyerle, "the phrase beginning with *as* is to be taken with *adradde* and the intervening material is parenthetical" (p. 233). In other words, their dread is "as" or "like" *affection of wonderfulnesse*, etc.

113 *a lady.* Skeat compares *Cons.* 1. pr. 1, line 3. See my Introduction iii b, for further commentary.

127 *O my nory.* Compare Chaucer's *Boece* III, pr. 9, line 159: *O my nory*, as Philosophy praises the aptness of her student (*alumnae* in the original, which Chaucer [and Usk] convert into a suckling, Philosophy being the wet nurse). Love as wet nurse becomes an important trope for Usk. See lines 187 and 202 below, and especially, lines 376–77, where his lady scolds him for forgetting "the olde soukyng whiche thou haddest of me."

133–34 *Nowe, good lady . . . are thy movynges.* Jellech sees a possible allusion to Canticles 4.10–12: Favus distillans labra tua sponsa, mel et lac sub lingua tua; et odor vestimentorum tuorum sicut odor thuris. Hortus conclusus, fons signatus! [Thy lips, my spouse, are as a dropping honeycomb, honey and milk are under thy tongue; and the smell of thy garments, as the smell of frankincense. My sister, my spouse, is a garden enclosed, a fountain sealed up.] See p. 154.

146 *For that me comforteth.* The sense is "Because [it] comforts me to think on passed gladness, it annoys me to be doing it again [experiencing gladness since I can assume it will become passed gladness again]."

152ff. See Matthew 18.12; Luke 15.4; John 10.11.

165ff. *Haste thou not radde*. Skeat observes: "Love was kind to Paris, because he succeeded in gaining Helen. Jason was false to Love, because he deserted Hypsipyle and Medea" (p. 454).

167 *false behest*. Leyerle comments: "Skeat proposes to emend *false* to *faire* in order to provide the contrast implied by *for*. A reading of *faste* would offer fewer paleographical difficulties than *faire* does. No emendation is needed, if *false* is taken as a repetition of *falsed* in order to gain emphasis" (pp. 235–36).

Sesars swonke. Th: *Sesars sonke*. Jellech observes: "The meaning is obscure. Skeat emended *sonke* to 'swynk,' but we cannot be sure that is correct. Suetonius' *Lives of the Caesars* (in Vincent of Beauvais' *Speculum Historiale* 6.38) reads 'Armorum et equitandi peritissimus, laboris ultra fidem patiens erat.' This 'endurance of effort' might have been transformed into 'Sesars swynk' in some alliterative version of Caesar's life, but no such work has been found. The earliest life of Caesar in English seems to be Lydgate's *Serpent of Division*" (p. 157). *Sonke* could be a misprint for *sonde*, ME "message" or "errand," with the possible meaning in *TL* then being, "How Caesar's errand or mission I abandoned it for no grief until he was throned. . . ." Or perhaps the reading should be *swonke*, which OED sees as an archaic term for "ostentation" or "presumption" (n.b., *swank*), in which case the sense is, "How Caesar's pomp I abandonded . . ." I have followed this possibility, as it makes the best sense of the passage. Leyerle (p. 236) offers a different reading, based in the *Polychronicon*.

169 *nompere*. Skeat suggests, "And chose a maid to be umpire between God and man" — alluding to the Virgin Mary (p. 455).

171 *whome*. Th: *home*. Skeat's emendation, followed by Jellech and Leyerle.

189 *wo is him*. Skeat suggests an allusion to Ecclesiastes 4.10.

189–90 *and to the sorye*. Compare *T&C* 1.12–14:

For wel sit it, the sothe for to seyne,
A woful wight to han a drery feere,
And to a sorwful tale, a sory chere.

203 *wolde ben deynous*. *Th*: *wolde endeynous*. Skeat's emendation, followed by Jellech and Leyerle.

210–11 *appetyte of desyre*. Compare St. Augustine's concept of the *pondus amoris* ("weight of love") in, e.g., *City of God* 11.28:

> For the specific gravity of a body is, in a manner, its love, whether a body tends downwards by reason of its heaviness or strives upwards because of its lightness. A material body is borne along by its weight in a particular direction, as a soul is by its love. (p. 463)

And see further *Conf.* 7.17 (p. 151).

220 *playde raket nettyl in docke out*. Compare *T&C* 4.460–61:

> "But kanstow playen raket, to and fro,
> Netle in, dok out, now this, now that, Pandare?"

224 *a*. Skeat notes that this is an unemphatic form of *have* — "thou wouldest have made me" (p. 455). See also line 231.

229 *voyde*. Skeat: "*voyde*, do away with; *webbes*; the *web*, also called *the pin and web*, or *the web and pin*, is a disease of the eyes" (p. 455).

237–38 *truste on Mars*. Skeat: "trust to Mars, i.e., be ready with wager of battle — alluding to the common practice of appealing to arms when a speaker's truthfulness was called in question" (p. 455). See line 668 below.

258ff. The narrator's recollection of his nightmare journey into the wilderness, where he encounters terrifying beasts that once were domestic but now have turned vicious and then takes refuge on a ship, bears a remarkable likeness to John Gower's allegorical allusion to the Peasant's Revolt, *Vox Clamantis*, Book I, especially lines 161–2059, where the poet in the fourth year of the reign of King Richard (i.e., 1381) encounters domestic beasts gone wild (that is, the rabble turned into vicious asses, oxen, swine, dogs, etc.) that assail him, driving him through the woods and then on to a ship, where he finds small comfort once the storm arises. Gower's victim does not find security in a great pearl at the bottom of the sea, as Usk's persona does, but he does find refuge through the Virgin Mary, *stella Maria maris* (I, 2083ff.), a pearl in her own right, who calms the rough waters and saves him from the fearful jaws of wild beasts and fishes. Rather than the Peasant's Revolt, Usk's allusion is to the political aggressions of the Merciless Parliament, through which his life is in jeopardy. That he seems to have read Gower's Latin poem, for whatever reason, is in itself remarkable, for the light it sheds on Gower, Chaucer, and Usk as a literary group. For reference to the *Vox Clamantis*, see G. C. Macaulay, *The Complete Works of John Gower* (Oxford: Clarendon Press, 1902), IV: The Latin Works, lines 1–2092 (pp. 22–78). For a translation of the passage, see Eric W. Stockton, *The Major Latin Works of John Gower* (Seattle: University of Washington Press, 1962), pp. 54–94.

261 *halke*. Skeat glosses as "nook"; MED offers "corner," "hiding place," and "cavity" as well, though the term remains troublesome. Analogy with the "full barn" trope earlier in the sentence clearly suggests the tight container of the nut, thus the shell. See James Orchard Halliwell, *A Dictionary of Archaic and Provincial Words, Obsolete Phrases, Proverbs, and Ancient Customs, from the XIV Century* (London: George Routledge and Sons, 1924), p. 465, where "hulk" is glossed as "a hull or husk."

264–66 *Oft the lothe thyng . . . of luste to travayle*. Observing that both Skeat and Schaar comment on these lines without coming to an acceptable conclusion, Jellech proposes the adding of "I" between *opynyon* and *whiche* and then emending *wolden* to *wolde* and *take* to *toke* to mean: "often the loath thing is done by excitation of another man's opinion; I which would fayne have my abiding [in one place] took in heart a lust to labor and see" (p. 168). Leyerle, like Jellech, rejects Skeat and Schaar. Construing *of lust* as a rare past participle, *oflust*, meaning "affected with longing," and construing *take* as a past participle, too, he would read: "in such a time of plenty, he who has a home and is wise, does not want to wander about seeking miracles, unless he is constrained or incited. Often the hateful thing is done at the incitement of other men, who willingly would have my staying taken to heart. Affected with a desire to travel, etc." (p. 243). In this reading, a new sentence begins with *Ofluste* (line 266), and "I" (line 268) is the subject of this sentence. I remain at this time skeptical of all proposals, though I have none better myself to offer.

265–66 . . . *abydynge* may here have a concrete meaning; if so, *whiche wolden fayne haue myn abydynge take in herte* etc. would mean: . . . "wanted me, who was staying at home, to take a mind to travel." *Wolden* seems to owe its *n* to the following *fayne*; otherwise we may let the passage stand as it is:

> In suche tyme of plentee he that hath an home and is wyse, list not to wander mervayles to seche, but he be constrayned or excited. Oft the lothe thing is doon, by excitacion of other mannes opinion, whiche wolde fayne have myn abydinge take in herte of luste to travayle. . . . (Schaar, p. 10)

266 *take in herte*. Skeat emends to *[Tho gan] take in herte*, which perhaps makes the syntax more gracious.

268 *ladels*. "applied to the cup of an acorn" (*OED* L, p. 581, "ladel," br. 3). Hence, "by small paths that swine and hogs had made, as lanes with acorns, [there] to seek out their mast [food]."

270 *gone to wylde*. "to grow wild." Skeat cites *gynne ayen waxe ramage*, in Book 1, line 273, for the like sense (p. 456).

275 *many*. Skeat: "*many* is here used in place of *meynee*, referring to the ship's company" (p. 456). See Siennicki, p. 91 especially.

Syght was the first. Compare 1 John 2:16: "For all that is in the world, is the concupiscence of the flesh, and the concupiscence of the eyes, and the pride of life."

283 For consistency of dialect, Skeat emends *wethers* to *weders*, and to ease the syntax adds *[of]* after *avowyng*. Leyerle follows Skeat; Jellech does not.

285 *as*. Skeat emends to *at*, and Leyerle concurs.

292 *my shyppe was out of mynde*. Skeat glosses: "I forgot all about my previous danger."

293–94 *a muskel in a blewe shel*. Jellech notes that "natural historians from antiquity conveyed to medieval encyclopaedists the tradition that the pearl was engendered by a drop of dew enclosed in a shellfish or cockle." See Appendix 1 below, for specific historical comments on pearls.

At the risk, I know, of eliciting scorn from some, I nonetheless feel obliged to call the reader's attention to the following datum. In the entire *TL*, as Thynne prints it (i.e., before Book 3 is re-arranged to accord with the acrostic), the only occurrence of the name "Usk" is in the word "mUSKel." In trying to understand Usk and what he wrote, I think it would be mistaken to ignore this datum.

298–99 *the man that sought . . . to bye that jewel.* I.e., the merchant-man in Matthew 13.45–46, who sold all that he had to buy the pearl of great price. Biblical commentaries equate the pearl in the parable with the soul.

304–07 *Your might . . . I wonder . . . knoweth.* Note how my punctuation recognizes Usk's loose ablative absolute.

312 *lady, myne desyre.* Skeat punctuates: *lady mine, desire*, which makes good sense too, though Usk normally refers to Margarite simply as *lady*, not *lady mine* (e.g., lines 292 and 315), and here it is *his* desire that is under scrutiny.

317 *of nothyng now may serve.* Skeat (p. 456): "is now of no use (to you)."

319 *under your wynges of protection.* A Marian analogue, where wings or robes signify the aegis of comfort. See John V. Fleming's discussion of the trope in "Anticlerical Satire as Theological Essay: Chaucer's *Summoner's Tale*," *Thalia*, 6 (1983), 5–22.

322 *A renyant forjuged.* Jellech asserts that *forjuged* is used to signify "exile." "For *renyant*, the *OED* gives a 'renegade, apostate,' from French *renay*. Thus, we would be closer to Usk's meaning by paraphrasing, 'a convicted traitor,' or merely 'criminal'" (p. 174).

341 *sir Daunger.* A personification in the *fin'amors* or "courtly love" tradition, referring to the Beloved's standoffishness or haughtiness. Leyerle suggests, in one of his major theoretical arguments about *TL*, that "Usk's usage [of *Daunger*] illustrates the tendency in late medieval work for the language of power and the language of love to

be applied to each other, In particular, Usk transfers the language of love to the subject of political power . . ." (p. 246). This latter point is perhaps the key to Leyerle's understanding of *TL*; see, further, p. 17n38, above.

348 *For he . . . suffer*. Skeat: "a perfect alliterative line." Skeat goes on to argue (p. 456) that the line is "imitated from *PPl* C.21.212"; but see my Introduction, section iv "Usk and his Contemporaries."

352 *harse*. Skeat emended the form to "harm." Jellech notes, however, that the *MED* "has not accepted Skeat's emendation, for it has an entry, *harse* n. (Compare OF *herce* a harrow). Grief, vexation. 1532 rev [c.1385] Usk *TL* (Skeat) 18/158" (p. 177).

355 *lyches*. Skeat emends to *leches*, presumably for dialect consistency. Probably the vowel /e/ had not yet moved upward to /i/ in the fourteenth century as it had done in Thynne's era.

370 *for of disease . . . vessel.* Th: *or of disease . . . nessel.* Skeat's emendation: "For *or* read *for*, to make sense; *for of disease*, for out of such disease come gladness and joy, so poured out by means of a full vessel that such gladness quenches the feeling of former sorrows. Here *gladnesse and joy* is spoken of as being all one thing, governing the singular verb *is*, and being alluded to as *it*" (p. 457). Jellech and Leyerle follow Skeat, as do I.

375 *O where haste thou be*. Compare the identical phrasing in *T&C* 4.496–97: "'O, where hastow ben hid so longe in muwe, / That kanst so wel and formely arguwe?'"

376 *soukyng*. Skeat emends needlessly to *soukinges*. Usk is alluding here to Philosophy's chastizing of Boethius who had been "norisched with my melk" (*Cons*. 1. pr. 2, lines 5–6). This section of Usk draws extensively on this passage. See notes to lines 380 and 382.

380 *astonyed.* The wording comes from Chaucer's *Boece* I, pr. 2, lines 12–15. See also *Boece* I, pr. 1, line 81.

382 *clothe*. See *Cons*. 1. pr. 2. lines 25–30, where Philosophy wipes the tears from Boethius's eyes — "the wawes of my wepynges," as Chaucer puts it (*Boece*, p. 399).

385–89 *ye . . . ye . . . ye . . . ye.* Compare *T&C* 3.15, 22–36 (emphasis added):

> *Ye* Joves first to thilke effectes glade,
>
> . . .
>
> *Ye* fierse Mars apaisen of his ire,
> And as yow list, *ye* maken hertes digne;
> Algates hem that *ye* wol sette a-fyre,
> They dreden shame, and vices they resygne;
> *Ye* do hem corteys be, fresshe and benigne;
> And heighe or lowe, after a wight entendeth,
> The joies that he hath, youre myght him sendeth.

387–88 *us beestes*. Skeat (p. 457) traces the power that governs beasts and heavenly bodies to Boethian Love controlling the universe (*Cons*. 2. m. 8).

390 *Yet al thynge desyreth ye wern . . . wele.* Skeat emends *wele* to *wol* and suggests: "Read *werne* (refuse) and *wol* (will) — 'yet all things desire that you should refuse help to no one who is willing to do as you direct him'" (p. 457).

396–97 *sythen . . . by an impossyble*. Jellech suggests that *contyngent, impossyble*, and *proposycion* are "terms from the vocabulary of the schoolmen" (p. 181). See Conley (1964). "The suggestion of future contingency anticipates the Anselmian discussion of God's providence in Book 3" (p. 181).

404–06 *Also false wordes . . . sothnesse*. Compare *HF* 2108–09: "Thus saugh I fals and soth compound / Togeder fle for oo tydynge"; see further Strohm (1989), p. 76.

407 *no*. Th: *uo*. Leyerle's emendation.

414 *maner*. Skeat emends to *maneres*.

418 *Acrisyus*. Skeat notes: "Acrisius shut his daughter Danaë up in a tower, to keep her safe; nevertheless she became the mother of Perseus, who afterwards killed Acrisius accidentally" (p. 457).

423 *so*. Skeat emends to *to*.

424–25 Lady Love's defense of Divine Providence for permitting evil to function on earth is similar to Lady philosophy's argument in *Cons*. Bks 4 and 5.

426 *welny people . . . efte*. Skeat emends to *wel ny [al] people . . . ofte*. Jellech glosses as "well-nigh." Leyerle claims that "*welny* is a form, well recorded in ME, of *villainy*, 'insult, indignity, discredit,' and may be kept" (p. 252), but he cites no sources. Another possibility might be some form of *wilne*, thus "willful," "desirous," or "obstinate." "Villainous" is probably the likeliest sense, though in a less perjorative implication than one would associate with the term in modern usage — i.e., deceitful, but without the twirling of moustaches.

431 *and who that . . . I helpen*. See Matthew 10.22: "he that shall persevere unto the end, he shall be saved."

432 *into blysse to wende*. Skeat supplies *don* before *blysse* and translates: "and I will cause him to come to bliss, as being one of my own servants." He then rewrites the syntax in what follows: *As [in] marcial doing in Grece, who was ycrowned? By god, nat the strongest . . . .* (p. 22).

433–34 *rathest come . . . play lest*. See 2 Timothy 4:7: "I have fought a good fight, I have finished my course, I have kept the faith."

435 Skeat inserts *[and]* before *therin* and *[is]* before *redy*.

436 *and into water*. Skeat: "and jumps into the water and immediately comes up to breathe, like an unsuccessful diver" (p. 457). But Leyerle objects and offers the alternative *repriseth*, "withdraws," as a possible emendation of *respireth* (p. 252).

441 *this countré*. Skeat: "a common saying"; see *T&C* 2.28, 42 (p. 457).

443 *healed with his hele*. Skeat (p. 457) and Jellech (p. 186) cite *HF*, line 290, as a parallel.

betwixe two thynges lyche. Compare *T&C* 3.404–6:

"Departe it so, for wyde-wher is wist
How that ther is diversite requered
Bytwixen thynges like, as I have lered."

446 *dyversyté cometh in by the contrarious malyce*. See St. Augustine, *City of God* 16.11.

448 *lawes*. Skeat emends to *lawe*.

450 *and to what*. Skeat emends to *and [founden] to what*.

455 *lawe of kynde*. Leyerle: "The gist of Love's legal argument as it applies to Usk's situation, is that the ordinance by which Usk was imprisoned is mere *mannes lawe* (*lex positiva*), which should be *underputte*, 'subordinated' to the law of Love, *lex naturalis*, which Usk professed to be following in those actions for which he was condemned" (p. 254).

462 *exployte*. Skeat: *exployte[s]*.

474 *thin*. Th: *than*. Leyerle's emendation.

475 *nothyng undertaketh . . . nothyng acheveth*. The proverb is common, as Leyerle observes (p. 256), but, as he also notes, and I would, too, Chaucer uses it twice in *T&C* (2.807–08; 5.784).

480 *a*. "have" (as before).

480–85 *I have this seven yere . . . fayled*. Genesis 29.17–30. Jellech notes that later exegetes read the story of Rachel and Leah in terms of the active life and the contemplative life, citing e.g., Richard of St. Victor, *Liber Exceptionum*, pp. 240–42; Usk, she observes, has adapted the "Biblical account to his own purposes, but his mode of interpreting it seems to show he was drawing on patristic concepts" (p. 190). Perhaps the most memorable adaptation of the story in medieval literature is Dante's, in *Purgatorio*, in the relationship between Matelda and Beatrice (*Purg.* 27.100–08); see also the commentary in Singleton 2.2, p. 659.

481 *Lya*, Leah. See Genesis 29.17.

484 *wepe with Rachel.* See Matthew 2.18.

485 *sone.* Skeat emends to *[come] sone*, which makes good sense; Leyerle concurs with Skeat. I have imagined *come* to be implicit in *sone*, though such an ellipsis perhaps stretches credibility too far.

486–87 *eyght yere: this eighteth mowe . . . of travayle.* Skeat emends *eyght* to *eight[eth]* needlessly (p. 458). See Chaucer's *BD*, line 37, where *eight* also means *eighth.* That Usk had this specific passage from Chaucer in mind in constructing his riddle on eight and reward through the agency of a lady (*the good faire White*, who has gone to her reward, though the narrator's *boote*, line 38, is no nearer in *BD*; and, in Usk, for Margarite, *kynrest and masseday* — a form of reward), see Russell A. Peck, "Theme and Number in Chaucer's *Book of the Duchess*," in *Silent Poetry*, ed. Alastair Fowler (London: Routledge & Kegan Paul, 1970), pp. 98–99. *Eight* is the number of eternity, marking the eighth sphere of the fixed stars, beyond the seven moving spheres. It is the Easter number (the *dies octavus*, the new beginning after Christ's seven days of labor in Jerusalem) and the number of Resurrection (first day after the Jewish Sabbath, Matthew 28.1, Mark 16.2, 9, Luke 24.1, John 20.1); likewise it is affiliated with massday (where the eighth day after seven becomes one again), baptism (octagonal font), Christ's circumcision marking His presentation into His new life (Luke 2.21), the Transfiguration (Luke 9.28) at the end of the eighth day of Jesus's ministry preaching by the Sea of Galilee, Christ's revelation to Thomas (John 20.26), the New Jerusalem and thus justice in the eighth age, after time ceases to be. It is a number of Pentecost (the eighth day after a week of weeks), hence a sign of new beginning, grace, and reward; and (apart from one) as the only cube in the decad, a sign of justice and justification. On the general numerological properties of eight, see Russell A. Peck, "Number as Cosmic Language," in *Essays in the Numerical Criticism of Medieval Literature*, ed. Caroline D. Eckhardt (Lewisburg: Bucknell University Press, 1980), p. 62; also Fowler, p. 53, and Meyer, p. 140.

486 *kynrest*. The *MED* offers "a general cessation of work, a holiday with particular reference to the ancient Jewish sabbatical year"; however, the only citation is this passage in *TL*. See numerological explanation in the previous note.

488–90 Thynne reduplicates *in this case . . .," quod she*, which I have deleted. Skeat does not acknowledge the dittography.

493 *the conysance of my lyvery*. On the nature of livery — "Liveried retainers were clad in a distinctive uniform that marked them out as the men of a particular lord" (Hicks, p. 63) — and its political importance in late Middle English culture, see, in addition to Hicks (pp. 63–65), Horrox (p. 68) and Strohm, "The Literature of Livery" (1992, pp. 179–85) in *Hochon's Arrow*.

498–99 *ben worshyp*. Skeat emends to *ben [to] worship[pe]*; Leyerle concurs.

501 *a bridge*. Skeat glosses: "to serve by way of retreat for such as trust them" (p. 458).

wolves. "destroyers"; here meant as a complimentary epithet.

503–05 *Jupiter . . . Rome is nowe stondyng*. Skeat: "This idea, of Jupiter's promotion, from being a bull, to being the mate of Europa, is extremely odd; still more so is that of the promotion of Aeneas from being in hell" (p. 458). I can find no source for this passage either. In my opinion, though, here as elsewhere (see, e.g., line 541), Usk may be inventing images for his own particular use.

504 *lowest degré*. Skeat observes: "not true, as Caesar's father was praetor, and his aunt married Marius" (p. 458). But compare *CT* VII.2671–73:

By wisedom, manhede, and by greet labour,
From humble bed to roial magestee
Up roos he Julius, the conquerour.

See, further, Suetonius (p. 34):

> Caesar's first home was a modest house . . . one story goes, he found certain features in [a house he built] to his dislike, so that, although poor at the time and heavily in debt, he tore the whole place down.

507 *that their jangles*. Th: *that are their janghes*. Skeat emends: *that [suche] are their jangles*. Leyerle disagrees and proposes "*jang[linge]s* for *jangles is*. The sense would be as follows: 'their pratings are not to count worth a blade of cress to your disadvantage'" (p. 258).

510 *fame*. Skeat emends to *[en]fame* so that the form corresponds with lines 512 and 513. Jellech and Leyerle concur.

516–17 *thy frende to thee*. Skeat emends: *they frende [is] to the*. Jellech and Leyerle concur.

517 *false kyssyng*. See Proverbs 27.6: "Better are the wounds of a friend, than the deceitful kisses of an enemy."

518 *maketh suche*. Skeat emends: *maketh [voyd] suche*. Jellech concurs; Leyerle emends *maketh* to *ma[t]eth*.

534–35 *by goodnesse or enfamé*. Th: *or by goodnesse enfame*. Skeat's emendation, followed by Jellech and Leyerle.

535 *For every*. Skeat emends *For [of] every*, which is more graceful (parallel), though not necessary.

541 *Zedeoreys* (or *ȝedeoreys*). Skeat notes that he "can find nothing resembling this strange name, nor any trace of its owner's dealings with Hannibal" (p. 458). I can find nothing either. Bressie argues that "Antiochus the Great is certainly meant. See Usk's probable source, Higden's *Polychronicon*, IV, 88–92" (p. 23). But it is not beyond possibility, in my opinion, that, given the personal remarks that follow, Usk invented this character and this "episode" in Roman history as a parallel to his own historical situation: for a while he was on Northampton's side, then he turned against

Northampton (to side with Brembre), and "by his wytte after was [Northampton] discomfyted" — only, as we know in hindsight, the wheel turned yet once more and crushed Usk. But see Leyerle who, following Bressie, writes: "The actions of Antiochus fit the reference in the *Testament* . . .: the name Antiochus was probably lost and his title, *Syria rex*, corrupted in transmission to the one word, *ȝedioreys*, which was then taken as his name" (p. 260).

547 *exitours*. Skeat: *ex[c]itours*.

558 *tho teeres lasshed*. Skeat emends to *tho [the] teres [that] lasshed*, thus changing *tho* from "those" to "though" and altering the syntax.

563 *Lachases*. See *T&C* 5.6–7: "shal dwellen in pyne / Til Lachesis his threed no lenger twyne." Lachesis is one of the three Fates in classical mythology, the others being Clotho and Atropos, who "spin" the thread of an individual's life. Like Boethius, Usk seems to be writing from prison, cognizant of the harm that awaits him. His extended defense of his behavior is not unlike that of Boethius, *Cons.* I. pr. 4, which is one of the longest sections in the *Consolation*. Reference to those who imprisoned him as *Senatoures* effects a similar circumstance to that of Boethius, who was betrayed by the Roman Senate.

564 *And ever I was sought*. Bressie (p. 21) suggests that Usk's defense proper begins here. Jellech offers the following paraphrase of the reasons Usk gives for changing sides (Jellech, p. 200, lines 564 through line 592):

> He was pressed to confess so that he would have his life and freedom. / He considered it his duty to help the city. / His soul would have been lost if he had died in falseness. / He did not deserve hatred except insofar as he upheld the errors of the Northampton group and kept their secrets. / All the Northampton faction were prejudiced against their opponents, so that they created broils in order to destroy them. / If he had not exposed the faction, the peace of the city of London, which he dearly loved, would have been broken. / Peace is enjoined on us by Scripture and the example of history.

See, further, Appendix 2 below.

568 *helpe to ben saved*. Jellech understands *to ben saved* as "ought to do so," the sense being that "any man who can legitimately help the commonalty to be saved ought to

do so" (p. 201). Skeat emends *helpe* to *wele*. I punctuate with a dash to suggest a broken thought that can easily be completed — i.e., "he ought to do so."

583ff. *perfyte peace*. See John 14.27 on the passing of the peace. Jellech notes that Dante in the *Monarchia*, I.4, also remarks: "'Peace be with you' was the salutation of the one who was the salvation of man. . . . And also his disciples and among them Paul, saw fit to preserve this custom" (p. 202).

584–89 *This peace . . . one body we shulde perfourme*. Jellech notes that Dante, *Monarchia*, I.4, "adduces the same example of the angel's song at Christ's nativity to argue that peace is necessary for society's perfection" (p. 202).

585 *Testament*. The reader should notice that Usk here uses the same word as figures in the title of his book — he does not use "covenant" or "pact," for example, but the word, "testament," that aligns his book with the Savior's benediction.

590 *Athenes*. "Athene was the goddess who maintained the authority of law and order, and in this sense was 'a god of peace.' But she was certainly also a goddess of battles" (Skeat, p. 459). Jellech observes that "the specific notions here of Athena as a god and as an upholder of peace do not have any traceable origin. The tradition seems to have emphasized Athens as a center of art and learning" (p. 203). But see also Downing, p. 490:

> [Athena's] central concern is the well-being of the community. "Cities are," it was said, "the gifts of Athena." She nurtures the children on whom the city's future depends and encourages its citizens in the arts and crafts so integral to civilized existence.

From such a perspective, it is not difficult to imagine Athena as "god of peace."

592 *certayne poyntes*. Jellech notes that several of these *poyntes* follow rather closely the articles declared in Usk's *Appeal*. See Appendix 2 below.

593 *thilke persones*. I.e., members of the Northampton faction.

593–95 *drawen to . . . prudence*. Jellech compares these lines with the Appeal: "tho they drewe to hem many craftes & mochel smale people that konne non skyl of governance ne of god conseyl" (p. 204). See Appendix 2, lines 149–50.

597–607 *whiche," quod they, "... and al other good menynges*. Jellech points out that the point of view of this speech is that of Northampton and his followers.

598–99 *and auctorité of execucion by comen election*. Jellech observes: "That is, election of the Common Council by crafts instead of by wards as in the past. This was one of the issues created by Northampton" (p. 204).

599–601 *for we, out ... in such subjection*. Jellech compares *Appeal*: "& yt was seide thus to the poeple that ever the grete men wolden have the poeple be oppression in lowe degree" (p. 205). See Appendix 2, lines 50–51.

605–07 *There ben cytezens ... good menynges*. Jellech: "The reference is to charges made by John More, sheriff under Northampton, that Sir John Philipot had borrowed money from the city during his mayoralty and never repaid it; see *Appeal* [Appendix 2, lines 54–59]. Other men were to be charged with usury, under a patent to chastise usurers, and so be discredited and exiled from the city, leaving Northampton's men free in charge" (p. 205). See *Appeal*, Appendix 2, lines 75–91.

608 *the mighty senatoures*. I.e., the leaders of the victuallers, such as Sir William Walworth, Sir John Philipot, and Sir Nicholas Brembre (Jellech, p. 206).

609–10 *free election*. Skeat adds *[was mad]* after *free eleccion* and *[that]* before *for greet*, which alters the sense needlessly. Usk's point is that the manipulated mob, by its clamorous voice, in effect controls the vote. As Leyerle notes (p. 264), "*that free election* [is] in apposition to *it* and [is the] subject of *fel*."

609–14 *And so, lady, ... withouten reason*. Jellech suggests that Usk's evident purpose here is to say that the outcome of the election was against the dissidents, but some part of the passage has been lost (p. 206). She reads the sense of the passage to be:

> So, when the free election was held, by clamor of many people because of great injury from misgovernance, they (i.e., Northampton and his associates) remained so steadfast in their choice that they underwent every kind of fate rather than allow the hated regimen to rule. Nevertheless, many of the common mass, who have consideration only to their wilful desires, without reason, held to the contrary (i.e., the Northampton faction lost their popular following).

611 *face*. Skeat (p. 459) emends to *fate*, observing, "We must read *fate*, not *face*; the confusion between *c* and *t* is endless." But *every maner face*, as sign of fickleness, makes good sense, given Usk's appeal against the clamorous mob. Jellech emends to *fate* (p. 206), as does Leyerle too (p. 43).

614 *thylke governour*. I.e., John de Northampton (Jellech, p. 207).

614–15 *faynynge toforne his undoynge for misrule in his tyme*. I.e., "pretending, before his undoing, on account of misrule in his time [i.e., inventing misrule as an excuse], arranged to have."

615–16 *shope . . . ben chosen*. Jellech compares *Appeal*, where Usk relates that Northampton sent a delegation, Usk amongst them, to the Duke of Lancaster asking him for a royal writ proclaiming a new election. They were refused. See Appendix 2, lines 118–33.

616 *rore have*. Skeat: *rore [to] have*, which is okay too.

617–20 *These thynges . . . furthered and holde*. Jellech observes: "The clause *these thynges . . . to the people* seems to be an ablative absolute, meaning 'when these things were made known among the princes and opened to the people, then there was brought about an improvement, with the result that every degree . . . 'etc." (p. 207).

621 *their moste soverayne juge*. I.e., the king.

632 *my selven apparaylen*. I would expand to *my selven [, how they] apparaylen*.

648 *out of denwere*. Leyerle solves this crux: "The form is a nonce spelling of ME *denier*, 'denial, refusal,' *MED* 2. The *MED* takes *denier* to be from OF *deniïer*, a variant of *denoiier*; Usk's spelling reflects the latter word with the *oi* represented by *w*. The phrase *out of denwere* thus means beyond 'denial'" (p. 256).

651 *submytten*. Skeat: *submitted*.

652 *But nowe than the false fame*. With Leyerle (p. 256) I agree that here *TL* participates directly in the medieval tradition of fame (Leyerle cites *Aeneid* 4.172ff. and Chaucer's *HF* 349–50); see, further, my Introduction, Section vi f, page 25, note 44.

668–69 *the prise leaned on thy syde*. Leyerle: "The sense is, 'You spoke truth because your adversaries have affirmed your words [by their refusal to join combat]. Even if you had lied [in the affirmations you had offered to prove by combat], they are still discomfitted. The lever leaned on your side so that fame will hold down infamy.' The image in the last sentence is of a *prise*, 'lever,' that raises a thing at one end while pressing down on the other. The final sentence in the passage is Love's commentary on the words *every wight* [line 666]. The reference of *he* . . . [line 669] is to *wight* in line [666]; *bringe up* means 'to invent or tell lies,' *MED* 6(b): 'He will be lying in no way'" (p. 266).

672 *without a stroke or fighting*. Schaar suggests the meaning to be: "without a single stroke"; the right reading, thus, must be: *without a stroke of fighting* (p. 10).

679 *maysters*. Th: *maystresse*. Jellech's emendation (p. 214), with which I concur.

685 *that sacrament of swearyng*. Jellech suggests that "to charge by oath" merely means "to swear," or "to pledge" (*MED* 10a), not "to be under oath." The suggestion here seems to be that Usk "was not perjured or forsworn by his oath — presumably the one binding him to Northampton, because it lacked either truth, judgment, or righteousness. It was on account of his being thought disloyal to Northampton and his friends that Usk was considered by his fellow citizens to have been unkind and unnatural. The issue is . . . one of social pressure and custom" (p. 215).

688 *trewe jugement*. Skeat argues that *trewe* is an error for *trewthe*; the statement is copied from Jeremiah 4.2: "Et iurabis . . . in veritate, et in iudicio, et in justitia" [And you shall swear . . . in truth, and in judgment, and in justice] (p. 460). So in line 693, we have *in jugement in trouth, and rightwisenesse*; and in lines 690–91, *for ofte tymes a man, to saye sothe, but jugement and justyce folowe, he is forsworne*.

691 *Herodes*. Herod swore to give Salome whatever she asked for. Her request was for the head of John the Baptist. See Matthew 14.7. Skeat inserts *[he]* before *dampned*.

692–93 *Also, to saye truthe . . . to sayne.* Skeat paraphrases: "it is sometimes forbidden to say truth rightfully — except in a trial — because all truths are not to be disclosed" (p. 460).

695 *that worde*. Skeat suggests Tobit 3.6: "expedit mihi mori magis quam vivere" [for it is better for me to die, than to live] (p. 460).

696 *fame*. Skeat: *[en]fame*, followed by Jellech and Leyerle.

702 *sklaundrynge*. Th: *sklaundynge*. Emended by all.

704 *shulden*. Skeat: *[they] shulden.*

706 *demest, therin thy selfe*. See Romans 2.1 — "For wherein thou judgest another, thou condemnest thyself."

728 *commens*. Possibly, a truncation of *commensal*, "sustenance" ("?as contributed by or to a community or group of people" — see the *MED* C, p. 446 "communes," branch 4).

729 *Selande*. Zealand (Zeeland) the southwesternmost province of the Netherlands, almost, to the naked eye, due east of London, across the Channel. Skeat suggests the port of Middleburg, in the isle of Walcheren: "The reference must be to some companions of the author who had fled to Zealand to be out of the way of prosecution" (p. 460). See, further, Leyerle, pp. 268–69.

730–31 *Yet, pardye, . . . renter*. Jellech: "Love's sardonic accusation is that Usk's associates took money set aside by his superiors for his expenses so he had to pay out of his own pocket. Usk was their 'renter' or 'landlord'" (p. 219).

732–33 *neyther . . . for to have*. Skeat places a semicolon after *unkyndnesse*, where Thynne prints a virgule (slash). Jellech rearranges the virgule to produce a "superior reading which needs no explanation [*neyther the ne them selfe myghten helpe/ of unkyndnesse nowe they beare the name. . .*]. *Unkyndnesse* or unnatural disloyalty seems to have been one of the main accusations made against Usk" (p. 220). I have followed Jellech.

736 *helest*. Skeat emends to *hele[de]st*. Jellech and Leyerle concur.

740 *Efte*. Th: *Ofte*. Skeat's emendation which Jellech and Leyerle support. Jellech writes: "*Ofte* in this position, [is] clearly an error, both in what the sense of the passage calls for [i.e., *Efte*] and in failing to conform to the acrostic" (p. 221). See Introduction, iii c.

sterne me these. Skeat: *steren me [with] these*. Jellech and Leyerle concur.

748 *flocke*. See Matthew 18.12.

751 *but in hoole*. Th: *but hoole*. Skeat's emendation, followed by Leyerle, but not Jellech. The story of Lot's life is found in Genesis 19.

758–59 *in their mouthes . . . habundaunce of the herte*. See Matthew 12.34.

759 *stones*. Th: *stones stones*. Emended by all.

763 *use Jacobes wordes*. Skeat suggests an allusion to the conciliatory conduct of Jacob towards Esau (Genesis 33.8, 10, 11): "Similarly the author is to be patient, and to say 'I will endure my lady's wrath, which I have deserved,' etc." (p. 461).

768 *shul*. Skeat: *[she] shul*. But no emendation is necessary. Headless clauses are not uncommon in ME usage.

768–70 *For ryght . . . commended*. Jellech notes that Skeat inserted "is" in front of *commended* and suggested that Thynne's *his* (line 768) might be an error for "her" (p. 224). Schaar rejected on paleographical grounds the possibility of mistaking *his* for "her" and suggested that Thynne's words *at his* were a misreading of a ms. "alle is." But, Jellech concludes "a misreading of *a t h* for 'alle' is as hard to support paleographically as Skeat's proposal. If we knew the origin of the saying we could perhaps make an intelligent emendation. I have left the sentence in its imperfect state" (p. 224) But although I am insecure about the "origin" of the phrase, I do think we should consider the remarkable similarity between this passage and the climax of the great alliterative poem *Patience*, when God speaks to Jonah and says "For he þat is to rakel to renden his cloþes / Mot efte sitte wiþ more unsounde to sewe hem togeder" (lines 526–27). Here the counsel is to patience — "don't rip up your clothes in a fit of pique." We might think of the sentence in *TL*, with the aid of the idea in *Patience*, as meaning something like: "For just as you tear your clothes in plain sight [of God], having reason to do so because of your error, so openly to repair them at his, God's, worship, without further reproof, is [to be] commended."

769 *at*. Schaar would emend to *alle*.

771–72 *so good savour . . causeth*. Skeat emended Thynne's *al errour* to *of errour* and thus omitted *distroyeng* as a gloss on *forgoyng*, though he noted that the terms are not synonymous. He glosses *forgoyng* as "abandonment." Jellech assumes that "*Forgoyng* and *distroyeng* do have overlapping meanings, in that sin or error can be both avoided and destroyed, and Usk's original phrase, now hopelessly corrupt, probably read, 'good savour to forgoyng and distroyeng of errour.' Skeat's omission of *distroyeng*, as a gloss, is inexcusable. There are no other glosses, there is apparently no one who could have made one, and no reason to gloss the not obscure word *forgoyng*" (p. 224). Although Jellech's sharp tone is perhaps deplorable, her position is certainly sound and fundamental, given the corruption of the text of *TL*: there really is no evidence of glossing or any other form of interpolation in *TL*, and so much needs to be duly recorded for the reader to know what editorial decisions are necessary.

774–75 *every thynges contrary in kynde*. On this very ancient idea, which I have called "epistemology by contraries" (Shoaf [1989], pp. 22–24), see, among many possible examples, *T&C* 1.637: "'By his contrarie is every thyng declared.'" Its origin is ultimately Platonic and neo-Platonic; a very good example can be found in *City of God* 11.18.

780 *Adam*. See Genesis 3.6.

781 *Noe*. See Genesis 9.21.

782 *Lothe*. See Genesis 19.35.

782 *Abraham.* See Genesis 22.1.

783 *Davydes.* See II Samuel 11.2–15.

784 *Hector.* Skeat notes that Hector, according to Guido delle Colonne in his *Destruction of Troy*, gave counsel against going to war with the Greeks, but was overborne by Paris (p. 461).

788 *He that is stylle.* In *Proverbia Sententiaeque Latinitatis Medii Aevi*, Walther records as number 24843a "Qui tacet, consentire videtur" (Part 4, *Q-Sil*, p. 291).

792–93 *howe necessary was Adams synne.* Skeat (p. 461) sees an allusion to the canticle "Exultet" sung upon Easter Eve, in the *Sarum Missal* (p. 118), "O certe necessarium Ade peccatum" [O truly necessary sin of Adam (p. 272 in the *Sarum Missal in English*)]. Commonly known as the *felix culpa* ("fortunate fall," "happy guilt" [*Sarum Missal in English*, p. 272, as well]), this idea is widespread in the Middle Ages and Renaissance — had Adam not fallen, Christ would not have been born God incarnate; for bibliography, see Shoaf (1993), p. 199n71.

793 *Salomon.* See II Samuel 12.24, on the conceiving and birth of Solomon.

809 *at the hardest suche fame into.* Jellech (p. 228) emends to *at the farthest . . . is.*

814 *reason hyndred.* Schaar emends *reason* to *renoun*: "*Reson* is not the proper word here; the corresponding passage in Chaucer's *Boece* (II, p. VII, 64 ff.) reads:

> *(to the whiche naciouns . . .) nat only the names of singuler men ne may nat strecchen, but eek the fame of citees ne may nat strecchen.*

The Latin text gives:

> *ad quas (nationes) . . . non modo fama hominum singulorum, sed ne urbium quidem peruenire queat.* (lines 26 ff)

The original reading of our passage, then, seems to be . . . *but also citees and realmes of prosperité ben letted to be knowe, and their renoun hindred*" (p. 12).

818 *London.* Skeat notes that *London* is substituted for "Rome" in Chaucer's *Boece* (p. 461), further evidence to suggest that Usk is working from Chaucer's translation, rather than the Latin.

819 *praysen . . . lacken.* Here and elsewhere (e.g., Book 2, line 742; Book 3, lines 210–11), Usk uses the ancient formula, *laudando et vituperando* ("praising and blaming"), that derives from epideictic rhetoric (see Curtius, p. 69n and p. 182). Although space prohibits a lengthy demonstration, I want nonetheless to register here my sense that Usk's reliance on this rhetorical tradition is one key to understanding *TL*, especially where the issue of fame is concerned (see the note to Book 1, line 652).

830 *ofte.* For Skeat *ofte* is a misprint for *of the*; Jellech and Leyerle concur.

834 *healed.* Conceivably the term is a corruption of *heilen* as a salutation of praise, as one might hope of rumors. Or perhaps it is a figurative form of *helen*, an agricultural metaphor for "planted," as in the "sowing" or "broadcasting" of seed. Or perhaps it is akin to a medieval metaphor for cure, i.e., "improved." Skeat says "*heled* (lit. hidden) is quite inadmissible; the right reading is probably *deled*, i.e., dealt round" (p. 462). Jellech proposes *heard*, "but the case is uncertain," she says (p. 230). Leyerle follows Skeat.

838–39 *for werkes of vertue asketh.* Th: *of werkes of vertue asketh.* Skeat emends to: *of vertue. [Trewly, vertue] asketh.*

849 *leneth.* Skeat emends to *leveth*, "cease." Jellech and Leyerle concur.

854 *olde proverbe.* Skeat compares the form of the proverb to Hazlitt's "Who-so heweth over-high, / The chips will fall in his eye." See also Gower, *CA* 1.1917–18; and Stevenson 57.1.

856 *ere.* Th: *are.* Skeat emends to *that.* I propose *ere* (before).

864–65 See *Boece* I. pr. 4. 260–62, where the saying is attributed to Pythagoras.

886–87 *I sette now the hardest*. Leyerle (p. 279) notes a similarity with *T&C* 2.367, "I sette the worste" (Pandarus to Criseyde).

891–92 *in this persone*. Skeat suggests *on this persone*, but Schaar notes, "the passage is still not in order. Love is continually speaking to the prisoner, and we cannot avoid reading [. . .] *thilk Margarite, that no routh had on thy persone* etc." (p. 12). Leyerle has *in th[y] persone*.

897 *For she hath hem*. Leyerle (pp. 280–81) argues at length that a dislocation of text has occurred here. His re-arrangement yields:

> shal beno*mm*en from thylke perle/ al the vertues that firste here were taken/ for she hath hem forfeyted/ by that on the my seruaunt in thy lyue she wolde not suffre to worche al vertues with order whiche to me was ordayned/ sothely none age/ none ouertournynge tyme/ but withdrawen/ by might of the hygh bodyes: Why than shuldest thou wene so any more. And if the lyste to loke vpon the lawe**<334vb>** **<335ra>** of kynde/ and hytherto had no tyme ne power to chaunge the weddyng/ ne the knotte to vnbynde of two hertes thorowe one assent in my presence/ togyther accorden to endure tyl dethe hem departe.

He then punctuates, heavily, to the following sense (p. 60):

> shal ben[i]men from thylke perle al the vertues that firste her were taken, for she hath hem forfeyted by that on the, my servaunt, in thy lyve, she wolde not suffre to worche al vertues [with order whiche to me was ordayned. Sothely none age, none ouertournynge but] withdrawen by might of the hygh bodyes. Why, than, shuldest thou wene so any more, and, if the lyste to loke upon the lawe of kynde, and hyt herto had no tyme ne power to chaunge the weddyng, ne the knotte to unbynde of two hertes thorowe one assent in my presence togyther accorden to enduren tyl dethe hem departe?

The reader can compare my own construction (next note) and quickly appreciate the staggering difficulty of "editing" *TL*.

898 *withdrawen by might*. Understand "all those virtues withdrawn (see *benommen*, line 896), if she so behaves, by might . . . etc."

899 *Why than shuldest.* Jellech: "That is, why should Usk any longer fear that he is loving above his degree?" (p. 238).

902 *hertes thorowe.* Skeat: *hertes [that] thorowe.*

905–06 *Do waye, do waye . . . nothyng of this.* Compare *T&C* 2.890–04 (emphasis added):

"But wene ye that every wrecche woot
The parfite blisse of love? Why, nay, iwys!
They wenen all be love, if oon be hoot.
Do wey, do wey, they woot no thyng of this!''

906 *consente of two hertes alone.* On the role of consent in marriage in the Middle Ages, see Baldwin, pp. 6–7, 75–76.

920 *haven the.* Skeat: *haven [by] the*, followed by Leyerle.

922 *He is.* Th: *he his.* Skeat's emendation, followed by Jellech and Leyerle.

925 *they.* Th: *thy.* Skeat's emendation, followed by Jellech and Leyerle.

926 *prophete.* David, in Psalm 95.5: "For all the gods of the Gentiles are devils."

929 *nowe reasonable.* Skeat: *now [art thou a] resonable*, followed by Leyerle.

936 *abjection.* Skeat: *objeccion*, followed by Jellech.

937 *last objection.* I.e., his poverty, see chapter 3, lines 331–32.

960–61 *Alas, thou that knyttest . . . amenden these defautes?* Compare *Boece* I. m 5.1–2, 31–35.

974 *and yet dyddest.* Skeat inserted "before that" in front of *any thing*, but, as Jellech observes, "the mere addition *that* [after *any thing*], possibly omitted by the printer by

repetition of *true were* in the following line, completes the meaning; i.e., 'you performed in that office by advice of superiors all the business that was transacted.'" (p. 245).

975 *ended*. Leyerle emends to *[ne]ded* (p. 284).

1012–15 Leyerle construes the sense as follows: "He (that false friend) was never separated easily from fair fortune." The point is that a false friend follows fortune. No emendation is needed. The next sentence follows the same logic, but is elliptical in sense. "Your own good (i.e., worldly adversity), therefore, leaves it (i.e., what is properly yours) yet with you" (p. 286).

1014 *never from that*. Schaar emends to *ever from thee*.

1020 *if that Margarite denyeth*. Schaar: "it is very probable that there is a simple transposition of letters, and that the correct reading is: *And if that Margarite deyneth now nat to suffre her vertues shyne to thee-wardes with spredinge bemes* etc. *Deynen*, moreover, is a word that exactly fits in with the idea of the unresponsive lady, the standard figure of Courtly Love" (p. 13).

1024 *lette us syngen*. Skeat suggests an imitation of the metres in Boethius, "which break the prose part of the treatise at frequent intervals" (p. 463).

Book 2

1 *Very*. Skeat identifies an acrostic in the first letters of initial words in the several chapters of Book II. In the Thynne text I have used a boldface font to represent what in the original are large block letters. Skeat observes,

> The initials of the fourteen Chapters in this Book give the words: VIRTW HAVE MERCI. Thynne has not preserved the right division, but makes *fifteen* chapters, giving the words: VIRTW HAVE MC*T*RCI. I have set this right, by making Chapter XI begin with 'Every.' [But see Leyerle, at the note to Book 2, line 1048.] Thynne makes Chapter XI begin with 'Certayn' [below, line 1048], and another Chapter begin with

'Trewly' [below, line 1127]. This cannot be right . . . the Chapter thus beginning would have the unusually small number of 57 lines. Chapter I really forms a Prologue to the Second Book [see Minnis, (1988), pp. 163–64], interrupting our progress. At the end of Book I we are told that Love is about to sing, but her song begins with Chapter II. Hence this first Chapter must be regarded as a digression, in which the author reviews what has gone before . . . and anticipates what is to come." (p. 463)

5 *chaungyng of the lyft syde to the ryght halve*. Jellech: "Although no direct reference is made, the allusion is to the turning of Fortune's wheel, so often iconographically represented as having on one side man's rising to prosperity and on the other his fall. Note this passage from the *Ayenbite of Inwyt*, ed. Richard Morris, EETS o.s. 23, p. 181:

> Efter þise uiȝtinge [fighting] comþ þe worlde and dame fortune mid al hare hueȝel [wheel]/ þet asayleþ þane man a riȝt half and a left half /. . . ." (p. 251)

7 *Of.* Th: *O*. My emendation.

wrongful steeryng. Skeat emends silently to *wonderful steering*.

10ff. *Grevously God wotte*. Schaar takes the passage to refer to Richard II. This "badly damaged passage might be restored as follows:

> Grevously, god wot, have I suffred a greet throwe that the Romayne emperour, which in unité of love shulde acorde with every other, <the> cause of <love> to avaunce, <this cause dereth>; and namely, sithe this empyre <nedeth> to be corrected of so many sectes in heresies of faith, of service, o<f> rule in loves religion.
>
> Through his very weakness, the monarch harms the cause of love by giving free rein to the powers of discord; only vigorous measures against these would conform with the spirit of love . . ." (pp. 14–15).

Skeat notes that there is "clearly much corruption in this unintelligible and imperfect sentence." The reference to "the Roman emperor" he calls "mysterious." Be that as it may, I agree with Jellech's rejection (p. 252) of Schaar's emendation and, like her, leave the passage as it is in Thynne. I speculate that the allusion may be to Constantine, the "Romayne emperour" who could be said to have "this empyre . . . corrected of so many sectes in heresie of faith," but this is only speculation which at this time I cannot substantiate. Leyerle proposes an entirely different solution (pp. 289–90).

12–13 *to be corrected*. Skeat: *[nedeth] to be corrected.*

13 *of rule*. Th: *o rule*. Emended by all.

15ff. *that sayne love*. Jellech notes that the four misplaced loves listed here are equivalent to the false goods enumerated by Lady Philosophy in Boethius, *Cons*. 3. pr. 2: wealth, renown, honor, and power (p. 253).

23 *But*. Skeat: *But [of]*.

27 *but*. Skeat: *but [men]*.

28 *wo without ende*. Compare Isaiah 5.20.

38–45 *But I, lovers clerke . . . be enduced*. Again Leyerle proposes a re-arranging of the text (pp. 291–92):

> But I louers clerk in al my connyng and with al my mightes/ trewly I haue no suche grace in vertue of myracles/ ne for no discomfyte falsheedes/ suffyseth not auctorytes alone/ sythen that suche heretykes and maintaynours of falsytes./ with that auctorite misglosed by mannes reason/ to graunt shal be enduced. wherfore I wotte wel sythen that they ben men/ and reason is approued in hem/ the clowde of erroure hath her reason bewonde probable resons/ whiche that catchende wytte rightfully may not with sytte. By my trauaylynge studye I haue ordeyned hem

He then punctuates as follows (p. 72):

> But I, lovers clerke, in al my connyng and with al my mightes, trewly, I have no suche grace in vertue of myracles. Ne for [t]o discomfyte falshessed, suffyseth not auctorytes alone, sythen that suche heretykes and maintaynours of falsytes, [with that auctorie misglosed by mannes reason, to graunt shal be enduced.] Wherfore, I wotte wel, sythen that they ben men and reason is approved in hem, the clowde of erroure hath her reason bewonde. Probable resons, which that catchende wytte rightfully may not withsytte, by my travaylynge studye, I have ordeyned hem.

This solution might very possibly be correct.

40 *ne for no discomfyte*. Schaar would emend *no* to *to*, observing: "the error here is obvious and easily eliminated: *ne for to discomfit falsheedes*, *no* being an easy mistake after *ne*" (p. 15). Leyerle adopts this emendation.

41 *suche*. Skeat: *suche [arn].*

42 *the clowde of erroure*. Jellech cites Boethius, *Cons*. 1. pr. 2.6: "mortalium rerum nube" (p. 256). Chaucer translates: "the cloude of mortal thynges" (p. 399).

44 *with that*. Skeat: *whiche that.*

46 *Nowe gynneth my penne to quake*. Compare *T&C* 4.13–14 (emphasis added): "And now *my penne*, allas, with which I write, / *Quaketh* for drede of that I moste endite."

50 *Certes, me thynketh the sowne*. Skeat: *Certes, me thynketh, [of] the sowne.*

59 *faith hath no meryte of mede*. Skeat sees this as a translation of "Fides non habet meritum ubi humana racio prebet experimentum," as quoted in *PPl* B.10.256a (p. 464). Alford (p. 65), like Skeat, identifies this quotation as St. Gregory's: this is "Gregory's Homily 26 on the Gospels (*PL* 76, p. 1197), quoted in the first lesson at matins on the Sunday after Easter (*Brev*. 1, p. dcclx)." My own sense, therefore, is that the latter source is just as likely to be Usk's as is *Piers*; and I would caution against putting much store by Skeat's "as quoted in."

66 *love in hymselfe is the most*. Compare 1 Corinthians 13.13.

67 *The sede of suche springynge*. Matthew 15.13; Mark 4.26–29, 30–32.

70 *cockle*. cockle, tares. Skeat sees a possible reference to the Lollards, as "puns upon the words *Lollard* and *lolia* were very rife at this period" (p. 464). We should proceed with caution here, however; the pun is possible, certainly, but inferences from it about Usk's persuasions are risky just because such puns "were very rife" — i.e., such evidence is very general, hardly specific (see further *The Riverside Chaucer*, p. 863).

71–74 *Neverthelater . . . thilke name*. According to Schaar,

> The general structure and idea of the whole sentence shows that the meaning intended must be: although the name of love, by foolish and malicious people, is given to things which do not deserve it, this fact nevertheless shows that the worship of this name goes deep and is essential to man. The corrupt clause must conform with this idea; and, I think, no extensive operations are necessary to restore this sense to the passage, which presents some rather insidious errors:
>
> *Never-the-later, yet how-so-it-be that men clepe thilke thing preciousest in kynde, with many eke-names, that <to> other thinges they foule yeven the ilke noble name, it sheweth wel that in a maner men have a greet lykinge in worshippinge of thilke name.*
>
> A *to*, then, was dropped and *that* erroneously repeated; the last letter of an original *they* seems to have dropped out; and the easy substitution of *f* for *s* restores the author's reproach. *Thilke thing*, refers, then, to the before-mentioned *cockle*; 'although people call such a thing the most precious in Nature, with many nicknames, so that they shamefully give that noble name to other things, this clearly shows that in a way people have great liking in worshipping that name.' (pp. 15–16)

Leyerle (p. 73) offers the following construal of this difficult sentence: "Never-the-later, yet, howe-so it be that menne cleape thilke [li]kynge, preciousest in kynde, with many eke-names, [and] other thynges tha[n] the soule yeven the ylke noble name, it sheweth wel that in a maner men have a great lykynge in worshyppynge of thilke name."

72 *thynge*. Th: *kynge*, which makes a kind of sense, as if it were an appeal to Richard. Skeat makes the emendation, and Schaar's analysis makes sense too. But see Leyerle's conjecture, in the preceding note.

78–80 *Every thynge . . . his fynal cause*. Jellech "I have made no emendations in this passage, but the thought sequence is erratic. A possible source of the difficulty is the repetition of *Euery thynge* [line 78] and *euery thynge* [line 79]. Rearrangement of the phrases so as to merge the repeated 'every thing' might give a clearer reading: 'Aristotle supposeth that the acts of every thyng to whom is owande occasyon done as for his ende ben in a maner his fynal cause'" (p. 260).

80 *fynal cause*. I update Skeat's note. See *OED* C, p. 225, "cause," branch 4: "Final cause" is a technical term "introduced into philosophical language by the schoolmen as a translation of Aristotle's fourth cause . . . the end or purpose for which a thing is done, viewed as the cause of the act; *esp*. as applied in Natural Theology to the design, purpose, or end of the arrangements of the universe."

81 *fynally to thilke ende*. Skeat glosses: "is done with a view to that result."

92 *putteth*. Leyerle (p. 74) emends and punctuates as follows: "But who is that, in knowyng of the orders of heven, [p]utteth his resones in the erthe?"

97ff. Here Schaar argues for three pages (pp. 16–18) that Usk uses Alan of Lille as a source.

108 *wened*. I suggest *[is] wened* for sense.

109ff. *I have me withdrawe*. Jellech (p. 264) suggests that "Love's withdrawal from an evil and unloving mankind is similar to the departure of Astraea [Justice] in Ovid, *Metamorphoses* 1.149–50."

111–12 *These thynges me greven . . . passed gladnesse*. Jellech cites *Cons*. 2. pr. 4. 3–4 and *Boece* 2. pr. 4. 7–9.

113 *They that wolden maystries*. Leyerle proposes (p. 296) that "the literal sense is 'in that age those, who wished me to have sway, in proper time were lodged in heaven on high above the sphere of Saturn.' . . . The phrase *above Saturnes spere [sic]* may refer either to the circle of the fixed stars, or to the Empyrean beyond."

113–16 Schaar would repunctuate to differentiate "then" and "now":

> "Those who wanted power possess me. But then . . . they lived in Heaven; now, however etc." . . . The end of the passage seems also to have suffered some slight corruption. . . . we must read "and yet sayn some that they me have in celler with wyne shet" [—] "they say that with wine, they have locked up Love in their cellars." *Shed* is an easy error after *wyne*. (pp. 18–19)

116 *shet*. Th: *shed*. Schaar's emendation, followed by Jellech and Leyerle.

122 *Somtyme toforn the sonne in the seventh partie was smyten*. Jellech observes, "Skeat notes that *seventh* is possibly an error for 'third,' and the allusion derived from Revelations 8.12, 'percussa est tertia pars solis,' and it is not difficult to see how such an error might have come about. If the original manuscript has the numeral 'iij' there would have been three strokes; if the number was not clear to the editor or printer, he may have read 'vij.' However, I have not made the change" (p. 266). Leyerle does make the change. Further confirmation of Skeat's speculation derives from the gloss on Revelations 8.12 in Hugh of St. Cher (7, fol. 392^v), for example, where the passage is interpreted in terms of reprobate clergy, lacking in charity; just so, a few lines hence in *TL* the object of Love's attack is simony — *but nowe the leude for symonye. . .* (line 130) — or the sale of Church office (most generally, any use of religion for personal profit and aggrandizement) as opposed to *servyce in holy churche honest and devoute* (line 129).

122–23 *crosse and mytre*, accoutrements of a bishop.

131 *is*. Th: *it*; Skeat: *is*. Jellech and Leyerle concur.

131–33 *Nowe is . . . encrease*. Skeat: "And each one gets his prebend (or share) all for himself, with which many thrifty people ought to profit" (p. 465).

131–34 Skeat observes the rimes: *achates*, *debates*; *wronges*, *songes*. He might have cited *forsake*, *take*, as well.

132 *for his wronges*.Skeat glosses: "on account of the wrongs which he commits"; also *personer*, better *parsoner* or *parcener*, participant, sharer; i.e., the steward, courtier, escheator, and idle minstrel, all get something (p. 465).

133 *and provendre*. Skeat: *and [hath his] provendre*. Jellech concurs, but not Leyerle. Leyerle (p. 297) glosses as "prebendary," the clergyman who holds a prebend, or stipend from his church.

134 *behynde*. Skeat: "behindhand — even these wicked people are neglected, in comparison with the *losengeour*, or flatterer" (p. 465).

146 *dolven*. Skeat glosses as "buried," observing: "because they (the poor) always crave an alms, and never make an offering, they (the priests) would like to see them dead and buried" (p. 466).

148 *forthe*. Skeat: *force*, which makes easier sense, but not definitively. I follow Leyerle who reads *forthe* as a noun, a variant of *fort*. Leyerle (pp. 298–99) argues that "the correct form was probably *forche*, 'the act of appearing in court, or of taking a legal step, separately rather than as a group.' This AF legal term . . . gave the compositor trouble and he replaced it with a common word nearly indistinguishable with it in handwriting, but meaningless in context. . . . [Leyerle next paraphrases the sense:] 'But among lawyers I dare not come. My activity, they say, makes them poor. They would on no account have me around, for then tort and individual cases in court would not be worth a haw nearby and would please no men; but these lawyers are oppressive and extortionate in power and activity.'"

148ff. Jellech emends *pleasen* to *pleaden* and this emendation supersedes Schaar's mistaken construals, which are based in the reading *pleasen* (Schaar, p. 19).

150 *ryme*. Skeat: "The reference is not to actual jingle of rime, but to a proverb then current. In a poem by Lydgate in MS. Harl. 2251 (fol. 26), beginning 'Alle thynge in kynde desirith thynge i-like,' the refrain to every stanza runs thus, 'It may wele ryme, but it accordith nought'; [see the *Minor Poems*, pp. 792–94, 'Ryme Without Accord']. The sense is that unlike things may be brought together, like riming words, but they will not on that account agree. So here: such things may seem, to all appearance, congruous, but they are really inconsistent" (p. 466). See above, lines 131–34.

151 *by me*. Jellech: "The phrase is ambiguous. It could mean 'by me, Love' or *me* might be the abbreviated form of 'men'" (p. 270).

166 *cease*. Jellech: "The meaning of *cease* in this passage would seem to be 'to renounce or abdicate a right or office.' The thought is that although the governed may have the

ability to govern and administer, still they should not try to exercise this ability until their heads call on them, notwithstanding the profit or pleasure such power might bring them" (p. 271).

172 *truly, he saith he com never of Japhetes childre*. Jellech: "The basic reference in this sentence and the lines following is to Genesis 9.25–27, and Noah's curse on the descendants of Canaan, son of Ham, because he was seen naked by Ham. The biblical story was given various allegorical interpretations by Christian exegetes, usually associating the line of Japhet, Noah's heirs and Shem with the faithful, or with the church, and the descendants of Ham or of Canaan variously with unbelievers, Jews, or the damned. . . . there seems to have been a vernacular tradition incorporating the interpretation Usk uses in this passage. The *Cursor Mundi*, lines 2133–35, interprets Noah's curse as dividing mankind into knight, freeman, and thrall:

> Knyth, and thrall, and freman,
> Oute of þes thre breþer began;
> O sem freman, o Iaphet knyght,
> Thrall of cham þe maledight." (p. 272)

See further Allen, pp. 77 and 117.

173 *Caynes*. Leyerle (p. 300) notices that "the context shows that the form *Caynes* . . ., despite its appearance, means 'of Ham.' The names Cain and Ham were confused in medieval orthography because of the Vulgate spelling Cham for Ham."

178 *in*. Th: *in in*.

178–93 Usk's eloquent defense of gentilesse as a matter of behavior rather than inheritance owes much to *Boece* III. pr. 6 and m. 6. But see also "Gentilesse: Moral Balade of Chaucer" and Chaucer's "Truth: Balade de Bon Conseyl" for similar wording and sentiment. The ideas are also prominent in the *Wife of Bath's Tale CT* III.1109ff and the *Roman de la Rose*, lines 6579–92.

180 *Perdicas*. Skeat: "Perdiccas, son of Orontes, a famous general under Alexander the Great. This king, on his death-bed, is said to have taken the royal signet-ring from his finger and to have given it to Perdiccas. After Alexander's death, Perdiccas held

the chief authority under the new king Arrhidaeus; and it was really Arrhidaeus (not Perdiccas) who was the son of a *tombestere*, or female dancer, and of Philip of Macedonia; so that he was Alexander's half brother. The dancer's name was Philinna, of Larissa." (p. 466). Jellech cites Trevisa, translating Higden's *Polychronicon*, as calling "Perdica, a tombester sone" (p. 273). See also Leyerle, p. 301.

189 *corare*. Skeat emends to *corage*. Jellech and Leyerle concur.

190 *clerkes*. Skeat emends to *cherles*.

191 *nempned*. Leyerle emends to *[d]empned.*

191–93 *And therfore he . . . gentylmen maketh*. Jellech compares the language of Boethius, *Cons*. 3. m. 5.1–4.

193–99 Jellech transfers the lines "And so speke . . . no maner mater," to Book 2, Chapter 3, below at line 281 between *desyren.* and *Trewly Nero*. She explains her decision thus: "These lines have been transferred from the end of the second chapter of this book because they obviously do not belong to that chapter's topic of *gentilesse*, and they are a fitting climax to Love's defense of women in [the third chapter]" (p. 283).

197 *so wene*. Leyerle (p. 302) emends to *sowene*, arguing that the word is the idiomatic *sowne* as in *sowne in*, meaning "tend toward, make for, be consonant with." "The sense is as follows: 'I will say nothing . . . that can tend toward anything against her sex.'"

206–09 *Ah good lady . . . aperen.* Schaar: "The corruption here is serious. . . . I propose the reading: *'Ah, good lady,' quod I, 'in whom victorie of strength is proved above al other thing, after the jugement of Esdram! Whos lordship <over> alle regneth? Who is, that right as emperour hem commaundeth? Whether thilke ben not women'* etc. This version seems to me to be as close as we can come to the sense of the context . . . and to the textual material extant. It would seem that the erroneous *lignes* was due to a contraction of syllables and to *i* in *lordship*, and that the following *is* was responsible for the ending" (p. 20). But see Leyerle, p. 303.

207 *jugement of Esdram*. 3 Esdras 4.15–17. Jellech notes: "The reference is to the story told in the apocryphal book of Esdras, of a banquet given by Darius, at which he held a contest to determine what is the strongest thing in the world. The person giving the wisest answer would be richly rewarded. One guest states that wine is strongest; another that the king is strongest; but the third, Zerubbabel, maintained that women are strongest, but Truth is victor in all things" (p. 276). The story is retold in Gower's *CA*, VII, 1783–1984.

210–11 *al the remenaunt ben no gendres*. I.e., the rest are neuter, and called gender only "of grace in facultie of grammer."

211ff. See 1 Esdras 4.15–17: "Women have borne the king and all the people that bear rule by sea and land . . . without women cannot men be."

222 *that desyre to a good asker*. Skeat: "That by no way can they refuse his desire to one that asks well" (p. 467).

223 *of your sectes*. Skeat: "of your followers, of those of your sex" (p. 467).

231 *so maked*. Skeat: "and that (i.e., the male sex) is so made sovereign and to be entreated, that was previously servant and used the voice of prayer. Men begin by entreating, and women then surrender the sovereignty" (p. 467).

232ff. *Anon as fylled is your lust*. These lines, Skeat argues, derive from *HF* 269–85; Jellech, however, contends that both Chaucer and Usk "used a common source" (pp. 70–77). See, further, Leyerle, p. 304.

234 *so*. Leyerle emends to *se*.

235–36 *every glyttryng thyng*. Skeat paraphrases, "All that glisters is not gold," and compares *CT* VIII.962 (p. 467).

239 *of*. Th: *on*. Skeat's emendation. Jellech and Leyerle concur.

242 *unhande*. Skeat: *on hande*. Jellech and Leyerle concur.

244 *blober*. Th: *bloder*. Skeat: *blobere*. Leyerle concurs, but not Jellech.

245 *is put into wenyng*. I.e., "she [each one of them] is led to suppose" (Skeat, p. 467).

246 *their wyl in*. I suggest *their wyl [others] in* for sense.

248ff. *a thirde for delyte*. Copied from *HF* 305–10 (Skeat, p. 468).

252 *Alas*. Skeat: "Expanded from *HF* 332–59; observe how some phrases are preserved" (p. 468).

258 *Ever their fame*. In addition to *HF*, compare *T&C* 5.1058–62:

> "Allas, of me, unto the worldes ende,
> Shal neyther ben ywriten nor ysonge
> No good word, for thise bokes wol me shende.
> O, rolled shal I ben on many a tonge!
> Thorughout the word my belle shal be ronge!"

radde. Skeat: *[ben] radde*.

268 *helper*. Skeat: "Faciamus ei adiutorium simile sibi" — Genesis 2.18 [Let us make him a help like unto himself].

this tree. I.e., Eve, womankind. See *City of God* 14.11: "or rather it was the man himself who was that tree . . ."

274 *Sarazins*. Saracens, or the infidel.

275–79 *If the fyre doth . . . wytte in sterynge*. See *City of God* 12.4:

> For what is more beautiful than a fire, with all the vigour of its flames and the splendours of its light? And what more useful, with its heat, its comfort, and its help in cooking? And yet nothing can cause more distress than the burns inflicted by fire. . . . So we

must not give a hearing to those who praise the fire's light and find fault with its heat, because they are not thinking of its natural properties, but are judging it by the standard of their own convenience or inconvenience. They like to see the fire; but they do not like being burned.

280–81 Jellech: "These lines [below] have been transferred from the end of the second chapter of this book because they obviously do not belong to that chapter's topic of *gentilesse*, and they are a fitting climax to Love's defense of women in this chapter:

> And so speke I in feminyne gendre in general/of tho persones at the reuerence of one/ whom euery wight honoureth/for her bountie and her noblesse ymade her to god so dere/that his moder she became/and she me hath had so great in worshyp/that I nyl for nothyng in open declare/that in any thynge ayenst her secte maye so wene: for al vertue and al worthynesse of plesaunce in hem hahoundeth. And although I wolde any thing speke/trewly I can not/I may fynde of yuel in her no maner mater." (p. 283)

282 *dames*. Compare *Cons*. 2. m. 6. 5–8 (Jellech).

284 *an herbe*. This proverb is copied from *HF* 290–91 (Skeat, p. 468).

294 *Thou desyrest*. Leyerle begins chapter 4 here.

294–300 Leyerle argues, over almost two pages (pp. 307–08), for a slight modification of the chapter division (that preserves the initial T dictated by the acrostic) and for other alterations in the passage to try to clarify its sense. He concludes that the gist of the passage is that "Love's point is that women's insistence on long service is not really a delay because it reinforces the innate desire of all men, even a wretch, for complete and faultless joy in everything done" (p. 308).

296–97 *Nowe . . . belongeth*. Schaar: "After the restoration of two small words we get the sense obviously required:

> *'Now' quod she, 'for thou shalt not wene that <to> womans condicions for fayre speche suche thing <ne> longeth.'*

An ironical sally, then, alluding to the previously mentioned contempt for woman [lines 259–61]." Compare Jellech, however: "There is some corruption here which is not to be resolved" (p. 285).

299 Skeat would strike out either *my* or *to me.*

302 *lyveth.* Skeat emends to *leveth*, which is certainly the sense.

306–07 *wight weneth.* Skeat: *wight, [which] weneth.*

308–10 *but than . . . syde.* Jellech: "The argument is derived from Boethius, *Cons.* 3. pr. 2. 5–10, except that Usk has substituted *love* for the *summum bonum*. Both Boethius and Usk are saying that a person is not going to have complete happiness if his happiness is lacking anything in any way. Also, if this happiness consists in love, then it follows that he who is supposed to have complete happiness should not lack happiness in love in any way" (p. 287).

308–10 *lacke . . . lacke.* "It is probable . . . that the second *lacke* is an erroneous repetition of the first, and that the correct reading should be: "Eke it foloweth than, that he that must have ful blisse <geteth> no blisse in love on no syde" (Schaar, p. 21).

311 *sohte.* Th: *sothe.* Leyerle's emendation.

313 *thinges.* Th: *thrages. Thrages* could be a variant of *thronges*, meaning "groups," or "dangers," or "anxieties." None complements the sense as well as "things," however; I follow Skeat's emendation. Leyerle: "The original was probably *thrates*, 'vexations'; the word originally had a sense of 'press or crowd of people,' which fits the context here very well" (p. 309).

turneth. Skeat: "It goes against the hair." Now we say, "against the grain" (p. 468).

316 *wot.* Th: *wol.* Skeat's emendation, followed by Jellech and Leyerle.

330–31 *cleaped resonable, manlych, and bestiallich. Resonable is.* Th: *cleaped bestiallich resonablich.* Skeat emends to: *cleaped bestiallich, resonablich, [and manlich. Resonablich] is.* Jellech reads: *cleaped/ bestiallich/ manlich and resonablich/ resonablich is.* I have emended the series to accord with the hierarchical order in which they are discussed. It is difficult to suggest a single source for Usk's argument here. Triplicities, on the one hand, and the basic idea of vegetative, animal, and rational creatures, on the other, are so ubiquituous in medieval thought that Usk could depend here on any one or a group of a vast array of sources. Readers may find it helpful to consult Lewis [1964], 152ff., "The Human Soul."

338 *holden for absolute*. Skeat: "considered as free, separate, or detached; as in *Boece* 5. pr. 6. 203" (p. 468).

338–39 *so lyveth in to*. Both Skeat and Jellech emend *lyveth* to *leveth* and *to* to *two*. Thynne's spelling probably reflects early sixteenth-century pronunciation, after the front medial vowel has moved upward. This seems the case in several instances.

357 *in name than preise." "Soth*. Leyerle's suggestion (p. 310) I consider superior to Schaar's: "The emendation of *soth* to *other* . . . [yields] the sense . . .: '"Truly," said I, "it is shame and baseness to him who desires reputation that more people do not praise him in name than praise another".'" In this reading, the text would continue with a new sentence, "Quod she, 'thou sayst soth . . . etc.'" Schaar would read: "more folk nat prayse his name than these" (p. 21).

377 *thy kyng*. Skeat: presumably, Richard II.

381 *wot*. Th: *wol*. Skeat's emendation, followed by Jellech and Leyerle.

384–85 On the importance of this announcement for understanding the possible transmission history of *TL*, see the Introduction vi f, "The Problem of the Broken Sequence of Book 3."

387 *of this purpose*. Leyerle (p. 91) emends and construes as follows: "Trewly, it was I, for haddest thou of me fayled, than [I] this purpose had never taken in this wyse."

389–90 *Sylver fyned . . . werkynge*. Compare Psalm 12.6.

391 *disease*. Th: *diseases*. Emended by all.

394–96 *But for as moche . . . the hert*. Skeat: "Love and the bliss already spoken of above [see *the parfyte blysse of love*, above, line 60] shall be called the 'knot in the heart.' This definition of 'the knot,' viz. as being the perfect bliss or full fruition of love, should be noted; because, in later chapters, the author continually uses the phrase 'the knot,' without explaining what he means by it. It answers to 'sovereyn blisfulnesse' in Chaucer's Boethius" (p. 468). See *Boece*, p. 412, and see my Introduction, pp. 10ff.

397 *inpossession*. Skeat: "*inpossession* is all one word, but is clearly an error. The right word is certainly *imposition*. The Lat. *impositio* was a grammatical term, used by Varro, signifying the *imposing* of a name, or the application of a name to an object. . . . It is just the word required. When Love declares that she shall give the name of 'the knot' to the perfect bliss of love, the author replies, 'I shall well understand the application of this name,' i.e., what you mean by it" (pp. 468–69). Further, on the ubiquitous *impositio ad placitum* ("imposition of the meaning of a word at the pleasure or discretion of the one doing the imposting"), see Eco and Lambertini, et al.; also Shoaf (1983), pp. 11, 33, and 247n22.

402 *admyt it*. Th: *admytted*. Skeat and Jellech's emendation, followed, with slight variation, by Leyerle.

409 *Aristotle*. Perhaps the reference is to the *Nicomachean Ethics*, 1.1, as Skeat suggests. But whether here or elsewhere, the basic Aristotelian idea, we may be sure, that that for the sake of which something is done or made, the end, is of more value than the means, informs Usk's thought: if health causes my habit of eating properly, then, in Aristotelian terms, health, the cause, is greater than the thing caused, my habit, because my habit is for the sake of health.

431–32 *Thilke knytten . . . the yvel*. Leyerle: "They accept the riches and not the evil" (p. 313). Schaar would change *yvel* to *lyve*, explaining:

> *Lyf* in the sense "person" or "body" is not uncommon. . . The same error, *yvel* for *lyve*, recurs in a passage later in the same chapter, where the author speaks of those who love a person not for her own sake, but for her property's (line 478). . . . The reading "that loven non lyve for dereworthinesse of the persone" is quite as indispensable here as in the other passage; it seems that the scribe or the printer was led astray by the spelling *lyve*, the word otherwise being spelt *lyf* in Usk [another instance of the spelling *lyve*, however, is found in line 1028] (p. 22).

434 *than*. Th: *that*. Skeat's emendation, followed by Jellech and Leyerle.

437 *thynges precious or noble that neyther han lyfe ne soule*. Compare *Boece* II pr. 5, 130–33, where Philosophy laments that some think themselves neither fair nor noble except by riches, "ostelementz that ne han no soules."

438 *whan they ben in gatheryng*. Jellech: "Such riches are more worthy when they are in the process of being gathered; in giving them away begins man's love of other men's praising" (p. 300).

439 *avaryce gatheryng*. "Avaricious gathering." The subject of *be* would be an impersonal "one," unexpressed (Jellech, p. 300).

442–43 *and in the gatheryng of hem make men nedy*. This is very typical anti-venality lore and can be found in many examples of venality satire (especially those referring to the image of the hydroptical avaricious, who thirsts the more the more he drinks — see Yunck, pp. 16 and 32): the evil of riches is that they excite endless desire for more riches. See also Little, pp. 35–41.

456 *to kynde suffiseth lytel thing*. Compare Chaucer's "Truth: Balade de Bon Conseyl," lines 2 and 10 — "Suffyce unto thy thing, though it be smal" and "Gret reste stant in litel besinesse."

489 *gravel and sande*. To understand the following extended metaphor, which is rather clumsy, the reader needs to realize that "gravel and sand" amount to a figure for riches, that arrive with the flow of the sea and depart with its ebb.

491 *the*. Th: *to*. Skeat's emendation, followed by Leyerle but not Jellech.

493–95 *And certes . . . ayen meve*. In a lengthy note (pp. 313–14), Leyerle proposes *warnysh*, "the state of being guarded," for *warnyng*, "probably an error resulting from the substitution of a common noun for a very rare one." Schaar suggests:

> *warning* was miswritten for the very rare word *warpinge*, "silt" . . . Being an obvious *lectio difficilior*, it is natural enough that it should be misunderstood by the scribe or

> the printer. . . . If we accept the reading warpinge . . . the sentence would read: "And certes, ful warping in love shalt thou never thorow hem get ne cover, that lightly with an ebbe, er thou be ware, it wol ayen meve." (pp. 22–24)

517 *contrarie*. Skeat emends to *[the] contrarie*, followed by Leyerle; Jellech follows Thynne.

522 *whiche thynge*. Skeat emends to *[of] whiche thing*, followed by Leyerle but not by Jellech.

526–27 *governour shulde*. Leyerle: ". . . apparently a misdivision for *governours hulde*; *hulde* is the past participle of *hilen*, 'concealed' *MED* 2, and modifies *rancours*" (p. 315).

528 *but*. Th: *by*. Leyerle's emendation.

have ben trusted. Jellech: "The sentence, *Thou wottest wel what I meane*, [line 529], is probably an oblique reference to the Northampton affair" (p. 309).

529–31 *"Ye," quod I, ". . . in doyng."* Jellech: "the meaning and syntax are perfectly clear without emendation: '. . . as dignity wrought such a harmful thing [as the *quentye thynges* of line 529], so, the substance of dignity being changed, they would rely on them to bring again a good effect'" (p. 309).

542 *hadden*. Jellech points out that the unexpressed subject of *hadden* is "dignities" (p. 310).

557 *Nero*. Skeat: "The name was evidently suggested by the mention of Nero immediately after the end of Boethius, *Cons*. 3. pr. 4 (viz. in met. 4); but the story of Nero killing his mother is from an earlier passage in Boethius, viz. 2. met. 6" (p. 469).

559 *kyng John*. Skeat observes that by asserting his "dignity" as king against prince Arthur, John brought about a war in which "the greater part of the French possessions of the crown were lost" (p. 469). By strict primogeniture, Prince Arthur should have succeeded to the throne instead of John; John may have killed Arthur (in the spring of 1203) after capturing him at Mirabeau in 1202, but the matter is uncertain. As Skeat

implies, John's warfaring in France was spectacularly unsuccessful — hence his nickname, "Lackland."

573 *such maner planettes.* "planets such as those," referring to the sun and moon mentioned just above (lines 564–67). The sun and moon were then accounted as being among the seven planets (Skeat, p. 469). Although Usk almost certainly did not know Dante's works firsthand, the reader may want to bear in mind that Dante engages in the *Monarchia* (3.4) the long-standing allegory of the sun and the moon (the two luminaries) for his arguments regarding the relationship between the Empire and the Papacy.

574–75 *that any desyre . . . shewe.* "that have any desire for such (ill) shining planets to appear any more in that way" (Skeat, p. 469).

590 *to contrarious.* Skeat: *[that] to contrarious.*

598–600 *And if reverence . . . grounded.* Jellech: "As Skeat has said, the difficulty begins in the clause *for that*, [line 599]. The subject of *ben shewed* is 'reverence nor worship.' The general sense of the period is, 'if worship or reverence are not in dignities and if reverence and worship are no more revealed in dignities that [*sic*; than] is goodness revealed in them (but goodness is not revealed in them), then it proves that goodness is not grounded in them by nature'" (p. 316). See, further, Leyerle, p. 319. Schaar, on the other hand, proposes: "And if reverence ne worshippe kyndely be not set in dignitees, and they more therein ben <not> shewed than goodnesse-for that in dignité is <not> shewed-it but proveth that goodnesse kyndely in hem is not grounded," observing,

> In this way we arrive at a syllogism, rather heavy but free from contradiction: if reverence and honour are not naturally placed in dignities, and if they are not shown to be there any more than goodness — for that is not shown to be in dignity — this only proves that goodness is not naturally rooted in them (i.e. dignities) either. For if a thing is naturally associated with another, we must be able to show that it is always there; if this cannot be shown (as in the case of honour, reverence, and goodness, in relation to dignities), it cannot be naturally "grounded" in it. (pp. 24–25)

605 *ne*. Th: *he*. Leyerle's emendation.

614 *that*. Th: *that that*. Skeat's emendation, followed by Jellech and Leyerle.

615–16 *What . . . shynynge*. Schaar proposes: "What bountee mowe the <moone> yeve that, with cloude, lightly leveth his shyninge," suggesting that "*moone* may have been dropped in an early MS, which would more easily explain the fact that *y* in *yeve* was attached to *the*" (p. 25).

618 *lefte syde*. Conventionally in the Middle Ages, the left is associated with evil and that which is to be shunned or evaded — see the essays in Needham, especially that by Hertz, pp. 3–31.

620 *of worthy*. Skeat: *of [men, to maken hem] worthy*.

629 *Henry Curtmantyl*. "Among his Anglo-Norman barons, he always wore the short Angevin cloak, which by contrast with their long robes earned him the name of Curtmantle" (Barber, pp. 56 and 264n3).

He had not so moche. "The attendants, knowing that his desperate state meant that there would be none of the traditional rewards for them, stripped the body, plundered all they could find, and left the despoiled corpse to be found by William the Marshal soon afterwards. One of the knights, William de Trihan, had to take off his cloak to cover the corpse, and even the faithful marshal was hard put to it to arrange matters as befitted a royal funeral" (Barber, p. 232).

674 *a sypher in augrym*. Jellech: "The zero in arithmetic, which has no power of meaning in itself, yet gives signification to other numbers. This was a stock definition in medieval arithmetic: 'nil cifra significat sed dat signare sequenti'" (p. 325). (See Steele, p. 5.)

679 *great*. Th: *graet*.

680 *for as the*. Skeat emends to: *for as, [if] the*.

683 *Thou haste knowe many*. It is difficult not to think here of "the turbulent London of Richard II" (Bird's phrase).

699 *Buserus*. Chaucer has *Busyrides* in *Boece* 2. pr. 6. 67; but *Busirus* in the Monk's Tale, *CT* VII 3293. The true name is *Busiris*, of which *Busiridis* is the genitive case (Skeat, p. 471).

Hugest. Skeat suggests this is an error for Hengest, and that the reference is to his slaughter of the Britons. But Jellech cites the example of "Hugest" for Boethius's example of Regulus (*Boece*, p. 417). On Hengest and related "origin myths" in early Britain, see Brooks (pp. 58–64), who notes that the numerous accounts may be "myth" (p. 58) but are nonetheless widely attested; there can be little doubt, then, that Usk could have come by familiarity with one account or another in his wide if superficial reading among various sources.

700–01 See Matthew 26.52: "Omnes enim, qui acceperint gladium, gladio peribunt" — [for all that take the sword shall perish with the sword].

707–09 *He is mighty . . . not withsytte*. Jellech: "He is powerful who can act without bringing anxiety or injury to himself, and he is impotent who cannot resist wretchedness; but then he who has power over you, if he wishes to impose wretchedness on you, you cannot resist it." Skeat believed something to be missing, but, as Jellech observes, the form and thought are whole (p. 328).

719–20 *Why there . . . as he shulde*. Jellech: "Skeat inserted 'for him' before *that loketh*. Schaar disagreed as to the comprehensibility of this change, and would insert at the same place, 'but for him,' so as to say 'Why, there is no way to the knot except for him who seeks for the high way.' However, neither emendation is supported by any principle of textual criticism. *No*, [line 719], may be an error for 'one' or 'oon' but no straightforward way of improving the passage suggests itself" (p. 329). For Schaar the only possible restoration is: "Why, there is no way to the knotte <but for him> that loketh aright after the hye way, as he shulde" (p. 25). I would venture the suggestion that we add *here for him*: "[Which is] why there is no way to the knot here [in the dimension of power] for him that looks aright after the high way as he should" — i.e., I think Skeat is close to the mark. Leyerle posits a similar solution.

741 *veyned*. Skeat emends to *weyved*; followed by Jellech and Leyerle.

744 *our*. Jellech emends to *your*, as does Leyerle, too, following her.

746–49 An excellent introduction to and overview of the theory of the elements will be found in Lindberg, pp. 55–56 and 332ff; on page 55 is a helpful diagram of the "square of opposition of the Aristotelian elements and qualities," which I reproduce here:

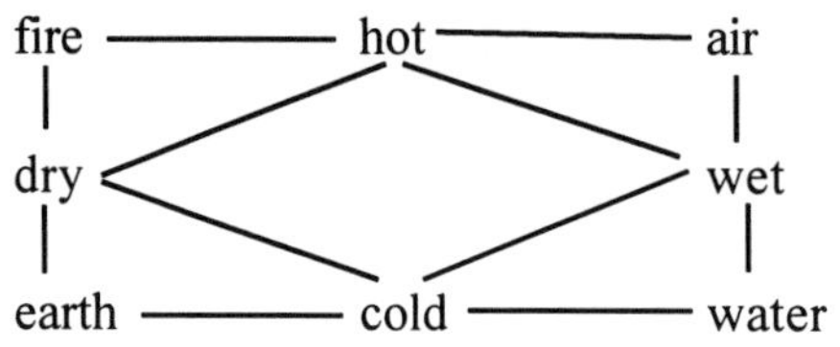

cold and dry = earth
cold and wet = water
hot and wet = air
hot and dry = fire

751 *cloudes*. Leyerle emends to *c[old]nes*.

753 *by*. Th: *my*. Skeat's emendation, followed by Jellech and Leyerle.

754 *eyre*. Th: *erth*, in both places in the line. Skeat labels Thynne's *erth* as "an obvious error" for *eyre*, and so emends both instances; followed by Jellech and Leyerle.

761 *oweth*. Skeat: *[it] oweth*, though the vergules (marked here by commas) suggest that emendation is unnecessary.

772–73 Schaar would read: "And if it be fayr, a mans name be eched by moche folkes praysing, <than it is> fouler thing that mo folk <it> not praysen" (p. 26).

775 *obstacles*. They are enumerated in Book 1, chapter 8, lines 809–14 (Skeat, p. 472).

777 *than renome*. Leyerle emends to *[and] renome*.

791–93 *And if . . . a foule syght*. Leyerle (p. 329), as part of a lengthy note, emends *hewe* to *heȝed* ("exalted") and modernizes as follows: "And if your eyes were as good as those of the lynx that can see through stone walls, both ugly and handsome in their inwardness would appear in no way exalted; that would be an ugly spectacle." Schaar suggests: "The transition from 'many stone walles' to 'bothe fayre and foule' has an abruptness unparalleled in Usk, and probably an addition should be made: "And if thyne eyen weren as good as the lynx, that may seen thorow many stone walles, <and> bothe fayre and foule, in their entrayles, of no maner hewe shulde apere to thy sight, that were a foule sight'" (p. 26).

799 *falowen*. Th: *folowen*. Skeat's emendation, followed by Jellech and Leyerle.

804–05 *al daye . . . fooles wende*. Jellech: "A proverbial expression; see Skeat, *Early English Proverbs*, 63" (p. 338). See too *T&C* 1.217.

806 *de polo antartico*. Th: *autartico*. Skeat's emendation, followed universally. Jellech (pp. 338–39) notes that the belief in a southern polar star corresponding to the North Star is also found in one version of *Mandeville's Travels* (pp. 132–34). The idea lived on into the fifteenth century among navigators; see Taylor (second ed.), pp. 124 and 161–62.

817 *a melodye in heven*. Jellech notes that belief in the melody of the harmony of the spheres was, of course, widespread until the eighteenth century. "In order to understand Usk's analogy between the harmony of lovers and the harmony of the spheres it is important to know that music of the spheres, both in its scientific and its spiritual interpretation, was not to be heard by ordinary ears under ordinary circumstances" (p. 340).

819 *joye*. Skeat emends, needlessly, to *joye[s]*.

820–21 *God made al thyng*. See Wisdom 11.21.

824–37 *Swetenesse . . . endure*. Jellech argues (pp. 341–42) for a rearrangement of several sentences here. Her proposed order would run as follows: lines 802–23 (as text now stands), 833–37, 824–33, 837 etc.:

> This blysse is a maner of sowne delycious in a queynte voyce touched and no dynne of notes: there is none impressyon of breakynge laboure. I canne it not otherwyse nempne for wantynge of privy wordes but paradyse terrestre ful of delycious melody withouten travayle in sown pe*r*petual servyce in ful joye coveyted to endure. Swetenesse of this paradyse hath you ravisshed it semeth ye slepten rested from al other diseases so kyndely is your hertes therin ygrounded. Blysse of two hertes in ful love knytte may not aright ben ymagyned: ever is their co*n*templacion i*n* ful of thoughty studye to plesaunce mater in bringynge comforte everyche to other. And therfore of erthly thinges mokel mater lightly cometh in your lerning. Knowledge of understondi*ng* that is nyghe after eye but not so nyghe the covetyse of knyttynge in your hertes: More soveraine desyre hath every wight in lytel herynge of hevenly connynge than of mokel materyal purposes in erthe. Right so it is in propertie of my servauntes that they ben more affyched in sterynge of lytel thynge in his desyre than of mokel other mater lasse in his conscience. Onely kynde maketh hertes in understondi*ng* so to slepe that otherwyse may it nat be ne*m*pned ne i*n* other maner names for lykyng swetnesse can I nat it declare al sugre *and* hony al mynstralsy *and* melody ben but soote and galle in co*m*parison by no maner p*ro*porcion to reken **<344rb><344va>**in respecte of this blysful joye. This armony this melody/ etc.

827 *plesaunce, mater*. Leyerle emends to *plesaun[t]e mater*.

829–30 *Knowledge . . . hertes*. Jellech: "the idea being expressed would be, 'and, therefore, with regard to earthly things, a great deal of material comes easily in your learning. Knowledge of understanding (i.e., comprehension) that is based on experience comes easily, but not the desire to be united in your hearts'" (p. 342).

829–37 Inexplicably these lines are missing from Jellech's edition: her text goes from "Knowledge of understonding" directly to "Onely kynde maketh" (pp. 342–43, continuous pagination). I speculate that in working out her re-ordering of lines (see note to lines 824–37), she inadvertently omitted this section which was in question. I base this speculation on the fact that her note on page 342 *does* contain her construal of the sentence "Knowledge of understonding . . .", which I cited in the previous note — i.e., presumably the omitted lines were there in a draft (they were annotated), but then were subsequently dropped inadvertently.

835–38 Schaar: "Usk must here have used a word for the process in the hearts that produces the wonderful harmony, for whose sweetness even Love cannot find adequate words: I can it not otherwyse nempne . . . but paradyse terrestre ful of delicious melody . . . Only kynde maketh hertes in understonding so to *stere*, that otherwyse may it not be nempned etc. Only Nature, who establishes eternal law and concord, makes hearts stir in mutual understanding, like strings of a sensitive instrument, so that a music of unspeakable beauty is produced, a harmony comparable only to the music of the spheres" (pp. 27–28).

839–40 *sugre . . . soote*. Skeat compares "sucre be or soot," *T&C* 3.1194.

851 *Flebring*. Skeat: "Mr. Bradley suggests *flekring* or *fleckering*, which is probable enough. The Middle English *flekren*, also spelt *flikeren*, meant not only to flutter, but to be in doubt, to vacillate, and even to caress. We may take it to mean 'light speech' or 'gossip'" (p. 473).

853 *innocentes*. Th: *innoctenes*. Skeat's emendation, accepted also by Jellech and Leyerle.

866–69 *Right so . . . to tourne*. Leyerle (pp. 119 and 333) emends *do* (line 868) to *to* and *out* (line 868) to *oweth*; he then modernizes as follows: "Just as the knot is greater than all other goods, so you can reckon all things less. And what belongs to the knot ought to turn into a cause of honor and desire for its greater part; otherwise, it is rebel and ought to void away from defending its superior."

871 *hem*. Schaar would read *<by> hem* (p. 28).

894 *he that is in heven felyth*. Compare *T&C* 3.1656–59:

> Pandare answerd, and seyde thus, "he
> That ones may in hevene blisse be,
> He feleth other weyes, dar I leye,
> Than thilke tyme he first of it seye.

900 *to weten . . . me ben ymoned*. Jellech: "Skeat erroneously read Thynne's *ymoned* as 'ymoved,' though the text clearly has *ymoned*. Then, after making this error he was

forced to make some sense of the line and altered *me* to 'men.' Schaar, seeing that there was still something lacking, proposed a new word order: 'a lytel other with me . . .,' but this syntax is still strained syntax. The correct reading removes all these difficulties. According to the *OED* the verb 'moan' is rare before the sixteenth century, but two instances are recorded" (p. 349).

903–09 *"O, for," quod she, . . . "were so ferde*. Jellech: "Skeat considered this 'the finest passage in the treatise, but not very original,' and referred his readers to parallel passages in *PPl* C.21.456–57 and to Boethius, *Cons*. 4. m.6. 25–29" (p. 349).

905 *yeres*. Skeat emends to *yere*.

912 *proverbe*. Th: *pronerbe*. Leyerle's emendation. See Proverbs of Hending: "When bale is hext (highest), then bote is next"(in Singer, p. 130). "For *hext* our author substitutes *a nyebore*, i.e., a neighbour, nigh at hand" (Skeat, p. 473).

923 *to suffre*. Leyerle (p. 336) plausibly suggests adding "change" — *to suffre [change], of whiche changes cometh . . .*

925–28 *Of which worchynges . . . taketh his name*. I replace Skeat's explanation of the "planetary hours" with North's, which is more economical. In understanding the "planetary hours," it helps to remember that the order in use was the *reverse* order of distance from the earth (which was considered the center of the planetary system): Saturn, Jupiter, Mars, Sun, Venus, Mercury, Moon.

> Suppose we divide the days, each into twenty-four hours. . . . If we give the first hour of Sunday to the governance of the Sun, the second hour of the same day to Venus, the third to Mercury, and so on through the cycle again and again, we shall eventually come to the first hour of the following day, which by the rules will turn out to be governed by the Moon [English Monday]. Continuing, we shall find that Mars governs the first hour of the third day [hence French Mardi], Mercury the first hour of the fourth [hence French Mercredi], then Jupiter [hence French Jeudi], and Venus [hence French Vendredi], and finally Saturn [English Saturday]. The names of the days of our week are a relic of this arrangement of so-called "planetary hours." (p. 29)

936 *Wherefore the*. Skeat: *wherfore [in] the*, followed by Leyerle but not Jellech.

940 *contingence*. Th: *contygence*. Emended by all.

956 *one of thre*. Skeat emends to *[of] one of thre*, and makes cross-reference to Book 2, chapter 4, line 328, above. Leyerle follows Skeat but Jellech does not.

964 *first sayde*. I.e., Book 2, chapter 4 (lines 333–35).

965 *But manly*. Skeat emends to *but [by] 'manly.'*

969 *is more . . . by clerkes*. Jellech reads: "is reckoned by clerkes to be the more reasonable way than is the manly way" (p. 358).

972 *wele*. Skeat emends to *wol*. Schaar observes: "the meaning, if *wel* is retained and *remembre* considered a subjunctive, appears to be: 'anyone who carefully contemplates the consequences of sensual enjoyment, is bound to admit that ultimately, they give melancholy and sorrow'" (p. 29).

973–75 *Right as . . . at her goynge*. Jellech compares Boethius, *Cons*. 3. m. 7. Schaar suggested that Thynne's "hadde" might be an error for *shadde*, which term conforms to the Latin "fundit" of Boethius [. . .] as well as to Chaucer's "hath sched" (*Boece*, p. 428).

975 *entreth*. Leyerle emends to *en[d]eth*.

975–76 *stynge . . . knot*. Schaar: "the bliss of the knot, after the sting of fleshly lust, cannot enter and disappear at the same time. Here also a slight emendation seems indispensable: '. . . and than stinge they at her goinge, wherthrough *endeth* and clene voydeth al blisse of this knot'" (p. 29).

986 *glorien*. Skeat supplies the head: *[they] glorien*. Leyerle follows Skeat.

990 *stongen*. As in line 986 Skeat loses the syntax by supplying the auxillary: *[is] stongen*. Leyerle follows Skeat.

1016 *at the*. Th: *at he*. Skeat's emendation, followed by Jellech and Leyerle.

1023–28 Heyworth (p. 143) would re-punctuate as follows:

> Ben these nat mortal thynges agon with ignorance of beestial wyt, and hast receyved reason in knowyng of vertue? What co*m*forte is in thy hert, the knowi*n*ge sykerly in my servyce be grou*n*ded. And woste thou nat wel, as I said, that deth maketh ende of al fortune? What than? Sta*n*dest thou in noble plyte, lytel hede or reckyng to take if thou let fortune passe dyng, or els that she fly wha*n* her lyst, now by thy lyve.

He comments: "The last sentence . . . is not a question but an answer to the preceding *What than?*" (p. 142).

1027 *reckyng*. Th: *rcekyng*. Emended by all.

1027–28 Schaar: "Love must rather be asking if it would not be a noble attitude to care little whether fortune passes away, either at our death or leaving us during our lifetime: 'Standest thou <not> in noble plyte, litel hede or recking to take,'" etc. (p. 30).

1028 *dying*. Th: *dyng*. Skeat's emendation, followed by Leyerle but not Jellech.

1028–31 *Pardy, a man . . . than thy lyfe?* Jellech sees an adaption here from Boethius, *Cons.* 2. pr. 4. 22–25:

> Cum igitur praecipua sit mortalibus vitae cura retinendae, o te, si tua bona cognoscas, felicem, cui suppetunt etiam nunc quae vita nemo dubitat esse cariora. (Therefore, since the sovereign care of mortals is to retain life, O you are a happy man if you know your goods, you to whom goods are at hand even now which no one doubts to be dearer than life.)
>
> Usk's unclear clause *if thou knowe thy goodes that thou hast yet be loued whiche nothynge may doute* is a translation of "si tua bona cognoscas tuas suppetunt etiam nunc quae vita nemo dubitat esse cariora," but the antecedent for both the relative pronouns *that* and *which* is the same — *goods*. Boethius's "nemo" may have become the unintelligible *nothyng* through faulty reading of an abbreviation. (p. 364)

1030 *be loved*. Leyerle emends to *be[n] l[e]ved*.

1039 *daunger*. Th: *dauuger*. Leyerle follows Skeat.

1043 *Lo*. Skeat mistranscribes: *to*.

1045 *whyle*. Leyerle emends to *w[e]le*.

1046 *for in this*. Th: *for this*. Skeat's emendation, followed by Jellech but not Leyerle.

1048 *"Certayn," quod I*. Thynne begins a new chapter here, but, since the initial letter "C" does not follow the acrostic, this chapter has been incorporated into chapter 10. (See Jellech, p. 366, and Skeat, p. 479).

amonge. In a major alteration of Thynne and Skeat, Leyerle (p. xxvii) intervenes here as follows (I quote only the essential part of a lengthy explanation):

> For the sake of the acrostic, Skeat puts the chapter divisions at a word beginning with E, *every*, at [line 1070 — i.e., 22 lines later]. A break at this point seems dubious because it divides Love's discourse on the *resonable lyf* and makes an awkward interruption in the middle of one of her remarks. . . . Chapter 11 is best started with the word *Amonge* [line 1048], emended to its common by-form *Emonge* to provide the necessary E for the acrostic. Thus the third word of the acrostic in Book II becomes
>
> | M | E | R | C | I |
> |---|---|---|---|---|
> | 10 | 11 | 12 | 13 | 14 |
>
> A further result is that Book II has 14 chapters in its edited version, not the 15 chapters in Thynne.

1055–56 *there thou hast myswent, eschewe the pathe*. Compare *T&C* 1.633–35 (emphasis added):

> "And there thow woost that I have aught *myswent*,
> *Eschuw* thow that, for swich thing to the scole is;
> Thus often wise men ben war by foolys."

1057 *confounded*. Th: *coufouded*. Leyerle's emendation.

1070 *Every soule*. Jellech notes there is no capital or ornate capital to mark a chapter division at this point in Thynne and follows Skeat in selecting this sentence as the beginning of a new chapter, because it is the only sentence in this portion of the text beginning with the letter "E" required by the acrostic (p. 369). But see Leyerle, above, note to line 1048.

1075–77 *These olde philosophers . . . th'other lyvenges*. Jellech: "Who these old philosophers were is not easy to say; presumably Boethius was one. The reference is to the idea that grace perfects nature; compare St. Thomas (pp. 142–43):

> We may say, accordingly, that in the state of pure nature man did not need a gift of grace added to his power, in order to love God above all things, although he did need the help of God in moving him to do so. But in the state of corrupt nature he needs further help of grace, that his nature may be healed." (p. 369)

Consult further Vitto, pp. 5–50.

1077 *Resonably have I lyved*. Skeat notes that "the author forgets that Love is supposed to be the speaker, and speaks in his own person" (p. 475).

1079 *connyng*. Skeat: *[his] conning*. Jellech: *the connynge*. Leyerle follows Skeat.

1085 *as in knowing a wake*. Jellech notes that something has gone wrong here. "I suspect that *in* should be 'his' and *a wake* should be 'awaketh' — as his knowing awakes" (p. 369).

1107 *if he*. Th: *he*. Skeat's emendation, followed by Jellech and Leyerle.

1110 *is*. Th: *as*. Skeat's emendation, followed by Jellech and Leyerle.

1114 *power and suffisaunce*. Th: *power suffisaunce*. Jellech's emendation. Skeat emends to *power with suffisaunce*. Leyerle concurs with Jellech.

1135 *servant*. Th: *servant* (with the *a* upside down). Leyerle calls attention to and corrects the upside-down *a*.

1135–37 *Plato*. Skeat suggests Seneca, *De Ira*, lib. i.c. 15, as the source (p. 145).

1146 *conclude*. The sense "confute" is found in the *OED* C, p. 665, "conclude," branch 4.

1153 *habyte maketh no monke*. "Cucullus non facit monachum," a common medieval proverb, Skeat observes (p. 475), of which Shakespeare is also fond — see *Twelfth Night* 1.5.56. See also Tilley, p. H586.

1156 *cordiacle*. Skeat (p. 475) sees *cordiacle* to be Thynne's misprint for *cardiacle*. See *CT* VI 313, and also the note to *CT* VI 313, where *cardiacle* is defined as quaking of the heart ("herte quakyng"). See, further, Appendix 1, p. 415 below.

1157 *praye to enforme*. Skeat emends to *praye [thee] to enforme*, followed by Leyerle but not Jellech.

1171–72 *If fyre . . . shal suffre*. Jellech: "If fire is in a place where there is something capable of being burned or heated, and the two — fire and the combustible material — are set at such a distance from each other that the fire can act, the combustible material will be acted upon" (p. 378).

1176 *wercheth*. Th: *wrethe*. Skeat's emendation, followed by Jellech and Leyerle.

1177–78 *and no . . . I fynde*. "And I cannot find any passive except you in all my Donet." Jellech notes that a *donet* is a "colloquial expression for a book of principles, after the Roman grammarian Donatus, who wrote a book of elementary Latin grammar, widely used in medieval schools" (p. 379).

1188 *muskle with a blewe shel*. See Appendix 1 below.

1189–90 *shel, by excellence*. Th: *shel excellence*. Skeat's emendation, followed by Jellech and Leyerle.

1200 *thus sayth kynde of this perle*. See Appendix 1 below.

1200–05 *This precious Margaryte . . . vertues loken*. See Appendix 1 below.

1205ff. *Al thyng that hath soule . . . .* Jellech remarks: "The relationship of the mussel, as an example of humility, to the good in man may have been suggested by Boethius's example of 'conchis maris' as creatures which feel but cannot move" (p. 382). She then continues: "The whole passage is extremely obscure." Indeed it is. It will help, however, to note that "meane" is quasi-technical in this passage. "It is not possible to passe from one extreme to another but by a meane" (cited in Lewis [1964], p. 166). "This is the old maxim from *Timaeus* $31^{b\text{–}c}$," Lewis continues; and the maxim will help us understand *TL* at this point. The point of the passage, its destination, so to speak, is the meekness or lowness of the mussel (lines 1201–02); and Usk is driving to this point with the idea of the different souls — vegetative, animal, rational. Each higher soul contains the lower soul(s), and this is the "mean"-ing by which one soul is "reduced" into another: because man has a rational soul, "in to god [he] is reduced" (line 1206). We see that "reduced" must also be a quasi-technical term; Skeat offers "connected," which is hardly wrong, but I think we can get a better grasp on the passage if we use instead "made to participate in." If we use these definitions and accept Skeat's emendation of *meue* to *mene* (line 1207), we can construe the passage, roughly (and only roughly) as follows:

> Everything that has a soul is made to participate in the good (or God) by mediation, an intermediary, as thus: in God, man is made to participate by his reasonable soul; and so further, creatures that may not move [like mussels] according to their place, are made to participate in man by the beasts' mediation [i.e., the animal soul, the soul to which motion is appropriate], the mediation of those creatures that move from place to place [in other words, between the creatures that do not move and man comes the "mean" or mediation of creatures that do move, the animal soul's category, which "contains" the vegetative soul and thus "reduces" it along with itself into man, who contains both animal and vegetative souls]: so that those bodies that have feeling souls [vegetative] and move not from their places hold the lowest degree of creatures endowed with vegetative souls; and such are made to participate in man by mediation. So it follows that the mussel as mother of all virtues holds the place of meekness.

1205 *good.* Leyerle emends to *G[o]d.*

1207 *beestes*. Skeat: "living things that cannot move, the very word used by Chaucer, *Boece* 5. pr. 5. 20" (p. 476).

1207 *meve*. Skeat emends to *mene*, which helps a little.

1211 *discendeth downe*. Skeat: "There is something wrong; either *discendeth* should be *discended*, or we should understand *and* before *to*; and perhaps *downe* should be *dewe*. . . . The reference seems to be to the Incarnation" (p. 476). Continuing my effort from the previous note, I would propose adopting Skeat's suggestion of *and* before *to* and his emendation of *dewe* for *downe*. We may then read:

> So it follows that the mussel as mother of all virtues holds the place of meekness *and* to its lowest degree descends *dewe* of heaven; and there by a manner of virgin birth are these Margarites/Pearls born, and afterward congealed.

I wish to insist that this reading is imperfect in both emendatory practice and syntactical construction. But, as the preceding and as the following notes suggest, it has at least the modest virtue of consistency of thought.

1213–14 *Made not mekenesse . . . a dewe*. Jellech finds these lines obscure: "There does not seem to be a subject for *Made* [line 1213]" (p. 383). But headless sentences are common in Middle English writing. Continuing my effort from the previous two notes, I would propose that Skeat is correct in his punctuation: *Made* is a verb in the interrogative position, and, *pace* Jellech, the subject of the sentence is *mekenesse*. We may then read:

> Did not meekness [itself, i.e., God incarnate] make the high heaven so low so as to enclose and catch out of it so noble a dew [i.e., Christ] that, after congealment [i.e., the Virgin birth] a Margarite/Pearl with endless virtue and everlasting joy, with a full vessel of grace, was given to every creature that in goodness would receive it?

My proposed readings depend ultimately on the iconography represented in the illumination that serves as the frontispiece to this edition. Basically, to evaluate my proposals, the reader needs to keep in mind the following (simplified) schema (see, further, Manning in Luria and Hoffman, pp. 330–36): the Virgin Mary is the mussel, the dew is the Trinity, principally in his Spiritship, and the Pearl is the Son as incarnate in the body of Mary, the whole schema functioning to insist, in this particular part of *TL*, on the meekness or lowliness of the site of the Incarnation (since this provides the optimum contrast with the previously discussed candidates — wealth, power, renown — for attaining the "knot in the heart"). Observe especially that the consistency achieved by this reading has another notable strand to it, or congruence with Usk's final definition of the Margarite (*Margarite a woman betokeneth grace lernyng or wisdom of God or els holy church*" — Book 3, chapter 9, lines 1123–24): the Pearl may be "both" the Son incarnate (Wisdom) *and* the Church, His Body/Members as left on earth (see Vona, p. 158 for a commentary that glosses the pearl as holy Church; see also Wailes, p. 123).

1220 *yet wolde I have better declared.* Skeat: This does not mean "I would have explained it better," but "I should like to have it better explained" (p. 476).

1225 *thilke jewel.* Skeat: *[of] thilke jewel*, followed by Leyerle but not Jellech.

1229 *wolde.* Skeat emends to *welde*, followed by Leyerle but not Jellech.

1233 *God.* Th: *good.* Skeat's emendation.

1236 *coutreplede.* Skeat emends to *countreplede.*

1244–51 *For trewly, al this . . . hath erred.* Jellech and others have quarreled with Skeat over these lines. He says (p. 476),

> this shews that Margarete does not mean a woman; for it is declared to be as precious as a woman, to whom it is likened.

I agree that Skeat is mistaken here. I think the matter has to be more carefully nuanced: Margarite is sometimes a woman, sometimes the Church, sometimes Christ incarnate, sometimes "grace/lernyng/or wisdom of God." We need to understand, I think, that Usk is finally incapable of resolving these terminologies into one — moreover, he may have not desired such resolution.

1253 *saw.* Th: *save.* Skeat's emendation, followed by Jellech and Leyerle. See also line 1272 where *saw* is *save* in Th.

1256–58 *everyche qualyté . . . badnesse.* Sanderlin (p. 70) notes that this sentence translates material from Anselm's *Conc.* (I.7). The following several sentences also depend on, sometimes paraphrase, *Conc.* I.7 (through line 1264).

1258 *Badde to be is naught*. This is the classic Augustinian formulation of evil as "privatio boni" — for a particularly clear expression of it, see *City of God* 11.22:

> There is no such entity in nature as "evil"; "evil" is merely a name for the privation of good. (p. 454)

See also, cited by Jellech (p. 387), *Cons*. 4. pr. 2 180–200 (*Boece*, p. 443).

1262 *beyng hath*. Skeat emends to *beyng [it] hath*.

1267 *that in every*. Th: *that every*. Skeat's emendation, followed by Jellech and Leyerle.

1271 *determission*. Skeat emends to *determinison* with which Leyerle concurs; Jellech reads *determinacion*, i.e., determination, conclusion.

1273 *yourselfe sayd*. I.e., at the beginning of this chapter.

1276 *nothynge but good*. Leyerle emends to *nothynge but G[o]d*.

1278 *goodly goodnesse*. Leyerle emends to *G[o]dly goodnesse*.

1280 *Austen saythe*. See *Civitas Dei* 12.5, and *De Natura Boni* 2.

1284 *Boece sheweth*. *Cons*. 3. pr. 10. 233–50 (*Boece*, p. 433).

1286 *God, knotte of al goodnesse*.This is a key moment in *TL*; see my Introduction, pp.10ff.

Every creature cryeth. See, e.g., St. Augustine, *Enarrationes in Psalmos* 144.10 (*Expositions* 6, p. 328):

> When thou has thought on the universal beauty of this world, doth not its very beauty as it were with one voice answer thee, "I made not myself, God made me?"

1287 *apeted . . . affection*. Leyerle (p. 349) emends *apeted* to *aptes* and then comments: "The words *aptes* and *affection* are used in special senses derived from [St. Anselm's] *De concordia*: *aptes* means 'aptitudes, inclinations'; and *affection* means 'the propensity or inclination of the will.'"

1288 *This*. Skeat: "*This* stands for *This is*, as usual" (p. 477).

1290 *badnesse*. Th: *baddesse*. Emended by all.

1290–91 *in the grounde . . .roted*. Leyerle addresses the confusion here by putting a full stop after *menynge*. A new sentence then begins with *In*, and *[good]* is inserted after *aleged*, with a semi-colon following *roted*.

1294–1307 *Al thyng . . . in vertue*. This long passage repays careful comparison with St. Augustine's arguments on opposition and harmony in the creation; see especially *City of God* 11.18–23, perhaps most especially 11.23: "A picture may be beautiful when it has touches of black in appropriate places. . ." (p. 455).

1296 *God hath in*. Skeat emends to *God hath [ordeyned] in*. Leyerle concurs; Jellech does not. Leyerle (p. 350), following Sanderlin, observes that lines 1296–99 depend on *Conc*. I.7.

1300 *betterer*. Skeat (p. 477): "'better,' but not necessarily a misprint. The form *bettyrer* occurs in the *Catholicon Anglicum* (p. 31)."

1308 *yeven by the ayre*. See Appendix 1 below.

1309 *ryght mokel*. Skeat emends to *[maken] right mokel*. "Although there is no paleographical justification for that particular word," Jellech notes, "some such verb of causation must be understood" (p. 392). Leyerle follows Skeat also.

1310–11 *Howe shulde ever goodnesse . . . wrothe*. See *City of God* 11.18:

> The opposition of such contraries gives an added beauty to speech; and in the same way there is beauty in the composition of the world's history arising from the antithesis of contraries — a kind of eloquence in events, instead of in words. (p. 449)

1316 *Pallas . . . Mercurye*. According to Leyerle, "the allusions are almost certainly to figures in Usk's London" (p. 351). He argues, at some length, for an identification of Pallas as Gaunt, Mercury ("the classical god of trade") as Brembre, and the *hym* of line 1315 as Northampton.

1318 *weneth*. Skeat emends to *weyveth*, followed by Leyerle but not Jellech.

1321 *adewe and a deblys his name is entred*. Jellech: "His name is assigned to God and to the devil; i.e., he is given over to them" (p. 393). Leyerle: "The sense seems to be: 'good-by and to the devil' his name is entered" (p. 351).

1334–39 Heyworth (p. 143) would re-punctuate as follows:

> But the sonne is not knowe but he shyne; ne vertuous herbes but they have her kynde werchynge; ne vertue but it stretche in goodnesse or profyte to another. Is no vertue than, by al wayes of reason (sythen mercy and pytie ben moste commended amonge other vertues) and they myght never ben shewed, refresshement of helpe and of comforte, but nowe at my moste nede. And that is the kynde werkynge of these vertues.

He then continues to explain (pp. 143–44):

> The sense, confused in Usk's prose, is that virtue unless manifested in action is no virtue; it cannot be passive, it must "strecche in goodnesse or profyte to another." Hence help and comfort cannot reasonably be accounted praiseworthy unless they are extended to someone (in this case the Dreamer) in the moment of his greatest need; mercy and pity (pre-eminent among virtues) dictate this.

1336ff. Schaar: "What must the author have said about their effects to be able to continue 'but now at my moste nede?' [line 1338]. Obviously: 'Than, by al wayes of reson, sithen mercy and pitee ben moste commended among other vertues, they might never ben <more> shewed, <with> refresshement of helpe and of comfort, but now at my moste nede etc.' If mercy and pity are the greatest virtues, it follows that their effects are never more clearly perceived than at the greatest need. *And*, then, seems to have been anticipated; *more* is necessary, and I suggest that a *with* has dropped out before *refresshement*" (pp. 30–31).

1348 *these*. Th: *chese*. Skeat's emendation, followed by Leyerle.

1352 *Proverbes*. See Proverbs 7.7–22.

1365 *unleful*. Skeat emends to *[of] unlefful*. Leyerle concurs; Jellech does not.

1366 *skleren and wymplen.* "veil and cover over." Skeat hesitantly suggests that Usk probably found the word *skleire*, a veil, in *PPl* C.9.5 (see also B.6.7, A.7.7), as that is the only known example of the substantive. The verb occurs here only (pp. 477–78).

1366–67 *Austen wytnesseth.* Jellech notes that no source in St. Augustine has been found for this reference (p. 398). James Marchand, in a private communication to me (April 21, 1996), suggests that *wytnesseth* here means "offers an example of" — a meaning arguably appropriate to the context: Augustine the rhetorician, in his youth, "right expert in resons and swete in his wordes," behaved like a heretic (a Manichean, most especially) until he could no longer bear the life he was leading (*Conf.* 7–8), and thus he "offers the example of a heretic." I am insecure in this reading but believe it is worth recording. Leyerle (p. 355), *pace* Jellech and me, suggests the source is *Confessions* 5.3–7, and especially 6, where Augustine narrates his encounter with the Manichean bishop Faustus of Mileve: "His discourse was eloquent and sweet, but his inadequacy in face of Augustine's questions revealed the discrepancy between his speech and his performance." Leyerle acknowledges that the allusion is "vague."

1374 *veyned.* Skeat emends to *weyved.* Jellech and Leyerle concur. See note to Book 2, line 741 above.

1377 *Syloe.* Siloam. Skeat: "It is a wonder where the author found this description of the waters of the pool of Siloam; but I much suspect that it arose from a gross misunderstanding of Isaiah 8.6, 7, thus:

> the waters of Shiloah that go softly . . . shall come up over all his channels, and go over all his banks.

In the Vulgate:

> aquas Siloë, quae uadunt cum silentio . . . ascendet super omnes riuos eius, et fluet super uniuersas ripas eius.

Hence *cankes* in [line 1380] is certainly an error for *bankes*; the initial *c* was caught from the preceding *circuit*" (p. 478).

1380 *bankes.* Th: *cankes.* Skeat's emendation, followed by Jellech and Leyerle.

Notes to Book 2

1381 *stormes*. Leyerle emends to *storme[th]*.

Skeat emends *Mercurius* to *mercurious [servants]*, explaining that "The children or servants of Mercury mean the clerks or writers. The expression is taken from *CT* III.697: 'The children of Mercurie and of Venus / Ben in hir wirking ful contrarious'" (p. 478). Jellech emends to *Mercuriens*, a formation analogous with *Veneriens* in the next line.

1381–90 *Mercurius . . . fayned love*. Leyerle argues at length (pp. 354–55) for a continuing political allegory, with thinly veiled references to Gaunt, Brembre, and Northampton.

1382 *Veneriens*. I.e., followers of Venus. Skeat compares *CT* III.609.

1392 *sote of the smoke*. Skeat suggests the soot of the smoke of the fire prepared for the sacrificed ox and cites Proverbs 7.22, "bos ductus ad uictimam" (p. 478). There might also be an allusion here to the defacement of Philosophy by the soot of time in *Boece*, I, pr. 1. 20–28.

1405–09 Heyworth (p. 144) would re-punctuate as follows:

> Were thou not goodly accepted in to grace? By my pluckynge was she to foryeuenesse enclyned. And after, I her styred to drawe the to house; and yet wendest thou vtterly for euer haue ben refused. But wel thou wost sythen, that I in suche sharpe disease might so greatly auayle. What thynkest in thy wyt? Howe ferre maye my wytte stretche? And thou lache not on thy syde, I wol make the knotte.

He comments (p. 144):

> . . . take the second *wit* in the sense "practical talent, clever management" (*OED* under *wit* sb. II 5b) and understand it as a question imputed to the Dreamer by the Lady. That is, "What are you thinking? Just how far my clever management extends?"

1408 *my*. Schaar would emend to *thy*, noting that the error would be very easy after *may*.

1410 *founde*. Th: *foude*. Skeat's emendation, followed by Leyerle.

1411 *holy oyle of peace*. Psalm 88.21.

1412 *leavyng*. Th: *leanyng*. Skeat's emendation, followed by Jellech and Leyerle.

Book 3

1 *Of nombre*. Jellech (p. 404) notes that this is a standard definition, derived ultimately from Boethius' *De Arithmetica*: "Numerus est unitatum collectio vel quantitatis acervas ex unitatibus profusa" [A number is a collection of unities, or a big mass of quantity issuing from unities (p. 76)].

4 *in thre tymes is devyded*. Recent studies of the extensive lore of the ages in English include Burrow (pp. 5–11; 66–92) and Dove (pp. 120–21). After St. Augustine, six is the norm for the number of ages prior to the Last Judgment in the later medieval period (Burrow, p. 80). I suspect that Usk has conflated the lores of three and six and has again proved somewhat atypical; however, in this case, his position — ages of deviation, grace, and joy — is certainly a very recognizable one in terms of the contemporary lore (see Burrow, p. 6 especially). *Deviacion* equates with life under the Old Law; *grace* is life after the Advent of Christ; *joy* is the life eternal after death. It is pertinent here to observe that *TL*, after it has been re-ordered through the Bradley-Skeat shift, as modified by Bressie, contains 33 chapters (not counting the Prologue) — see Medcalf's summary, pp. 44–45 above, for a quick count.

5 *Deviacion*. Th: *Demacion*, where the three consecutive minims for *u [v]* and *i* have been read as *m*. Skeat's emendation, followed by Jellech and Leyerle.

9 *Grace*. Not capitalized in Thynne. I have followed Skeat so that the designation of the second time is parallel with the first — *Deviacion*. So too *Joye* in line 13.

19 *that*. Th: *is*. Skeat's emendation, followed by Jellech and Leyerle, though Leyerle keeps Thynne's *is* (i.e., *[that] is cryed*).

20 *whiche is faylinge*. Schaar would read: *whiche is <eke yeven to> faylinge*, with the gloss "Which is also given to weakness without its deserving it." The actual wording he continues, "may of course have been different, but I think this must have been Usk's meaning" (p. 32).

20 *faylinge*. Leyerle emends to *[av]aylinge*.

20–21 *whiche is faylinge without deserte*. Skeat glosses *deserte* as "merit"; he suggests that the phrase is out of place here, and perhaps belongs to the preceding clause, after *shewed* in line 19 (p. 479).

21 *and*. Leyerle emends to *in*.

26 *whit*. Th: *with*. Leyerle's emendation, following Skeat. Later in the line he emends *jewel* to *jewel[es]*.

26–27 *us Englissh people*. Skeat (p. 479) suggests that "Usk says the English alter the name *Margarite-perle* to *Margery-perle*, whereas Latin, French, and many other languages keep the true form."

29 *Margery perles the*. Leyerle, following Skeat, emends: *Margery perles [by] the*.

33 *the more Britayne*. That is, greater Britain (i.e., England, Scotland, and Wales), as distinguished from lesser Britain (Brittany). See Appendix 1 below. The same lore is found in Gibbon, *The Decline and Fall of the Roman Empire* 1, chapter 1 (p. 33); Suetonius reports that "pearls seem to have been the lure that prompted [Caesar's] invasion of Britain; he would sometimes weigh them in the palm of his hand to judge their value" (p. 34).

34–37 On the capacity of pearls to control passion and staunch bleeding, see the Peterborough Lapidary (Evans and Serjeantson, pp. 107–08). The Lapidary identifies pearl as "Margarita." See, further, Appendix I below (p. 415).

35 *Another is good*. Schaar suggests that the sentence should begin: *Another good is: it is profitable helthe ayenst passions* etc. (p. 32). Leyerle follows Schaar, but uses a comma instead of the colon.

38 *speces*. Jellech notes that *speces* as used here by Usk is one of the scholastic neologisms of Middle English uncovered by John Conley and listed by him in his article ([1964], p. 209). So too *opinyon* in line 41 (p. 409).

40–41 *good lyvyng*, according to Jellech, means "living . . . the life of a good man; ethics" (p. 409).

50–51 *arsmetrike . . . astronomye*. Usk here is drawing on the tradition of the seven liberal arts, composed of the trivium and quadrivium. On the quadrivium, or "four ways" to knowledge (i.e., arithmetic, geometry, music, and astronomy) see Wagner, pp. 2–6 and 150–53.

54 *prudence, justyce, temperaunce, and strength*. On the four cardinal virtues (Prudence, Justice, Temperance, and Fortitude), see Piltz, p. 181.

59 *One is arte*. Jellech suggests that the completing phrase, "of logic," may have dropped out, although the *MED* does enter *art* (1.c) as being used alone to mean dialectics or rhetoric (p. 411). Skeat remarks that "it was usual to introduce here the *trivium*, or second group of the seven arts . . . which contained logic, grammar, and rhetoric. For the two former he has substituted 'art,' the general term" (p. 479).On the trivium, or "three ways" (to knowledge), see Wagner, pp. 6–9 and 23, especially.

64 *Ordre of homly thinges*. I.e., domestic economy (Jellech, p. 411).

73ff. *twey*. Skeat (p. 479) differentiates *natural* and *reasonable* as the *twey*. The third is *moral*. Hence, he suggests, the following scheme.

Philosophy	relating to the body	*natural*: the quadrivium *reasonable*: the trivium
	relating to the soul	*moral*: the cardinal virtues
Law	law: *natural*	
	right: *reasonable*	
	custom	written: *constitution* unwritten: *usage*

See further Piltz, p. 197.

75 *lawe, right, and custome*. Jellech points out that the division of law into three kinds goes back at least to Isidore of Seville, *Etymologiae* v.10, and became a common-

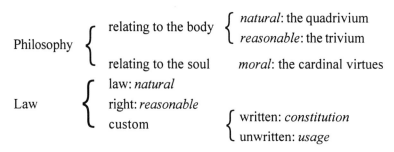

place of medieval political thought (p. 413). See Gilby, pp. 60–61. *Lawe* equates with natural law and *right* with civil law. See further King, p. 141; Pennington, p. 424; and Canning, pp. 454–56.

78 *constitution* is a technical legal term, equating with "statutes." See Jellech, p. 413.

85 *strength.* Th: *strentgh.* Emended by all.

87 *Cause, forsothe, in ordaynyng of lawe.* As Jellech notes, the "theory set forth here of the origin of law in men's evil wills is Augustinian" (p. 414); for a helpful overview, see Markus, pp. 108–11, especially 110.

90 *harme for harme.* Skeat: "That is, so that harm, (as punishment) for harm, should restrain evil-doers by the bridle of fear" (p. 480).

96 *and unworthy.* Skeat: "even if they be unworthy."

professe and reguler. Skeat observes, "the 'professed' were such as, after a year of probation, had been received into a monastic order; the 'regular' were such as were bound by the three monastic vows of poverty, chastity, and obedience" (p. 480).

97 *obedyencer.* One bound by obedience; used adjectivally; Skeat compares Low Latin *obedientiarius* (p. 480).

102 *at the lest.* Th: *the lest.* Leyerle's emendation.

104 *sleight.* Skeat emends to *sleigh.*

106 *I so.* Skeat emends to *I [am] so.*

111 *sende me water.* Jellech sees allusions to Exodus 17.1–7 and Psalm 114.8 (p. 416).

116 *redy refrete.* Jellech sees a "continual refrain" in "his ghost or spirit's meditations" (p. 417).

116–17 *commyng about I not than.* Skeat glosses "recurring I know not when," where *than* reads as *whan,* to make sense.

117 *coude I endite.* Th: *coude endite.* Skeat's emendation, followed by Jellech and Leyerle.

yet at dore. Jellech suggests an allusion to Revelations 3.7. The statement is in the way of a prayer with the antecedent for *whiche,* line 118, being *key of David* which is an image of Christ, as Leyerle observes (pp. 361–62). Jellech thinks the clause would be better placed following *vnshyt* (p. 417). See also John 10.9.

117–19 Schaar inserts *the* between *at* and *dore* and places the phrase *and He bring me in* between *closeth* and *whose* (p. 32).

118 *whiche that childrens.* The allusion is to Matthew 21.16.

119 *wel.* Skeat emends to *wol,* followed by Jellech and Leyerle.

119–20 *whose spirite . . . lyketh.* The figure of David equates with Christ or the Holy Spirit. The reference here is to John 3.8 and I Corinthians 12.11 (see Jellech, p. 417).

123 *frenship plesance.* Skeat emends to *fren[d]ship [in] plesance,* followed by Leyerle.

126 *wyte that the.* Leyerle emends to *wi[te]th that [to] the.*

128 *wyttes in many.* Th: *wyttes many.* Skeat's emendation, accepted by Leyerle but not Jellech. Schaar emends *in* to *of.*

135 *and me wondreth . . . in the lawe.* Jellech wonders what the verb "pass in" means. "Possibly it is the same as 'pass over' or 'skip over.' In his reply to Love Usk seems to quibble on a sense of 'pass' as 'to ford' or 'to walk through water'" (p. 419).

141 *innocent.* Th: *innocet.* Silent emendation in Skeat, followed by Jellech, but noted and followed by Leyerle.

142–43 *lybel of departicion*. A bill (or writ) of separation; taken from *libellum repudii* in Matthew 5.31, which Wyclif translates by "a libel of forsakyng" (Skeat, p. 480). See Henryson's *Testament of Cresseid*, line 74, for a comparable literary usage.

143–44 *Ye, ye . . . of desertes*. Skeat reads the sentence as follows: "I find, in no law, (provision for) recompensing and rewarding in a bounteous way, those who are guilty, according to their deserts" (p. 480). Jellech opposes this reading, complaining that it "does not alter the tenor of the sentence as we have it in Thynne, but that meaning [i.e., in Thynne] goes against the tenor of the preceding and following statements of Love" (p. 420). Here I would intervene against Jellech but not necessarily for Skeat. It is possible to construe this and the following sentence as transitions, very abrupt and unprepared for in the preceding sentences, to a consideration of conversions and how the same law that condemns the guilty can also acknowledge and reward the guilty who have converted. The examples, then, that follow would illustrate this principle. Note that in this construal, Jellech's complaint that Skeat's "reading of *in goodnes* as 'in a bounteous way' does not conform to any meaning of the term recorded in the *MED*," becomes irrelevant since we need read the phrase only as "reward in [i.e., with] goodness" to follow the construction I am proposing.

145ff. *Paulyn*. Th: *Pauly*, followed by Leyerle. Skeat emends to *Pauly[n]*, i.e., Paulinus, but suggests there is some mistake. "Perhaps he refers to L. Aemilius Paullus, brother of M. Aemilius Lepidus the Triumvir. This Paullus was once a determined enemy of Caesar, but was won over to his side by a large bribe" (p. 480). Jellech follows Skeat.

147–50 *This lawe . . . treason*. Jellech cites Schaar, who makes two plausible suggestions for its emendation: "First, he judges *this lawe* to refer to a passage about laws against conspiracies which has been lost, since there is no earlier reference for *is acompted in to*. Using Higden's account of the Civil War as a guide to Usk's possible attitude towards those events, he concludes that for Usk the conspiracy was on the part of Caesar, and that it was Cato who was considered to have thwarted the betrayal of the republic by Caesar. Consequently, Schaar would emend the passage as follows: 'This law in Rome hath yet his name of measuring, in mede, the bewraying of [a] conspiracy. Ordayned by the senatours, the deth [of] Julius Cesar is acompted into Catons rightwisness; for ever in trouth florisshes his name among the knowers of

reason.' I have incorporated Schaar's proposals into my text, except for the indefinite article 'a' which is often not used by Usk, though it seems necessary to modern ears" (p. 420). Leyerle and I, also, in the main, concur with Schaar.

150 *treason*. Th: *reason*. Leyerle's emendation.

150–52 *Perdicas*. Skeat: "Perdiccas, according to the romances, succeeded Alexander the Great; see note to Book 2, [line 180]. I do not find the anecdote referring to Porus. It is not improbable that the author was thinking of Philip the physician, who revealed to Alexander 'a privy hate' entertained against that monarch by Parmenion; see the *Wars of Alexander*, lines 2559–83" (p. 480).

152–55 Heyworth (pp. 144–45) would re-punctuate. He argues that

> The author's meaning is clarified if *reward* is allowed the rare sense "estimation, worth" recorded by *OED* (under *reward* sb[1] I 3) only in two texts from the fourteenth century, and the punctuation slightly modified.
>
> Wherfore euery wight, by reson of lawe, after his rightwysenesse apertely his mede may chalenge, *and* so thou that maynteynest lawe of kynde *and* therfore disease hast suffred in th*e* lawe. Rewarde is worthy to be rewarded *and* ordayned, *and* apartly thy mede might thou chalenge.
>
> That is, everyone may claim his reward to the extent that he has earned it by virtue of his goodness; so may the Dreamer, who has maintained nature's laws and suffered for his pains. Moral worth deserves to be rewarded and clearly the Dreamer is justified in claiming what is due to him.

154 Schaar would omit *rewarde* and change *is* to *art* (p. 34).

155–58 Heyworth (pp. 145–46) would re-punctuate. He comments:

> The Dreamer is here restating the law that the Lady has just enunciated: that by virtue of his goodness a man may claim the reward due to him . . .; that worth ought to be rewarded. . . . His restatement is: "Wel deseruynge in to worship of a wight without nedeful compulsion ought medefully to be rewarded." That is, merit in voluntarily doing honour to a person deserves to be rewarded. . . . Repunctuation helps to make the meaning clearer.

> Certes, q*uo*d I, this haue I wel lerned. *And* euer hensforward I shal drawe me therafter in onehed of wyl to abyde, this lawe bothe maynteyne *and* kepe (*and* so hope I best entre in to your grace): Wel deseruynge in to worship of a wight without nedeful compulsion ought medefully to be rewarded.

Leyerle modernizes this last sentence as follows: "Uncompelled and meritorious conduct in honor of a person ought to be rewarded richly."

158 *nedeful*. Th: *nedefnl*. Leyerle's emendation.

compulsion ought. Skeat emends to *compulsion [that] ought*; Schaar supplies *and* in place of Skeat's *that*, noting, "it is the speaker, not the subject, who expects reward" (p. 35).

160 *avauntage*. Th: *avautage*. Leyerle's emendation.

161 *may*. Skeat emends to *many*, suggesting a parallel structure with line 160; followed by Jellech and Leyerle. But *may* makes satisfactory sense.

166 *right as mater*. Skeat cites Guido delle Colonne's *Historia Troiae*: "sicut ad formam de forma procedere materiam notum est" [just as one observes matter move from form to form] (pp. 480–81). See the note to *Legend of Good Women*, line 1582 ("As mater apetiteth forme alwey"), where the version "sicut appetit materia semper formam" [just as matter always hungers for form] is given.

173 *do by*. Skeat emends to *do [it] by*.

178 *and right*. Skeat: "if right-doing were not in the original working" (p. 481).

180 *recche*. Th: *recth*. Skeat's emendation, followed by Jellech and Leyerle.

183 *parte be*. Skeat emends to *part [that] be*.

191 *muste do good nedes*. Skeat: "must necessarily do good" (p. 481).

194–95 *Aristotel . . . in understanding*. Skeat refers to *Nicomachean Ethics* I.1.2 and 5; but Jellech notes that by Usk's time this was standard medieval moral doctrine. See further Piltz, p. 179.

195–97 *and he that . . . must nedes be bad*. Jellech: "The contrasts Usk seems to make are sufficiently clear, although the syntax is not. In line [195] I have emended Thynne's verb phrase 'doth away,' meaning 'to turn away from,' to *doth alway*, because Thynne's reading would not provide any contrast between the act and the ends for which it is done. Also, in line [195], Thynne's 'he that' seems a certain instance of dittography, because there are only two kinds of good acts under consideration, not three. One kind is to do good and not take account of the ends for which it is done, which merely cancels out the goodness. The other kind is to do good, but not in a good manner or by a good means so that the direction of the end is perverted" (p. 425).

196 *goodly and draweth*. Th: *goodly draweth*. Skeat's emendation, followed by Jellech and Leyerle.

199 *doth nat goodly*. Th: *doth goodly*. Skeat's emendation.

203 *ever*. Th: *even*. Skeat's emendation, followed by Jellech and Leyerle. *Even* does make some sense, however.

210 *commended*. Th: *eommended*. Leyerle's emendation.

213 *Clerkes . . . is blessed*. Jellech cites St. Augustine, *De Trinitate* 13.8: "Quia beatus nolens nemo fit" [because no one becomes blessed against his will] (p. 427).

215 *ne service in that is*. Skeat emends to *ne service [is] in that [that] is*; followed by Jellech and Leyerle.

218 *may after-rewarde*. Th: *after reward*. Skeat's emendation, followed by Jellech and Leyerle.

229–30 *so mote . . . it nat betyde.* Jellech: "*So mote it be nedes* and *otherwyse may it nat betyde* are definitions offered for the terms 'necessary' and 'necessity'" (p. 428).

234 *desyreth.* Jellech emends to *deserveth.*

237–38 *if it . . . or of mede.* Compare Boethius, *Cons.* 5. pr. 3. 73–88.

239–43 *Me thynketh . . . stande togyther.* "This passage introduces the chief issue of this third book of the *Testament*, whether God's foreknowledge can be reconciled with man's free will. The statement is from St. Anselm, *De Conc.* Q.I.l, 507b" (Jellech, p. 429). (See Appendix 3.)

239–69 See *Conc.* 1.1 (Appendix 3, pp. 432–33).

248–49 *lyberté of arbetry of arbitrement.* Skeat emends silently to *liberté of arbitrement.* Leyerle emends *of* to *or*, which may well be right.

248–50 *First, if . . . sothe to understonding.* Jellech notes that "this statement follows closely the latter half of St. Anselm's opening sentence of the *De Conc.* Q. I.l. With some exceptions, this chapter is a close paraphrase of St. Anselm's Chapters 1, 2, and part of 3, of Question 1" (see Appendix 3).

251 *repugnaunce.* Th: *repuguaunce.* Emended by all.

253–54 *whom foloweth necessité of thinges commyng.* Jellech: "The antecedent of *whom* is *prescience*; the Latin reads 'quam sequi necessitas futurorum rerum videtur'" (p. 432).

255–56 *Bothe . . . I admyt.* Jellech: "Usk's immediate capitulation to Love's assertion is undramatic and a contradiction of the doubt which he expressed at the end of Chapter 2. Nor does he follow St. Anselm in accepting the two propositions as not contradictory. Since Anselm's argument is rather paradoxical, it may not have been fully understood by Usk. Anselm asserts that there is another impossibility included in the two propositions; i.e., free will assumes something happens without necessity, but since God has foreknowledge and since God's foreknowledge assumes that what God knows is necessarily the future, the paradoxical conclusion is that there is something in the future without necessity by necessity. Anselm did not develop or resolve the issue, but left it open. Usk, however, makes definite the vagueness of his original and consequently is misled" (p. 432).

262 *wheder.* Th: *whedto.* Schaar notes that *wheder* is Skeat's emendation of the corrupt *whedto* in Thynne's text. "It seems that *wheder* was substituted for *wherof (ergo)*, and that a negation corresponding to *nequaquam* should be restored: *and wherof, to every wight that hath good understanding, is seen these thinges <in no wise> to be repugnaunt* etc. After the second *necessité* a full stop is required" (p. 36).

267–69 *God beforne wote . . . love dedes.* Here Usk substitutes his own case of love and destiny for St. Anselm's topics of man's righteousness and sinfulness. See Jellech, p. 433. See also Leyerle, p. 370.

273 *so it foloweth.* Skeat misreads, *so followeth.*

273–74 *And so . . . and shal be.* Jellech suggests that the phrase "without necessity" was "either dropped by the printer or inadvertently omitted by Usk. It is essential for the sense: And so it follows, whether you love or do not love, either case is and shall be without necessity" (p. 434).

276 *through.* Th: *though.* Skeat's emendation, followed by Jellech and Leyerle.

281 *if no love.* Skeat emends to *if [I] no[t] love*; Leyerle, to *if [I ne] love.*

284–385 See *Conc.* 1.2 (Appendix 3, pp. 433–35).

289–90 *Right so . . . or els none.* Jellech: "Just as if I say that you are a lover or else not a lover through necessity" (p. 436).

291–92 *whiche shal nat be.* Jellech: "That which it will not be" (p. 436).

292 *whiche shal be.* Jellech: "That which it will be" (p. 436).

292–94 *That same thynge . . . any other thing.* Jellech: "It is possible that Usk did not understand the Latin construction here and transferred his confusion to the English version. The Latin is, 'hoc ipsum namque praescit Deus, qui praevidet aliquid futurum ex sola voluntate, quod voluntas non cogitur, aut prohibetur ulla alia re.' The Latin 'qui praevidet' has become *which he beforne seeth* instead of 'who foresees' and no syntactical relationship between *any thyng commende* and the preceding verb is expressed in the English" (p. 436). See Appendix 3 below, p. 433.

296 *inconvenyent.* Leyerle emends to *inconvenyen[ce].*

298–300 *Also farthermore . . . it is pronounced.* Jellech: "Furthermore, whoever considers properly his understanding of [the word] 'prescience,' in the same way that anything is said to be before known, [will realize] it is also pronounced or declared to be coming, or in the future" (p. 437).

302 *if I sey if it shal be.* Skeat reads: *if I sey, it shal be.* Leyerle: *if I sey, 'If it shal be [of necessyté it shal be].'*

306–07 *the thyng toforne put.* In the general murkiness of language here, one key, centered in this phrase, *the thyng toforne put*, will be of considerable help to the reader. It is the order of the grammar — *dyversité in settyng of wordes maketh dyversité in understandynge* (lines 313–14). If something is, it is necessary — *if loue is put to be it is said of necessyté to be*; but necessity does not make it that it is — *nat for that necessité constrayneth or defendeth love to be or nat to be*. Or, as we find it a few lines later, *and it is nat the same to saye, love to be passed, and love passed to be passed* (lines 311–12) — i.e., the "setting of the words" is crucial: love passed *must* be passed.

307 *that thyng shal be.* Leyerle adds: *[of necessite it shal be].*

310 *commyng to al.* Leyerle: *commyng to [be] al.*

341 *And yet.* Leyerle emends to: *and yet [after it is present].*

342 *whiche to her, Margarite, thee hath bounde*. "which has bound you to her, Margarite." Th reads *boude* for *bounde*. Both Skeat and Jellech read *bounde*.

343 *for*. Th: *ferre*. Schaar argues that *ferre* in Usk's text was miswritten for *for*, translating St Anselm's *quia*. "The authentic reading, it can hardly be doubted, should be: 'Trewly, som doing of accion nat by necessité is comminge, for toforn it be, it may be that it shal nat be comminge'" (p. 36).

355 *right as this terme*. Th: *Right these termes*. Jellech's emendation. Skeat emends: *right [so] this terme*, linking the clause to the previous sentence, as does Leyerle, who changes *this* to *th[e]*.

356 *that thyng*. Skeat emends to *that [a] thing*.

357 *that*. Skeat: "that which."

357–58 *foloweth with . . . constrayned*. Leyerle emends to: *folow[yng], w[hic]h nothyng [constrayneth] to be*.

357 *with nothyng*. Skeat: "yet not so as to be constrained by anything else" (p. 481).

358–417 See *Conc*. 1.3 (Appendix 3, pp. 435–37).

359–61 Schaar notes, "as has been demonstrated often enough on the preceding pages, words and clauses have frequently dropped out during the copying of the text, and, I think, something has been lost in that way here as well. The passage, it seems, should be thus restored: "For if I say, 'tomorowe love is comming in this Margarites herte,' nat therfore thorow necessité shal the ilke love be; yet it may be that <toforn it be,> it shal nat be, although it were comming" (p. 37).

361 *that it shal nat be*. Leyerle, following Schaar, emends to: *that [toforn it be], it shal nat be*.

370–71 *one is . . . Another is*. Leyerle observes that "the distinction . . . is between *forgoing necessity* . . ., Anselm's *praecedens necessitas*, which is causative, and *folowyng necessite* . . ., Anselm's *sequens necessitas*, which is not" (p. 373).

371 *nedeful is*. Skeat emends to *nedeful [it] is*.

375 *commynge*. Leyerle thinks some portion of the text is probably lost at this point.

389 *For why . . . nat be*. Schaar finds it more likely that Usk wrote *now than that god wol may nat <nat> be*, and that one negation was either dropped by haplography [shortened writing] or consciously eliminated by a scribe or printer, unfamiliar with philosophical argument (p. 37). Leyerle follows Schaar and adds the double negative.

400–01 *Right so . . . wyl is necessarye*. Jellech observes: "There is some corruption here. The Latin construction is very simple: 'ita non est peccatum voluntatis necessarium, sicut velle non est necessarium' (see Appendix 3, p. 436). Skeat added 'in' before *maner*, but this is no clarification. I have let the passage stand as is" (p. 448). Leyerle follows Skeat.

402 *through*. Th: *though*. Skeat's emendation, followed by Jellech and Leyerle.

403–04 *right so . . . to wylne*. Jellech: "This translation is confusing. It means, as the thing which free will wishes, it also may and may not wish. That is, in order to be *free* the will must have an option to choose or not to choose, but it is necessary for the will to choose something" (p. 448).

405–06 *for impossyble . . . to him*. Jellech suggests that "between *impossyble*, line [405], and *to him*, line [406], two and a half lines of text have been repeated in Thynne: *to him it is one thyng and the same to wylne he may not wylne but thilk to wylne nedeful is: for impossyble ~~to him it is one thyng and the same to wylne he may not wylne but thilk to wylne nedeful is: for impossyble~~ to him it is one thyng and the same to wylne and not to wylne*. In addition some equivalent portion of St. Anselm's text in translation has been omitted after *he may not wylne*, line 404: "antequam velit quia libera est; et cum jam vult, non potest non velle." "Sed eam velle necesse est" follows and the translation is duly included in Thynne. Possibly the similarity between this clause and the clause *thilke to wylne nedeful is* (line 406) was the source of the errour" (p. 449). Leyerle's emendation of lines 403–06 is as follows: "*Right so thilke thynge that fre wyl wol: and [he] maye and not may not wylne, and nedeful is that to wylne. [For he maye not wylne toforne he wol, as wyl is fre, and whan than he wol] he maye [not] not wylne, but thilke to wilne nedeful is* [etc.]." Leyerle also calls this passage "a *locus desperatus*" (p. 376):

> . . . Thynne's text is little more than bewildering nonsense. . . . Anselm's *De concordia* is not easy to understand in itself and Usk's version of it is often baffling unless read beside the original, and sometimes then as well. At line . . . [424] of this chapter the manuscript from which Thynne's text was set had the major displacement of leaves discussed in the Introduction . . .; consequently, any attempt by the printer to get a general sense of the chapter's argument was futile. In view of these circumstances, the corruption of Thynne's text is not surprising. . . . [T]he editor must acknowledge that his proposals are little more than first aid to what must be considered a *locus desperatus*.

408 *and that he wol not*. Leyerle emends to *and that [it be not, that] he wol not*.

or. Th: *of*. Skeat's emendation, followed by Jellech and Leyerle.

409–10 *than by wyl . . . togyther be*. Jellech: "The phrase *than by wyl not constrayned* seems to be Usk's explanatory insertion into the argument. The sentence following is hopelessly corrupt. The Latin is, 'befariam est necessarium, quia et voluntate cogitur fieri, et quod fit non potest simul non fieri.' In Usk the negation of the final infinitive *be* is missing; as is the main clause" (p. 449).

413 *seeth*. Th: *syght*. Skeat's emendation, followed by Jellech and Leyerle.

414–15 *al maner thynges ben*. Skeat: *al maner thinges [that] ben*. Leyerle: *al, [and] man[y] thynge ben*.

415–16 *might have ben never they*. Skeat: *[it] might have ben [that] never they*. Leyerle: *might have ben, never th[at]*.

418–19 *Hereby . . . lybertie of wyl*. Jellech: "There is a mixture of constructions here, of a noun clause dependent on *ben knowe*, 'everything is not from necessity,' and an accusative-infinitive construction, 'all things not be from necessity.' Hence, the non-agreement between subject and verb. *For*, line [419], means 'but'" (p. 451).

418–38 See *Conc.* 1.4 (Appendix 3, p. 437).

424 *movable tyme. There is*. Here, as do Jellech and Leyerle, I intervene in Thynne's text to re-order it in conformity with the Bradley-Skeat shift, as modified by Bressie (see the Introduction, vi f, "The Problem of the Broken Sequence of Book 3," for extended comment). As a consequence of this intervention, the reader can no longer follow Thynne except by observing the boldface folia numbers in the lower half of the page and skipping across the breaks to connect Thynne's consecutive foliation. I will alert the reader to each break in my notes as well as marking it in the boldface foliation. Finally, I would like to cite Leyerle's important observation that "here the Bradley shift follows the order of [St. Anselm's] *De concordia*, conclusive proof of the accuracy of the shift at this point" (p. 379). The reader can test this assertion, with which I concur, by checking the relevant passages in Appendix 3 below (p. 437).

432–35 *whiche thyng . . . for free arbitrement*. Jellech: "This sentence is a straightforward calque [translation by modelling the target language on the original language] on the Latin, with much resultant confusion in the English. However, the Latin is not very coherent either. I would translate St. Anselm:

> The conclusion is, if it is not too absurd even to state, either it is not by necessity or it is not anything which God knows or foreknows to be or not to be. Therefore [= Usk *and yet*] nothing prevents anything from being known or foreknown by him in our wills or from being done in our acts, or from being in the future through free will. (p. 453; see Appendix 3)

442–60 See *Conc.* 1.4 (Appendix 3, p. 438).

447 *first alone*. Jellech: "'Alone' in the sense of 'solitary' is not suitable here. A substantive derived from OF *aloigner*, 'to move,' may have been the original word, misread or misunderstood by the printer. The OF noun 'aloinement,' and the verb "aloinen"

entered Middle English" (p. 454). Leyerle offers a very different explanation: "the word *commyng*, from line [446], is understood after *first*. Love's point in this discussion is that whether motion is coming or going is a matter of perspective. In its circular motion, the sun in going from a given position is also coming back to it" (p. 380).

462–63 *Job . . . passe*. Skeat (p. 481) cites Job 14.5: "Constituisti terminos eius, qui praeteriri non poterunt" [thou hast appointed his bounds which cannot be passed].

462–554 See *Conc*. 1.5 (Appendix 3, pp. 438–39).

464 *dying*. Th: *doyng*. Skeat's emendation.

466–67 *ne He seeth . . . of necessyté*. Jellech: "This sentence is an inaccurate calque on the Latin, '[Deus] dicitur constituisse apud se immutabiliter quod apud hominen priusquam fiat mutari potest.' An English rendering would read:

> *God is said to have ordained for himself immutably what can be changed amongst men before it happens.*

Usk's version loses the contrast between what has been set down as requisite for God and what is the case for man" (p. 456; see Appendix 3). Leyerle, following Schaar, emends *nothing wheder* to *nothing [but the sothe], wheder*.

470 *conformes*. Skeat cites the Vulgate (Romans 8.29, 30): "*Nam quos praesciuit, et praedestinauit* conformes *fieri imaginis Filii sui*" — For whom he foreknew, he also predestinated to be made *conformable* to the image of his Son (p. 481).

473 *magnifyed*. Compare Romans 8.30.

475 *nowe as mokel . . . wynter*. Jellech glosses: "And now a moment is as great as seven thousand winters" (p. 457).

490–92 *But right as . . . very knowynge*. Jellech: "This is an incomplete and confused rendering of the Latin, which contrasts the temporal present, even when projected to include every place and everything which is in existence anywhere, with the eternal present which contains everything which has ever existed in time, all at once" (p. 458; see Appendix 3). Leyerle solves the problem by emending *coveyteth* to *co[nteyn]eth* and *both* to *b[e]th.*

499 *at the God.* Jellech emends to *at God* and glosses "with God" (p. 459); Leyerle follows Jellech.

502 *temporel, without.* Skeat places *and* before the preposition *without.* Leyerle follows Skeat. Jellech notes that the subject is still *al thynges* and that "there is nothing in St. Anselm to correspond to this clause''(p. 460).

505 *to thy.* Leyerle, following Skeat, emends to *[in] thy.*

507–08 *for at thilk . . . thilke seintes.* Th: *for al thilk . . . thilke sentences.* Leyerle's emendation. Skeat reads: *for al [at] thilk . . . [of] thilke sentence*; Jellech: *for al at thilk . . . at thilk sentence.*

511 *in wordes.* Th: *worde is.* Jellech's emendation, followed by Leyerle. Skeat reads: *[in] worde.*

520–21 *in whiche . . . your actes.* Jellech suggests that a key word, *true*, has been lost here; i.e., . . . "your wylles and your actes true'' (p. 461).

525 *nat.* Th: *no arte.* Skeat suggests (p. 482), with a "(?)," the gloss "in no way"; but then he goes on to suggest that *ne arte* is "surely an error for *nat*, as *writest nat* is repeated in line [525]." Jellech and Leyerle follow Skeat's suggestion, as do I.

526 *or els wylne to write.* Jellech: "Or it is not necessary for you to wish to write" (p. 462).

528–29 *for somthyng is . . . it nat be.* Jellech: "Apparently nothing more was attempted here by Usk than an approximation of the Latin, but the rendering has become badly confused. The changes which I have made are only those errors which the printer might have made under influence of the surrounding text: 'for somthyng is in the everlastynge presence that in temporal tyme it was nat in tyme in eterne presence shal it nat be'" (p. 462). Leyerle (p. 182) emends as follows: *For somthynge [is nat in temporal tyme that] is in the everlastynge presence [and somthynge that was] in temporal tyme, it was nat in eternyte, [and somthynge that will be in temporal] tyme, in eterne presence shal it nat be: than no reason defendeth that somthyng [may] be in tyme temporal movyng that in eterne is immovable.* Schaar (p.39) would read: *For <if> somthing is in the everlastinge presence, than in temporal tyme it was nat; <if it was> in <temporal> tyme, in eterne presence shal it nat be*; that is "if anything is in eternity, it was not in time; if it was in time, it shall not be in eternity."

532 *immovable*. Th: *movable*. Skeat's emendation, followed by Jellech and Leyerle.

535 *is in eternyté*. Th: *is eternyté*. Skeat's emendation, followed by Jellech and Leyerle.

536 *ne*. Leyerle, following Skeat, omits.

537–41 *A so . . . in his present maner*. Jellech: "Skeat drily calls attention to the obscurity of Usk's explanation and the incongruity of Love's enthusiasm for her pupil's perspicuity. Schaar attempted to remedy the apparent defects in Usk's explanation by going back to St. Anselm's work to see what is missing in ours. Schaar did not see the error 'deemed' for *denied* in line [538]. Moreover, Schaar did not realize the extent to which Usk is paraphrasing in these lines, so that his proposed emendations are too extensive to be genuine. I do not believe that emendation is required so much as syntactical expansion of Usk's paraphrase. Of course, access to the Latin treatise (see Appendix 3) is invaluable because at least one knows what he was trying to say. I would read these sentences as follows:

> It seems to me that things coming or else past here in your temporal time ought not to be denied to be in eternity ever now and present. And yet it does not follow that anything which was or will be (in time) is not there [in eternity] in any manner, past or else future: we shall completely deny that, because there [in eternity] it is without ceasing in its manner of the present." (p. 464)

Schaar would add *it there to be passed or coming* between *deny* and *for* in line 540, observing that the missing words may easily have been dropped by haplography "since the words *there to ben passed or els comming* had just before been written" (p. 40).

538 *denied.* Th: *demed.* Skeat follows Thynne, but Jellech emends to *denied* (followed by Leyerle), which makes good sense, presupposing a misreading of three consecutive minims.

540 *than.* Leyerle emends to *tha[t].*

541 *be able.* Th: *able.* Skeat's emendation, followed by Jellech and Leyerle.

542 *cloude in unconnyng.* Conceivably a verbal echo of the "cloud of unknowing."

547 *afore.* Th: *and for.* Skeat's emendation, followed by Jellech and Leyerle.

548 *For right.* Skeat: "for nothing at all exists there (i.e., in eternity) after the manner of that which is temporal" (p. 482).

554 *that God al thyng.* Th: *that al thyng.* Skeat and Leyerle add *God*, as head of the clause; Jellech adheres to Thynne.

554–58 See *Conc.* 1.7 (Appendix 3, pp. 440–41).

555 *ben to ben.* Leyerle emends to *have beyng.* Skeat glosses *ben to ben* as "are to come because of God's knowledge" (p. 482).

559–60 *the noble philosophical poete in Englissh.* Jellech: "Ever since the discovery that Chaucer was not the author of *TL* . . . this reference has been taken to allude to Chaucer. Skeat makes the interesting point that the metaphysical question of greatest importance in *Troilus and Criseyde* is not the origin of evil, which is Usk's topic at this point, but predestination. From Usk's reference here to Chaucer as an authority on the origin of evil it would seem that he misread or misunderstood the Troilus" (p. 466). *Pace* Skeat and Jellech (and Bressie, too), Leyerle argues, correctly, I think, that (p. 387)

> Usk's request . . . is for information on two problems: one concerns the problem of evil and the other concerns God's foreknowledge. Love replies by sending him in lines [569–73] back to II.13 and II.14 in the *Testament*, chapters that contain a discussion of the nature of evil; see, especially, II.13.1ff. . . . The reference to *Tr* can thus be seen as one to matters about foreknowledge.

560 *whiche*. Leyerle emends to *[spe]che*.

565 *starieres*. Skeat: *storiers*, gen. pl. of *storier*, a teller of a story. Leyerle emends to *storiers*.

569 *of two the laste*. Jellech suggests chapters 13 and 14 of Book 2.

573 *to be*. Leyerle, following Skeat: *to be [lykned]*.

577 *muste come the spire*. Jellech: "The tree allegory describing the lover's growth in steadfastness was foreshadowed at Book 2, chapter 11 [lines 1141–44]. Usk's use of the metaphor of the tree may have been inspired by St. Anselm's lengthy analogy (*De Conc*. Q.III.6 [see Appendix 3, p. 442]) of the garden of the human heart and the reception of God's word as seed" (p. 469). See below note to lines 806–07.

586 *seconde booke*. Skeat: Book 2, chapter 11 (lines 1106ff.).

588 *setling*. Th: *setteles*. Skeat's emendation, followed by Jellech and Leyerle.

591 *frendes*. Leyerle: *f[erdn]es*. Schaar emends to *feendes* (p. 41).

591–93 *my wyl maye ben turned* . . . Leyerle speculates that "this autobiographical reference would suggest that Book III was not written while Usk was in confinement. There are no references to the prison in the book, except possibly one at III.1 [128], *disesely habitation*" (pp. 388–89). With this speculation, compare Medcalf who argues, at great length ([1997], pp. 232ff.), for a major change in and resumption of *TL* between Book 2, toward the end, and Book 3, transpiring perhaps as late as 1387 (p. 234):

> Finally, imprisoned by the Lords Appellant, when his new political motive, the king's service, had become the reason why execution for treason was close upon him, he was driven to those profound considerations of value, vocation, commitment, and the analogy between human and divine love which are the intellectual glory of the *Testament*. The joins and inconsistencies in the book [*viz*., 3] are unrevised, presumably, because he suffered execution. (p. 237)

If Medcalf is correct in his bold hypothesis — and his arguments are too complicated and subtle for me to paraphrase adequately here — then a great many received opinions about Usk and *TL* will have to be subjected to fresh examination.

595 *hou*. Th: *thou*. Leyerle's emendation. Jellech and Skeat read *thou*.

596 *is thy*. Leyerle emends to *is [of] thy*.

601 *deme*. Leyerle: *de[in]e*. This emendation (meaning "disdain to") is perhaps sound, given the trouble the compiler for Usk had in reading sequences of minims. But though it makes clearer sense, it is not absolutely necessary. Moreover, *jugement* in line 604 lends support to *deme*.

612 *lovynge*. Leyerle: *l[e]vynge*.

613–40 See *Conc*. 3.11 (Appendix 3, pp. 441–42).

613 *lykened*. Leyerle: *ly[nk]ed*. Leyerle's emendation picks up the knot metaphor nicely, but *lykened* makes good sense and ties in with metaphors of similitude, which are also prominent.

614 *wylles*. Leyerle: *will[e]*, which is more idiomatic (and probably right) though less quaint, and the plural is repeated in the same line, which Leyerle is likewise obliged to emend.

615 *Right as ye han in your body*. Leyerle offers the following clarification (p. 390):

> Because Usk does not define his terminology clearly, a brief summary of the argument may be helpful. As the body has instruments of use, such as eyes to see and feet to walk, so the soul has its instruments. One instrument of the soul is reason and another is will. Each instrument of the soul has use and also propensities, Anselm's *aptitudines*, which Usk renders as *aptes*. Anselm refers to the *aptitudines voluntatis*, the propensities of the will, by the word *affectiones*, which Usk renders as *affections*. Thus the will is an instrument of the soul and can be considered in three ways: it can be referred to simply as the will itself, or by its affections, or by its use.

616 *wyttes*. The *five wits* are the five senses. See further Piltz, pp. 204–07.

616, 617 *aparte*. Leyerle emends to *ap[t]e* (see note to line 615), which makes sense, but loses the pun on "separate," "appropriate," and "open." *Apte* is the term in line 622, however, which strengthens Leyerle's case. But his emendation of *apetytes* to *ap[t]es* in line 624 is quite unnecessary.

624 *apetytes*. "Sanderlin has pointed out (p. 71n4) Usk's mistranslation of *apetytes* for the Latin 'aptitudinibus' in the *De conc.*" (Jellech, p. 474).

625 *terme of equivocas*. Skeat: "terms of like signification, *terme* being an error for *termes*. Answering to Lat. *uerba aequiuoca*, words of like signification" (p. 482). See further Piltz, p. 97.

629 *whan ye*. Leyerle: *whan [ye reason, and eye is instrument of seeing whiche ye usen whan] ye*.

632–37 *And thus is instrument wyl* . . . Leyerle observes that "there are three instances in [these lines] of the past participle *affectum* rendered as if it were the noun *affectio*; as a result, Usk's text makes little sense" (pp. 392–93). The reader should consult Anselm's original, *Conc.*, 3.11, in Appendix 3, pp. 441–42 below.

636–37 *For affection* . . . *to wake*. Jellech suggests that a person never wants to be sick, or never wants always to be awake (p. 475).

641 *purposed*. Th: *pursosed*.

649 *use ye ne ought*. Leyerle: *n[o si]ght*. Between *ye* and *ne* ends the first shift of the text. As Leyerle notes "here, as at 3.4. [424], the shifted text follows the order of *De concordia*" (p. 395). At this point, Thynne's text must be rearranged again.

660 *But utterly* . . . *ben rewarded*. "But in order to be rewarded with grace to get thy desired bliss" (Jellech, p. 477).

672 Schaar inserts <*and*> before *away* and *grace* (p. 42).

683–85 *for though . . . unbyde*. Schaar: "Obviously, the second sentence is the concrete case in question, illustrated by the metaphor in the first. The clauses in the second sentence must therefore be paralleled in the first, and we must read: *I trowe right, for though thy wil out of reson shulde not tourne, thy wil in one reson shulde not onbyde*. The meaning seems to be: just as, though drunkenness is forbidden, people need not always be without drink, so, although your will ought not to lose its contact with reason, it need not necessarily be reasonable in one way only, but so as to make you satisfied, provided you remain virtuous" (p. 42). See also *T&C* 3.715–18:

"In every thyng, I woot, ther lith mesure.
For though a man forbede dronkenesse,
He naught forbet that every creature
Be drynkeles for alwey, as I gesse."

688 *Thou might not chaunge*. Schaar (p. 43) proposes punctuating here so that *thou might not change* begins a new sentence: *Trewly, that wil and reson shulde be knit togider, was free wil of reson: after tyme thyne herte is assentaunt to them bothe. Thou might not chaunge, but if thou from rule of reson varye*.

711 *envy*. Leyerle: *en[em]y*.

714 *wyners*. Skeat notes that the word *welked* occurs twice in *CT* VI.738, IV.277; and *wiver* once, *T&C* 3.1010. Leyerle follows Skeat's suggestion and emends to *wy[v]ers*.

722 *kynde*. Th: *kindly*. Jellech's emendation, followed by Leyerle.

728 *evydence*. Th: *evydece*. Emended by all.

732 *som*. Th: *no*. Jellech's emendation, followed by Leyerle.

734–35 *Why . . . t'other*. Skeat: "Why, as soon as one has sprung up on high, does not the other spring up also?" Here "one" and "the other" seem to refer to "will" and "bliss" (p. 482).

739–40 *anon as . . . to receyve*. "As soon as that will proffers itself to be shown and revealed, the bliss should hasten to it, to receive the will" (Jellech, p. 484).

742 *Great weight on hye onlofte*. See Book 1, line 211, and note above.

his. Th: *this*. Skeat's emendation, followed by Jellech and Leyerle.

742–44 The lines echo the eagle's speech in Chaucer's *HF*, lines 729–56. See also Aristotle's *Physics* 8.4, but especially Boethius's *Cons.*, 3. pr. 11.95–187.

752 *if*. Schaar would emend to *in* (p. 40).

759–75 See *Conc.* 3.6 (Appendix 3, pp. 442–43).

760–64 *but suche . . . in traveyle*. Leyerle rearranges the passage as follows: *But suche as nought in norisshynge to mannes kynde serven, or els suche as tournen soone unto mannes confusyon in case that therof they ataste, [men might leave, though they were] comen forthe out of the earth by their owne kynde, withouten any mannes cure or any busynesse in traveyle*.

761–62 Schaar would insert *to* between *kynde* and *serven* (p. 41).

767 *yit*. Th: *it*. Skeat's emendation, followed by Leyerle. Jellech emends to *that*.

774 *in*. Not in Th. Skeat's addition, followed by Leyerle.

787 *amended*. Th: *ameded*.

791–93 *Certes, such . . . it to rewarde*. Jellech: "There is some corruption here. The thought is, that bliss gotten quickly will be rewarded accordingly by brief duration, while bliss obtained slowly and laboriously will endure. At line [791] there was no antecedent for Thynne's *hem*, which I have emended to *him*; i.e., bliss" (p. 489).

792 *thee wel*. Leyerle reads *the w[y]l*, which may be better. Skeat and Jellech follow Th: *the wel*, where *the* may be the definite article rather than a pronoun, with *wel* as "weal."

793 *right can . . . it to rewarde*. "Right, or justice, can send such bitterness afterward to even out the reward for merit" (Jellech, p. 489).

797 *blysse endelesse*. Skeat reads: *blysse [ben] endelesse*, followed by Leyerle, but not Jellech.

805 *wel*. Th: *wol*. Skeat's emendation, followed by Jellech and Leyerle.

806–07 *Thou hast herde . . . wexyng*. Skeat (p. 483) argues, vigorously, that "the idea of this Tree is copied from *PPl* C.19.4–14." But as the article by Dronke amply demonstrates, there are many other, possibly more proximate sources for the image in *TL* (see also above, note to line 577). My own position is currently one of suspicion: I can show Usk's familiarity with *T&C* to a very fine degree; not so his familiarity with *PPl* — I am therefore still sceptical that he knew *Piers*, even as I am strongly inclined to believe that even if he did, he was nowhere near being so intimate with it as he was with *T&C* and *Cons./Boece*. See further the Introduction, Section iv, "Usk and his Contemporaries."

807 *wyse this*. Leyerle inserts *[is]*.

826–28 *as gledes . . . overleyn*. See *T&C* 2.538–39: "And wel the hotter ben the gledes rede, / That men hem wrien with asshen pale and dede."

842–43 *Voice without . . . in hert*. Skeat: "The reference appears to be to Aristotle, *De Interpretatione* . . . Chapter 1. *Voice* seems to mean 'a word unrelated to a sentence,' i.e., not related to something else as forming part of a sentence" (p. 483). Skeat's opinion, then, is that Usk means the distinction between mere words and propositions, propositions being Aristotle's express subject in *Peri hermenias* (4; p. 121); only of propositions can one speak of truth or falsity. Hence, Usk continues: ". . . in ful sentence of *trewe menyng* . . ." (p. 483 — emphasis added). See further Shoaf (1983), pp. 9–11 and Isaac on the fortunes of the *Peri hermenias*.

852 *avoyde*. Schaar: "There is nothing here to be avoided, either with or without difficulty, but there is obviously something which it is not easy to wait for: *Alas! than, after suche stormes, how hard is it to abyde, til efte wedring and yeres han maked her circute cours al about, er any frute be able to be tasted!*" (p. 43).

866 *That, fole*. At this point, Thynne's text must be rearranged again.

868 *A marchaunt*. Compare Chaucer, *CT* VIII.947–50.

870 *on the oke smyte*. Skeat (p. 483) rightly compares Chaucer, *T&C* 2.1380–84, which reads:

"Thenk here-ayeins: whan that the stordy ook,
On which men hakketh ofte, for the nones,
Receyved hath the happy fallying strook,
The greete sweigh doth it come al at ones."

N.b., the close verbal echoes here in both works: *happy, sweigh, come al at ones*.

871 *falleth the lethy water*. Skeat cites Ovid, *Ex Ponto* 4.10.5.

876–77 *my thynketh . . . rewarde for my longe traveyle*. The language here reflects perhaps the complaint in *BD*, lines 36–38: "hit be a sicknesse / That I have suffred this eight yeer; / And yet my boote is never the ner." See Book 1, lines 486–87 where Usk draws upon this same passage. See also lines 879–910, and the idea that reward comes through peace which becomes possible through Margaryte's goodness, an idea similar to Blanche's gracious therapy of the distraught dreamer in *BD*.

881 *your selven sayd*. Skeat compares Book 3, chapter 2 (lines 217–21).

890–91 *it is not to put to him*. "It is not imputed to him" (Jellech, p. 498).

898–99 *kyndely drawen homewarde*. See *BD*, lines 1314ff.

899–900 *al is holy her to wyte*. "It is all to be accounted to her wholly" (Skeat, p. 483). *To wyte* usually has a bad sense, as implying blame. Hence, Jellech would emend *wyte* to *quyte* and construe "her" as "for her" so as to read: "it is entirely for her to repay the love that you have" (p. 499).

910 *this lady*. I.e., "Heavenly Love suddenly took up its place in his heart." "This of course puts an end to the dialogue, but in Thynne's misarranged print the lady speaks to him again, as if it were *out of his heart!*" (Skeat, p. 483).

918 *lyves*. Skeat emends to *lynes*, i.e., written lines of writing, which he imagines to be imprinted on his understanding (p. 483); see lines 919 and 923–24.

928–43 See *Conc*. 3.3 (Appendix 3, pp. 443).

928ff. *It is no maner doute*. . . . Jellech: "The abstraction Love has been substituted for Anselm's example of Justice" (p. 502).

932 *wyl wylne*. Skeat inserts *may* between the two words; Leyerle inserts *to*.

937 *nothynge*. Th: *nothyuge*. Leyerle's emendation.

942ff. Schaar: "The last sentence is an interpolation of Usk's own, continuing an argument borrowed from St Anselm . . .. There seems to be a slight corruption . . .. The passage, to all appearances, emphasizes the fact that 'will' and 'not will' do not go together; thus it is a commentary on the preceding statement that anyone who is not willing may not have 'loving' (for this implies free will): *Pardé, every conseyt of every resonable creature otherwyse wol not graunte:wil in affirmative with not willing by no way mowe accorde.* This continuation shows that Grace added to free will is the way to 'loving': *And although this loving wol come in myn herte by freenesse of arbitrement, as in this booke fully is shewed, yet owe I not therfore as moche alowe my free wil as grace of that Margaryte to me lened"* (p. 44).

943–76 See *Conc*. 3.4 (Appendix 3, p. 443–44).

950 *his owne gylte by fre wyl that leseth*. Jellech: "Through his own guilt by free will so that he loses" (p. 504).

953–56 See *Conc*. 3.5 (Appendix 3, p. 444).

959 *Trewly*. Th: *Trewy*.

grace. Th: *gra e*.

961 *accepted*. Leyerle: *acc[om]pted* on grounds that the term anticipates line 971.

963 *consydereth*. Skeat emends to *considereth [howe]* and Leyerle concurs.

968 *havynge*. Th: *havyuge*. Leyerle's emendation.

975 *so no man to her blysse shal ben folowed*. Jellech: "This unclear clause has no counterpart in the Latin. *Man* is probably an error for 'men' — 'so no men to their bliss. . . .' Still, *shal ben folowed* makes no sense; if it were not for the passive, 'folowe' might have the meaning 'reach or arrive at' (*MED* 6.c); compare Chaucer, *Boece* 4. p. 2. 152, where 'folowen' means 'to attain'" (p. 507).

976–86 See *Conc*. 3.12 (Appendix 3, p. 445).

981–82 *good savour*. Skeat cites 2 Corinthians 2.15–16: "Quia Christi bonus odor sumus Deo, in iis qui salui fiunt; . . . aliis quidem odor mortis in mortem" [For we are the good odour of Christ unto God, in them that are saved, . . . to the one indeed the odour of death unto death (but to the others the odour of life unto life)] (p. 484).

986–1051 See *Conc*. 3.13 (Appendix 3, pp. 445–47).

1003 *ne had*. Skeat prints *had*, disregarding *ne*, which is inserted after the word *denyded* in line 1002.

herte. Jellech emends to *hete* (also in line 1004); followed by Leyerle.

1009 *God*. Th: *good*. Skeat's emendation, followed by Leyerle.

1014 *God*. Not in Th. Skeat's addition, followed by Jellech and Leyerle.

1015 *thylke two*. Leyerle identifies the *two* through emendation: *[wylles, or affections]*, which he places after *two*.

1024–25 *fyl man unto lykenesse of unreasonable bestes*. On "unlikeness" to God (i.e., likeness to beasts) as punishment for the Fall, see Shoaf (1983), p. 250n4 and the sources cited there. The idea finds particularly vivid expression in St. Augustine's *Confessions* (7.10; p. 147) as the "regio dissimilitudinis," or "land of unlikeness"; see also his commentary on Psalm 95 (*Expositions* 4, pp. 383–85).

1026ff. *But yet wyl of blysse* . . . Leyerle argues at length (pp. 410–12) that

> this passage is an account of why Usk withdrew his support from Northampton and appealed him for treason presented in terms of Anselm's discussion of free will, justice and grace. . . The point is clear enough in outline, if not in the veiled statement in the *Testament.* Usk presents his appeal of Northampton for treason as a return by means of grace received from the *Margarite perle* to the full freedom of his will, that is, of his capacity to leave off injustice and *bestyal appetytes* and chose [*sic*] justice. To explain this political shift of allegiance in terms of Anselm's theological philosophy is an unusual and remarkably sophisticated argument without parallel in Middle English literature.

1028–29 *in his owne comodyté*. "in what is suitable for him." Skeat defines *comodites* as "desires that are suitable" (p. 484). Leyerle says that "*comodytees* means 'advantages'" (p. 410).

1029 *where*. Th: *were*. Skeat's emendation, followed by Leyerle. Jellech emends to *trewe*.

1034 *And frenesse of arbytrement*. Jellech: "There is some corruption here. The Latin translates 'man cannot wish for uprightness through free choice when he does not have uprightness, however much he was powerful to keep uprightness when he did have it'" (p. 513). See Appendix 3.

1036 *Wyl of commodyté*. Jellech: "That aspect of the will which is the instrument or means for desiring satisfactory things" (p. 513).

1048 *flesh*. Th: *flyes*. Skeat's emendation, followed by Jellech and Leyerle.

1050 *their*. Th: *they*. Leyerle's emendation; he cites the *their* in [line 1051] as proof of the emendation's validity.

1052–54 See *Conc*. 3.14 (Appendix 3, p. 447).

1056–68 See *Conc*. 2.2 (Appendix 3, p. 448).

1057 *badnesse*. Th: *hadnest*. Schaar's emendation, followed by Jellech and Leyerle. Skeat emends to *hath desteness*.

1057–59 Schaar: "Usk's argument is here very obscure, and it would be useless to try and get complete sense and coherence out of it, the obscurity being doubtless mainly due to the author's own confusion. The reason why he has been led astray seems to be his attempt to combine some reflections on Grace and destiny with a remark of St. Anselm's that predestination is true not only of good things, but of evil things as well. . . . Usk's conjunctions, then, are the chief cause of the incoherence in his passage. There are, however, other weak points in it, but for these it is less probable that Usk should be blamed. . . . the correct reading seems to be 'god badnesse made' etc. It seems more probable, further, that *missayth* (Thynne: *missaythe*) is a copyist's error than a mistranslation of *emollit*; but it is difficult to suggest a convincing emendation of this detail of Usk's passage. In Thynne *mis* is printed at the end of one line, *saythe* at the beginning of the next, and it is possible that some letters are missing. Perhaps the author wrote *mis allayth*, 'puts an end to wrong-doing,' a paraphrase of *(hominem) emollit*" (p. 45).

1059 *missaythe*. Schaar emends to *mis allayeth*; Leyerle emends to *[ne]iss[h]ythe*, "softens." Leyerle's emendation depends on *Conc*. 2.2 (See Appendix 3, pp. 447–48).

into temptacion. The reference is to Romans 9.18.

1062 *leneth*. Th: *leveth*. Skeat's emendation, followed by Jellech and Leyerle.

1066 *chapitre*. Skeat suggests Book 3, chapter 3 (p. 484).

Notes to Book 3

1068–78 See *Conc.* 2.3 (Appendix 3, pp. 448–49).

1073 *falleth, fre wyl.* Skeat emends to *falleth [through] fre wyl*; Leyerle supplies *fro* as the medial word. I punctuate, however, to recognize Usk's loose ablative absolute construction.

1077–78 Schaar: "Skeat's additions do not agree with the statement that both actions were done out of free will; no emendation seems necessary, and *for if that with free wil there had it not willed, neyther had wrought that he perfourmed* is a literal and awkward translation of St Anselm's 'quia si non sponte voluisset, neuter quod fecit fecisset'" (p. 44).

1080 *seyntes.* Th: *sentence.* Jellech's emendation, followed by Leyerle.

1085 *and the grettest.* At this point, Thynne's text must be rearranged one final time.

1090 *pamflet.* Leyerle (p. 415):

> A *pamflet* is a small treatise occupying fewer pages than would make a book. The word is, apparently, a generalized use of *Pamphilet*, a familiar name of a twelfth-century Latin amatory poem *Pamphilus seu de amore.* Usk's use is the first in English, and it may have a sense still connected with its source: "a short work about love."

1098 *of.* Not in Th. Supplied by Skeat and Leyerle.

1115 *booke amender.* A request for prayers and for the reader's indulgence was a conventional conclusion of the medieval writer. See C.S. Lewis (1964), p. 195.

1125–26 *spyrite that yeveth lyfe.* Compare John 6.63.

1127 *The letter sleeth.* See 2 Corinthians 3.6.

1128–29 *God graunt us . . . .* Skeat: "Printed as prose in Thynne; but two riming verses seem to be intended. If so, *al-le* is dissyllabic" (p. 484).

Appendix 1

The Pearl
(***TL*** 2.12 and 3.1)

I list here several accounts, beginning with Pliny, whose remarks are repeated throughout the medieval and early modern period. I proceed to Albert the Great, who closely follows Pliny. I then include Marbod of Rennes's *De Lapidibus*, probably the most important lapidary of the Middle Ages. I then proceed to Trevisa's translation of Bartholomæus Anglicus's *De Proprietatibus Rerum* and to *The Peterborough Lapidary* as examples of Middle English texts. And I also include McCulloch's commentary on the pearl since it is a useful brief overview.

For the origin of the pearl in dew penetrating the oyster, the best witness I can provide the reader is the frontispiece to this edition. This beautiful illumination tells the entire story. Under the rays of the sun striking both the pearl and the Virgin, the oyster receives the dew that begets the pearl and the Virgin receives the Trinity that begets the Christ. Notice in particular the progression indicated by the closed oyster in between the open oyster and the Virgin — it has received the dew and is "gestating" the pearl as the illumination draws our eye toward the Virgin who becomes both "mussel" and mother. For allegorical developments and extensions of this image, see the many patristic comments collected in Vona and the further discussion in Ohly's two articles. In English, Manning's study is an excellent introduction to the basic allegory of the dew and the Incarnation, with references to essential sources in Scripture and commentaries on Scripture.

List of Works Cited

Albert the Great. *Man and the Beasts: de Animalibus (Books 22–26)*. Trans. James J. Scanlan, M.D. Binghamton: MRTS, 1987.

Anglicus, Bartholomæus. *De Proprietatibus Rerum*. Trans. John Trevisa. *On the Properties of Things*. Ed. M. C. Seymour. 3 vols. Oxford: Clarendon Press, 1975.

Ebenbauer, Alfred *et al.*, eds. *Strukturen und Interpretationen: Studien zur deutschen Philologie gewidmet Blanka Horacek zum 60. Geburtstag*. Philologica Germanica 1. Vienna: Wilhelm Braumüller, 1974.

Luria, Maxwell S., and Richard L. Hoffman, eds. *Middle English Lyrics*. New York: Norton, 1974.

McCulloch, Florence. *Mediaeval Latin and French Bestiaries*. Second ed. University of North Carolina Studies in the Romance Languages and Literatures 33. 1960. Chapel Hill: University of North Carolina Press, 1962.

———. "Mermecolion — A Mediaeval Latin Word for 'Pearl Oyster'." *Mediaeval Studies* 27 (1965), 331–34.

Manning, Stephen. "'I Sing of a Myden.'" *PMLA* 75 (1960), 8–12; rpt. in Luria and Hoffman. Pp. 330–36.

Marbod of Rennes (1035–1123). *De Lapidibus*. Trans. C. W. King and John M. Riddle. Wiesbaden: Franz Steiner Verlag, 1977.

Ohly, Friedrich. "Die Geburt der Perle aus dem Blitz." In Ebenbauer *et al.* Pp. 263–78.

———. "Tau und Perl, Ein Vortrag." In Schmidtke and Schupert. Pp. 263–78.

Pliny. *Natural History*. In 10 vols. First ed. Trans. H. Rackham. 1940. Cambridge: Harvard University Press, 1983. [See especially III. 235–47.]

Schmidtke, Dietrich, and Helga Schuperte, eds. *Festschrift fur Ingeborg Schrobler zum 65. Geburtstag*. Tübingen: Niemeyer, 1973.

Vona, Costantino. "La *Margarita Pretiosa* nella interpretazione di alcuni scrittori ecclesiastici." *Divinitas* 1 (1957), 118–60.

Appendix 1

Pliny, *Natural History*, 9.54 (III, 235–37; 239–41; 243)

The first place therefore and the topmost rank among all things of price is held by pearls. These are sent chiefly by the Indian Ocean, among the huge and curious animals that we have described as coming across all those seas over that wide expanse of lands from those burning heats of the sun. And to procure them for the Indians as well, men go to the islands — and those quite few in number: the most productive is Ceylon, and also Stoidis, as we said in our circuit of the world, and also the Indian promontory of Perimula; but those round Arabia on the Persian Gulf of the Red Sea are specially praised.

The source and breeding-ground of pearls are shells not much differing from oyster-shells. These, we are told, when stimulated by the generative season of the year gape open as it were and are filled with dewy pregnancy, and subsequently when heavy are delivered, and the offspring of the shells are pearls that correspond to the quality of the dew received: if it was a pure inflow, their brilliance is conspicuous but if it was turbid, the product also becomes dirty in colour. Also if the sky is lowering (they say) the pearl is pale in colour: for it is certain that it was conceived from the sky, and that pearls have more connexion with the sky than with the sea, and derive from it a cloudy hue, or a clear one corresponding with a brilliant morning. If they are well fed in due season, the offspring also grows in size. If there is lightning, the shells shut up, and diminish in size in proportion to their abstinence from food, but if it also thunders they are frightened and shut up suddenly, producing what are called "wind-pearls," which are only inflated with an empty, unsubstantial show: these are the pearls' miscarriages. Indeed a healthy offspring is formed with a skin of many thicknesses, so that it may not improperly be considered as a hardening of the body; and consequently experts subject them to a cleansing process. I am surprised that though pearls rejoice so much in the actual sky, they redden and lose their whiteness in the sun, like the human body; consequently sea-pearls preserve a special brilliance, being too deeply immersed for the rays to penetrate; nevertheless even they get yellow from age and doze off with wrinkles, and the vigour that is sought after is only found in youth. Also in old age they get thick and stick to the shells, and cannot be torn out of these except by using a file. Pearls with only one surface, and round on that side but flat at the back, are consequently termed tambourine pearls; we have seen them clustering together in shells that owing to this enrichment were used for carrying round perfumes. For the rest, a large pearl is soft when in the water but gets hard as soon as it is taken out. . . .

56. There is no doubt that pearls are worn away by use, and that lack of care makes them change their colour. Their whole value lies in their brilliance, size, roundness, smoothness and weight, qualities of such rarity that no two pearls are found that are exactly alike: this is doubtless the reason why Roman luxury has given them the name of "unique gems," the word *unio* not existing in Greece, and indeed among foreign races, who discovered this fact, the only name for them is *margarita*. There is also a great variety in their actual brilliance; it is brighter with those found in the Red Sea, whereas those found in the Indian Ocean resemble flakes of mica, though they excel others in size. The highest praise given to their colour is for them to be called alum-coloured. The longer ones also have a charm of their own. Those that end in a wider circle, tapering lengthwise in the shape of perfume-caskets, are termed "probes." Women glory in hanging these on their fingers and using two or three for a single-earring, and foreign names for this luxury occur, names invented by abandoned extravagance, inasmuch as when they have done this they call them "castanets," as if they enjoyed even the sound and the mere rattling together of the pearls. . . .

57. . . . It is established that small pearls of poor colour grow in Britain, since the late lamented Julius desired it to be known that the breastplate which he dedicated to Venus Genetrix in her temple was made of British pearls.

Albert the Great, *de Animalibus* (p. 361)

16. MARGARITAE (Pearl shellfish) belong to the class of hard-shelled mollusks and live in shells lined with a pearly iridescence. When they come to the shoreline, these oysters absorb the dew that descends from the heavens; if it is a clear morning dew and the body of the oyster is well cleansed and vigorous, the creature conceives and forms a pearl from this absorbed dew, and the product is well rounded and shot through with a resplendent whiteness that rivals the color of the moon. If it is an evening dew produced in overcast weather, and the body of the oyster is poorly cleansed and defective, the shellfish conceives and forms a dirty pearl; up to now a pearl has not been found to exceed half an ounce in weight. Pearls are called "uniones" because at most two are found together in the same shell, but in most instances only one is found. If the oyster is in a state of fear from lightning, hail, or some other reason while the seed-pearl is developing, the final pearl will be somewhat flattened from its usual sphericity and lacking in its customary color. While still in the water, a pearl is soft in consistency, but after

exposure to air it hardens to a stony durability. Oysters emerge in droves to absorb the pearl-inducing dew. Pearls that are dropped into vinegar grow soft and eventually dissolve.

Within the scope of our own observations, pearls are found in three sites: at the point of closure of the oyster's shells; within the substance of the oyster itself; and among the stones under which the oysters lurk. The best pearls come from the Orient.

When ground to a powder and taken as medicine, pearls cure stomach disorders; they fortify the chastity of those who wear or eat them; and they strengthen the heart.

Marbod of Rennes, *De Lapidibus* (p. 84)

Tollitur a conchis species memoranda marinis
Unio dictus ob hoc, quod ab una tollitur unus,
Non duo vel plures unquam simul inveniuntur.
Cujus ad ornatum laudatur candida forma
Cum deceat vestes, deceat nichilominus aurum.
Conchae, temporibus certis, referuntur hiantes
In coelum, patulae rores haurire supernos
Ex quibus orbiculi candentes concipiuntur.
De matutino fit clarior unio rore,
Ros vespertinus fetus soles edere fuscos;
At juvenes conchae dant baccas candidiores.
Obscurat fetus concharum grandior aetas.
Quanto rorantis fuerit plus aeris haustum,
Tanto majorem gignit roratio baccam.
Ultra seminucem sed crescere nulla putatur.
Quod si celsa miscent tonitru convexo corusco,
Conchae diffugiunt subita formidine clausae.
Sic intercepto conceptio deperit hausta.
Et fit abortivum quod coeperat inde creari,
Insignes baccas praedam Maris India gignit,
Gignit et insignes antiqua Britannia baccas.

[The sea-born shell conceals the Union round,
Called by this name as always single found.
One in one shell, for ne'er a larger race,
Within their pearly walls the valves embrace.
Prized as an ornament its whiteness gleams,
And well the robe, and well the gold beseems.
At certain seasons do the oysters lie
With valves wide gaping towards the teeming sky,
And seize falling dews, and pregnant breed
The shining globules of th' ethereal seed.
Brighter the offspring of the morning dew,
The evening yields a duskier birth to view;
The younger shells produce a whiter race,
We greater age in darker colours trace.
The more of dew the gaping shell receives,
Larger the pearl its fruitful womb conceives;
However favoring airs its growth may raise,
Its utmost bulk ne'er half an ounce outweighs,
If thunders rattle through the vaulted sky
The closing shells in sudden panic fly;
Killed by the shock the embryo pearls they breed,
Shapeless abortions in their place succeed.
These spoils of Neptune th' Indian ocean boasts;
But equal those from ancient Albions's coasts.]

Bartholomæus Anglicus, *De Proprietatibus Rerum* (II, 856)

. . . [After repeating the standard lore from Pliny, he continues] And haue vertue of comfort by alle þe kynde þerof, as some men meneþ, oþer, for þey ben bysprongen wiþ certeyn kynde, it comforteþ lymes and membres for it clenseþ hem of superfluites of humours and fastneþ þe lymes. And helpeþ aȝeins þe cardiacle passioun and aȝeins swownyng of herte and aȝeins feblenesse þat comeþ of fluxe of medicyne, and helpeþ also aȝeins rennynge of blood and aȝeins fluxe of þe wombe, as Plato seiþ. . . [He continues with the standard lore about generation from dew].

Appendix 1

***The Peterborough Lapidary* (Peterborough 33. MS F, fol. 14)**

[Adapted into METS format from Joan Evans and Mary S. Serjeantson, ed., *English Medieval Lapidaries*. EETS o.s. 190. (London: Oxford University Press, 1960), pp. 107–08.]

CXIV. Margarita is chef of al stons that ben wyght and preciose, as Ised seyth. And it hathe the name margarita for it is founde in shellis which ben cokelis or in mosclys and in schellfyssh of the see; this bredyng is schellfyssh, and it is genderd of the dewe of heven, which dewe the schell fissh receyveth in certen tymes of the yer, of the which dew margarites comen. Some ben cleped unyons, and they han a conable name, for ther is oonly one ifonde and never two togeder; and the whight margarites ben better then the yelow, and tho that ben conceyved of the morow dew ben made dym with the eyr of eventyde: hucusque Isodorus. Also some ben fonde which ben perced kenly, and they ben better then that other; and some ben persed by crafte, as Plato seyth. And they ben best wyght, cler and rownde; and they han vertu of comfort by al kend therof; and somme seyne that they comforten lymes and membris, for it clenseth him of superfluite of homours and fasten the lymes, and helpen agen the cordiacle passioun and agens swonyng of hert, and agens febilnes of Flux by cause of medecyne, and also agens rennyng of blod, and agens the flyx of the wombe, as Plato seyth. And also in Plato it is seyd that margarites ben gendred of the morow dewe, and some more and some lesse, but it is trowed that no margarite groweth past half a fote. Also it is seyd that when lightnynge or thundringe falleth, when the margarite sholde bred of the dew that it resseyveth, the schel closeth be most soden strength and the gendringes faileth and is cast owt. The best and most noblyst margarites comen owt of Inde and of old Brytayn.

***Mediaeval Latin and French Bestiaries* (McCulloch, pp. 154–55)**

[The abbreviations (sigla) refer to groups of manuscripts from the eighth century onward that McCullough has based her comments on. Abbreviations: Y=MSS based on Munich Lat. 19417; B=MSS based on Bern. Lat. 233, f.1–13; B-Is=Bern. Lat. 233, f.1–13, with additions from Isidore; H=Latin MSS of a bestiary attributed to Hugh of St. Victor; PT=MSS based on the added French bestiary by Phillipe de Thaon.]

The Pearl

PEARL and AGATE.
margarita, unio, perla, concha, concha sabea, mermecolion, achates; union.

To find pearls divers tie an agate to a rope which is dropped into the sea. The stone comes to a pearl, remains there, and the diver follows the rope to its treasure.

According to Y (23) before dawn at sea the stone which is called oyster *(sostoros)* opens its mouth and swallows dew, the rays of the sun, moon, and stars. From this the pearl is born.

The essential part of the long allegory as recorded in B-Is (37) is found at the beginning, which says that the pearl signifies the Virgin Mary, who ascended to the temple of God and there received the words (celestial dew) of Gabriel. The opening of the shell symbolizes the Virgin who said "Ecce ancilla Domini. . . ." PT adds that as the shell opens and closes without a break, so did the Virgin conceive and give birth.

Isidore's account (xii.7.49) is followed in some later bestiaries which call the pearl *oceloe.* This word has numerous spellings and its origin is somewhat uncertain. In H (ii.35) pearls are called *uniones,* though the common people say *perlae.* Of these a certain kind are called *marmaetholion (mermecolion),* for which the Greek word is *concha sabea.* In manuscripts of the common B or B-Is version this passage begins "Item lapis est in mari qui dicitur latine mermecolion, grece concha sabea, quia concavus est et rotundus." What *concha sabea* means or why the name that was attached to the Ant-Lion, *mermecolion*, found also applied to the pearl remains so far unexplained. [But see her later article.]

The role of the agate in finding pearls is unknown before the *Physiologus,* but in Arrian's *Indica* (viii.8) Megasthenes reports that should the king pearl be captured, the others are easily caught. The birth of the pearl from dew is recorded in classical Indian poetry.

Two descriptions of the pearl are found in PT (3015–3062), which include some statements similar to those in Pliny (ix.35.54,56), where the pearl is called *unio* as in PT and where the island of Taprobane (Ceylon, PT *Tapne*) is said to be very fertile in pearls. PT adds that if one drinks the pearl mixed with dew it will cure any illness but death.

The only miniature seen of the agate's use in finding pearls is Bern 318, fol. 20v., which shows two men in a boat while a third dives into the water, guiding himself with a rope. In Bodl. 602, fol. 35 [*sic*] [see frontispiece] the two valves of an oyster are open to receive drops of dew from the sky and rays from the sun. Beside a closed oyster, to illustrate the allegory, is a graceful drawing of the Virgin holding her young Son.

Appendix 2

The Appeal of Thomas Usk against John Northampton (1384)
(*TL* 1.6–8)

I print here the text as found in *A Book of London English 1384–1425*, ed. R. W. Chambers and Marjorie Daunt (Oxford: Clarendon, 1931), pp. 22–31, with the heading supplied by Strohm (1992), p. 146. The text is from MS Public Records Office, Miscellanea of the Exchequer 5/26. I reproduce Chambers and Daunt's typographical markers of emendations and omissions. I indicate page numbers in their edition inside bold-face brackets. Finally, I print their glosses of a few difficult phrases as footnotes to my copy.

Appell[um] . . . Vsk f[a]c[tu]m coram Joh[ann]e Charn[eye] . . . London.

The * * * the vij^{t} day in the eyghte yer of the regne of our lord the king R[ic]hard [Scde] I, Thomas Vsk, in the presence of John . . . . co . . . . of london knowleched thes wordes & wrote hem with myn owne [honde]. * * * * To f . . . . eue . . . . . . [con]seil in the tyme of John Norhampton mair ther sholde [kome] . . . in to a . . . . that ys to seye in J[ohn] Willynghames tav*er*ne in the Bowe, ... es of xx of the **[C&D 23]** craftes that hielde with hym, a man or two that for thilk yer was chose [to] be in the comun conseyl, & . . . . John More, m*er*cer, Ric*hard* Norbury, m*er*cer, & Will*iam* Essex, drap*er*, and I also, Thom*as* Vsk, to write thair billes, & ther sholde al . . . . e be s * * * * * so th[at] atte comun conseil these, that tho wer p*re*sent, myghten be on voys accorde vpon the p*ur*pos to-forn take, & ther vpon they sholde atte day of comun co*n*seil crie ayein [the p*ur*pos to-forn take] * * * * and be * * * p*ur*pos that thilk John Norh*am*pton, John More, Richard Norbury & Will*iam* Essex wolden, wer it fals wer it trewe, & did * * * * be cause that S*ir* Will*iam* Walworth & other suche worthy p*er*sones as aldermen & com*un*ers weren in the contrarie opynion of the or[dinances of John] Norh*am*pton, yt was accorded be the forseyde John More, Richard Norbury, & Will*iam* Essex that the mair myghte take to hys conseyl whom th[at] he wolde, as for hys tyme, & leue hem that so wolde contrarie hym, & that of tho craftes that heilden a-yeins hym shulden come but tho that weren p*re*sented be the selue craft & no mo; but of other craftes that hielden with hym sholde kome as many as he wolde, & so he loked to haue so many holdyng w*ith* hym that the tother syde myght noght avayle & her-of I appele the forseyde John Norh*a*mpton, John More, Ric*hard* Norbury, & Will*ia*m Essex.

Also it was ful p*ur*posed be John Norh*a*mpton & hys conseyl, that ys to seye John More, Richard Norbury, & Will*ia*m Essex & be al the craftes that hielden with hym, that four poyntȝ shulden, with al the lordship & Frendeship that they myghten, [C&D 24] be kept & stablisshed; that ys to seyn, that the aldermen sholden be remoued fro yer in to yer, & that the comun conseyl sholde kome be craftes, & that ther sholde no vitailler bere office judicial, & that al s*tra*ng[e] vitaillers sholden with thair vitailles frelich kome to the Cite, to selle thair vitailles as wel be retaile as in other wyse, hauyng no reward to the F*ra*nchise. And, truly, the ful entent was that al the ordinances that wer ordeyned in hys tyme, wer they neuer so badde, sholden haue be meigtened euer more aft*er*ward with strength of meigtenance of the poeple a-yeins any mayr that wolde haue do the contrarie. And, in thys wyse, whan the worthy & wysest of the town had left such vnthrifty conseilles, the forseyde mair, John Norh*a*mpton, John More, & Ric*hard* Norbury, & Will*ia*m Essex, drogh to hem the comun poeple for to stonde be thes purposes to lyue & to dye. And ate euery conseyl was John More, Ric*hard* Norbury, & Will*ia*m Essex, &, otherwhile, Adam Bame; but the mair wolde otherwhile do be hys own avys, and also on Willyngh*a*m, a scryuen, & on . . . . . . Marchaund, clerk, writen many thynges in myn absence, & atte some tymes wer ther mo[r]e pryuier than I. And, c*er*teinly, the ful purpos of the p*er*sones to-forn nempned was to haue had the town in thair gou*er*naile, & haue rulid it be thair avys, & haue holden vnder, or elles de-voyded owt of towne, al the p*er*sones that had be myghty to haue wyth-seyde hem, &, the remenant, that had no*n* such myght, to haue holden hem vnder for euer; & her-of I apele John Norh*a*mpton, John More, Ric*hard* Norbury & Will*ia*m Essex.

Also, for the elde officers of the town loued noght the opinions of the forseyde mair, al the elde officers sholden haue be remoued by p*ro*ces of tyme, & sette in her place suche as wolden haue meigtened & loued hise opinions, for they seyden that thilk p*er*sones that hielden the contrarie of hys menyng wer Enemys to alle gode menyng. And that was euer-more an excitation to the pore poeple to make hem be the more feruent & rebel a-yeins the grete men of the town, & ayeins the officers [C&D 25] ek, & yt was seide thus to the poeple that euer the grete men wolden haue the poeple be opp*re*ssion in lowe degre, for whiche wordes, & be thair meigtenance, the dissension ys arrise be-twene the worthy p*er*sones & the smale people of the town; & her-of I apele John Norhampton, John More, Ric*hard* Norbury & Will*ia*m Essex.

Also, ayeins the day of the s*econ*de eleccion of John Norh*a*mpton mair, be-cause that Sir John Philpot had be a-yeins the badde doynges to-for seyde, John More was on of the chief cause to p*ro*cur that a bille sholde be put vp be the com*un*es conseyl, to aske of the forseyde S*ir* John the mone that he had borwed in tyme of hys mairalte; and it was ment that he sholde haue ther-by ben i-jugged of al maner of estat of office in the town for euer; & her-of I appele John More.

Also, a-yeins the forseyde s*econ*de eleccion, [ther] was made mochel ordinance be John More, Ric*hard* Norbury, Adam Bame, Will*ia*m Essex, & many a[lso] mo, & be me Thom*as* Vsk, to make ful [c*er*tei]n the co*mun*es atte that day shulde chese the forseyde John Norh*a*mpton to be mair & no*n* other, to that entent that al hys ordinances mighten be co*n*fermed be our lord the kyng in hys statut, to haue dured euer-mor; so that thilk ordinances sholden bothe haue be stablisshed be statut, & be meigtened ek be myght of people, as yt ys to-forn write; & her-of I apele John More, Ric*hard* Norbury, Adam Bame, & Will*ia*m Essex.

Also, ayeins the parlement than next folwyng, the mair, John Norh*a*mpton, made me, Thom*as* Vsk, go to the com*un*es to enfo*r*me hem of the [ord]inance a-yeins the Fisshmong*er*s, & for to haue thair wil ther-of amonges the other, that they sholde chese for the com*un*es to the [parlem]ent Ric*hard* Norbury & Will*ia*m Essex, & he wolde ordeigne amonges the aldermen [C&D 26] to chese John More & Thom*as* Carleton, for the [sam]e entent, that ys to seyn, they wer ordeyned; & so they diden p*ur*suwe thyng*es* a-yeins the F*ra*nchise of london for euer; & her-of I [appele] John Norh*a*mpton.

[Also, a]tte thilk p*ar*lement, was p*ur*suwed a patent to the mair for to chastise vsurers, yf any man wolde pleigne, or elles be enditeme*n*t, be whiche patent yt was fully as-sented ferst to haue don execucion vpon any man that had be p*ro*ued giltyf ther jnne acte, [or ther]of p*ar*tie; & in thys wise, be fals *com*passement & ymaginacion to-forn cast, many of the worthiest of the town sholde haue [be] ther-by enpesched, & be execucion ydo so vpon hem, that they sholde noght haue bore nomore estat in the town; and now [I] wot wel that, vnder colour ther-of, shulde haue be broght a-boute mochel of the euel menyng, to haue vndo the worthy membres of the town that had be a-yeins hym, & for no*n* other entent of wel menyng but only for malice, to put ovte of the town al the worthiest was thilk patent p*ur*chaced, & be suche fals p*ur*posyng & ymaginacions of destrucion sholden the worthi p*er*sones of the town have ben for-jugged ovt of towne; wher-for it was cast al redy of officers bothe for the mairalte, aldermanries, & shirreuehod, & suche other degrees, for yeres komyng, so that the adu*er*sairs of John

Norh*am*pton sholde noght haue be in non offices her-after, wher thorw me may wel se the destruxion of the [t]own w*ith*-jnne a litel p*ro*ces of tyme, as for to haue so many thrifty men owt of towne; & ther-of I apele John Norh*a*mpton, John More, Ric*hard* Norbury, and Will*ia*m Essex.

Also, atte p*ro*curement of John More, Walter sybile John horn & Adam Carlett wer endited, & altheigh ther wer take many inquisicio[ns], we that serued our lord the king best wer returned; & truly, Rob*er*t F*ra*nceys & other, I not whiche now, wolden haue endited S*ir* Nichol Brem[bre] of meigtenance **[C&D 27]** of Thom*as* Farndon, and John More ferst was ther-to assented, & afterward he letted it, so that it nas noght execut; & her-of I apele John More.

Also, ofte to-forn that S*ir* Nichol Brembr*e* was chose mair, the mair, John Norh*a*mpton, John More, & Richard Norbury, senten Will*ia*m Essex & me, Thom*as* Vsk, to the goldsmithes halle to speke with men of the comun co*n*seyl for chesyng of the mair, & also ther-for weren al [that weren] of the commun conseyl take me be John Norhampton, that I, Thom*as* Vsk, sholde speke to hem that I knewe. And ther, atte Goldsmithes [halle, amo]nges hem that wer assembled, it was accorded that c*er*tein p*er*sones of diu*er*s craftes, [th]o that wer entred for the comun conseyl, sholde be [called] atte eleccion day in to the comun co*n*seil for to helpe to the eleccion of John Norh*a*mpton, [&] the smale poeple was drawe in to be [p*ar*tie therof], to that entent that fully thair hertes sholde stonde with John Norh*a*mpton, & that yf, in tyme komyng, a-nother mair, that wer [to be chose], wolde oght do a-yeins hym, he myghte haue hem redy to meigtene hym [ayei]ns al that they wolde seye a-yeins hym, &, if he had ben mair, I wot wel he wolde haue meigtened al hys ordinances, or elles haue sette al the town in a rore; & her-of I appele John Norhampton, John More, Ric*hard* Norbury, & Will*ia*m Essex.

Also, the night to-for the day of the eleccion of the mair, John More warned al hys sergeantȝ & hys men to be armed on the [morwe atte] yeldehalle. For he kyde he & hys felawe wolde kepe the dores that day, to that entent that ther sholde no*n* haue kome jn but onl[y that] wolde haue chose John Norh*a*mpton to be mair; & her-of I appele John More. **[C&D 28]**

Also, that day that [Sir] Nichol Brembre was chose mair, a-non after mete kom John Norhampton to John Mores hows, & thider kom Ric*hard* Norbury & Will*ia*m Essex, & ther it was a[ccor]ded that the mair, John Norh*a*mpton, sholde sende after the p*er*sones that thilk time wer in the comun co*n*seil of craftes, & aft*er* the wardeyns of craftes, so that thei sholde kome to the goldsmithes halle on the morwe after, & ther the mair sholde speke with hem, to loke & ordeigne how thilk eleccion of S*ir* Nichol Brembr*e* myght be letted; &, nad it be for dred of our lord the kyng, I wot wel eueri man sholde haue be in others top.[1] And than sente he Ric*hard* Norbury, Rob*ert* Rysby & me, Tho*mas* Vsk, to the Neyte, to the duk of lancastr*e*, to enforme hym in thys wyse: "S*ir*, to day, ther we w[olde]n haue go to the eleccion of the mair in goddes peas & the kynges, ther kom jn an orrible companye of criers, no man not wh[ic]he & [t]her, w*ith* oute any vsage but be strength, chosen S*ir* Nichol Brembr*e* mair, a-yein our maner of eleccion to-forn thys vsed; wher-fore we preye yow yf we myght haue the kynges writ to go to a Newe eleccion." And the duk seide: "Nay, c*er*tes, writ shul ye no*n* haue, auise yow amonges yowr selue." & her-of I appele John Norh*a*mpton, John More, Ric*hard* Norbury, & Will*ia*m Essex.

Also, atte Goldsmithes halle, when al the people was assembled, the mair, John Norh*a*mpton, reherced as euel as he koude of the eleccion on the day to-forn, & seyde that truly: "S*ir*s, thus be ye shape for to be ouer-ronne, & that," q*uo*d he, "I nel noght soeffre; lat vs rather al be ded atones than soeffr*e* such a vylenye." & than the com*un*es, vpon these wordes, wer stered, & seiden truly they wolde go to a-nother eleccion, & noght soeffr*e* thys wrong, to be ded al ther-for attones in on tyme[2]; and than be the mair, John Norh*a*mpton, was euery man boden gon hom, & kome fast a-yein strong in to Chepe w*ith* al her craftes, & I wene ther wer a-boute a xxx craftes, & in Chepe they sholden haue sembled to go to a newe eleccion, &, truly, had noght the aldermen kome to trete, & maked that John Norh*a*mpton bad [C&D 29] the poeple gon hoom, they wolde haue go to a Newe eleccion, & in that hete haue slayn hym that wolde haue letted it, yf they had myght; and her-of I appele John Norh*a*mpton.

And, vpon al thys matirs be-forn seide, tho that John Norh*a*mpton atte tat tyme mair, John More, & Richard Norbury, & William Essex & otherwhile Adam Bame, seyen that the worthy p*er*sones wer drawe fro hem for willesful goue*r*naile & fiebel co*n*seyl, & that they had made refus of hem to-forn tyme,[3] tho they drewe to hem many craftes & mochel smale poeple that konne no*n* skyl of goue*r*nance ne of gode conseyl & be confederacie, congregacion, & couyne, p*ur*posed & to-forn cast for to meigtene be myght thair fals & wykked menyng, vnder colour of wordes of comun p*ro*fit euer more

[1] "in conflict with each other"

[2] "if they all died for it together there and then"

[3] "they had already rejected them"

[charg]ed the people fro day in to other to be redy to stonde be hem in that euel p*ur*posed matirs[4]; & so, as wel sithe he was noght mair as to-forn, they han euerich of hem on hys syde stired, co*n*fedred, & co*n*spired the matirs to-forn ne*m*pned, saue Adam Bame, sithen that he was noght mair, that I wot of, hath noght ent*re*meted hym. And also the forseide John Norh*a*mpton, John More, Ric*hard* Norbury, & Will*iam* Essex, so fer forth wolden depraue the worthy men of towne that the people was, & ys, the more enbolded to be rebel a-yeins thair gou*er*no*ur*s that bien now, & that shul bien in tyme komyng, be her fals informacion & excitacion, couyns, & gadrynges, & co*n*federacies atte that tyme maked & euer sithen co*n*tinued, as it ys to-forn seyde; & so be hem, & be ther p*rocur*ementy, & co*n*federacies, & excitacions, the debates & the grete stryf, that yet ys regnyng in the cite, ys komen jn p*ri*ncipalich be John Norh*a*mpton, John More, Ric*hard* Norbury, & Will*iam* Essex; so that ys in poynt to truble al the realme; & the cite hath stonde in grete doute & yet doth. To which euel menyng I was a ful help*ere* **[C&D 30]** & p*ro*motour in al that euer I myght & koude, wher-for I aske g*ra*ce & m*er*cy of my lyge lord the kyng, & aft*er*ward of the mair, & of al the worthy aldermen, & of al the gode com*un*es of the town, as he that wol neuer more t*re*space a-yeins the town in no degre. And, truly, Adam Bame was noght so comunly, ne so bysy on thys p*ur*pos [& co*n*fed*er*aci]es as [wer] the tother; & her-of I apele the forseyde John Norh*a*mpton, Ric*hard* Norbury, John More, & Will*iam* Essex.

And euer sithen that he was noght mair the forseide John Norh*a*mpton, John More, Ric*hard* Norbury & Will*iam* Essex han ben [a]boute * * * * * to drawe the poeple to be to hym ward & hym self most y-maked assembles & gadringes of co*m*panyes to sto[nd]e w[ith] h[ym] * * * * he b[ad] me Thom*as* Vsk to the Bowe amonges other folk that he had gadred, & ther he shewed a bille that was maked a[yeins hym & he] procured that co*m*panye to stonde be hym and with oute seche thynges as wol[d]e [put?] * * * * that * * sholden . . . . . . neghbo*urs* to stonde be hym in ryght & in wrong & haue [soe]ffred no man of London * * * * hym * * * * * Rob*er*t Franceys, John Lyncoll goldsmithes & I Thom*as* Vsk haue made al * * * go * * * londe or m . . . . * * duk of lancastre to enfourme hym that John Northampton was the beste ma[ir] that euer [was] * * * * al that we myg[ht] * * * * S*ir* Nichol Brembr*e* & hys gou*er*nance to hym & * * will to vs wardes * * * p*ar*lement alwey bisied vs to helpe that John N[orh*a*mpton] * * * kome to hys . . . ser * * * den that the men * * * * [arrested?] * * * cause * * * * lok * * * * of

[4] "in those evilly conceived plots"— *that* with a plural noun and the sense "those" is common

w . . . . . [en]formed **[C&D 31]** the duk how * * * * . . ade arme * * the wal of * * * * al the * * * * we * * * * stered the lord * * * * to speke w[ith] * * ted me to helpe faste w*ith* my p*re*sence * * therto that he sholde haue al * * * was euer a-boute to haue holpe that * * * * r And of al thys matirs I crie to my [lyge] lo[rd] the kyng euer- more of g*ra*ce & of mercy & aft*er* to my * * * * p*er*sones of London & truly I wol [neuermore] * * * * but euer stonde be the town & be the worthy * * * ght may do next my lige [lorde] wol * * be redy [at] al tymes wher I shal to a vowe * * * * * * now me thynketh the * * * gode & trewthe & al maner of felicite to the cite * * * * that * be * * * * informacion And therof euer as verrey repentant as I kan * * * * I haue desired & hervpon I apele John Norh*a*mpton Ric*hard* Norbury * *

Appendix 3

St. Anselm's *De Concordia* (Sections Relevant to *TL*)

Grateful acknowledgment is hereby made to the Edwin Mellen Press for permission to reprint sections from *De Concordia Praescientiae et Praedestinationis et Gratiae Dei cum Libero Arbitrio* from *Anselm of Canterbury, Complete Treatises*, edited and translated by Jasper Hopkins and Herbert Richardson (Lewiston: New York, 1974–76), II (1976), 181–223.

In some ways, this Appendix is bound to be misleading. Like the others, it is designed to provide information. However, the information it provides is a translation of a major Latin work of the early Middle Ages (St. Anselm died in 1109 CE). If Appendix 1 also contains translations from Latin, these, being translations of different versions of the same lapidary lore, are by their nature utilitarian and thus no imminent threat to deleteriously replace the topic to hand. But Anselm's *De Concordia* is a major philosophical/theological work which deserves attention in its own right in its original Latin. Hence the translation here can promote a false sense of security which I hope to have dispelled by these remarks.The translations quoted here should not, of course, be understood to be a substitute for the Latin text with which Usk worked.

To prepare this Appendix, I have in the main followed Sanderlin, having checked his work and found it generally reliable. However, I do not reproduce all of his arguments. The information he provides on Usk's manipulations of *De Concordia*, as distinct from the principal translations, I have included primarily in my notes in abbreviated form at the relevant site in *TL*. I do want, though, to quote his summary (pp. 70 and 72) of Usk's major changes to *De Concordia* and his analyses of Usk's procedure with the text:

> . . . Usk changes this term *rectitude* [a key term of St. Anselm's argument], meaning the *end* assigned to free choice, to the word *love*, meaning an *act* of the will and referring especially to his own will's love of the Margaret. Similarly, he substitutes "lovinge wil" for "recta voluntas," with the same purpose of adapting St. Anselm's discussion to his own allegory of the Margaret. . . . [He turns] St. Anselm's treatise into dialogue form

> by assigning to himself in the *Testament* the objections and counter arguments that are given in the *De concordia*, leaving the positive teaching to be spoken by Love. . . . [The disorder in Book 3] is caused by the substitution of the term *love* for *rectitude*; by the patchwork character of the translation with clumsy or non-existent transitions; by the limitations of the English philosophical vocabulary of the fourteenth century.

With this position, compare that of Medcalf (pp. 188–90), for whom, recall, *TL* is "the first book of original philosophy in English" (Introduction, note 17):

> . . . the study of Usk as a translator of Anselm at the level of word correspondence will remain particular and perilous. . . . conformity to Anselm is no guide. . . . This would suggest a rule that you may emend our text of Usk to follow Anselm more literally unless where it seems that Usk would want to make the text more conversational or to make it refer to love.

It is not my concern here to test this "rule" — although I will say that it "feels" right to me (the reader will already have seen that I find Usk frequently inventive in unpredictable ways). Still, I urge the reader, even if Medcalf's warm defense of Usk seems disputable, to keep his "rule" in mind, if only as a check against premature conclusions.

Sanderlin's analysis shows that Usk uses some 45% of *De Concordia.* My own rough statistics show that this 45% amounts to slightly more than the same percentage of *TL* 3. (*TL* 3 [containing 17,653 words] is only slightly shorter than *De Concordia* [containing 18,301]). Obviously, then, the relationship is extensive and ideally should receive detailed separate study. My sense of the matter is that Usk sometimes follows St. Anselm quite closely, but that at other times he is independent if not inventive. On balance, I admire his effort. *De Concordia* is not an "easy" text. Moreover, it is often densely figurative — Anselm develops an image of the seed as word and word as seed (*De Concordia* 3.6) as complex and provocative in its context as Dante's is in its (*Inferno* 33.7ff.). Usk may occasionally appropriate the figuration — for example, his tree image is probably borrowed from St. Anselm (see the notes to Book 3, lines 577 and 806–07) — but he is always involved in appropriating St. Anselm's arguments to his purposes. What I mainly wish to do here with this observation and these very brief comments is prepare readers to understand *TL* 3 a bit more easily than would otherwise be possible and urge them at the same time to practice an adequate scepticism toward any premature conclusions about *TL* and *De Concordia.*

To follow the list, use the line numbers of Book 3, at the left, to find Usk's version of the passage from *De Concordia.* Conversely, in the notes I list the passage from *De Concordia* and the page numbers in the Appendix. I include the page numbers of the Hopkins-Richardson translation in bold-face parentheses in case readers wish to consult it. I provide no more of the Latin than what is included by Hopkins and Richardson, and I do not annotate *De Concordia* at all.

***De Concordia* 1.1 (pp. 181–83)**
Compare *TL*, lines 239–69

(181) Admittedly, free choice and the foreknowledge of God seem incompatible; for it is necessary that the things foreknown by God be going to occur, whereas the things done by free choice occur without any necessity. Now, if these two are incompatible, then it is impossible that God's all-foreseeing foreknowledge should coexist with something's being done by freedom of choice. In turn, if this impossibility is regarded as not obtaining, then the incompatibility which seems to be present is completely eliminated.

Therefore, let us posit as existing together both God's foreknowledge (from which the necessity of future things seems to follow) and freedom of choice (by which many actions are performed, we believe, without any necessity); and let us see whether it is impossible for these two to coexist. If this coexist- **(182)** ence is impossible, then some other impossibility arises from it. For, indeed, an impossible thing is one from which, when posited, some other impossible thing follows. Now, on the assumption that some action is going to occur without necessity, God foreknows this, since he foreknows all future events. And that which is foreknown by God is, necessarily, going to occur, as is foreknown. Therefore, it is necessary that something be going to occur without necessity. Hence, the foreknowledge from which necessity follows and the freedom of choice from which necessity is absent are here seen (for one who rightly understands it) to be not at all incompatible. For, on the one hand, it is necessary that what is foreknown by God be going to occur; and, on the other hand, God foreknows that something is going to occur without any necessity.

But you will say to me: "You still do not remove from me the necessity of sinning or the necessity of not sinning. For God foreknows that I am going to sin or foreknows that I am not going to sin. And so, if I sin, it is necessary that I sin; or if I do not sin, it is necessary that I do not sin." To this claim I reply: You ought to say not merely "God foreknows that I am going to sin" or "God foreknows that I am not going to sin" but "God foreknows that it is without necessity that I am going to sin" or "God foreknows that it is without necessity that I am not going to sin." And thus it follows that whether you sin or do not sin, in either case it will be without necessity; for God foreknows that what will occur will occur without necessity. Do you see, then, that it is not impossible for God's foreknowledge (according to which future things, which God foreknows, are said to occur of necessity) to coexist with freedom of choice (by which many actions are performed without necessity)? For if this coexistence were impossible, then something impossible would follow. But no impossibility arises from this coexistence.

Perhaps you will claim: "You still do not remove the constraint of necessity from my heart when you say that, because of God's foreknowledge, it is necessary for me to be going to sin without necessity or it is necessary for me to be not going to sin without necessity. For *necessity* seems to imply coercion or restraint. Therefore, if it is necessary that I sin willingly, I interpret this as indicating that I am compelled by some hidden power to will to sin; and if I do not sin, [I interpret this as indicating that] I **(183)** am restrained from willing to sin. Therefore, it seems to me that if I sin I sin by necessity, and if I do not sin it is by necessity that I do not sin."

De Concordia 1.2 (pp. 183–85)

Compare *TL*, lines 284–358

(183) And I [reply]: We must realize that we often say "necessary to be" of what is not compelled-to-be by any force, and "necessary not to be" of what is not excluded by any preventing factor. For example, we say "It is necessary for God to be immortal" and "It is necessary for God not to be unjust." [We say this] not because some force compels Him to be immortal or prohibits Him from being unjust, but because nothing can cause Him not to be immortal or can cause Him to be unjust. Similarly, then, I might say: "It is necessary that you are going to sin voluntarily" or "It is necessary that, voluntarily, you are not going to sin"—just as God foreknows. But these statements must not be construed to mean that something prevents the act of will which shall not occur, or compels that act of will which shall occur. For God, who foresees that some action is going to occur voluntarily, foreknows the very fact that the will is neither compelled nor prevented by anything. Hence, what is done voluntarily is done freely. Therefore, if these matters are carefully pondered, I think that no inconsistency prevents freedom of choice and God's foreknowledge from coexisting.

Indeed, (if someone properly considers the meaning of the word), by the very fact that something is said to be *foreknown,* it is declared to *be* going to occur. For only what is going to occur is foreknown, since knowledge is only of the truth. Therefore, when I say "If God foreknows something, it is necessary that this thing *be* going to occur," it is as if I *were* to say: "If this thing will occur, of necessity it will occur." But this necessity neither compels nor prevents a thing's existence or nonexistence. For because the thing is presumed to exist, it is said to exist of necessity; or because it is presumed not to exist, it is said to not-exist of necessity. [But our reason for saying these things is] not that necessity compels or prevents the thing's existence or nonexistence. For when I say "If it will occur, of necessity it will occur," here the necessity follows, rather than precedes, the presumed existence of the thing. The sense is the same if we say "What will be, of necessity will be." For this necessity signifies **(184)** nothing other than that what will occur will not be able not to occur at the same time.

Likewise, the following statements are equally true: (1) that some thing did exist and does exist and will exist, but not out of necessity, and (2) that all that was, necessarily was, all that is, necessarily is, and all that will be, necessarily will be. Indeed, for a thing to be past is not the same as for a past thing to be past; and for a thing to be present is not the same as for a present thing to be present; and for a thing to be future is not the same as for a future thing to be future. By comparison, for a thing to be white is not the same as for a white thing to be white. For example, a staff is not always necessarily white, because at some time before it became white it was able not to become white; and after it has become white, it is able to become not-white. But it is necessary that a white staff always be white. For neither before a white thing was white nor after it has become white can it happen that a white thing is not-white at the same time. Similarly, it is not by necessity that a thing is temporally present. For before the thing was present, it was able to happen that it would not be present; and after it has become present, it can happen that it not remain present. But it is necessary that a present thing always be present, because neither before it is present nor after it has become present is a present thing able to be not-present at the same time. In the same way, some event — e.g., an action — is going to occur without necessity, because before the action occurs, it can happen that it not be going to occur. On the other hand, it is necessary that a future event be future, because what is future is not able at the same time to be not-future. Of the past it is similarly true (1) that some event is not necessarily past, because before it occurred, there was the possibility of its not occurring, and (2) that, necessarily, what is past is always past, since it is not able at the same time not to be past. Now, a past event has a characteristic which a present event or a future event does not have. For it is never possible for a past event to become not-past, as a present event is able to become not-present, and as an event which is not necessarily going to happen has the possibility of not happening in the future. Thus, when we say of what is going to happen that it is going to happen, this statement must be true, because it is never the case that what is going to happen is not going to happen. **(185)** (Similarly, whenever we predicate something of itself, [the statement is true]. For when we say "Every man is a man," or "If he is a man, he is a man," or "Every white thing is white," or "If it is a white thing, it is white": these statements must be true because something cannot both be and not be the case at the same time.) Indeed, if it were not necessary that everything which is going to happen were going to happen, then something which is going to happen would not be going to happen — a contradiction. Therefore, *necessarily,* everything which is going to happen is going to happen; and if it is going to happen, it is going to happen. (For we are saying of what is going to happen that it is going to happen.) But ["necessarily" here signifies] subsequent necessity, which does not compel anything to be.

***De Concordia* 1.3 (pp. 185–87)**
Compare *TL*, lines 358–417

(185) However, when an event is said to be going to occur, it is not always the case that the event occurs by necessity, even though it is going to occur. For example, if I say "Tomorrow there will be an insurrection among the people," it is not the case that the insurrection will occur by necessity. For before it occurs, it is *possible* that it not occur even if it is going to occur. On the other hand, it is sometimes the case that the thing which is said to be going to occur does occur by necessity — for example, if I say that tomorrow there will be a sunrise. Therefore, if of an event which is going to occur I state that it must be going to occur, [I do so] either in the way that the insurrection which is going to occur tomorrow is, necessarily, going to occur, or else in the way that the sunrise which is going to occur tomorrow is going to occur by necessity. Indeed, the insurrection (which will occur but not by necessity) is said necessarily to be going to occur — but only in the sense of subsequent necessity. For we are saying of what is going to happen that it is going to happen. For if the insurrection is going to occur tomorrow, then — necessarily — it is going to occur. On the other hand, the sunrise is understood to be going to occur with two necessities: (1) with a preceding necessity, which causes the event to occur (for the event will occur because it is necessary that it occur), and (2) with a subsequent necessity, which does not compel anything to occur (for because the sunrise is going to occur, it is — necessarily — going to occur).

(186) Therefore, when of what God foreknows to be going to occur we say that it is necessary that it be going to occur, we are not in every case asserting that the event is going to occur by necessity; rather, we are asserting that an event which is going to occur is, necessarily, going to occur. For something which is going to occur cannot at the same time be not going to occur. The meaning is the same when we say "If God foreknows such-and-such an event" — without adding "which is going to occur." For in the verb "to foreknow" the notion of future occurrence is included, since to foreknow is nothing other than to know the future; and so if God foreknows some event, it is necessary that this event be going to occur. Therefore, from the fact of God's foreknowledge it does not in every case follow that an event is going to occur by necessity. For although God foreknows all future events, He does not foreknow that all of them are going to occur by necessity. Rather, He foreknows that some of them will occur as the result of the free will of a rational creature.

Indeed, we must note that just as it is not necessary for God to will what He does will, so in many cases it is not necessary for a man to will what he does will. And just as whatever God wills must occur, so what a man wills must occur — in the case, that is, of the things which God so subordinates to the human will that if it wills them they occur and if it does not will them they do not occur. For since what God wills is not able not to occur: when He wills for no necessity either to compel the human will to will or to prevent it from willing, and when He wills that the effect follow from the act of human willing, it is necessary that the human will be free and that there occur what it wills. In this respect, then, it is true that the sinful deed which a man wills to do occurs by necessity, even though the man does not will it by necessity. Now, with respect to the human will's sin when it wills to sin: if someone asks whether this sin occurs by necessity, then he must be told that just as the will does not will by necessity, so the will's sin does not occur by necessity. Nor does the human will act by necessity; for if it did not will freely, it would not act — even though what it wills must come to pass, as I have just said. For since, in the present case, to sin is nothing other than to will what ought not [to be willed]: just as willing is not necessary, so sinful willing is not necessary. Nevertheless, it is true that if a man wills to sin, it is **(187)** necessary that he sin — in terms, that is, of that necessity which (as I have said) neither compels nor prevents anything.

Thus, on the one hand, free will is able to keep from willing what it wills; and, on the other hand, it is not able to keep from willing what it wills — rather, it is necessary for free will to will what it wills. For, indeed, before it wills, it is able to keep from willing, because it is free. And while it wills, it is not able not to will; rather, it is necessary that it will, since it is impossible for it to will and not to will the same thing at the same time. Now, it is the will's prerogative that what it wills occurs and that what it does not will does not occur. And the will's deeds are voluntary and free because they are done by a free will. But these deeds are necessary in two respects: (1) because the will compels them to be done, and (2) because what is being done cannot at the same time not be done. But these two necessities are produced by freedom-of-will; and the free will is able to avoid them before they occur. Now, God (who knows all truth and only truth) sees all these things as they are — whether they be free or necessary; and as He sees them, so they are. In this way, then, and without any inconsistency, it is evident both that God foreknows all things and that many things are done by free will. And before these things occur it is possible that they never occur. Nevertheless, in a certain sense they occur necessarily, and this necessity (as I said) derives from free will.

***De Concordia* 1.4 (pp. 187–88)**
Compare *TL*, lines 418–38

(187) Moreover, that not everything foreknown by God occurs of necessity but that some events occur as the result of freedom-of-will can be recognized from the following consideration. When God wills or causes something, He cannot be denied to know what He wills and causes, and to foreknow what He shall will and shall cause. ([It makes no difference here] whether we speak in accordance with eternity's immutable present, in which there is nothing past or future, but in which all things exist at once without any change (e.g., if we say only that He wills and causes something, and deny that He has willed or has caused and shall will or shall cause something), or whether we speak in accordance with temporality (as when we state that He shall will or shall cause that which we know has not yet occurred).) Therefore, if **(188)** God's knowledge or foreknowledge imposes necessity on everything He knows or foreknows, then He does not freely will or cause anything (either in accordance with eternity or in accordance with a temporal mode); rather, He wills and causes everything by necessity.

Now, if this conclusion is absurd even to suppose, then it is not the case that everything known or foreknown to be or not to be occurs or fails to occur by necessity. Therefore, nothing prevents God's knowing or foreknowing that in our wills and actions something occurs or will occur by free choice. Thus, although it is necessary that what He knows or foreknows, occur, nevertheless many events occur not by necessity but by free will — as I have shown above.

De Concordia 1.4 (p. 188)
Compare *TL*, lines 442–60

(188) Indeed, why is it strange if in this way something occurs both freely and necessarily? For there are many things which admit of opposite characteristics in different respects. Indeed, what is more opposed than coming and going? Nevertheless, when someone moves from one place to another, we see that his movement is both a coming and a going. For he goes away from one place and comes toward another. Likewise, if we consider the sun at some point in the heavens, as it is hastening toward this same point while always illuminating the heavens: we see that the point to which it is coming is the same point from which it is going away; and it is constantly and simultaneously approaching the point from which it is departing. Moreover, to those who know the sun's course, it is evident that in relation to the heavens, the sun always moves from the western sector to the eastern sector; but in relation to the earth, it always moves only from east to west. Thus, the sun always moves both counter to the firmament and — although more slowly [than the firmament] — with the firmament. This same phenomenon is witnessed in the case of all the planets. So then, no inconsistency arises if (in accordance with the considerations just presented) we assert of one and the same event (1) that, necessarily, it is going to occur (simply because it *is* going to occur) and (2) that it is not compelled to be going to occur by any necessity — except for the necessity which (as I said above) derives from free will.

De Concordia 1.5 (pp. 188–91)
Compare *TL*, lines 462–554

(188) Now, Job says to God with reference to man: "You have established his end, which cannot be escaped." On the basis of **(189)** this verse someone might want to prove — in spite of the fact that sometimes someone does seem to us to cause his own death by his own free will — that no one has been able to hasten or delay the day of his death. But his objection would not tell against that which I have argued above. For since God is not deceived and sees only the truth — whether it issues from freedom or from necessity — He is said to have established immutably with respect to Himself something which, with respect to man, can be altered before it is done. This is also what the Apostle Paul says about those who, in accordance with [God's] purpose, are called to be saints: "Whom He foreknew He predestined to become conformed to the image of His Son, so that His Son would be the firstborn among many brethren. And whom He predestined, these He also called. And whom He called, these He also justified. And whom He justified, these He also glorified." Indeed, within eternity (in which there is no past or future but is only a present) this purpose, in accordance with which they have been called to be saints, is immutable. But in these men this purpose is at some time mutable because of freedom of choice. For within eternity a thing has no past or future but only a present; and yet, without inconsistency, in the dimension of time this thing was and will be. Similarly, that which within eternity is not able to be changed is proved to be, without inconsistency, changeable by free will at some point in time before it occurs. However, although within eternity there is only a present, nonetheless it is not the temporal present, as is ours, but is an eternal present in which the whole of time is contained. For, indeed, just as present time encompasses every place and whatever is in any place, so in the eternal present the whole of time is encompassed at once, as well as whatever occurs at any time. Therefore, when the apostle says that God foreknew, predestined, called, justified, and glorified His saints, none of these actions is earlier or later for God; rather everything must be understood to exist at once in an eternal present. For eternity has its own "simultaneity" wherein exist all things that occur at the same time and place and that occur at different times and places.

But in order to show that he was not using these verbs in their temporal sense, the same apostle spoke in the past tense of even those events which are future. For, temporally speaking, God had not already called, justified, and glorified those who He fore- **(190)** knew were still to be born. Thus, we can recognize that for lack of a verb [properly] signifying the eternal present, the apostle used verbs of past tense; for things which are temporally past are altogether immutable, after the fashion of the eternal present. Indeed, in this respect, things which are temporally past resemble the eternal present more than do things which are temporally present. For eternally present things are never able not to be present, just as temporally past things are never able not to be past. But all temporally present things which pass away do become not-present.

In this manner, then, whenever Sacred Scripture speaks as if things done by free choice were necessary, it speaks in accordance with eternity, in which is present immutably all truth and only truth. Scripture is not speaking in accordance with the temporal order, wherein our volitions and actions do not exist forever. Moreover, just as when our volitions and actions do not exist, it is not necessary that they exist, so it is often not necessary that they ever exist. For example, it is not the case that I am always writing or that I always will to write. And just as when I am not writing or do not will to write, it is not necessary that I write or will to write, so it is not at all necessary that I ever write or will to write.

A thing is known to exist in time so differently from the way it exists in eternity that at some point the following statements are true: (1) in time something is not present which is present in eternity; (2) in time something is past which is not past in eternity; (3) in time something is future which is not future in eternity. Similarly, then, it is seen to be impossible to be denied, in any respect, that in the temporal order something is mutable which is immutable in eternity. Indeed, being mutable in time and being immutable in eternity are no more opposed than are not existing at some time and always existing in eternity — or than are existing in the past or future according to the temporal order and not existing in the past or future in eternity.

For, indeed, the point I am making is not that something which always exists in eternity never exists in time, but is only that there is some time or other at which it does not exist. For example, I am not saying that my action of tomorrow at no time exists; I am merely denying that it exists today, even though it always exists in eternity. And when we deny that something which is past or **(191)** future in the temporal order is past or future in eternity, we do not maintain that that which is past or future does not in any way exist in eternity; instead, we are simply saying that what exists there unceasingly in its eternal-present mode does not exist there in the past or future mode. In these cases no contradiction is seen to raise an obstruction. Thus, without doubt and without any contradiction, a thing is said to be mutable in time, prior to its occurrence, although it exists immutably in eternity. [In eternity] there is no time before it exists or after it exists; instead, it exists unceasingly, because in eternity nothing exists temporally. For there exists there, eternally, the fact that temporally something both exists and — before it exists — is able not to exist (as I have said). It seems to me to be sufficiently clear from what has been said that free choice and God's foreknowledge are not at all inconsistent with each other. Their consistency results from the nature of eternity, which encompasses the whole of time and whatever occurs at any time.

***De Concordia* 1.7 (p. 193)**
Compare *TL*, lines 554–58

(193) Since God is believed to foreknow or know all things, we are now left to consider whether His knowledge derives from things or whether things derive their existence from His knowledge. For if God derives His knowledge from things, it follows that they exist prior to His knowledge and hence do not derive their existence from Him; for they can only exist from Him in accordance with His knowledge. On the other hand, if all existing things derive their existence from God's knowledge, God is the creator and the author of evil works and hence is unjust in punishing evil creatures — a view we do not accept.

***De Concordia* 3.11 (pp. 214–16)**
Compare *TL*, lines 613–59

(214) But since this last consideration concerns the will, I deem it necessary to say in more detail about the will something which shall not be useless, it seems to me. In our bodies we have five senses and [various] members, each of which, distinctly, is adapted for its own special function. We use these members and **(215)** senses as instruments. For example, the hands are suited for grasping, the feet for walking, the tongue for speaking, and sight for seeing. Similarly, the soul too has in itself certain powers which it uses as instruments for appropriate functions. For in the soul there is reason, which the soul uses (as its instrument) for reasoning; and there is will, which the soul uses for willing. Neither reason nor will is the whole of the soul; rather, each of them is something within the soul. Therefore, since the distinct instruments have their essence, their aptitudes, and their uses, let us distinguish in the will — in regard to which we are discussing these matters — the instrument, its aptitudes, and its uses. In regard to the will we can call these aptitudes *inclinations (affectiones).* Indeed, the instrument-for-willing is modified by its own inclinations. Hence, when a man's soul strongly wills something, it is said to be inclined to will that thing, or to will it affectionally.

Assuredly, the will is seen to be spoken of equivocally — in three senses. For (a) the instrument-for-willing, (b) the inclination of this instrument, and (c) the use of this instrument, are distinguishable. The instrument-for-willing is that power-of-the-soul which we use for willing — just as reason is the instrument-for-reasoning, which we use when we reason, and just as sight is the instrument-for-seeing, which we use when we see. The inclination *(affectio)* of the instrument-for-willing is that by which the instrument is so inclined to will some given thing (even when a man is not thinking of that which he wills) that if this thing comes to mind, then the will wills [to have] it either immediately or at the appropriate time. For example, the instrument-for-willing is so inclined to will health (even when a man is not thinking of it) that as soon as health comes to mind, the will wills [to have] it immediately. And the instrument-for-willing is so inclined to will sleep (even when a man is not thinking of this) that when it comes to mind, the will wills [to have] it at the appropriate time. For the will is never inclined in such way that it ever wills sickness or that it wills never to sleep. Likewise, in a just man the instrument-for-willing is so inclined to will justice (even when a man is asleep) that when he thinks of justice he wills [to have] it immediately.

On the other hand, the use of this instrument is something which we have only when we are thinking of the thing which we will.

(216) Now, the word "will" applies to the instrument-for-willing, to the inclination of this instrument, and to the use of this instrument. (1) Indeed, we call the instrument *will* when we say that we direct the will toward various things (e.g., now toward willing to walk, now toward willing to sit, now toward willing something else). A man always possesses this instrument even though he does not always use it. The case is similar to his having sight, in the sense of the instrument-for-seeing, even when he does not use it (e.g., when he is asleep). But when he does use it, he directs it now toward seeing the sky, now toward seeing the earth, now toward seeing something else. Moreover, the case is similar to our always possessing the instrument-for-reasoning, viz., reason, which we do not always use and which, in reasoning, we direct toward various things. (2) But the inclination of the instrument-for-willing is called *will* when we say that a man always possesses the will for his own well-being. For in this case we label as *will* that inclination (of the instrument) by which a man wills his own well-being. [The same thing is true] when in this way we say that a saint — even when he is sleeping and is not thinking about living justly — continually has the will to live justly. Moreover, when we say that one person has more of the will to live justly than another person, the only thing we are calling *will* is the instrument's inclination, by which a man wills to live justly. For the instrument itself is not greater in one person and less in another.

***De Concordia* 3.6 (p. 206)**
Compare *TL*, lines 759–75

Without any cultivation on man's part the earth produces countless herbs and trees by which human beings are not nourished or by which they are even killed. But those herbs and trees which are especially necessary to us for nourishing our lives are not produced by the earth apart from seeds and great labor and a farmer. Similarly, without learning and endeavor human hearts freely germinate, so to speak, thoughts and volitions which are not conducive to salvation or which are even harmful thereto. But without their own kind of seed and without laborious cultivation human hearts do not at all conceive and germinate those thoughts and volitions without which we do not make progress toward our soul's salvation. Hence, those men upon whom such caretaking is bestowed the apostle calls "God's husbandry." Now, the word of God constitutes the seed of this husbandry . . .

De Concordia 3.3 (pp. 201–02)
Compare *TL*, lines 928–43

(201) Assuredly, there is no doubt that the will wills rightly only because it is upright. For just as sight is not acute because it sees acutely but sees acutely because it is acute, so the will is not upright because it wills rightly but wills rightly because it is upright. Now, when it wills uprightness-of-will, then without doubt it wills rightly. Therefore, it wills uprightness only because it is upright. But for the will to be upright is the same as for it to have uprightness. Therefore, it is evident that it wills uprightness only because it has uprightness. I do not deny that an upright will wills an uprightness which it does not have when it wills more uprightness than it already has. But I maintain that the will is not **(202)** able to will any uprightness unless it has the uprightness by which to will uprightness.

Let us now consider whether someone who does not have uprightness-of-will can in some way have it from himself. Surely, he could have it from himself only by willing it or without willing it. But, indeed, it is not the case that by willing it someone is able to obtain it by his own efforts, because he is able to will it only if he has it. On the other hand, no one's mind accepts the view that someone who does not have uprightness-of-will can acquire it by himself without willing it. Therefore, a creature can in no way have uprightness from himself. But neither can one creature have it from another creature. For just as one creature cannot save another creature, so one creature cannot give to another creature the necessary means for salvation. Thus, it follows that only by the grace of God does a creature have the uprightness which I have called uprightness-of-will.

De Concordia 3.4 (pp. 203–04)
Compare *TL*, lines 943–76

(203) Assuredly, even though uprightness is kept by free choice, still its being kept must be imputed not so much to free choice as to grace; for free choice possesses and keeps uprightness only by means of prevenient and of subsequent grace.

However, grace so follows its own gift that the only time grace ever fails to bestow this gift — whether it is something large or something small — is when free choice by willing something else forsakes the uprightness it has received. For this uprightness is never separated from the will except when the will wills something else which is incompatible with this uprightness — as when someone receives the uprightness of willing sobriety and rejects it by willing the immoderate pleasure of drinking. When a man does this, it is by his own will; and so, through his own fault he loses the grace which he received. For when free choice is under attack to abandon the uprightness it has received, grace even assists free choice — either by mitigating the assailing temptation's appeal, or by completely eliminating its appeal, or by increasing free choice's affection for uprightness. In fact, since everything is subject to the ordinance of God, all of what happens to a man which assists free choice to receive or to keep this uprightness of which I am speaking must be imputed to grace.

I have said that all justice is uprightness-of-will kept for its own sake. Hence, it follows that everyone who has uprightness- **(204)** of-will has justice and is just (since everyone who has justice is just). But it seems to me that eternal life is promised not to all who are just, but only to those who are just without any injustice. For these are properly and unqualifiedly called just in heart and upright in heart. For [there is a case where] someone is just in some respect and unjust in another respect (for example, a man who is both chaste and envious). The happiness of the just is not promised to such individuals, since even as true happiness exists without any deficiency, so it is given only to him who is just without being at all unjust.

***De Concordia* 3.5 (p. 205)**

Compare *TL*, lines 953–56

Therefore, grace and free choice are not incompatible but cooperate in order to justify and to save a man — even as, although natural functioning procreates an offspring only by means of a mother and not without a father, nevertheless no accurate account excludes either a father or a mother from an offspring's generation.

Appendix 3

De Concordia 3.12 (p. 219)
Compare *TL*, lines 976–86

In itself, to be sure, uprightness is a cause of no evil merit but is the mother of every good merit. For uprightness favors the spirit as it strives against the flesh; and uprightness "delights in the law of God in accordance with the inner man," i.e., in accordance with the spirit [which strives against the flesh]. However, [even] if evil sometimes seems to follow from uprightness, it does not proceed from uprightness but proceeds from something else. Indeed, because of their uprightness the apostles were a good odor unto God. But the fact that unto certain men the apostles were "the odor of death unto death" did not proceed from their justice but from evil men's wickedness. Now, the will for willing what is beneficial is not always evil, but is evil when it consents to the flesh as it strives against the spirit.

De Concordia 3.13 (pp. 219–22)
Compare *TL*, lines 986–1051

(219) But in order to understand this matter more clearly, we must investigate how the will [for what is beneficial] became so corrupt and so prone to evil. For we must not believe that in our first parents God created it prone to evil. Now, when I stated that because of sin human nature became corrupt and acquired appetites similar to those of brute animals, I did not explain how such a will arose in man. Indeed, base appetites are one thing; a corrupt will that assents to these appetites is another thing. Therefore, it seems to me, we must ask about how such a will became the lot of man.

The cause of such a will as this shall readily become apparent to us if we consider the original condition of rational nature. The intention of God was to create rational nature just and happy in order that it would enjoy Him. Now, it was able to be neither just nor happy without the will-for-justice and the will-for- **(220)** happiness. Assuredly, the will-for-justice is itself justice; but the will-for-happiness is not happiness because not everyone who has the will-for-happiness has happiness. However, everyone believes that happiness — whether angelic happiness is meant or the happiness which Adam had in Paradise — includes a sufficiency of suitable benefits and excludes all need. For although the happiness of angels is greater than the happiness of man in Paradise, still Adam cannot be denied to have had happiness. For, indeed, nothing prevents Adam from having been happy in Paradise and free of all need, in spite of the fact that angelic happiness was greater than his. (By comparison, an intense heat is free of all cold; and, nevertheless, there can be another more intense heat. And cold is free of all heat, even though there can be a more intense cold.) To be sure, having less of a thing than does another is not always identical with being in need; to be in need is to be deprived of something when it ought to be possessed — a condition which was not true of Adam. Where there is need there is unhappiness. God created rational nature for knowing and loving Him; but it is not the case that He created it unhappy when it had no antecedent guilt. Therefore, God created man happy and in need of nothing. Hence, at one and the same time rational nature received (1) the will-for-happiness, (2) happiness, (3) the will-for-justice (i.e., uprightness which is justice itself), and (4) free choice, without which rational nature could not have kept justice.

Now, God so ordained these two "wills," or inclinations, that (1) the will-as-instrument would use the will-which-is-justice for commanding and governing (though being itself instructed by the spirit, which is also called mind and reason), and that (2) without any detriment it would use the other will to the end of obedience. Indeed, God gave happiness to man — not to speak of the angels — for man's benefit. But He gave man justice for His own honor. [He gave] justice in such a way that man was able to abandon it, so that if he did not abandon it but kept it perseveringly, he would merit being elevated to fellowship with the angels. But if man did abandon justice, he would not thereafter be able to regain it by himself; nor would he attain to the happiness of the angels. Rather, he would be deprived of that happiness which he possessed; and falling into the likeness of brute animals, he would be subjected with them to corruption and to the appetites I have often mentioned. Nevertheless, the will-for-happiness would remain in **(221)** order that by means of man's need for the goods which he had lost he would be justly punished with deep unhappiness. Therefore, since he abandoned justice, he lost happiness. And the will which he received as being good and as being for his own good is fervent with desire for benefits which it is unable to keep from willing. And because it is unable to have the true benefits which are suitable for rational nature but which rational nature has lost, it turns itself to benefits which are false and which pertain to brute animals and which bestial appetites suggest. And thus when the will inordinately wills these benefits it either (1) shuns uprightness, so that it does not accept uprightness when uprightness is offered, or else (2) it casts uprightness away after having received it. But when the will wills these benefits within proper bounds, it neither shuns nor casts away uprightness.

So the will-as-instrument was created good, with respect to the fact that it has being; moreover, it was created just and having the power to keep the justice it received. And in the above manner it was made evil by free choice. [It was made evil] not insofar as it exists but insofar as it was made unjust as a result of the absence of justice, which was freely abandoned and which it was always supposed to have. Moreover, it now became powerless to will the justice it had deserted. For it is not the case that by free choice the will can will justice when it does not have justice — as it is the case that by free choice the will can keep justice when it has justice. Furthermore, the will-for-the-beneficial, a will which was created good insofar as it is something, became evil (i.e., unjust) because it was not subordinate to justice, without which it ought to will nothing. Therefore, since the will-as-instrument freely became unjust: after having abandoned justice, it remains (as regards its own power) a servant of injustice and unjust by necessity. For it is unable by itself to return to justice; and without justice the will is never free, because without justice the natural freedom of choice is idle. The will was also made the servant of its own inclination for the beneficial, because once justice has been removed, the will is able to will only what this inclination wills.

I predicate "to will" of both the instrument and its inclination; for the instrument is *will,* and the inclination is *will.* And without impropriety "to will" is predicated of both these wills. For the instrument, which wills by means of its inclination does indeed **(222)** will; and the inclination, by means of which the instrument wills, also wills. (Similarly, "to see" is predicated both of the man who sees by means of sight and of the sight by which the man sees.) Hence, we can without absurdity say that the inclinations of this will which I have called the soul's instrument are, so to speak, "instruments" of this instrument, because it does something only by means of them. Therefore, when the "instrument"-for-willing-justice (i.e., when uprightness) has been lost, the will-as-instrument cannot at all will justice, unless justice is restored by grace. Therefore, since the will-as-instrument ought to will nothing except justly, whatever it wills without uprightness, it wills unjustly. None of the appetites which the apostle calls the flesh and concupiscence are evil or unjust with respect to the fact that they exist; rather they are called unjust because they are present in a rational nature, where they ought not to be found. For, indeed, they are not evil or unjust in brute animals, because they ought to be present there.

***De Concordia* 3.14 (p. 222)**
Compare *TL*, lines 1052–54

From what has already been said above, one can recognize that the reason a man does not always possess justice (which he ought always to have) is that he cannot at all acquire or regain it by himself.

De Concordia 2.2 (p. 197)
Compare *TL*, lines 1056–68

(197) . . . we must notice that predestination can be said [to apply] not only to good men but also to evil men -– even as God is said to cause (because He permits) evils which He does not cause. For He is said to harden a man when He does not soften him, and to lead him into temptation when He does not deliver him. Hence, it is not inappropriate if in this manner we say that God predestines evil men and their evil works when He does not correct them and their evil works. But He is more properly said to foreknow and to predestine good works, because in them He causes both what they are [essentially] and the fact that they are good. But in evil deeds He causes only what they are essentially; He does not cause the fact that they are evil — as I have already said above. We must also realize that just as foreknowledge is not properly said to be found in God, so predestination is not either. For nothing is present to God either earlier or later, but all things are present to Him at once.

De Concordia 2.3 (pp. 197–98)
Compare *TL*, lines 1068–78

(197) Let us now consider whether some things which are going to occur as a result of free choice can be predestined. Surely, we ought not to doubt that God's foreknowledge and predestination do not conflict. Instead, just as He foreknows, so also He predestines. In the discussion about foreknowledge we saw clearly that, without any inconsistency, some actions which are going to occur as a result of free choice, are foreknown. Therefore, reason and plain truth also teach that, without any inconsistency, some actions which are going to occur by means of free choice, are likewise predestined. For God neither foreknows nor predestines that anyone will be *just* by necessity. For he who does not keep justice by means of his free will is not just. Therefore, although things foreknown and predestined must occur, it is nonetheless **(198)** equally true that some things foreknown and predestined occur not by the necessity which precedes a thing and causes it, but by the necessity which succeeds a thing — as I have said above. For although God predestines these things, He causes them not by constraining or restraining the will but by leaving the will to its own power. But although the will uses its own power, it does nothing which God does not cause — in good works by His grace, in evil works not through any fault of His but through the will's fault. (As I promised, this shall become clearer when I shall speak about grace.) And just as foreknowledge, which is not mistaken, foreknows only the real thing as it will occur — either necessarily or freely — so predestination, which is not altered, predestines only as the thing exists in foreknowledge. And although what is foreknown is immutable in eternity, it can nevertheless be changed in the temporal order at some point before it occurs. Similarly, the case is in every respect the same for predestination.

Therefore, if these statements which have been made are examined closely, it is evident from them that predestination does not exclude free choice and that free choice is not opposed to predestination. For, indeed, all the considerations by which I have shown above that free choice is not incompatible with foreknowledge show equally that it is compatible with predestination. Therefore, whenever something happens by the agency of free will (e.g., when one man wrongs another man and as a result is killed by this other), it is unreasonable for certain people to give vent loudly to the words: "Thus it was foreknown and predestined by God; and hence it was done by necessity and could not have been done otherwise." Indeed, neither the man who provoked the other by a wrong nor the other who avenged himself did this by necessity. Rather, [each acted] voluntarily, because if each had not freely willed to, neither one would have done what he did.

Glossary

a *a; have*
a peyred *damaged*
a thishalfe god *here below*
achates *purchases*
acomered *encumbered*
affyched *fixed*
aforne *before*
after as *according as*
after mede *reward*
algates *anyway*
almesse *those deserving of alms*
almoygner *alms-man, who distributes the alms of another*
alowe *applaud*
alyes *friends, allies*
amonesteth *admonishes*
an *an; and*
and *and; if*
anguys *excruciating, anxious*
anon *soon*
apayred, apeyred *denigrated [lit., damaged]*
apeched *impeached*
aperte *open*
appropred *proper, appropriate*
aptes *aptitudes*
arbitrement *free will*
arered *raised up, raised*
arn *are*
as yerne *quickly*
assoyle *solve, answer*
asterte *make to move or go away, start*
asured *painted or enameled with azure (lapis lazuli)*
aver *(v) payment; (n) true*
augrym *mathematics, arithmetic*
auter *altar*
azure *lapis lazuli*

bandon *control*
be *be; by*
be swynke *work for*
berafte out of *deprived of, booted from, expelled*
bote *remedy*
boystous *rough, plain*
brotel *changeable*
burjons *buds*
buxome *obedient*

carpen *speak of*
catchende *apprehending*
catel *wealth, possessions, chattels, belongings*
chere *countenance, demeanor, look, looks; aspect*
cleape *call*
clepyng *calling, naming*
clippynges *hugs*
coarted *coerced, compelled*
cockle *weeds*
colours *figures of rhetoric*
commensal *a companion of the dining table*
con, conne *know how to, can, know, be able to, would know how to,*

connyng *intelligence, knowledge, shrewdness, wit, understanding*
cordiacle *heart attack, or failure*
cresse *trifle (lit., crease)*

daunger *haughtiness, peril, resistance*
defend *prevent, forbid, prohibit, hinder*
demen *judge*
deynous *disdainful*
disease *discomfiting*
dolven *cultivated, buried*
don *do; cause*

efte *after*
eke names *nickname*
endite *compose, write*

fallas *fallacy, deceitful*
famulers *familiars*
ferde *fear, afraid, intimidation*
ferdenesse *fear or awe*
fere *companion, mate, friend or companion*
fette *fetched*
forgoyng *abandonment*
forjuged *condemned*
forleten *abandoned*
fyne *end*

gabbest *chatter*
glosed *deceived, flattered*
gloseth *flatters*
graffed *dug, planted*
groubed *dug around the roots of a plant*
gubernatyfe *governmental*
guerdon *reward*

haboundeth *abounds*
han *has, have*
happes *circumstances*
happyous *fortuitous*
hautayn *haughty*
hawe *trifle, worthless plant*
hayn *hatred*
heigheth *hastens*
hem *them*
her(e) *her, their; here; hear*
hestes *promises; commands*
hete *be called; heat*
his *his, its*
horisons *beseechings, prayers*
hote *be called*

inrest *inner most*
inseer *insightful viewer, reader*
inwytte *conscience, intuition*
iwys *indeed*

jangelers *tattle-tellers*
jape *jest, joke*

knette *knit (as in a net)*
knytten *make the knot of*
kynde *nature*
kyndely *naturally*

lache *seize*
lacke *blame*
lerne *teach*
let *hinder*
let games *hinderers*
leude *lay, uneducated, rude, unlearned, ignorant, uncultured, uninformed, infirm*
leudenesse *ignorance, lack of learning*
leve *believe*
lore *learning, teaching*
lorn *lost*
losengeour *flatterer*
lyches *physicians*
lysse *relief*

magre (maugre) *disdain, spite*
mased *amazed*
maugre *in spite of, displeasure*
maystreshyp *mastery*
me *me; myself; men*
me lyketh *I like*
me lyste *it pleases me*
me might *one might*
me semed *it seemed to me*
me weneth *I suppose*
me were leaver *I would prefer*
mean *intercessor, intermediary*
meane *means, mediatory*
mede *reward (usually monetary), wealth*
meded *satisfied*
meyny *groups, troop, entourage*
miscleapyng *misnaming*
mo *more; many*
moeble *moveables, wealth*
mokel *much, many, great*
moned *commiserated with*
mores *superiors; greater*
mote *must*
mow *may*
muskel *mussel*
mykel *much, great*

nedes *necessarily*
nempne *name*
nempned *named, counted*
nere *were not*
never the later *nevertheless*
neyghe *approach*
nories, nory *disciples (lit., ones being nursed or nourished)*
noriture *nurture*
nygh *near, nearly*
nyl *will not*
nys *it is not, is not*

of *of, on, in; off*
onbyde *abide*
oned *reconciled*
onehed *singleness, unity*
outforth *externally*

parde *indeed*
partable *not whole*
paynyms *pagans, heathens*
persel *part*
pert *open*
peysen *weigh*
platly *plainly, openly*
playne *complain*
plite *plight, condition*
preve *prove*
pynande *grievous*
pyne *pain*

queynt *ornate, involved, curious, quenched, weird, over-wrought, difficult*
queyntyses *contrivances*
quyte *requite*

rathe *soon*
rathest *soonest*
rede *counsel, advise*
renome *renown*
reve *steal, take away, take it away*
rewth *pity*
rownyng *whispering*
ryche *splendid, adorned, well-endowed; lavish; powerful, noble*

sawes *wise sayings, teachings*
seare *dry, depressing*
secre *secrecy or intimacy*
sely *fortunate, innocent, felicitous*
selynesse *fortune, felicity*
semelych *decorous*
setlyng *plant*

shende *ruin, destroy*
shope, shopen *arranged*
shreude, shreudnes, shreudnesse *wicked, misdeeds, shrewishness*
shrewes *wicked person, rascal, villain; devil*
skylles *reasons, arguments, reasonings*
slydyng *variable*
somdele *somewhat*
sothe *truth, fidelity, truthfulness, true*
sottes *idiots*
spede *prosper*
spire *shoot, sprout*
spyl, spylle *destroy, decline*
steered, stered *manipulated, guided, directed*
sterte *moved*
stondmele *at regular intervals, sometimes*
stoundes *times, turns*
styl *secretive, politic*
stynte *cease, ceased*
styred *directed, steered*
surquedry *pride*
swynke *labor*
syker *certain, sure, secure*
syth *since*
sythen *since, ago*

tene *sorrow, grief, trouble*
that *that, where, what*
the *the; you*
the lyste *it pleases you*
there *there, where*
thilk(e) *those same, that same, the same, those, that very*
tho *then; those*
thoughtful *anxious*
throwe out *thorough*
to forne *heretofore, before*
tofore *heretofore*
travaylyng *laboring*
trayson *betrayal*
trow *believe*

unbyde *abide, await*
unconnyng *ignorant, unable, ignorance*
unknytte *unravel*
unleful *inappropriate*
unlusty *undesirable*
unneth *scarcely, hardly*
unsely *unfortunate, miserable, Misery, Misfortune, Infelicity*
unwetyng *unknowing*
uphap *perhaps*

wanhope *despair*
wantrust *despair*
ward(es) *guardianship, keeping, care, custody*
ware *aware*
warne *deny*
wayters, *hinderers, watchmen, inhibitors, interferers*
weaked *wicked*
wele *fortune, prosperity*
welfulnesse *prosperity*
wemme *stain*
wende *expected, expected [to], assumed*
wene *suspect, expect or assume; suppose or think; make assumptions or allegations; understand*
werche *work, cause*
werchynge *effect, working, living*
wernynges *warnings*
werre *war*
wete *to know*
wexe *grow*
wight *person, creature*
wilne *(n) will; (v) desires*
wist *knew, known*
wite, wist, wyste *know(n)*
with sytte *resist*

withsay *contradict*
wol *will, desires*
worche *work*
wote, wost(e) *know*
wreche *vengeance, retribution*
writte *written*
wylne *desire, wish*
wyse *manner; a wise person*
wyte *blame*

yave *gave*
yede *went*
yelde *yield*
yere *year*
ylke *same*
ynempned *named*
ynowe *enough*
yolde *paid back*
you lyste *it pleases you*
yvels *ills*
ywis *certainly*

Other Volumes in the Middle English Texts Series

The Floure and the Leafe, *The Assemblie of Ladies*, and *The Isle of Ladies*, ed. Derek Pearsall (1990)

Three Middle English Charlemagne Romances, ed. Alan Lupack (1990)

Six Ecclesiastical Satires, ed. James M. Dean (1991)

Heroic Women from the Old Testament in Middle English Verse, ed. Russell A. Peck (1991)

The Canterbury Tales: Fifteenth-Century Continuations and Additions, ed. John M. Bowers (1992)

Gavin Douglas, *The Palis of Honoure*, ed. David J. Parkinson (1992)

Wynnere and Wastoure and *The Parlement of the Thre Ages*, ed. Warren Ginsberg (1992)

The Shewings of Julian of Norwich, ed. Georgia Ronan Crampton (1994)

King Arthur's Death: The Stanzaic Morte Arthur and *The Alliterative Morte Arthure*, ed. Larry D. Benson and Edward E. Foster (1994)

Lancelot of the Laik and *Sir Tristrem*, ed. Alan Lupack (1994)

Sir Gawain: Eleven Romances and Tales, ed. Thomas Hahn (1995)

Sir Perceval of Galles and *Ywain and Gawain*, ed. Mary Flowers Braswell (1995)

The Middle English Breton Lays, ed. Anne Laskaya and Eve Salisbury (1995)

Four Middle English Romances: Sir Isumbras, Octavian, Sir Eglamour of Artois, Sir Tryamour, ed. Harriet Hudson (1996)

Medieval English Political Writings, ed. James Dean (1996)

The Poems of Laurence Minot, 1333–1352, ed. Richard H. Osberg (1996)

The Book of Margery Kempe, ed. Lynn Staley (1996)

Amis and Amiloun, *Robert of Ciseyle*, and *Sir Amadace*, ed. Edward E. Foster (1997)

The Cloud of Unknowing, ed. Patrick Gallacher (1997)

Robin Hood and Other Outlaw Tales, ed. Stephen Knight and Thomas Ohlgren (1997)

The Poems of Robert Henryson, ed. Robert Kindrick (1997)

Moral Love Songs and Laments, ed. Susanna Fein (1998)

The Troy Book, ed. Robert Edwards (1998)

To order please contact:

MEDIEVAL INSTITUTE PUBLICATIONS
Western Michigan University
Kalamazoo, MI 49008–3801
Phone (616) 387–8755 FAX (616) 387–8750
http://www.wmich.edu/medieval/mip/mipubshome/html

Other TEAMS Publications

Documents of Practice Series:

Love and Marriage in Late Medieval London, by Shannon McSheffrey (1995)

A Slice of Life: Selected Documents of Medieval English Peasant Experience, edited, translated, and with an introduction by Edwin Brezette DeWindt (1996)

Sources for the History of Medicine in Late Medieval London, by Carole Rawcliffe (1996)

Regular Life: Monastic, Canonical, and Mendicant Rules, selected with an introduction by Douglas J. McMillan and Kathryn Smith Fladenmuller (1997)

Commentary Series:

Commentary on the Book of Jonah, by Haimo of Auxere, translated with an introduction by Deborah Everhart (1993)

Medieval Exegesis in Translation: Commentaries on the Book of Ruth, translated with an introduction by Lesley Smith (1996)

Nicholas of Lyra's Apocalypse Commentary, translated with an introduction and notes by Philip D. W. Krey (1997)

To order please contact:

MEDIEVAL INSTITUTE PUBLICATIONS
Western Michigan University
Kalamazoo, MI 49008–3801
Phone (616) 387–8755 FAX (616) 387–8750
http://www.wmich.edu/medieval/mip/mipubshome/html